**1711–1776**
**DAVID HUME**
Scottish Historian/Empiricist

**1632–1704**
**JOHN LOCKE**
English Founder of Empiricism

**1588–1679**
**THOMAS HOBBES**
English Political Theorist

**1053–1109**
**ST. ANSELM**
Christian Theologian

**1515–1582**
**ST. TERESA OF AVILA**
Spanish Mystic

| 600 CE | 700 CE | 800 CE | 900 CE | 1000 CE | 1100 CE | 1200 CE | 1300 CE | 1400 CE | 1500 CE | 1600 CE | 1700 CE |

**1473–1543**
**COPERNICUS**
**(MIKOLAJ KOPERNIK)**
Polish Astronomer

**1225–1274**
**ST. THOMAS AQUINAS**
Italian Scholastic
Philosopher

**1483–1546**
**MARTIN LUTHER**
Founder of
Lutheran Church

**1564–1642**
**GALILEO**
Italian Astronomer/
Physicist

**1596–1650**
**RENÉ DESCARTES**
French Rationalist Philosopher

**1632–1677**
**BARUCH (BENEDICT) SPINOZA**
Dutch Rationalist Philosopher

**1642–1727**
**SIR ISAAC NEWTON**
English Philosopher/Mathematician

**1646–1716**
**GOTTFRIED LEIBNIZ**
German Rationalist

**1685–1753**
**GEORGE BERKELEY**
Irish Philosopher/Clergyman

**1712–1778**
**JEAN-JACQUES ROUSSEAU**
French Philosopher

# EXPERIENCING PHILOSOPHY

## Anthony Falikowski
Sheridan College

PEARSON

Prentice
Hall

Upper Saddle River, NJ 07458

**Library of Congress Cataloging-in-Publication Data**

Falikowski, Anthony F.
    Experiencing philosophy/Anthony Falikowski.—1st ed.
      p. cm.
    Includes bibliographical references and index.
    ISBN 0-13-012267-X (pbk.)
    1. Philosophy–Introductions. I. Title.
    BD21.F337  2003
    100—dc21              2002027073

VP/Editorial Director: Charlyce Jones Owen
AVP/Director of Production and Manufacturing:
  Barbara Kittle
Acquisitions Editor: Ross Miller
Assistant Editor: Wendy Yurash
Editorial Assistant: Carla Worner
Editorial/production supervision: Mary Araneo
Marketing Manager: Chris Ruel

Prepress and Manufacturing Buyer: Brian Mackey
Creative Design Director: Leslie Osher
Interior Designer: Laura Gardner
Cover Art Director: Jayne Conte
Cover Designer: Bruce Kenselaar
Cover Art: Jerry Uelsmann
Photo Permission Coordinator: Debbie Hewitson

This book was set in 10/12 ACaslon Regular by Clarinda and was printed and bound
by R.R. Donnelley & Sons, Inc. The cover was printed by Coral Graphics.

© 2004 by Pearson Education, Inc.
Upper Saddle River, New Jersey 07458

Printed in the United States of America

10 9 8 7 6 5 4 3 2 1

ISBN 0-13-012267-X

Pearson Education LTD., London
Pearson Education Australia PTY, Limited, Sydney
Pearson Education Singapore, Pte. Ltd
Pearson Education North Asia Ltd, Hong Kong
Pearson Education Canada, Ltd., Toronto
Pearson Educación de Mexico, S.A. de C.V.
Pearson Education—Japan, Tokyo
Pearson Education Malaysia, Pte. Ltd
Pearson Education, Upper Saddle River, New Jersey

Dedicated with love:
To Heather, a kindred spirit of Nietzsche,
To Michelle, existentialism's prototype,
To Michael, an aesthete clothed in a toga of Greek rationalism,
And to my wife Pamela, who gives principled morality
new definition.

# CONTENTS

Note to the Instructor   xii
Features   xv
Message to Students   xviii
Acknowledgments   xx

## CHAPTER 1

### WHAT IS PHILOSOPHY? WHAT'S IN IT FOR ME?   2

Take It Personally   5

**KNOW THYSELF**
My Preconceptions about Philosophy   7

Philosophy and Philosophers: Caricatures, Myths, and Realities   8
The Philosopher's Profile   9
Wisdom: The Object of Love   11
The Practical Value of Philosophy   12
Therapeutic Applications of Philosophy: Back to the Future   16
Philosophy's Relevance in an Age of Information and Emerging Technologies   20
Fields of Philosophy   21
    Metaphysics   22
    Epistemology   22
    Logic   23
    Ethics   23
    Axiology   24
    Social/Political Philosophy   24
    Foundational and Disciplinary Philosophies   24
    Philosophies of Life   25
Approaches to Philosophy   26
    Masculine versus Feminine Approaches   26
    World Philosophies: Eastern, Western, and Ethno-racial   26
    Rational versus Nonrational Philosophy   28
Historical Periods of Philosophy   32

**ORIGINAL SOURCEWORK**
Bertrand Russell, *The Problems of Philosophy*   33

**STUDY GUIDE**   36
Key Terms   36
Progress Check   37
Summary of Major Points   37
Source References   38
Philosophy in Cyberspace   39
Endnotes   39

## CHAPTER 2

### PHILOSOPHIES OF LIFE   40

Take It Personally   43

**KNOW THYSELF**
The Philosophy of Life Preference Indicator   44

Stoicism: A Prescription for Peace of Mind   48
    Stoicism's Cynical Origins   48
    The Stoic Universe   50
    How to Live in a Fated Universe   51
    Freedom and Value   52
    Purpose of Life   52
    Emotions in Life   55
    How to Progress Morally   55

**ORIGINAL SOURCEWORK**
Marcus Aurelius, *The Meditations of Marcus Aurelius*   56

Existentialism: Born Free, Let Me Be Me   61
    Methods   62

**KNOW THYSELF**
The Purpose in Life Test   63

    Philosophers Associated with Existentialism   66
    Existentialism as a Revolt   67
    Essence versus Existence   69

Individuality and Subjective Experience  **70**
Freedom of Choice  **71**

**ORIGINAL SOURCEWORK**
Jean-Paul Sartre, *The Humanism of Existentialism*  **72**

**PHILOSOPHICAL SEGUE**
Fate, Free Will, and Determinism  **74**

Hedonism: Pleasure Is the Measure  **82**
Psychological versus Ethical Hedonism  **83**
Aristippus of Cyrene  **84**
Epicurus  **86**

**ORIGINAL SOURCEWORK**
Epicurus, *Letter to Menoeceus*  **94**

Buddhism as a Philosophy of Life  **97**
The Four Noble Truths  **99**
The Noble Eight-Fold Path  **106**

**ORIGINAL SOURCEWORK**
John Koller, *Basic Characteristics of Buddhist Culture*  **114**

**STUDY GUIDE**  115
Key Terms  **115**
Progress Check  **117**
Summary of Major Points  **118**
Source References  **119**
Philosophy in Cyberspace  **120**
Endnotes  **120**

**CHAPTER 3**

**PHILOSOPHICAL ARGUMENT . . . THAT SOUNDS LOGICAL!**  122
Take It Personally  **125**
Attitude Adjustments for Argument  **127**
Benefits of Argument  **128**

**ORIGINAL SOURCEWORK**
Plato, *"Euthyphro" featuring the Socratic Method*  **129**

**KNOW THYSELF**
How Rational Am I?  **137**

Opinions versus Arguments  **139**
Opinions  **139**
Arguments  **140**
Factual Statements versus Value Judgments  **140**
Factual Statements  **141**
Value Judgments  **141**
Deductive Arguments  **143**
*Modus Ponens* (MP)  **143**
*Modus Tollens* (MT)  **145**
Syllogisms  **145**
Inductive Logic  **151**
Argument from Past Experience  **151**
Argument by Analogy  **152**
Argument by Inductive Generalization  **152**
Faulty and Fallacious Reasoning  **153**
Validity  **153**
Evaluating Arguments  **154**
Informal Logical Fallacies  **156**
*Ad Hominem* Fallacy  **156**
Straw Man Fallacy  **157**
Circular Reasoning/Begging the Question Fallacy  **157**
Two Wrongs Fallacy  **158**
Slippery Slope Fallacy  **158**
Appealing to Authority Fallacy  **159**
Red Herring Fallacy  **159**
Guilt by Association Fallacy  **160**

**STUDY GUIDE**  162
Key Terms  **162**
Progress Check  **163**
Summary of Major Points  **164**
Source References  **165**
Philosophy in Cyberspace  **165**
Endnotes  **165**

# CHAPTER 4

## EPISTEMOLOGY, METAPHYSICS, AND GOD 166

Take It Personally 170

**KNOW THYSELF**
**My Philosophical Presuppositions about Knowledge and Reality 173**

Preliminary Questions and Definitions 175
Plato's Metaphysical Epistemology 176
    Divided Line Theory 178
    Theory of Forms 181
    Simile of the Sun 183

**ORIGINAL SOURCEWORK**
Plato, *Simile of the Sun* 183

    Allegory of the Cave 185

**ORIGINAL SOURCEWORK**
Plato, *Allegory of the Cave* 186

Rationalism: René Descartes 189
    Historical Context 189
    The Quest for Certainty Using
        Methodological Doubt 192

**ORIGINAL SOURCEWORK**
René Descartes, *First Meditation Concerning Things that Can Be Doubted* 195

    *Cogito Ergo Sum*—I Think, Therefore
        I Am 197

**ORIGINAL SOURCEWORK**
René Descartes, *Second Meditation of the Nature of the Human Mind, and That It Is More Easily Known than the Body* 197

**ORIGINAL SOURCEWORK**
René Descartes, *The Wax Example* 200

British Empiricism: Locke, Berkeley, and Hume 203

Historical Background of Empiricism 204
John Locke 205
Bishop George Berkeley 209
David Hume's Radical Skepticism 214

**ORIGINAL SOURCEWORK**
David Hume, *Skeptical Doubts Concerning the Operations of the Understanding* 223

**ORIGINAL SOURCEWORK**
Patricia Hill Collins, *An Afrocentric/Feminist Standpoint Challenges the Tradition of Positivism* 226

Immanuel Kant's Synthesis of Rationalism
    and Empiricism 229
    The Roles of Reason and Experience
        in Knowledge 230
    The Copernican Revolution in
        Epistemology 233
    *A Priori* Elements of Knowledge 234
    Kantian versus Platonic Forms 236
    The Categories of "Cause" and
        "Substance" 237
    Types of Judgments 238

**ORIGINAL SOURCEWORK**
Immanuel Kant, *The Distinction between Analytic and Synthetic Judgments* 241

    Metaphysics and the Regulative Function of
        Transcendental Ideas 244

**ORIGINAL SOURCEWORK**
Benjamin Whorf, *The Language of the Hopi Provides a Metaphysics Without Space and Time* 248

**PHILOSOPHICAL SEGUE**
**Proofs for the Existence of God 250**

    Anselm's Ontological Proof 252
    St. Thomas Aquinas's "Five Ways"—Proofs
        for the Existence of God 253

**ORIGINAL SOURCEWORK**
Thomas Aquinas, *Whether God Exists?*  **261**

**STUDY GUIDE**  **263**
Key Terms  **263**
Progress Check  **264**
Summary of Major Points  **265**
Source References  **267**
Philosophy in Cyberspace  **268**
Endnotes  **268**

CHAPTER 5

**ETHICS AND MORAL DECISION
MAKING**  **270**
Take It Personally  **274**

**KNOW THYSELF**
**The Ethical Perspective Indicator**  **278**

Character Ethics: Plato  **282**
 Plato's Teleology  **282**
 Vision of the Soul  **283**
 Moral Balance and Plato's Functional
  Explanation of Morality  **283**

**KNOW THYSELF**
**Platonic Character Type Index (PCTI)**  **285**

Plato's Character Types  **288**

**ORIGINAL SOURCEWORK**
Plato, *Virtue and Justice in the Individual
and in the State*  **289**

Utilitarian Ethics: Jeremy Bentham  **297**
 The Problem of Pleasure  **298**
 Is-Ought Fallacy  **299**
 Theory of Sanctions  **299**
 The Hedonic Calculus  **301**

**ORIGINAL SOURCEWORK**
Jeremy Bentham, *An Introduction to the Principles
of Morals and Legislation*  **306**

Deontological Ethics: Immanuel Kant  **308**
 The Rational Basis of Morality  **308**
 Concept of the Good Will  **309**
 Notion of Duty  **311**
 Moral Duties to Oneself and Others  **313**
 Maxims and Moral Behavior  **314**
 Kantian Formalism and the Categorical
  Imperative  **314**
 Hypothetical versus Categorical
  Imperatives  **316**
 Autonomy versus Heteronomy of the
  Will  **317**

**ORIGINAL SOURCEWORK**
Immanuel Kant, *Fundamental Principles of the
Metaphysics of Morals*  **318**

Feminine Ethics: Carol Gilligan and Nel
 Noddings  **320**
 Male Bias in Moral Research  **320**
 Gilligan's Morality of Care  **324**
 Nel Noddings and Feminine Ethics  **327**
 Romanticizing Rationality: Reasons to Reject
  Principled Morality  **327**
 Relation as Ontologically Basic  **329**
 Brief Outline of Noddings's Care-Based
  Ethic  **329**

**ORIGINAL SOURCEWORK**
Nel Noddings, *Caring: A Feminine Approach to
Ethics and Moral Education*  **331**

Existentialist Ethics: Friedrich Wilhelm
 Nietzsche  **335**
 God Is Dead  **336**

**ORIGINAL SOURCEWORK**
Friedrich Wilhelm Nietzsche, *The Gay
Science*  **336**

 Will to Power  **338**
 Master versus Slave Morality  **339**
 Traditional (Herd) Morality and the
  Revaluation of All Values  **342**
 The Superman/Übermensch  **344**

Objectivist Ethics: Ayn Rand **347**
    Ethical Egoism **347**
    Objectivist Ethics **347**
    Altruism Is Inhumane **348**
    Values and Virtue **351**
    Rational Selfishness **352**

**ORIGINAL SOURCEWORK**
Ayn Rand, *The Objectivist Ethics* **354**

**PHILOSOPHICAL SEGUE**
**Religion and Ethics: Islamic, Hindu, and Christian Perspectives 356**

    Islamic Ethics **357**

**ORIGINAL SOURCEWORK**
Riffat Hassan, *Islamic View of Human Rights* **359**

    Hindu Ethics **360**

**ORIGINAL SOURCEWORK**
A.K. Malhotra, *Transcreation of the Bhagavad Gita* **362**

    Christian Ethics **365**

**ORIGINAL SOURCEWORK**
Brian Berry, *Roman Catholic Ethics: Three Approaches* **366**

**STUDY GUIDE** 369
Key Terms **369**
Progress Check **370**
Summary of Major Points **372**
Source References **372**
Philosophy in Cyberspace **374**
Endnotes **374**

**CHAPTER**

**POLITICAL PHILOSOPHY** 376
Take It Personally **379**

**KNOW THYSELF**
**My Political Outlook** 380

Political Philosophy versus Politics and Political Science **383**
Plato's Republic **386**
    The Individual and the State **387**
    Plato's Class System **389**
    Imperfect Societies **392**
    Women, Marriage and Family in the Republic **395**

**ORIGINAL SOURCEWORK**
Plato, *The Nature of Woman* **396**

Social Contract Theorists: Hobbes and Locke **399**
Thomas Hobbes **401**
    State of Nature **401**
    Laws of Nature **403**
    The Commonwealth—Hobbes's *Leviathan* **404**
    The Social Contract **406**
    Conditions on the Sovereign **406**

**ORIGINAL SOURCEWORK**
Thomas Hobbes, *Of the Causes, Generation, and Definition of a Commonwealth* **407**

John Locke **409**
    Locke's State of Nature and Natural Law **410**
    Property Rights **411**
    Political Society and Government **413**
    Social Compact **414**
    Limits on Government **415**
    Divisions of Power **416**
    The Dissolution of Government **417**

**ORIGINAL SOURCEWORK**
John Locke, *Of the Ends of Political Society and Government* **417**

Karl Marx **421**
    Marx's Metaphysics and Dialectical Materialism **424**
    Class Conflict **426**
    Alienation as a Byproduct of Capitalism **429**
    Idolatry/Fetishism of Commodities **432**
    Division of Labor **433**
    After Capitalism **435**

ORIGINAL SOURCEWORK
Karl Marx, *Economic and Philosophical Manuscripts* **436**

**STUDY GUIDE**   438
Key Terms   **438**
Progress Check   **439**
Summary of Major Points   **440**
Source References   **442**
Philosophy in Cyberspace   **443**
Endnotes   **443**

**Appendix: Answers to Progress Checks**   445
**Photo Credits**   447
**Index**   448

# NOTE TO THE INSTRUCTOR

*Experiencing Philosophy* is a textbook written and designed to be used in introductory philosophy courses. It could also be adopted in humanities and liberal arts courses, in general education courses, or in critical thinking courses. It can be used in institutions having a first year "foundations" component in their academic program or in vocational schools where there's a wish to broaden the student's intellectual horizons.

The book begins with the assumption that philosophy is not simply something you know or do but something you experience! There is a human side to philosophy that, unfortunately, is too often neglected in traditional approaches to philosophical teaching. I believe philosophy needn't be seen as something that is completely theoretical and dry or something that is totally impractical and outdated; rather, the study of philosophy has the potential to transform lives. Acceptance of a metaphysical belief in God or a philosophical commitment to materialistic atheism, for example, will take individuals down very different roads in life. In this book, I will explore philosophy with frequent references to its personal and practical relevance, making efforts to present the subject in its rich diversity to an audience that demands accessibility. Convoluted, impenetrable language will therefore be regarded as an academic vice, not as a virtue of philosophic expression.

*Experiencing Philosophy* is an "applied" text of sorts. Though the personal and applied nature of the book does not adequately present itself in the table of contents, the practical "experiential relevance" shows up in the "Know Thyself" diagnostics, in the "Take It Personally" chapter introductions, in the "Meditative Moment" journal writing opportunities, as well as in the features entitled "Philosophers in Action" and "Discussion Questions for Critique and Analysis." These last two elements in the book provide occasions for students to actually "do" philosophy and thereby experience it in practice for themselves. Note, however, that by making this book practical and personally relevant, I do not wish to compromise on aca-demic respectability. I have written it to be theoretically sound and philosophically sophisticated. You should find it technically accurate and appropriately detailed. As part of my content coverage, I have also included the actual writings of philosophers discussed in a repeating feature throughout the book entitled, "Original Sourceworks." Any one excerpt will be relatively short so as not to discourage beginning students, but, cumulatively, the original writings will constitute a significant exposure to some of the major works with which all introductory philosophy students should be familiar. For the most part, though, significant topics and important philosophers' writings will be paraphrased, summarized, and explained for those students who would find an entire course based on the classical works inappropriate. In writing this book, I recognize that there are levels of difficulty; I also recognize that not everyone who studies philosophy plans to major in it. The truth is a majority don't. Furthermore, I appreciate the fact that beginning students should not be expected to master material often assigned in philosophy graduate courses—something I was once expected to do! To capture the point metaphorically, let us say that before one can run a marathon, one must first learn to walk.

In recognition of learner needs, this text will contain a substantial pedagogical apparatus designed to encourage and motivate students as well as to maximize their chances of success. I don't want your students' first philosophy course to be their last. Little is accomplished if the syllabus is covered, but because of "technical difficulties," regarding meaning and comprehension, nobody cares to learn or remember what was taught. Systematically covering the contents of philosophy, but failing to motivate and inspire students to pursue it further, is like saying, "the operation was a success, but the patient died!" In this book, we'll be focusing on the "philosophical patient" as much as on following the strict operational procedures demanded by the doctors of philosophy! My aim is to make philosophy "student-friendly"—to give it S.O.U.L.—a *S*tudent *O*rientation for *U*nderstanding and *Learning*. My goal here is to make this text interesting and exciting for students. I hope to challenge and inspire them. Anyone using this book can expect to do the same.

In Chapter 1, we begin with a discussion of the nature, purpose, and scope of philosophy, examining a number of myths and misconceptions about philosophy, and exploring its personal and therapeutic value. In this section, we make efforts to motivate students in their studies by pointing out that philosophy can help to clarify values and assist them in making important life decisions. We observe that, through an examination of perennial wisdom, people can find greater direction and achieve an enhanced sense of personal well being. In this regard, it's claimed that philosophy may in fact turn out to be the most important and practical subject the student will ever study—truly a startling claim for many. As part of the introduction to philosophy, we also cover the major sub-disciplines and discuss the various approaches to philosophy that have been taken in the past.

Chapter 2 is titled "Philosophies of Life." In order to immediately engage students with the practical "existential relevance" of philosophy, they are invited to reconsider their own personal philosophies in light of some others that have been developed throughout the ages. We learn in this section how differing philosophical ideas and worldviews are captured by hedonism, stoicism, existentialism, and Buddhism—four starkly contrasting visions of reality. We also see how life takes on different value priorities, depending on which philosophical worldview is adopted. In this chapter, students are encouraged to reflect on their own goals and perceptions of the world. An awareness is generated of how people's unconscious philosophical assumptions can have real life consequences.

In Chapter 3, we find a coverage of logic and its place in philosophical thinking. So many introductory textbooks often make the point that philosophy is more of a method of thinking than a body of knowledge and then, surprisingly, neglect to deal with the method or forget to give students a chance to practice it. In this book, students are indeed encouraged to "do" philosophy, especially when completing reasoning exercises and evaluative critiques. Focusing on the human side of philosophy, I also underscore the necessity of making certain attitude adjustments if people are to "do," or engage in, philosophy properly. I discuss the benefits of philosophical argument and explain how arguing is different from opinionating. In this chapter, we look at inductive and deductive logic, learning the differences between validity, soundness, and truth. We also go on to examine a number of informal logical fallacies that make use of emotional and psychological appeals. Students are given opportunities here to practice their logical reasoning skills necessary for further philosophical analysis and debate.

Once students understand what philosophy is all about, once they can begin to think as philosophers using valid logic and sound reasoning, and having engaged in a preliminary examination of their own personal philosophies, we move ahead full-steam in Chapter 4 to explore epistemology and metaphysics, including a section on God. A coverage of Plato, Descartes, the British empiricists, and Immanuel Kant reveals how claims regarding the nature of knowledge (epistemology) are often based on beliefs and assumptions about reality and the physical universe (metaphysics). Discussing rational proofs for the existence of God will help students on a personal level, especially if they are grappling with religious questions at this time in their lives.

In Chapter 5, we proceed to the study of ethics and moral philosophy. Perspectives to be covered include: Character Ethics, Utilitarian Ethics, Deontological Ethics, Feminine Ethics, Existentialist Ethics and Ethical Egoism. This coverage will expose students to ancient and modern thinkers, to male and female theorists, and to rational and nonrational approaches. A segue feature in this chapter will also introduce students to the relationship between religion and ethics. Upon successful completion of this chapter, students will be able to make better informed and rationally justifiable moral decisions—certainly an important practical life skill.

Chapter 6, the final one, takes us into the territory of political philosophy. Plato's utopian society is discussed as are the social contract theorists—Hobbes and Locke—thinkers whose collective works reflect the philosophical foundations of Western liberal democracy. In addition, a perspective critical of capitalist liberal democracy, namely Marxism, is also covered. Marx works very effectively as an intellectual alarm clock waking us from our dogmatic capitalist slumbers. A coverage of Chapter 6 should enable students to better appreciate alternative political systems. It should also help to inject a dose of calm rational objectivity when discussing political issues and ideologies. Successful efforts in this regard will have the effect of liberating students from political bias or ethnocentric dogmatism and thereby enable them to function better as citizens of the world.

In selecting the content to be dealt with in this introductory textbook, I was very cognizant that not all important subjects and thinkers could be covered. Not only does the writing of a book impose its own time and space limitations, but twelve- to sixteen-week college semesters determine how much materi-

al can be meaningfully covered by anyone using any book. Courses designed to be massive "information-dumps" and little else have proven to be pedagogically suspect. It seemed to me, then, that the objective in textbook writing should not be to present absolutely everything but to select topics and to develop skills that will prepare students for real-life philosophical reflection and for further studies in the field of philosophy. It is my firm belief that *Experiencing Philosophy* does this and that it does it in a way that is student-centered, both interesting and useful for neophyte philosophers. I wish you well in your teaching endeavors and hope that this book enriches your professional experience in the classroom or lecture hall. It constitutes a labor of love to be offered to all those who truly enjoy sharing philosophy with others!

# FEATURES

## TAKE IT PERSONALLY

To illustrate how philosophy can be useful and relevant to the individual, each chapter of *Experiencing Philosophy* begins by placing the material to be covered in a personal context. Students are shown how philosophical questions and concerns are often built into their daily life experiences. Grounding philosophical inquiry in the context of real life serves to motivate students and thereby helps instructors to teach more effectively.

## KNOW THYSELF DIAGNOSTICS

This book takes seriously, as did Socrates, the Delphic Oracle's dictum to "*Know thyself.*" To this end, students are provided self-diagnostics in each of the chapters to explore further their own philosophical values, ideals, and beliefs pertaining to truth, reality, ethics, the existence of God, the nature of knowledge, metaphysics, and the best system of political organization. By means of these diagnostics, students are given a chance to identify their underlying personal philosophies of life and to compare them with other worldviews that have been articulated over the centuries. Students are also able to assess their current logical thinking abilities so that they can establish how much work they will need to do in order to think rationally like philosophers.

## PHILOSOPHICAL PROFILES

The student-centeredness of *Experiencing Philosophy* is evidenced again by putting names and faces with the ideas covered in the book. Pictures of influential and historically important philosophers are presented along with biographical information. Abstract ideas contained within the book are tied to real people with interesting real-life personal histories. This helps to bring the textbook material alive.

## PHILOSOPHERS IN ACTION

Philosophy is often described as more of a method of thinking than as a body of knowledge. From this perspective, philosophy is something you "do," not something you know. With this in mind, students are given many opportunities to practice doing philosophy. Students using this text are frequently asked to think critically and analytically in response to questions posed in the *Philosophers in Action* feature. These questions require them to conduct thought experiments, analyze concepts, as well as to discuss and debate controversial points.

## MEDITATIVE MOMENTS

Students are encouraged to keep a journal to record their thoughts in response to questions raised in the *Meditative Moment* features found in each of the chapters. By answering these questions, students learn to appreciate not only the intrinsic value of intellectual inquiry, but also the instrumental worth of philosophy when it comes to dealing with their own existential predicaments—especially where matters of character, happiness, conflict, meaning, and peace of mind are concerned. The kinds of self-reflections encouraged by the *Meditative Moment* features serve to promote self-knowledge and, in part, a personal wellness function contributing to individual psycho-hygiene.

## QUOTATIONS

Inspirational and thought-provoking quotations are sprinkled throughout the text as a way of generating interest. They may be taken to heart by some readers or remembered for purposes of finding personal meaning and direction in life. At other times, the quotations may be useful to capture the essence of points that are made in a much more detailed way in the main text. These "philosophical zingers," as one might call them, will certainly give us all pause for thought.

## SHOWCASE BOXES

Various figures are presented in *Showcase Boxes* throughout the text as a way of illustrating and underscoring important points. These boxes can also add relevance sometimes by relating philosophical theory to real-world experiences and current events. Tables, figures, and charts are especially helpful to visual learners.

## PHILOSOPHICAL SEGUES

At several places in the text, digressions called Philosophical Segues are introduced. One deals with *Fate, Free Will, and Determinism*, another with *Proofs for the Existence of God*, and a third with *Religion and Ethics*. These segues address topics relevant to the chapters in which they are found, but in an abbreviated fashion. Given the length restrictions imposed by any introductory text, not all thinkers and topics can be fully covered. The segue features enable one to touch on important subjects, without devoting entire chapters to them. Contributing to the teachability of the text, the segues may themselves provide convenient detours for instructors wishing to digress from the main text from time to time in order to pursue topics of personal interest at greater length.

## BUILT-IN STUDENT STUDY GUIDE

*Experiencing Philosophy* is designed to maximize the chances for student success. Before students can properly analyze, discuss, and debate subtle and esoteric philosophical points, they must first master the basic vocabulary and be able to grasp the fundamental concepts. The built-in study guide is designed to help them do this. By enabling students to gain knowledge and an understanding of the fundamental ideas contained within any one chapter, they are then better prepared to "do" philosophy when it comes to conceptual analysis, theoretical application, or critical normative evaluation. To learn more about how to use the study guide, read my "Message to Students." Listed below are the elements comprising this valuable learning tool.

Chapter Overview
Learning Outcomes
Focus Questions
Boldfaced Key Terms
List of Key Terms
Chapter-End Progress Check
Summary of Major Points
Source References

Philosophy in Cyberspace
Endnotes

## INCLUSIVENESS AND RESPECT FOR DIVERSITY

Though this book focuses on the Western rational tradition in philosophy, clearly other perspectives exist. Philosophy finds a home in Eastern, Middle Eastern, African, Latin American, and Native North American cultures as well, and in a way that doesn't always give priority to rationality and discursive thought. Comparative distinctions are made at the outset of this text between the reasoned approach of the Western rational tradition and the more non-rational, ritualistic, meditative, and symbolically laden approaches we find in other ethno-cultural world-views. So that students are not mistakenly led to believe that all of philosophical inquiry has been conducted exclusively by "dead white males," philosophical profiles of modern and contemporary female philosophers like Ayn Rand, Martha Nussbaum, and Julia Annas are also included. So too are descriptive outlines and profiles of thinkers like Siddhartha Gautama (The Buddha). Students thereby learn that not all philosophers are necessarily Caucasian and of European descent. By featuring people of different backgrounds, genders, and ethno-cultural origins, *Experiencing Philosophy* makes honest and sincere efforts to be inclusive and to respect diversity in a way that does not misrepresent the rich tradition of western philosophy.

## ORIGINAL SOURCEWORKS ACCOMPANIED BY DISCUSSION QUESTIONS FOR CRITIQUE AND ANALYSIS

*Experiencing Philosophy* seeks to balance accessibility and relevance with academic rigor. While introducing some beginning students to philosophy entirely by means of original source readings might be regarded as inappropriate for a variety of reasons, doing so without any exposure at all to the primary works of the philosophers could be seen as equally misguided. To say that one has completed an introductory course in philosophy but has not read any philosophy in the original seems wrong somehow. In efforts to strike an appropriate balance for beginning students, the bulk of this text will be comprised of theoretically sound descriptive outlines of philosophers and their theories. In addition, however, numerous original source-works—usually shorter excerpts from them—will be included as well, to give users of the book exposure to the "real thing." Discussion Questions for Critique and Analysis accompany each reading. These questions afford students the opportunity to "do" more philosophy and to practice their logical/critical/analytical thinking skills.

## ANCILLARIES

### INSTRUCTOR'S MANUAL WITH TEST-ITEM FILE

*Experiencing Philosophy* comes with an instructor's manual to facilitate teaching and evaluation. The manual includes overhead-masters for each of the chapters. These masters provide a convenient backdrop for formal lectures and serve as a useful talking-point guide. In the manual, you will also find more activities and exercises designed to promote critical and analytical thinking skills on the part of students. You will also discover test questions in a variety of formats that you can include in your evaluation scheme.

### COMPUTERIZED TEST ITEM FILE

A computerized version of the test-item file is also available for both MacIntosh and PC systems. Test questions can easily be composed and selected allowing for multiple versions of the same test to be made.

## COMPANION WEBSITE

Prentice Hall's exclusive *Companion Website* (TM) offers unique tools and support that make it easy for students and instructors to integrate this online study guide with the text. The site is a comprehensive resource that is organized according to the chapters within the text and features a variety of learning and teaching modules:

## FOR STUDENTS:

Study Guide Modules contain multiple choice and true/false quizzes, and other features designed to help students with self-study.

Reference Modules contain *Web Destinations* and *Net Search* options that provide the opportunity to quickly reach information on the Web that relates to the content in the text.

Communication Modules include tools such as *Life Chat* and *Message Board* to facilitate online collaboration and communication.

Personalization Modules include our enhanced *Help* feature that contains a text page for browsers and plug-ins.

## FOR INSTRUCTORS:

The Syllabus Manager(TM) tool provides an easy-to-follow process for creating, posting, and revising a syllabus online that is accessible from any point within the companion website.

The *Companion Website* makes integrating the internet into your course exciting and easy. Join us online and enter a new world of teaching and learning.

# MESSAGE TO STUDENTS

*Experiencing Philosophy* is a textbook written with you, the student, in mind. It contains a built-in Study Guide designed to promote success by helping you to gain knowledge and understanding of the basic concepts covered in the book. This guide incorporates the SQ3R system of learning. SQ3R is an acronym for *Survey, Question, Read, Recite, and Review*. Included below are the steps you should follow when using the system.

## STEP ONE: *SURVEY*

Each chapter of the book begins with an *Overview* and list of *Learning Outcomes*. Survey these things to find out what is included in the chapter and what you will be expected to know and do upon successful completion of it. Think of outcomes as objectives or aims to be achieved. Your study of the chapter is not really done until you show mastery of all the outcomes listed up front in any particular chapter.

## STEP TWO: *QUESTION*

Every chapter of *Experiencing Philosophy* contains *Focus Questions*. As you might guess, they are intended to focus your attention while you read. Knowing what to look for helps you to be selective and to separate what needs to be known from what is nice to know or what is relatively insignificant.

## STEP THREE: *READ*

Once you know what to look for and what you are supposed to accomplish by your study of the chapter, you can then begin reading. Note that reading philosophy is not like reading the newspaper or a popular paperback novel. Philosophy contains a lot of technical vocabulary and terms with which you may not be familiar. It is advised that you read each section slowly, repeatedly, and with a philosophical dictionary nearby. You may find it helpful to highlight important sections of the text with a marker or pen. Do not be discouraged if a first reading leaves you bewildered sometimes. Philosophy requires you to pay attention to difficult matters and think in a way that is not always encouraged by popular culture or mainstream society. While reading, take notice of the **boldfaced** terms. They indicate that an especially important concept or idea is being addressed. Follow-up of many points is made possible by the inclusion of *Endnotes*, in which expanded clarifications may be given and original sources identified.

## STEP FOUR: *RECITE AND REVIEW*

After completing your reading, begin the review and recitation process. Look over the list of *Key Terms* and make sure you can define each one. You may wish to go back to the sections of the chapter you highlighted and make notes from them by paraphrasing what was written in a language that you can remember and understand. Chapter headings and subtitles can serve as organizational guides for note-taking. As part of the recitation and review process, you should also refer to the *Summary of Key Points*. Captured in each of the chapter summaries is the essential content to be grasped. Once you have studied your notes in light of the summaries provided, you can then go back to review the list of learning outcomes at the beginning of the chapter. Do you know what you should know, and can you do what you should be able to do? Completion of the *Progress Check* at the end of each chapter can help to verify your conclusions. Check your answers to the Progress Checks using the Appendix at the end of the book. If you are still unclear, then you can do outside research referring to the *Source References* given for each chapter. You can also surf the Web. Helpful sites pertaining to each chapter are listed at the end of each chapter in *Philosophy in Cyberspace*. In the event your outside readings and web site explorations do not answer your questions and concerns, raise them with other students, with the instructor of your course, or with your tutorial leader.

Note that mastery of more advanced philosophical reasoning will require you to practice logical/

analytical thinking skills covered in Chapter 3 and addressed in several of the pedagogical features included in the book, e.g., *Philosophers in Action, Meditative Moments*, and *Discussion Questions for Critique and Analysis*. This last feature accompanies each of the original philosophical sourceworks presented in the text.

In conclusion, allow me to suggest that success in the study of philosophy is going to require a lot of hard work and active involvement on your part. Quick or cursory reading and mere passive listening during lectures is not likely to be enough to ensure that you achieve at optimum levels. The SQ3R learning method integrated into this text requires you to interact with the material that is presented. It prepares the way for higher-order philosophical inquiry and critical/analytical discussion by facilitating a mastery of basic knowledge and understanding. While this method of learning cannot guarantee success, it can pave the way for the first step toward it. Good Luck!

# ACKNOWLEDGMENTS

Publishing a book is no easy task. It requires an enormous amount of work, not to mention the long-term commitment and cooperation of an entire professional team. I'd like to begin by thanking Ross Miller, the Philosophy and Religion Acquisitions Editor at Prentice Hall/Pearson Education. Ross placed enormous trust in my vision for this book and, in effect, served as the developmental editor when the need arose. He did an admirable job. Carla Worner, Ross's assistant, also made the whole process more enjoyable and efficient by her frequent e-mail communications with me. I feel we've become "cyber-friends" over the past couple of years. Thanks go to Wendy Yurash, assistant editor, as well. She looked after arrangements for the Instructor's Manual that philosophy instructors will no doubt find very handy. Thanks go to Mary Araneo as well. Over a period of many months, she worked very closely with me in the development and production of this book. Serena Hoffman, the copy editor for the book, taught me humility without knowing it perhaps. She made it abundantly clear by her revisions that even after lengthy university study, I still haven't mastered the placement of the comma! Serena was able to masterfully make editorial changes without sterilizing the manuscript of its style and intent—for this I am grateful. I also appreciate the creative design that Laura Gardner brought to this project. She did a great job making *Experiencing Philosophy* a visually inviting experience. Further, numerous reviewers were kind enough to read preliminary drafts of the book and provide their critical feedback. Of course, it goes without saying that they are not to be held responsible for any deficiencies that may still remain. Thanks go to Gary Kessler, California State University, Bakersfield; Isabel Luengo, MiraCosta College; Roger P. Ebertz, University of Dubuque; Jennifer McErlean, Siena College; Timothy Davis, Community College of Baltimore County, Essex; John Beversluis, Butler University; Patricia Guinan, Truman State University; Sherry Blum, Austin community College; and John Laughlin, Averette College.

I would be remiss if I did not thank my friends and colleagues at Sheridan College who always showed interest in my progress and support for this project, especially Paul Angelini and Mikal Radford, both dedicated teachers of philosophy. And finally, I wish to acknowledge the contributions that many hundreds of my students have made indirectly in helping me to shape the presentation of ideas contained in this book. Their searching curiosity and youthful enthusiasm provided me with motivational fuel for this project. My sincerest thanks to all.

# EXPERIENCING PHILOSOPHY

CHAPTER

# WHAT IS PHILOSOPHY?
# WHAT'S IN IT FOR ME?

# CHAPTER OVERVIEW

**Take It Personally**

KNOW THYSELF
My Preconceptions about Philosophy

**Philosophy and Philosophers: Caricatures, Myths, and Realities**

**The Philosopher's Profile**

**Wisdom: The Object of Love**

**The Practical Value of Philosophy**

**Therapeutic Applications of Philosophy: Back to the Future**

**Philosophy's Relevance in an Age of Information and Emerging Technologies**

**Fields of Philosophy**
  Metaphysics
  Epistemology
  Logic
  Ethics
  Axiology
  Social/Political Philosophy
  Foundational and Disciplinary Philosophies
  Philosophies of Life

**Approaches to Philosophy**
  Masculine versus Feminine Approaches
  World Philosophies: Eastern, Western, and Ethno-racial
  Rational versus Nonrational Philosophy

**Historical Periods of Philosophy**

PHILOSOPHICAL PROFILE
**BERTRAND RUSSELL**

ORIGINAL SOURCEWORK:
Bertrand Russell, *The Problems of Philosophy*

**STUDY GUIDE**
Key Terms ■ Progress Check
Summary of Major Points
Sources References ■ Philosophy in Cyberspace
Endnotes

# LEARNING OUTCOMES

*After successfully completing this chapter, you will be able to:*

Describe various caricatures associated with philosophers

Provide a general profile of the Western rational philosopher

Define wisdom

Explain the practical value of philosophy

Point to the therapeutic applications of philosophy

Show how philosophy is relevant in an information and technology age

Outline the internal boundaries of the philosophical domain

List the historical periods of philosophy

# FOCUS QUESTIONS

1. What thoughts come to mind when the subject of philosophy is raised? What images are evoked? Are they accurate and soundly based? Why or why not?

2. What do philosophers try to be like? What do they do?

3. What is meant by wisdom? What good is it?

4. What practical value could philosophy possibly have? How is it relevant for us in the twenty-first century?

5. What constitutes the discipline of philosophy? What are its subdisciplines?

# TAKE IT PERSONALLY

As someone who has already experienced the joys of philosophy for many years, I'm excited anticipating what is in store for you as we embark together on our travels into the philosophical domain. This journey into the realm of philosophy promises to be one of the most rewarding explorations you will ever undertake. Although the philosophical landscape can sometimes be slippery and tortuous, previous climbs to the tops of metaphysical mountain peaks reveal breathtaking horizons stretching across alternative realities and differing conceptions of the universe. Our philosophical quest will be no trivial pursuit, but one of significant import. In fact, philosophy may turn out to be *the* most relevant, practical, and important course you will ever take in your lifetime! The questions and issues raised in this book will not disappear with fad and fashion. They will not become dated or obsolete like last year's computer software. The philosopher's tune is not like the rock musician's "one hit wonder." Philosophy's soothing and sometimes haunting eternal themes have echoed for centuries and will continue to play in our minds throughout our lives—quietly in good times, but with startling bombast in situations of calamity and disappointment.

We are embarking here on a very important task, young inquisitor, one that takes us down many difficult but previously traveled roads. Proceed with caution, then, respecting the twists and turns ahead. Your safe journey to philosophical enlightenment depends upon it. St. Teresa of Avila, a Christian mystical writer, prepares us for our journey to enlightenment, or what she calls heaven, with the following words:

> Do not be frightened, [sons and] daughters, by the many things you need to consider in order to begin this divine journey which is the royal road to heaven. A great treasure is gained by traveling this road; no wonder we have to pay what seems to us a high price. The time will come when you will understand how trifling everything is next to so precious a reward.
>
> . . . to those who want to journey on this road and continue until they reach the end, which is to drink from this water of life, I say that how they are to begin is very important—in fact, all important. They must have a great and very resolute determination to persevere until reaching the end, come what may, happen what may, whatever work is involved, whatever criticism arises, whether they arrive or whether they die on the road, or even if they don't have courage for the trials that are met, or if the whole world collapses.[1]

Finding the "resolute determination to persevere" that St. Teresa talks about may not be easy, especially given the misguided preconceptions many people have regarding philosophy and those who engage in its practice. I suppose that as a philosopher, I could try to prove to you, using reason and logic alone, that philosophy does matter and that it should be important to you, whether you believe it or not. Because I have already tried this strategy—not surprisingly with something less than perfect success—I appreciate how opting for this approach is analogous to trying to get people to believe in a creator-God by simply offering them logical proofs for God's existence. Anyone with deep religious convictions probably already knows that faith goes far beyond mere rational assent. Some might even argue that a genuine belief in God requires a personal encounter with the Divine at some existential, heart-felt level, perhaps in a conversion experience. In this case, the experience of God serves as the proof.

In the same vein, let me suggest that an appreciation of the value of philosophy and its practical relevance to you will gradually unfold as we proceed through this text. I'll let your experience of philosophy be the judge of its ultimate worth, asking only that you not make up your mind in advance before sampling the many tasty philosophical delicacies that will be offered to you for your intellectual consumption along the way. The proof that philosophy is worthwhile will be in the philosophical food for thought you'll be invited to sample. I'm confident that you'll enjoy philosophy, for so much of it relates directly to your experience of everyday life.

To illustrate this point, let me ask whether you have ever wondered what you should do with your life or what sort of person you should strive to become? If so, then you may find some helpful direction in Chapter 2, where we cover different philosophies of life. You may also find guidance in Chapter 5, dealing with ethics, where character and virtue are discussed. Further, do people who dress like clones and act like sheep bother you for some unknown reason? You might find some deep insights on this matter in sections of the book dealing with Marxist alienation and Nietzsche's slave morality. How about your annoyance when it comes to all the fighting you witness on television talk shows? Is it bothersome that people just seem to be screaming their opinions at each other without really listening and without actually putting forward any reasoned thought in a legitimate debate? Well then, have a look at Chapter 3, where you learn to distinguish between unfounded opinions and valid arguments. You needn't be one of the screaming opinionators. Learn how to put your own proper arguments together, displaying, if not the wisdom of Socrates, then at least his humility!

And what about an afterlife? Is this all there is, or is there another reality beyond the material realm of sensory experience? Check out Plato in the metaphysics chapter, for example, to discover what he says about the spaceless, timeless realm of forms. Further, does God exist? How can you know for sure? Read about St. Anselm and St. Thomas Aquinas, who provide proofs that there is indeed a God. You might also wish to consider those proofs in light of what atheistic philosophers say. Maybe religion is just an "opium of the people," as Karl Marx charges, or perhaps God is nothing more than a psychological invention of fearful and neurotic individuals? You'll get the opportunity to think about such things later in the text.

Finally, are you completely convinced that American capitalism is unconditionally good, or that economic globalization should be encouraged? Are there moral consequences at stake? Is it possible that human rights are being violated? If so, then what constitutes a violation of rights? What is justice? What is the individual's proper relation to the state? You can read more about rights and justice in the final chapter on political philosophy to find out. In the process, you can become a more informed, rational citizen. The point, as I hope you can plainly see by the questions just raised, is that philosophical concerns are an inextricable part of life. You can make vain efforts to ignore them in your daily living, but in the end they cannot be escaped. It's highly unfortunate, therefore, that so much confusion surrounds the nature and purpose of philosophy. If we properly understand philosophy and use it to our advantage, much in life could be improved.

Before we proceed any further, I invite you to complete the *Know Thyself* diagnostic that follows. It will enable you to get a preliminary indication of how

 **KNOW THYSELF**

## My Preconceptions about Philosophy

**AIM** The purpose of this self-diagnostic is to help you develop an awareness of your preconceptions about philosophy. Just as attitudes like anger or suspicion can interfere with productive dialogues, so too can uncritically accepted misunderstanding of philosophy interfere with proper learning and application. In order to be fully open to the experience of philosophy, any prejudgments about it should first be exposed and then critically examined.

**INSTRUCTIONS** Below are ten statements pertaining to philosophy. Indicate which are true (T) and which are false (F). When you have completed this task, follow the scoring instructions.

T    F    1. The vast majority of philosophers today are hermits and monks, either living in monasteries, caves, deserts, or mountainside retreats.

T    F    2. If you are a philosopher, you must be an atheist, since reason necessarily contradicts faith.

T    F    3. Philosophy is essentially useless and outdated, serving no practical purpose.

T    F    4. Most philosophers are either unemployed or else they drive taxicabs.

T    F    5. Women are precluded from becoming philosophers today because, historically, there has been so much discrimination against women in the field.

T    F    6. In order to be a philosopher, you must have a beard, smoke a pipe, and wear elbow patches on your jacket.

T    F    7. Philosophers are rarely grounded in reality, usually living impractical lives with their heads in the clouds.

T    F    8. Philosophers are a dysfunctional bunch because they are hyper-critical and like to argue about everything.

T    F    9. Philosophers are always wise individuals.

T    F    10. Practically speaking, the study of philosophy will get you nowhere.

## SCORING AND INTERPRETATION

All of the preceding statements about philosophy and philosophers are *false*. To the extent you agreed with any of them, you may have fallen prey to some popular, uncritically held misconceptions of what philosophers do and what philosophy is all about. Not to fear, however, for the rest of this chapter will dispel any of your misguided preconceptions and help you to gain a clearer, more accurate understanding of philosophical inquiry.

accurate or inaccurate your current understanding of philosophy is. In case you have developed any distorted views, the sections that follow the self-diagnostic should help to clarify the true nature and purpose of philosophy, its history, sub-disciplines, and approaches, as well as its personal and practical relevance. Let the experience of philosophy begin!

## PHILOSOPHY AND PHILOSOPHERS: CARICATURES, MYTHS, AND REALITIES

For first-time travelers into the philosophical domain, directions can be found by turning to the wisdom of the philosophical immortals, those whose ideas have stood the test of time and whose rational reflections have changed our conceptions of reality, human nature, truth, beauty, and the Good. Don't be discouraged by the anti-intellectual crowd or by defensive individuals fearful of embarking on the philosophical journey. They have opted for ignorance over illumination and have tended to trivialize the pursuit of wisdom by stereotyping and caricaturing those most actively engaged in it. These caricatures and stereotypes portraying the philosopher's weird "irrelevance" are often amusingly perpetuated in popular culture by cartoonists, comedians, and Hollywood movie makers. For instance, the term *philosopher* has come to evoke, in many minds, the stereotypic image of a bearded old man, a detached hermit who wanders the desert wilderness or dwells in a mountainside cave. Perhaps the term *philosopher* conjures up a mental picture of someone who works in an ivory tower, occupying a comfortable wingback chair in an oak-walled den or library. Of course, pipe in mouth and book in hand are mandatory, along with a distant pensive gaze. Still another image may be that of a sandaled and toga-clad ancient Greek making a nuisance of himself by asking unquestioned authorities unanswerable questions.

In spite of such stereotypes and caricatures, you can rest assured, as a beginning student in philosophy, that philosophers are not necessarily male, aging, toga-clad, or bearded. They may also be young, female, stylishly dressed, and smooth skinned. Their dwelling place is probably not a cave or desert, but a neighborhood apartment or house. Although lots of philosophers do, in fact, make a living today teaching at colleges and universities (sometimes referred to as the "ivory tower"), other "closet philosophers" have been known to discuss philosophical issues at such unlikely places as pubs, parties, and family gatherings. In short, philosopher types are unpredictable. They are varied in appearance and may show up almost anywhere. For all you know, the student sitting next to you in class may, in fact, be a closet philosopher ready to come out at the first invitation. Don't let the trendy clothes, pierced body parts, and youthful appearance deceive you. So, to all of you closet philosophers, I extend your long-awaited invitation to step out of the darkness and into the light so that we may embark on the philosophical quest. Let's all join together in our efforts as we face the amazing adventure that awaits us!

*"The unemployment line isn't as happy as it used to be. It's no longer just for philosophy majors. Now even useful people are unemployed."*
"THE SIMPSONS"

# THE PHILOSOPHER'S PROFILE

If it's erroneous to see philosophers as hermits, cave dwellers, or toga-clad renegades, then we're still left wondering who or what a philosopher is. Throughout this book, we will examine a variety of different philosophies, and I will introduce you to different paradigmatic philosophers who support them. Until then, however, let me give you a rough sketch of the Western philosopher's characterological profile.

Our first clue about the philosopher's identity comes from the origins of the word **philosophy** itself. Etymologically, *philosophy* derives from the Greek words *philos,* meaning love, and *sophia,* meaning the exercise of one's intelligence in practical affairs. However, as John Passmore explains, most English-speaking philosophers have chosen to translate *sophia* more narrowly as wisdom.[2] Consequently, we often speak of philosophy as the love of wisdom and philosophers as **lovers of wisdom;** so, by definition, that is what they are. But having said this, we still don't know what the typical philosopher is like as a person or what the ideal philosopher should be like.

Recognizing that philosophers are not clones of one another and that they express a variety of styles and orientations, permit me, nonetheless, at the risk of making my own gross generalizations, to describe them in the following fashion. I believe most philosophers, at least in the **Western rational tradition,** would accept my depiction of them.[3] To begin with, professionally trained philosophers aspire to be **reasonable** individuals. In fact, reason is the primary tool used in conducting their work. It is their *modus operandi.* I'm not suggesting that all philosophers can be described as rationalists or that reason is necessarily given primacy of place for all of them, only that philosophers tend to take a rational approach to life and human inquiry. By using this rational approach, they seek to make sense of themselves, others, and the world. Through use of reason, philosophers aim to arrive at clear understandings of things by reducing vagueness and ambiguity as much as possible. If philosophers didn't, or couldn't, make sense to each other—that is, if their use of language were so imprecise and their reasoning so scatological that nobody could figure out what they were saying—then philosophical discourse would be impossible. Even "nonrational" existentialist philosophers (see Chapter 2) and feminist critics of rational morality (see Chapter 5) must still use language and rational thought to express their objections to the supremacy of pure rationality. Paradoxically, then, reason must be used to criticize its own applications.

The remarks just made point to the critical function of philosophers. Philosophers, as a group, tend to be **critically minded.** They choose to adopt a **questioning attitude** toward most things, accepting little on authority or blind faith. Philosophers are a **curious** bunch who frequently ask, "Why?" demanding **rational justifications** for the positions people take on issues and for the actions they perform. The ancient philosopher Socrates asked many questions and was often considered a gadfly, irritating everybody he met with his inquiries. Although most philosophers are not as irritating as Socrates was for unthinking people, they do bug us sometimes, due to a kind of positive addiction manifested as an unquenchable thirst for knowledge and understanding. Their questions just never seem to end. Don't get me wrong; the critical mindedness of philosophers is not intended to be unproductively confrontational or dangerously subversive, but rather to reflect caution and a desire for clarity and precision in thought. Unlike some disturbed people who are opposed to, and critical of, most things simply for the sake of opposition, philosophers are critical with a legitimate purpose. They do not want unfounded assumptions to go unchallenged. They do not want unsubstantiated or unverified factual claims to pass notice; nor do they wish illogical conclusions to follow from invalid reasoning. Philosophers are not only lovers of wisdom but **seekers of truth.** They are awed by life and everything it entails.

As seekers of truth, philosophers make efforts to be **open-minded.** They are prepared to entertain propositions which, at first glance, may seem disturbing, counter-intuitive, or wrong (for example, God is dead.). Philosophers also raise basic questions about reality, truth, beauty, and goodness. Is the material world all there is? Does beauty exist in things themselves, or does it exist only in the eye of the beholder? Are morality and knowledge merely matters of opinion or things the truth of which can be objectively determined? Philosophers are willing to inquire into what many of us might accept unreflectively as self-evident truths. For instance, you might loudly declare your firm conviction in a classroom debate that all human beings are created equal. But how do you know this for sure? Were human beings, in fact, created by a supreme being who bestowed equality upon them, or have they evolved according to evolutionary laws of nature? If, as equals, we all have the same rights, then what is a right? Do we share all rights or only basic rights? What then is a basic right? Which rights do we not share? Do some of us have rights that others don't? Can rights be taken away once they are given to us? Are rights earned, or are they somehow inherent in our being? How big or broad is a right? Is it ever justifiable to violate somebody's rights? Why? As you can tell from this line of questioning, philosophers don't take things for granted just because they make us feel good, because the majority holds a particular point of view, or because common sense dictates their existence. Philosophers are like intellectual miners, digging deeply beneath the surface of life to find diamonds of truth that must be polished by the friction of argument and analysis before they can radiate their true brilliance.

A number of attitude adjustments necessary to conduct proper philosophical argument and debate are discussed in a later chapter on logic and philosophical method, but for now, suffice it to say that philosophers like to probe, analyze, reflect, consider alternatives, question authority, display healthy scepticism and doubt, while remaining objective, impartial, respectful of others, and cognizant of differing and divergent points of view. Certainly, the ideal Western rational philosopher can be described as detached and unbiased, someone who suspends judgment before all the philosophical facts are in. As we travel along on our philosophical journey, you will get to know many different philosophers, as well as their ideas and methods, a little better, and you should begin to develop an appreciation of philosophers that is more elaborate than the thumb-nail sketch I have provided you here.

# WISDOM: THE OBJECT OF LOVE

Now that you have some idea of what philosophers are like, we can turn to **wisdom,** the object of their affection. In *The Encyclopedia of Philosophy,* Brand Blanshard defines wisdom in the following way:

> Wisdom in its broadest and commonest sense denotes sound and serene judgment regarding the conduct of life. It may be accompanied by a broad range of knowledge, by intellectual acuteness and by speculative depth, but it is not to be identified with any of these and may appear in their absence. It involves intellectual grasp or insight, but it is concerned not so much with the ascertainment of fact or the elaboration of theories as with the means and ends of practical life.[4]

Blanshard's conception of wisdom reminds us again of philosophy's usefulness. Wisdom concerns the practical conduct of life—how we choose to live our lives on an everyday basis. Wisdom requires that we exercise good judgment when making choices and important life decisions. As Blanshard explains, wisdom can be accompanied by **knowledge** and **intelligence,** but not necessarily so. Having a high IQ doesn't necessarily make you wise. You could be a clever crook who uses your "smarts" to cheat other people out of what is rightfully theirs. You could also use those same smarts in imprudent ways or as an evil genius. Ted Kaczynski, the infamous Unabomber, who spent nearly two decades mailing bombs to innocent people in the United States, was described by many as brilliant, yet despite his obvious intelligence as a Harvard graduate, he displayed demonically bad judgment and made many wrong choices. Clearly, the lesson we learn from Kaczynski is that being smart doesn't necessarily make you wise. Needless to say, perhaps, is that intelligent people are not necessarily excluded from wisdom. Intelligent people can indeed be wise as well, even if Kaczynski wasn't.

Blanchard also distinguishes between wisdom and knowledge. He understands that knowing a lot doesn't necessarily make you wise either. You may have extensive knowledge of theoretical physics or a photographic memory, for example, and be able to recall so much information that you become a walking encyclopedia, yet this still wouldn't be a confirmation of wisdom. You could memorize the great ideas of all the important philosophers throughout history and ace all of your philosophy exams and still be a fool. Wisdom would be reflected by your ability to put that knowledge and all those ideas to practical use.

Having distinguished wisdom from knowledge and intelligence, perhaps we should note that wisdom is often connected to **experience,** although again, not necessarily so. As previously suggested, wisdom goes beyond mere book learning and intellectual activity. It is associated with maturity, life experience, and the virtue of putting into practice what is truly valuable. Of course, experience guarantees nothing. Some young people are "wise beyond their years," while others are remarkably foolish, given their age. Experience is a great teacher, but unfortunately, not every student of life learns the lessons it has to teach.

Wisdom has an all-encompassing feature; people displaying wisdom seem to have a **sense of perspective.** They are somehow able to find unity in separate

*The point has been made that perennial wisdom crops up again and again in different cultures and during different epochs. What, if any, wisdom do you know of that has been captured by writers, philosophers, religious thinkers, poets, political theorists, historians, psychologists, social analysts, and/or by your own experience? What is it about this wisdom that you find particularly useful? Why? What difference has this wisdom made in your personal life? Write down your thoughts in a personal journal. You're invited to do so for all other meditations in this book.*

and seemingly disconnected things. Hence, wise people tend not to live compartmentalized, fragmented lives. They present solid priorities, which somehow rationally cohere into a distinguishable worldview or **integrated mode of existence.** As a result, wise people's lives are far less subject to whim and fancy. They are not like leaves tossed about by the winds of life, since at a deep level, they are solidly rooted, cognizant of their purpose and mission in the world. However, wise people are not always happy and effervescent souls, as life can sometimes be unkind, but you will probably notice a joyful serenity in the demeanor of those people you would describe as wise.

Finally, a study of intellectual history reveals a **perennial wisdom** that crops up again and again in different cultures and at different epochs. We call this the "wisdom of the ages." This wisdom takes on different expressions depending on time and place, but it often reflects remarkably similar insightful truths. As we proceed in this text, you'll come across some of this perennial wisdom as embedded in different philosophies of life and as expressed by various philosophers in their theories and philosophical outlooks. Personally, I have enjoyed contemplating such things, as they give occasion for fruitful thought and self-reflection. They also disturb and challenge us, waking us from our dogmatic slumbers. I suppose that's the value of wisdom—it awakens us to new visions of reality and to fresh perceptions of life.

## THE PRACTICAL VALUE OF PHILOSOPHY

In view of the preceding discussion of wisdom's usefulness, please allow me to question one widely accepted commonsense notion—namely, that philosophy has little or no practical value. Tell people you're studying philosophy or, heaven forbid, majoring in it, and you'll often be asked, "Why study that?" or "What's that going to get you?" The underlying assumption would seem to be that "only those subjects that will get you a job or help you to earn more money are worth pursuing." Whether this assumption is acceptable merits some serious philosophical examination. In fact, aren't critics of philosophy simply burying their own viewpoint in the unstated, but presupposed, claim that, "only job-related pursuits have worth?" Isn't this a value judgment that needs to be rationally justified? Aren't anti-philosophers actually guilty of engaging in the activity they condemn? Aren't they really making a philosophical claim of their own while enjoying the luxury of not having to defend it? I think so.

The point is that philosophy is so central to life that it cannot be ignored, circumvented, or escaped. Even rejections of philosophy are themselves philosophical in nature. When Edie Brickell, the rock star, tells you in one of her songs that philosophy is little more than "talk on a cereal box" and that she would rather be "shoved in the shallow water, before she gets too deep," doesn't her creative but cavalier dismissal of profound and serious philosophical thought require reasons? Isn't Edie advocating a shallow lifestyle that is open to question? Again, I think so. Could it be possible that Edie is one of our closet philosopher types who hasn't come to acknowledge and accept her own philosophical orientation? Maybe. In any event, if you really need a job-related reason to justify your philosophical pursuits, turn now to a newspaper feature written by Thomas Hurka, a Canadian philosophy professor who provides the "cash value" some of you might insist on.

## HOW TO GET TO THE TOP—STUDY PHILOSOPHY

THOMAS HURKA

How should Canada or the United States educate students to compete successfully in the business world. Some provincial governments think it is by teaching them business.

The Alberta government has announced plans for an "unprecedented" expansion of business education at its three universities. Already, 120 extra students are studying management at the University of Calgary.

Recent evidence suggests this approach is mistaken. We will produce better managers if we educate them first in traditional subjects in the arts and sciences. We may do best of all if we educate them in philosophy.

Each year, thousands of undergraduates write admissions tests for the prestigious graduate programs. There's the Law School Admissions Test (LSAT), the Graduate Management Admission Test (GMAT) for business study, and the Graduate Record Examination (GRE) for other fields. A 1985 study for the U.S. Department of Education compared tests of students from different disciplines, with surprising results.

Consider the GMAT, used for admission to MBA programs [Masters of Business Administration] and, ultimately, to the highest levels of management. Undergraduate business students, whom you would think would be especially well prepared for this test, do badly on it, scoring below average for all test takers. The best results are by math students, followed by philosophy students and engineers.

This is typical. Business students score below average on almost all the tests, as do, excepting engineers, all other students in applied or occupational fields. The best results come from students in the natural sciences and humanities. The study concludes that, on tests measuring aptitude for advanced professional study, "undergraduates who major in professional and occupational fields consistently underperform those who major in traditional arts and science fields."

The most consistent performers are philosophy students. They are first out of 28 disciplines on one test, second on another, and third on a third. On their weakest test they are still 4.6 percent above the average, the best performance on a weakest test of any group.

Although data here are less consistent, the superior performance of arts and science students continues after university. According to a book by sociologist Michael Useem, they have more difficulty finding beginning managerial jobs than those with business or professional degrees because they lack specific skills in finance or engineering. When they are hired, it is usually lower in the company hierarchy. Once hired, however, they advance more rapidly than their colleagues.

On average, arts and science graduates end their careers level with business and engineering graduates, having closed the gap. In some companies with less of an engineering or MBA "culture," they pass them. An AT&T study showed that, after 20 years with the company, 43 percent of liberal arts graduates had reached upper-middle management compared with 32 percent of business majors and 23 percent of engineers. The Chase Manhattan Bank found that 60 percent of its worst managers had MBAs, while 60 percent of its best managers had BAs. At IBM, nine of the company's top 13 executives had liberal arts degrees.

What explains the success of arts and science students? Many arguments for liberal education cite a contemporary cliché—that we live in a time of unprecedented change. If the world is in flux, an applied education will soon be out of date. Better the breadth and flexibility given by general studies.

A better explanation points to what cannot change: the basic elements of reasoning and problem-solving. The study of admissions tests found that students do best "who major in a field characterized by formal thought, structural relationships, abstract models, symbolic languages, and deductive reasoning." The more abstract a subject, the more it develops pure reasoning skills; and the stronger a person's reasoning skills, the better he or she will do in any applied field.

This fits the data from business. Corporations report that, though technical skills are most important in low-level managerial jobs, they become less so in middle and top jobs, where the key traits include communications skills, the ability to formulate problems, and reasoning. Liberal arts education may be weak in the pre-requisites for beginning managerial jobs, but provides just what's needed for success at the top.

This doesn't mean there's no place for business education. Canadian industry needs specialized business skills, and our universities should supply them. But in the increasingly competitive world economy there will be a premium on vision, creativity and analytical power, traits better fostered by liberal education.

This points to the recommendation now heard most from chief executive officers: first an arts and science degree in a field like English, physics, or philosophy, then an MBA. First some general intellectual skills, then the specific knowledge needed to apply them in business.

So to train successful business leaders, Canada should strengthen education in the arts and sciences. And this will have another effect. Students educated in the liberal arts will be better rounded individuals, knowing more of the natural world or the history of their culture, and better at reasoning about morality and politics. At the very least, a nice side-effect.

Used by permission from Thomas Hurka Article,
originally published in the Globe and Mail; Jan. 2, 1990, p. A8

In stark contrast to rock star, Edie, most philosophers find **intrinsic value** in the study of philosophy. The value of pursuing knowledge or wisdom *for its own sake* is not something the vast majority of philosophers need to be arm-twisted about. Indeed, for some philosophers, deliberate efforts to make philosophy practical or applied are not appreciated. I can only guess their objection to making philosophy practical is not based so much on rational objection but more on the fear that the profound and important endeavors of philosophers will be watered down or distorted to appeal to the masses who demand instant intellectual gratification, and therefore gross oversimplifications of philosophical subtleties will ensue. In the academic world, there is often tension between **pure and applied research.** The former is usually given more status than the latter. Sometimes, "applied" efforts are looked upon with derision as somehow less academic. But the pursuit of philosophy is valuable in itself, and it is also **instrumentally valuable** as a means to an end. Nicely capturing my sentiment about the value of putting philosophical theory into personal practice is the Armenian-Russian mystic George Gurdjieff, who writes: *Books are like maps, but there is also the necessity of traveling.*

The suggestion made earlier that philosophy is inescapable doesn't mean that we are somehow imprisoned by it. Indeed, the study of philosophy can be a liberating experience. As the saying goes, "The truth shall set you free." By studying philosophy, we can burst the bubble of **subjective bias** and release all of our hot air pretensions. Philosophy can help us to emerge from our socially conditioned **ethnocentrism** to see other cultures and worldviews in objective terms. How many people do you know whose lives are severely constricted by their narrow-minded or, even worse, close-minded attitudes? Some people simply refuse to know, inquire, or understand. Communicating with such people

> Theory without application feels empty.
> Application without theory is blind.
> Reason is their devoted matchmaker,
> Laboring in the temple of the mind.
>
> FALIKOWSKI

## PHILOSOPHERS IN ACTION

**AIM:** Philosophy is sometimes described as an activity, not as a body of knowledge. Let's "do" some philosophy now, even before we cover the section on philosophical reasoning in Chapter 3. Our less-than-professional efforts here will be rationalized by our enthusiasm and eagerness to start engaging in philosophical discussion.

**INSTRUCTIONS:** First, break up into pairs, or if you prefer, split the class into two groups. One individual or group will take the affirmative side, while the other individual or group will take the negative side of the proposition: "*Philosophy should be a required course for all post-secondary students.*" Each side will be given a few minutes to prepare its position. Arguments in favor of the proposition will be offered first; then arguments opposed will be presented. Subsequently, the affirmative side will be afforded an opportunity to critique the negative, and the negative side will be given last word to critique the arguments made by the positive side. Once finished, have the instructor facilitate full-class discussion, evaluating the merits of both affirmative and negative positions. Decide which arguments turned out to be better. This will require objectivity and rational detachment—virtues of the true philosopher!

is quite difficult, as you may have already discovered. Do you wish to be like them? Do you wish to be blind to reality, shielded from the truth and willfully ignorant of life? Is this freedom and the good life? Is this Edie Brickell's "shallow water" or simply some kind of defensive retreat from human existence? Philosophical questioning offers you intellectual freedom. It is your way out of the prison of darkness and your guiding light to existential liberation!

## THERAPEUTIC APPLICATIONS OF PHILOSOPHY: BACK TO THE FUTURE

Many years ago, when I began my undergraduate university studies as a psychology major, I was interested in matters of human nature, morality, emotion, mental dysfunction, and the meaning of life. It wasn't very long into my psychology program before I began studying hormones and human physiology, neural synaptic transmissions, mechanisms of perception, rats in Skinner boxes, dominance hierarchies in primates, and so on. To use a philosophical term, I felt quite **alienated** as a result. At the time, I didn't see much of a connection between the kind of insight and self-understanding I was looking for and studying reinforcement schedules used to condition rats. I'm not suggesting that scientific, experimental psychology has no value; it certainly does. Nonetheless, for me, it was unsatisfying. In retrospect, I see I was hungering for something in my life, which in the end turned out to be the fruits of philosophical inquiry. Philosophers asked the same questions I experienced as most pressing in my early adult life. As a seeker of sorts, trying to make sense of myself, others and the world around me, philosophy became the key to wisdom and understanding. My elective course in introductory philosophy opened the door to a whole new way of seeing life. After only preliminary study, I realized that a subject so important had never been taught to me before in high school, and I felt cheated. I thought everybody should study philosophy as a required course. Had the adult world conspired to hide something from me, or was it that only a few enlightened individuals had access to the sweet wisdom that philosophy clearly had to offer? I didn't know for sure. What I did know is that after the study of philosophy, I would never be the same. Philosophy was to become a exercise of self-transformation, an experience of existential rebirth and, for a lost soul like me, a way out of the woods. (By the way, after graduating in psychology, I transferred to the philosophy program.)

For centuries, philosophers have recognized the healing and therapeutic powers of philosophy. The therapy here is not so much ministered to the body, as to the mind—what the ancients sometimes referred to as "soul." Some philosophers, certainly those belonging to the **Hellenistic tradition** (Epicureans, Skeptics, and Stoics, circa 400 BCE–350 C.E.) thought of philosophy as a way of dealing with the most painful problems of human life. As Martha Nussbaum reminds us in her excellent book, *The Therapy of Desire: Theory and Practice in Hellenistic Ethics,* the Hellenistic philosophical schools in Greece and Rome:

> . . . practiced philosophy not as a detached intellectual technique dedicated to the display of cleverness, but as an immersed and worldly art of grappling with human misery. They focused their

*"Vain is the word of a philosopher which does not heal any suffering of man. For just as there is no profit in medicine if it does not expel the diseases of the body, so there is no profit in philosophy either if it does not expel the suffering of the mind. "*
EPICURUS

attention, in consequence, on issues of daily and urgent human significance—the fear of death, love and sexuality, anger and aggression—issues that are sometimes avoided as embarrassingly messy and personal by the more detached varieties of philosophy.[5]

The therapeutic dimension of Hellenistic philosophy points again to philosophy's surprising practicality in real life. The thinking of philosophers such as Epicurus and Marcus Aurelius can help people to reduce stress and anxiety, especially where things like misfortune and inappropriately expressed passions are concerned. However, just so you don't develop any misunderstandings about the therapeutic role of philosophy, and just so you don't confuse it with psychology or psychotherapy, I should quickly add at this juncture that twentieth-century philosophers, both in Europe and North America, have made relatively little use of Hellenistic philosophy, as compared to philosophers from any other Western philosophical period since the fourth century BCE.[6] Most Western philosophers in the twentieth century have approached topics like ethics in a more detached and theoretical way, trying to keep personal matters to the side. In view of this tendency, the present focus on philosophy's practical and therapeutic function appears strangely new and innovative—again, largely because it does not reflect the prevailing interests, activities, and preoccupations of most contemporary philosophers.

As mentioned, for centuries Hellenistic philosophers were very much concerned with the practical matters of life, and for hundreds of years following the Hellenistic era, philosophers continued trying to make a difference in people's lives, certainly where morality and religious belief were concerned. Immanuel Kant's efforts to give morality a solid and secure foundation were certainly no useless endeavor (see Chapter 5). The role of stoicism in Christian philosophy is also undeniable. Thus, in truth, the practical therapeutic role of philosophy is neither new nor innovative. One could even make the case that to neglect the practical contributions of the ancients, and to ignore the enduring influence of their therapeutic mission is, in fact, to provide a distorted (twentieth century) picture of what the history of philosophy is all about. Indeed, in view of some very recent developments within the field, it appears that a number of philosophers are now willing to revisit the Hellenistic period to see where philosophy might be going in this new millennium. For example, Tom Morris, a former Notre Dame professor and founder of The Morris Institute for Human Values has written:

> We live in a time suddenly hungry for wisdom. In a culture that has been celebrating material success for a century, we're ready for a reassessment of what really matters. As we move into a new millennium, we're witnessing a new global openness to ancient wisdom, a personal concern for meaning on a broad scale, and a widespread quest to understand what truly constitutes the good life.
>
> We want to get our bearings. Money, fame, power, and status have been found elusive by some, empty by others. They structure our societies and permeate our minds, but never deliver all they promise. And so we find ourselves searching for something more.
>
> The ancient stoic thinkers had something more. These practical philosophers say that inner strength is the secret to personal effectiveness; that inner peace is, for most of us, the missing link to

personal happiness; and that a nobility of self-possession and emotional self-control can make all the difference for living a life in full command of its own resources, and with a full enjoyment of its deepest inner rewards. The stoics saw what we need. And they left us powerful advice about how to find it in our own lives.[7]

In 1981, a modern version of therapeutic philosophy was developed in the form of **philosophical counseling** by German philosopher Gerd. B. Achenbach. After opening his practice in Bergisch Gladbach, near Cologne, he founded the German Association for Philosophical Practice (*Gesellschaft für Philosophische Praxis*). This association currently publishes its own journal and now consists of members from countries as diverse as Austria, Holland, Switzerland, Norway, Italy, Canada, Israel, and South Africa. In 1988, The Philosopher's Hotel was opened in Amsterdam by Ad Hoogendijk and Ida Jongsma; it hosts many activities and provides introductory courses for beginning philosophical counselors. In Canada, Petra von Morstein, from the University of Calgary, has been practicing philosophical counseling for several years and has organized a working group on the topic. In the United States, Louis Marinoff, at The City College of New York, has fairly recently established the American Philosophical Practitioners Association, where he offers training programs for philosophers wishing to engage in counseling and consulting services. The American Society for Philosophy, Counseling and Psychotherapy (ASPCP) has been formed by Kenneth Cust at Central Missouri State University and meets in conjunction with the American Philosophical Association's annual conference. Both the APPA and the ASPCP hope to have philosophical counseling legally recognized in the future as a new *bona fide* profession.

The philosophical practitioners' movement is beginning to gain momentum at the beginning of the twenty-first century. At this time, it is by no means mainstream without controversy, nor is it without its skeptics and immune to criticism. However, notwithstanding the difficulties and growing pains that accompany the development of any new profession, we can still appreciate the efforts of philosophical practitioners trying to apply philosophy to immediate experience, with the express purpose of improving the quality of human life—a noble cause indeed! With the passage of time, as greater numbers of philosophers descend from the "ivory towers" and take their wisdom to the streets of life, we predict that more and more people with serious existential dilemmas will be using the services of philosophical consultants.

Illustrating how philosophy can make a difference in your life is one of the main objectives of this book. To get a better idea of what is occurring in Europe, turn now to the newspaper article entitled. *Philosophers Set up Consultation Service.*

## PHILOSOPHERS SET UP CONSULTATION SERVICE

BY GALINA VROMEN G & M DEC. 28/89
REUTER AMSTERDAM, NETHERLANDS

Taking a page from psychotherapists, Dutch philosophers are opening private practices and charging clients up to $50 an hour to kick around ideas.

"There's a new generation of philosophers who want to take part in society, not just work in an ivory tower. We are making use of philosophical tradition to exchange thoughts with clients over whatever subject they want," explained Ad Hoogendijk, who in 1987 became one of the first Dutch philosophers to set up a practice.

Hoogendijk has been joined by a dozen others who talk with clients about everything from the meaning of life to a career change. He predicted the number would jump to about 100 in three years.

Unlike some psychologists, practicing philosophers do not try to probe deep into the past of the individual to understand childhood-ingrained behavior or subconscious actions and suggest modifications.

Rather, they try to bring the wisdom of their discipline to help people see their problems from a new perspective.

"I try to help people answer very basic questions like: Who are you? What do you want? It's a kind of re-orientation to structure their desires," Hoogendijk explained in an interview.

"I don't try and fit a person into a pre-existing theory but take what they say about themselves at face value and try to act as a midwife to let them articulate what they have inside," he explained in his Amsterdam office.

About 80 percent of his clients are at some type of major emotional crossroads—businessmen worried about approaching retirement, women upset when their grown children leave home, and youths unsure what to study at university.

"I ask people to make up a life plan of their desires and ideals that can be the basis of a revitalization plan. Often people have made choices in life on the basis of what they think is available, not on their ideals," Hoogendijk said.

He usually meets a client for about four or five sessions.

While a psychologist faced with a depressed patient might recommend months or years of treatment, Hoogendijk takes another tack.

Faced with just such a client, he tries to offer him a perspective on his views, engaging in discussion about the high value modern culture places on happiness and how thinkers in the past have put a high value on melancholia.

He does not talk about the fine points of Aristotelian logic or Jean-Paul Sartre's existentialism.

But he said his philosophical training had helped turn asking questions into his key tool and his thinking has been enriched by the sages he has read.

"There is a famous saying that Plato and Aristotle said it all, and it's true," he noted. But his reading of Spinoza, Marcuse, Karl Marx and Hannah Arendt have also informed his counselling, he said.

Hoogendijk came to the idea of starting a philosophical practice from his contact with a colleague, Gerd Achenbach, who first set up an office in 1981 in the Cologne suburb of Refrath in West Germany.

But the idea has caught on more in the Netherlands than in West Germany, he said.

One of his colleagues, Eite Veening, said he began his practice in the northern city of Groningen in 1987 because he was disturbed by "how much sloppy thinking there was around."

He said he was not interested in "curing" patients by helping them sort out their emotions but in helping them intellectually puzzle out their values and thought processes.

"I try to get people to understand their own ethics and what the best choice would be for them in a situation," said Veening.

"If you can get yourself to do what is best or not is another thing. If you find you can't, well then maybe that's more a matter for a psychologist," he explained.

Article by: Galina Vromen, article published in "The Arts" section of the Globe and Mail, Dec. 28, 1989, used by permission from Reuters

## PHILOSOPHY'S RELEVANCE IN AN AGE OF INFORMATION AND EMERGING TECHNOLOGIES

At the outset of the twenty-first century, I think it is fairly safe to say that we are still firmly ensconced in the **information age.** Internet access, electronic superhighways, fax machines, and cellular telephones are just a few of the things that make the worldwide transmission of information quick and efficient. It seems, sometimes, that we're relentlessly moving at a frenzied pace to acquire and process ever-increasing amounts of information. Computers become faster, hard drives increase their capacity, while modems send and receive data in amounts and at speeds that boggle the mind. Everyday, as we approach the altar of information technology, many of us are humbled and awestruck by the miracles performed there. The gurus of digital animation create graphic images and virtual realities never dreamed of before or thought only possible by divine intelligence. In our frozen and dazed state, brought on by the glare of computer pixel lights, many of us do not always appreciate the philosophical questions associated with the frenzied rush to know more and more. Surely, gathering and organizing information has positive value, but to what end? Professors often lament the fact that students can research and gather information from the World Wide Web but do not understand the information they've gained. Furthermore, there's no guarantee, even if you understand the information you've acquired, that you'll know how to put it to use wisely. As suggested before, it's possible to gain all the knowledge in the world and still be a fool. It's curious, isn't it, how preoccupied we are with acquiring information (electronically and otherwise), but how little we focus on understanding what we've acquired, and how little emphasis we place on putting to proper use what we know. Information without understanding and wise application is oftentimes useless and sometimes potentially dangerous. Insofar as philosophy can help us make sense of the information we dig up and assist us in putting that information to good use, it is indeed highly practical, relevant, and important. History reveals to us that

*There is no truth . . . to the promise that technology does away with human drudgery . . . it merely does away with human purpose.*

GEORGE GRANT

misapplications of knowledge and technology can have disastrous consequences. Without trying to overly dramatize the situation, let me suggest that philosophical wisdom may be required to save future generations and maintain the security of the world.

Faced with the many innovative technologies emerging in the new millenium, philosophers are constantly being called out of the halls of academe to help scientists and researchers with real-life ethical and philosophical problems. For example, with the new genetic engineering techniques evidenced by the cloning of Dolly the sheep, the question has arisen whether humans too should be cloned. Should cloning research continue to be funded, or should a moratorium be called? Just because we are able to do something technologically, does this necessarily mean that it should be done?

In the case of other reproductive technologies, such as *in vitro* fertilization and artificial insemination, should we now encourage, or at least countenance, childbirth outside the boundaries of traditional marriage? For example, should lesbian women involved in homosexual relationships be allowed to be artificially inseminated or undergo *in vitro* fertilization with purchased sperm from the local sperm bank in order to have families and raise children of their own? Today, this is possible, but is it right? Who should decide? Should the government? How about the private individuals involved? Do the rights of the yet unborn children matter? Is encouraging the advance of reproductive technology in an era of world overpopulation and diminishing resources for health care a good thing?

All these questions point again to the quandary that just because we are able to do certain things doesn't necessarily mean that we should. As you'll learn later in the book, you can't justifiably derive a philosophical or ethical "ought" from an "is" of experience. This constitutes a kind of reasoning error or logical mistake called the **is-ought fallacy.** Normative issues (that is, matters of value and morality) require rational, philosophical treatment, not scientific or technological solutions. Science and technology cannot decide what is right and wrong. It would appear that, yet again, philosophy serves as a practical aid in the affairs of everyday life.

> *"We move about the earth with unprecedented speed, but we do not know, and have not thought, where we are going, or whether we shall find any happiness there for our harassed souls."*
>
> WILL DURANT

# FIELDS OF PHILOSOPHY

Another way to understand and approach philosophy, apart from focusing on its practical and therapeutic dimensions, is to examine philosophy in terms of its specialized fields of inquiry. A survey of the literature reveals some variation on how philosophy, as a subject of study, should be divided and organized. Six major specializations and two generic subdivisions capture most philosophical endeavors. The six major fields are **metaphysics, epistemology, logic** (sometimes included under epistemology), **ethics, axiology** (aesthetics and the study of non-moral values), and **social/political philosophy** (sometimes classified as part of axiology). Less fundamental, perhaps, but still important are the philosophical subdivisions I call **foundational and disciplinary philosophies** and the

**philosophies of life.** Several philosophies of life will be discussed in the next chapter, and you'll be better able there to appreciate why I consider them less basic or fundamental than the six major specializations. For now, let me say the reason is that life philosophies incorporate ideas, values, principles, and understandings that ultimately come from the primary branches. For instance, as part of your personal philosophy of life, you may or may not believe in God (metaphysics); you may argue that no knowledge of anything beyond sensory experience is possible (epistemology); that the purpose of rational argument is simply to win, gain control, and persuade opponents (logic); that nobody has the right to make value judgments on the behavior of others (ethics); and that beauty is in the eye of the beholder (axiology-aesthetics). Of course, taking a position in one area of philosophy may influence what position you can reasonably take in another one. If your metaphysical stance is that only the material universe exists and nothing else, then by logical default there can be no immaterial heaven, hell, God, or immortal soul. Morality can have no supernatural foundation or divine architect behind it.

Notwithstanding the fact that fields of philosophical inquiry can sometimes overlap and have mutual implications, for purposes of description and clarification, we will treat them now as if they were separate and distinct. In later chapters, we will examine a number of the major fields more closely. Presently, let's get a broad overview of that subject of study we call philosophy.

## Metaphysics

Popular usage of the term *metaphysics* might lead you to conclude that it has something to do with spiritualism and the occult. After all, metaphysical book stores do specialize in selling things like astrological charts, ouija boards, and crystals. However, this is *not* what philosophical metaphysics concerns itself with. In the context of academic philosophy, metaphysics is the study of ultimate reality, human existence, personhood, freedom, God, causality, space, and time. The following questions are inherently metaphysical: What is the world made of? Is there something beyond the physical? Is there an unchanging reality behind the world of perception and appearance? Do humans have free will, or are they determined? Is there a God and, if not, what are the implications? Do minds exists? Do souls? If so, what are they like? And finally, is there a purpose to life, life after death, or a reason behind the existence of all things as we experience them?

## Epistemology

The term *epistemology* derives from the Greek, *episteme,* and means the theory or study of knowledge. Philosophers are fascinated by the nature and limits of knowledge. They ask themselves what we, as humans, can know with certainty. How is knowledge possible? Is there such a thing as absolute knowledge, or is all knowledge relative to the individual? What are the possible sources of knowledge? How is knowledge similar to, or different from, belief? What constitutes truth? Is reason the only way to truth or are there other avenues leading to it (such as divine revelation)?

# Logic

Philosophers are very much interested in logic, which can be defined as the science of reasoning. Logic addresses itself to forms of argument and laws of correct thought. I particularly like the way Thomas White defines it:

> Logic is the branch of philosophy devoted to determining what counts as solid, disciplined, reasoned thinking. In fact, the ancient Greek philosopher Aristotle sees it as so basic that he calls it not so much a part of philosophy as the "instrument" we use to do philosophy.

White also says:

> In much the same way that we have building codes to ensure that a house is built well, there is also a "thinking code," that is, guidelines and rules for what makes an argument pass "philosophical inspection." We find this code in that part of philosophy called *logic*.[8]

Later in this text we will learn what constitutes valid logic and sound reasoning. We will look at some of the differences between inductive and deductive reasoning before examining some informal logical *fallacies* (unacceptable forms of reasoning using diversionary tactics and psychological appeals). Mastering logic is important for, as Aristotle reminds us, logic is the primary tool for "doing philosophy," understanding the discipline more as an activity than as a body of knowledge to be memorized.

# Ethics

Ethics, as a branch of philosophy, can generally be understood as the study of morals in human conduct. Ethicists are preoccupied with concepts such as good and bad, right and wrong, praise and blame. They also focus on considerations of moral obligation, principles of moral conduct, ultimate life values, virtue, the justification of behavior, and ideal character. Over the centuries, numerous moral theories have been articulated and used as normative bases for ethical decision making.

In addition to dealing with specific moral issues, some philosophers like to analyze the moral theories themselves, looking for internal inconsistencies, vagueness, ambiguity, and equivocation. These same philosophers may also examine and evaluate the ultimate foundations of particular ethical systems of thought, asking, for example, "Should faith or reason form the foundation of morality?" Because they are one step removed from normative inquiry and the practical application of principles to specific moral issues, they are called *meta*-ethicists. Whereas the moral philosopher could ask if capital punishment is right, the meta-ethicist would ask what is meant by the concept of right, or question the standard used to determine rightness.

## Axiology

Axiology is a field of philosophical inquiry dealing with values. A major component of axiology is **aesthetics.** Aesthetics concerns itself with artistic values, beauty, and aesthetic appreciation. In the realm of aesthetics, people make value judgments about visual art, music, dance, and theater. Is beauty merely in the eye of the beholder? Are there objective standards by which to judge artworks? Can we say justifiably that classical music is better than country and western or hiphop? These constitute just a tiny sampling of the kinds of questions that philosophers concerned with aesthetics might ask.

## Social/Political Philosophy

Sometimes divided into two categories, social/political philosophy can be seen as that part of philosophy drawing our attention to conceptions of how to live well together in society, as well as to the philosophical foundations of the state and its political institutions. Social/political philosophers examine the individual's relation to the state and argue in favor or against specific social policies (for example, forced busing and integrated schools, quota systems, corporate welfare, public funding for stem-cell research, preferential admissions, and graduated income tax). Social/political philosophers also analyze different forms of government and social arrangements to help establish what is best or ideal. As you can probably intuit, the questions raised by social/political philosophers are likely to have ethical implications, especially where rights and social responsibilities are concerned. These philosophers ask the following sorts of questions: Is it ever justified to violate the rights of the individual or minority group for the benefit of the majority? Is capitalism inherently corrupt? What is the best form of government? What principles should constitute the basis of a free and well-ordered society? Are all people created equal? Should we recognize the collective rights of Native North Americans and give them preferred treatment in order to rectify past injustices?

## Foundational and Disciplinary Philosophies

Foundational and disciplinary philosophies serve as the theoretical and conceptual bases for different human activities and academic subjects of study. For example, the practice of education is typically founded on a particular educational philosophy; how we run a business may be tied to our business philosophy; and how we participate in athletic events may hinge on our philosophy of sport. As an educator, you might value cooperation and therefore stress teamwork and group projects as a way of achieving your educational goals. As a business owner, you might apply the philosophy that "the customer is always right," even when it inconveniences you or cuts into your profits. As an athlete, you might choose to quietly "look out for number one," sacrificing the welfare of the team for the sake of personal advantage. Whatever the activity or human endeavor, the underlying philosophy gives purpose, order, and direction to it. It defines what's acceptable and what's not; what should be done and what shouldn't.

Academic discipline-related philosophies (like the philosophy of science, law, or psychology) spell out the implicit assumptions, methods, and principles of inquiry used by scholars in the field. Embedded in such things, you'll often find ethical, epistemological, and metaphysical presuppositions that make disciplinary philosophies derivative just like philosophies of life. For instance, the philosophy of psychological behaviorism adheres to the metaphysical notion of determinism. Proponents of behaviorism, like the late B.F. Skinner, do not believe in free will and hence do not accept conventional understandings of moral responsibility. Also, since the mind cannot be directly observed and scientifically studied, using the empirical methods of science, behaviorists like Skinner ignore it for all intents and purposes. For Skinner, what we generally understand by the so-called mind does not exist.

## Philosophies of Life

There are probably as many philosophies of life as there are intelligent thinking beings in the world. Your own philosophy may or may not be well thought out. It may or may not be something to which you pay much attention. Regardless, your personal philosophy reveals itself in much of what you say and do. Probably the best indicator of your personal philosophy is captured by your current lifestyle. What do you own? What do you want? What do you aspire to achieve? How do you spend your time? What do you consider most important? What are your ideals? What do you hate? For what things are you willing to sacrifice or even die? On what issues will you not bend? How do you see yourself as a person? Answers to these and other like questions form your philosophical worldview. Perhaps you fall under the category of "hedonist," like the rock star Madonna. You may recall she self-identifies philosophically in one of her hit songs as a "material girl living in a material world." By contrast, maybe you're a "stoic," wishing to find peace of mind above all else. In the next chapter, we examine different philosophies of life and give you an opportunity to reflect on your own. Maybe it's time for you to reconsider your lifestyle or to engage in a wholesale philosophical reorientation.

> **“ There is perhaps nothing worse than reaching the top of the ladder and discovering that you're on the wrong wall. ”**
>
> JOSEPH CAMPBELL

Reprinted with permission of King Features Syndicate, Inc.

## APPROACHES TO PHILOSOPHY

Still another way to understand and appreciate philosophy is by examining different approaches that have been taken toward it. In this section, you will see how gender, ethno-racial, historical, and methodological considerations can influence the way we conceptualize philosophy and engage in the enterprise.

## Masculine versus Feminine Approaches

It was suggested earlier that philosophy can serve a liberating function, freeing us from our prejudices, ignorance, and subjectivity. It's a bit embarrassing, therefore, to have to admit that, in the past, many male philosophers have been guilty of their own gender bias and cognitive egocentrism. This is evidenced by the fact that women have traditionally been ignored in treatises on the history of philosophy. In at least one significant historical introduction, released by a major publisher as recently as 1987, not a single female philosopher was listed in the table of contents.[9] With the growing interest in women's thought and feminist political activism, however, the role of women within the field of philosophy is sure to expand. Alison Jaggar, for example, has made a significant philosophical contribution by reexamining the role of emotion in a newly re-framed feminist epistemology. As will be discussed in Chapter 5, Carol Gillian has questioned the use of male norms as a basis of evaluating the adequacy of ethical judgment and determining the maturity levels of moral development in children and adolescents. We can await then, with great anticipation, the fresh new insights that a feminist perspective has to offer, and we can look forward to a future philosophy that is enriched by it. (To learn more about another woman's contribution to moral philosophy, turn to the section in this book on Ayn Rand's ethical egoism, pp. 346 to 356. There you'll find a discussion and rejection of collectivist ethics.)

## World Philosophies: Eastern, Western, and Ethno-racial

Western rational thought has a proud and venerable tradition, and most of the philosophers covered in this introductory text belong to it. When making reference to philosophers like Plato, Aristotle, Kant, Nietzsche, or Seneca, for example, we're talking about **Western** thought. As a student of philosophy, you should be aware, however, that there are many other philosophical traditions different from our own; unfortunately, space limitations imposed by this book prevent me from giving you an adequate treatment of them. For better or for worse, I've decided to emphasize the Western philosophical tradition. Nonetheless, I must draw your attention briefly to other world philosophies besides the ones reflecting our European and Anglo-American heritage. In China and Japan, for instance, hundreds of millions of people profess some form of religious philosophy, be it Buddhism, Taoism, or classical Confucianism. (See Chapter 2 for a brief treatment of Buddhism.) In India and in parts of southeast Asia, you again have different philosophical worldviews, Hinduism in particular. In the

Middle East, Islam and Judaism are the prevailing religious philosophies guiding the lives of millions. In North America, the Native peoples have found philosophical direction in the **Medicine Wheel** (Figure 1.1). As a teaching tool, the concept of The Medicine Wheel has been used for centuries to help individuals gain self-knowledge and spiritual enlightenment. The wisdom of the

# SPIRITUALLY-BASED PHILOSOPHICAL TRADITIONS

The First Nations people of North America have developed their own spiritually-based philosophical traditions independently from European, Middle Eastern, African, and Asian influences. In Saskatchewan, for example, the Moose Mountain Medicine Wheel, a 2000-year-old physical structure, is believed to have spiritual and astrological significance.

As a teaching tool, the concept of the medicine wheel has been used for centuries by Native Indians across North America to help them gain self-awareness and spiritual enlightenment. However, little is recorded about it. Knowledge and information about the medicine wheel has been transmitted orally from one generation to the next. The best way for you to learn more is by speaking to a tribe elder at the nearest Indian reservation. Because of its oral tradition, details and descriptions of the medicine wheel differ between regions and tribes. In her discussions of the medicine wheel. Mary E. Loomis (1991) shares with us Native teachings as revealed to her by Harley Swiftdeer, a Cherokee medicine man.

Loomis tells us that the medicine wheel is first of all a circle. On the circle are placed the so-called Powers of the Four Directions: North, South, East, and West. Native spiritualists believe everything that exists can be organized according to these powers. For example, if you look at the medicine wheel included here, you will note that each direction has a color associated with it (white, black, yellow, and red). These colors represent the four races of humanity. The rainbow center represents people of mixed race.

Each direction on the wheel provides specific life lessons for us to learn. The sun and fire of the East Power illuminate possibilities and spark the imagination. The Power of the West, using earth and blackness, teaches us the value of introspection and connection

with the earth. The South Power, with plants that nourish us, teaches us to be trusting and innocent, while the Power of the North, using animal symbols, teaches us about perfection, wisdom, and logic. At the center of the wheel is found sexual energy. This catalytic energy is a creative force that combines masculine and feminine potentials in harmonious balance. Using the medicine wheel, we can learn to balance and harmonize the emotional, physical, mental, spiritual, and sexual components of the human character. The medicine wheel can facilitate the development of psychological wholeness and health.

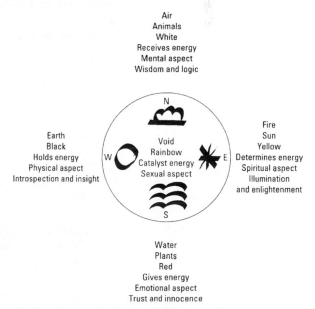

**FIGURE 1.1** The Medicine Wheel: Powers of the Four Directions
SOURCE: From Mary E. Loomis, *Dancing the Wheel of Psychological Types* copyright 1991 by Mary E. Loomis, p. 5. Reprinted by permission of the publisher, Chiron Publications.

Medicine Wheel has been transmitted orally from generation to generation, so very little about it can be found in written form.[10]

Africans, too, have their own philosophical approach. Like Native North Americans, they have adopted an oral tradition as well, often demeaned by Western thinkers who grant greater legitimacy to recorded discursive argument. African **ethnophilosophy** tends to be more emotive, intuitive, and spiritual than Western varieties of thought. For the past several decades, African philosophers have been trying to come to terms with past colonial oppression. They have faced a "deconstructive" challenge, trying to understand and respond to what some regard as a harmful Eurocentrism inherited from European colonists who culturally imposed themselves on indigenous Africans. They have also confronted the "reconstructive" challenge of trying to revitalize the modern reality of Africa's broken historical and cultural heritage. African American philosophers are now asking: What does and does not genuinely belong to African philosophy? Is it different from Western philosophy? And what does philosophizing as a black person really mean?

## Rational versus Nonrational Philosophy

While the majority of Western philosophers are committed to the ideals of reason, religious existentialists such as Søren Kierkegaard contend that subjective truth cannot properly be understood by rational objectivity, and that certain higher levels of being are beyond reason, requiring "irrational" leaps of faith to arrive at them. As mentioned, feminists like Carol Gilligan are also critical of rational morality, seeing in it a male bias. With this understanding, Gilligan uses the concepts of "care" and "relation" to explain another basis of morality, one that is not reserved exclusively for women but is more reflective of their tendencies given their biology and social conditioning.

Like feminists and existentialists, many other world philosophies, as we've learned, take a *nonrational approach,* as well. Not all of philosophy is based on discursive reasoning, proceeding in a linear fashion from premises to logical conclusions. Specifically, we find traditions that make extensive use of symbols in their spiritual practices and in their philosophical efforts to understand the universe. The Native North American Medicine Wheel, already mentioned, is one such symbol. From the Middle East comes mystical Judaism with its Kabbalah, or *Tree of Life*—a diagram that functions as a kind of map illustrating the particular patterns and laws by which God is said to have created the manifest universe. (Figure 1.2). The "Sign of the Presence of God" has been used by Middle Eastern Islamic Sufi mystics to promote moral healing (Figure 1.3). An adaptation of the Sign, called the *enneagram,* is now used by Jesuits and other mystically inclined Christians to understand the human condition in terms of man's fall from grace.[11] The symbol illustrates and explains how we all inevitably detach from our human "essence" and what we must do to recapture our true selves in God (Figure 1.4). Contemporary developers of the enneagram, like Oscar Ichazo and Claudio Naranjo, have made efforts to synthesize its traditional wisdom with modern psychiatry to get a better understanding of human character.

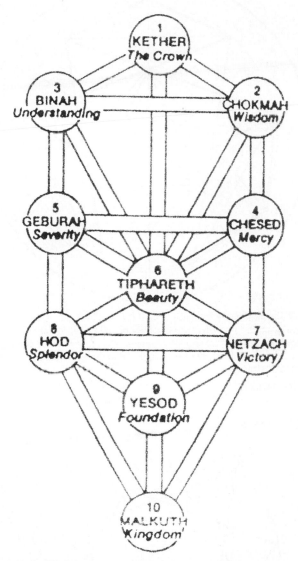

**FIGURE 1.2** The Kabbalah

Kabbalah means "given by the tradition," and the term refers to the oral, mystical, and esoteric traditions of the Jewish people. Many of its ideas and themes are present in other systems of thought, for example, Indian philosophy, Platonism, and Gnosticism. In the Kabbalah, the biblical tradition converges with these other systems "to produce a comprehensive philosophical and psychological vision of the nature of God and humankind that was only imperfectly represented in prior traditions."

SOURCE: "The Theosophical Kabbalah" at the following website: www.newkabbalah.com/newkabbalah.html.

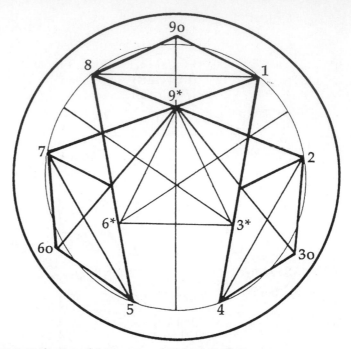

**FIGURE 1.3** The Sign of the Presence of God (Wajh Allah)
The design was given this name by the Naqshbandi Sufi Order in Central Asia. It is used to help the "spiritual warrior" attain moral healing. The more familiar enneagram, which symbolizes nine character types, derives from this sign. You can learn more about this by reading LALEH BAKHTIAR.

SOURCE: Laleh Bakhtiar, *Moral Healer's Handbook: The Psychology of Spiritual Chivalry* Chicago, Il: 60618: KAZI Publications, 1994 (COVER DESIGN).

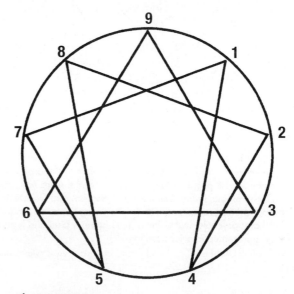

**FIGURE 1.4** *The Enneagram*
The enneagram is a symbol used to promote character development. Each number captures a different character type that constructs reality in accordance with type-specific fears, desires, and assumptions about the world. Use of the enneagram helps one to achieve spiritual liberation, knowledge of oneself, and understanding of others.

Eastern religious philosophies such as Buddhism are also nonrational, as they make concerted efforts to "still the mad monkey of the mind." Meditative practices and disciplined ritual take on a much more prominent role than do rational analysis and critique. In short, there are many different ways of "doing" philosophy, experiencing it, or engaging in it. Whether reason, meditation, character self-analysis, or something else should be your vehicle to philosophical enlightenment is a question that only you can answer. For our introductory purposes here, we'll be emphasizing the rational approach first, though, as I said, a coverage of Buddhism is included in Chapter 2, Philosophies of Life. Chapter 5 also includes a section on Hindu ethics which is religiously, not rationally, based.

## PHILOSOPHERS IN ACTION

*Experience Meditation:* Before we become fully engaged in the typically Western rational pursuit of philosophical wisdom, let us pause and still "the mad monkey of the mind" for a moment with some Eastern-inspired meditation. The practice is actually quite simple. All you need to do is focus your attention on a particular word or phrase, (for example, "om" or "in-out"), repeating it slowly in rhythm with your natural breathing. As an alternative, you could choose to gaze at a candle flame, a sunset, a morning sunrise, or a geometric figure of what Hindus call a *mandala*. Still another strategy is simply to pay attention to your breath as you naturally inhale and exhale.

The idea in all these cases is to narrow your focus and limit the stimuli bombarding your nervous system. To the extent you are successful, you will calm your mind in the process. Hindu gurus, highly trained in meditative practices, claim to be able to reach higher levels of cosmic consciousness transcending all rational forms of knowledge. Since we are neither gurus nor highly trained, we will be content for now just to still the mind for a few minutes. Your experience of meditation should quickly reveal to you how busy and agitated your mind really is, and how difficult such an apparently simple practice can be. If you're still unsure about what to do for your first meditation, you could try the following:

1. First, find a quiet spot, dim the lights, and sit comfortably with a relatively straight back. Unfold your arms and uncross your legs.
2. Close your eyes and then take three or four deep breaths.
3. Pick a word, phrase, or affirmation that is quite simple or has special meaning to you. ("Forgive all," "I can do it," "Om").
4. Start to breathe through your nose, repeating the word or phrase in your mind in time with your breathing. Some people find counting breaths is useful. As you inhale, count *one;* when you exhale, count *two;* on the next inhalation count *three,* and so forth until you reach ten. Then start over again. See if you can make it to ten without mental distraction. If and when distractions occur, release them and let them pass by. Don't feel like you've done something wrong or that the meditation hasn't worked. Be gentle with yourself.
5. Continue the meditation for about five minutes. Slowly regain normal awareness and then peacefully go about the rest of your day.[12]

*For Discussion:* What was your experience of meditation like? Were you able to "still the mad monkey of the mind" and achieve inner calm? Describe that calm or explain what prevented you from attaining it.

# HISTORICAL PERIODS OF PHILOSOPHY

Efforts to understand Western philosophy have sometimes led individuals to carve it up historically. There are different periods into which particular philosophers fit. Plato and Aristotle, for instance, would fall under the category of **ancient philosophy,** which ranges from the sixth century BCE to approximately the third century C.E. Religious philosophers such as St. Augustine and St. Thomas Aquinas can be placed together under **medieval philosophy,** a period running from the fourth century to roughly the sixteenth century. **Modern philosophy** can include people like Immanuel Kant and John Stuart Mill. It extends from about the end of the sixteenth century through to the nineteenth century. **Contemporary philosophy** incorporates twentieth-century thinkers such as Jean-Paul Sartre, Simone de Beauvoir, Bertrand Russell, and those involved in philosophy during the infancy of the twenty-first century. Contemporary philosophers tend to be classed as either **analytic** or **continental,** a distinction based on the interests displayed and methods used. **Analytical philosophers** focus on **conceptual analysis,** while **continental philosophers**—existentialists and phenomenologists, for example—concentrate on matters of being, authenticity, freedom, and meaning. Still more recently, **postmodernism** has appeared as a newest school of philosophical thought. Essentially, it rejects most of the cultural certainties on which life in the West has been structured over the past couple of centuries.

For those of you particularly interested in the nature of philosophy, you may wish to read the following excerpt from Bertrand Russell before moving on to the next chapter, where you will find a smorgasbord of philosophical worldviews from which to choose, and in terms of which to direct your life.

## PHILOSOPHICAL PROFILE

**BERTRAND RUSSELL**

### Bertrand Russell

Bertrand Russell, a British philosopher, mathematician, and social reformer, was born in Trelleck, Wales, in 1872. He was educated at Cambridge University, where he studied mathematics, logic, and philosophy. He became a Fellow of Trinity College at Cambridge and subsequently a Lecturer in philosophy. He was dismissed from his position in 1916, however, because of his agnosticism and pacifist views. Several years later, he was offered reinstatement to his position, but declined.

Russell also studied social/political thought in Berlin, where he wrote *German Social Democracy* in 1896. His first important book, *The Principles of Mathematics,* was completed in 1903. In collaboration with Alfred North Whitehead, Russell produced *Principia Mathematica* in 1910. Russell went on to deal with many social, moral, political, and ethical issues. Some books on these topics include: *The Practice and Theory of Bolshevism; Why I am Not a Christian; Education and the Social Order; Marriage and Morals; Religion and Science;* and *On Education, Especially in Early Childhood.*

Russell's views on educational philosophy were put into practice in his experimental Beacon Hill School started in 1927. In 1938, Russell moved to the United States, first teaching at the University of Chicago and then at the University of California at Los Angeles. In 1940, he accepted an invitation to join the philosophy department at the City College of New York. Unfortunately, a local judge found him unfit for the position, believing he had to protect "public health, safety and morals." Over his lifetime, Russell's irreverence was to offend several generations of moralists and religious conservatives; nonetheless, he became a philosopher with an enormous audience and widespread popularity. Russell was awarded the Nobel Prize for Literature in 1944. He died in 1970. The Russell archives are currently housed at McMaster University in Hamilton, Ontario, Canada.

Source: Peter A. Angeles, The HarperCollins Dictionary of Philosophy (New York: Harper-Perennial, 1992); and Paul Edwards, William Alston, and A.N. Prior, HarperCollins Dictionary of Philosophy, pp. 235–58.

## ORIGINAL SOURCEWORK

## The Problems of Philosophy

### BERTRAND RUSSELL

Having now come to the end of our brief and very incomplete review of the problems of philosophy, it will be well to consider, in conclusion, what is the value of philosophy and why it ought to be studied. It is the more necessary to consider this question, in view of the fact that many men, under the influence of science or of practical affairs, are inclined to doubt whether philosophy is anything better than innocent but useless trifling, hair-splitting distinctions, and controversies on matters concerning which knowledge is impossible.

This view of philosophy appears to result, partly from a wrong conception of the ends of life, partly from a wrong conception of the kind of goods which philosophy strives to achieve. Physical science, through the medium of inventions, is useful to innumerable people who are wholly ignorant of it; thus the study of physical science is to be recommended, not only, or primarily, because of the effect on mankind in general. This utility does not belong to philosophy. If the study of philosophy has any value at all for other than students of philosophy, it must be only indirectly, through its effects upon the lives of those who study it. It is in these effects, therefore, if anywhere, that the value of philosophy must be primarily sought.

But further, if we are not to fail in our endeavor to determine the value of philosophy, we must first free our minds from the prejudices of what are wrongly called "practical" men. The "practical" man, as this word is often used, is one who recognizes only material needs, who realizes that men must have food for the body, but is oblivious of the necessity of providing food for the mind. If all men were well off, if poverty and disease had been reduced to their lowest possible point, there would still remain much to be done to produce a valuable society: and even in the existing world the goods of the mind are at least as important as the goods of the body. It is exclusively among the goods of the mind that the value of philosophy is to be found; and only those who are not indifferent to these goods can be persuaded that the study of philosophy is not a waste of time.

Philosophy, like all other studies, aims primarily at knowledge. The knowledge it aims at is the kind of

Source: Bertrand Russell, The Problems of Philosophy (Oxford: Oxford University Press, 1912), pp. 46–50.

knowledge which gives unity and system to the body of the sciences, and the kind which results from a critical examination of the grounds of our convictions, prejudices, and beliefs. But it cannot be maintained that philosophy has had any very great measure of success in its attempts to provide definite answers to its questions. If you ask a mathematician, a mineralogist, a historian, or any other man of learning, what definite body of truths has been ascertained by his science, his answer will last as long as you are willing to listen. But if you put the same question to a philosopher, he will, if he is candid, have to confess that his study has not achieved positive results such as have been achieved by other sciences. It is true that this is partly accounted for by the fact that, as soon as definite knowledge concerning any subject becomes possible, this subject ceases to be called philosophy and becomes a separate science. The whole study of the heavens, which now belongs to astronomy, was once included in philosophy; Newton's great work was called "the mathematical principles of natural philosophy." Similarly, the study of the human mind, which was, until very lately, a part of philosophy, has now been separated from philosophy and has become the science of psychology. Thus, to a great extent, the uncertainty of philosophy is more apparent than real: those questions which are already capable of definite answers are placed in the sciences, while those only to which, at present, no definite answer can be given, remain to form the residue which is called philosophy.

This is, however, only a part of the truth concerning the uncertainty of philosophy. There are many questions—and among them those that are of the profoundest interest to our spiritual life—which, so far as we can see, must remain insoluble to the human intellect unless its powers become of quite a different order from what they are now. Has the universe any unity of plan or purpose, or is it a fortuitous concourse of atoms? Is consciousness a permanent part of the universe, giving hope of indefinite growth in wisdom, or is it transitory accident on a small planet on which life must ultimately become impossible? Are good and evil of importance to the universe or only to man? Such questions are asked by philosophy, and variously answered by various philosophers. But it would seem that, whether answers be otherwise discoverable or not, the answers suggested by philosophy are none of them demonstrably true. Yet, however slight may be the hope of discovering an an-

swer, it is part of the business of philosophy to continue the consideration of such questions, to make us aware of their importance, to examine all the approaches to them, and to keep alive that speculative interest in the universe which is apt to be killed by confining ourselves to definitely ascertainable knowledge.

Many philosophers, it is true, have held that philosophy could establish the truth of certain answers to such fundamental questions. They have supposed that what is of most importance in religious beliefs could be proved by strict demonstration to be true. In order to judge of such attempts, it is necessary to take a survey of human knowledge, and to form an opinion as to its methods and its limitations. On such a subject it would be unwise to pronounce dogmatically; but if the investigations of our previous chapters have not led us astray, we shall be compelled to renounce the hope of finding philosophical proofs of religious beliefs. We cannot, therefore, include as part of the value of philosophy any definite set of answers to such questions. Hence, once more, the value of philosophy must not depend upon any supposed body of definitely ascertainable knowledge to be acquired by those who study it.

The value of philosophy is, in fact, to be sought largely in its very uncertainty. The man who has no tincture of philosophy goes through life imprisoned in the prejudices derived from common sense, from the habitual beliefs of his age or his nation, and from convictions which have grown up in his mind without the cooperation or consent of his deliberate reason. To such a man the world tends to become definite, finite, obvious; common objects rouse no questions, and unfamiliar possibilities are contemptuously rejected. As soon as we begin to philosophise, on the contrary, we find as we saw in our opening chapters, that even the most everyday things lead to problems to which only very incomplete answers can be given. Philosophy, though unable to tell us with certainty what is the true answer to the doubts which it raises, is able to suggest many possibilities which enlarge our thoughts and free them from the tyranny of custom. Thus, while diminishing our feeling of certainty as to what things are, it greatly increases our knowledge as to what they may be; it removes the somewhat arrogant dogmatism of those who have never travelled into the region of liberating doubt, and it keeps alive our sense of wonder by showing familiar things in an unfamiliar aspect.

Apart from its utility in showing unsuspected possibilities, philosophy has a value—perhaps its chief value—through the greatness of the objects which it contemplates, and the freedom from narrow and personal aims resulting from this contemplation. The life of the instinctive man is shut up within the circle of his private interests: family and friends may be included, but the outer world is not regarded except as it may help or hinder what comes within the circle of instinctive wishes. In such a life there is something feverish and confined, in comparison with which the philosophic life is calm and free. The private world of instinctive interests is a small one, set in the midst of a great and powerful world which must, sooner or later, lay our private world in ruins. Unless we can so enlarge our interests as to include the whole outer world, we remain like a garrison in a beleaguered fortress, knowing that the enemy prevents escape and that ultimate surrender is inevitable. In such a life there is no peace, but a constant strife between the insistence of desire and the powerlessness of will. In one way or another, if our life is to be great and free, we must escape this prison and this strife.

One way of escape is by philosophic contemplation. Philosophic contemplation does not, in its widest survey, divide the universe into two hostile camps—friends and foes, helpful and hostile, good and bad—it views the whole impartially. Philosophic contemplation, when it is unalloyed, does not aim at proving that the rest of the universe is akin to man. All acquisition of knowledge is an enlargement of the Self, but this enlargement is best attained when it is not directly sought. It is obtained when the desire for knowledge is alone operative, by a study which does not wish in advance that its objects should have this or that character, but adapts the Self to the characters which it finds in its objects. This enlargement of Self is not obtained when, taking the Self as it is, we try to show that the world is so similar to this Self that knowledge of it is possible without any admission of what seems alien. The desire to prove this is a form of self-assertion, and like all self-assertion, it is an obstacle to the growth of Self which it desires, and of which the Self knows that it is capable. Self-assertion, in philosophic speculation as elsewhere, views the world as a means to its own ends; thus it makes the world of less account than Self, and the Self sets bounds to the greatness of its goods. In contemplation, on the contrary, we start from the not-Self, and through its greatness the boundaries of Self are enlarged, through the infinity of the universe the mind which contemplates it achieves some share in infinity.

For this reason greatness of soul is not fostered by those philosophies which assimilate the universe to man. Knowledge is a form of union of Self and not-Self; like all union, it is impaired by dominion, and therefore by any attempt to force the universe into conformity with what we find in ourselves. There is a widespread philosophical tendency towards the view which tells us that man is the measure of all things, that truth is man-made, that space and time and the world of universals are properties of the mind, and that, if there be anything not created by the mind, it is unknowable and of no account for us. This view, if our previous discussions were correct, is untrue; but in addition to being untrue, it has the effect of robbing philosophic contemplation of all that gives it value, since it fetters contemplation to Self. What it calls knowledge is not a union with the not-Self, but a set of prejudices, habits, and desires, making an impenetrable veil between us and the world beyond. The man who finds pleasure in such a theory of knowledge is like the man who never leaves the domestic circle for fear his word might not be law.

The true philosophic contemplation, on the contrary, finds its satisfaction in every enlargement of the not-Self, in everything that magnifies the objects contemplated, and thereby the subject contemplating. Everything, in contemplation, that is personal or private, everything that depends upon habit, self-interest, or desire, distorts the object, and hence impairs the union which the intellect seeks. By thus making a barrier between subject and object, such personal and private things become a prison to the intellect. The free intellect will see as God might see, without a *here* and *now*, without hopes and fears, without the trammels of customary beliefs and traditional prejudices, calmly, dispassionately, in the sole and exclusive desire of knowledge—knowledge as impersonal, as purely contemplative, as it is possible for man to attain. Hence also the free intellect will value more the abstract and universal knowledge into which the accidents of private history do not enter, than the knowledge brought by the senses, and dependent, as such knowledge must be, upon an exclusive and personal point of view and a body whose sense-organs distort as much as they reveal.

The mind which has become accustomed to the freedom and impartiality of philosophic contemplation will preserve something of the same freedom and impartiality in the world of action and emotion. It will view its purposes and desires as parts of the whole, with the absence of insistence that results from seeing them as infinitesimal fragments in a world of which all the rest is unaffected by any one man's deeds. The impartiality which, in contemplation, is the unalloyed desire for truth, is the very same quality of mind which, in action, is justice, and in emotion is that universal love which can be given to all, and not only to those who are judged useful or admirable. Thus contemplation enlarges not only the objects of our thoughts, but also the objects of our actions and our affections: it makes us citizens of the universe, not only of one walled city at war with all the rest. In this citizenship of the universe consists man's true freedom, and his liberation from the thralldom of narrow hopes and fears.

Thus, to sum up our discussion of the value of philosophy: Philosophy is to be studied, not for the sake of any definite answers to its questions, since no definite answers can, as a rule, be known to be true, but rather for the sake of the questions themselves; because these questions enlarge our conception of what is possible, enrich our intellectual imagination, and diminish the dogmatic assurance which closes the mind against speculation; but

above all because, through the greatness of the universe which philosophy contemplates, the mind also is rendered great, and becomes capable of that union with the universe which constitutes its highest good.

## DISCUSSION QUESTIONS FOR CRITIQUE AND ANALYSIS

1. In what sense is philosophy "practical"? If there are no final, definite answers to philosophical questions, then why ask them, and why seek to inquire into them? What would Russell say? How would you respond?

2. What does philosophy aim at?

3. In what sense can philosophy be "self-enlarging"?

4. If, as Russell argues, the value of philosophy derives from its indirect effects on people's lives, then what happens if very few people are affected—a very real possibility in view of widespread allegations that philosophy is irrelevant in today's world? Does it make sense to argue that the value of philosophy is dependent on who and how many are affected or how deeply they're moved? Discuss.

# STUDY GUIDE

## KEY TERMS

philosophy  **9**
lovers of wisdom  **9**
Western rational tradition  **9**
reasonable  **9**
critically minded  **9**
questioning attitude  **9**
curious  **9**
rational justifications  **9**
seekers of truth  **10**
open-minded  **10**
wisdom  **11**
knowledge  **11**
intelligence  **11**
experience  **11**

depth  **11**
sense of perspective  **11**
integrated mode of existence  **12**
perennial wisdom  **12**
intrinsic value  **15**
pure and applied research  **15**
instrumentally valuable  **15**
subjective bias  **15**
ethnocentrism  **15**
alienated  **16**
Hellenistic tradition  **16**
philosophical counseling  **18**
information age  **20**
is-ought fallacy  **21**

metaphysics  **21**
epistemology  **21**
logic  **21**
ethics  **21**
axiology  **21**
social/political philosophy  **21**
foundational and disciplinary
    philosophies  **21**
philosophies of life  **22**
aesthetics  **24**
Western  **26**
Medicine Wheel  **27**
ethnophilosophy  **28**
ancient philosophy  **32**

medieval philosophy   **32**        analytic philosophers   **32**          postmodernism   **32**
modern philosophy   **32**          continental philosophers   **32**
contemporary philosophy   **32**    conceptual analysis   **32**

## PROGRESS CHECK

**Instructions:** Fill in the blanks with the appropriate responses listed below:

historical periods          liberate                social/political philosophy
knowledge                   depth                   ethics
instrumental                rational                wisdom
Hellenistic tradition       conceptual analysis     therapeutic value
Western rational philosophy irrational leap         logic
epistemology                practical use           Medicine Wheel
foundational                axiology

1. Philosophy means the love of _____.
2. Philosophers belonging to the _____ are curious, detached, objective, and critically minded.
3. Wisdom is not the same thing as _____ or intelligence.
4. Wisdom is captured by one's ability to put information and intelligence to _____.
5. Wise people exhibit _____ and a sense of perspective.
6. Because philosophy can help to reduce tensions and anxiety resulting from such things as moral indecision and meaninglessness, it has _____.
7. Philosophy has both intrinsic and _____ value.
8. The study of philosophy can _____ one from ethnocentrism and subjective bias.
9. The _____ deals most directly with the healing powers of philosophy.
10. _____ is the study of knowledge

11. _____ is the study of values (aesthetic and non-moral).
12. The philosophy of sport is an example of a _____ philosophy.
13. _____ is the science of reasoning.
14. _____ is the study of morals in human conduct.
15. _____ is the study of the philosophical foundations of society and its institutions.
16. Not all world philosophies are _____ in nature.
17. The _____ is a conceptual device used by Native North Americans as a tool for living wisely.
18. Some religious philosophers believe that a(n) _____ of faith is required to live life at the highest level of human existence.
19. Philosophy can be understood by dividing it up into _____.
20. Contemporary analytic philosophers focus on _____.

## SUMMARY OF MAJOR POINTS

1. What comic images and caricatures does the term philosopher evoke?
   - bearded old man
   - detached hermit
   - cave dweller
   - ivory-tower professor
   - toga-clad Greek
   - wandering nuisance
2. How could Western rational philosophers be more accurately portrayed?
   - lovers of wisdom
   - seekers of truth

- reasonable
- critically minded
- questioning
- curious
- objective, impartial
- respectful of others
- cognizant of differing and divergent points of view
- detached, unbiased

3. What is wisdom?
   - Related to, but not the same as, intelligence and knowledge
   - The ability to put one's knowledge and intelligence to good practical use
   - Sometimes achieved by experience, though not necessarily so
   - A sense of depth and perspective
   - Reflected in an integrated mode of existence and in joyful serenity
   - Perennial: arises again and again in different contexts and times

4. What is the practical value of philosophy?
   - Unavoidable, so must be dealt with
   - Intrinsically valuable: pleasure and insight from the pursuit of wisdom
   - Instrumentally valuable: personally therapeutic and socially useful
   - A liberating experience
   - Removes subjective bias and ethnocentrism
   - Enhances wisdom and understanding
   - Offers guidance, direction, and meaning

- Helps people to cope with moral indecision, matters of purpose, lifestyle development, and psychological self-management
- Offers insight into the wise application of technology

5. What are the various specializations within the discipline of philosophy?
   - Metaphysics: The study of ultimate reality, human existence, personhood, God, freedom.
   - Epistemology: The theory of the nature and limits of knowledge
   - Logic: The science of reasoning
   - Ethics: The study of morals in human conduct
   - Axiology-Aesthetics: Philosophical inquiry dealing with (artistic) values
   - Social/Political: The study of the philosophical foundations of society and its political institutions
   - Foundational and Disciplinary: Theoretical and conceptual bases for different human activities and academic subjects of study
   - Philosophies of Life: The underlying principles and values of one's lifestyle, belief system, and chosen actions

6. What are some basic approaches to philosophy?
   - Masculine versus Feminine
   - Eastern, Western, Ethno-racial (Native, African, etc.)
   - Rational versus Nonrational
   - Historical (divided into ancient, medieval, modern, contemporary, and postmodernistic)

# SOURCE REFERENCES

**Angeles, Peter A.,** *The HarperCollins Dictionary of Philosophy* (New York: HarperPerennial, 1992).

**Copleston, Frederick,** *A History of Philosophy*, Vols. 1–9 (New York: Image Books, 1993).

**Edwards, Paul, William Alston, and A.N. Prior** *The Encyclopedia of Philosophy*, Vol. 7 (New York: Macmillan Publishing Co., Inc.) The Free Press, 1967.

**Garry, Ann, and Marilyn Pearsall, eds.,** *Women, Knowledge and Reality—Explorations in Feminist Philosophy* (New York: Routledge, 1996).

**LaHav, Ran, and Maria da Venza Tillmanns, eds.,** *Essays on Philosophical Counselling* (Lanham: University Press of America, 1995).

**Loomis, Mary,** *Dancing the Wheel of Psychological Types* (Wilmette, IL: Chiron Publications, 1991).

**Nussbaum, Martha C.,** *The Therapy of Desire: Theory and Practice in Hellenistic Ethics* (Princeton, NJ: Princeton University Press, 1994).

**Russell, Bertrand,** *A History of Western Philosophy* (London: Unwin Paperbacks, 1979).

**Shogan, Debra, ed.,** *A Reader in Feminist Ethics* (Toronto: Canadian Scholars' Press, 1993).

**Solomon, Robert C., and Kathleen Higgins, eds.,** *World Philosophy: A Text with Readings* (New York: McGraw-Hill, 1995).

# PHILOSOPHY IN CYBERSPACE

*Poiesis:* **Philosophy On-Line Serials**
www.nlx.com/posp
An electronic reference and publishing service that offers online access to the full text of hundreds of current, recent, and back issues of a growing number of philosophy journals.

**Morris Institute for Human Values**
www.morrisinstitute.com/mihv_frms.html

Material on this website encourages people to become more philosophical about their lives, and wiser in their choices.

**American Philosophical Practitioners Association**
www.appa.edu
Learn more about philosophical counseling and other practical applications of philosophy.

# ENDNOTES

1. St. Teresa of Avila, *The Way of Perfection, The Collected Works,* (Rockford, IL: TAN Books + Publishers, 1997), pp. 117–18.
2. John Passmore, "Philosophy" in *The Encyclopedia of Philosophy,* Vol. 6, (New York: Macmillan Publishing Co., Inc. & The Free Press, 1972), p. 216.
3. The expession, "Western rational tradition" is used with a caution that not all Western philosophers give the same weight and credence to reason. Native North Americans have built a philosophical worldview as conveyed by the Medicine Wheel. Existentialists are not irrational, but they do not have the same faith in rational objectivity that other philosophers do. Further, Eastern mystics seek to transcend the limitations of reason by meditation.
4. Brand Blanshard, "Wisdom," *The Encyclopedia of Philosophy,* Vol. 8, (New York: Macmillan Publishing Co., Inc. & The Free Press, 1967), p. 322.
5. See Martha Nussbaum, *The Therapy of Desire: Theory and Practice in Hellenistic Ethics* (Princeton: Princeton University Press, 1994), p. 4.
6. Ibid.
7. This selection was taken from a rough draft manuscript entitled, *The New Stoics Book.* It has been altered and re-titled, *Inner Resilience and Outer Results.* Go to the Tom Morris' website to learn more: http://www.morrisinstitute.com/mihv_book_03.html.
8. Thomas I. White, *Discovering Philosophy: Brief Edition,* Prentice Hall, Upper Saddle River, NJ, 07458, 1996, p. 22.
9. Albert Hakim, *Historical Introduction to Philosophy* New York: Macmillan Publishing Company, 1987.
10. To learn more about the Medicine Wheel as interpreted by a Cherokee medicine man, Harley Swiftdeer, refer to mary Loomis', *Dancing the Wheel of Psychological Types.* (Wilmette, IL: Chiron Publications, 1991).
11. To learn how the enneagram has been used within Islam, see Laleh Bakhtiar's, *Traditional Psychoethics and Personality Paradigm* (1993); also see *Moral Healer's Handbook: The Psychology of Spiritual Chivalry* (1994). Both books are available through Kazi Publications, Chicago, Illinois. To learn how the enneagram has been used outside of Islam, see Dan Riso and Russ Hudson, *Understanding the Enneagram,* rev. ed., Boston: 2000, pp 34–35.
12. This meditation is adapted from *Meditation for Dummies* Stephan Bodian, and published by IDG Books, 1999. Foster City, CA.

CHAPTER 2

# PHILOSOPHIES OF LIFE

# CHAPTER OVERVIEW

**Take It Personally**

KNOW THYSELF
**The Philosophy of Life Preference Indicator**

**Stoicism: A Prescription for Peace of Mind**
    Stoicism's Cynical Origins

PHILOSOPHICAL PROFILE
**SOCRATES**

    The Stoic Universe
    How to Live in a Fated Universe
    Freedom and Value
    Purpose of Life
    Emotions in Life
    How to Progress Morally

ORIGINAL SOURCEWORK:
Marcus Aurelius, *The Meditations of Marcus Aurelius*

**Existentialism: Born Free, Let Me Be Me**
    Methods

PHILOSOPHICAL PROFILE
**JEAN-PAUL SARTRE AND SIMONE DE BEAUVOIR**

KNOW THYSELF
**The Purpose in Life Test (Abbreviated Version)**

    Philosophers Associated with Existentialism
    Existentialism as a Revolt
    Essence versus Existence
    Individuality and Subjective Experience
    Freedom of Choice

ORIGINAL SOURCEWORK:
Jean-Paul Sartre, *The Humanism of Existentialism*

PHILOSOPHICAL SEGUE:
**Fate, Free Will, and Determinism**

**Hedonism: Pleasure Is the Measure**
    Psychological versus Ethical Hedonism
    Aristippus of Cyrene
    Epicurus

PHILOSOPHICAL PROFILE
**CONTEMPORARY SCHOLARS OF HELLENISTIC PHILOSOPHY**

ORIGINAL SOURCEWORK:
Epicurus, *Letter to Menoeccus*

**Buddhism as a Philosophy of Life**

PHILOSOPHICAL PROFILE
**SIDDHARTHA GAUTAMA—THE BUDDHA**

    The Four Noble Truths
    The Noble Eight-Fold Path

ORIGINAL SOURCEWORK:
John Koller, *Basic Characteristics of [Asian] Buddhist Culture*

**STUDY GUIDE**
Key Terms ▪ Progress Check
Summary of Major Points ▪ Source References
Philosophy in Cyberspace ▪ Endnotes

# LEARNING OUTCOMES

*After successfully completing this chapter, you will be able to:*

Identify philosophical worldviews that more or less approximate your own.

Outline the history and origins of stoicism.

Briefly describe the stoic's cosmology (conception of the universe).

Gain insight into how one should live in a fated universe.

Account for the role of emotions in life for the stoic.

Explain how one should live morally in a stoic world.

Elucidate the philosophical unorthodoxy of existentialism.

Gauge the extent to which you find meaning and purpose in your life.

Discuss some of the major themes embedded in existential philosophy.

Distinguish between psychological and ethical hedonism.

List the basic tenets of Cyrenaic hedonism.

Outline Epicurean philosophy, distinguishing between types of pleasure.

Describe *Ataraxia* as the ultimate end of life and the impediments to achieving it.

Comment on the roles of virtue and friendship in *Ataraxia*.

Articulate Buddha's Four Noble Truths.

Understand how to reduce suffering using the Noble Eight-Fold Path.

# FOCUS QUESTIONS

1. What makes developing a personal philosophical worldview so difficult in contemporary society?

2. How is luxurious living viewed by the stoics as well as by their predecessors, Socrates and the cynics? Why are these views held?

3. Does a belief in God make much practical difference to one's philosophical worldview? If so, how?

4. How do the various philosophies covered in this chapter deal with problems of human purpose and meaning in life?

5. What are some practical and contemporary applications of stoic, existential, Buddhist, and hedonistic philosophy?

6. How is existentialism different from traditional or orthodox philosophy?

7. What concepts are central to the philosophy of existentialism?

8. What is hedonism? What variations of it do we find?

9. In what ways is Epicureanism different from Cyrenaic hedonism?

10. How is Buddhism therapeutic?

# TAKE IT PERSONALLY

Have you ever been overwhelmed by the many choices you've been faced with in life? Have your options been so numerous that you simply couldn't decide? Could it be that you've already made some important decisions but are now worried about future consequences likely to result from them? Am I talking about shopping at the mall, buying a car, picking an academic program, or choosing next year's vacation destination? No, I'm referring to the *purpose and meaning of your life*. Knowing what's ultimately worthwhile, choosing what to do, and deciding how to live are not easy tasks.

Every day, especially through advertising and the media, we are bombarded with endless messages telling us how we ought to live our lives: Buy this! Go there! Look like so! Play for fun! Beat the competition! Stay in school! Go to work! Feed the hungry! Pig out! Get even! Turn the other cheek! Take control! Serve others! Chill! Get pumped! For many of us, these countless and conflicting messages leave us wondering, "What, exactly, is the good life?" "What am I here for?" and "How should I live in order to find happiness and self-fulfillment?" Such questions, while deceptively simple in statement, are exceedingly difficult to answer. In fact, they belong to a class of timeless disturbing questions that philosophers have asked for centuries. Throughout the ages, thinkers have been raising such questions, debating the many possible answers to them. In some instances, these answers have coalesced to form different philosophical worldviews, which people have used to find personal guidance and direction.

In what follows, we look at several historically significant philosophies of life that philosophers have articulated. Specifically, we look at stoicism, existentialism, hedonism, and Buddhism. I chose these four because of their personal relevance as well as their starkly contrasting outlooks. Do you think, for example, that everything happens for a reason and that the world makes sense? If so, you might be surprised to learn that the ancient stoic philosophers claimed much the same centuries ago. Reading about the stoics will give you occasion to reflect upon your cosmological belief, hopefully clarifying it in the process. On the other hand, maybe you think that all of this destiny, fate, or preordained purpose stuff is for the birds, that there is no God to determine anything, and that, essentially, life is irrational and absurd. Well, then, the coverage of atheistic existentialist philosophy here should help you understand this philosophical stance of yours a little better. What exactly are the personal and ethical implications of believing that life makes no inherent sense, that no moral order exists, and that there is no underlying purpose to anything? Read on to find out.

Now, how about lifestyle? Do you buy into the notion of the American Dream: a spouse, two kids, a dog, and a house in the suburbs? Is this your definition of the good life, or would you prefer to indulge yourself, live for the moment, and satisfy your every wandering desire? Is this what good living is *really* all about? Believe it or not, a number of philosophers, known as Cyrenaic hedonists, would largely concur with you on this point. In this chapter you'll come to appreciate the value of pleasure and learn more about its types and pursuit.

On the other hand, you may have come to the conclusion that living for things like pleasure, money, or status is really a morally bankrupt proposition,

> **"*I should like to examine further, for no light matter is at stake, nothing less than the rule of human life.*"**
>
> SOCRATES, BOOK 1,
> *THE REPUBLIC*

leading only to gross dissatisfaction in the end. Perhaps you grew up in a highly secured mansion or were protected in a gated community, lest any "undesirables" penetrate your protective bubble of idealistic suburban existence. If this rings true for you, then you might be interested to learn about the life and philosophy of Siddhartha Gautama— better known in the West as the Buddha. Buddha escaped the walls of the luxurious palace that his father built to protect him. He gave up his worldly attachments and chose to live simply, with a compassionate heart, devoting himself entirely to helping the suffering people of the world find nirvana and peace of mind. He renounced the material values of his princely station in life and became the Enlightened One. Maybe you're looking for a little enlightenment yourself, especially given the apparently terrible conditions that surround you. If you're experiencing mental agitation or dissatisfaction resulting from frustrated desires, perhaps you'll find solace in the teachings of the Buddha. He has much guidance and direction to offer you.

As we proceed through this chapter, no one philosophical outlook will be presented as "the way to go." That decision will ultimately be yours. You may, or may not, be influenced by what you are about to learn. Whatever the case, the following discussion should at least get you thinking about your personal philosophy of life, however clear or unclear it is at this time. The naked truth is that you are responsible for your life and whatever direction it takes. Even allowing others, whoever they may be, to tell you what to do is still a personal choice for which you are accountable. It would be prudent, then, to make an intelligent and informed choice, don't you think? The quality of your life hinges on it. Oh, by the way, did I ever suggest that philosophy might be an important subject of study?

To learn which philosophy of life presented here most resembles your current worldview, complete the *Know Thyself* diagnostic which follows: *The Philosophy of Life Preference Indicator.*

## KNOW THYSELF

### The Philosophy of Life Preference Indicator

This chapter examines four philosophies of life—stoicism, existentialism, hedonism, and Buddhism—which offer us ancient and modern, Eastern and Western, theistic and atheistic, as well as rational and nonrational perspectives that have direct and immediate practical relevance to your personal life. The purpose of this self-diagnostic is to help you establish your level of agreement or disagreement with the assumptions, values, and beliefs, embedded in various philosophical viewpoints so that you might become clearer about your own thinking and personal worldview.

**INSTRUCTIONS** Below are a number of statements that reflect one of four philosophies covered in this chapter. Next to each statement, indicate your level of agreement or disagreement using this scale:

1 = strongly disagree
2 = disagree somewhat
3 = undecided
4 = agree somewhat
5 = strongly agree

After completing this task, follow the scoring instructions.

_____ 1. Pleasure is the principal motive for living.

_____ 2. Life makes no sense; it has only the meaning we give it.

_____ 3. It is not important to win favor with powerful and influential people.

_____ 4. Human existence is imperfect in a very deep way, filled with all types of suffering.

_____ 5. It is important to gain self-mastery over one's desires.

_____ 6. The value of individuality or individual expression is extremely high.

_____ 7. It is wrong to deny yourself enjoyment and pleasure.

_____ 8. The root cause of human suffering is desire or craving.

_____ 9. Live for the moment; tomorrow may never come.

_____ 10. Everything that happens, happens for a reason.

_____ 11. It is bothersome when people play roles and conform to societal expectations.

_____ 12. Grasping at the pleasures of life ultimately increases suffering.

_____ 13. Life is difficult; then you die.

_____ 14. The individual is the measure of pleasure; there are no objective standards.

_____ 15. Coincidences are not random, but meaningful.

_____ 16. In order to find happiness, we must eliminate selfish craving.

_____ 17. Emotions often get in the way of life; they should be controlled.

_____ 18. You're ultimately free to make life anything you will it to be.

_____ 19. _Pommes-frites_ (French fries) in Paris are better than boiled potatoes in Idaho.

_____ 20. Peace of mind ultimately derives from compassion and showing loving-kindness toward others.

_____ 21. "Eat, drink and be merry" should be everyone's motto in life.

_____ 22. Peace of mind through acceptance of life is the greatest good any individual can achieve.

_____ 23. People are responsible for their actions; you shouldn't blame your past, your parents, or anybody or anything else for what you do.

_____ 24. Giving and receiving are ultimately connected: "What goes around, comes around."

_____ 25. Individuals are quite different and unique; there is no single human nature.

_____ 26. Life is all about minimizing pain and maximizing fun and enjoyment.

_____ 27. Everything that has happened to you until now has been a perfect preparation for where you're at in your life currently.

_____ 28. Enlightenment requires that we reduce suffering in our lives through wisdom, morality, and concentration.

# SCORING INSTRUCTIONS

Statement numbers are listed under each of the philosophical headings below. Next to each statement number, write in the value you gave it using the scale provided. Record your results in the "Philosophy of Life Sphere" (Figure 2.1).

| Stoicism | Existentialism | Hedonism | Buddhism |
|---|---|---|---|
| 3. | 2. | 1. | 4. |
| 5. | 6. | 7. | 8. |
| 10. | 11. | 9. | 12. |

| 15. | 13. | 14. | 16. |
| 17. | 18. | 19. | 20. |
| 22. | 23. | 21. | 24. |
| 27. | 25. | 26. | 28. |
| _____ | _____ | _____ | _____ |

Totals

My highest total is _____ under the philosophy of _____ .

**FIGURE 2.1** Philosophy of Life Sphere.

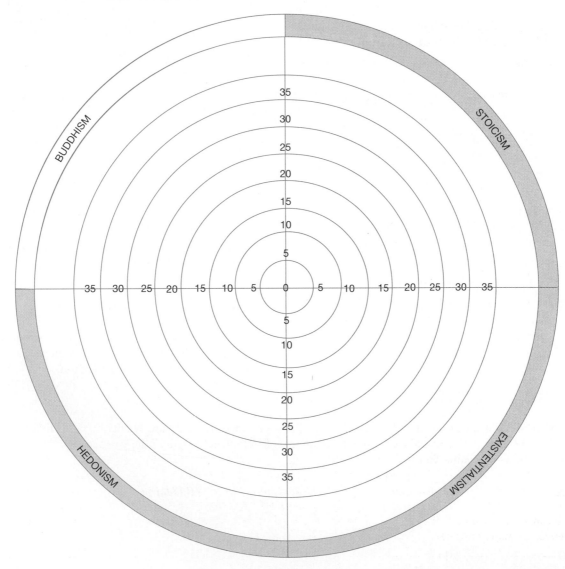

*Debriefing:*  By completing this informal instrument, you have been able to compare your own values, beliefs, and philosophical presuppositions with four major worldviews. Be cautioned that your highest score doesn't necessarily make you a stoic, an existentialist, a hedonist, or a Buddhist—though you could be. It may be that your pre-reflective philosophy is simply similar to one of them. As you go through the chapter, consider more seriously your agreements and disagreements with the philosophies of life outlined. Nothing final or scientifically conclusive is intended by this self-diagnostic. It merely serves as a tool to stimulate thought. You should note that the statements I've included under existentialism reflect "atheistic" existentialism, while those under hedonism are consistent with the views of a philosopher named Aristippus. Including statements consistent with religious existentialism and the hedonism of other thinkers such as Epicurus would have blurred the relatively clear cut distinctions I have tried to incorporate into this measure. Therefore, as you learn about variations in hedonistic and existential philosophy, your identified preferences may change somewhat. Read below the brief descriptions of each philosophy of life. Greater detail for each position is provided in the chapter.

# Philosophy of Life Descriptions

### Hedonism:

Cyrenaic hedonism, the type used for purposes of this comparative diagnostic, states that *pleasure is the principal motive for living.* Pleasure is always good, regardless of its source. There are no qualitative distinctions among pleasures. All pleasures are equally good. The only way to distinguish between pleasures is by their intensity. The greatest or most intense pleasure is the best. The pursuit of pleasure gives meaning to life. We ought to pursue our natural desires openly, without guilt or apology, and learn to enjoy ourselves. It is wrong to deny ourselves pleasure. The only pleasurable pursuits that are wrong are those which are enslaving and prevent the pursuit of other pleasures.

### Stoicism:

Stoics believe that true goodness does not lie in pleasure or in external objects, but in the state of the soul. *Peace of mind is found in wisdom and self-control,* by which people restrain passions and desires that disturb them in daily life. Stoicism adheres to the notion of fate or destiny, attributing the ultimate design of the universe to a divine being. Your mission in life is not to choose your role, but to play well the one you've been assigned.

### Existentialism:

Atheistic existentialism is a philosophy focusing on concepts such as *individuality, freedom, and human existence.* For the existentialist, there is no such thing as human nature. We are simply thrust into the world without reason, and once there, we are held responsible for creating ourselves and making ourselves what we are. This is not an option, for we are "condemned to be free." Efforts to conform, follow, or fit in are merely attempts to escape the frightening realities of our uniqueness, free will, and the absurdity of life. No God has made us, and no objective moral laws can tell us what to do. We are abandoned and alone in the world. We find meaning by living freely and responsibly in ways true to ourselves.

### Buddhism:

Buddhism is an Eastern religion but often regarded in the West as a philosophy of life because it involves no worship of a creator God, as with Christianity, Judaism, and Islam. Based on the teachings of Siddhartha Gautama, Buddhism tries to reduce suffering in life through *spiritual discipline and meditative practices.* Enlightenment is achieved through psychological detachment, loving-kindness, and the development of a compassionate heart—all reflective of "Buddha consciousness." According to this worldview, nothing is fixed; all volitional actions have consequences (Karmic results). That which we call the ego or self is impermanent, and hence, ultimately unreal.

# STOICISM: A PRESCRIPTION FOR PEACE OF MIND

## Stoicism's Cynical Origins

**Stoicism** is a school of philosophy that flourished in ancient Rome and Greece for approximately five centuries. It was founded by the merchant **Zeno** of Citium in Cyprus who, in the aftermath of being shipwrecked, took up philosophical studies in Athens. Initially, he became a pupil of the cynic Crates, a Socratic model of sorts, but later went on to found his own school. Only fragments of Zeno's writings remain.

The term *stoic*, a name for adherents to Zeno's philosophy, is derived from the fact that he lectured at the great central square of Athens, at the location of the *Stoa Poikile* or *Painted Porch* (colonnade). At first called Zenonians, followers of Zeno later came to be dubbed **Stoics,** or "men of the porch." Other notable stoics include the slave **Epictetus,** the Roman emperor **Marcus Aurelius,** and the statesman **Seneca. Chrysippus,** following Zeno and Cleanthes, eventually took over the Athenian Stoa academy and is sometimes considered the co-founder of this school of thought. He is credited with over 700 writings, but unfortunately, none exist today. Some historians have argued that, "Without Chrysippus, there wouldn't have been any Stoicism."

Stoic philosophy owes its origins to **cynicism,** whose Greek architect, **Antisthenes,** had been a disciple of **Socrates.** Antisthenes was so impressed by Socrates that he walked almost five miles a day just to hear him speak. Antisthenes was apparently less impressed with Socratic ideas than with Socrates himself. While Antisthenes did agree with Socrates that life should be based on reason, it was more Socrates's character and lifestyle that drew Antisthenes to him. Socrates showed contempt for fashion. He had no desire to impress people with shallow appearances. Rather, he opted for ragged functional clothing, choosing to walk without shoes. It was said that Socrates could go long periods of time without eating or sleeping. He displayed a physical toughness and forthright honesty that made a significant impact on Antisthenes.[1]

After the death of Socrates, Antisthenes founded a school that came to be called the **Cynosarges,** which means "the silver dog." The term *cynic* was derived from Cynosarges and later was applied to perhaps the most famous cynic in history, namely **Diogenes.** As the story goes, Diogenes lived in a wine barrel, preferring the company of dogs to the weakening corruptions of luxurious and sophisticated living. For him, trying to win favor with important and influential people was degrading. While many of us dream of the day when we can participate in "high society," from the cynic's perspective, high society is by its very nature corrupt. As one writer sums it up:

> . . . manners are hypocritical and phony; material wealth weakens people, making them physically and morally soft; the desire for success and power produces dishonesty and dependency; flattery, fashion, and convention destroy the individual and make him or her vulnerable to the whims of fortune.[2]

*"Men are disturbed not by things, but by the view which they take of them."*

Epictetus

Withdrawing from society, cynics came to regard luxury and wealth as a trap, ultimately resulting in frustrating, but avoidable, complications. Cynics argued that happiness was possible only to the extent that one could develop self-discipline. The aim was to gain rational control over one's desires. If one chose to remain uncorrupted, then contact with conventional society had to be minimized.

The sarcastic hostility displayed by some of the early cynics toward social conventions eventually led them into disrepute. Their legacy, perhaps, is that when someone is described as "cynical" today, we think of a person who is arrogant and condescending toward others or their intended actions. Whereas the ideal or archetypical philosophical cynic offered reasoned argument and penetrating social critique, so-called cynics of today are more likely to spew their venom of contemptuous scorn much more indiscriminately and, quite possibly, in a psychologically dishonest fashion. As you can probably well appreciate, rejecting people or their proposals out of fear, insecurity, or hatred is a lot different from principled rational objection. It is important, therefore, not to confuse the philosophical cynic with the Main-Street cynical "rebel without a cause"—someone who simply hates life or hates himself.

## PHILOSOPHICAL PROFILE

### Socrates

**Socrates** (circa 470–399 B.C.E.) is one of the greatest philosophers belonging to the Western rational tradition. He has been a model and source of inspiration for many philosophers throughout the centuries, including the stoics and the cynics who came before. Socrates actually wrote no philosophy himself, though **Plato,** one of his students, did incorporate many Socratic ideas into his writings. As many commentators point out, it is sometimes difficult to clearly distinguish between Plato's original thought and what he borrowed from Socrates. Alfred North Whitehead, a famous twentieth-century philosopher, once suggested that all of philosophy is but a series of footnotes to Plato. To the extent this is true, and insofar as Plato was strongly influenced by Socrates, perhaps Western rational philosophy should extend its series of footnotes a little further back to Plato's mentor.

**SOCRATES**

Socrates had a reputation for being indifferent to fashion and what we sometimes call today the "creature comforts" of life. He believed in minimizing wants and in self-mastery. For him, self-control, not self-indulgence, leads to pleasure. Thus, he sought to overcome weakness of will and to promote rationality in life. It is from Socrates that we get the saying: "*The unexamined life is not worth living.*" Unfortunately for him, because of his disturbing philosophical questioning, Socrates was charged with the crime of impiety and eventually condemned to death. Refusing, on principle, opportunities to escape his imprisonment, Socrates carried out his death sentence by drinking poisonous hemlock surrounded by friends and colleagues. He died for what he believed in.

Stoics shared the cynics' admiration for Socrates. They accepted the fundamental cynical premise that excessive desires are a prescription for unhappiness, and that the best form of life is characterized by detachment, courage, dignity, and self-control. Though Socrates was neither a cynic nor a stoic, he was a model for both.

## PHILOSOPHERS IN ACTION

Individually, or in small groups, try to name any philosophical thinkers or great leaders whose lives have prematurely ended in tragedy. What ideals or principles did these people stand for? How did they act? How did others respond to them? Were any of these individuals considered a social threat like Socrates? If so, why? If philosophy is irrelevant and useless, as many claim, then why would any of these philosophical thinkers be considered dangerous? Discuss.

> **❝Events do not just happen, but arrive by appointment. ❞**
> EPICTETUS

## The Stoic Universe

A great source of anxiety in the modern world derives from the prospect that life could be meaningless, that things might occur by fluke happenstance, and that the future offers only chaos and dangerous unpredictability. In an uncertain world, people can often feel hopelessly alone and abandoned. If, indeed, you feel this way yourself, you might find some sort of psycho-spiritual help in the therapeutic philosophy of the stoics.

According to the stoics, we live in an **ordered universe.** This means the universe is rational, structured, and shaped by design. Nothing that happens is random or serendipitous. For example, when two old friends bump into each other on the street, apparently by chance, they really don't; their meeting is evidence of what Carl Jung calls **synchronicity,** or meaningful coincidence. There is a reason behind it. Epictetus puts it so: *Events do not just happen, but arrive by appointment.* As Chrysippus argued, everything that happens is **fated,** predetermined, and according to plan. For stoics, the power behind the plan is God. Be careful, however, how you interpret the notion of God. Depending on your religious belief system, if you have one, you may tend to see God in essentially superhuman terms, as some kind of extraordinary being. Some Christians believe we are created in God's image as humans, only less than perfect. The stoics, by contrast, made God synonymous with Zeus, creative fire, ether, the Word (Logos), World Reason, Fate, Providence, Destiny, and the Law of Nature. In fact, in their **monistic universe,** there is no difference between God and all the things in the world; they are one. Thus, God, Zeus, the Logos (or whatever you choose to call this elemental force) is not somehow above or beyond us. God is **immanent** in everything. God is the determining element in all physical objects and events. As for humans, because we possess the power of reason, we have the spark of divinity emanating from our original Source. Under the guidance of the divine Logos, the universe displays a rational order. Everything is connected and happens for a reason—one that is divinely ordained (see Table 2.1).

## How to Live in a Fated Universe

From the philosophical notion of stoic determinism follow a number of practical, moral, and behavioral prescriptions for action. These prescriptions ultimately derive from the belief that God orders all things for the best. This stoic belief offers us a great measure of reassurance. Whatever is, or whatever happens, is or does so by design and with a purpose. Nothing in the stoic universe is out of place. This, of course, raises the problem of evil in the world, to which stoicism has the following reply: Good cannot exist without evil; evil throws the good into greater relief in the same way that the contrast of light and shadow

**TABLE 2.1**   Periods and Proponents of Stoicism

| Early Stoa (Third Century B.C.E.) | |
| --- | --- |
| Zeno (336–264 B.C.E.) | Founder of Stoicism; lectured at the Painted Porch (*Stoa Poikile*) in Athens; emphasized strength of character in ethical and political action |
| Cleanthes of Assos (331–232 B.C.E.) | Successor to Zeno; poet and religious visionary |
| Chrysippus of Soloi (279–206 B.C.E.) | Third leader of the stoa at Athens; successor to Cleathes; advocated living in accordance with reason; saw emotions as great obstacles to happiness that required eradication |
| **Middle Stoa (second and first centuries B.C.E.)** | |
| Panaetius of Rhodes (185–110 B.C.E.) | Softened asceticism of early stoa; attached moral value to external goods; spoke in terms of gradual moral progress |
| Posidonius of Apamea (135–51 B.C.E.) | Pupil of Panaetius; brought rigor and detail to the stoic system; developed stoic belief in the indivisibility of cosmos |
| **Late Stoa (first and second century C.E.)** | |
| Seneca (4 B.C.E.–65 C.E.) | Most sympathetic to Posidonius, minister of Nero; writer of tragedies; developer of stoic ethics: tranquility and social duty |
| Epictetus (50–138 C.E.) | Freed slave; member of Nero's bodyguard; distinguished between what we can and cannot control; believed in innate moral predispositions |
| Marcus Aurelius (121–180 C.E.) | Last of the great stoics; emphasized inward self-control and useful citizenship in the cosmopolis |

SOURCE: Paul Edwards, ed., *The Encyclopedia of Philosophy*, Vol. 7 (New York: Macmillan and Free Press, 1967), pp. 19–22.

*Take some time to think about a setback or disappointment in your life. It could have occurred at home, with your friends, at work or at school perhaps. What happened exactly? Why was the incident so upsetting? How could it serve, or has it served, as a preparation for your current and future life? Do you think the stoics were correct in saying that everything happens for a reason? Why or why not? Continue to record your thoughts in your meditative journal.*

**❝*Live according to Nature.*❞**
STOIC MAXIM

is pleasing in a picture. In a similar vein, Chrysippus said: "Comedies have in them ludicrous verses which, though bad in themselves, nevertheless lend a certain grace to the whole play."[3] Furthermore, apparent evil that befalls the good may be turned into a blessing in disguise. Individuals may overcome tragedies and transform them into personal triumphs. Physical diseases may stimulate medical research that ends in cures. Today's misfortunes may also become the open doorways for tomorrow's successes.

I'm reminded here of a former student of mine who transferred to General Arts and Science after flunking out of a sports injury management course. She was severely anxious and depressed by her removal from the program. In time, this student discovered she had an aptitude for philosophy, and as a result, she decided to proceed with future university studies to become a lawyer. The last time we spoke, she was delighted by this "twist of fate" which, at the outset, was painful but now seemed for the best. Her "failure" was simply a preparation for a new beginning, though she couldn't appreciate this fact at the time of her ejection. Just think, every joy, success, setback, disappointment, trauma, or failure that you've experienced constitute, in a stoic universe, simply the perfect preparation for what you're doing right now in your life.

## Freedom and Value

Because things happen as they should, in the **cosmology** of the stoics, no act is evil or reprehensible in itself. As stoics point out, it is "the intention, the moral condition of the agent from whom the act proceeds, that makes the act evil; the act as a physical entity is indifferent."[4] Moral evil manifests itself when the human will is out of harmony with right reason. Personal freedom in a stoic universe does not come from doing anything you want, but by choosing to act according to nature. A form of **interior freedom** is possible when individuals alter their **judgments** on events and **attitudes** toward them, perceiving them and welcoming them as the expressions of God's will. The stoic's advice is that we develop a psychological posture of **courageous acceptance.** Although we cannot control world events, we have complete (interior) freedom to respond emotionally and psychologically. We cannot choose life's roles (being born male or female, into a rich or poor family); we can only choose how well to play the roles assigned us. As I read on a bumper sticker once: *Attitude is everything.* (I didn't know a stoic was driving the car ahead of me—likely one of those closet-philosopher types I talked about in Chapter One!)

## Purpose of Life

In the stoic universe, the ultimate goal of life is to live according to nature. Doing so will lead to a state of spiritual peace and well-being, sometimes referred to as **stoic apathy** (from *apatheia*) or at other times as *eudaimonia.* The notion of *eudaimonia,* sometimes loosely translated as happiness, should not be interpreted in psychological terms, however, but rather in a normative fashion. The *eudaimon,* one who has achieved happiness, is someone who flourishes from stoic apathy, living the virtuous life. This person, whose human will accords with Divine Reason, lives life according to nature. Nothing else besides virtue has value in itself. External goods are neither parts of *eudaimonia,* nor necessary for it.[5] Things like health, wealth, pleasure, or absence of pain are, in fact, morally indifferent to the virtuous life. *Eudaimonia* is possible with or without them. One person can be sick and poor and still be virtuous. Another can be healthy and wealthy and yet be disturbed as well as miserably corrupt. Of course, given the choice, health is to be preferred over sickness, wealth over poverty, and freedom from pain over suffering. We should all try to conduct our affairs and influence events in our lives to enhance the former in each case and to minimize the latter.

Things like health and wealth do possess a "second grade worth" within the stoic hierarchical scale of values. What the stoic recognizes, however, is that such things are ultimately beyond our control. You may choose to live a healthy lifestyle, for instance, but suddenly be hit by a car, leaving you permanently disabled. You may also have made prudent financial investments for years, only to discover one morning that the stock market has crashed and left you personally bankrupt. As devastating as such events may seem, according to stoicism, they should not be cause for psychological disturbance. They only affect you if you let them, and you only let them if you allow yourself to become attached to worldly things. Personally, I find this stoic insight immensely liberating. Just think, nothing that happens in your life—no misfortune, accident, trauma, or tragedy—can ever prevent you from living life as it should be lived.

When "the good life" is equated with the virtuous life, which accords with the Logos or God's will, a certain self-possession and **emotional detachment** from worldly affairs can manifest itself in tranquility and peace of mind. If you are currently upset by life, then, from a stoic vantage point, you probably exhibit bad thinking and poor character development, confusing what you can and cannot control, placing value in things that have no intrinsic, ultimate worth. If you are unhappy, it is not because something has happened to you or because something has failed to happen; it is because *you* are the problem. To illustrate how the problem is "in you" not "out there," consider the fact that not everybody is upset by the same insult. You may become infuriated, while someone else could be left unaffected. News of a job loss could depress you but exhilarate someone elated by the prospect of challenging new opportunities. Insults and bad news affect different people in different ways. The upset is therefore not in the insult or the bad news, but in the person. What is important to recognize is that nothing or nobody can make you glad, mad, or sad without your permission. When it comes to your attitudes and emotions, the stoic maintains that you are ultimately in control. Marcus Aurelius says: *If you are pained by any external thing, it is not the thing that disturbs you, but your judgment about it. And, it is in your power to wipe out this judgment now.*

*Things themselves touch not the soul, not in the least degree.*

MARCUS AURELIUS

The psychologically healing powers of stoic wisdom have managed to trickle down into contemporary society through psychotherapeutic practices of stress management. **Albert Ellis,** the internationally recognized developer of **Rational-Emotive Behavior Therapy,** has found through research and clinical practice that people feel largely the way they do because of how they think. Ellis says that, " . . . what we label our emotional reactions are mainly caused by our conscious and unconscious evaluations, interpretations and philosophies."[6] When we feel anxious, worried, or stressed, it is frequently due to the irrational assumptions we make and the foolish beliefs to which we cling. Consistent with stoic thinking, Ellis argues that things and events, in themselves, don't *make us unhappy;* rather our interpretations of them do. Therefore, if we could identify our irrational assumptions and beliefs and then abandon them, we would then begin to live a more rational lifestyle, one with significantly less stress and less negative emotion. By clinging to irrationality, we become architects of our own emotional disturbance and "dis-ease."

To illustrate how this is so, Ellis has conceptualized an A–B–C Model of psychological functioning, which he incorporated into his therapeutic methods (Figure 2.2). The *A* represents the activating event—the real-life occurrence that is potentially stressful, although not necessarily so. The activating event could be a failure, loss, hurt, or anything else that could produce stress in your life. Intuitively, some of us think that such events automatically cause a stress response. However, the emotional consequence *C*—of failure, loss, or hurt—is not necessarily determined by such things. Coming between the activating event (*A*) and the ultimate emotional response or consequence (*C*) is the belief (*B*) about what just happened (*A*). The cognitive interpretation and appraisal of the activating event will ultimately determine the emotional response. Figure 2.2 also serves to underscore the insight of Epictetus the stoic that *Men are not disturbed by things, but by the view which they take of them.*

**FIGURE 2.2** Albert Ellis's "A–B–C" model.

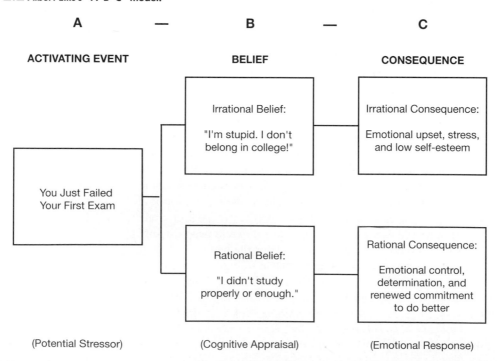

| A | — | B | — | C |
|---|---|---|---|---|
| **ACTIVATING EVENT** | | **BELIEF** | | **CONSEQUENCE** |

You Just Failed Your First Exam

Irrational Belief:
"I'm stupid. I don't belong in college!"

Irrational Consequence:
Emotional upset, stress, and low self-esteem

Rational Belief:
"I didn't study properly or enough."

Rational Consequence:
Emotional control, determination, and renewed commitment to do better

(Potential Stressor)    (Cognitive Appraisal)    (Emotional Response)

# Emotions in Life

Given the lengthy history of stoicism and its many variations from different periods and geographic locations (Athens and Rome), academic interpretations regarding the stoic position on **emotion** are not entirely consistent. Some analysts claim the stoics rejected all emotions to the extent it was humanly possible; others contend that such a claim is only a half-truth, asserting that what the stoics wished to abolish were the "excessive passions" that led to mental disturbance.[7] The discrepancy seems to come from the fact that interpreters cite different sources in their translations from the Greek that either distinguish, or fail to distinguish, between the notions of *emotion* and *passion*. Where there is a total dismissal of emotion, the distinction appears not to be made; where emotion is countenanced, the difference is recognized. On this latter interpretation, some emotions are acceptable, while others become **excessive passions.** Excessive passions are unreasonable and unnatural. However, a parent's love for a child, for instance, is an acceptable emotion that is natural and consistent with the divine order. Feelings of love for humanity and the attractions of friendship are also natural, so not necessarily to be avoided. By contrast, fear is an exaggerated emotion (a passionate disturbance), to be eliminated because it is contrary to reason. When people experience fear of the future, they may exhibit physical symptoms such as jittery hands or heart palpitations. These physical effects of fear result because of the belief that something bad is about to happen. However, in a fated stoic universe, nothing that happens can be described as bad, for it occurs as a function of God's will. Even things like death, pain, and ill-repute are morally indifferent. The experience of fear is the result of exaggerating their importance and believing that they will bring real harm when, in truth, they leave our essential moral being unaffected.

Other disturbing passions to be avoided include lust for revenge, envy, jealousy, grief, and even pity. The desire for revenge contains a disquieting element of hatred, whereas envy, grief, and jealousy possess some fairly obvious negative qualities of their own, leading to their own 'dis-ease.' As for pity, although it may sound like an admirable emotion, it too should be eliminated for it is based on the (false) belief that something "bad" has happened to someone else. Since no sorrow or resentment should follow from one's own suffering, it should not accompany another's. In the grand scheme of things—that is, from a universal and timeless perspective beyond one's own personal concerns and particular circumstances—all that happens is for the best and by design.

# How to Progress Morally

Stoic wisdom offers us not only tranquility and freedom from fear, but also some suggestions for achieving such things. If we wish to develop morally as persons, we must behave in certain ways. First of all, we should live by the Socratic injunction to "Know Thyself." Seneca and Epictetus recommend that we engage in daily self-examinations, monitoring our thoughts, feelings, and actions.[8] This will help us to substitute good habits for bad ones. In this regard, we should try to avoid temptations and wayward companions. We must become masters in our own psychological homes—controlling, avoiding, or eliminating those excessive emotions contributing to passionate disturbances in our lives. Recognizing the role of divine Providence in all events and seeing how most things desired by people in life are morally indifferent, we should also learn to forgive those who we erroneously thought hurt us or took from us what we once believed was valuable, but now recognize as worthless. From the stoic perspective, it is advantageous to set before our eyes some ideal of virtue (for example, Socrates) and then try to live up to it. As aspiring stoics, we should order our desires and perform our duties in accordance with right reason. Epictetus would recommend that we become indifferent to external goods. If we choose to seek happiness in goods that do not depend entirely on ourselves, we fall into the abyss of nonstop psychological dissatisfaction. Temperance and abstinence are more likely to result in happiness than efforts directed toward never-ending want gratification. Further stoic insights into how life should be lived can be gained in The Meditations of Marcus Aurelius.

## ORIGINAL SOURCEWORK

## *The Meditations of Marcus Aurelius*

**MARCUS AURELIUS**

**V**

In the morning when thou risest unwillingly, let this thought be present—I am rising to the work of a human being. Why then am I dissatisfied if I am going to do the things for which I exist and for which I was brought into the world? Or have I been made for this, to lie in the bedclothes and keep myself warm?—But this is more pleasant.—Dost thou exist then to take thy pleasure, and not at all for action or exertion? Dost thou not see the little plants, the little birds, the ants, the spiders, the bees working together to put in order their several parts of the universe? And art thou unwilling to do the work of a human being, and dost thou not make haste to do that which is according to thy nature?—But it is necessary to take rest also.—It is necessary: however nature has fixed bounds to this too: she has fixed bounds both to eating and drinking, and

yet thou goest beyond these bounds, beyond what is sufficient; yet in thy acts it is not so, but thou stoppest short of what thou canst do. So thou lovest not thyself, for if thou didst, thou wouldst love thy nature and her will. But those who love their several arts exhaust themselves in working at them unwashed and without food; but thou valuest thy own nature less than the turner values the turning art, or the dancer the dancing art, or the lover of money values his money, or the vainglorious man his little glory. And such men, when they have a violent affection to a thing, choose neither to eat nor to sleep rather than to perfect the things which they care for. But are the acts which concern society more vile in thy eyes and less worthy of thy labour?

2. How easy it is to repel and to wipe away every impression which is troublesome or unsuitable, and immediately to be in all tranquility.

Source: Marcus Aurelius, *The Meditations of Marcus Aurelius*. Trans. George Lang. New York: P.F. Collier & Son, 1909–1914.

3. Judge every word and deed which are according to nature to be fit for thee; and be not diverted by the blame which follows from any people, nor by their words, but if a thing is good to be done or said, do not consider it unworthy of thee. For those persons have their peculiar leading principle and follow their peculiar movement; which things do not thou regard, but go straight on, following thy own nature and the common nature; and the way of both is one.

4. I go through the things which happen according to nature until I shall fall and rest, breathing out my breath into that element out of which I daily draw it in, and falling upon that earth out of which my father collected the seed, and my mother the blood, and my nurse the milk; out of which during so many years I have been supplied with food and drink; which bears me when I tread on it and abuse it for so many purposes.

5. Thou sayest, men cannot admire the sharpness of thy wits.—Be it so; but there are many other things of which thou canst not say, I am not formed for them by nature. Show those qualities then which are altogether in thy power: sincerity, gravity, endurance of labour, aversion to pleasure, contentment with thy portion and with few things, benevolence, frankness, no love of superfluity, freedom from trifling magnanimity. Dost thou not see how many qualities thou art immediately able to exhibit, in which there is no excuse of natural incapacity and unfitness, and yet thou still remainest voluntarily below the mark? Or art thou compelled through being defectively furnished by nature to murmur, and to be stingy, and to flatter, and to find fault with thy poor body, and to try to please men, and to make great display, and to be restless in thy mind? No, by the gods: but thou mightest have been delivered from these things long ago. Only if in truth thou canst be charged with being rather slow and dull of comprehension, thou must exert thyself about this also, not neglecting it nor yet taking pleasure in thy dullness.

6. One man, when he has done a service to another, is ready to set it down to his account as a favour conferred. Another is not ready to do this, but still in his own mind he thinks of the man as his debtor, and he knows what he has done. A third in a manner does not even know what he has done, but he is like a vine which has produced grapes, and seeks for nothing more

after it has once produced its proper fruit. As a horse when he has run, a dog when he has tracked the game, a bee when it has made the honey, so a man when he has done a good act, does not call out for others to come and see, but he goes on to another act, as a vine goes on to produce again the grapes in season.—Must a man then be one of these, who in a manner act thus without observing it?—Yes.—But this very thing is necessary, the observation of what a man is doing; for it may be said, it is characteristic of the social animal to perceive that he is working in a social manner, and indeed to wish that his social partner also should perceive it.—It is true what thou sayest, but thou dost not rightly understand what is now said; and for this reason thou wilt become one of those of whom I spoke before, for even they are misled by a certain show of reason. But if thou wilt choose to understand the meaning of what is said, do not fear that for this reason thou wilt omit any social act.

7. A prayer of the Athenians: Rain, rain, O dear Zeus, down on the plowed fields of the Athenians and on the plains.—In truth we ought not to pray at all, or we ought to pray in this simple and noble fashion.

8. Just as we must understand when it is said, That Æsculapius prescribed to this man horse-exercise, or bathing in cold water, or going without shoes, so we must understand it when it is said, That the nature of the universe prescribed to this man disease or mutilation or loss or anything else of the kind. For in the first case prescribed means something like this: he prescribed this for this man as a thing adapted to procure health; and in the second case it means, That which happens to [or suits] every man is fixed in a manner for him suitably to his destiny. For this is what we mean when we say that things are suitable to us, as the workmen say of squared stones in walls or the pyramids, that they are suitable, when they fit them to one another in some kind of connection. For there is altogether one fitness [harmony]. And as the universe is made up out of all bodies to be such a body as it is, so out of all existing causes necessity [destiny] is made up to be such a cause as it is. And even those who are completely ignorant understand what I mean, for they say, It [necessity, destiny] brought this to such a person.—This then was brought and this was prescribed to him. Let us then receive these things, as well as those which Æsculapius prescribes. Many, as a matter of course, even among his

prescriptions, are disagreeable, but we accept them in the hope of health. Let the perfecting and accomplishment of the things, which the common nature judges to be good, be judged by thee to be of the same kind as thy health. And so accept everything which happens, even if it seem disagreeable, because it leads to this, to the health of the universe and to the prosperity and felicity of Zeus [the universe]. For he would not have brought on any man what he has brought, if it were not useful for the whole. Neither does the nature of anything, whatever it may be, cause anything which is not suitable to that which is directed by it. For two reasons, then, it is right to be content with that which happens to thee; the one, because it was done for thee and prescribed for thee, and in a manner had reference to thee, originally from the most ancient causes spun with thy destiny; and the other, because even that which comes severally to every man is to the power which administers the universe a cause of felicity and perfection, nay even of its very continuance. For the integrity of the whole is mutilated, if thou cuttest off anything whatever from the conjunction and the continuity either of the parts or of the causes. And thou dost cut off, as far as it is in thy power, when thou art dissatisfied, and in a manner triest to put anything out of the way.

9. Be not disgusted, nor discouraged, nor dissatisfied, if thou dost not succeed in doing everything according to right principles; but when thou hast failed, return back again, and be content if the greater part of what thou doest is consistent with man's nature, and love this to which thou returnest; and do not return to philosophy as if she were a master, but act like those who have sore eyes and apply a bit of sponge and egg, or as another applies a plaster, or drenching with water. For thus thou wilt not fail to obey reason and thou wilt repose in it. And remember that philosophy requires only the things which thy nature requires; but thou wouldst have something else which is not according to nature. It may be objected, Why, what is more agreeable than this [which I am doing]? But is not this the very reason why pleasure deceives us? And consider if magnanimity, freedom, simplicity, equanimity, piety are not more agreeable. For what is more agreeable than wisdom itself, when thou thinkest of the security and the happy course of all things which depend on the faculty of understanding and knowledge?

10. Things are in such a kind of envelopment that they have seemed to philosophers, not a few nor those common philosophers, altogether unintelligible; nay even to the Stoics themselves they seem difficult to understand. And all our assent is changeable; for where is the man who never changes? Carry thy thoughts then to the objects themselves, and consider how short-lived they are and worthless, and that they may be in the possession of a filthy wretch or a whore or a robber. Then turn to the morals of those who live with thee, and it is hardly possible to endure even the most agreeable of them, to say nothing of a man being hardly able to endure himself. In such darkness, then, and dirt, and in so constant a flux, both of substance and of time, and of motion, and of things moved, what there is worth being highly prized, or even an object of serious pursuit, I cannot imagine. But on the contrary it is a man's duty to comfort himself, and to wait for the natural dissolution and not to be vexed at the delay, but to rest in these principles only: the one, that nothing will happen to me which is not conformable to the nature of the universe; and the other, that it is in my power never to act contrary to my god and dæmon: for there is no man who will compel me to this.

11. About what am I now employing my own soul? On every occasion I must ask myself this question, and inquire, what have I now in this part of me, which they call the ruling principle? and whose soul have I now? that of a child, or of a young man, or of a feeble woman, or of a tyrant, or of a domestic animal, or of a wild beast?

12. What kind of things those are which appear good to the many, we may learn even from this. For if any man should conceive certain things as being really good, such as prudence, temperance, justice, fortitude, he would not after having first conceived these endure to listen to anything which should not be in harmony with what is really good. But if a man has first conceived as good the things which appear to the many to be good, he will listen and readily receive as very applicable that which was said by the comic writer. Thus even the many perceive the difference. For were it not so, this saying would not offend and would not be rejected [in the first case], while we receive it when it is said of wealth, and of the means which further luxury and fame, as said fitly and wittily. Go on then and ask if we should value and think those things to be good, to which after their first

conception in the mind the words of the comic writer might be aptly applied—that he who has them, through pure abundance has not a place to ease himself in.

13. I am composed of the formal and the material; and neither of them will perish into non-existence, as neither of them came into existence out of non-existence. Every part of me then will be reduced by change into some part of the universe, and that again will change into another part of the universe, and so on forever. And by consequence of such a change I too exist, and those who begot me, and so on forever in the other direction. For nothing hinders us from saying so, even if the universe is administered according to definite periods [of revolution].

14. Reason and the reasoning art [philosophy] are powers which are sufficient for themselves and for their own works. They move then from a first principle which is their own, and they make their way to the end which is proposed to them; and this is the reason why such acts are named Catorthóseis or right acts, which word signifies that they proceed by the right road.

15. None of these things ought to be called a man's which do not belong to a man, as man. They are not required of a man, nor does man's nature promise them, nor are they the means of man's nature attaining its end. Neither then does the end of man lie in these things, nor yet that which aids to the accomplishment of this end, and that which aids toward this end is that which is good. Besides, if any of these things did belong to man, it would not be right for a man to despise them and to set himself against them; nor would a man be worthy of praise who showed that he did not want these things, nor would he who stinted himself in any of them be good, if indeed these things were good. But now the more of these things a man deprives himself of, or of other things like them, or even when he is deprived of any of them, the more patiently he endures the loss, just in the same degree he is a better man.

16. Such as are thy habitual thoughts, such also will be the character of thy mind; for the soul is dyed by the thoughts. Dye it then with a continuous series of such thoughts as these: for instance, that where a man can live, there he can also live well. But he must live in a palace—well then, he can also live well in a palace. And again, consider that for whatever purpose each thing has

been constituted, for this it has been constituted, and toward this it is carried; and its end is in that toward which it is carried; and where the end is, there also is the advantage and the good of each thing. Now the good for the reasonable animal is society; for that we are made for society has been shown above. Is it not plain that the inferior exist for the sake of the superior? but the things which have life are superior to those which have not life, and of those which have life the superior are those which have reason.

17. To seek what is impossible is madness: and it is impossible that the bad should not do something of this kind.

18. Nothing happens to any man which he is not formed by nature to bear. The same things happen to another, and either because he does not see that they have happened or because he would show a great spirit he is firm and remains unharmed. It is a shame then that ignorance and conceit should be stronger than wisdom.

19. Things themselves touch not the soul, not in the least degree; nor have they admission to the soul, nor can they turn or move the soul: but the soul turns and moves itself alone, and whatever judgments it may think proper to make, such it makes for itself the things which present themselves to it.

20. In one respect man is the nearest thing to me, so far as I must do good to men and endure them. But so far as some men make themselves obstacles to my proper acts, man becomes to me one of the things which are indifferent, no less than the sun or wind or a wild beast. Now it is true that these may impede my action, but they are no impediments to my affects and disposition, which have the power of acting conditionally and changing: for the mind converts and changes every hindrance to its activity into an aid; and so that which is a hindrance is made a furtherance to an act; and that which is an obstacle on the road helps us on this road.

21. Reverence that which is best in the universe; and this is that which makes use of all things and directs all things. And in like manner also reverence that which is best in thyself; and this is of the same kind as that. For in thyself also, that which makes use of everything else, is this, and thy life is directed by this.

22. That which does no harm to the state, does no harm to the citizen. In the case of every appearance of

harm apply this rule: if the state is not harmed by this, neither am I harmed. But if the state is harmed, thou must not be angry with him who does harm to the state. Show him where his error is.

23. Often think of the rapidity with which things pass by and disappear, both the things which are and the things which are produced. For substance is like a river in a continual flow, and the activities of things are in constant change, and the causes work in infinite varieties; and there is hardly anything which stands still. And consider this which is near to thee, this boundless abyss of the past and of the future in which all things disappear. How then is he not a fool who is puffed up with such things or plagued about them or makes himself miserable? for they vex him only for a time, and a short time.

24. Think of the universal substance, of which thou hast a very small portion; and of universal time, of which a short and indivisible interval has been assigned to thee; and of that which is fixed by destiny, and how small a part of it thou art.

25. Does another do me wrong? Let him look to it. He has his own disposition, his own activity. I now have what the universal nature wills me to have; and I do what my nature now wills me to do.

26. Let the part of thy soul which leads and governs be undisturbed by the movements in the flesh, whether of pleasure or of pain; and let it not unite with them, but let it circumscribe itself and limit those affects to their parts. But when these affects rise up to the mind by virtue of that other sympathy that naturally exists in a body which is all one, then thou must not strive to resist the sensation, for it is natural: but let not the ruling part of itself add to the sensation the opinion that it is either good or bad.

27. Live with the gods. And he does live with the gods who constantly shows to them that his own soul is satisfied with that which is assigned to him, and that it does all that the dæmon wishes, which Zeus hath given to every man for his guardian and guide, a portion of himself. And this is every man's understanding and reason.

28. Art thou angry with him whose arm-pits stink? art thou angry with him whose mouth smells foul? What good will this anger do thee? He has such a mouth, he has such arm-pits: it is necessary that such an emanation must come from such things—but the

man has reason, it will be said, and he is able, if he takes pains, to discover wherein he offends—I wish thee well of thy discovery. Well then, and thou hast reason: by thy rational faculty stir up his rational faculty; show him his error, admonish him. For if he listens, thou wilt cure him, and there is no need of anger. [Neither tragic actor nor whore.[1]]

29. As thou intendest to live when thou are gone out, . . . so it is in thy power to live here. But if men do not permit thee, then get away out of life, yet so as if thou wert suffering no harm. The house is smoky, and I quit it. Why dost thou think that this is any trouble? But so long as nothing of the kind drives me out, I remain, am free, and no man shall hinder me from doing what I choose; and I choose to do what is according to the nature of the rational and social animal.

30. The intelligence of the universe is social. Accordingly it has made the inferior things for the sake of the superior, and it has fitted the superior to one another. Thou seest how it has subordinated, co-ordinated and assigned to everything its proper portion, and has brought together into concord with one another the things which are the best.

31. How hast thou behaved hitherto to the gods, thy parents, brethren, children, teachers, to those who looked after thy infancy, to thy friends, kinsfolk, to thy slaves? Consider if thou hast hitherto behaved to all in such a way that this may be said of thee:

Never has wronged a man in deed or word.

And call to recollection both how many things thou hast passed through, and how many things thou hast been able to endure: and that the history of thy life is now complete, and thy service is ended: and how many beautiful things thou hast seen: and how many pleasures and pains thou hast despised; and how many things called honourable thou hast spurned; and to how many ill-minded folks thou hast shown a kind disposition.

32. Why do unskilled and ignorant souls disturb him who has skill and knowledge? What soul then has skill and knowledge? That which knows beginning and end, and knows the reason which pervades all substance and through all time by fixed periods [revolutions] administers the universe.

33. Soon, very soon, thou wilt be ashes, or a skeleton, and either a name or not even a name; but name is

sound and echo, and the things which are much valued in life are empty and rotten and trifling, and [like] little dogs biting one another, and little children quarrelling, laughing, and then straightway weeping. But fidelity and modesty and justice and truth are fled

Up to Olympus from the wide-spread earth.
*Hesiod, Works, etc.,* v. 197.

What then is there which still detains thee here? if the objects of sense are easily changed and never stand still, and the organs of perception are dull and easily receive false impressions; and the poor soul itself is an exhalation from blood. But to have good repute amid such a world as this is an empty thing. Why then dost thou not wait in tranquility for thy end, whether it is extinction or removal to another state? And until that time comes, what is sufficient? Why, what else than to venerate the gods and bless them, and to do good to men, and to practise tolerance and self-restraint; but as to everything which is beyond the limits of the poor flesh and breath, to remember that this is neither thine nor in thy power.

34. Thou canst pass thy life in an equable flow of happiness, if thou canst go by the right way, and think and act in the right way. These two things are common both to the soul of God and to the soul of man, and to the soul of every rational being, not to be hindered by another; and to hold good to consist in the disposition to justice and the practice of it, and in this to let thy desire find its termination.

35. If this is neither my own badness, nor an effect of my own badness, and the common weal is not injured, why am I troubled about it? and what is the harm to the common weal?

36. Do not be carried along inconsiderately by the appearance of things, but give help [to all] according to thy ability and their fitness; and if they should have sustained loss in matters which are indifferent, do not imagine this to be a damage. For it is a bad habit. But as the old man, when he went away, asked back his foster-child's top, remembering that it was a top, so do thou in this case also.

When thou art calling out on the Rostra, hast thou forgotten, man, what these things are? Yes; but they are objects of great concern to these people—wilt thou too then be made a fool for these things? I was once a fortunate man, but I lost it, I know not how. But fortunate means that a man has assigned to himself a good fortune; and a good fortune is good disposition of the soul, good emotions, good actions.

## NOTES

1. This sentence is imperfect or corrupt, or both.

## DISCUSSION QUESTIONS FOR CRITIQUE AND ANALYSIS

1. What lifestyle does Marcus Aurelius recommend to us? Is it the one we ought to prefer? Why or why not?

2. Marcus Aurelius says that, "Things themselves touch not the soul, not in the least degree." What does this mean exactly? Do you agree or disagree? Why?

3. What are some contemporary obstacles to stoic serenity? How best should we deal with these obstacles?

# EXISTENTIALISM: BORN FREE, LET ME BE ME

**Existentialism** is a philosophical movement that some prefer to see as an attitude or outlook rather than as a formal philosophy. We regard it as a philosophy of life for our purposes here. Existentialism is difficult to define precisely because there doesn't exist any common body of doctrine to which all existentialists would subscribe. For example, within the existential movement, you find **atheists** and **theists** (primarily Christian and Jewish), as well as **political conservatives, Marxists, humanitarians,** at least one **fascist,** and those who are

> **66** *Whatever its ultimate meaning, the universe into which we have been thrown cannot satisfy our reason—let us have the courage to admit it once and for all.* **99**
>
> GABRIEL MARCEL

**anti-political.** Some are optimistic, while others tend toward pessimism. Certain existentialists have emphasized issues of **freedom** in their writing, whereas others have focused on **absurdity** or on the world of the **interpersonal.** To complicate things even further, some philosophers associated with existentialism predate the use of the term itself, and others simply refuse to be called existentialists at all. To belong to a "school of thought" and be labeled as a member, or to subordinate one's individuality and adhere to some shared philosophical doctrine, would not be very "existential." You'll understand why shortly.

## Methods

Existentialism adopts some **unorthodox methods** of investigation for probing the human condition; consequently, some don't see existentialism as a legitimate philosophy. Existential insights are often best communicated in

## PHILOSOPHICAL PROFILE

**JEAN-PAUL SARTRE AND SIMONE DE BEAUVOIR**

### Existentialists

#### JEAN-PAUL SARTRE

Jean-Paul Sartre was a famous novelist, playwright, and major philosopher of the twentieth century. He virtually held court over French intellectual life for a couple of decades. After completing a high school diploma, he began six years of study at the Sorbonne in Paris for his "agregation," the exam that would launch his academic career as a philosophy teacher. In 1928, Sartre failed the agregation, coming last in his class. This setback resulted, fortunately, in his meeting Simone de Beauvoir. Sartre and de Beauvoir were to develop a loving friendship that would last until his death. Sartre's major philosophical opus is *Being and Nothingness;* his literary works include *Nausea, No Exit,* and *Saint Genet.*

#### SIMONE DE BEAUVOIR

Simone de Beauvoir was born in 1908. She was educated at the Sorbonne, where she studied philosophy. De Beauvoir enjoyed a productive and prosperous career as a philosophy professor and novelist, perhaps the foremost in her time. Until 1949, de Beauvoir was primarily recognized as a talented writer and close companion to Jean-Paul Sartre. She read and critiqued most of Sartre's works. In that same year, the release of *The Second Sex* made her arguably one of the most important and controversial theorists of the twentieth century. De Beauvoir provided us with a conception of existential ethics, something Sartre never did. Though she did greatly emphasize freedom, like Sartre she paired it with morality, making her own original and important contribution to philosophical research. See her *Ethics of Ambiguity.* Other works by de Beauvoir include *The Coming of Age, A Very Easy Death, The Blood of Others, America Day by Day,* and *Marquis de Sade.* De Beauvoir passed away in 1986.

**aphorisms, dialogues, parables,** and other **literary forms** such as novels and plays. Poignant existential statements are often found in poetic verse and in visual art, and not necessarily in the context of systematic rational argument and debate. Also, given that prominent existentialists like **Jean-Paul Sartre** practiced his philosophy in Parisian cafés, far removed from the hallowed halls of academe and the lecture podium of the university professor, many initially regarded existentialism as little more than a passing fad. The unorthodox existential approach to philosophical inquiry is certainly different from traditional philosophy and often the source of much confusion and bewilderment. Nonetheless, existentialism remains a useful umbrella term under which it is possible to gather together a number of **recurrent themes** and philosophical preoccupations.

It is undeniable that the existential movement has had its effects on contemporary society, and that its profound insights can have personal relevance. Some basic existential questions pertaining to you include the following: *"What am I to do?" "To what can I commit my life?" "What does my life mean?"* To determine if, or to what extent, you possibly suffer from a sense of meaninglessness in your life and are unable to answer the last question, complete the *Know Thyself* self-diagnostic entitled "The Purpose in Life Test–Abbreviated Version" developed by James C. Crumbaugh and Leonard Maholick (1969).

## KNOW THYSELF

### The Purpose in Life Test (Abbreviated Version)

## BACKGROUND AND AIMS

"The Purpose in Life Test" is an attitude scale based on the insights of the psychiatrist Viktor Frankl and his system of existential counseling known as "Logotherapy." *Logos* is a Greek term denoting the idea of meaning, so his work is a kind of meaning therapy, helping people to escape the "existential vacuum"— a sense of futility and emptiness that pervades the lives of so many individuals today. According to Frankl, the primary motive in people is the "will-to-meaning," in contrast to Sigmund Freud's "will to pleasure" and Alfred Adler and Friedrich Nietzsche's "will-to-power" (see Chapter 5). Frankl believes that human beings possess within themselves the urge to find meaning and purpose in life. Failure to do so results in a form of existential frustration, or even more seriously, in "noögenic neurosis"—a breakdown created by a compounding of neurotic symptoms with an inability to find meaning in human existence. It should be noted that the existential vacuum is not a neurosis or abnormality as such, but rather a pervasive human condition resulting from modern society's tendency toward dehumanization. Only in neurotically predisposed people does the more serious noögenic neurosis develop. "The Purpose in Life Test" helps to detect the presence of an existential vacuum. Other clinical tests and procedures are required to identify the more serious presence of noögenic neurosis.

## Purpose of Life Test (PIL)

James C. Crumbaugh, Ph.D, and Leonard T. Maholick, M.D.

# PART A

For each of the following statements, circle the number that would be most nearly true for you. Note that the numbers always extend from one extreme feeling to its opposite kind of feeling. "Neutral" implies no judgment either way; try to use this rating as little as possible.

1. I am usually:

| 1 | 2 | 3 | 4 | 5 | 6 | 7 |
|---|---|---|---|---|---|---|
| completely bored | | | (neutral) | | | exuberant, enthusiastic |

2. Life to me seems:

| 7 | 6 | 5 | 4 | 3 | 2 | 1 |
|---|---|---|---|---|---|---|
| always exciting | | | (neutral) | | | completely routine |

3. In life I have:

| 1 | 2 | 3 | 4 | 5 | 6 | 7 |
|---|---|---|---|---|---|---|
| no goals or aims at all | | | (neutral) | | | very clear goals and aims |

4. My personal existence is:

| 1 | 2 | 3 | 4 | 5 | 6 | 7 |
|---|---|---|---|---|---|---|
| utterly meaningless, without purpose | | | (neutral) | | | very purposeful and meaningful |

5. Every day is:

| 7 | 6 | 5 | 4 | 3 | 2 | 1 |
|---|---|---|---|---|---|---|
| constantly new | | | (neutral) | | | exactly the same |

6. If I could choose, I would:

| 1 | 2 | 3 | 4 | 5 | 6 | 7 |
|---|---|---|---|---|---|---|
| prefer never to have been born | | | (neutral) | | | like nine more lives just like this one |

7. After retiring, I would:

| 7 | 6 | 5 | 4 | 3 | 2 | 1 |
|---|---|---|---|---|---|---|
| do some of the exciting things I have always wanted to | | | (neutral) | | | loaf completely the rest of my life |

8. In achieving life goals I have:

| 1 | 2 | 3 | 4 | 5 | 6 | 7 |
|---|---|---|---|---|---|---|
| made no progress whatsoever | | | (neutral) | | | progressed to complete fulfillment |

9. My life is:

| **1** | **2** | **3** | **4** | **5** | **6** | **7** |
|---|---|---|---|---|---|---|
| empty, filled only with despair | | | (neutral) | | | running over with exciting good things |

10. If I should die today, I would feel that my life has been:

| **7** | **6** | **5** | **4** | **3** | **2** | **1** |
|---|---|---|---|---|---|---|
| very worthwhile exciting | | | (neutral) | | | completely worthless |

11. In thinking of my life, I:

| **1** | **2** | **3** | **4** | **5** | **6** | **7** |
|---|---|---|---|---|---|---|
| often wonder why I exist | | | (neutral) | | | always see a reason for my being here |

12. As I view the world in relation to my life, the world:

| **1** | **2** | **3** | **4** | **5** | **6** | **7** |
|---|---|---|---|---|---|---|
| completely confuses me | | | (neutral) | | | fits meaningfully with my life |

13. I am a:

| **1** | **2** | **3** | **4** | **5** | **6** | **7** |
|---|---|---|---|---|---|---|
| very irresponsible person | | | (neutral) | | | very responsible person |

14. Concerning people's freedom to make their own choices, I believe people are:

| **7** | **6** | **5** | **4** | **3** | **2** | **1** |
|---|---|---|---|---|---|---|
| absolutely free to make all life choices | | | (neutral) | | | completely bound by limitations of heredity and environment |

15. With regard to death, I am:

| **7** | **6** | **5** | **4** | **3** | **2** | **1** |
|---|---|---|---|---|---|---|
| prepared and unafraid | | | (neutral) | | | unprepared and frightened |

16. With regard to suicide, I have:

| **1** | **2** | **3** | **4** | **5** | **6** | **7** |
|---|---|---|---|---|---|---|
| thought of it seriously as a way out | | | (neutral) | | | never given it a second thought |

17. I regard my ability to find a meaning, purpose, or mission in life as:

| **7** | **6** | **5** | **4** | **3** | **2** | **1** |
|---|---|---|---|---|---|---|
| very great | | | (neutral) | | | practically none |

18. My life is:

| **7** | **6** | **5** | **4** | **3** | **2** | **1** |
|---|---|---|---|---|---|---|
| in my hands and I am in control of it | | | (neutral) | | | out of my hands and controlled by external factors |

19. Facing my daily task is:

| **7** | **6** | **5** | **4** | **3** | **2** | **1** |
|---|---|---|---|---|---|---|
| a source of pleasure and satisfaction | | | (neutral) | | | a painful and boring experience |

20. I have discovered:

| **1** | **2** | **3** | **4** | **5** | **6** | **7** |
|---|---|---|---|---|---|---|
| no mission or purpose in life | | | (neutral) | | | clear-cut goals and a satisfying life purpose |

Copyright
PSYCHOMETRIC AFFILIATES
Box 807
MURFREESBORO, TN 37133-0807
(615) 898-2565 890-6296          Test * 168

## INTERPRETATION OF RESULTS

The Purpose in Life Test has established norms for scoring which, unfortunately, cannot be included here. These norms help you to determine more precisely if you are indecisive, if you clearly lack meaning, or if there is a definite presence of meaning in your life at this time. Generally speaking, the higher your score, the greater the meaning in your life. As you can see from the test itself, the highest possible score is 140. Add the numerical values for all 20 questions and compare your score. Remember, your raw scores should really be compared with established norms to accurately assess the presence of meaning. Your raw scores are for preliminary consideration only. (To obtain the full test with its norms for scoring, contact Psychometric Affiliates, Box 807, Murfreesboro, TN., 37133-0807)

## Philosophers Associated with Existentialism

**Søren Kierkegaard** (1813–1855) is generally regarded as the father of existentialism, though elements of existential thinking can be found in the works of earlier writers such as **Michel de Montaigne** (1533–1592) and **Blaise Pascal** (1623–1662). When discussing existentialism, other notable names certainly come to mind: **Friedrich Nietzsche** (1844–1900), **Karl Jaspers** (1883–1969), **Gabriel Marcel** (1889–1973), and of course, **Jean-Paul Sartre** (1905–1980), who coined the term in 1946 in his famous essay (variously translated from the French as) *The Humanism of Existentialism.* **Simone de Beauvoir,** lover and colleague of Sartre, was certainly a significant existentialist too. She critically read and approved many of Sartre's works and became a celebrated writer herself. A noted feminist, she authored *The Second Sex* and *The Ethics of Ambiguity.* **Martin Heidegger's** (1899–1976) works are often discussed under existentialism, given that he exerted such an important influence on it. Nevertheless, he expressly indicated that he wished to be disassociated from Sartre.[9] **Albert Camus,** winner of the Nobel Prize for Literature in 1957, is usually tagged with the existentialist label as well, though he always refused it.[10] A good example of existential fiction is his *L'Étranger* (*The Stranger* or *The Outsider*). Also see **Fyodor Dostoyevsky's** *Notes from Underground* (1864) and **Franz Kafka's** *The Trial* (1925) for further examples of existential literary works. The more usual philosophical methods of logic and rational analysis are covered in the next chapter.

## Existentialism as a Revolt

If existentialism is unorthodox in its approach, this is largely because it represents a revolt against **rationality** and **philosophical system-building.** Perhaps one commonality shared by all existentialists is the belief that human existence cannot be dissected into discrete categories and neatly packaged as an interlocking system. Certainly, existentialists appreciate the fact that reason and rational inquiry are appropriate to mathematics and the natural sciences, but that such approaches are able to produce only disappointing vague generalities regarding real live persons. If you've ever read about a personality theory in your psychology class, for example, and then asked, "But how does this apply to me?" then you've experienced the existential disappointment I'm referring to here. As a protest against rationalism and the kinds of elaborate systems found in the works of thinkers such as **Plato** and **Hegel,** existentialists argue that the individual self is lost in **abstract universals.** As far back as Plato, many rational philosophers have held the view that everyday experience cannot provide a secure and sound foundation for knowledge. Plato argued that the material world is, in fact, a shadow world of illusion, and that ultimate reality or truth can be found only beyond the experienced spatio-temporal plane in the **realm of forms** (see the section on Plato in Chapter 4, dealing with metaphysics and epistemology). From the perspective of Platonic rationality, the body is to be held in contempt, since it houses the corrupting emotions and disquieting passions. **Perception** is regarded as untrustworthy, while reason and deductive thinking are elevated to the throne. Since, for Plato, truth must be universal, immutable, and eternal, and because sense perception is notoriously inaccurate and frequently deceptive, no certainty can be found in the world of everyday experience. It should be viewed with suspicion.

From an existential perspective, unquestioned adherence to reason and rational inquiry does violence to humanity by obliterating the **uniqueness of individuals** and their **subjective experience.** If you've ever been offended because someone drew conclusions about you based on some kind of broad sociological generalization, then you've experienced first-hand existential violence committed against your uniqueness and individuality. Your being upset at being "typed" or "classed" or "scientifically figured-out" manifests the same spirit of protest that the existentialists display toward dogmatic faith in science and rationality as methods for understanding human existence.

> **Probably a crab would be filled with a sense of personal outrage if it could hear us class it without apology as a crustacean, and thus dispose of it. "I am no such thing," it would say, "I am myself, myself alone."**
> WILLIAM JAMES

# VIKTOR FRANKL'S LOGOTHERAPY AND THE WILL-TO-MEANING

The late Viktor Frankl, a noted psychiatrist, adopted a number of existential insights and incorporated them into a form of psychological counseling called *logotherapy*. Like the stoics, he was able to see the overlap between psychological health and personal philosophy. During his lifetime of work, Frankl was able to identify a kind of spiritual malaise prevalent in contemporary society. He called it the *existential vacuum*. According to Frankl, we are all born with a fundamental need to make sense of the world, and we manifest this need in a will-to-meaning. Unfortunately, this basic need is often frustrated or left unsatisfied, with the result that we begin to suffer from a type of existential frustration. If this existential frustration is constant and excessive, then what results is a new type of psychological disturbance labeled noögenic neurosis (noögenic derives from the Greek, *noetic,* meaning perceptible to the mind; thinkable, as opposed to visible).

Frankl believed that meaninglessness comes essentially from a couple of sources. To begin with, unlike other animals, we are not governed by drives and instincts. Evolutionary biology has seen to it that we can, as autonomous beings, override biological urges. Therefore, biology no longer tells us what we must do. Secondly, in contrast to earlier times, traditions and traditional values relating to authority and the nuclear family are on the wane. What was once unquestionably valued is now oftentimes viewed with doubt and skepticism. Moral guidelines and acceptable practices are no longer clear. Therefore, we no longer know for sure what we should do. Not knowing what we must do (by force of instinct), nor knowing what we should do (according to traditional values and norms), we no longer know what we wish to do or what is truly rewarding and meaningful for us in life. The result is that we fall prey to the existential vacuum, feeling a sense of emptiness and futility.

To remedy the existential vacuum, Frankl recommends that we get beyond ourselves through a process of *self-transcendence*. He suggests we look for meaning outside of our petty egoistic preoccupations. For him,

Viktor E. Frankl, M.D., Ph.D., 1905–1997, neurologist and psychiatrist; founder of Logotherapy and Existential Analysis

meaning is found in love, work, and potentially, though not necessarily, through suffering. It is when we invest ourselves in something other than ourselves that we find meaning. We all need a mission in life. By serving a cause greater than ourselves or by loving another, we can live a fulfilling life. Also, by overcoming misfortune or illness in our own unique style, we can lend dignity to life and transform any tragedy into a personal triumph. As Frankl points out, no animal besides man can do this. Rather than live as if we were personally entitled to happiness, Frankl says, ". . . *man should not ask what he may expect from life, but rather understand that life expects something from him.*"

# Essence versus Existence

In the context of existentialism, much is made of the distinction between **essence** and **existence** and which comes first. Religious existentialists like Kierkegaard believe in God and so grant creative authority to this grand architect of the universe. If there is a God, then he (or she, if you prefer) envisioned the world and made human beings by design. To put it another way, the idea of humankind preceded the actual existence of any single human being. God knew, as it were, what human nature or the essence of humanity would be like before any real live existing beings were created. Thus, in a godly universe, essence precedes existence. A divine plan proceeded the project of producing reality. Humans were created in God's image.

In contrast to religious existentialists, atheistic ones like Jean-Paul Sartre adopt the opposite position, namely that existence precedes essence. This means that there is no all-powerful and all-knowing God that has made us who we are. All other-worldly essences are rejected. We were not born perfect, but neither were we born imperfect, stained with original sin. We are not good, nor are we evil by nature. Whatever we are, we are that by choice. To paraphrase Sartre, we are nothing else but what we make of ourselves.

The atheistic existential universe is very different from the stoic universe we learned about earlier. In the cosmology of the stoic, we found a reality that is ordered, fated, and purposeful. We are taught by the stoics to quiet the disturbing passions and to control the emotions in order to live a tranquil life in accordance with nature. Peace of mind is found not by choosing one's role (that is the task of God or the divine Logos), but by playing it well without complaint. A certain serenity can be found in the belief that the universe unfolds itself by design, and that whatever happens does so for a reason.

In the atheistic existential universe no such stoic comfort is to be found. Suffering serves as the origin of human consciousness and becomes the starting point for existential philosophy. Existentialists deny the thesis of *causal determinism* or fate, most clearly where psychological matters are concerned. For instance, traumatic events in your past don't necessarily "make" you behave in this way or that. What someone said cannot "force" you to become mad, glad, or sad. The values you live by are not written in the sky or somehow indelibly ingrained on your mind. How you respond to what others have said or done is a choice. Whatever has value has it only because you bestow personal worth upon it. In existential reality, nothing is good or bad in itself. Who would make it so? In a godless universe, everything is permissible, and it is you who are personally responsible for everything you think, say, feel, or do. Since existence precedes essence and there is no creator God to preside over the universe, life is therefore meaningless in itself. Rather than display rational order, life is absurd and chaotic, without purpose or design. Simply put, the universe doesn't make sense. Everything that happens is contingent and unpredictable. Thus, when a particular misfortune befalls you, it's silly to ask "why" it happened or what "meaning" is contained in the event. Being in the wrong place at the wrong time just happens—period. If there's any meaning, it is invented by you, not imposed from above. There are no hidden messages in life that some kind of divine presence transmits to you in times of struggle and adversity. Human beings themselves are the creators of meaning. The lessons of life are self-taught.

In view of the preceding discussion, it should be clear that atheistic existentialists reject other-worldly religious realms or anything resembling Plato's picture of ultimate reality as perfect, unchanging, and comprising pure essences or forms. Existence is not somehow less real than essence for, in fact, essences don't exist—either within or separate from human reality. The psychological point is that if existence precedes essence, then we as individuals carry the burden of making meaning in life. In itself, human existence is contingent and insecure. There is no "answer" or ultimate meaning to be discovered "out there" somewhere.

## Individuality and Subjective Experience

The belief that systems, universals, and general categories cannot explain the nature of human existence leads existentialists to emphasize the **uniqueness** of individuals. Though we are human, no two of us are exactly the same. Even identical twins are distinguishable by virtue of their behavioral patterns, differing beliefs, and so on. For existentialists, the fundamental drive within us is the urge to exist and to be recognized as individuals. By creating a sense of individuality, we find meaning and significance in life. To reduce human beings to the **cogito** (or thinking thing) of René Descartes is limiting and unperceptive. (For a discussion of Descartes's *Cogito*, see Chapter 4.) Human beings are not pure thinkers but existing individuals with passions, commitments, fears, hopes, and dreams. Human existence is full, vital, rich, self-conscious, and something for which we, as individuals, are personally responsible. As part of its protest against traditional rational philosophy, existentialism glorifies the individual and subjective experience. It encourages us to go our own ways and to become truly unique individuals. It also cautions us against the dehumanizing influences of modern society. In an age of mass production, mass markets, impersonal bureaucracies, personal subjugation in service to science and technology, and the pressure to follow fads and conform to others' standards and expectations, the **individual** continues to be under attack as much today as he or she was in the time of Kierkegaard and Nietzsche. The fight to be yourself and express yourself in the world has never been more difficult. Existentialists would encourage you to resist being swallowed up by the crowd. They advocate that you

## PHILOSOPHERS IN ACTION

Is the existentialist's preoccupation with individual uniqueness legitimate or merely reflective of some neurotic desire to be considered "special." Explain why. If the existentialist is correct that no objective reality exists and that no general statements can be made about human beings, then what are the consequences for morality? Discuss.

do not follow the herd or mindlessly go along with the masses. To do so is to rob yourself of your special uniqueness as an individual—a fatal mistake for living an authentic and genuine lifestyle, the kind in which you express yourself in a personally responsible way. In this regard, e.e. cummings writes: "*To be nobody but yourself—in a world which is doing its best, night and day, to make you everybody else—means to fight the hardest battle which any human being can fight, and never stop fighting.*"

## Freedom of Choice

Another major theme of great importance to the existentialists is **freedom of choice.** For existentialists, to be conscious is to be free. The only thing we're not free about is the choice to be unfree. Even if we wish to follow the totalitarian leader or conform to the crowd, we have still "chosen" to give up our individuality and personal freedom. Some people would argue that coercive circumstances can seriously limit freedom, but for the existentialist, you can still exercise a fair degree of it, even under duress. Let's suppose, for instance, that you are held up at gunpoint by a would-be thief demanding that you surrender your wallet. Whatever you do, the consequences are precariously uncertain. Nonetheless, you still have a choice. You could give over your wallet or refuse. In a very real example much like this one, a potential victim was actually confronted in the night by a robber but refused to give up his billfold. Fortunately for him, the robber was a coward and ran away at the refusal. Of course, the innocent man could just as easily have been killed. The point is that he was ultimately free to choose. He chose to take a risk and won. (Such risks are generally not recommended!) We must therefore be careful to distinguish between having difficult choices and having no choices at all. Making a free choice at gunpoint is difficult, though not impossible.

Fortunately for most of us, the choices we have to make on a daily basis are not so dangerous. In fact, life becomes so routine sometimes, we're not even aware that we're making choices at all. When the phone rings, we automatically pick it up, or when the light turns red, we stop. Yet in both cases, it's important to note that we do have choices to make. Just because you reflexively and unthinkingly pick up the phone when it rings doesn't mean you have to do so; if you would rather be left alone, you could let it ring forever. If you are in an emergency and rushing to the hospital, you could also choose to run a red light. If securing the health and safety of someone is more important to you than concern about violating a traffic regulation, then you will choose to break the law to get to your destination quicker. Of course, if a police officer lacking compassion catches you, you may also be ticketed. Again, the point is that environmental stimuli like red lights and telephone rings don't cause your behavior or determine you in any way. You are free. Indeed, Sartre suggests that "you are condemned to be free." There is no way out of personal responsibility for your actions. The "blame-game" is therefore not something you can honestly play. You are personally accountable for everything you do.

In the existentialist's universe of **possibility** and **contingency,** human freedom is guaranteed. It is the central fact of human existence. The only authentic and genuine way of life becomes, therefore, the one chosen by the individual. Responses, attitudes, purposes, values, feelings, beliefs, and thoughts are consciously or unthinkingly chosen by persons themselves. Saying "I did X because that's the way I was raised," or "You made me mad; that's why I'm screaming," are instances of attempted escapes from personal responsibility and hence, from freedom. If you chose not to value what someone said or did, then they couldn't "make" you mad. If you chose to reject what you were taught when growing up, then you wouldn't behave as conditioned. Even emotion is not outside the control of our wills. We are responsible for how we feel and respond to the world. When we are able to make our individual choices with full awareness that nothing else determines them for us, we are then in a position to live with **authenticity.**

One last point to be made about existential freedom involves its relationship to the concept of **negation.** Don't assume this term to imply anything evaluative or pejorative. Rather, put it into the context of existence—what is and what is not. An essential component of existential freedom is the ability to conceive of what is *not* the case, what does not yet exist. Social fairness and equality, for example, may not now exist between the genders or among the various ethnic and racial groups living in a particular society, but we can imagine what life would be like if such things did obtain. If fact, by imagining to ourselves what is not now the case, we could commit our lives to working toward making it the case. Unlike purely instinctive organisms that only react to stimuli, we can act freely, consciously, and intentionally to realize our visions, hopes, and aspirations. Consciously being able to make the possible a reality is a distinctively human characteristic. It is what makes us human. Thus, while having no escape from freedom in an absurd and contingent world may instill dread in the hearts of some, for others, this same freedom may serve as the impetus for taking personal action and living responsibly. How freedom is viewed is a choice—your choice!

Let us now consolidate our learning about the foundations of atheistic existentialism by turning to an excerpt from Sartre's *The Humanism of Existentialism.* You can also refer to a discussion of existentialist ethics in Chapter 5, where Friedrich Nietzsche's work is presented.

## ORIGINAL SOURCEWORK

*The Humanism of Existentialism*

**JEAN-PAUL SARTRE**

## PART I

What is meant by the term *existentialism?*

Most people who use the word would be rather embarrassed if they had to explain it, since, now that the word is all the rage, even the work of a musician or painter is being called existentialist. A gossip columnist in *Clarlés* signs himself *The Existentialist,* so that by this time the word has been so stretched and has taken on so broad a meaning, that it no longer means anything at all. It seems that for want of an advanced-guard doctrine analogous to surrealism, the kind of people who

Source: Jean-Paul Sartre, *The Humanism of Existentialism.*
New York: Philosophical Library Inc., 1947.

are eager for scandal and flurry turn to this philosophy which in other respects does not at all serve their purposes in this sphere.

Actually, it is the least scandalous, the most austere of doctrines. It is intended strictly for specialists and philosophers. Yet it can be defined easily. What complicates matters is that there are two kinds of existentialists; first, those who are Christian, among whom I would include Jaspers and Gabriel Marcel, both Catholic; and on the other hand the atheistic existentialists among whom I class Heidegger, and then the French existentialists and myself. What they have in common is that they think that existence precedes essence, or, if you prefer, that subjectivity must be the starting point.

Just what does that mean? Let us consider some object that is manufactured, for example, a book or a paper-cutter: here is an object which has been made by an artisan whose inspiration came from a concept. He referred to the concept of what a paper-cutter is and likewise to a known method of production, which is part of the concept, something which is, by and large, a routine. Thus, the paper-cutter is at once an object produced in a certain way and, on the other hand, one having a specific use; and one can not postulate a man who produces a paper-cutter but does not know what it is used for. Therefore, let us say that, for the paper-cutter, essence—that is, the ensemble of both the production routines and the properties which enable it to be both produced and defined—precedes existence. Thus, the presence of the paper-cutter or book in front of me is determined. Therefore, we have here a technical view of the world whereby it can be said that production precedes existence.

When we conceive God as the Creator, He is generally thought of as a superior sort of artisan. Whatever doctrine we may be considering, whether one like that of Descartes or that of Leibniz, we always grant that will more or less follows understanding or, at the very least, accompanies it, and that when God creates He knows exactly what He is creating. Thus, the concept of man in the mind of God is comparable to the concept of a paper-cutter in the mind of the manufacturer, and, following certain techniques and a conception, God produces man, just as the artisan, following a definition and a technique, makes a paper-cutter. Thus, the individual man is the realization of a certain concept in the divine intelligence.

In the eighteenth century, the atheism of the *philosophers* discarded the idea of God, but not so much for the notion that essence precedes existence. To a certain extent, this idea is found everywhere; we find it in Diderot, in Voltaire, and even in Kant. Man has a human nature; this human nature, which is the concept of the human, is found in all men, which means that each man is a particular example of a universal concept, man. In Kant, the result of this universality is that the wild-man, the natural man, as well as the bourgeois, are circumscribed by the same definition and have the same basic qualities. Thus, here too the essence of man precedes the historical existence that we find in nature.

Atheistic existentialism, which I represent, is more coherent. It states that if God does not exist, there is at least one being in whom existence precedes essence, a being who exists before he can be defined by any concept, and that this being is man, or, as Heidegger says, human reality. What is meant here by saying that existence precedes essence? It means that, first of all, man exists, turns up, appears on the scene, and, only afterwards, defines himself. If man, as the existentialist conceives him, is indefinable, it is because at first he is nothing. Only afterward will he be something, and he himself will have made what he will be. Thus, there is no human nature, since there is no God to conceive it. Not only is man what he conceives himself to be, but he is also only what he wills himself to be after this thrust toward existence.

Man is nothing else but what he makes of himself. Such is the first principle of existentialism. It is also what is called subjectivity, the name we are labeled with when charges are brought against us. But what do we mean by this, if not that man has a greater dignity than a stone or table? For we mean that man first exists, that is, that man first of all is the being who hurls himself toward a future and who is conscious of imagining himself as being in the future. Man is at the start a plan which is aware of itself, rather than a patch of moss, a piece of garbage, or a cauliflower; nothing exists prior to this plan; there is nothing in heaven; man will be what he will have planned to be. Not what he will want to be. Because by the word "will" we generally mean a conscious decision, which is subsequent to what we have already made of ourselves. I may want to belong to a political party, write a book, get married; but all that is only a manifestation of an earlier, more spontaneous choice that is called "will." But if existence really does precede essence, man is responsible for what he is. Thus, existentialism's first move is to make every man aware of what he is and to make the full responsibility of his existence rest on him. And when we say that a man is responsible for himself, we do not only mean that he is responsible for his own individuality, but that he is responsible for all men.

The word subjectivism has two meanings, and our opponents play on the two. Subjectivism means, on the one hand, that an individual chooses and makes himself; and, on the other, that it is impossible for man to transcend human subjectivity. The second of these is the essential meaning of existentialism. When we say that man chooses his own self, we mean that every one of us does likewise; but we also mean by that that in making this choice he also chooses all men. In fact, in creating the man that we want to be, there is not a single one of our acts which does not at the same time create an image of man as we think he ought to be. To choose to be this or that is to affirm at the same time the value of what we choose, because we can never choose evil. We always choose the good, and nothing can be good for us without being good for all.

If, on the other hand, existence precedes essence, and if we grant that we exist and fashion our image at one and the same time, the image is valid for everybody and for our whole age. Thus, our responsibility is much greater than we might have supposed, because it involves all mankind. If I am a workingman and choose to join a Christian trade-union rather than be a communist, and if by being a member I want to show that the best thing for man is resignation, that the kingdom of man is not of this world, I am not only involving my own case—I want to be resigned for everyone. As a result, my action has involved all humanity. To take a more individual matter, if I want to marry, to have children; even if this marriage depends solely on my own circumstances or passion or wish, I am involving all humanity in monogamy and not merely myself. Therefore, I am responsible for myself and for everyone else. I am creating a certain image of man of my own choosing. In choosing myself, I choose man.

## DISCUSSION QUESTIONS FOR CRITIQUE AND ANALYSIS

1. In a universe where "existence precedes essence," does moral responsibility make any sense? Comment.

2. Is Sartre presenting us with a gloomy and necessarily pessimistic philosophy? Why or why not?

# PHILOSOPHICAL SEGUE

## Fate, Free Will, and Determinism

Our trek into the philosophical domain began in this chapter with an expansive view of an ordered stoic universe. We found security and peace of mind in the knowledge that nothing that happens is random or out of place. We also learned how, in the stoic's world, the divine Logos is immanent in all physical objects and events. We saw how things happen for a reason which, in the end, is for the best. Fate, which determines life, and Providence, which assures us it's good, are but different aspects of God. The moral lesson we were able to take away from this stoic belief is that we should not balk at what life has to offer, but rather adopt an attitude of courageous acceptance, assenting to reality as an expression of God's will. There is a teleological purpose to all that happens.

No sooner did we gain some peaceful stoic reassurance about the universe and our place in it, when the existentialists exploded our cosmic complacency to bits. The atheist Sartre put "existence before essence," denying human beings a providential Godhead who would create, benevolently control, and look after things in the world. Suddenly, life became horribly confused in a whirlwind of existential doubt, chaos, and absurdity. With no God and no maker of humankind, no such thing as a predictable human nature could be counted upon. No ultimate reason could be provided for why things happened as they did and not in some other fashion. It felt as if we were thrown into the dark abyss or a maelstrom of meaninglessness, without any destiny or any real reason for being. What was particularly horrifying was the fact that, without God or some kind of divine intelligence to structure reality, all possibility of any objective morality blew away like dust in the wind. Our stoic calm was abruptly replaced by a dreadful existential *angst* resulting from the realization that we are condemned to be free.

Now, if we may regain some stoic composure for just a moment, recall that philosophies of life are derivative of other primary branches of philosophical inquiry. (See Fields of Philosophy in Chapter 1.) This fact has certainly been illustrated in our treatments of stoicism and existentialism thus far. These life philosophies offer us very different metaphysical worldviews, making starkly contrasting assumptions, especially with respect to human freedom. Whether you buy into the stoics' cosmological determinism or the existentialists' absurd and chaotic reality, it is extremely important that you understand the implications of your commitment, for so much hinges on it, both personally and philosophically.

## EXISTENTIAL FREE WILL

If, for instance, you agree with Sartre, that to be human is to be free, then an awesome burden of responsibility is placed upon your shoulders. You cannot hide behind excuses and blame others for what you say, do, think, or feel. To do this would require you to live inauthentically, in bad-faith, to use the existentialist expression. For existentialists, our intended actions belong exclusively to us. We have not been somehow programmed in advance; nor are we fulfilling some kind of preordained purpose. Nothing can control our attitudes or our will. There is simply nowhere to hide. We are naked and exposed, and the whole world is watching to see how we're going to respond to life's challenges.

In the atheistic existentialist universe, not only are we responsible for who we are and what we do; we are also saddled with the task of constructing meaningful lives for ourselves. Without a God, there is no divine mission to complete, neither is there an ultimate meaning inherent in human experience for us to discover. Whatever meaning exists is self-created by us as solitary individuals. No objective standards can be used to assure us that we're on the right track or that the ultimate meaning of life has been found. Anxiety and dread are thus likely to arise as we look at the dark sky of existential nothingness and infinite possibility. Such feelings remind us that we must choose our futures without even so much as a psychological north star to guide us on our journeys. Anything is possible, and this horrifies us. No wonder Sartre concluded that freedom is like a prison sentence—with no chance of parole until you die, I might add!

## DEFINITIONS OF FREEDOM

To say that human beings are free or unfree presupposes that we have some understanding of freedom upon which to base our conclusion. Philosophers, existentialist and otherwise, have tried in many places to define freedom. In the *Encyclopedia of Philosophy*, we find it explained in terms of two things: "absence of coercion" and "freedom to." These definitions tend to be more sociopolitical than metaphysical in nature, but are nonetheless useful for purposes of understanding our philosophical worldviews. They remind us that philosophical considerations often overlap, and that subdisciplines within philosophy are not always as separate and distinct as we might like them to be for our intentions of theoretical exposition. Freedom is not only an existential, metaphysical concept, but a sociopolitical one as well.

Now, if one is said to be free by virtue of the fact that there is an absence of coercion, then we can take it that no constraints have been imposed by another person or group of persons. On this definition, individuals are free to the extent they can choose their own goals and decide upon their own courses of action. Freedom, here, implies choice between or among alternatives. Individuals are not forced or compelled to act as they would not choose to act, by the will of another person, by the state, or by an authority of some sort. This absence of coercion is also referred to as "negative freedom" or "freedom from."

What negative freedom entails is deliberate and informed choice. However, if you are given alternatives, but these alternatives have somehow been manipulated, then others have determined your choice and coerced you indirectly, robbing you of true freedom. The coercion here is simply more subtle. You might even think you are choosing freely when, in fact, somebody has stacked things in his, her, or its favor. Ignorance of alternatives or misinformation about them thus curtails freedom.

Freedom has a positive aspect: "freedom to" or "freedom for." In sociopolitical contexts, claims to freedom are usually claims to a particular liberty like freedom of thought and expression, freedom of association, freedom of assembly, or freedom of movement. Positive freedom can also refer to the liberty involved in the exercise of some interest or form of activity. This might entail freedom in the use or disposal of one's property or freedom in the choice of an employer or occupation.[11] More about such freedoms and liberties will be discussed in the final chapter of the book dealing with political philosophy. For now, let's go back to stoicism for a moment and other deterministic views that challenge the notion that we are free.

## FATALISM

Supposing that you're not sympathetic to the existentialist worldview, and to the extent you find yourself agreeing with stoicism, you might be a little surprised to discover that you can be labeled a *fatalist*. Fatalists are people who hold to the doctrine that all events occur in accordance with a fixed and inevitable destiny—one that the individual neither controls nor affects. On this account, God is the Logos, the rational principle pervading everything. Though your twenty-first century, sophisticated scientific understanding might lead you to other conclusions, stoics conceptualized the Logos as an all-permeating cosmic fire whose fiery vapor manifests itself in the flaming spheres of the heavens, in the warmth and vitality of plants and animals, and in the Divine Spark of the human soul expressing itself in rational thought. For the ancient stoics, little sparks of the divine fire, the *Logoi,* are dispersed throughout the world like seeds, to guide the growth and development of each thing.

According to some interpretations, the fatalism of stoics offers no chance or contingency in the universe, as everything is determined down to the smallest detail. In this scenario, events could not be any other way. No matter what happens, the end is inevitable. If your time has come to die, for instance, nothing you can do can change this. Yet other interpretations of stoicism, while conceding that fate exists, stress that it is painted in broad brush strokes, allowing individuals to have some influence on the course of events in their lives. Epictetus, the stoic slave, writes the following in the *Enchiridion:*

> If then you desire . . . great things, remember that you must not (attempt to) lay hold of them with small effort; but you must leave alone some things entirely, and postpone others for the present.[12]

The advice proffered by Epictetus seems to suggest that we have at least some degree of influence over our actions and their results. If true, then it would be prudent, to distinguish between what is in our control from what is beyond it. We can still influence our futures, even if we cannot totally control them. Being born male or female, for example, was obviously beyond your control; deciding what kind of man or woman you will become would appear to be within your control. This second, looser interpretation of stoic fatalism, would thus allow for a small degree of personal freedom within a larger fatalistic scheme.

## SCIENTIFIC CAUSAL DETERMINISM

For a very long time before the modern era, philosophers like the stoics operated on a teleological model of the universe, one that focused on the idea of *purpose.*[13] The assumption was made that the universe was a perfect creation of a supreme intelligence. Ancient thinkers sought to build teleological systems to explain the reasons why the world functioned as it did. What happened wasn't a fluke but a product of "cosmological determinism."

With the arrival of modern science, however, philosophers ceased to ask about purposes and began to inquire into *causes.* Over time, a mechanistic paradigm replaced the earlier teleological model. Scientists discovered that the motions of heavenly bodies obeyed identifiable laws that could be expressed mathematically. As the scientific method continued to develop, observation, experiment, and inquiry into the physical laws of the universe took the place of metaphysical speculation. The world was compared to a vast machine whose parts were seen as interconnected and working together in unison.[14] With this transition, the future was not left to fate, destiny, or some kind of Divine Logos, but to science, which became a predictive discipline, able to tell us in advance what was going to occur in the physical universe.

In Chapter 4, dealing with metaphysics, you'll learn how René Descartes (1560–1650) tried to salvage free will in a determined universe by arguing for the notion of a *mind-body dualism*. He believed that mechanistic principles like those governing the movements of celestial bodies applied only to the material realm—that is, to physical objects and processes in nature—but that God gave human beings a free will, which made moral responsibility possible. If human beings were unfree and if their actions were completely determined, then to hold them morally praiseworthy or blameworthy for their actions wouldn't make any sense. For Descartes and others, a great deal of effort was spent trying to reconcile causal, scientific explanations with beliefs in God and free will.

Another philosopher concerned with the apparent conflict between science and faith was Thomas Hobbes (1588–1679). He was a materialist who rejected any notion of an immaterial soul or spirit. He also argued that all human action represents the behavior of matter and thus should be understood in accordance with the same laws we ascribe to matter.[15] Like objects in the world, human nature operates according to the laws of physics, so even all of our ideas, sensations, and psychological processes are nothing more than motions or manifestations of matter in the brain. The view that human beings could be regarded as the original source of their own voluntary motion or that acts of will could arise without causes was rejected as unintelligible.[16] According to Hobbes's metaphysical materialism, all events in the world, even mental events, were determined. Things don't just happen by chance; any perceived uncertainty or unpredictability about future events merely reflects a gap in our knowledge or an inability to understand, not something about events themselves, which always follow the laws of nature. For Hobbes, the greater our understanding about the laws that govern complicated systems of human motion, the more our behavior will be as predictable as an astronomical event.[17] Human nature is no different from the rest of material nature, so the methods of physical science are appropriate for both, and the kinds of predictions we can make about one, we should, in principle, be able to make about the other.

## DETERMINISM VERSUS FATALISM

A point of clarification might be necessary here, insofar as Hobbes and the stoics both believe in an ordered universe. Recall that the stoics adhere to a doctrine of "cosmological determinism," which states that the future is already fixed by a providential God. We call this determined future *fate*. In Hobbes's universe of metaphysical materialism, events are also determined; however, they are not fixed or fated in advance. The principle of universal causation states that every event has a cause, and that whatever happens in the universe is determined according to the laws of nature—not because the Logos or God planned it that way. No event is inevitable (determined in advance by fate or predestination). Determinism insists only that *if* certain conditions obtain, *then* a certain kind of event will take place. If those conditions are not present, then the event won't occur. For example, if we raise the temperature of a pot of water on the stove to a sufficiently high degree, it will boil and steam. If we leave it at room temperature, it won't. What the water will do depends on antecedent conditions. If we know precisely what the antecedent conditions are, we know what will happen.

Surprisingly, perhaps, Hobbes's metaphysical materialism does not automatically turn him into an atheist. Indeed, he actually accepts the idea that nature itself has an ultimate cause, namely God. Nonetheless, he remains consistent with his materialistic assumptions, suggesting that we cannot know God. To see or understand God as a nonphysical substance would be meaningless—spirit would have to be conceived in terms of very minute and transparent particles. Particles, no matter how tiny or transparent, are still physical, something presumably God is not. Thus, the best we can do, according to Hobbes, is simply to affirm that God exists. We cannot actually understand what God is, for we can only know what is based on what our senses tell us. Since we can have no sense experience of God, Hobbes concludes that the problem of God becomes a matter for theologians, not for philosophers and scientists.[18] With this one nifty maneuver, Hobbes is able to allow for a belief in God in a purely physical, mechanistically determined universe—an act of genius, perhaps, or maybe just an instance of philosophical tap-dancing around a controversial and unresolved issue.

Baron D'Holbach (1723–1789), a determinist like Hobbes but also an exponent of atheistic materialism, had little reservation about rejecting God, or human freedom for that matter. He wrote:

> Man is a being purely physical; in whatever manner he is considered, he is connected to universal nature, and submitted to the necessary and immutable laws that she imposes on all beings she contains, according to their peculiar essences or to particular species. Man's life is a line that nature commands him to describe upon the surface of the earth, without his own consent; his organization does in no way depend upon himself; his ideas come to him involuntarily; his habits are in the power of those who cause him to contract them; he is unceasingly modified by causes, whether visible or concealed, over which he has no control, which necessarily regulate his mode of existence, give the hue to his way of thinking, and determine his manner of acting. He is good or bad, happy or miserable, wise or foolish, reasonable or irrational, without his will being for any thing in these various states. Nevertheless, in despite of the shackles by which he is bound, it is pretended he is a free agent, or that independent of the causes by which he is moved, he determines his own will, and regulates his own condition.[19]

# PSYCHOLOGICAL DETERMINISM

More contemporary rejections of free will in human behavior can be found in the twentieth-century psychological theories of B.F. Skinner and Sigmund Freud. Skinner was a behavioral determinist who claimed that human conduct was governed by laws, and that it could be shaped according to certain contingencies of reinforcement. Thus, an action that is followed by a positive reinforcement or a more satisfying state of affairs is more likely to occur in the future, and an action that is punished or followed by a less satisfying state of affairs is less likely to occur. This is essentially what is meant by the so-called "law of effect"—a deterministic principle of human behavior originally articulated by Edward Thorndike and later used by Skinner and other behaviorists in conducting their empirical research. The implication of behavioral determinism is that people do what they do and become what they are as a function of experiential learning. The illusion of freedom comes from inconsistency in the reinforcements we receive throughout our lives. There is no single "Big Brother" watching us every moment to reinforce consistently those behaviors that are desired. The fact that our parents, friends, religious leaders, and bosses reinforce different and often opposite behaviors accounts for what looks like randomness or freedom in human action. However, in principle, we could condition people into becoming whatever we want them to become by controlling the environmental circumstances and all contingencies of reinforcement in their lives. Behavior is not free, fated, or predetermined; it is a matter of conditioning.

J.B. Watson (1878–1958), another of the founding fathers of psychological determinism, made the following disturbing remark, which reinforces the idea that human beings are simply a product of their environment, and their behavior is nothing more than a product of conditioning:

> Give me a dozen healthy infants, well-formed, and my own specified world to bring them up in and I'll guarantee to take any one at random and train him to become any kind of specialist I might select—doctor, lawyer, artist, merchant-chief, and yes even beggarman and thief, regardless of his talents, penchants, abilities, vocations, and race of his ancestors.[20]

Finally, on the subject of psychological determinism, allow me to bring Sigmund Freud into the picture. The originator of psychoanalysis, Freud held that the *unconscious,* a psychological structure of the human personality, was responsible for many of our actions and thoughts. According to Freud, during our early development as children, it is virtually inevitable that many of our instinctual urges will be left unsatisfied or be repressed in order to meet the demands of civilized society. These frustrated and unexpressed instinctual drives do not just disappear, however, but rather find themselves repressed in the unconscious part of the mind, along with unresolved conflicts and memories of traumatic experiences. If these conflicts and traumas are not somehow resolved or properly dealt with some time in early development, they can manifest in adulthood as neurotic symptomatology, even psychosis. For Freud, addictions, phobias, compulsions, obsessions, and other dysfunctions do, in fact, have a psychogenic cause—most often in the developmental history of the individual. Even silly mistakes like "slips of the tongue" were deemed by Freud to be caused by unconscious determining forces. When your friends laugh suspiciously at some of the things you do or say, accusing you of a *Freudian slip,* they are implicitly accepting Freud's notion of psychological determinism.

For Freud, complete freedom from unconscious influence was impossible. Consciousness can never be entirely transparent to itself, despite what existentialists assume. Using techniques of psychoanalysis, the best we can hope for is to gain more access into the unconscious recesses of the mind, affording us greater insight into our own personal psychodynamics, and thereby, a higher degree of rational control over our lives. The more we become aware of those unconscious influences determining our behavior, the freer we become.

As an atheistic psychological determinist, Freud made no assumptions about theology or transcendental metaphysics. Relying on his extensive medical knowledge of biological science and training in physiological research, he assumed that all phenomena are determined by the laws of physics, chemistry, and biology. As biological animals in nature, human beings were, in his estimation, subject to these laws as well. His instinct theory and much of what followed from it was based on a scientific "energy model" that was then current. Freud believed that by studying the "biology of the mind" and using the methods of science in this endeavor, psychoanalysis could diagnose people's problems to help them regain their psychological health.

## ECONOMIC DETERMINISM

One last theory I wish to mention here questioning the whole notion of free will is the economic determinism of Karl Marx (1818–1883). We'll revisit Marx in Chapter 6 for a much more elaborate treatment of his work, but for now, we'll briefly touch on the implications of his theory for human freedom.

Karl Marx was an atheist and material determinist. Sometimes regarded as the father of sociology, he set out to explain all human phenomena by the methods of science. Though other thinkers of the eighteenth-century Enlightenment like David Hume, for instance, had tried to do the same, Marx stands out with respect to his claim to have found the truly scientific method for studying the historical development of human societies.[21] He maintained that there are general socioeconomic laws operating in human history, and that all the major social and political changes throughout the ages can be explained by applying these laws to the prevailing conditions of the time.[22] For Marx, the laws that serve to explain sociopolitical events in the past could also be used to predict the future evolution of society. For instance, in his view, capitalism will predictably create conditions fostering disparities in wealth; the rich will get richer and the poor will get poorer until conditions become so desperate for the poor that they will finally rise up in violent revolution against the existing social order. The result will be communism. Whether Marx's predictions about social revolution will ever come true remains to be seen, though they appear highly unlikely at this time. However, about the growing disparities in wealth, one could argue they have, in fact, already occurred.

What is particularly disturbing to those who pride themselves on being autonomous, free-thinking individuals is Marx's claim that socioeconomic conditions of class, material production, and ownership of property, actually determine our very consciousness—our ideas, values, choices, beliefs, aspirations, habits, relations with others, and even our biological functions (see Chapter 6).

Whether you believe individualism is good or that state interference in the economy is bad will hinge on the social conditioning you've received. What gets conditioned—either directly by indoctrination or indirectly by advertising and the media—will reflect the prevailing interests of the dominant ruling classes within society. To the extent Marx is correct, your ideas may not really be your own in one respect. Perhaps they reflect little more than the materially self-interested "propaganda" spread by the "corporate global oligarchy," to use a phrase often bandied about these days by international economic summit protesters.

On this startling and controversial note, our *Philosophical Segue* into *Fate, Free Will, and Determinism* comes to an end. Apart from introducing you to a few metaphysical ideas that overlap the first two philosophies of life presented in this chapter, I hope this detour has enriched your understanding, piqued your interest, and caused you to think more deeply and seriously about the issues discussed. As we proceed next with our treatment of hedonism and Buddhism, you might try to uncover further metaphysical assumptions pertaining to human nature, freedom, God, and laws governing life or the workings of the universe. Continued good luck on your journey. I hope you're enjoying the experience so far!

## HEDONISM: PLEASURE IS THE MEASURE

> *The achievement of his own happiness is man's highest moral purpose.*
> AYN RAND

The third philosophy of life we'll cover in this chapter is called **hedonism.** I somehow suspect that you will already have some vague familiarity with it. In fact, a cursory glance at popular culture might easily lead you to conclude that hedonism is the prevailing philosophy of the day, if not the last half-century. Before we get a more technical and detailed understanding of what philosophical hedonism entails, let's begin by defining it broadly as the doctrine that pleasure is worth pursuing and, that in the end, *pleasure is the ultimate goal of life.*

Whether or not you are a hedonist yourself, it's difficult to deny that vast amounts of time, energy, and money are spent on the pursuit of pleasure. Theme parks across the nation are visited annually by millions with the express purpose of having fun and seeking thrills. Millions more attend sporting events to cheer on their favorite teams. Race tracks and gambling casinos, not to mention state and provincial lotteries, hold out the hope that you too could win large sums of money and buy anything you want, making your life much happier than presumably it is right now. Travel agents, as well, hold out the promise of pleasure and excitement by showing you pictures of exotic vacation destinations, luxurious hotel rooms, and sumptuous meals that promise to bring you pleasure and relaxation. On this note, I've heard many people say that they live for weekends, a time when work ends and the fun begins. Others fantasize about their early retirement and the prospect of endless hours on the golf course or at the beach, doing nothing but soaking up the midday sun. In a humorous vein, I've listened to fun-loving adults who joke about the time of death saying, "The one with the most toys wins!" Others find the greatest pleasure in sexual activity, in cultivating friendships, or in shopping for clothes and luxury items. Surely, all this pervasive and frenetic pursuit of pleasure points to the hedonistic tendencies in mainstream society. What you may not know, however, is that hedonists have existed for centuries and have had much to say on the subject of pursuing pleasure as the ultimate end of life.

## Psychological versus Ethical Hedonism

It is important for purposes of philosophical understanding to note that there are two different types of hedonism: psychological and ethical. **Psychological hedonism** is a motivational theory. It explains *why* we do the things we do. According to the psychological hedonist, actions and desires are determined by their pleasure-producing properties. People are motivated to produce one state of affairs over another if, and only if, they think it will be more pleasant, or less unpleasant, for themselves. Psychological hedonists wish to reduce, and if possible, to eliminate pain and displeasure as much as they want to give rise to its opposite. Richard Brandt describes this concept of psychological hedonism as the "goal is pleasure" theory.[23]

Another variation of psychological hedonism is called *motivation by pleasant thoughts*.[24] This theory asserts that people will choose to do A rather than B, or will prefer A to B (whether an action or situation) if, and only if, the thought of A (with its expected consequences) is more attractive, or less repugnant, than the thought of B (with its expected consequences). In slightly different terms, if you can't imagine yourself doing "this" over "that" because "this" would likely have such horrible consequences, or at least less attractive ones compared with "that," then "that" is what you will choose to do. The thought of "that" and its expected pleasurable or preferred consequences determines your choice.

A third form of psychological hedonism is called *conditioning by pleasant experiences*. This is a theory about the causal conditions of a person's wants and values. It states that whatever you want or value at any given moment in life can be correlated with past enjoyments and rewards. Positive reinforcements associated with values in earlier experience serve to explain, at least in part, why those values are now cherished and why they influence present behavior. A person's values are therefore conditioned by that person's earlier enjoyments. For instance, if you crave chocolate, it is because you've enjoyed it in the past. But if the chocolate you were fed was always waxy or bitter, then you might not desire it now. Past enjoyments and experiences of pleasure thus influence the wants and values that determine our current behavior. We always act to get what we want, and what we want is the most pleasurable or most satisfying, given the situation.

While all three forms of psychological hedonism are intended as descriptions of actual motivation, **ethical hedonism** is not an explanation of why we value or want the things we do. Rather, ethical hedonism is a *moral theory* that suggests that if you don't pursue pleasure in life, you should. It's wrong not to. From the perspective of ethical hedonism, pleasure is the only thing that is intrinsically valuable—that is, valuable in itself. A corollary to this idea is the proposition that only displeasure is intrinsically undesirable, or undesirable in itself. In whatever we do, we should always strive to create states of affairs that produce pleasure and reduce pain or displeasure. If what you're doing right now (namely reading) is painful, then you should stop. However, if failing philosophy would cause more pain than the pain of reading on, then you should continue.

Associated with states of affairs (situations or circumstances) are **states of mind.** The ethical hedonist makes the value judgment that pleasant states of mind are desirable in themselves and that unpleasant states of mind are undesirable in themselves. Combining the notion of states of mind with states of affairs we get the following ethical conclusion: One state of affairs is more desirable in itself than another state of affairs if, and only if, it contains more pleasant states of mind than the other.[25] Thus, the quantity of value in any state of affairs is measured by the quantity of pleasure in it. Our moral obligation in any situation is to choose the state of affairs that will produce the greatest pleasure.

Ethical hedonism, understood as a theory of value and a moral prescription for living, has been defended by a long line of distinguished philosophers from the early Greeks to the present. Some see pleasure as ethical egoists, arguing that pleasure should be maximized for oneself. Others have been more altruistic in their hedonism, arguing that the right thing to do is to maximize the pleasure or happiness of the greatest number of people.

## Aristippus of Cyrene

Aristippus (430–350 B.C.E.) was the first Western philosopher we know of to make a direct and uncompromising statement of hedonism. Originally living in Cyrene, a town in what is now Libya in North Africa, he traveled to Athens and became a close friend of Socrates. Like his friend, he was interested almost exclusively in practical ethics, the end of which Aristippus believed to be the enjoyment of present pleasures. After spending a number of years in Aegina, Aristippus relocated to the court of Dionysius of Syracuse where, from 389 to 388 B.C.E., he earned his living teaching and writing. At the court, he also came into contact with Plato. Eventually, Aristippus returned to his home in Cyrene, where he opened his own school of philosophy, promoting what we now call **Cyrenaic hedonism,** named after his home town. Unfortunately, his writings have either been lost or destroyed by the ravages of time, so only lists of his works remain. A number of his hedonistic ideas have nonetheless survived and immortalized Aristippus, making him relevant for us even today.

The ideas of Aristippus can be summarized into a number of basic tenets. (Consider whether you agree with any of them.) First, according to Aristippus, pleasure is the principle motive for living. **Pleasure** is always to be considered good, regardless of where it originates. Second, no qualitative distinctions can be made among pleasures themselves. **Intensity** is the only criterion that can be used to determine which action or state of affairs is best. Those things producing the greatest or most intense pleasure should be preferred. However, since physical, sensory pleasures are more intense than mental or emotional ones, they become, for Aristippus, the best of all. Pursuing physical, sensory pleasure is therefore a higher good than the pursuit of knowledge, goodness, or truth. Third, Aristippus contends that pleasure contributes greatly to the **meaning of life.** He recommends that we follow our natural desires without guilt or apology. Our mission in life is to learn how to enjoy ourselves most fully. Through the pursuit of sensory pleasures we can make our individual lives exciting, dynamic, and worth living. Don't take this to mean that Aristippus suggested that we should become enslaved by our cravings and appetites. He is not implying this at all. Rather, he advocates Socratic self-control, which he interpreted not as self-denial, but as rational control over pleasure instead of slavery to it. For Aristippus, no pleasure or personal enjoyment can be wrong. No passion is evil in itself. Pleasures are misguided or sick only when we lose control and are victimized by them. Loss of self-control can lead to less pleasure in the long run, so self-restraint can sometimes be necessary.

A key element of Cyrenaic hedonism was the character example of Aristippus himself. Superimposed on a Socratic self-control and freedom from debilitating desires was an uninhibited capacity for enjoyment. Aristippus could revel in luxury or be content with the simplest needs, choosing each as he deemed fit and as the circumstances demanded.[26] For Aristippus, since all acts were indifferent except in their capacity to provide immediate pleasure, the science of life translated into a calculated adaptation of the self to one's circumstances, along with the ability to use people and situations for self-gratification.

Another tenet of Cyrenaic hedonism is that **actual pleasures** are more desirable than **potential pleasures.** Some people deny pleasures to themselves now in the hope of gaining greater pleasures later on. Such a strategy is not recommended by the Cyrenaics. You may deprive yourself now and save an entire lifetime to enjoy your retirement, only to die shortly after you finish work. You may give up things now for promises of future rewards, only to find those promises empty and misleading. Furthermore, what happens if you no longer want what you worked so long and so hard to achieve, once you get it? Disappointment and regret may follow. Thus, it is better to enjoy yourself today than to dream of potential pleasures in the future.

The notion that all pleasures are equal and that they differ only in intensity points to the subjective element in Cyrenaic hedonism. Since pleasures cannot be objectively compared as better or worse, if watching the cable Comedy Channel is just as good as reading Shakespeare or playing chess, then the individual becomes the measure of pleasure. Whatever pleases me the most at any given moment is the highest good there can be.[27]

A last point to be made about Cyrenaic hedonism involves participation in society. According to Aristippus, participation in public life gives rise to avoidable hassles. Involved citizenship is almost certain to interfere with one's pursuit of pleasure. To remain free and detached from sociopolitical entanglements was therefore good, so that the individual could fulfill his or her ultimate obligation, namely, to enjoy every moment in life.

> **"*Pleasure is the absence of pain in the body and trouble in the soul.*"**
>
> EPICURUS

# Epicurus

**Epicureanism** is another expression of hedonistic philosophy given form and substance by its originator, **Epicurus** (341–270 B.C.E.), after whom it was obviously named. Epicurus was born in Samos in Asia Minor in 341 B.C.E. He was a voluminous writer, having produced over 300 works, most of which are lost today. Fortunately, **Diogenes Laertius** provided us with summaries of Epicurean doctrine. The Latin poet **Lucretius** also expressed many Epicurean ideas in his poem *De Rerum Natura (On the Nature of the Universe).*[28] Sayings of Epicurus are found as well in the works of **Seneca** and **Cicero.**

Epicurus chose to focus his attention on ethics, considering mathematics and all purely scientific pursuits as essentially useless, given that such studies have little connection with the conduct of everyday life. Though Epicurus studied with followers of **Plato** and **Aristotle,** he rejected both in the end as overly theoretical and irrelevant when it comes to the practical concerns of daily living. In reaction to both Plato and Aristotle, as well as to the stoics, who had all set up their own schools of philosophy, so too did Epicurus in 306 B.C.E.[29] He called his school **The Garden,** which was very appropriate given its secluded surroundings in Athens. The Garden served as a retreat from the sociopolitical and philosophical turmoil of Athens. Everyone was welcome at The Garden and was treated equally. Epicurus admitted men, women, courtesans, slaves, and aristocrats, making no distinctions among people based on social status, gender, or race—a very progressive policy for the thinking and values of the day. The Garden developed a reputation not only for its operating philosophy, but also for its good living and pleasant social surroundings.

Disciples of Epicurus, called Epicureans, actively competed with other philosophers for the hearts and minds of followers.[30] They ventured out into the great centers of the eastern Mediterranean to establish new communities modeled after The Garden. Epicureanism even took hold in the Roman Empire, where it reached its height of influence from 60 to 30 B.C.E.

Today, lots of people describe themselves as Epicureans, though often in a mistaken way. Many of us tend to equate the Epicurean with the *aesthete*—someone who lives a life devoted to the pursuit of beauty, physical pleasures, and the expression of discriminating and exquisite taste. Eating exotic foods, surrounding oneself in luxurious beauty, wearing only the finest clothes, and traveling to remote and exclusive destinations are often thought of as expressions of Epicureanism. The fact is that all of these things are more akin to Cyrenaic hedonism or the aestheticism of an Oscar Wilde than to what Epicurus promoted.[31]

## Momentary versus Enduring Pleasures

To appreciate the pleasures that Epicurus would actually have us seek, it is first necessary to distinguish between **momentary pleasures** and **enduring pleasures.**[32] Although Epicurus grants that all pleasure is good and all pain is evil, it's not the case that pleasure should always be chosen over painful or unpleasant activities. As Epicurus says, "Every pleasure is therefore good on account of its own nature, but it does not follow that every pleasure is worthy of being chosen; just as every pain is an evil, and yet every pain must not be avoided." For example, a particular pleasure might be very intense for the moment, but it might also lead to ill health or enslavement to a habit, thereby producing greater pain. Unprotected sex (intercourse without a condom) with a risky partner may lead to momentary orgasmic ecstasy, but it could also result in a sexually transmitted disease, an enduring pain for such a brief episode of pleasure. So too, for a momentary high, some people will experiment with addictive drugs, only to find that they become enslaved to the high feeling and the ceaseless craving that must then be continually satisfied before panic and frenzied preoccupation for physical satisfaction set in. From an Epicurean perspective, the pleasures of dangerous sex and addictive drugs should not be chosen, even if pain results from "missing out" or from not experiencing the physical high. On the other hand, sometimes pains should be chosen over pleasures. Undergoing surgery in a hospital is often painful, yet it produces the greater good—health—in the long run. Suffering momentary pain or short-lived pain thus may be the best choice for long term well-being. Living the good life, then, is not about the mindless pursuit of immediate pleasure; the exercise of practical wisdom is required. Practical wisdom enables one to measure pleasures against pains, accepting pains that lead to greater pleasures and rejecting pleasures that lead to greater pains.[33] Epicurus's willingness to delay immediate gratification for longer term benefits and the value he places on the exercise of practical wisdom both point to a kind of hedonism that can be distinguished from Aristippus's Cyrenaic version, which used intensity of pleasure as the main criterion of evaluative judgment. Unlike Aristippus, Epicurus would not necessarily conclude that the most immediate and intense pleasures are *always* the best.

## Kinetic versus Static (Catastematic) Pleasures

In the pursuit of pleasure, Epicurus would have us make a second distinction among pleasures, namely between **kinetic pleasures** and **static pleasures.** In the former case, pleasure is experienced through some kind of action. Drinking a cold glass of orange juice or ice water on a hot, sticky day is quite satisfying. The body's craving for liquid, experienced as a need or lack, is removed, and drinking feels good. Likewise, the felt need for food (hunger) can be removed by eating. In short, there is kinetic pleasure whenever a want or pain is removed. Kinetic pleasures accompany motion and cease when the motion or activity ceases.[34]

Static (or catastematic) pleasures are not pleasures found in movement or in activity but in the pleasurable states resulting when pains, lacks, deficiencies, or frustrations have been removed. Static pleasure is the state of having no pain, whereas, kinetic pleasure is the pleasure of getting to this state. Static pleasures give rise to a stable condition capable of indefinite prolongation. They are therefore characterized by an enduring state not found in kinetic pleasures, which are momentary or short-lived, lasting only as long as the accompanying action.

## *Ataraxia:* The Ultimate End of Life

For Epicurus, the ultimate end of life is static pleasure, not kinetic.[35] He calls this end **ataraxia,** the state of not having **tarachai,** or troubles (often translated as tranquility).[36] Freedom from pain in the body is called **aponia.** Reading Epicurus, his commentators, and some of his critics makes it difficult to know exactly whether *aponia* is meant to be included under *ataraxia* or whether the absence of bodily pain is something different to be added to it separately.[37] In any case, whether *aponia* is separate from or part of *ataraxia,* the fact still remains that such ends are static, not kinetic. Being free from pain in the body and free from disturbance and anxiety in the soul are both states, not actions.

To say that *ataraxia* (including *aponia*) is a state of being is not to suggest that it involves a total absence of activity. *Ataraxia* is not about doing nothing or remaining motionless in some kind of transcendental blissful state. When *ataraxia* is achieved, one is functioning normally without painful interference. The goal of *ataraxia* is positive and substantial. It is about unimpeded activity of the human organism in its natural condition. In a state of Epicurean *ataraxia,* individuals use all their faculties without strain and without obstruction from fear, hunger, and disease. In *ataraxia,* the mind (or reason) works with an awareness of bodily functioning. It aims to keep things working smoothly.

The specialized use of reason in logic and mathematics is considered only instrumentally valuable by Epicurus. Such use is not necessary for *ataraxia,* nor for a fulfilling life. According to Epicurus, the natural child, in its untutored state, would not desire logic and math as something pleasurably good.[38] The Epicurean does not, therefore, glorify the contemplative life or the life of reason as Plato and Aristotle did, for example. Mental pleasures are not any better or higher than bodily pleasures. Both are natural. On this note, Epicurus instructs us to follow our **natural desires.**[39] As Julia Annas puts it, "Natural desires . . . do not produce mental rather than bodily pleasures; rather, the natural/not natural distinction cuts right across that of mental and bodily. Natural desires are those we cannot help having, so that in fulfilling them we are following, rather than forcing, our nature."[40] Thus, bodily desires for food and drink are, for Epicurus, as natural as the mental desire for tranquility of the soul (what some of us today would call peace of mind).

## PHILOSOPHICAL PROFILE

### Contemporary Scholars of Hellenistic Philosophy

Philosophy is sometimes criticized for being the study of "dead white males." It is important for you to understand, however, that many philosophers who have made valuable contributions to philosophical scholarship are female, alive, and currently engaged in important writing and research. Two such philosophers are Julia Annas and Martha Nussbaum, both experts in Hellenistic philosophy, which incorporates skepticism, hedonism, and stoicism, the latter two of which

are covered in this chapter. Read below to learn more about these contemporary
Hellenistic scholars, who are referred to repeatedly in this chapter.

## JULIA ANNAS

Julia Annas (Ph.D. Harvard), Regents Professor of Philosophy, was at St. Hugh's
College at Oxford University for fifteen years before going to the University of
Arizona. She specializes in almost every facet of ancient Greek philosophy, in-
cluding metaphysics, epistemology, ethics, and psychology. Her current research
interests are in Platonic ethics. She is a fellow of the American Academy of
Arts and Sciences and the former editor of the annual journal *Oxford Studies in
Ancient Philosophy*. Her books include: *An Introduction to Plato's Republic, The
Modes of Skepticism* (with Jonathan Barnes), and *Hellenistic Philosophy of Mind*.
An excellent book of hers, dealing with stoicism and Epicureanism, is *The
Morality of Happiness*.

## MARTHA NUSSBAUM

Martha Nussbaum received her B.A. from New York University and her M.A.
and Ph.D. degrees from Harvard. Currently, she is Ernst Freund Professor of
Law and Ethics at the University of Chicago. She has also taught at Harvard
and Oxford Universities. From 1986 to 1993, Nussbaum was a research adviser
at the World Institute for Development Economics in Helsinki, a part of the
United Nations University. She has chaired the Committee on International
Cooperation of the American Philosophical Association and has been a member of the association's national board, currently chairing the Committee on
the Status of Women. Nussbaum has written an excellent treatise on stoic,
skeptic, and Epicurean themes entitled *The Therapy of Desire: Theory and Practice in Hellenistic Ethics*. Other books written by Nussbaum include *Aristotle's "De
Motu Animalium," The Fragility of Goodness: Luck and Ethics in Greek Tragedy and
Philosophy*, and *Love's Knowledge: Essays on Philosophy and Literature*.

**MARTHA NUSSBAUM**

If we are to fulfill our natural desires, it is important that we not rely on
**empty beliefs,** that is, on those that are false and harmful. Vain or unnatural desires based on empty beliefs do not come from nature but rather are products
of teaching and acculturation. Their falsity results from the incorrect evaluative
beliefs that ground them. Empty beliefs have a tendency to be vain and self-
defeating, since they typically reach out for boundless objects that can provide
no stability or long-term satisfaction. Natural desires, by contrast, can be well-
satisfied because they do have limits. By trying to satisfy artificial and limitless
desires, we end up sabotaging our own *ataraxia*.[41] Suppose, for instance, you
hunger for food and experience this as a lack. Simple bread could ease your
hunger pangs, but if you believe that, given your station in life, you truly deserve
Russian caviar which is unavailable, then even if you eventually quiet your body
with bread, you will still remain troubled in your soul with frustrated cravings.
You will believe that you didn't get what you deserve and be upset by this belief.

*"Frugal meals deliver a pleasure that is equal to that of an expensive diet, when once all the pain of need is removed; and bread and water give the very summit of pleasure, when a needy person takes them in."*

EPICURUS

Needing food is natural; yearning for caviar is not. Though eating caviar may be pleasurable (if you like that sort of thing), not every pleasure is worthy of being pursued or troubled about if it's not available. Believing you deserve caviar and developing a craving for it are things you have been taught and acculturated to, not things natural to the human organism. If we don't rid ourselves of empty beliefs like the one about caviar, we may end up removing the pains and lacks that we cannot help but have, but do so in ways that give rise to further pains and lacks.

In his **Letter to Menoeceus,** Epicurus classified the various kinds of human desires. Some are **vain desires,** meaning that they are not rooted in nature. Becoming famous or owning jewels are things you may desire, but they do not come with being born human. Such vain desires are conditioned by false beliefs of what is required to make one happy.

**Natural desires,** by contrast, may be either necessary or unnecessary. The desire for sex is natural, yet many people live a celibate life without much, if any, frustration. Desiring delicious foods is also natural but unnecessary, for we could easily live on a bland diet. Those desires that are both natural and necessary are required for comfort, happiness, and life itself. Epicurus believes that practical wisdom and friendship contribute greatly to happiness; things like shelter from the elements and adequate clothing contribute to comfort, while food and water are necessary to sustain life.

Distinguishing between what is natural and necessary from what is empty, vain, and unnecessary, Epicurus and his followers chose to live simple and frugal lives. It is truly a misreading of Epicureanism to suggest that it advocates that we all "Eat, drink, and be merry." In truth, Epicurus recommended suppression of desires that go beyond natural needs and moderation in those desires of the natural sort. Neither overindulgence of natural desires (gluttony with regard to food), nor strict asceticism (anorexia or physically wasting away) can lead to a pleasurable life.

For Epicurus, happy is the person who displays **prudence** (practical wisdom), **simple tastes, bodily health, freedom from physical need, powers of discrimination** (to distinguish between natural and vain desires) and **tranquility of the soul.** Because happy people are not deluded by vain and empty beliefs, constantly trying to satisfy limitless and unnecessary cravings, they possess a sober **self-sufficiency.** See Figure 2.3 for a classification of Epicurean desires.

## Impediments to *Ataraxia*

The road to achieving *ataraxia* is not an easy one according to Epicurus. Society and the acculturation process do severe damage to human desire and natural, unimpeded functioning. To begin with, religious teachers in Epicurus's day taught people to fear the gods and to fear death because of an uncertain afterlife. In ancient Greece, the gods were thought to intervene in the lives of humans. They could reward people as easily as they could take revenge on them. Thus, humans were constantly trying to appease the gods in order not to elicit their vengeful wrath. Although this belief in "the gods" may seem antiquated or

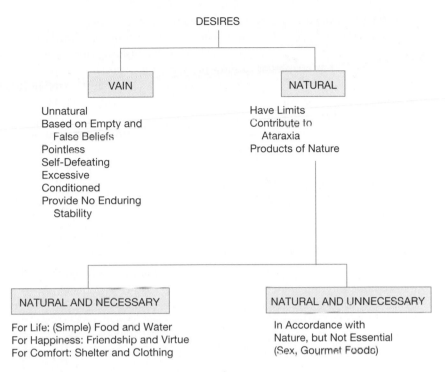

DESIRES

VAIN

Unnatural
Based on Empty and
    False Beliefs
Pointless
Self-Defeating
Excessive
Conditioned
Provide No Enduring
    Stability

NATURAL

Have Limits
Contribute to
    Ataraxia
Products of Nature

NATURAL AND NECESSARY

For Life: (Simple) Food and Water
For Happiness: Friendship and Virtue
For Comfort: Shelter and Clothing

NATURAL AND UNNECESSARY

In Accordance with
Nature, but Not Essential
(Sex, Gourmet Foods)

**FIGURE 2.3** **A classification of Epicurean desires.**

even barbaric given the monotheistic traditions of Christianity, Islam, and Judaism, I know from personal experience that people still "make deals" with God, promising to do "whatever" to achieve their goal. Others continue to morbidly fear death, worrying about the prospects of hell if life is not lived according to God's will. The belief that God rewards and punishes or that He intervenes in our lives is even evident in professional sports. Watch athletes on television after they score touchdowns or win games; prayers of thanks are frequently offered, as if God blessed the fortunate player or the team. We're left wondering how God feels about the losers. Are they being punished for something they did? Maybe God is a Buffalo Bills' fan and hates the Miami Dolphins. Seriously though, it's interesting, that never having met God, people still project human qualities and intentions onto this deity. When we pray for things to happen, aren't we just reducing God to an errand boy whose task it is to satisfy our desires? When we fear God, aren't we choosing to see Him as a vengeful judge who sentences his creations to an eternity in hell if they do not do His bidding? In view of these beliefs, I think the fear of God and the fear of death are no less real today than they were during the times of Epicurus.

   If Epicurus were living now, I suspect he would strongly recommend that we stop making false assumptions about God and attributing to God our own imperfect, human qualities. Epicurus might speculate that seeing God as judgmental is nothing more than a human projection of our own feelings of guilt. No matter what utterances we make about God, what is certain is that they are not based on any true perceptions derived from actual sensory experience. We have never seen or met God. In whatever way we conceptualize Him (or Her), we are merely projecting our own human qualities upon this divinity. Epicurus would thus instruct us to show piety and reject popular superstitious beliefs about God—beliefs largely created out of fear. We ought to accept the blessedness and immortality of God (the gods) and recognize that He, She, or They are too preoccupied to trouble themselves with the problems of this world. As for our own mortality, we should be undisturbed, for with death comes the end of all physical sensation. Rather than yearn for the impossible (life forever), we should enjoy our present life all the more, understanding that our lifetime is not limitless. Every moment is precious and should be enjoyed to the fullest. Desiring the impossible and fearing the inevitable can only disturb the soul.

## Virtue in the Pleasant Life

The role **virtue** plays for Epicurus in the development of *ataraxia* and the pleasant life is not entirely unambiguous. Some passages taken from Epicurus's writings seem to suggest that virtue possesses only a secondary instrumental value next to pleasure. In other words, if acting virtuously contributes to pleasure, then we should act virtuously. However, if virtuous acts stand in the way of personal pleasure, then virtuous acts should be overridden. In one passage, Epicurus states:

> It is because of pleasure that we choose even the virtues, not for their own sake, just as we choose medicine for the sake of health. (Diogenes X, 138)

In another passage, though, Epicurus says something quite different:

> . . . it is impossible to live pleasantly without also living prudently, honestly, and justly; [nor is it possible to lead a life of prudence, honor, and justice] and not live pleasantly. For the virtues are closely associated with the pleasant life and cannot be separated from them.

I guess as long as there are different analysts and commentators on Epicurus's works, there will be conflicting opinions about what he really meant. Julia Annas, a scholarly expert on Epicurus, suggests that it's possible that hostile critics of Epicurus have tended to downplay the inextricable link he makes between virtue and pleasure, and that they have quoted Epicurus out of context and with the most damaging interpretation of his apparent inconsistencies. A more lenient interpretation allows for the inconsistencies to serve a rhetorical, albeit innovative, way for Epicurus to awaken his listeners to Epicurean insights. As Annas points out, and as some passages seem to support, pleasure and virtue appear to be inseparable for Epicurus, if life is taken as a whole. Each one entails the other. According to some interpretations, it would appear that the virtues become part of happiness, and that part of the pleasant life is formed by acting and living according to the virtues.[42]

## The Role of Friendship

*Ataraxia,* as the final end of life, must be complete and self-sufficient, or else it is not the final end. In this respect, virtue must, for Epicurus, be included under *ataraxia,* for virtuous acts are pleasurable and *ataraxia* incorporates all that is pleasurable. As friendship, too, is pleasurable, any concept of *ataraxia* that is complete and self-sufficient must include it as well.

The value placed on **friendship** by Epicurus is evident from how The Garden was organized. Remember, it was a placid, apolitical world devoted to the values of companionship and solidarity. Life in The Garden community was to replace prior familial, societal, and civic relationships in order that all might grow together in philosophy. People were expected to leave their former positions in society and join in common purpose at The Garden. On the subject of friendship from an Epicurean perspective, Cicero wrote:

> Isolation and a life without friends are full of hidden traps and fears, so that reason itself advises us to secure friendships; when these are obtained our spirits are strengthened and cannot be parted from the hope of getting pleasures.
>
> So, since we cannot in any way keep a continuing pleasantness in life without friendship, and since we cannot have friendship itself unless we love our friends equally with ourselves—this is in fact brought about in friendship, and friendship is linked with pleasure. (Cicero, *De Finibus* I, 66–68)

As Cicero points out, Epicurean friendship would have us love our friends as much as ourselves and have equal concern for their pleasures as our own. Friendship is not about using others to get pleasure for oneself; we get genuine pleasure from being concerned about, and caring for, others. Thus, our final end, *ataraxia,* must include friendship.

## PHILOSOPHY IN PRACTICE

### "Sigmund Freud's Debt to Epicurus"

> *The poets and philosophers before me discovered the unconscious. What I discovered was the scientific method by which the unconscious can be studied.*
>
> **SIGMUND FREUD**

In a marvelous book entitled *The Therapy of Desire: Theory and Practice in Hellenistic Ethics,* Martha C. Nussbaum points to Epicurus's greatness as a psy-chologist. In fact, she attributes the discovery of the unconscious to him. In The Garden, Epicurus emphasized memorization and repetition of Epicurean principles as a way of internalizing his teachings and giving them the transformative power required to overcome society's harmful teaching of false and empty beliefs. Epicurus understood how socially conditioned beliefs, causing disturbances in life, do not all lie on the surface of consciousness and may even show up in dreams. Epicurus held that the self is not entirely transparent to itself and that false beliefs and vain desires can exercise their influence, often without our conscious awareness. As a consequence, he saw the limitations of a purely rational, critical, or dialectical scrutiny of the self. Rational understanding does not guarantee personal change. Knowing what is good does not necessarily mean that one will do it, according to Epicurus, no matter what the rationalist Socrates thought. False beliefs are often buried deep in the soul and exert their troubling influence beneath the level of the conscious mind. By rote memory and repetition of Epicurean principles (based on natural and necessary desires), those vain desires based on empty and false beliefs could be driven down so deeply that their influence would be minimized.

To help followers of The Garden become aware of their vain desires and false beliefs, Epicurus started something new in the Greek philosophical tradition—the ritual of confession or personal narrative. Philodemus, a student of Epicurus, wrote:

> The pupil must show him his failings without concealment and tell his defects

in the open. For if he considers him the one guide of correct speech and deed, the one whom he calls the only savior and to whom saying 'with him at my side,' he gives himself over to be therapeutically treated, then how could he not show the things in which he requires therapeutic treatment, and receive his criticism?

Through confession and personal narrative, that is, by having the disturbed person describe his or her actions, thoughts, desires, and even dreams, Epicurus hoped to grasp the totality of the philosophical patient's disturbing symptoms and open them up for analysis and diagnosis, much like Freud used free association to uncover repressed conflicts and unconscious motivations. Freud's recognition of the unconscious and his use of indirect means (like dream analysis) to gain access to the unconscious would appear, then, to have been predated by Epicurus many centuries before!

So that you might now formulate your own interpretations and draw your own conclusions about Epicureanism, let us now turn to the Original Sourcework entitled, *Letter to Menoeceus,* wherein Epicurus shares with us his conception of the happy life.

## ORIGINAL SOURCEWORK

## *Letter to Menoeceus*

**EPICURUS**

Epicurus to Menoeceus, greetings:

Let no one be slow to seek wisdom when he is young nor weary in the search of it when he has grown old. For no age is too early or too late for the health of the soul. And to say that the season for studying philosophy has

not yet come, or that it is past and gone, is like saying that the season for happiness is not yet or that it is now no more. Therefore, both old and young alike ought to seek wisdom, the former in order that, as age comes over him, he may be young in good things because of the grace

Source: Epicurus, *Letter to Menoeceus,* Trans. Robert Drew Hicks, 1925.

of what has been, and the latter in order that, while he is young, he may at the same time be old, because he has no fear of the things which are to come. So we must exercise ourselves in the things which bring happiness, since, if that be present, we have everything, and, if that be absent, all our actions are directed towards attaining it.

Those things which without ceasing I have declared unto you, do them, and exercise yourself in them, holding them to be the elements of right life. First believe that God is a living being immortal and blessed, according to the notion of a god indicated by the common sense of mankind; and so believing, you shall not affirm of him anything that is foreign to his immortality or that is repugnant to his blessedness. Believe about him whatever may uphold both his blessedness and his immortality. For there are gods, and the knowledge of them is manifest; but they are not such as the multitude believe, seeing that men do not steadfastly maintain the notions they form respecting them. Not the man who denies the gods worshipped by the multitude, but he who affirms of the gods what the multitude believes about them is truly impious. For the utterances of the multitude about the gods are not true preconceptions but false assumptions; hence it is that the greatest evils happen to the wicked and the greatest blessings happen to the good from the hand of the gods, seeing that they are always favorable to their own good qualities and take pleasure in men like themselves, but reject as alien whatever is not of their kind.

Accustom yourself to believing that death is nothing to us, for good and evil imply the capacity for sensation, and death is the privation of all sentience; therefore a correct understanding that death is nothing to us makes the mortality of life enjoyable, not by adding to life a limitless time, but by taking away the yearning after immortality. For life has no terrors for him who has thoroughly understood that there are no terrors for him in ceasing to live. Foolish, therefore, is the man who says that he fears death, not because it will pain when it comes, but because it pains in the prospect. Whatever causes no annoyance when it is present, causes only a groundless pain in the expectation. Death, therefore, the most awful of evils, is nothing to us, seeing that, when we are, death is not come, and, when death is come, we are not. It is nothing, then, either to the living or to the dead, for with the living it is not and the dead exist no longer.

But in the world, at one time men shun death as the greatest of all evils, and at another time choose it as a respite from the evils in life. The wise man does not deprecate life nor does he fear the cessation of life. The thought of life is no offense to him, nor is the cessation of life regarded as an evil. And even as men choose of food not merely and simply the larger portion, but the more pleasant, so the wise seek to enjoy the time which is most pleasant and not merely that which is longest. And he who admonishes the young to live well and the old to make a good end speaks foolishly, not merely because of the desirability of life, but because the same exercise at once teaches to live well and to die well. Much worse is he who says that it were good not to be born, but when once one is born to pass quickly through the gates of Hades. For if he truly believes this, why does he not depart from life? It would be easy for him to do so once he were firmly convinced. If he speaks only in jest, his words are foolishness as those who hear him do not believe.

We must remember that the future is neither wholly ours nor wholly not ours, so that neither must we count upon it as quite certain to come nor despair of it as quite certain not to come.

We must also reflect that of desires some are natural, others are groundless; and that of the natural some are necessary as well as natural, and some natural only. And of the necessary desires some are necessary if we are to be happy, some if the body is to be rid of uneasiness, some if we are even to live. He who has a clear and certain understanding of these things will direct every preference and aversion toward securing health of body and tranquillity of mind, seeing that this is the sum and end of a blessed life. For the end of all our actions is to be free from pain and fear, and, when once we have attained all this, the tempest of the soul is laid; seeing that the living creature has no need to go in search of something that is lacking, nor to look for anything else by which the good of the soul and of the body will be fulfilled. When we are pained because of the absence of pleasure, then, and then only, do we feel the need of pleasure. Wherefore we call pleasure the alpha and omega of a blessed life. Pleasure is our first and kindred good. It is the starting-point of every choice and of every aversion, and to it we come back, inasmuch as we make feeling the rule by which to judge of every good thing.

And since pleasure is our first and native good, for that reason we do not choose every pleasure whatsoever, but will often pass over many pleasures when a greater annoyance ensues from them. And often we consider pains superior to pleasures when submission to the pains for a long time brings us as a consequence a greater pleasure. While therefore all pleasure because it is naturally akin to us is good, not all pleasure is should be chosen, just as all pain is an evil and yet not all pain is to be shunned. It is, however, by measuring one against another, and by looking at the conveniences and inconveniences, that all these matters must be judged. Sometimes we treat the good as an evil, and the evil, on the contrary, as a good.

Again, we regard independence of outward things as a great good, not so as in all cases to use little, but so as to be contented with little if we have not much, being honestly persuaded that they have the sweetest enjoyment of luxury who stand least in need of it, and that whatever is natural is easily procured and only the vain and worthless hard to win. Plain fare gives as much pleasure as a costly diet, when once the pain of want has been removed, while bread and water confer the highest possible pleasure when they are brought to hungry lips. To habituate one's self, therefore, to simple and inexpensive diet supplies all that is needful for health, and enables a man to meet the necessary requirements of life without shrinking, and it places us in a better condition when we approach at intervals a costly fare and renders us fearless of fortune.

When we say, then, that pleasure is the end and aim, we do not mean the pleasures of the prodigal or the pleasures of sensuality, as we are understood to do by some through ignorance, prejudice, or willful misrepresentation. By pleasure we mean the absence of pain in the body and of trouble in the soul. It is not an unbroken succession of drinking-bouts and of revelry, not sexual lust, not the enjoyment of the fish and other delicacies of a luxurious table, which produce a pleasant life; it is sober reasoning, searching out the grounds of every choice and avoidance, and banishing those beliefs through which the greatest tumults take possession of the soul. Of all this the beginning and the greatest good is wisdom. Therefore wisdom is a more precious thing even than philosophy; from it spring all the other virtues, for it teaches that we cannot live pleasantly without living wisely, honorably, and justly; nor live wisely, honorably, and justly without living pleasantly. For the virtues have grown into one with a pleasant life, and a pleasant life is inseparable from them.

Who, then, is superior in your judgement to such a man? He holds a holy belief concerning the gods, and is altogether free from the fear of death. He has diligently considered the end fixed by nature, and understands how easily the limit of good things can be reached and attained, and how either the duration or the intensity of evils is but slight. Fate, which some introduce as sovereign over all things, he scorns, affirming rather that some things happen of necessity, others by chance, others through our own agency. For he sees that necessity destroys responsibility and that chance is inconstant; whereas our own actions are autonomous, and it is to them that praise and blame naturally attach. It were better, indeed, to accept the legends of the gods than to bow beneath that yoke of destiny which the natural philosophers have imposed. The one holds out some faint hope that we may escape if we honor the gods, while the necessity of the naturalists is deaf to all entreaties. Nor does he hold chance to be a god, as the world in general does, for in the acts of a god there is no disorder, nor to be a cause, though an uncertain one, for he believes that no good or evil is dispensed by chance to men so as to make life blessed, though it supplies the starting-point of great good and great evil. He believes that the misfortune of the wise is better than the prosperity of the fool. It is better, in short, that what is well judged in action should not owe its successful issue to the aid of chance.

Exercise yourself in these and related precepts day and night, both by yourself and with one who is like-minded; then never, either in waking or in dream, will you be disturbed, but will live as a god among men. For man loses all semblance of mortality by living in the midst of immortal blessings.

## DISCUSSION QUESTIONS FOR CRITIQUE AND ANALYSIS

1. Is philosophical study for everybody? Why?

2. Is happiness all about getting what you want according to Epicurus? What exactly does he say about wants? What are your reasons for agreeing or disagreeing with him?

3. What prescriptions for life do we get from Epicurus's letter to Menoeceus? Which ones do you accept or take issue with? Explain.

# BUDDHISM AS A PHILOSOPHY OF LIFE

As we turn now to Buddhism, we find yet another philosophy which, like Hellenistic stoicism, has great personal and practical relevance. It too has therapeutic applications for better functioning in the world. One needn't be a practicing Buddhist to benefit from the insights it has to offer. If nothing else, a study of Buddhist philosophy affords an opportunity to engage in a process of self-reflection, reevaluating the directions our lives have taken thus far. In what follows, we will briefly cover **The Four Noble Truths** revealed to Buddha at the time of his enlightenment. We will also take a look at **The Noble Eightfold Path** which constitutes **The Middle Way** of living—the one recommended by Buddha for release from selfish craving. Without such release, true and lasting happiness is not possible, according to Buddhist teachings.

> *"Suffering I teach— and the way out of suffering."*
> THE BUDDHA

## PHILOSOPHICAL PROFILE

### Siddhartha Gautama — The Buddha

The person we have come to know as the Buddha was born circa 563 B.C.E. as Siddhartha Gautama, the only son of a ruling king in what is now Nepal. The details of Siddhartha's life are sketchy since no complete biography of the Buddha was compiled until centuries after his death. Much of the information we have comes from tradition and myth, and it's difficult, therefore, to distinguish between fact and legend. What we do know is that his people were called the Sakyas; for this reason, the Buddha is sometimes referred to as *Sakyamuni,* or "the sage of the Sakyas." "Buddha" is not a personal name but an honorific title meaning the "awakened one." Siddhartha Gautama (his clan name) did not actually become the Buddha until his mid-thirties, when he achieved enlightenment.

As the son of a royal ruler, the young Siddhartha led a life of luxury and pleasure. Legend has it that soon after his birth, a wise sage came to visit and noticed that there were 32 special markings on Siddhartha's tiny body. For the sage, this was a sign that Siddhartha was destined for glory. He would either become a universal monarch or great religious teacher. Siddhartha's father, Suddhodana, was not entirely thrilled by this. The king wanted his son to succeed him, since if the prince abandoned his position in the royal palace, Suddhodana would be without an heir. Believing that the ugly, unpleasant, and painful things of life would turn Siddhartha's mind toward religion, Suddhodana decided that he should raise his son in a completely protected environment of comfort, beauty, and pleasure. Three splendid marble palaces were built—one for each of the hot, cool, and rainy seasons. Siddhartha was confined to the upper stories of these palaces and provided with every kind of pleasure and luxury to prevent boredom from setting in. He lazed around the palace in fine silks, ate the most delicious foods, and enjoyed armies of musicians, dancing girls, and the most sensuous courtesans who were on hand to amuse and entertain him. Shielded from him were illness and old age. Presumably, if Buddha never experienced the

**SIDDHARTHA GAUTAMA—THE BUDDHA**

pains and miseries of life, he would never be drawn to religion and could therefore fulfill his father's wishes. At age 16, Siddhartha married his cousin Yasodhara, who eventually bore him a son (Rahula) when he was 29.

Before the birth of his son, Siddhartha had already fallen prey to restless boredom, notwithstanding all of the efforts of his father. Ironically perhaps, unproductive self-indulgence simply could not make life satisfying for him. With his hired guardian, friend, and charioteer, Channa, Siddhartha made secret trips outside the palace walls. Channa became a tour guide of sorts, answering many of Siddhartha's questions about the harsh realities of life beyond his protected environment. It was during these secret trips that Siddhartha saw "the four signs" that would change his life forever.

On the first trip, Siddhartha encountered an old man; on the second trip, a sick man; and on the third trip, a corpse being carried away for cremation. Because Siddhartha had lived such a cloistered life for almost 30 years, these three encounters were quite traumatic for him. He had no concept of the true human condition: that all human beings are susceptible to sickness, old age, and death—including Siddhartha himself. Disturbed by this, he wondered how anyone could find happiness since, in the end, there is no escape from suffering and loss, with all of the associated sadness and disappointment. After witnessing the first three signs, all the pleasures and delights of palace life quickly lost their charm. Siddhartha had lost his innocence.

On a fourth trip outside the palace walls, Siddhartha and Channa came upon a wandering holy man. Alone, dressed in rags and possessing nothing, this ascetic monk displayed a demeanor that thoroughly impressed Siddhartha. He seemed to possess a peaceful tranquility that other people lacked, however great their possessions or station in life. The monk appeared to be detached from the worries of the world, serene and quietly purposeful. This was the fourth sign. Shortly after witnessing it, Siddhartha knew deep within himself that he would have to leave the comforts of home and live as a monk. On the very night that his son Rahula was to be born, Siddhartha rose from bed, woke Channa, saddled up his horse, and rode to the River Anoma, which divided the land of the Shakyas from the neighboring kingdom of Magadha. On the banks of the river, Siddhartha removed his jewelry, cut off his hair, exchanged his silken robe for the ragged yellow one of a wandering holy man, and then said his good-byes to Channa. Siddhartha walked off alone in his spiritual quest for the solution to the problem of suffering.

Renouncing earthly attachments, he embarked on his search by first adopting a lifestyle of radical asceticism: fasting, meditation, simple clothes, and plain food. He showed so much discipline in his fasting that Siddhartha almost wasted away. Eventually, he abandoned asceticism as fruitless and instead adopted "a middle path" between a life of self-indulgence (exemplified by palace life) and one of self-denial.

One day, at a place now called Bodh Gaya in the modern Indian state of Bihar, Siddhartha sat at the base of what was to become known as The Bodhi Tree or Tree of Wisdom, swearing to remain there until answered about the problem of suffering or dead. Meditating and gradually rising through a series of higher states of consciousness, he finally attained the enlightenment for which he had been searching. Siddhartha had undergone a transformation, turning a spoiled and naive young man into "the awakened one"—the one we call the Buddha.

In the Deer Park at Isipatana Buddha preached his first sermon regarding The Four Noble Truths. He also spoke about The Middle Way that he had discovered between the extremes of sensual indulgence and self-mortification. For the next 45 years, the Buddha was to wander from place to place, gathering disciples and organizing them into a monastic community known as the *sangha*.

At around the age of 80, the Buddha was having a meal at the humble home of a lowly blacksmith. He took ill soon thereafter. As an accidental result of eating either poisonous mushrooms or tainted pork, Buddha died (circa 480 B.C.E.).

The teachings of Buddha were handed down orally for hundreds of years until monks began to transcribe them in the first century B.C.E. More recently, the Pali Text Society has collected and edited them into the so-called "Three Baskets": the rules for monks (*Vinaya Pitaka*), the basic teachings of the Buddha (*Sutta Pitaka*) and a commentary (*Abhidhamma Pitaka*). Today the teachings of Buddha serve as an inspiration and guide for millions throughout the world.

> *When the iron bird flies, and horses run on wheels, the Tibetan people will be scattered like ants across the world, and the Dharma [Buddha's teachings] will come to the land of red-faced people.*
>
> PADMA SAMBHAVA, EIGHTH CENTURY INDIAN GURU

## The Four Noble Truths

Introducing the topic of Buddhism into any casual conversation probably elicits, in many minds, the image of bald-headed monks in yellow robes wandering about in some distant foreign land where the inhabitants look different, speak different languages, and practice strange and different customs. From the vantage point of the modern Western mind-set, the Buddhist monk probably looks about as weird as the toga-clad philosopher haunting the streets of ancient Athens—somewhat bothersome and irrelevant to day-to-day affairs. Yet a closer inspection of Buddhism reveals that it is eminently practical. It does not begin by posing grand metaphysical questions like, "Who made the world?" or "What is the meaning of life?"[43] Nor does it expect its adherents to suspend reason, critical judgment, or commonsense experience. Its teachings are not dogmatic articles of faith that must be accepted blindly and without question. Furthermore, Buddhism is not presented as a universally prescriptive model of truth. As devotees admit, Buddhism may not, in fact, be appropriate for you at all. In a spirit of tolerance and understanding, his Holiness, the Fourteenth Dalai Lama—the current spiritual leader for millions of Buddhists—writes:

> A teaching may be very profound but if it does not suit a particular person, what is the use of explaining it? In this sense, the **Dharma** [Buddhist teaching] is like medicine. The main value of

medicine is that it cures illness; it is not just a question of price. For example, one medicine may be very precious and expensive, but if it is not appropriate for the patient, then it is of no use.

Since there are different types of people in the world, we need diffcrent types of religion.[44]

Rather than present itself as dogmatic and otherworldly, then, Buddhism starts with the down-to-earth fact that human existence is imperfect in a very deep way.[45] Understood as a way to wisdom, Buddhism offers us a method for retraining our minds so that we may experience a self-transformation, one that improves the quality of our lives. In this respect, Buddhism is very much a **therapeutic philosophy.** Indeed, The Four Noble Truths, which make self-transformation possible, follow a medical pattern. We shall learn more about this pattern as we discuss each of The Four Noble Truths in turn.

## First Noble Truth

This, monks, is the Noble Truth of Suffering; birth is suffering; decay is suffering; illness is suffering; death is suffering; presence of objects we hate is suffering; separation from objects we love is suffering; not to obtain what we desire is suffering. In brief, the five aggregates which spring from grasping, they are painful.

The Buddha

**Diagnosis of Humanity's Problem**   In the first sermon delivered in the Deer Park at Benares, after his enlightenment under the Bodhi Tree (see Philosophical Profile), Buddha diagnoses the basic problem of human life as **suffering.** In his teachings, Buddha gives a systematic analysis of the nature and causes of suffering, providing numerous means for overcoming it.[46] In his statement of the First Noble Truth, Buddha lists various types of suffering, which most of us can easily recognize and understand (decay, illness, death). The point should be appreciated, however, that suffering goes much deeper than these examples might have you conclude. Suppose, for instance, that you are currently experiencing a great deal of pleasure in your life. You may not think you are a victim of suffering at all, and Buddha's assessment that life is suffering may seem counterintuitive to you. Before you summarily dismiss the venerable Buddha as some kind of bleak pessimist, however, let us take a closer look at the pleasures you (and the rest of us) might be enjoying right now.

First of all, isn't it true that the objects and activities we enjoy carry with them an element of **attachment?** Don't we often say things like, "I'm very attached to this or that," or "I don't know what I would do without him or her," meaning some possession or person has sentimental value? Isn't it also true that we consciously or unconsciously experience anxiety from the possibility of separation from the object, person, or activity to which we're so attached? Have you ever rejected the idea of owning a pet, for example, because you dread the day it will inevitably die, leaving you sad and unhappy? In other words, have you ever anticipated the short-lived and precarious nature of your pleasures? Haven't your pleasures always been alloyed with fear and insecurity at some level—conscious or unconscious? Buddhists understand that the anxiety that results from change and the possibility of separation is like a hidden cancer in any pleasure, and therefore, a source of suffering.[47] Whereas one can easily appreciate how illness or death can be a clear source of suffering, understanding how attachment to pleasure-producing things can be painful is not so obvious.

Pleasure can lead to suffering in yet another way. Many pleasures are not only self-perpetuating but also self-accelerating. Getting pleasure from engaging in some activities may not diminish the drive for the particular pleasure but rather strengthen it. Enjoying a cold alcoholic beverage on a hot day may be pleasurable, yet experience teaches us that one drink can often lead to another, and then to another, and still another, until one becomes physically ill or one passes out. Some people find drinking alcohol so pleasurable that they become attached to certain beer labels and whiskey brands, psychologically identifying with them all the way down the rocky road to addiction—something not so pleasurable.

On a somewhat less dramatic note, have you ever found the more pleasure one achieves, the more one wants. I once heard a very wealthy businessman discuss his kitchen renovation, which cost an exorbitant amount of money. Given that his kitchen had looked virtually new and was very tastefully designed, an onlooker asked why the renovation was being undertaken, since there was no real practical need for it. The rich man answered, "When you get to my station in life, it's not what you need, but what you want!" Now, before you find yourself impressed by the luxury and choice that wealth can bring, ask yourself what motivated the rich man to renovate the kitchen. Was it not dissatisfaction, boredom, displeasure, or unhappiness with what he had? Is this not a form of suffering? How long will it be, we could ask, before the new kitchen ceases to provide pleasure; the previous one certainly couldn't sustain his enthusiasm. Will the pleasure produced by subsequent renovations successfully hide the suffering below? The Buddhist insight here is that grasping at the pleasures of life ultimately increases suffering. The drive for pleasure is simply too shallow and insignificant to be fulfilling. It cannot provide true happiness.[48]

The notion of suffering can reflect a wide spectrum of possibilities. Suffering can be mental or physical. It can relate to petty dislikes and frustrations, or more seriously, to conflict, anxiety, and anger. Sometimes, suffering results from dull feelings of malaise stemming from the perception that things are never quite right or how we would like them to be.[49] Also, as we've learned, even beautiful, pleasurable experiences can have melancholy undertones because we know they will not last forever. The proverbial saying reminds us that *all good things must come to an end.*

What prevents us from healing on our human journeys is that we staunchly resist the dark side of life. No matter how dissatisfied we are by our pursuit of pleasure, we continue to believe that with just a few changes and minor adjustments, we can overcome the obstacles to our happiness and enjoy heaven on earth. The Buddhist, however, would describe this approach to life

> *"Avoid attachment to both what is pleasant And what is unpleasant. Losing the pleasant causes grief. Dwelling on the unpleasant also causes grief."*
> THE BUDDHA

as **willful blindness**—a refusal to face the facts of the human condition.[50] Life is suffering. This is not pessimistic, but an accurate reflection of how things are.

### Man and His Shadow

There was a man
who was so disturbed
by the sight of his own shadow
and so displeased with his own footsteps
that he determined to get rid of both.
The method he hit upon was to run away from them.
So he got up and ran.
But every time he put his foot down
there was another step,
while his shadow kept up with him
without the slightest difficulty.
He attributed his failure
to the fact that he was not running fast enough.
So he ran faster and faster, without stopping,
until he finally dropped dead.
He failed to realize that if he merely stepped into the shade,
his shadow would vanish,
and if he sat down and stayed still, there would be no more footsteps.

*Chuang Tzu*

Source: Thomas Merton, *The Way of Chuang Tzu,* Copyright © 1965 by The Abbey of Gethsemani. Reprinted by permission of New Directions Publishing Corp.

## Second Noble Truth

[Suffering] originates in that craving which causes the renewals of becomings, is accompanied by sensual delight, and seeks satisfaction now here, now there; that is to say, craving for pleasures, craving for becoming, craving for not becoming.

**Craving—The Cause of Human Suffering**   In the First Noble Truth, Buddha diagnoses the "disease" of humanity as the universal plague of suffering. In the Second Noble Truth, he isolates its cause. For Buddha, the cause of suffering stems from a generalized mentality of poverty. We feel we are deficient, lacking or missing something in our lives; hence, we crave. Indeed, suffering originates in **craving.** Craving can take many forms, some subtle, some not so subtle. We may have an obsessive lust for money or physical pleasure. We may crave health in times of illness or immortality when facing death. We may desire to develop a self or possess an ego which we can satisfy, massage, inflate, or develop a positive concept around. We may also lust after the truth or desire to do good. Whatever form our craving takes, it reflects a gnawing dissatisfaction with what is and an associated grasping for something outside of ourselves. This incessant craving ensures that we can never be at rest.[51] Like the young child who screams for the scissors that would hurt it, we crave those things that in the end cause only suffering and pain. No matter what, we insist on being possessive, greedy, and above all, self-centered. We all seek to satisfy our "**self**"—a self whose egocentric cravings can never be fully or finally satiated.

On this note, it should be pointed out that things in the world do not of themselves cause suffering. It is the *self*, aware of changes in its condition, that suffers. Bricks and water don't experience pain. Suffering occurs when objective factors (events and situations) related to the self change, or do not change, as desired. It is the self that craves changes or craves to avoid them. When what is craved is not obtained, then suffering arises.

For Buddha, then, craving is associated with the ego, or self. It is the ego-self that forms attachments and identifications with objective factors in the external world. When such things are threatened, the self suffers. Another way to say this is that our self-centeredness, or desire to create and satisfy ourselves, produces suffering because of its *partiality*. If, for example, I am bored (suffering) listening to you, it's because I wish you were addressing a topic of interest to *me*. It is my *self* that gets bored. Likewise, if I'm envious about the attention my sister is receiving from my parents, it's because I crave more attention for *me*. If I did not crave the attention I felt I deserved, I would not be upset but rather delighted for her.[52] We can plainly see, then, how attachment to the ego-self constitutes a large part of our malady. We are attached to the self, which suffers because it craves.

## Third Noble Truth

> This monks, is the Noble Truth concerning the Cessation of Suffering; verily, it is passionless, cessation without remainder of this very craving; the laying aside of, the giving up, the being free from, the harboring no longer of, this craving.
>
> Buddha

**Identification of a Cure**    After diagnosing humanity's illness as suffering, and isolating its root cause, therapist-Buddha offers us good news in the Third Noble Truth, declaring that a remedy exists. Suffering can be extinguished by putting to an end the selfish craving that causes it. The cessation of suffering leads to a kind of supreme bliss or inner peace called **Nirvana.** "*Nirvana* is liberation, everlasting freedom, fulfillment, and enlightenment itself."[53] The concept of

*Nirvana* has connotations of "blowing out" or "extinguishing"—the idea is that when it is attained, selfish craving is blown out like a flame. Heated and flickering emotions are replaced by a cool and undisturbed peacefulness.

The concept of *Nirvana* can be difficult to understand, for it cannot be grasped by sense experience; neither can the mind get hold of it by operating in terms of the usual categories of thought. *Nirvana* falls outside of our normal field of experience and can only be known through direct insight. This is reminiscent of Plato's "acquaintance with the forms"—a kind of special wisdom available only to the "philosopher rulers," those who have undergone intensive moral and intellectual training qualifying them to govern the ideal society. This philosophical enlightenment lies beyond rational understanding (see the section on Plato's epistemology and metaphysics in Chapter 4, pp. 176 to 188).

Fortunately for us, therapist-Buddha offers us a prescription for achieving *Nirvana.* This prescription requires the annihilation of the self-consciousness, judgmentalism, greed, and fear that characterize the **ego.**[54] By severing our attachments, by showing compassion and loving-kindness, and by learning to control our thoughts, attitudes, and behaviors, we can escape the treadmill of suffering. As one writer puts it: "*Nirvana* is always trying to seep through the small chinks in our ego's armor. You can widen these openings by relinquishing some of the defenses and barricades of your personality, your holding on, your repetitive, addictive habitual behavior—in short, your psychological conditioning."[55] What we must do to achieve *Nirvana* is specified in the Fourth Noble Truth.

## Fourth Noble Truth

> [Concerning the path which leads to the cessation of suffering, Buddha taught] It is this Noble Eight-fold Path, that is to say, right view, right thought, right speech, right action, right livelihood, right effort, right mindfulness, and right concentration.
>
> The Buddha

**Prescription for Nirvana**   Having declared that a remedy for suffering exists, the Buddha presents us in the Fourth Noble Truth with directions leading away from the dissatisfaction of conditional existence and toward the end of craving—*Nirvana.*[56] These directions require us to take *The Noble Eight-Fold Path to Enlightenment.* Following Buddha's instructions enables us to purify our hearts and minds by living an impeccable and enlightened life. The Noble Eight-Fold Path is all about living the *Dharma* (Buddha's teachings) daily in everything we do. It captures *The Middle Way* between asceticism and self-indulgence. You might view The Noble Eight-Fold Path as a guideline for a way of life, designed to transform us by changing our way of seeing things (our consciousness). The path prescribed by Buddha can help us to abandon our egocentric sense of identity, replacing the self-centered *me* with a compassionate heart.

In essence, The Noble Eight-Fold Path constitutes a systematic strategy to uproot the defilements or foul corruptions that generate suffering in our lives.[57] By developing **morality,** we can restrain defilements in their coarsest form, namely their outflow in unwholesome actions. Through methods of **concentration,** we can remove more refined defilements that manifest as distracting and restless thoughts. With the help of **wisdom** we can also eradicate defilements presenting themselves as subtle latent tendencies, "by penetrating with direct insight the three basic facts of existence, summed up by the Buddha in the three characteristics of **impermanence, suffering, and egolessness.**"[58] The Noble Eight-Fold Path constituting The Middle Way comprises the following elements:

1. Right View      ⎫
2. Right Thought  ⎬ Wisdom

3. Right Speech       ⎫
4. Right Action       ⎬ Morality
5. Right Livelihood ⎭

6. Right Effort              ⎫
7. Right Mindfulness   ⎬ Concentration
8. Right Concentration ⎭

Note that The Noble Eight-Fold Path is *not* to be thought of as hierarchical stages that one passes through sequentially, abandoning lower ones as more advanced ones are achieved. The eight factors specify the ways in which morality, wisdom, and concentration are to be cultivated in an integrated and continuous basis.[59]

## THE EGO-SELF AS FICTION

Contained in the cause of suffering is the notion of *self.* It is only when objective factors in the world are related to a self that suffering occurs. The self may crave them or crave to avoid them. When the self cannot obtain what is craved, there is suffering. In this context, it makes sense to ask what it means to attribute a "self" to a person. Who or what is the "I" or "self" that craves? According to Buddha, a self, as such, doesn't really exist. It is the craving for one that gives rise to suffering. This craving results in the invention and projection of a self. "This self, being attached to the factors making up a person, suffers when the identification is threatened by changes in the factors to which it is attached, whether these be the factors of that person, other persons, or other objects and activities in the world."[60]

According to Buddha, if we analyze what it actually means to be a person, we find that the person is really just a bundle of:

1. Activities constituting what we call the bodily or physical self
2. Sensing activities
3. Perceiving activities
4. Action impulses
5. Activities of consciousness

These activities are forever changing from one moment to the next. In our efforts to attach a permanent self to these ever-changing activities, we create a fiction—one produced by ignorant craving,—and it is this craving for a fictitious self that underlies all suffering.[61] Changing conditions and impermanent objective factors constantly threaten the satisfaction of our cravings, and hence, our ego-identifications with them. One might say in this context that: "Although nothing lasts, suffering is everywhere, and the 'me' that suffers isn't even real."[62] For Buddha, our mission in life is not to become a "somebody," but to become a selfless, egoless nobody. If this sounds unappetizing, perhaps it is because you are still attached to the illusion of the self.

# The Noble Eight-Fold Path
## The Training of Wisdom

The first two elements of The Noble Eight-Fold Path deal with wisdom, which involves correct understanding and the resolution to act in accordance with this understanding. Don't be misguided into thinking wisdom is some kind of intellectual or theoretical knowledge; it is not. Wisdom derives from viewing things just as they are through a kind of "direct seeing." In this kind of wisdom, there is an illumination of things as they are in themselves, something not limited by concepts and labels. The illumination of wisdom enables us to experience the relative and conditional nature of all things and to appreciate how suffering is caused by selfish grasping. We are wise when we resolve to overcome suffering by setting aside all of our selfish cravings. When wisdom is achieved, egoistic desires, ill-will, hatred, and violence are all abandoned.[63]

**Step One—Right View** To follow The Noble Eight-Fold Path, one must first be aware of the teachings of Buddha, and then come to accept them through experimental confirmation—not blind faith. As part of this acceptance, one develops the wisdom of clear vision, seeing the world as insubstantial and impossible to grasp. The first step reminds us to look at the world without any delusions, fabrications, or distortions about ourselves. Buddha was one of the first *spiritual psychotherapists,* so to speak, requiring us to engage in a kind of **reality testing,** looking out for **denial** and any other egoistic defensive distortions we might engage in as we produce delusional systems of thought.[64] The Buddha would have us move away from fantasy and illusion to directly see things as they really are.

**Step Two—Right Thought or Right Intentions** Following The Noble Eight-Fold Path requires that we develop **right intentions,** or to put it another way, correct motivation.[65] In Step Two, we are asked to purify our thoughts and attitudes so that we may become totally straightforward and honest with ourselves. You see, none of us possesses a perfect understanding of what makes us tick. Through the practice of Buddhism, one gradually uncovers all sorts of blind spots and subtle forms of self-centeredness.[66] The more we uncover, the more we become freed from our self-imposed bondage, becoming more able to express loving-kindness, empathy, and compassion toward all creatures. Before achieving right thought, we fall prey to self-absorption, which acts as a veil of delusion destroying everything. Our self-absorption is so deeply ingrained that we can be fooled by its subtle manifestations. For instance, even insecurity is a type of self-absorption—only an inverted expression of it. Worry and anxiety about our lim-

The Radiant Buddha said:
Regard this fleeting world like this:
Like stars fading and vanishing at
    dawn,
like bubbles on a fast moving
    stream,
like morning dewdrops evaporating
    on blades of grass,
like a candle flickering in a strong
    wind,
echoes, mirages, and phantoms,
    hallucinations,
and like a dream.

"THE EIGHT SIMILES OF ILLUSION,"
*From the Prajna Paramita Sutras*

itations or our inabilities is still worry about the self and what the self cannot do. If we didn't care about the self and how embarrassed we might become as a result of failure or exposed weakness, then we wouldn't have become insecure in the first place. So too with self-denial. Going through elaborate rituals of self-denial is to give importance to something that is significant enough that it must be denied—another example of inverted self-absorption.

When we have right thoughts or right intentions, things like winning, achieving, and looking good don't matter. When we understand how "selfish pleasures" are contaminated with ambivalent feelings, melancholy, and other disturbing defilements like anger, envy, and revenge, they no longer taste so sweet. What is really in our interest is to be less self-conscious and less selfish. As John Snelling puts it:

> The unreformed (i.e., selfish) mind, like a mill in perpetual motion, is constantly devising plans, plots and strategies for advancing its own cause, outflanking rivals and undoing enemies. Or else it indulges itself in egoistic and hedonistic fantasies.[67]

When we achieve right thought, we switch over to other-directed mental modes. We adopt those that are more altruistic and benign. Rather than engage in self-promotion, we focus on being of service to the world.

## The Training of Morality

As we have seen thus far, there is no rigid or universally prescriptive moral code in Buddhism. Also, Buddhism does not seek to make evaluative judgments, which could arouse shame or guilt. For Buddhists, moral transgressions should be met with correction and instruction (to overcome ignorance), not with punishment, condemnation, and blame.[68] When we fail to live up to an ethical principle, we should resolve to do better next time. Recognizing that we still have a long way to go before overcoming our faults breeds a healthy humility.

**Step Three—Right Speech**   If you truly wish release from suffering, then you should consider following Buddha's instructions regarding right speech. As everyone well knows, words can be used in a variety of ways: as gifts, weapons, magic, prayer, poetry, or song.[69] Words enable us to put our thoughts and ideas into concrete terms. They enable us to define our priorities, express our views, and state our intentions. Through the use of your words, you declare and confirm to the world and to yourself, what you think is important. The compassionate Buddha would have us use words ideally as a reflection of our wish to help others. We should think kindly and speak in a gentle fashion.[70] Words do indeed have power, and how you use them indicates how you have chosen to use yours.

**Right speech** requires that we "speak the truth and tell no lies." Never knowingly tell falsehoods to gain an advantage for yourself or others. Words spoken with guile or masked intentions muddy the clear waters of truth and complicate what is actually very simple. Like political spin-doctors who distort the truth to the advantage of their chosen leaders, we, as individuals, also embark on egotistical advertising campaigns, embellishing the truth to present ourselves in the best possible light. The consequence is that we create false personas that leave us feeling incomplete and alienated from our authentic selves.[71] Ironically, perhaps, self-congratulatory words used to inflate the ego do violence to the (higher) self. In our relationships, we should therefore always try to be honest and forthright. We should try to let go of our elaborate defense mechanisms and be truthful and open about who we are and how we feel.

Another dimension of right speech involves refusing to gossip. Telling tales about others is a masked way for us to feel superior and part of the in-crowd. However, when we tell tales or make unkind jokes behind people's backs, we only create greater distance between ourselves and them. We treat them disrespectfully as objects of our amusement. Thus, we must resist the urge to speak unkindly about others in their absence, as doing so is not kind.

Buddha also instructs us to "use words in helpful, not harmful ways." We should refrain from causing trouble with talk that is hurtful or unnecessarily disruptive.[72] Pronouncing judgment on others, increases interpersonal distance and alienation. Judgmentalism will also obscure our higher view and distort our direct appreciation of how things really are. Judgmental words and self-righteous tones seldom, if ever, help in any situation. So, to repeat a Tibetan proverb: "Don't notice the tiny flea in the other person's hair and overlook the lumbering yak on your own nose."[73]

Still on the subject of right speech, Buddha says we should "avoid harsh abusive language; always speaking kindly." You cannot find inner peace using abusive speech, which is associated with hostility and anger. Expressing arrogance and sarcasm may give you momentary pleasure, but at the expense of your long-term well-being. The challenge is to use words in ways that reflect acceptance, love, and compassion.[74] A further challenge is to maintain a "noble silence" when appropriate. Sometimes the best thing or most helpful thing to say is nothing.

**Step Four—Right Action**   In a lovely book entitled *Awakening the Buddha Within,* Lama Surya Das sums up the fourth step of The Noble Eight-Fold Path with the following words: "The practice of Right Action is about cultivating goodness and virtue in the way we treat others; it's about creating harmony in our world, our home, in this very life, right now."[75] For practicing Buddhists like Lama Surya Das, life is an art form, and we are the artistic creators.

## PHILOSOPHERS IN ACTION

Does Buddhism make sense to you as a practical philosophy of life? How, or why not? What, if anything, about Buddhism do you like most? What, if any, Buddhist notion is most challenging or most difficult for you to accept? After thinking about this, imagine a conversation between Siddhartha Gautama and the hedonist Aristippus. What would they say to each other? Would they agree with each other's philosophy? Explain and elaborate, creating a kind of discussion or debate that might transpire between them. You might even wish to stage a theatrical scene for the benefit of the class!

Though we are personally responsible for our own volitional actions, Buddhist teaching offers us five precepts that can be used in moral life. Blind obedience to these precepts is discouraged, since wisdom and discernment must accompany them. By pondering these precepts, we can come to see why refraining from certain actions is good. We can prepare the ground for our personal self-transcendence and enlightenment. We can "clear the weeds from the soil," a wonderful metaphor to capture the idea of ordering the outer life before turning to the inner life.[76] The Five Precepts ask us to:

1. Refrain from harming living things.
2. Refrain from taking what is not given.
3. Refrain from misuse of the senses.
4. Refrain from wrong speech.
5. Refrain from taking drugs or drinks that tend to cloud the mind.

Each of the Five Precepts seems to have a fairly obvious, superficial meaning, but it should be understood that they all have deeper connotations. For example, the first precept is not just an injunction against hurting or killing, but it implies an awareness of the sanctity of life. It involves a reverence and respect for all life forms that we should incorporate into our daily behavior. In the second precept, we are instructed to refrain from taking what is not given. Yes, we should not steal what does not belong to us. Moreover, we should not take more than our fair share or steal the spotlight as we try to become the center of attention. We should live patiently and generously without grasping to satisfy our own selfish desires.

The third precept would have us refrain from misuse of the senses. No doubt there is a directive about sexual misconduct here, but much more. We should refrain from any personal habits that lead to excess (for example, obesity), muscular deterioration, or any pollution of the body and its organs.[77] In the fourth precept, we should avoid lying, slander, gossip, and malicious talk. On the other hand, we should exhibit right speech when getting to know people or when communicating in conversation, advertising, or political speeches. (Dirty political campaigns involving personal attacks violate this fourth precept.) In the fifth precept, we are guided not to impair our mental functioning, for to do so is to create obstacles for enlightenment and illumination. As one writer puts it: "Anyone seriously interested in attaining the state of enlightened wisdom will refrain from indulgences that impair the clarity of mental vision, shroud doubts and uncertainties in a kind of euphoria, and encourage seeing things other than as they are."[78]

**Step Five—Right Livelihood**   As college students, you are no doubt giving much thought to your future, especially where employment is concerned. What will be your chosen occupation? Will you pick the best job or most appropriate career? How will you know that you've made the right choice?

Again, the practical Buddha offers some guidance for you in this aspect of your life. Step Five asks us to express love in the world through our work. We should not compromise our integrity by becoming involved in vocational activities that are likely to cause harm to people, animals, or the environment. Sure, it is difficult to avoid corruption in today's competitive world; for this reason we should avoid livelihoods that are deceitful, unwholesome, or corrupting in any fashion. Examples of professions that would harm others include sexual procurement, trading in firearms, selling liquor, dealing drugs, or killing for hire. Only occupations that enable you to earn a living while at the same time promoting peace and well-being are in accord with the requirement of right livelihood.[79] Maybe your mission is to bring joy and laughter into the lives of others by becoming a comedian (who uses right speech). Or perhaps you should become a philosopher, advancing wisdom and understanding around the world? Who knows?

> *"The mind is restless, unsteady, hard to guard, hard to control. The wise one makes it straight, like a fletcher straightens an arrow. The mind is mercurial, hard to restrain, alighting where it wishes. It is good to tame and master this mind, for a disciplined mind brings happiness."*
>
> THE BUDDHA

## The Training of Concentration

**Step Six—Right Effort**   To live according to the teachings of the Buddha is going to require right effort. As the old Ringo Starr tune reminds us, "It don't come easy; you know it don't come easy." **Right effort,** in this context, means spiritual effort—working to elevate ourselves and to develop more wholesome states. We are striving to go deeper and live more fully. By our own efforts, we hope to open and awaken our hearts and minds, our bodies and souls.[80] Through meditation training, through introspection and contemplation, through mindfulness and through awareness practices, the devotee to Buddhism uses the tried and tested inner science of spiritual awakening and transformation.[81] Clearly, effort is required to release old habits and patterns of behavior. It also takes effort to strengthen our mind so that it is not overcome by ignorance or easily swayed by craving or aversion. Accompanying all of this effort, we will certainly need commitment, patience, courage, and enthusiasm.

The method for exploring inner reality can start with "awareness of respiration." This is the technique practiced by Buddha himself. You have to learn to focus your mind and fixate on a single object of attention (your breathing). By doing this you make the mind an instrument for examining the subtlest realities about yourself. Paying attention to the breath is a basic centering and grounding exercise you can practice anywhere. By training to pay attention, we can focus and pay attention to ourselves.

**Step Seven—Right Mindfulness**   The human condition has sometimes been likened to a waking dream. From day to day, we live our lives largely distracted or lost in trains of unreflective thought and fantasy.[82] Absent to immediate experience, we are by-passed by life without our conscious awareness. We mindlessly fall into bad habits and repetitive patterns of behavior. With all the predictability of conditioned Pavlovian dogs, we may become habitual grumblers who use any pretext to launch into angry and embittered diatribes.[83]

Fortunately, there are ways of awakening to experience. Even if for only a few moments at a time, we can learn to detach from the ongoing drama of our lives and objectively examine the habitual patterns of behavior that entrap us. By doing this, we can begin to loosen their compulsive hold on us. In the process of *dis*-identifying with them, we can also start to see how those habitual thoughts, feelings, and actions are not *us*. They come along accidentally and so can be extinguished with effort. We are not necessarily slaves to our conditional existence.[84]

By means of **right mindfulness,** we learn to awaken to reality and take what Lama Surya Das calls "the escalator to enlightenment." To live in a conscious, fully awake state, we must slow down, quiet the mad monkey of the mind, and be present in the moment. In our frenzy to get a job done, or to go here or there, or to meet with so-and-so, we forget to stay in touch with who we are, what we are, and what we are doing.[85] We miss the truth of our experience as it passes us by from one moment to the next.

Going through life in a daze may, at first glance, not seem so bad. However, there are negative consequences to being only semiconscious. For instance, our lack of mindfulness can make us careless. How many times have you hurt someone else without thinking or without even noticing that you did? Not only can we hurt others by being asleep to reality, but we can also do damage to ourselves. If we fall asleep at the illumination switch of our lives, we leave ourselves vulnerable to all sorts of accidents, both physical and emotional. If we are not truly "with" our loved ones, not really "present" to them, we may discover one day that they have become distant and alienated from us. Make sure, then, that you mind your mindfulness!

**Step Eight—Right Concentration**   The final step of The Noble Eight-Fold Path is **right concentration.** In contrast to focusing on the breadth, in order to develop awareness of the present moment, right concentration demands that we maintain this awareness on an ongoing basis. Using right concentration, we harness energy so that every part of our being is integrated and working harmoniously toward the ultimate goal of enlightenment.[86] Lama Surya Das puts it so: "Buddha taught that in order to concentrate we need a combination of Right Effort and Right Mindfulness." Concentration thus integrates all of the factors and aspects of mindful awareness into a coherent and vividly present, functioning whole. Right concentration involves recollection, remindfulness, vigilance, alertness, and perseverance; it thus brings us full circle back to the wisdom of Right View and authentic understanding.

Through right concentration, a person experiences oneness and completeness in which everything fits. We feel "together," not "scatterbrained," entangled by numerous disjointed activities and thoughts. We are at one with the world.

Within Buddhism, four stages of concentration, which enable us to purify our mental activities as a means of achieving happiness, have been identified.[87]

1. The first stage involves getting rid of lust, ill-will, laziness, worry, anxiety, and doubt. These unwholesome mental activities are replaced by feelings of joy and happiness.
2. In stage two, one is able to see through and get beyond all mental activities, while still keeping an awareness of joy and happiness.
3. In the third stage of right concentration, one goes beyond the mental activity responsible for feelings of joy and attains an equanimity pervaded by happiness.
4. In the fourth and final stage of right concentration, complete equanimity and total awareness are achieved, both beyond happiness and unhappiness.

*"These awakened ones, Dedicated to meditation Striving actively and vigorously, Attain NIRVANA, the ultimate security."*
THE BUDDHA

## Karma and Rebirth

It is important for adherents of Buddha's teachings to follow The Noble Eight-Fold Path because of its implications for **karma** and **rebirth.** Karma is the **law of moral causation,** which refers to all the willed actions of body, speech, and mind. According to this law, all such actions plant seeds which in time bear fruit, so to speak, spawning further consequences. Karmic consequences follow from actions that are either wholesome, unwholesome, or neutral. Lying, for example, is an unwholesome action producing unpleasant results. Giving money to charity or helping a neighbor, by contrast, are wholesome actions producing pleasant consequences. Of course, neutral actions are intentional but have no beneficial or harmful effects either way.

Although karma is usually discussed as something one inherits from their actions in previous lives or what one passes on to future lives, there is a current dimension to it as well. You might wish to think of karma as something that "comes back on you." For instance, maybe you told a lie or committed a misdeed that could come back to haunt you. Perhaps a sudden outburst of anger soured your relationship with somebody for days, weeks, or even years. Maybe a brilliant political career was ruined by a momentary moral lapse. Gary Condit and Bill Clinton come to mind here. Whatever the case, karma does not involve a punishing judge heaping on retribution; it's about the individual creating the consequences of his or her own future. Buddha teaches:

> . . . if a person speaks or acts with unwholesome mind, pain pursues him, even as the wheel follows the hoof of the ox that draws the cart. (The Dhammapada)

Another way of explaining karma is to say, "What goes around comes around." In this respect, "giving is indeed receiving." Give unwholesomeness, and you get it back in return. Give wholesomeness, and you receive it in kind.

The notion of karma extends beyond current existence to past lives and future ones. For instance, your own karma has determined such matters as the species into which you were born (human), your beauty, intelligence, longevity, wealth, and social status.[88] What you do in this life will, in turn, affect the karma of your next life. If you have been born with "bad karma," not to worry. There is a modifiability of the karma you've inherited. Furthermore, if you have already engaged in some unwholesome activities to this point in your life, it is not necessarily true that bad karma will result. It can be mitigated. On the subject of the modifiability of karma, Nyanaponika Thera writes:

> . . . a particular karma, either good or bad, may sometimes have its result strengthened by supportive karma, weakened by counteractive karma, or even annulled by destructive karma.[89]

For Thera, a bad action, or any karmic actions for that matter, must be viewed from the total qualitative structure of the mind from which the action issues:

> . . . it is an individual's accumulation of good or evil karma and also his dominating character traits, good or evil, which affect the

karmic result. They determine the greater or lesser weight of the result and may even spell the difference between whether or not it occurs at all.[90]

Appreciating that karmic results are modifiable frees us from the bane of determinism. It teaches moral and spiritual responsibility for oneself and others. It helps us to recognize that karmic action affects the doer of the deed. Even if bad words and deeds, or the thoughts that give rise to them, fail to harm others, they will not fail to have a damaging effect on the doer.[91]

On a final cautionary note, don't confuse *rebirth* with *reincarnation*—the idea that there is a single soul that transmigrates or commutes from body to body down through the aeons.[92] The ego-identity of self-consciousness that you identify as "I" or "me" is not going to be transferred to an ant or weasel in the next life. Rebirth—a causal connection between one life and another—is perhaps best captured by metaphor: See rebirth as a flame that is passed from one candle to the next. It is not exactly the same flame that moves on down the line, but it is not entirely different either. Another useful image involves billiard balls. As one ball strikes another, it stops dead on impact. The second ball moves on to strike a third and then stops dead; the third ball continues the process. There is a single movement passed on through a sequence of temporary vehicles.[93] The "you" with which you identify in life is simply one of these temporary vehicles.

## BUDDHA: THE HIGHER REALITY THERAPIST

William Glasser, the internationally famed psychiatrist who initially developed Reality Therapy, aims to help people live more productively by enabling them to get what they want out of life, namely, more power, fun, freedom, and love. You could say "attachments" to people and things are generally accepted and that the counseling process is designed essentially to work on effective strategies to get basic needs met. Of course, Buddha is not concerned about getting what one wants, but with removing attachments to those selfish cravings that ultimately lead to suffering. The reality Buddha is concerned with is beyond physical and material want satisfaction. Buddha would not have us satisfy our every want or desire; rather, he would have us transcend them if we wish to achieve personal enlightenment.

As a higher reality therapist, Buddha has his own program of personal development—The Four Noble Truths and The Noble Eight-Fold Path. He uses them as part of his medical model, as we've learned. As a spiritual practitioner, what Buddha did was:

1. First, diagnose the universal ailment of humankind as suffering.
2. Isolate its root cause, namely craving.
3. Identify the remedy to restore spiritual health.
4. Finally, prescribe an eight-fold course of action for purposes of psychospiritual rehabilitation.

The life and teachings of the Buddha serve again to underscore a basic premise of this book—that philosophy is relevant for us because it has practical and therapeutic applications. To further appreciate the relevance of Buddhism, turn now to the following reading, which examines Buddhism's influence on Asian culture.

ORIGINAL SOURCEWORK

*Basic Characteristics of Buddhist Culture*

**JOHN KOLLER**

The religious-philosophical teachings of Buddhism outlined in the preceding pages have left their mark on much of Asian civilization. Buddhism, much more so than most religions, has permeated the cultures with which it has been associated. Consequently, in Sri Lanka, Burma, Cambodia, Thailand, and Laos, where Thervada Buddhism has held sway, and in Tibet, China, Korea, Japan, and Vietnam, where Mahayana Buddhism has been influential, we find rather distinctive Buddhist cultural traits. Prominent among these cultural characteristics are the following: (1) emphasis on human dignity, (2) an attitude of non-attachment, (3) tolerance, (4) a spirit of compassion and nonviolence, (5) an inclination to meditation, and (6) a practical orientation.

*Human Dignity:* In Buddhist cultures human beings have not been subordinated to things and machines. Human beings are regarded as self-creative, capable of determining their fate by their own efforts. What greater dignity can be bestowed upon persons than to recognize that they control their own life and destiny? In theistic religions persons are usually subordinated to God, regarded as something fashioned by God to suit His own aims. In a materialistic culture, on the other hand, humans are often subordinated to nature and external things. But according to the teachings of Buddhism, these alternatives represent the projection of, and ensnarement by, our own ignorance. It is entirely up to us whether we will subordinate ourselves to God, nature, or other persons.

*Non-Attachment:* Because of their conviction that there are no enduring selves or things in the world, Buddhists do not attach themselves either to ego or to things in the world. Recognizing that impermanence is the mark of this world of suffering existence, they refuse to cling to absurd conceptions of permanence. As a result, they are unruffled by change, face the future with equanimity, and do not lament over what has gone by. A spirit of ready acceptance of life marks most Buddhist cultures.

*Tolerance:* Buddhism is a way of practical realization of the truth of non-suffering attainable by self-discipline and mental purification. It is not based on the commands of jealous gods and is not affected by claims to exclusiveness that grow out of such jealousy. Consequently, it is tolerant both of other religions, and of differing individual interpretations of Buddhist teachings. Despite the many differences found among Buddhists in different countries of the world, they all recognize each other as Buddhists. Furthermore, they do not look upon non-Buddhists as inferior, without a hope of happiness, and for whom salvation is impossible because they live outside the fold of Buddhism. The sickness and suffering that dogs human beings accrues to the individual person, and it is the individual person who must make the Way from suffering to peace and happiness. This recognition lies at the bottom of the respect for individual differences in all spheres of life that is so characteristic of Buddhist cultures.

*Nonviolence:* In the twenty-five hundred years since its beginnings, Buddhism has spread throughout Asia and has made its way even to the other continents, claiming over four hundred million followers at the present time. During this time no wars have been fought and no blood shed in the propagation of the teaching. Violence is contrary to the teachings and practice of Buddhism. It is a common conviction of Buddhists everywhere that anger and violence are only appeased and removed by kindness and compassion. The compassion demonstrated by Gautama as he traveled around the countryside teaching the causes and cessation of suffering has permeated all of Buddhism, and in Mahayana occupies the central place in the religion, in the form of the *Bodhisattva* ideal. It is a relatively easy thing to say, "Love thine enemies," but a much more difficult thing to do in the face of the enemies' anger, hatred, and violence. Nevertheless, the Buddhist record on this score is excellent, as is seen by the relative lack of war, revolution,

Source: John M. Koller, *Oriental Philosophies*, 2nd ed. New York: Charles Scribner's Sons, 1985.

or violence in predominantly Buddhist cultures. In this century savage fighting in Southeast Asia has certainly brought a great deal of violence to this part of the world. But even here the Buddhist influence has worked to alleviate much of the violence and suffering that war causes. And we should remember that most of this fighting was precipitated by foreign powers.

*Meditation.* As a result of the Buddhist emphasis on self-discipline and self-purification, it is common practice for Buddhists everywhere to concentrate on emptying themselves of everything impure and conducive to suffering. The meditative techniques involved in these practices, despite the great variety of forms or degrees, are all essentially a matter of self-cultivation and self-discipline. Their aim is to enable a person to participate directly in reality without the intermediaries of false selves, desires, and ambitions estranging one from reality. The mark of these meditative practices in Buddhist lands is a calm peacefulness that characterizes the majority of the people.

***Practical Orientation:*** Practice in meditation produces an attitude that strikes an observer as very practical and down-to-earth. No doubt, this is due, at least in part, to the Buddhists' ability to immerse themselves in the activity of the present moment. When one is at peace with oneself and not pulled by a thousand desires and nagged by ten thousand doubts, it is possible to freely and complete engage in the activities at hand. For example, a Buddhist does not ordinarily regard eating, working, and playing as simply activities to be gotten over with in order to get on to the "real business of life." Rather, these are counted as the sum and substance of life itself. Consequently, these things are regarded as important, and participation is wholehearted, occupying the total attention of the person. Yet people do not cling to these activities and become long-faced and heavy-hearted when there is not quite enough to eat, or the work is hard.

Learning from the past and planning for the future are, of course, essential for improving the quality of life in all spheres. But learning from the past and planning for the future are themselves activities of the present moment, and should not be confused with living in the past or the future. There can be no real happiness in brooding over the future which has not yet come. Nor can happiness be found in lamenting the past. The Buddhists' recognition of this fact and, in consequence, their relatively complete engagement and immersion in the activities of the immediate present results in an attitude that is extremely practical.

## DISCUSSION QUESTIONS FOR CRITIQUE AND ANALYSIS

1. How do Buddhist teachings and practice emphasize the dignity of human beings?

2. How has Buddhism affected Asian culture?

# STUDY GUIDE

## KEY TERMS

*Stoicism*

Zeno **48**
stoics **48**
Epictetus **48**
Marcus Aurelius **48**
Seneca **48**
Chrysippus **48**
cynicism **48**
Antisthenes **48**
Socrates **48**
Cynosarges **48**
Diogenes **48**

Socrates **49**
Plato **49**
ordered universe **50**
synchronicity **50**
fated **50**
monistic universe **50**
immanent **51**
cosmology **52**
interior freedom **52**
judgments **52**
attitudes **52**

courageous acceptance **52**
stoic apathy **52**
*eudaimonia* **52**
emotional detachment **53**
Albert Ellis **54**
rational-emotive behavior therapy **54**
emotion **55**
excessive passions **55**

## Existentialism

atheists  **61**
theists  **61**
political conservatives  **61**
Marxists  **61**
humanitarians  **61**
fascist  **61**
anti-political  **62**
freedom  **62**
absurdity  **62**
interpersonal  **62**
unorthodox methods  **62**
aphorisms  **63**
dialogues  **63**
parables  **63**
literary forms  **63**
Jean-Paul Sartre  **63**

recurrent themes  **63**
Søren Kierkegaard  **66**
Michel de Montaigne  **66**
Blaise Pascal  **66**
Friedrich Nietzsche  **66**
Karl Jaspers  **66**
Gabriel Marcel  **66**
Jean-Paul Sartre  **66**
Simone de Beauvoir  **66**
Martin Heidegger  **66**
Albert Camus  **67**
Fyodor Dostoyevsky  **67**
Franz Kafka  **67**
rationality  **67**
philosophical system-building  **67**
Plato  **67**

Hegel  **67**
abstract universals  **67**
realm of forms  **67**
perception  **67**
uniqueness of individuals  **67**
subjective experience  **67**
essence  **68**
existence  **68**
uniqueness  **70**
*cogito*  **70**
individual  **70**
freedom of choice  **71**
possibility  **71**
contingency  **71**
authenticity  **72**
negation  **72**

## Hedonism

psychological hedonism  **83**
ethical hedonism  **83**
states of mind  **84**
Cyrenaic hedonism  **84**
pleasure  **84**
intensity  **84**
meaning of life  **85**
actual pleasures  **85**
potential pleasures  **85**
Epicureanism  **86**
Epicurus  **86**
Diogenes Laertius  **86**
Lucretius  **86**

Seneca  **86**
Cicero  **86**
Plato  **86**
Aristotle  **86**
The Garden  **86**
momentary pleasures  **86**
enduring pleasures  **86**
kinetic pleasures  **87**
static pleasures  **87**
*ataraxia*  **88**
*tarachai*  **88**
*aponia*  **88**
natural desires  **88**

empty beliefs  **89**
*Letter to Menoeceus*  **90**
vain desires  **90**
natural desires  **90**
prudence  **90**
simple tastes  **90**
bodily health  **90**
freedom from physical need  **90**
powers of discrimination  **90**
tranquility of the soul  **90**
self-sufficiency  **90**
virtue  **92**
friendship  **93**

## Buddhism

The Four Noble Truths  **97**
The Noble Eight-Fold Path  **97**
The Middle Way  **97**
Dharma  **99**
therapeutic philosophy  **100**
suffering  **100**
attachment  **100**
willful blindness  **102**
craving  **103**
self  **103**

*Nirvana*  **104**
ego  **104**
morality  **105**
concentration  **105**
wisdom  **105**
impermanence  **105**
suffering  **105**
egolessness  **105**
reality testing  **106**
denial  **106**

right intentions  **106**
right speech  **107**
right action  **108**
right livelihood  **109**
right effort  **110**
right mindfulness  **110**
right concentration  **111**
karma  **112**
rebirth  **112**
law of moral causation  **112**

# PROGRESS CHECK

**Instructions:** Fill in the blanks with the appropriate responses listed below

| | | |
|---|---|---|
| suffering | natural | ethical hedonism |
| friendship | virtue | blame |
| aphorisms | vain | ordered |
| craving | Socrates | revolt |
| causal determinism | synchronicity | existence |
| Aristippus | existentialism | absurd |
| *Nirvana* | Diogenes | pleasure |
| enduring | Epicurus | worldviews |
| immediate | essence | self-control |
| Middle Way | Zeno | psychological hedonism |
| courageous acceptance | unorthodox | Viktor Frankl |
| ego | crowd | emotional detachment |
| fear | *ataraxia* | subjectivity |
| uniqueness | limits | nature |

1. Philosophies of life offer us different perspectives or _____.

2. The founder of stoicism was _____ of Citium.

3. _____ was a model for both cynics and stoics alike.

4. The most famous cynic in history is _____, who lived in a wine barrel.

5. The stoic universe is one which is rational and _____.

6. A term for meaningful coincidence is _____.

7. Since life is fated and an expression of God's will, according to the stoics, it is best that we develop an attitude of _____.

8. The purpose of life for the stoic is to live according to _____.

9. If we are not to be adversely affected by events in the world, we must develop _____.

10. _____ is a philosophical movement that some prefer to see as an attitude or outlook, rather than as a formal philosophy as such.

11. Existential insights are sometimes best captured by _____ and other literary forms, not by rational deductive argument.

12. The reason some philosophers have problems with existentialists is due to their _____ methods.

13. Existentialism is a _____ against rational, philosophical system building.

14. Existentialists underscore the importance of _____ and the _____ of individuals.

15. Atheistic existentialists believe that _____ precedes _____.

16. Existentialists reject the thesis of _____ or fate.

17. Without God to give it order and meaning, the existentialist's universe is _____ and chaotic.

18. The existentialist would warn you against being swallowed up by the _____.

19. If it is true that we are completely responsible for our actions, thoughts, and emotions, then we can't _____ others for what we do or how we feel.

20. _____, the noted psychiatrist, used many existential insights in the development of logotherapy.

21. _____ is the thesis that human beings pursue pleasure and are motivated to do so.

22. _____ is the thesis that you ought to pursue pleasure and it is wrong for you not to do so.

23. _____ of Cyrene gave hedonism its strongest and most direct statement.

24. According to Cyrenaic hedonists, _____ is the principal motive for living.

25. For Cyrenaic hedonists, the only pleasures that should be avoided are those which are enslaving or cause us to lose _____.

26. Aristippus believed that _____ or actual pleasures are better than potential pleasures located in the future.

27. _____, another hedonist, founded his own philosophical school of thought at The Garden.

28. The selection of _____ pleasures over immediate ones may sometimes mean that one must opt for short-term pain for longer-term gain.

29. For Epicurus, the ultimate end of life is _____, a static pleasure reflected by tranquility of the soul.

30. According to Epicurus's classification, desires can either be _____ or vain.

31. Epicureans believe that peace of mind is disturbed by _____ of the gods and worry about the afterlife.

32. On some interpretations of Epicurus's writings, _____ is part of the pleasant life.

33. *Ataraxia* is an Epicurean notion that includes _____ and concern for others.

34. _____ desires are based on empty beliefs that are conditioned, false, and self-defeating.

35. Natural desires have _____ and can be satisfied.

36. The First Noble Truth of Buddhism states that life is _____.

37. _____ is the source of human misery and unhappiness, according to Siddhartha Gautama.

38. With the attainment of _____, the hot flames of selfish desire are blown out like a lamp, resulting in a detached peacefulness for the individual.

39. To achieve enlightenment, it is necessary to follow the _____ captured by The Noble Eight-Fold Path.

40. In order to eliminate selfish craving, we must come to recognize the impermanence of the _____.

# SUMMARY OF MAJOR POINTS

1. What is the historical background of stoicism?
   - flourished in ancient Rome and Greece for about five centuries (third century B.C.E.–second century C.E.)
   - founded by Zeno; cofounded by Chrysippus
   - well-known stoics: Epictetus, Marcus Aurelius, Seneca
   - influenced by Socrates and the cynics

2. What is the stoic universe like?
   - ordered, rational, structured, and shaped by design
   - synchronistic, fated
   - monistic (God is immanent in all things)

3. How should we live in a fated universe?
   - Be reassured; God orders things for the best.
   - See beyond evils and misfortunes; in a larger context, they make sense.
   - Appreciate your freedom to choose your attitudes and make your judgments.
   - Develop an attitude of courageous acceptance.
   - Live according to nature.
   - Try to develop stoic apathy to live in *eudaimonia.*
   - Look upon the world with emotional detachment to develop peace of mind.
   - Abolish excessive passions.

4. How do we progress morally?
   - Know thyself.
   - Engage in daily self-examinations.
   - Monitor your thoughts, feelings, and actions.
   - Substitute good habits for bad ones.
   - Avoid temptations and wayward companions.
   - Become master in your own psychological home.
   - Eliminate disturbing passions and excessive emotions.
   - Forgive others.
   - Live up to some ideal of virtue (Socrates, Jesus, Buddha).
   - Perform your duties in accordance with right reason.

5. Why is existentialism difficult to define?
   - something like an attitude or outlook; not a formal system
   - different perspectives (atheist, theist, apolitical, Marxist)
   - unorthodox methods (literary and artistic)

6. Who are the major philosophers associated with existentialism?
   - Friedrich Nietzsche, Karl Jaspers, Gabriel Marcel, Jean-Paul Sartre, Simone de Beauvoir, Martin

Heidegger, Albert Camus, Fyodor Dostoyevsky, and Franz Kafka.

7. How is existentialism a revolt?
   * It is a reaction against pure rationality and philosophical system-building.
   * It emphasizes subjective experience.
   * It uses literary forms and other unorthodox methods.

8. What are some central themes of existentialism?
   * essence versus existence
   * freedom of choice
   * individuality and subjective experience
   * possibility and contingency
   * authenticity
   * negation
   * personal responsibility

9. What forms of hedonism are there?
   * psychological versus ethical
   * Cyrenaic versus Epicurean

10. Who founded Cyrenaic hedonism? What did he believe?
   * Founder is Aristippus (430–350 B.C.E.)
   * Pleasure is the principle motive for living.
   * Pleasure is always good; pain is always bad.
   * Pleasures cannot be compared; intensity of pleasure determines its value.
   * The meaning of life is found in the pursuit of pleasure.
   * Control only those pleasures which become enslaving.
   * Actual pleasures are preferable to potential pleasures.
   * One should avoid public life to maximize personal pleasure.

11. Who is Epicurus? What did he found?
   * Epicurus is a hedonistic philosopher.

* He founded The Garden as a challenge to the Stoa, Plato's Academy, and Aristotle's Lyceum.

12. What are some basic tenets of Epicureanism?
   * Enduring pleasures are better than momentary pleasures.
   * Kinetic pleasures (of motion) are different from static pleasures (states).
   * *Ataraxia* is achieved when one functions normally without painful interference; it is freedom from bodily pain and tranquility of the soul.
   * *Ataraxia* derives from the satisfaction of natural and necessary desires; vain desires are unnatural and based on empty and false beliefs; these latter desires cannot be satisfied and therefore offer no enduring stability.
   * Pleasantness in life is also tied to virtue and friendship.

13. What are the obstacles to achieving *ataraxia,* or an enjoyable tranquil life?
   * Society and the acculturation process condition false beliefs, creating vain desires.
   * People have wrongly learned to fear God and the afterlife.

14. How are the teachings of the Buddha therapeutic?
   * The Buddha diagnoses the perennial problem of humanity as suffering.
   * Second, he isolates the cause of suffering as selfish craving.
   * Third, he identifies the remedy to restore psychospiritual health.
   * Fourth, he prescribes an eight-fold course of action for personal healing involving right views, right thought, right speech, right action, right livelihood, right effort, right mindfulness, and right concentration.

## SOURCE REFERENCES

Annas, Julia, *The Morality of Happiness* (New York: Oxford University Press, 1993).

Barrett, W., *Irrational Man* (New York: Anchor Books, 1958).

Bercholz, Samuel, and Sherab Chodzin Kohn, eds., *Entering the Stream: An Introduction to Buddha and His Teachings* (Boston: Shambala, 1993).

Blackham, H.J., *Six Existentialist Thinkers*, 1951.

Brandt, Richard, "Hedonism," in Paul Edwards, ed., *The Encyclopedia of Philosophy*, Vol. 3 (New York: Macmillan and Free Press, 1967), pp. 432–435.

**Burtt, E.A., ed.,** *The Teachings of the Compassionate Buddha: Early Discourses, The Dhammapada and Later Basic Writings* (New York: Signet, 1955).

**Copleston, F.,** "Greece and Rome: From the Pre-Socratics to Plotinus," *A History of Philosophy,* Vol. 1 (New York: Image Books, 1993).

**Dalai Lama,** *The Four Noble Truths.,* trans. Geshe Thupten Jinpa (Hammersmith, London: Thorsons, 1997).

**DeLacy, P.H.,** "Epicurus" in Edwards, *The Encyclopedia of Philosophy,* pp. 3–5.

**Ellis, Albert,** *Reason and Emotion in Psychotherapy* (New York: Lyle Stuart, 1962).

———, *Humanistic Psychotherapy: The Rational-Emotive Approach* (New York: Julian Press, 1973).

**Eliot, Charles W., ed.,** *The Meditations of Marcus Aurelius,* trans. George Long, (Danbury: Harvard Classics Series, Grolier Enterprises, 1980).

**Gaskin, John, ed.,** *The Epicurean Philosophers* (Rutland, VT: Charles E. Tuttle, 1995).

**Grene, Marjorie,** *Introduction to Existentialism* (Chicago: Midway, 1984).

**Hadas, Moses, ed.,** *The Stoic Philosophy of Seneca* (New York: Norton, 1958).

**Koewn, Damien,** *Buddhism: A Very Short Introduction* (New York: Oxford University Press, 1966).

**Koller, John M.,** *Oriental Philosophies,* 2nd ed., (New York: Charles Scribner's Sons, 1985).

**Lawhead, William,** *The Voyage of Discovery: A History of Western Philosophy* (Belmont CA: Wadsworth, 1996).

**MacQuarrie, John,** *Existentialism: An Introduction, Guide and Assessment* (New York: Penguin Books, 1973).

**Nussbaum, Martha,** *The Therapy of Desire: Theory and Practice in Hellenistic Ethics* (Princeton: Princeton University Press, 1994).

**Russell, Bertrand,** *A History of Western Philosophy* (Boston: Unwin Paperbacks, 1984).

**Sandbach, F.H.,** *The Stoics,* 2nd ed., (Indianapolis: Hackett Publishing, 1994).

**Sartre, John Paul,** *Existentialism and Humanism* (London: Methuen, 1948).

**Soccio, Douglas,** *Archetypes of Wisdom: An Introduction to Philosophy,* 3rd ed. (Belmont, CA: Wadsworth, 1998).

**Snelling, John,** *The Buddhist Handbook: A Complete Guide to Buddhist Teaching and Practice* (London: Rider, 1998).

**Surya Das, Lama,** *Awakening the Buddha Within* (New York: Broadway, 1997).

**Tart, Charles,** *Living the Mindful Life* (Boston: Shambala, 1994).

**Velasquez, Manuel,** "Buddhist Ethics" in *Philosophy: A Text With Readings,* 6th ed. (Belmont, CA: Wadsworth, 1997), pp. 493–98.

**White, Nicholas, trans.,** *The Handbook of Epictetus* (Indianapolis: Hackett Publishing, 1983).

## PHILOSOPHY IN CYBERSPACE

**Freud: A Philosophy of Life**
www.marxists.org/reference/subject/philosophy/works/at/freud.htm
Read Freud's statement of a philosophy of life as presented in Lecture XXXV found in his *New Introductory Lectures on Psychoanalysis (1993).*

**Writing Your own Philosophy of Life**
www.mentalhelp.net/psyhelp/chap3/chap3p.htm

Develop a personal philosophy of life with help from this website which provides examples for your consideration.

**International Network for Life Studies**
www.lifestudies.org/cross-cultural.html
Learn more about cross-cultural approaches to life philosophies in the contemporary world.

## ENDNOTES

1. Douglas Soccio, *Archetypes of Wisdom,* 3rd ed. (Belmont, CA: Wadsworth, 1998), p. 215.
2. Ibid., p. 216.
3. Quoted in Copleston, *A History of Philosophy,* Vol. 1, p. 392 (New York: Image Books), 1993.
4. Ibid., p. 390.
5. Martha Nussbaum, *The Therapy of Desire: Theory and Practice in Hellenistic Ethics* (Princeton: Princeton University Press, 1994), p. 360.
6. Albert Ellis, Humanistic Psychotherapy: The Rational-Emotive Approach (New York: Mc-Graw Hill), 1974, p. 56.
7. See, for example, F.H. Sandbach, *The Stoics* (Indianapolis: Hackett Publishing, 1994), pp. 59–60; also Soccio, *Archetypes,*
pp. 226–27. Sandbach reminds us about Marcus Aurelius, who learned from Sextus to be entirely passionless, yet full of affection. Soccio quotes Seneca in claiming that stoicism rejects all emotion, seeing it as a disease that has no half-way cure.
8. For a discussion of this point, see Copleston, *A History of Philosophy,* Vol. 1, p. 433.
9. See Harold Titus, Marilyn Smith, and Richard Nolan, *Living Issues in Philosophy,* 7th ed. (New York: D. Van Nostrand, 1979), p. 339.
10. David Zane Mairowitz and Alain Korkos, *Camus for Beginners* (Duxford, Cambridge: Icon Books, 1998).
11. See P.H. Partridge, "Freedom," in Paul Edwards, ed., *The Encyclopedia of Philosophy* Vol. 3 (New York: Macmillan and Free Press, 1967), pp. 221–25.

12. Epictetus, cited in Soccio, *Archetypes,* p. 216.
13. Diane Barsoum Raymond, *Existentialism and the Philosophical Tradition* (Upper Saddle River: Prentice Hall, 1991).
14. Ibid., p. 295.
15. Ibid., p. 296.
16. See Richard Taylor, "Determinism," in Edwards, *The Encyclopedia of Philosophy,* Vol. 2, pp. 359–73.
17. William Lawhead, *The Voyage of Discovery,* pp. 236–37.
18. Ibid., p. 234.
19. Baron D'Holbach, *System of Nature,* p. 110.
20. Quotation from Leslie Stevenson and David L. Haberman, *Seven Theories of Human Nature* (New York: Oxford University Press, 1974), p. 93.
21. Leslie Stevenson and David L. Haberman, *Ten Theories of Human Nature,* 3rd ed., (New York: Oxford University Press, 1988), p. 135.
22. Ibid.
23. See Edwards, *The Encyclopedia of Philosophy,* Vol. 3, article on hedonism by Richard Brandt, pp. 432–35.
24. Ibid.
25. Ibid.
26. I.G. Kidd, Edwards, *The Encyclopedia of Philosophy,* Vol. 3, p. 148.
27. Soccio, *Archetypes.*
28. See John Gaskin, ed., *The Epicurean Philosophers* (London: Everyman Library, 1995).
29. Soccio, *Archetypes,* p. 200.
30. Gaskin, *Epicurean Philosophers.*
31. Aetheticism flourished in the nineteenth century in England and France. Advocates of this philosophy were called aesthetes. Aesthetes made a religion of enjoying pleasurable moments. They forcefully opposed the injection of moral values into any calculation of possible pleasures. Aesthetes put themselves beyond morality, which represented "bad taste," preaching, repression, restraint, and self-sacrifice. From the aesthetic viewpoint, the subjective experience of beautiful moments was regarded as the highest pleasure. See Soccio, *Archetypes,* Chap. 8.
32. See Copleston, *A History of Philosophy,* Vol. 1, pp. 407–408.
33. P.H. DeLacy, Edwards, *The Encyclopedia of Philosophy,* Vol. 3. pp. 3–5.
34. Ibid., p. 5
35. A point made by Julia Annas, *The Morality of Happiness* (New York: Oxford University Press, 1993), p. 238.
36. Ibid.
37. Ibid., p. 336.
38. Nussbaum, *The Therapy of Desire.*
39. Annas, *Morality,* p. 337.
40. Ibid., p. 337.
41. Nussbaum, *Therapy of Desire.*
42. Annas, *Morality,* pp. 339–41.
43. John Snelling, *The Buddhist Handbook: A Complete Guide to Buddhist Teaching and Practice,* 3rd ed., (London: Rider, 1998), p. 51.
44. The Dalai Lama, *The Four Noble Truths* (London: Thorsons, 1997), p. 6.
45. Snelling, *Buddhist Handbook.*
46. John M. Koller, *Oriental Philosophies,* 2nd ed. (New York: Charles Scribner's Sons, 1985).
47. Ibid., p. 138.
48. Ibid.
49. Snelling, *Buddhist Handbook,* pp. 52–53.
50. Ibid.
51. Ibid., p. 53.
52. This example comes from Soccio, *Archetypes,* p. 327.
53. Lama Surya Das, *Awakening the Buddha Within: Tibetan Wisdom for the Western World* (New York: Broadway Books, 1997), p. 84.
54. Soccio, *Archetypes,* p. 327.
55. Lama Surya Das, *Awakening,* p. 88.
56. Ibid.
57. Bhikku Bodhi, "The Buddha's Teaching," in Samuel Bercholz and Sherab Chodzin Kohn, eds., *Entering the Stream: An Introduction to the Buddha and His Teachings* (Boston: Shambhala, 1993), p. 64.
58. Ibid.
59. Damien Keown, *Buddhism: A Very Short Introduction* (New York: Oxford Press, 1966), p. 57.
60. Koller, *Oriental Philosophies,* p. 140.
61. Ibid.
62. Soccio, *Archetypes,* p. 325.
63. Koller, *Oriental Philosophies,* p. 141.
64. Lama Surya Das, Awakening, p. 98.
65. Snelling, *Buddhist Handbook,* p. 56
66. Ibid.
67. Ibid., pp. 56–57.
68. Ibid., p. 57.
69. Lama Surya Das, *Awakening,* p. 172.
70. Ibid.
71. Ibid., p. 174.
72. Ibid., p. 175.
73. Ibid., p. 176.
74. Ibid., p. 178.
75. Ibid., p. 198.
76. This point is made in Manuel Velasquez, *Philosophy: A Text with Readings,* 6th ed., (Belmont, CA: Wadsworth, 1997), p. 495.
77. Ibid., p. 496.
78. Ibid., pp. 496–97.
79. Koller, *Oriental Philsophies,* p. 144.
80. Lama Surya Das, *Awakening,* p. 266.
81. Ibid.
82. Snelling, *Buddhist Handbook,* p. 67.
83. Ibid.
84. Ibid.
85. Lama Surya Das, *Awakening,* p. 298.
86. Ibid., p. 335.
87. Koller, *Oriental Philosophies,* pp. 142–144
88. James Paul McDermott, "Buddhism," *Microsoft "Encarta" 98 Encyclopedia,* © 1993–1997 Microsoft Corp.
89. Nyanaponika Thera, "Karma and Its Fruits," in Bercholz and Kohn, *Entering the Stream,* p. 123.
90. Ibid., p. 125.
91. Ibid., p. 127.
92. Snelling, *Buddhist Handbook,* p. 73
93. Ibid., p. 72.

# CHAPTER

## PHILOSOPHICAL ARGUMENT . . . THAT SOUNDS LOGICAL!

# CHAPTER OVERVIEW

**Take It Personally**

    Attitude Adjustments for Argument

    Benefits of Argument

**ORIGINAL SOURCEWORK:**

Plato, *Euthyphro*, featuring The Socratic Method

**KNOW THYSELF:**

**How Rational Am I?**

**Opinions versus Arguments**

    Opinions

    Arguments

**Factual Statements versus Value Judgments**

    Factual Statements

    Value Judgments

**Deductive Arguments**

    *Modus Ponens* (*MP*)

    *Modus Tollens* (*MT*)

    Syllogisms

**Inductive Logic**

    Argument from Past Experience

    Argument by Analogy

    Argument by Inductive Generalization

**Faulty and Fallacious Reasoning**

    Validity

    Evaluating Arguments

**Informal Logical Fallacies**

    *Ad Hominem* Fallacy

    Straw Man Fallacy

    Circular Reasoning/Begging the Question
      Fallacy

    Two Wrongs Fallacy

    Slippery Slope Fallacy

    Appealing to Authority Fallacy

    Red Herring Fallacy

    Guilt by Association Fallacy

## STUDY GUIDE

Key Terms ■ Progress Check
Summary of Major Points ■ Source References
Philosophy in Cyberspace ■ Endnotes

# LEARNING OUTCOMES

*After successfully completing this chapter, you will be able to*

Assess your current level of logical reasoning ability

Explain the differences between opinions and arguments

Distinguish between factual statements and value judgments

Present various types of valid and invalid deductive arguments, recognizing the differences between form and content

Identify examples of valid and invalid reasoning

Create and complete syllogisms

Outline the process of inductive logic

Identify faulty and fallacious reasoning, distinguishing among the concepts of validity, truth, and soundness

Test value premises

Define and identify some common informal fallacies

List some "Do's and Don'ts" when it comes to philosophical argument

# FOCUS QUESTIONS

1. What is philosophical argument?
2. How is arguing different from opinionating?
3. What are some benefits of philosophical argument?
4. What are some valid and invalid forms of logic used in philosophical debate?
5. How do inductive and deductive logic differ?
6. In what ways can normative arguments be evaluated?
7. What are some common informal fallacies? How do they work?

# TAKE IT PERSONALLY

It's been said that there are two unavoidable things in life: death and taxes. I would like to add a third item, namely, **disagreement**. If you think about it, it is virtually impossible to avoid having disputes with others. Whether friends are discussing sports, entertainment, culture, religion, politics, art, education, business, morality, or in this context, philosophy, we almost always find conflicting points of view. Take the previous chapter, for example. Aristippus, the hedonist, presented the view that pleasure is good in itself and that it should be pursued without guilt. The venerable Buddha recommended, by contrast, that we loosen our worldly attachments to things, recognizing the impermanence of the ego. He reminded us that pleasures are always alloyed with negative emotions like fear, which result from the realization at some level that those things we take pleasure in will eventually change, decay, wither, or cease to be. Besides, the "me" that takes pleasure in things doesn't really exist in the first place, making our garden of earthly delights something of an illusion. And how about those existentialists and stoics! They clearly disagreed about freedom. Sartre claimed that individuals are utterly free, whereas the best the lenient stoics would offer us was a small degree of personal influence in an otherwise fated universe. The more stringent stoic position didn't even allow for that, maintaining that every little occurrence, however insignificant, is totally determined. If we ask, "Determined by what or by whom?" the stoic would reply saying by God or the Divine *Logos*. Tell that to the atheist Sartre, who would disagree!

As we proceed through this book, many more controversial issues and disputed philosophical positions will be raised. In Chapter 4, conflicting ideas will be presented on the sources and nature of knowledge. In Chapter 5, dealing with morality, you will encounter theorists who disagree among themselves about what should serve as the foundation for ethical action and decision making. Should it be virtue, utility, duty, relational care, survival, or personal self-interest? In Chapter 6, dealing with political philosophy, alternative conceptions of the state and the individual's proper relation to it will be presented: What degree of control should the state have over the individual? Should society sanction a class system, or should everyone be treated as equals? Historically, philosophers have disagreed among themselves when trying to answer such questions. Of course, it's important that you arrive at some sound conclusions yourself, and that you learn to do so using logical procedures of thought. As you begin to master logic and the associated skills pertaining to critical analytical thinking, I invite you to reconsider your personal worldview and encourage you to reevaluate the philosophies of life covered in Chapter 2. I also recommend that you keep your "critical eye" open when exploring all of the theories and approaches yet to come.

By now you may have noticed that trying to answer philosophical questions or resolve philosophical disputes is as difficult as it is exhausting. Part of the reason is that philosophical questions have no final answers, and philosophical disputes, no ultimate resolutions. Questions like: "What constitutes human nature?" or "Is there a God?" or "What is most important in life?" are not likely to be answered once and for all by scientists, medical doctors, lawyers, astronomers, or experts of any description. Such questions have been asked for

> *"There is nothing in which an untrained mind shows itself more hopelessly incapable than in drawing the proper conclusions from its own experience."*
> JOHN STUART MILL

centuries and will continue to be raised in the future. The human condition seems to demand that each generation attempt to find its own answers to such disturbingly important questions. Jonathan Glover, a contemporary English philosopher, once described doing philosophy as something akin to trying to stay afloat in a leaky boat. The rotting planks must be replaced so we don't sink, but since we're at sea, we don't wish to down the vessel in the process of making our repairs—tricky business! Similarly, on our voyage of philosophical discovery, some assumptions, values, beliefs, and ideas that have kept us "afloat" in the past are now rotting and thus require us to make some repairs to our existential "life-boats." Finding the right planks and making the proper connections will take significant time and effort, not to mention some of St. Teresa's "resolute determination to persevere" discussed in the introductory chapter.

Because the task of staying philosophically afloat is so difficult, and because so many people have never received formal training in philosophical argumentation, discussions about important, controversial life issues pertaining to religion, morality, metaphysics, or the nature of human existence, for example, often degenerate into mindless opinionating and explosions of heated emotion. As a result, people frequently avoid disputed subjects, preferring to keep things light. We're reminded here of someone else mentioned in Chapter 1— our pop-star friend Edie Brickell, who, you may remember, wanted us to "shove her in the shallow water" before she got too deep. Individuals like Edie would rather keep human discourse on a superficial level. Edie's underlying assumption seems to be that if you say nothing important or controversial, everybody will get along just fine. When things get too serious, nobody will have a good time. This is unfortunate, for as Edie's kindred spirit, Cindy Lauper, another fading pop-star, proclaims in a song, *Girls just wanna have fun* (boys too, some would add). Now, if you wish to believe this notion personally, stand for nothing important; agree with all points of view, however contradictory or adverse their implications for you or for others, and never discuss anything significant. If you adopt this psychologically defensive life strategy, your interpersonal communications will admittedly be friendly, but in the end, less rewarding and meaningful than they otherwise could be—or do you disagree? Furthermore, refusing to take a position on significant issues could make you the object of moral scorn for people who conclude, "If you accept everything, then you stand for nothing!" Such contempt is expressed most poignantly by the medieval Italian poet Dante, who wrote: *The hottest places in hell are reserved for those who, in times of great moral crisis, maintain their neutrality.*"

If mindless superficiality and ethical fence-sitting are not attractive options, and if you wish to make rational and responsible choices regarding important decisions in your life, given all of the conflicting moral and philosophical viewpoints that are out there, then it will be necessary for you to learn how to argue and think philosophically. Among all the different philosophical planks and platforms to choose from, we must select those which will enable us to make the repairs and alterations required for our rational and enlightened travels throughout life. In order to determine what's worth accepting and what needs modifying or rejecting, we have to learn to weigh the value of opposing ideas and philosophical positions by determining their meaningfulness, coherence, and justifiability.

We have to become rational, critical, and analytical in our perspective. "Doing philosophy" requires that we engage in a structured process of thought using accepted norms of logic, which underscores the fact that philosophy is more of a method than a body of knowledge. Very shortly we'll look into this method of thinking, but before we do, let's continue to take philosophical argument personally, bearing in mind that some attitude adjustments may be in order.

## Attitude Adjustments for Argument

If people are going to argue in constructive ways about what's true, valuable, or justified, it's important to cultivate a particular mind-set. We should welcome properly conducted arguments, not avoid them. This does not mean that we should get into serious arguments with everyone we meet, as this would be highly impractical and time consuming. On the other hand, opportunities for meaningful discussion should not be missed. Rather than become defensively belligerent about conflicting viewpoints, we should see them as opportunities for intellectual growth. If these viewpoints are presented in an honest and sincere fashion, then they pose legitimate challenges that we can use for building philosophical insight. If our opponent's disagreements are ill-founded, we can bring this to light. If they are justified, then we are given an opportunity to modify our views or abandon our positions entirely. It's an admirable philosophical trait to be able to change your thinking under the weight of contrary evidence or in response to legitimate criticism. Refusal to do so makes you irrational or stubbornly dogmatic.

As well as opening up to arguments, we should try to develop an attitude of **rational disinterestedness**—remaining as objective and impartial as possible. This attitude requires that we stop trying to impose our viewpoints on others. Properly conducted argument is not really about winning and losing; nor is it a matter of looking good at someone else's expense or "one-upping" another person. The problem is that many people view argument and debate as a competition where there are winners and losers. Because losing an argument can be personally embarrassing or a threat to self-esteem, some people will say or do almost anything rather than lose a disputed point. For instance, in the middle of a heated discussion, have you ever invented facts or statistics to support your arguments? Be honest, now! Have you ever said things you do not really believe or cannot support as a way of winning and not losing face? If you have, then you can appreciate how psychological factors can affect rational thinking processes. If you or the person you're arguing with are making things up, then no wonder arguments are often seen as useless and something to avoid. Before we can engage in productive debate, we have to get our "psychological acts" in order. This is part of the human experiential dimension of philosophy that so often gets overlooked.

An important recommendation for us comes from the example of Plato's teacher, Socrates. Centuries ago, Socrates was declared to be the wisest man in Athens by the Oracle at Delphi. Aware of his ignorance, Socrates set out to disprove the Oracle by finding someone wiser. After searching long and hard, he concluded that everyone he encountered was ignorant, just like him. If he possessed greater wisdom, it must have come from the awareness of his own ignorance. Others were apparently unaware of theirs. They pretended to know what they did not. In light of this historical example, you may wish to reduce your own pretensions to knowledge. If you have no ignorance to hide because you freely and openly admit when you do not know something, then you greatly reduce the need to communicate defensively. If you reduce defensiveness, you can then engage in more fruitful dialogue without having to "prove" yourself or convince everybody that you are always right. Rather than trying to one-up others or embarrass them, you should display **Socratic humility,** making efforts to listen carefully and then responding intelligently and thoughtfully to what others have said. Constructive attitudes toward disagreement can provide enormous benefits. Let's see what some of those benefits are.

## Benefits of Argument

If engaged in properly, philosophical argument can open minds. It can rid us of ignorance and the evils of blind prejudice. Without argument, people are free to rest on a bed of unexamined beliefs. Lies may be taken for truths. Gross injustices may be accepted as normal or what nature intended. For instance, before some thoughtful and morally sensitive people began to question and to seriously disagree with the values of their contemporaries, women and blacks were regarded as inferior beings and were unfairly denied their basic human rights. In part because of the philosophical challenges raised in protest, they are now considered equal and, in principle, share the same basic entitlements as the rest of us. We see clearly in this case how argument, disagreement, and rational criticism can serve a social purpose. Such things can expose and rectify prejudicial injustices. In short, philosophical argument has positive social value.

Argument also has advantages for personal growth. When challenged by argument, we are not allowed the questionable luxury of mindless response. Saying things without thinking becomes more difficult when people disagree with us. This should not discourage us, for by engaging in productive dialogue with those who dispute what we claim or believe, we may, in the end, strengthen our viewpoints, modify them to make them more acceptable, or discard them when they are no longer supportable. In fact, when people argue and disagree with us, we might see this as a kind of compliment. If our views were regarded as totally insignificant, or if we were not taken seriously by others, then nobody would waste their time on us. When someone chooses to debate with us, we can assume that the other individual has at least heard and acknowledged us.

The spirit of Socratic humility, which I recommend we all adopt in our philosophical discussions, is perhaps best captured in the writings of Plato, especially in the Platonic dialogues where the character of Socrates is featured. In the dialogue entitled *Euthyphro,* Socrates engages a man by that name in conversation. The setting for the dialogue is the *agora,* or central marketplace of Athens. Socrates has been charged with the crime of "impiety" by a young man named Meletus. The sentence for this crime is death. Coincidentally, Euthyphro has charged his own father with the murder of a slave, which at the time was a religious offense that was considered a form of "pollution" or "impiety," which, if not ritually purified, would offend the gods. In charging his father, Euthyphro believes that he is acting on his own knowledge about the gods and their wishes, and so about the general topic of impiety. Socrates wishes to gain this special knowledge of impiety from Euthyphro so that he can mount a defense for himself. Unfortunately, Euthyphro cannot answer Socrates's questions about impiety to Socrates's satisfaction or even his own. Euthyphro is unable to make clear what impiety is, even though he has charged his father with the crime. When Socrates presses Euthyphro to express his knowledge of impiety, he leaves with the excuse of business elsewhere.[1]

Turn now to the excerpt from the Platonic dialogue *Euthyphro* to get a flavor of philosophical discussion from the master Socrates himself. Basic elements of the Socratic Method, typically found in the Platonic dialogues are listed in the showcase feature that follows.[2] You may wish to apply the Socratic method in your next philosophical discussion, but do so with Socratic humility, of course!

## THE SOCRATIC METHOD

1. Engage someone in a conversation about a controversial issue.
2. Turn the conversation in the direction of some concept or term having philosophical significance or central importance to the issue discussed.
3. Ask for a definitional clarification of the key philosophical concept or term.
4. Uncover the inadequacies of the definition provided and help your opponent to develop a new, more adequate one.
5. Critically examine the new improved version of the previously unacceptable definition, showing how it fails or is inconsistent.
6. Repeat steps 4 and 5 several times until a clear definition is articulated to everyone's satisfaction. (In the Platonic dialogues, the other party engaged by Socrates often becomes irritated or upset in the end, usually finding an excuse for terminating the conversation or suggesting that the search for a proper definition continue at some other time.)

## ORIGINAL SOURCEWORK

### *"Euthyphro," featuring the Socratic Method*

**PLATO**

*Soc.* And what is piety, and what is impiety?

*Euth.* Piety is doing as I am doing; that is to say, prosecuting any one who is guilty of murder, sacrilege, or of any similar crime—whether he be your father or mother, or whoever he may be—that makes no difference; and

not to prosecute them is impiety. And please to consider, Socrates, what a notable proof I will give you of the truth of my words, a proof which I have already given to others:—of the principle, I mean, that the impious, whoever he may be, ought not to go unpunished. For do not

Source: Plato, Euthyphro, (trans.) Benjamin Jowett

men regard Zeus as the best and most righteous of the gods?—and yet they admit that he bound his father (Cronos) because he wickedly devoured his sons, and that he too had punished his own father (Uranus) for a similar reason, in a nameless manner. And yet when I proceed against my father, they are angry with me. So inconsistent are they in their way of talking when the gods are concerned, and when I am concerned.

*Soc.* May not this be the reason, Euthyphro, why I am charged with impiety—that I cannot away with these stories about the gods? and therefore I suppose that people think me wrong. But, as you who are well informed about them approve of them, I cannot do better than assent to your superior wisdom. What else can I say, confessing as I do, that I know nothing about them? Tell me, for the love of Zeus, whether you really believe that they are true.

*Euth.* Yes, Socrates; and things more wonderful still, of which the world is in ignorance.

*Soc.* And do you really believe that the gods, fought with one another, and had dire quarrels, battles, and the like, as the poets say, and as you may see represented in the works of great artists? The temples are full of them; and notably the robe of Athene, which is carried up to the Acropolis at the great Panathenaea, is embroidered with them. Are all these tales of the gods true, Euthyphro?

*Euth.* Yes, Socrates; and, as I was saying, I can tell you, if you would like to hear them, many other things about the gods which would quite amaze you.

*Soc.* I dare say; and you shall tell me them at some other time when I have leisure. But just at present I would rather hear from you a more precise answer, which you have not as yet given, my friend, to the question, What is "piety"? When asked, you only replied, Doing as you do, charging your father with murder.

*Euth.* And what I said was true, Socrates.

*Soc.* No doubt, Euthyphro; but you would admit that there are many other pious acts?

*Euth.* There are.

*Soc.* Remember that I did not ask you to give me two or three examples of piety, but to explain the general idea which makes all pious things to be pious. Do you not recollect that there was one idea which made the impious impious, and the pious pious?

*Euth.* I remember.

*Soc.* Tell me what is the nature of this idea, and then I shall have a standard to which I may look, and by which I may measure actions, whether yours or those of any one else, and then I shall be able to say that such and such an action is pious, such another impious.

*Euth.* I will tell you, if you like.

*Soc.* I should very much like.

*Euth.* Piety, then, is that which is dear to the gods, and impiety is that which is not dear to them.

*Soc.* Very good, Euthyphro; you have now given me the sort of answer which I wanted. But whether what you say is true or not I cannot as yet tell, although I make no doubt that you will prove the truth of your words.

*Euth.* Of course.

*Soc.* Come, then, and let us examine what we are saying. That thing or person which is dear to the gods is pious, and that thing or person which is hateful to the gods is impious, these two being the extreme opposites of one another. Was not that said?

*Euth.* It was.

*Soc.* And well said?

*Euth.* Yes, Socrates, I thought so; it was certainly said.

*Soc.* And further, Euthyphro, the gods were admitted to have enmities and hatreds and differences?

*Euth.* Yes, that was also said.

*Soc.* And what sort of difference creates enmity and anger? Suppose for example that you and I, my good friend, differ about a number; do differences of this sort make us enemies and set us at variance with one another? Do we not go at once to arithmetic, and put an end to them by a sum?

*Euth.* True.

*Soc.* Or suppose that we differ about magnitudes, do we not quickly end the differences by measuring?

*Euth.* Very true.

*Soc.* And we end a controversy about heavy and light by resorting to a weighing machine?

*Euth.* To be sure.

*Soc.* But what differences are there which cannot be thus decided, and which therefore make us angry and set us at enmity with one another? I dare say the answer does not occur to you at the moment, and therefore I will suggest that these enmities arise when the matters of difference are the just and unjust, good and evil, honourable and dishonourable. Are not these the points about which men differ, and about which when we are unable satisfactorily to decide our differences, you and I and all of us quarrel, when we do quarrel?

*EUTH.* Yes, Socrates, the nature of the differences about which we quarrel is such as you describe.

*SOC.* And the quarrels of the gods, noble Euthyphro, when they occur, are of a like nature?

*EUTH.* Certainly they are.

*SOC.* They have differences of opinion, as you say, about good and evil, just and unjust, honourable and dishonourable: there would have been no quarrels among them, if there had been no such differences—would there now?

*EUTH.* You are quite right.

*SOC.* Does not every man love that which he deems noble and just and good, and hate the opposite of them?

*EUTH.* Very true.

*SOC.* But, as you say, people regard the same things, some as just and others as unjust,—about these they dispute; and so there arise wars and fightings among them.

*EUTH.* Very true.

*SOC.* Then the same things are hated by the gods and loved by the gods, and are both hateful and dear to them?

*EUTH.* True.

*SOC.* And upon this view the same things, Euthyphro, will be pious and also impious?

*EUTH.* So I should suppose.

*SOC.* Then, my friend, I remark with surprise that you have not answered the question which I asked. For I certainly did not ask you to tell me what action is both pious and impious: but now it would seem that what is loved by the gods is also hated by them. And therefore, Euthyphro, in thus chastising your father you may very likely be doing what is agreeable to Zeus but disagreeable to Cronos or Uranus, and what is acceptable to Hephaestus but unacceptable to Here, and there may be other gods who have similar differences of opinion.

*EUTH.* But I believe, Socrates, that all the gods would be agreed as to the propriety of punishing a murderer: there would be no difference of opinion about that.

*SOC.* Well, but speaking of men, Euthyphro, did you ever hear any one arguing that a murderer or any sort of evil-doer ought to be let off?

*EUTH.* I should rather say that these are the questions which they are always arguing, especially in courts of law: they commit all sorts of crimes, and there is nothing which they will not do or say in their own defence.

*SOC.* But do they admit their guilt, Euthyphro, and yet say that they ought not to be punished?

*EUTH.* No; they do not.

*SOC.* Then there are some things which they do not venture to say and do: for they do not venture to argue that the guilty are to be unpunished, but they deny their guilt, do they not?

*EUTH.* Yes.

*SOC.* Then they do not argue that the evil-doer should not be punished, but they argue about the fact of who the evil-doer is, and what he did and when?

*EUTH.* True.

*SOC.* And the gods are in the same case, if as you assert they quarrel about just and unjust, and some of them say while others deny that injustice is done among them. For surely neither God nor man will ever venture to say that the doer of injustice is not to be punished?

*EUTH.* That is true, Socrates, in the main.

*SOC.* But they join issue about the particulars—gods and men alike; and, if they dispute at all, they dispute about some act which is called in question, and which by some is affirmed to be just, by others to be unjust. Is not that true?

*EUTH.* Quite true.

*SOC.* Well then, my dear friend Euthyphro, do tell me, for my better instruction and information, what proof have you that in the opinion of all the gods a servant who is guilty of murder, and is put in chains by the master of the dead man, and dies because he is put in chains before he who bound him can learn from the interpreters of the gods what he ought to do with him, dies unjustly; and that on behalf of such an one a son ought to proceed against his father and accuse him of murder. How would you show that all the gods absolutely agree in approving of his act? Prove to me that they do, and I will applaud your wisdom as long as I live.

*EUTH.* It will be a difficult task; but I could make the matter very clear indeed to you.

*SOC.* I understand; you mean to say that I am not so quick of apprehension as the judges: for to them you will be sure to prove that the act is unjust, and hateful to the gods.

*EUTH.* Yes indeed, Socrates; at least if they will listen to me.

*SOC.* But they will be sure to listen if they find that you are a good speaker. There was a notion that came into my mind while you were speaking; I said to myself: "Well, and what if Euthyphro does prove to me that all the gods regarded the death of the serf as unjust, how do I know anything more of the nature of piety and impiety? for granting that this action may be hateful to the gods, still piety and impiety are not adequately defined by these distinctions, for that which is hateful to the gods has been shown to be also pleasing and dear to them." And therefore, Euthyphro, I do not ask you to prove this; I will suppose, if you like, that all the gods condemn and abominate such an action. But I will amend the definition so far as to say that what all the gods hate is impious, and what they love pious or holy; and what some of them love and others hate is both or neither. Shall this be our definition of piety and impiety?

*EUTH.* Why not, Socrates?

*SOC.* Why not! certainly, as far as I am concerned, Euthyphro, there is no reason why not. But whether this admission will greatly assist you in the task of instructing me as you promised, is a matter for you to consider.

*EUTH.* Yes, I should say that what all the gods love is pious and holy, and the opposite which they all hate, impious.

*SOC.* Ought we to enquire into the truth of this, Euthyphro, or simply to accept the mere statement on our own authority and that of others? What do you say?

*EUTH.* We should enquire; and I believe that the statement will stand the test of enquiry.

*SOC.* We shall know better, my good friend, in a little while. The point which I should first wish to understand is whether the pious or holy is beloved by the gods because it is holy, or holy because it is beloved of the gods.

*EUTH.* I do not understand your meaning, Socrates.

*SOC.* I will endeavour to explain: we, speak of carrying and we speak of being carried, of leading and being led, seeing and being seen. You know that in all such cases there is a difference, and you know also in what the difference lies?

*EUTH.* I think that I understand.

*SOC.* And is not that which is beloved distinct from that which loves?

*EUTH.* Certainly.

*SOC.* Well; and now tell me, is that which is carried in this state of carrying because it is carried, or for some other reason?

*EUTH.* No; that is the reason.

*SOC.* And the same is true of what is led and of what is seen?

*EUTH.* True.

*SOC.* And a thing is not seen because it is visible, but conversely, visible because it is seen; nor is a thing led because it is in the state of being led, or carried because it is in the state of being carried, but the converse of this. And now I think, Euthyphro, that my meaning will be intelligible; and my meaning is, that any state of action or passion implies previous action or passion. It does not become because it is becoming, but it is in a state of becoming because it becomes; neither does it suffer because it is in a state of suffering, but it is in a state of suffering because it suffers. Do you not agree?

*EUTH.* Yes.

*SOC.* Is not that which is loved in some state either of becoming or suffering?

*EUTH.* Yes.

*SOC.* And the same holds as in the previous instances; the state of being loved follows the act of being loved, and not the act the state.

*EUTH.* Certainly.

*SOC.* And what do you say of piety, Euthyphro: is not piety, according to your definition, loved by all the gods?

*EUTH.* Yes.

*SOC.* Because it is pious or holy, or for some other reason?

*EUTH.* No, that is the reason.

*Soc.* It is loved because it is holy, not holy because it is loved?

*Euth.* Yes.

*Soc.* And that which is dear to the gods is loved by them, and is in a state to be loved of them because it is loved of them?

*Euth.* Certainly.

*Soc.* Then that which is dear to the gods, Euthyphro, is not holy, nor is that which is holy loved of God, as you affirm; but they are two different things.

*Euth.* How do you mean, Socrates?

*Soc.* I mean to say that the holy has been acknowledge by us to be loved of God because it is holy, not to be holy because it is loved.

*Euth.* Yes.

*Soc.* But that which is dear to the gods is dear to them because it is loved by them, not loved by them because it is dear to them.

*Euth.* True.

*Soc.* But, friend Euthyphro, if that which is holy is the same with that which is dear to God, and is loved because it is holy, then that which is dear to God would have been loved as being dear to God; but if that which dear to God is dear to him because loved by him, then that which is holy would have been holy because loved by him. But now you see that the reverse is the case, and that they are quite different from one another. For one (theophiles) is of a kind to be loved cause it is loved, and the other (osion) is loved because it is of a kind to be loved. Thus you appear to me, Euthyphro, when I ask you what is the essence of holiness, to offer an attribute only, and not the essence—the attribute of being loved by all the gods. But you still refuse to explain to me the nature of holiness. And therefore, if you please, I will ask you not to hide your treasure, but to tell me once more what holiness or piety really is, whether dear to the gods or not (for that is a matter about which we will not quarrel) and what is impiety?

*Euth.* I really do not know, Socrates, how to express what I mean. For somehow or other our arguments, on whatever ground we rest them, seem to turn round and walk away from us.

*Soc.* Your words, Euthyphro, are like the handiwork of my ancestor Daedalus; and if I were the sayer or pro-pounder of them, you might say that my arguments walk away and will not remain fixed where they are placed because I am a descendant of his. But now, since these notions are your own, you must find some other gibe, for they certainly, as you yourself allow, show an inclination to be on the move.

*Euth.* Nay, Socrates, I shall still say that you are the Daedalus who sets arguments in motion; not I, certainly, but you make them move or go round, for they would never have stirred, as far as I am concerned.

*Soc.* Then I must be a greater than Daedalus: for whereas he only made his own inventions to move, I move those of other people as well. And the beauty of it is, that I would rather not. For I would give the wisdom of Daedalus, and the wealth of Tantalus, to be able to detain them and keep them fixed. But enough of this. As I perceive that you are lazy, I will myself endeavor to show you how you might instruct me in the nature of piety; and I hope that you will not grudge your labour. Tell me, then—Is not that which is pious necessarily just?

*Euth.* Yes.

*Soc.* And is, then, all which is just pious? or, is that which is pious all just, but that which is just, only in part and not all, pious?

*Euth.* I do not understand you, Socrates.

*Soc.* And yet I know that you are as much wiser than I am, as you are younger. But, as I was saying, revered friend, the abundance of your wisdom makes you lazy. Please to exert yourself, for there is no real difficulty in understanding me. What I mean I may explain by an illustration of what I do not mean. The poet (Stasinus) sings—

Of Zeus, the author and creator of all these things,
You will not tell: for where there is fear there is also
reverence. Now I disagree with this poet. Shall I tell you in what respect?

*Euth.* By all means.

*Soc.* I should not say that where there is also reverence; for I am sure that many persons fear poverty and disease, and the like evils, but I do not perceive that they reverence the objects of their fear.

*Euth.* Very true.

*Soc.* But where reverence is, there is fear; for he who has a feeling of reverence and shame about the commission of any action, fears and is afraid of an ill reputation.

*Euth.* No doubt.

*Soc.* Then we are wrong in saying that where there is fear there is also reverence; and we should say, where there is reverence there is also fear. But there is not always reverence where there is fear; for fear is a more extended notion, and reverence is a part of fear, just as the odd is a part of number, and number is a more extended notion than the odd. I suppose that you follow me now?

*Euth.* Quite well.

*Soc.* That was the sort of question which I meant to raise when I asked whether the just is always the pious, or the pious always the just; and whether there may not be justice where there is not piety; for justice is the more extended notion of which piety is only a part. Do you dissent?

*Euth.* No, I think that you are quite right.

*Soc.* Then, if piety is a part of justice, I suppose that we should enquire what part? If you had pursued the enquiry in the previous cases; for instance, if you had asked me what is an even number, and what part of number the even is, I should have had no difficulty in replying, a number which represents a figure having two equal sides. Do you not agree?

*Euth.* Yes, I quite agree.

*Soc.* In like manner, I want you to tell me what part of justice is piety or holiness, that I may be able to tell Meletus not to do me injustice, or indict me for impiety, as I am now adequately instructed by you in the nature of piety or holiness, and their opposites.

*Euth.* Piety or holiness, Socrates, appears to me to be that part of justice which attends to the gods, as there is the other part of justice which attends to men.

*Soc.* That is good, Euthyphro; yet still there is a little point about which I should like to have further information, What is the meaning of "attention"? For attention can hardly be used in the same sense when applied to the gods as when applied to other things. For instance, horses are said to require attention, and not every person is able to attend to them, but only a person skilled in horsemanship. Is it not so?

*Euth.* Certainly.

*Soc.* I should suppose that the art of horsemanship is the art of attending to horses?

*Euth.* Yes.

*Soc.* Nor is every one qualified to attend to dogs, but only the huntsman?

*Euth.* True.

*Soc.* And I should also conceive that the art of the huntsman is the art of attending to dogs?

*Euth.* Yes.

*Soc.* As the art of the ox herd is the art of attending to oxen?

*Euth.* Very true.

*Soc.* In like manner holiness or piety is the art of attending to the gods?—that would be your meaning, Euthyphro?

*Euth.* Yes.

*Soc.* And is not attention always designed for the good or benefit of that to which the attention is given? As in the case of horses, you may observe that when attended to by the horseman's art they are benefited and improved, are they not?

*Euth.* True.

*Soc.* As the dogs are benefited by the huntsman's art, and the oxen by the art of the ox herd, and all other things are tended or attended for their good and not for their hurt?

*Euth.* Certainly, not for their hurt.

*Soc.* But for their good?

*Euth.* Of course.

*Soc.* And does piety or holiness, which has been defined to be the art of attending to the gods, benefit or improve them? Would you say that when you do a holy act you make any of the gods better?

*Euth.* No, no; that was certainly not what I meant.

*Soc.* And I, Euthyphro, never supposed that you did. I asked you the question about the nature of the attention, because I thought that you did not.

*Euth.* You do me justice, Socrates; that is not the sort of attention which I mean.

*Soc.* Good: but I must still ask what is this attention to the gods which is called piety?

EUTH. It is such, Socrates, as servants show to their masters.

SOC. I understand—a sort of ministration to the gods.

EUTH. Exactly.

SOC. Medicine is also a sort of ministration or service, having in view the attainment of some object— would you not say of health?

EUTH. I should.

SOC. Again, there is an art which ministers to the ship-builder with a view to the attainment of some result?

EUTH. Yes, Socrates, with a view to the building of a ship.

SOC. As there is an art which ministers to the house-builder with a view to the building of a house?

EUTH. Yes.

SOC. And now tell me, my good friend, about the art which ministers to the gods; what work does that help to accomplish? For you must surely know if, as you say, you are of all men living the one who is best instructed in religion.

EUTH. And I speak the truth, Socrates.

SOC. Tell me then, oh tell me—what is that fair work which the gods do by the help of our ministrations?

EUTH. Many and fair, Socrates, are the works which they do.

SOC. Why, my friend, and so are those of a general. But the chief of them is easily told. Would you not say that victory in war is the chief of them?

EUTH. Certainly.

SOC. Many and fair, too, are the works of the husbandman, if I am not mistaken; but his chief work is the production of food from the earth?

EUTH. Exactly.

SOC. And of the many and fair things done by the gods, which is the chief or principal one?

EUTH. I have told you already, Socrates, that to learn all these things accurately will be very tiresome. Let me simply say that piety or holiness is learning, how to please the gods in word and deed, by prayers and sacrifices. Such piety, is the salvation of families and states, just as the impious, which is unpleasing to the gods, is their ruin and destruction.

SOC. I think that you could have answered in much fewer words the chief question which I asked, Euthyphro, if you had chosen. But I see plainly that you are not disposed to instruct me—clearly not: else why, when we reached the point, did you turn, aside? Had you only answered me I should have truly learned of you by this time the—nature of piety. Now, as the asker of a question is necessarily dependent on the answerer, whither he leads—I must follow; and can only ask again, what is the pious, and what is piety? Do you mean that they are a, sort of science of praying and sacrificing?

EUTH. Yes, I do.

SOC. And sacrificing is giving to the gods, and prayer is asking of the gods?

EUTH. Yes, Socrates.

SOC. Upon this view, then piety is a science of asking and giving?

EUTH. You understand me capitally, Socrates.

SOC. Yes, my friend; the reason is that I am a votary of your science, and give my mind to it, and therefore nothing which you say will be thrown away upon me. Please then to tell me, what is the nature of this service to the gods? Do you mean that we prefer requests and give gifts to them?

EUTH. Yes, I do.

SOC. Is not the right way of asking to ask of them what we want?

EUTH. Certainly.

SOC. And the right way of giving is to give to them in return what they want of us. There would be no, in an art which gives to any one that which he does not want.

EUTH. Very true, Socrates.

SOC. Then piety, Euthyphro, is an art which gods and men have of doing business with one another?

EUTH. That is an expression which you may use, if you like.

SOC. But I have no particular liking for anything but the truth. I wish, however, that you would tell me what benefit accrues to the gods from our gifts. There is no doubt about what they give to us; for there is no good thing which they do not give; but how we can give any good thing to them in return is far from being equally clear. If they give everything and we give nothing, that must be an affair of business in which we have very greatly the advantage of them.

*EUTH.* And do you imagine, Socrates, that any benefit accrues to the gods from our gifts?

*SOC.* But if not, Euthyphro, what is the meaning of gifts which are conferred by us upon the gods?

*EUTH.* What else, but tributes of honour; and, as I was just now saying, what pleases them?

*SOC.* Piety, then, is pleasing to the gods, but not beneficial or dear to them?

*EUTH.* I should say that nothing could be dearer.

*SOC.* Then once more the assertion is repeated that piety is dear to the gods?

*EUTH.* Certainly.

*SOC.* And when you say this, can you wonder at your words not standing firm, but walking away? Will you accuse me of being the Daedalus who makes them walk away, not perceiving that there is another and far greater artist than Daedalus who makes them go round in a circle, and he is yourself; for the argument, as you will perceive, comes round to the same point. Were we not saying that the holy or pious was not the same with that which is loved of the gods? Have you forgotten?

*EUTH.* I quite remember.

*SOC.* And are you not saying that what is loved of the gods is holy; and is not this the same as what is dear to them—do you see?

*EUTH.* True.

*SOC.* Then either we were wrong in former assertion; or, if we were right then, we are wrong now.

*EUTH.* One of the two must be true.

*SOC.* Then we must begin again and ask, What is piety? That is an enquiry which I shall never be weary of pursuing as far as in me lies; and I entreat you not to scorn me, but to apply your mind to the utmost, and tell me the truth. For, if any man knows, you are he; and there-fore I must detain you, like Proteus, until you tell. If you had not certainly known the nature of piety and impiety, I am confident that you would never, on behalf of a serf, have charged your aged father with murder. You would not have run such a risk of doing wrong in the sight of the gods, and you would have had too much respect for the opinions of men. I am sure, therefore, that you know the nature of piety and impiety. Speak out then, my dear Euthyphro, and do not hide your knowledge.

*EUTH.* Another time, Socrates; for I am in a hurry, and must go now.

*SOC.* Alas! my companion, and will you leave me in despair? I was hoping that you would instruct me in the nature of piety and impiety; and then I might have cleared myself of Meletus and his indictment. I would have told him that I had been enlightened by Euthyphro, and had given up rash innovations and speculations, in which I indulged only through ignorance, and that now I am about to lead a better life.

## DISCUSSION QUESTIONS FOR CRITIQUE AND ANALYSIS

1. Socrates begins by asking Euthyphro the question, "What is piety?" Is he satisfied with Euthyphro's answer? Why or why not?

2. Socrates apparently has some concerns about bringing in the gods for purposes of ethical justification. Why so? How do the gods pose problems for Euthyphro's definition of piety?

3. Euthyphro accuses Socrates of logical trickery, which prevents him from giving a clear and firm definition of piety. Is this charge against Socrates a fair assessment or a defensive response on the part of Euthyphro? Explain your answer.

## KNOW THYSELF

### How Rational Am I?

## AIM

Before we begin to cover matters of logic and philosophical reasoning in earnest, let's first determine your current level of reasoning. The ability to think philosophically presupposes a number of subskills addressed in this diagnostic. For instance, if you are going to think like a philosopher, you must be able to distinguish between mere opinions and *bona fide* arguments; you must know the difference between factual statements and value judgments and be able to identify them. Furthermore, philosophical argumentation requires the proper use of logic. Philosophers must be able to spot invalid, unsound, and fallacious reasoning if they wish to argue in a rational fashion. By completing this diagnostic, you will be able to get a sense of how much work you'll need to do before being able to properly engage in philosophical discussion and debate. After completing the chapter study, you may wish to do this self-diagnostic again to gauge your progress.

## PART ONE

**INSTRUCTIONS**   The statements below are either factual, reflecting what is true or false in principle, or else they are value judgments requiring rational justification. Place an *F* next to the factual statements and a *V* next to the value judgments.

_____ 1.  It is good to do what is in your rational self-interest.

_____ 2.  Marcus Aurelius was an existentialist.

_____ 3.  Karl Marx was banished from several countries during his lifetime.

_____ 4.  Martin Luther King professed a philosophy of nonviolence.

_____ 5.  The Oracle at Delphi declared that Socrates was the wisest man in Athens.

_____ 6.  Trying to avoid anxiety by following fads or fitting in with the group is wrong.

_____ 7.  You shouldn't worry about the future.

_____ 8.  Jean-Paul Sartre is an atheist.

_____ 9.  Hedonism is a morally corrupt philosophy of life.

_____ 10.  People ought to seek philosophical enlightenment, as the Buddha did.

**Answer Key:**
1. V   2. F   3. F   4. F   5. F
6. V   7. V   8. F   9. V   10. V        Score /10

## PART TWO

Philosophers need to be able to distinguish between opinions and arguments. Opinions are merely unsupported statements or assertions, often indicative of one's feelings or unreflective conclusions. Arguments have a structured flow, starting from premises and leading to conclusions that can be inferred from them.

**INSTRUCTIONS**   Distinguish between arguments and opinions. Place *A* next to reasoned arguments and *O* next to opinions.

_____ 1.  Toll roads ought to be banned. I hate having to stop and pay money at what seems like every ten-mile interval.

_____ 2.  Look here. Unrestricted immigration has to be stopped. Unlimited increases in the number of immigrants will surely cause higher levels of unemployment, and we all know that whatever causes that should be eradicated as quickly as possible.

_____ 3.  People who favor cosmetics research using animals are no better than Hitler. They intentionally harm living beings for their own selfish purposes. No doubt, those engaged in animal research are earning a handsome profit at the expense of great suffering on the part of God's little defenseless creatures.

_____ 4. What's wrong with those people in Washington and at the Pentagon? This whole "star wars" business of intercontinental missile defense is propagated by paranoid military strategists. Don't they know all this will cost billions of dollars of taxpayers' money? We don't need this initiative! We never did.

_____ 5. Globalization is a bad thing. Countries have a right to protect their national sovereignty for the good of their citizens. Whatever violates or threatens that right is wrong. All that economic globalization does is undermine the ability of countries to exercise their right to self-determination by putting undue political power in the hands of transnational corporations.

**Answer Key:**
1. O  2. A  3. O  4. O  5. A     Score:     /5

## PART THREE

"Doing Philosophy" requires you to be able to think deductively. In this part of the self-diagnostic, see how good you are in providing the missing premises and conclusions in the logical deductive arguments that follow. Notice how the premises and conclusions found below are derived from the various philosophies of life covered in the previous chapter.

**INSTRUCTIONS** Fill in the missing statements for each of the arguments below.

1. Major Premise: _____
   Minor Premise: Seneca is a stoic.
   Conclusion: Therefore, Seneca values peace of mind.

2. Value Premise: That which pollutes the mind should be avoided.
   Factual Premise: _____
   Conclusion: Therefore, alcohol should be avoided.

3. If there is a God, then all misfortune is fated. There is a God.
   _____

4. If I make pleasure my number one priority, then I'll be happy.
   _____
   Therefore, I didn't make pleasure my number one priority.

5. _____
   If I am free, then I am responsible for my actions. Therefore, if there is no God, then I am responsible for my actions.

**Answer Key:**
1. Stoics value peace of mind.
2. Alcohol pollutes the mind.
3. Therefore, all misfortune is fated
4. I am not happy.
5. If there is no God, then I am free.     Score:     /5

## PART FOUR

From the vantage point of rational philosophy, individuals should try to remain objective, logical, and impartial whenever constructing arguments or debating them with others. Unfortunately, individuals sometimes use rhetorical devices called _informal fallacies_ to divert attention, cloud the truth, or intimidate others in order to persuade others or win disputes.

**INSTRUCTIONS** Place an _F_ next to any of the following examples that are instances of fallacious reasoning. Place an _A_ (for acceptable) next to those statements that do not make any illegitimate psychological or emotional appeals.

_____ 1. It's perfectly acceptable to cheat on exams; everybody else does.

_____ 2. We should always treat people respectfully as ends in themselves, never merely as a means to achieving our own ends.

_____ 3. Homosexuality is morally wrong because it says so in the Bible.

_____ 4. Don't accept anything he says; he's just an idiot!

_____ 5. When held to account for why the quality of education has deteriorated, the politician responded by giving a budget report showing an increase in educational spending.

**Answer Key:**

1. *F* – Two wrongs fallacy; one wrong doesn't justify another.
2. *A* – This principle is objective, rational, consistent, and reversible, not to mention that it is a statement of Immanuel Kant's Categorical Imperative (see Chapter 5).
3. *F* – Appeal to authority; nobody has a moral duty to be a Christian or Jew, so the Bible carries no moral weight.
4. *F* – *Ad hominem* fallacy; attacking the person rather than the person's argument is improper reasoning.
5. *F* – Red herring fallacy; here, attention is diverted from quality issues to budget issues in order to avoid addressing the concern about deterioration.                       Score:    /5

Total Score:       /25 (multiply your score by 4 to get a grade out of one hundred)

**Interpretation** In view of the fact that this diagnostic is only suggestive, don't place too much confidence in the final result. Nonetheless, your grade does provide you with some preliminary basis for deciding how well you are able to reason at this time.

# OPINIONS VERSUS ARGUMENTS

## Opinions

In the preceding section, we examined the personal dimensions of argument, looking at the attitude adjustments required and the benefits that accrue from legitimate philosophical debate. In this section, we turn our attention to the formal dimensions of arguments themselves, distinguishing them from opinions.

Most of us intuitively understand what's meant by an **opinion.** *The New Webster Encyclopedia Dictionary of the English Language* defines it as: "A judgment or belief formed without certain evidence; belief stronger than impression, less strong than positive knowledge." In view of the uncertainty surrounding opinions, we should be careful about accepting them. Not all opinions should be given equal weight, as some are more acceptable than others. Judges and lawyers, for instance, may issue opinions on the legality of particular public policies (for example, hiring quotas). Medical doctors may offer considered opinions on the advisability of surgery or the best therapeutic procedures for a patient. Such professional opinions are usually based on extensive research, expert knowledge, and careful thought. Although these opinions do not always turn out to be right, it is usually reasonable to accept them. When multiple professional opinions conflict, we tend to go with majority rule.

By contrast to expert legal and medical opinion, we often hear expressions of personal opinion in which we tend to place far less confidence, probably because we perceive them to be thoughtless, emotionally charged, and sometimes biased, bigoted, or discriminatory. In some ways, everyday thoughtless opinions are cheap. We can all afford to have them on any subject, even if we know very little or nothing about the subject itself. Personal opinions are especially abundant when the issue is a controversial one, like the moral status of the developing human fetus, for example.

In contrast to professional opinions, personal ones are often not accompanied by any reasons or concrete evidence. In this case, no **grounds** are given for adopting them; so hence, no process of thought supports or justifies them. Such

> *". . . isn't anyone with a true but unthinking opinion like a blind man on the right road?"*
> PLATO

> *"Too often we enjoy the comfort of opinion without the discomfort of thought."*
> JOHN F. KENNEDY

personal opinions are simply blurted out in a spontaneous, knee-jerk fashion. They may be intended, either consciously or unconsciously, to fill space in idle conversation, to express emotions, or to elicit reactions from others. To the extent that personally stated opinions initiate discussion and give rise to serious thought, they are worthwhile. In many cases, they can serve as the first step toward genuine philosophical argument and debate, acting as a catalyst for further analytical deliberation. Unfortunately, all too often discussions begin and end with statements of unreasoned opinion. Emotions are vented and viewpoints are stridently expressed, but little progress is made by way of further insight, understanding, or clarification of the issues involved. Sadly, as alluded to before, many people take great pleasure in forcing their opinions upon others, winning shouting matches, name calling, and making others look foolish or stupid. The truth is that screaming and one-upmanship do not take us very far down the road of sober thought and rational understanding.

> *A great many people think they are thinking when they are merely rearranging their prejudices.*
> — WILLIAM JAMES

## Arguments

From a purely rational, philosophical perspective, an **argument** is not an interpersonal event, a contentious dispute, or a confrontation of egos; rather, it is a series of related statements leading to a conclusion. Earlier statements, acting as assumptions or major premises, are tied together with factual claims or minor premises in such a way that logical conclusions can be inferred or derived from them. By concentrating on the form of someone's argument, its validity and soundness, and not on the person with whom we disagree, we can divest ourselves of the unpleasant feelings and contaminating psychological variables that often disrupt rational debate. We can proceed to examine controversial philosophical positions with impartial objectivity. In a moment, we'll learn to construct arguments ourselves, but before we do, another subskill we must master as a prerequisite for arguing properly is distinguishing between factual statements and value judgments.

## FACTUAL STATEMENTS VERSUS VALUE JUDGMENTS

A great deal of the acrimony we either witness or experience ourselves when debating important controversial issues often comes from a failure by one or more of the conflicting parties to clearly distinguish between **factual statements** and **value judgments.** These two kinds of statements are qualitatively different and, hence, need to be handled in different ways. When this fact/value confusion arises, what happens is that people begin to argue at different levels and miss each other's point. A clear illustration of this argumentative miscommunication can be found in the debate over capital punishment. Some people favor executing murderers because they believe it will deter murder in the future—a "matter of fact" to be proven either true or false statistically. Others, however, are opposed to capital punishment because they believe killing a human being is always wrong under any circumstances—a "matter of value" to be rationally or ethically justified. Even if we could prove conclusively with statistics that capital punishment does, in fact, deter murder, opponents here would not likely be dissuaded. For them, it is wrong to kill anyone (even a murderer) "on principle," regardless of the consequences. From this illustration, you can see how arguments at cross-purposes can result when disputants fail to recognize that they are not addressing the same kind of claims. Here, it would be useful for the disputants to get on the same wavelength, as it were, and discuss the value of deterrence in the first place. If that value cannot be reasonably justified, then any factual claims regarding the deterrence characteristics of capital punishment would become irrelevant.

## Factual Statements

A factual statement is a statement that is true or false and can be so determined by empirical means. Note that it is true *or* false. Ironically, perhaps, a factual statement or claim can sometimes be false. For instance, "There are Venusians on Venus" is a factual claim, but one that is likely untrue. The claim makes an empirical assertion about what purportedly is the case. Whether this statement is actually true or false depends on what we find there. If, after traveling to Venus, we performed an exhaustive search and found no Venusians, then we could conclude with a fair degree of certainty that the statement was false. If, however, we were surprised to find Venusians living in bubbled domes, then the factual statement would indeed be true.

The simple point about factual statements is that sensory experience and observation can serve to determine their truth or falsity. Scientific methods of experimentation can also be used to test whether something actually is the case. Whenever you make a claim about the way things are, therefore, you are making a factual statement. Of course, if you are making an assertion about the way things were, not about the way things are, you could refer to old newspapers, magazines, past statistics, historical documents, and so on to determine the accuracy and truth of your claim. If, on the other hand, you are making a claim about how things will be in the future, you could always wait to see how things turn out. You could also do some kind of statistical, scientific, or empirical study to prove your point or to support your prediction about what you claim will be the case. Whether your factual claim deals with past, current, or future events, the point is that empirical methods can be used to verify them as true or false, or more or less probable.

## Value Judgments

Value judgments are very different in kind from factual claims. First of all, they are normative as opposed to empirical. They make a statement about what *should* or *should not* be done, or what is good or bad, right or wrong, praiseworthy or blameworthy, better or worse, obligatory or prohibited. Examples of value judgments include: "Liberal democracy is better than fascism," "Country music is good; classical music is boring," "You shouldn't trespass," "Single motherhood is unacceptable," "You ought to give to charity," and "People who pay their fair share of income tax are suckers." A feature of normative statements (value judgments) is that they cannot be "proven" or "verified" in the same way that empirical, factual statements can. You can't look into a microscope or perform an experiment to see whether one form of music is better or worse than another. Whether people should scribble graffiti on walls cannot be decided by observing what they actually do. If most kids in a particular neighborhood vandalize with graffiti, maybe they shouldn't. If most people don't donate to charity, maybe they should. The point is that telling me what people actually do does not tell me whether what they are doing (or not doing) is right.

In the context of philosophy, we try to justify value judgments by appeals to reason. Value judgments relating to particular actions, events, policies, and people can be judged against our accepted ideals, principles, and normative standards. Whether or not the standards that we base our value judgments on are acceptable is a matter of rational consideration. If our general principles and standards are unjustifiable, then any specific value judgments issuing from them will also be unacceptable. If they are vague, then we will not know for sure whether they apply in a given case. If our standards are inconsistent, then our value judgments will not make any sense. We could say, therefore, that the acceptability of a particular value judgment hinges on the justifiability of the normative principle or standard on which it is based and on the proper application of that principle or standard in any given instance. Thus, if we say that_____is a bad person, we probably have in mind some standard or ideal of what constitutes a good person. Perhaps "good people" are honest and kind. In view of the fact that_____is dishonest and unkind, we make a negative character evaluation.

Turn now to the *Philosophers in Action* feature to practice distinguishing between factual statements and value judgments yourself.

## PHILOSOPHERS IN ACTION

### Distinguishing between Factual Statements and Value Judgments

Being able to distinguish between factual statements and value judgments is important to philosophical argument. As you've learned, factual statements are those that can be proven to be either true or false in principle by sensory observation, by experience, or by some type of empirical investigation. Value judgments, by contrast, tell us what is good or bad, right or wrong, praiseworthy or blameworthy, better or worse, obligatory or prohibited. See if you can identify the factual statements (E) and value judgments (V) in the list below. The answer key follows the exercise.

_____ 1. Introductory philosophy is a good course.

_____ 2. Most students select job-related programs of study.

_____ 3. The Catholic Church condemns abortion.

_____ 4. Imported cars are better than domestic ones.

_____ 5. Immigration to this country should be reduced.

_____ 6. The earth is flat.

_____ 7. On average, taller people earn more money than shorter people.

_____ 8. Corporations do not pay enough taxes.

_____ 9. Before traveling abroad, you should see your own country first.

_____10. Most practicing Christians condemn homosexuality.

**Answer Key:**
1. V   2. F   3. F   4. V   5. V
6. F   7. F   8. V   9. V   10. F

# DEDUCTIVE ARGUMENTS

Now that we have learned to distinguish between factual claims and value judgments, let us proceed to see how they fit into various forms of philosophical argument. If this book were designed for a course in logic, it would then be appropriate to examine the many subtleties and intricate forms of deductive reasoning. Since, however, as philosophical beginners, we are looking at logical thinking as a means of improving our critical thinking and practical decision-making skills, we will limit our discussion here to a few of the more common and basic forms of **deductive logic.** We will also discuss some invalid forms of reasoning before we move on to a brief treatment of inductive reasoning, another type of thinking that is important to master for critical, analytical purposes.

To understand the nature of deductive philosophical arguments, it is helpful to distinguish between their **form** and **content.** Arguments—whether moral, epistemological, or political, for example—typically address some subject or issue. It may be a practice (artificial insemination), an event (a meeting of NATO), or an act (civil disobedience) that provides the content of the argument. Regardless of the issue under debate, if the arguments involved are to be considered valid, they must display an acceptable **logical form.** Underlying the content embedded in any rational argument is a formal structure that can be abstracted. The more common forms have been given standardized names, some of which have strange sounding Latin origins like the first one we will examine: *modus ponens.*

> ***"If you want to know whether you are thinking rightly, put your thoughts into words. In the very attempt to do this, you will find yourselves, consciously or unconsciously, using logical forms. "***
> JOHN STUART MILL

## Modus Ponens (MP)

Many of the arguments that you will read in philosophical writings or hear expressed in everyday conversations contain the ***modus ponens*** (***MP***) form. Arguments of this type have been determined to be valid, and so this logical form can be used to test arguments for their validity. Of course, the *MP* argument is not the *only* valid form of reasoning, and therefore an argument not displaying the *MP* form is not necessarily invalid. As you will see, there is more than one type of **valid reasoning.** Below are two *MP* arguments containing different content but identical forms.

(1)   Whenever the economy goes into a recession, church attendance increases. Since we are currently in an economic recession, we can conclude that church attendance has increased or that it will do so shortly.

(2)   If a person is a Democrat, then the person is liberal minded. Linda is a democrat, so we can conclude that Linda is liberal minded.

If we abstract from the content of these two very different arguments, we can see that they still share the same formal structure expressed below. (*Note*: There is nothing significant about the selection of the letters "p" and "q"; the letters could have been "x," "y," or "z.")

If p, then q                    (Alternative notation)                    p → q
p                                                                          p
So, q                                                                      ∴  Q

***Example One:***
Whenever the economy goes into a recession (p), then church attendance increases (q).
Since we are currently in an economic recession (p).
So, (q) we can conclude that church attendance has increased.

***Example Two:***
If a person is a Democrat (p), then the person is liberal minded (q).
Linda is a democrat (p).
So, (q) Linda is liberal minded.

When using the *MP* form of argument, you should be careful not to make any mistakes. In this logical form, the proper thing to do is to affirm the antecedent. In the opening statement, "If p, then q," "p" becomes the **antecedent** and "q" the **consequent.** If you affirm the consequent, an invalid faulty form of argument results. Formally, affirming the consequent looks like this:

If p, then q                    (or)                    p → q
q                                                        q
So, p                                                    ∴  p

If we provide some content to the formal expression above, we can easily see how affirming the consequent constitutes an invalid form of reasoning.

If you won the lottery (p), you would be happy (q).
Since you're happy (q),
You must have won the lottery (p).

In the example above, where the consequent is affirmed, we find an example of invalid reasoning. Sure, it may be the case that winning the lottery would make you happy, but being happy alone does not make it *necessarily true* that you won the lottery. You may be happy because you just passed your first philosophy test or because you just bought your first car. In valid deductive logic, the conclusion *necessarily* follows from preceding premises, something not so in this case.

When testing arguments for their validity, one thing you can try to do is construct an obviously invalid counterexample containing the identical logical form of the first example. Clearly seeing how the counterexample is invalid will enable you to appreciate what's wrong in the first instance. If, say, you still can't understand what's logically wrong with the lottery argument, then perhaps the following BMW counterexample will help to illustrate the flaw. Both arguments have identical forms (they both affirm the consequent), though their content is different.

If I bought a new BMW (p), I would be broke (q).
I am broke (q).
So, I must have bought a new BMW (p).

As you can well imagine, it is quite possible to be broke without buying a new BMW. Being broke does not necessarily indicate that you bought this automobile. Maybe a business deal fell through or a business bankruptcy caused you to lose money. Thus, affirming the consequent in *MP* reasoning results in invalid logic. The conclusion does not necessarily follow from preceding premises (or statements) included in the argument.

## Modus Tollens (MT)

*Modus tollens* (**MT**) is a second form of valid logic. In a *MT* argument, an inference results by **denying the consequent.** Formally, *MT* is expressed in the following fashion:

| | | |
|---|---|---|
| If p, then q | (or) | $p \rightarrow q$ |
| not q | | $- q$ |
| So, not p | | $\therefore \ - p$ |

If it rains (p), then the streets get wet (q).
The streets did not get wet (q).
So, it has not rained (not p).

The invalid form of MT reasoning would involve **denying the antecedent.**

| | | |
|---|---|---|
| If p, then q | (or) | $p \rightarrow q$ |
| not p | | $- p$ |
| So, not q | | $\therefore \ - q$ |

The form above is invalid, since it is possible that the streets are wet from something other than rain. Perhaps a fire hydrant burst or someone hosed down the road. The conclusion that the streets are not wet does not necessarily follow from the fact it is not raining. In case you still can't see how the preceding argument is invalid, examine the similar counterexample below. It will help you to intuit better how denying the antecedent in *MT* logic constitutes invalid logic.

If it rains (p), there are clouds (q).
It is not raining (not p).
So, there are no clouds (not q).

Again we see in this argument that an unnecessary conclusion follows from the two preceding premises. Experience teaches us that we can have cloudy days without rain. We cannot necessarily conclude, therefore, that there are no clouds just because it is not raining.

## Syllogisms

An extremely important form of deductive argument often used in philosophical debate is the **syllogism.** The syllogism actually comes in many forms, but we will limit ourselves to hypothetical and disjunctive syllogisms, categorical syllogisms (those involving class membership), and syllogisms involving practical value reasoning.

*"Watch your Ps and Qs."*
SOME LOGICAL ADVICE

## Hypothetical Syllogisms

Hypothetical syllogisms are comprised of a series of "if-then" statements following in a string. This string contains two premises and a conclusion. It is because this type of syllogism contains "conditional" premises that it is referred to as hypothetical. An example of a hypothetical syllogism is the following:

> If you obtain a pass on this test (p), you will successfully complete your last course (q). On top of that, if you successfully complete your last course (q), you will earn your diploma (r). So, if you pass the test (p), you will earn your diploma (r).

Expressed formally,

| | | |
|---|---|---|
| If p, then q | (or) | $p \rightarrow q$ |
| If q, then r | | $q \rightarrow r$ |
| Therefore, if p then r | | $\therefore \quad p \rightarrow r$ |

The invalid form of a hypothetical syllogism is:

If p, then q
If p, then r
Therefore, if q then r

To appreciate why the form above is invalid, see the example below:

If you study (p), you will pass the final exam(q).
If you study (p), you will graduate (r).
Therefore, if you pass the final exam(q), you will graduate (r).

The invalid hypothetical syllogism above concludes that passing the final exam guarantees your graduation simply because you have studied; surely, this does not necessarily follow. It is possible to study, pass the final exam, and still fail the course and, thus, fail to graduate.[3] Following is another example of an invalid hypothetical syllogism.

If you go to Disneyland (p), you will have fun (q).
If you go to Disneyland (p), you will drive for many hours (r).
Therefore, if you have fun (q), you will drive for many hours (r).

## Disjunctive Syllogisms

Like the hypothetical syllogism, the disjunctive syllogism is made up of three statements. Unlike the former, however, which deals with a logical chain of consequences, this one involves an either/or choice. This choice may be expressed symbolically by "V." To express "either p or q," one could write "p V q." An example of a disjunctive syllogism is the following:

> Either Mary has made the right decision (p), or she has made the wrong decision (q). Since she has not made the wrong decision (not q), she has therefore made the right one (p).

Expressed formally,

| | | | |
|---|---|---|---|
| Either p or q | (or) | p V q | |
| not q | | - q | |
| Therefore, p | | ∴ p | |

If Mary had made the wrong decision, then the disjunctive syllogism would be altered so:

| | | | |
|---|---|---|---|
| Either p or q | (or) | p V q | |
| not p | | - p | |
| Therefore, q | | ∴ q | |

Sometimes the conjunction "or" means not one *or* the other, but *both*. "Or" can be inclusive or exclusive. When it is inclusive, an invalid form of the disjunctive syllogism (called **affirming the inclusive disjunct**) can be expressed so:

| | | |
|---|---|---|
| Either p or q | (or) | Either p or q |
| p | | q |
| Therefore, not q | | Therefore, not p |

To understand why affirming the inclusive disjunct is invalid, consider the following example:

Either Fred gets paid a lot (p), or he inherited lots of money (q).
Fred gets paid a lot (p).
Therefore, he did not inherit lots of money (q).

In this invalid form of reasoning, one starts by stating that either p or q—meaning that only one and not the other can be true. In fact, *both* disjuncts could be true at the same time. Maybe Fred does get paid well and perhaps he has inherited lots of money as well. P does not preclude q or vice versa. The "or" here is *inclusive*, which allows both disjuncts in the first premise to be true. If the disjuncts were *exclusive*, that is if both p and q could not be true at the same time, then we could say: "If p, not q" or If q, not p." Here is an example of a disjunctive syllogism that is exclusive:

It cannot be that mother is both alive (p) and dead (q).
Because she is alive (p).
She cannot be dead (q).

Expressed formally:

It cannot be both p and q
p
So, not q

**TABLE 3.1** Some Valid and Invalid Forms of Deductive Logic

| Valid Logical Forms | | Invalid Logical Forms | |
|---|---|---|---|
| **Modus Ponens**<br>If p, then q<br>p<br>So, q | | **Affirming the Consequent**<br>If p, then q<br>q<br>So, p | |
| **Modus Tollens**<br>If p, then q<br>not q<br>So, not p | | **Denying the Antecedent**<br>If p, then q<br>not p<br>So, not q | |
| **Hypothetical Syllogism**<br>If p, then q<br>If q, then r<br>So, if p, then r | | **Hypothetical Fallacy**<br>If p, then q<br>If p, then r<br>If q, then r | |
| **Disjunctive Syllogism**<br>Either p or q    (or)<br>not q<br>So, p | Either p or q<br>Not p<br>So, q | **Affirming the Inclusive Disjunct**<br>Either p or q    (or)<br>p<br>So, not q | Either p or q<br>q<br>So, not p |

## PHILOSOPHERS IN ACTION

### Evaluating Arguments

For each of the reasoning examples below, indicate whether the logic is valid (V) or invalid (I). Following each example, provide the logical form contained in it. Refer to the Answer Key to check your responses for correctness.

_____ 1. If George lost his wallet, then he lost his student identification. If he lost his student identification, then he will not be allowed to join any varsity teams. Therefore, if Fred lost his wallet, then he will not be allowed to join any varsity teams.

Logical Form:_____

_____

_____

_____ 2. Either I am going to school, or I am going to earn a lot of money. I am going to

school. Therefore, I am not going to earn a lot of money.

Logical Form:_____

_____

_____

_____ 3. If we go to war, I will be very upset. I am very upset. So, we went to war.

Logical Form:_____

_____

_____

_____ 4. If you lie to people, then they will not trust you. People do trust you. So you have not lied.

Logical Form:_____

_____

_____

**Answer Key**

1. V   Valid hypothetical syllogism
       Form: If p, then q
       If q, then r
       Therefore, if p then r

2. I   Invalid: affirming the inclusive disjunct; one
       can both go to school *and* earn lots of money.
       Form: Either p or q
       p
       Therefore, not q

3. I   Invalid: affirming the consequent; you can
       become upset for reasons other than going
       to war.
       Form: If p, then q
       q
       So, p

4. V   Valid – *Modus Tollens* form
       Form: If p, then q
       not q
       So, not p

## Categorical Syllogisms or Syllogisms of Class Membership

When it comes to proper reasoning, not all of it is of the "if . . . . then" variety. Sometimes we make conclusions based on inferences from assumptions and preceding premises pertaining to acts, events, or individuals belonging to a particular class, group, or category. In such cases, **categorical syllogisms of class membership** are used. See below:

| | | |
|---|---|---|
| Major Premise: | All A are B | A is B |
| Minor Premise: | All C are A | C is A |
| Conclusion: | Therefore, all C are B | ∴ C is B |

Adding some content to this formal structure, we come up with the following example:

| | |
|---|---|
| Major Premise: | All men (A) are mortal (B). |
| Minor Premise: | Socrates (C) is a man (A). |
| Conclusion: | Therefore, Socrates (C) is mortal (B). |

Another variation of a class membership syllogism is provided below.

All A are B.
Some C are A.
Some C are B.

*Content Example:*
All bankers (A) are conservative (B).
Some people (C) are bankers (A).
Therefore, some people (C) are conservative (B).

An invalid form of class syllogism can be expressed in the following symbolic fashion:

All A is B.
All C is B.
Therefore, all C is A.

At first glance, you might be a bit bewildered as to how the syllogism above is invalid. After all, if all As are Bs and all Cs are Bs, then why shouldn't all As be Cs? Adding some content to the invalid logical form above, you can easily see that the conclusion does not follow from the preceding premises.

All cats (A) are animals (B).
All dogs (C) are animals (B).
Therefore, all dogs (C) are cats (A).

## Practical Syllogisms

What I am calling a **practical syllogism** is basically the same in form as a syllogism of class membership. Again, it contains three statements having a conclusion derived from two preceding premises. The difference is that in the case of a practical syllogism, the first statement or **major premise** is a *normative assertion* or some kind of *value judgment.* Hence, the major premise of a practical syllogism is not empirically true or false or analytically true—that is, true by definition. The major premise of a practical syllogism, called the **value premise,** cannot be proven true by sensory observation or scientific study. Rather, it can be justified only by rational processes of thought. Since normative assertions involving principles of right conduct, standards of goodness, and so on, cannot be based on *what is the case,* for what is may frequently be unjustified, evil, or immoral, the ultimate basis of justification for the value premise is reason, not experience. Using reason, we can test the adequacy of the value premises that serve as the starting points of our arguments.

The equivalent of the **minor premise** in the class syllogism is the practical syllogism's **factual premise.** As the term implies, the factual premise makes some type of empirical claim about the world; it is either true or false in principle. Although we may be unable at present to prove the truth or falsity of a particular factual premise given our limited knowledge, experience, or technology, it must be possible to do so in principle.

Finally, the **conclusion** of a practical syllogism is also expressed as a value judgment. It typically makes a statement about what is better or worse, obligatory or prohibited, good or bad, right or wrong, and praiseworthy or blameworthy. Below are two examples of practical syllogisms:

***Example One:***
Value Premise: All acts that harm human health (S) are wrong (P).
Factual Premise: Polluting the lakes (Q) is an act that harms human health (S).
Conclusion: Polluting the lakes (Q) is wrong (P).

Formally expressed:

All S is P          (or)          S is P
Q is S                            Q is S
Therefore, Q is P                 ∴ Q is P

*Example Two*

| | |
|---|---|
| Value Premise: | Criminals (S) should be punished (P). |
| Factual Premise: | Tax evaders (Q) are criminals (S). |
| Conclusion: | Tax evaders (Q) should be punished (P). |

Now that you understand the formal structure of practical and categorical syllogisms, apply that understanding and knowledge to the logical exercise in the Philosophers in Action feature.

## PHILOSOPHERS IN ACTION

### Completing Syllogisms

Below you will find incomplete syllogisms. Fill in the missing statements and indicate next to each syllogism whether it is practical (P), that is, value-related, or value-neutral (VN).

——— 1.  Deceiving the public is wrong.

    ———————.

    Advertisers are wrong.

——— 2.  All Russians live by the principles of Lenin and Marx.
    Vladimir is a Russian.

    ———————.

——— 3.  All acts of violence are inherently evil.

    Stabbing someone to death is an act of violence.

    ———————.

——— 4.  ———————.
    Ralf is a bachelor.
    Ralf is an unmarried man.

——— 5.  Triangles are three-sided figures.

    ———————

    That is a three-sided figure.

**Answer Key**

1.  P Advertisers deceive the public.
2.  VN Therefore, Vladimir lives by the principles of Lenin and Marx.
3.  P Therefore, stabbing someone to death is inherently evil.
4.  VN All bachelors are unmarried men.
5.  VN That is a triangle.

# INDUCTIVE LOGIC

In addition to deductive logic, philosophers sometimes use **inductive logic** to support factual, empirical claims. Inductive logic comes in numerous forms. We look briefly at three of them for introductory purposes.

## Argument from Past Experience

Unlike deductive logic, which leads to necessary conclusions, inductive logic can yield only probable ones. Inductive conclusions are, therefore, weaker or stronger and need not be accepted or rejected in an all-or-nothing fashion. Thus,

> *A necessity for one thing to happen because another has happened does not exist. There is only logical necessity.*
>
> LUDWIG WITTGENSTEIN

in contrast to forms of deductive logic, examples of inductive logic are never said to be valid or invalid. To see why, let us take the following illustration. Suppose, for instance, that we are told that Wendy has lied on her job application, on her income tax return, and to her husband. We might then conclude that she has lied about her medical history required to purchase a new life insurance policy. Because she has lied before in many other instances, we conclude that she has lied this time as well. In this case, we are using past experience to support a current conclusion. Since our inductive conclusion is based on the facts of experience, however, and because these facts are never complete, and because new facts may have the effect of weakening, changing, or contradicting today's assumptions, we can never be absolutely sure about our conclusion. Perhaps Wendy has experienced some kind of religious or moral conversion that has led to a complete character transformation. Maybe Wendy was a liar since her youth, but is now an honest and responsible citizen. Many empirical variables could weaken the soundness of the inductive inference made here.

## Argument by Analogy

A second form of inductive reasoning involves **argument by analogy.** "Analogical arguments proceed from the similarities of two or more things in certain respects to their similarity in some additional respect."[4] Analogical arguments have the following form.

Items, A, B and C have characteristics X and Y.
A and B have characteristic Z.
Therefore, C probably has characteristic Z also.

This analogical form of inductive reasoning is the type used to argue for the probable existence of life on other planets. If significant similarities can be found between Earth and other celestial bodies, and if Earth supports life, then one might wish to argue by analogy that those other celestial bodies also support life. Notice again, there is no absolute certainty or deductive necessity about this conclusion; there is only lesser or greater probability.

## Argument by Inductive Generalization

A third form of inductive reasoning is argument by inductive generalization. When we make an inductive generalization, we make a statement about all, some, or none of a class based on our empirical examination of only a part of that class. It is important not to confuse inductive generalizations with generalized descriptions. Suppose, for instance, that we surveyed an introductory ethics class on its views about abortion and found that 88 percent of class members were against it. In stating this, one would be presenting only a generalized description of what is the case for that group. If we were to conclude, however, that 88 percent of all post-secondary students in North America were opposed to abortions, then we would be making an inductive generalization.

As you can well appreciate in the example above, inductive generalizations can easily be prone to error unless certain precautions are taken. For example, when making inductive generalizations, it is important to work from *large samples.* Basing a conclusion about millions of students in North America on a limited sample of one class is no guarantee that the findings are truly *representative* of the whole group about which a conclusion is being made.

Furthermore, large samples alone do not guarantee that generalizations based on them will be representative. If the larger sample we need were drawn exclusively from Catholic colleges, say, then the results might tend to be more reflective of the specific religious views held by a special subgroup of students and not representative of the entire post-secondary student population of North America. The views of students at Catholic colleges might not represent those of the majority attending secular institutions. In addition to being large, then, samples must also be *fair.* All members within a class (in this case, post-secondary students in North America) must have an equal chance of being selected or included in the survey sample. Otherwise, inductive generalizations are likely to be *skewed.* Arguments by inductive generalization based on biased or skewed samples are less acceptable than those based on fair and large ones that are more representative of the group under discussion. See Table 3.2 for a comparison between inductive and deductive logical thinking.

## FAULTY AND FALLACIOUS REASONING

So far in this chapter, we have examined different forms of inductive and deductive logic. Implicit in much of the discussion have been notions of **validity, truth** and **soundness.** In this section, we will examine these three important logical concepts to enrich your understanding of the logical processes of thinking.

## Validity

In everyday conversations, you often hear people say things like, "That's a valid point," or "That's a valid statement" or perhaps, "Your criticism is valid." In strict logical terms, however, "points," "statements," and "criticisms" are not valid. Arguments are. Factual statements may be true or false or more or less likely; criticisms may be justified or unjustified; and good points may be based on accurate

> *"Faced with the choice between changing one's mind and proving there is no need to do so, almost everyone gets busy on the proof."*
> JOHN KENNETH GALBRAITH

**TABLE 3.2**   Comparing Inductive and Deductive Arguments

| Example of Deductive Argument | Example of Inductive Argument |
| --- | --- |
| All birds have wings. Every swan is a bird. Therefore, every swan has wings. | Every swan that has ever been observed has wings. Therefore, every swan has wings. |
| If the form of the argument is valid and the premises are true, then the conclusion must also be true. | If the premises are true, then the conclusion is likely, though not necessarily true. (A negation of the conclusion does not constitute a logical contradiction.) |
| Deductive arguments are either valid or invalid. | Inductive arguments are better or worse. |

observations. But when it comes to logic, validity refers to the form of the argument within which a particular point or statement becomes a relevant part.

Validity should be clearly distinguished from another logical notion, namely, *soundness*. The concept of soundness also refers to arguments, but not narrowly and exclusively to their logical form. A sound argument is one that is valid in form, contains true (or acceptable) premises, and leads to a necessary conclusion. An **unsound argument,** by contrast, can be valid in form, but because its premises are untrue or unacceptable, the conclusion is false or one that must be rejected. In formal argument, then: *truth* refers to the veracity of the individual statements contained within the syllogism itself; validity refers to an argument's form or structure; and soundness involves a combination of truth and validity. An argument is sound, therefore, if it is comprised of true premises, is valid in form, and leads to a necessary conclusion. Having said this, remember that necessary conclusions are found only in deductive logic, not in inductive reasoning. Thus, soundness is a concept appropriately applied to the former and not the latter type of thinking process. Inductive logic is better or worse by degree.

It is interesting and ironic, perhaps, to note that valid arguments may sometimes have to be rejected on rational grounds. To appreciate why, look at the example that follows.

| | | |
|---|---|---|
| Major Premise: | All birds (A) are black (B). | All A is B. |
| Minor Premise: | Prince Philip (C) is a bird (A). | C is A |
| Conclusion: | Prince Philip (C) is black (B). | Therefore, C is B |

What you have here is a valid syllogism of class membership. The logical form of the argument is found to the right of it. What is obvious about this valid syllogism is that the conclusion is obviously false. Prince Philip is not black. You should note as well that the minor premise makes a claim that is likewise false; Prince Philip is not a bird. Even further, we could dispute the major premise of the argument, because we know that some birds are blue and others are red, so even if Prince Philip were a bird, the conclusion would still not be necessarily true. He could be a cardinal or blue jay. This example serves to underscore the point that when valid arguments containing unacceptable premises lead to false conclusions, then those arguments are unsound and must be rejected. By contrast, when arguments are valid in form, and when they possess true premises that lead to necessary and true conclusions, they are sound and certainly more acceptable.

## Evaluating Arguments

Given what you know now about validity, truth, and soundness, what you should do when evaluating a particular argument is, first, determine whether the conclusion follows from the preceding premises. *Is the form of the argument valid?* Second, *determine if the preceding premises are true or highly likely.* A factual, empirical claim resulting from a process of inductive reasoning may be included as a premise in the broader deductive argument you are evaluating. If the inductive reasoning is weak, then the premise need not be accepted, and the argument can be judged as unsound. If the empirical evidence does not support the factual claim, then it need not be accepted again. Still further, if the claim is based on the faulty use of statistical procedures, then you have another good reason to reject the argument that contains the claim in question, valid or not.

If in your critical analysis of a specific argument, it turns out that the logic is valid in form and the factual premise is true or acceptable, then the third thing you should do is *evaluate the major premise upon which the entire argument is based.* This is especially important when dealing with practical syllogisms that contain normative (value-related) principles and assumptions. In contrast to some syllogisms that start off with logically true statements (All bachelors are unmarried men), practical syllogisms contain value premises that may not be intuitively obvious or analytically true. The difficulty for us is that their acceptability cannot be empirically proven. Fortunately, they can be rationally tested.

To test the acceptability of a major value premise, you can begin by asking: "Is the value premise logically coherent?" A value premise suggesting, for example, that "We should make promises with the intention of breaking them" doesn't make any sense. Such a principle reflects deceptive intent or plain lying, not promise making at all. Value premises can also be deemed meaningless or incoherent if they cannot reasonably and consistently be universalized. For instance, if we suggest that: "People should accept help, but never offer it," such a principle would fall apart when universalized. If absolutely everyone refused to offer help, then there would never be any help to accept, rendering the principle irrational and incoherent. Another principle that becomes irrational and incoherent when universalized is the following: "Everybody else but me should pay their income taxes." If such a principle were universalized, then nobody would pay taxes and "everybody else" wouldn't even exist. Whenever you test a value premise by asking: "What if everyone accepted and acted upon this principle?" you are using the **universalizability** criterion. (To learn more about this, see Chapter 5's section on Immanuel Kant's ethics.)

Sometimes what we need to do when evaluating arguments is critically examine a particular value premise in view of the **higher-order principle** that supports it. A value premise stating that trespassing is wrong, for example, could be justified by the higher-order principle that we shouldn't violate others' rights. Since trespassing involves violating someone's property rights, the conclusion can be drawn that such action is unacceptable. Thus, more narrowly expressed value premises can be justified by more broadly stated ones. Ultimate higher-order principles relating to things like justice, goodness, fairness, and honesty do not usually require justification. They serve as the basis of justifications themselves. Of course, if a higher-order principle is incoherent, inconsistent, or self-contradictory, then any particular value premise that follows from it needn't be accepted.

Lastly, if a principle or value premise is considered acceptable in one case, then it should apply to other similar cases. Making sure it does involves using what might be called the **new cases test.** However, if other similar instances can be provided where the value premise does not apply or intuitively cannot be justified, then it is not acceptable as a starting point in anyone's rational deliberations. Let's practice evaluating some value premises at this point by turning to the *Philosophers in Action* feature.

## PHILOSOPHERS IN ACTION

### Testing Value Premises

**INSTRUCTIONS** Evaluate the value premises stated below. Discuss your evaluations with classmates. Are they acceptable from a rational, philosophical point of view? Why or why not?

1. You should take advantage of others when it is in your material self-interest.
2. Killing is always wrong.
3. It's all right to cut across your neighbor's lawn on your way to work.
4. Visible ethnic and racial minorities should not be allowed into this country.
5. Everyone but me should fill out his or her income tax forms honestly.
6. You should never use people solely as a means to get what you want out of life.

# INFORMAL LOGICAL FALLACIES

People who fail to appreciate the benefits of argument often feel threatened when their viewpoints are challenged. If there has been a lot of ego investment in a particular philosophical position or a deep involvement of personal feelings, improper forms of reasoning called **informal logical fallacies** may be used to perform the emotional rescue of the threatened self. Informal fallacies are irrational. They are designed to persuade us emotionally and psychologically, not rationally. People who use them try to divert attention from the real issues and arguments under discussion to something more favorable to them. Informal fallacies can also be used as forms of intimidation. Defensive people worried about being wrong may respond aggressively toward others. Putting someone else on the defensive requires you to be less defensive about yourself. Essentially, informal fallacies work through diversion and attack. As instruments of persuasion and rhetoric, they are, unfortunately, sometimes very effective. As ways of correct thinking, however, they are always wrong. Logical fallacies are sometimes committed unconsciously and without malicious intent. Some people are simply unaware of their poor reasoning. Let us now look at some common fallacies you will need to guard against in your own logical self-defense.[5]

## *Ad Hominem* Fallacy

When you disagree with someone, the proper response is to criticize your opponent's position. If, instead of debating the issues, you attack your opponent personally, you then commit the ***ad hominem* fallacy.** For example, a wasteful person who resents the inconvenience brought about by recycling might refuse to support the arguments presented by environmental advocacy groups on the grounds that all environmentalists are "1960s losers." Of course, the merits of an argument should not be judged by when its advocates were born or what generation they come from. Recycling is either a good or bad idea, to be decided independently of irrelevant considerations.

## Straw Man Fallacy

In formal debate or in informal conversations with others, we do not always like what we hear. In response, we may sometimes misrepresent what others have said so we can make their arguments appear obviously unacceptable. If we do this and then proceed to argue against the unsatisfying versions we've created ourselves to reject their original but unaddressed positions, we commit the **straw man fallacy.**

A caution may be in order here. Occasionally, it happens that recipients of messages do not accurately understand what was intended by the message. They may then respond to what was never said. This kind of honest mistake may reflect a communication problem of listening or comprehension. It is unlike the straw man fallacy, where one person deliberately misrepresents the arguments of another. We get into foggy territory when misrepresentations occur unconsciously in psychological efforts to reduce anxiety. Conscious or unconscious, however, straw man fallacies are irrational distortions of the truth.

## Circular Reasoning/Begging the Question Fallacy

Have you ever been involved in an argument that seemed to go around in circles? If you have, perhaps someone was using **circular reasoning,** also known as the **fallacy of begging the question.** In circular reasoning, people use the conclusion they are trying to establish as a starting premise of their argument. In other words, people assume to be true in the beginning what they intend to prove logically at the end. Thus, the "logical" argument does not take you anywhere except back to what was assumed to be true at the outset. The following is an example of circular reasoning in a religious context.

*B. LEVER:* God exists.

*I. M. AGNOSTIC:* How do you know God exists?

*B. LEVER:* Because it says so in the Bible.

*I. M. AGNOSTIC:* How do you know the Bible is telling you the truth?

*B. LEVER:* Because it's the inspired word of God.

In this example, B. Lever *begins by concluding* that God exists. In fact, he uses the Bible to prove this. However, the authority of the Bible carries absolute truth value or weight only if one already accepts the premise or presupposition that God inspired it in the first place. In other words, to use the Bible as proof that God exists, one must assume from the very beginning that God actually does exist as the inspirational Source—but this is the disputed point under debate! If B. Lever begins by assuming to be true at the beginning of his argument what he is trying to prove in the end, then nothing has, in fact, been proven, and we have just gone around in a big circle. I do not mean to suggest that rational proofs cannot be offered for the existence of God, only that circular ones do not work. (To learn more about other efforts to prove that God exists, read the *Philosophical Segue* in Chapter Four entitled: "Proofs for the Existence of God.")

## Two Wrongs Fallacy

Committing the **two wrongs fallacy** involves defending a particular wrongdoing by drawing attention to another instance of the same behavior that apparently went unchallenged and was, therefore, accepted by implication. For instance, I remember that back in my student days, there were traditional initiation rituals for freshmen at the University of Toronto. One ritual required first-year students to commit minor acts of vandalism (painting a certain statue in Queen's Park). Confronted about the justifiability of such acts, a student (guess who) responded by saying that freshmen had been committing these acts for years. Apparently, for this poor misguided soul the previous years' vandalism served as a justification for his own wrongdoing. Trying to justify one wrongdoing by referring to an instance of another is not rational or justified. If you don't believe this, try convincing a highway patrol officer not to give you a ticket for speeding, arguing that you were just keeping up with the other speeders in traffic. Good Luck!

## Slippery Slope Fallacy

People who commit the **slippery slope fallacy** display this form of ill logic when they object to something because they incorrectly assume that it will necessarily lead to other undesirable consequences. For example, you may object to smoking marijuana. You could reason that such behavior will necessarily lead to harder drug usage, addiction, and eventually to a life of crime. Because crime is wrong, you conclude that smoking marijuana is therefore wrong.

Notice that in this hypothetical example, the major objection is to crime, the presumed necessary and inevitable result of smoking marijuana. The conclusion drawn here, however, is neither necessary nor inevitable. After experimenting once, you could choose to avoid marijuana in the future. Or you might decide to use it only very occasionally in a recreational way. Or you could become a crusader against mood-altering drugs. The point is that smoking marijuana is a separate and distinct act from harder drug use, addiction, and crime. Each must be considered independently and evaluated on its own terms. Although it may be that many drug-addicted criminals began their lives of crime by smoking marijuana, not everybody who smokes marijuana becomes a criminal addict. Many law-abiding, non-addicted people have experimented with marijuana; therefore, there is no necessary **causal connection** between marijuana and criminality. One does not have to lead to the other. If you can find a break in the causal chain that presumably links two unrelated acts, you can uncover the presence of a slippery slope.

## Appealing to Authority Fallacy

When people get into debates and disagreements, they frequently commit the **fallacy of appealing to authority** to justify their positions. Some appeals to authority are proper, while others are not. Proper appeals can be made to support factual claims within larger arguments. If, in the previous example about marijuana, someone had wanted to condemn its use on medical grounds, scientific and empirical research data could have been presented to support claims about marijuana's adverse physical effects. As long as the data presented were based on the recognized contributions of medical researchers in the field and were accepted after peer review and evaluation, such data could have been justifiably used to support factual claims embedded in the broader argument.

When questions of value are at issue, however, it is much more difficult, and usually unjustifiable, to make authoritative appeals. Normative assumptions and principles of conduct (People should always behave in their own self-interest.) cannot be proven true or false by empirical observation or by scientific experiment. Whether or not people actually behave in their own self-interest cannot tell us whether or not they should. Where matters of value are concerned, authoritative appeals cannot be made in rationally acceptable ways. It is ill-advised, for example, to make appeals to religious authority when justifying moral claims. Since nobody has a moral duty to belong to any one religion, judgments issued by religious authorities need not necessarily carry any weight for the nonreligious or for those outside one's faith community. Furthermore, the fact that different religious authorities and faith communities disagree among themselves on basic issues of moral principle means that authoritative appeals become problematic. If we don't wish to foster religious intolerance and bigotry in a pluralistic democratic society, authoritative appeals must be discouraged.

## Red Herring Fallacy

The **red herring fallacy** is another favorite form of ill logic used in debates. The name of this fallacy comes from the sport of fox hunting. In this sport, hunters on horseback follow a pack of hounds tracking a fox's scent. To save the fox from being caught, dried and salted red herring is drawn across the fox's tracks ahead of the pack. The herring is then pulled in a direction away from the fox. The dogs are diverted by the stronger, fresher scent of the herring, allowing the fox to escape and run another day.

In the red herring fallacy, a controversial claim or position is defended by taking the offensive. This tactic involves setting up a new issue that has only a tenuous connection with the original one. Because the weaknesses of the orig-

MEDITATIVE MOMENT

*Think about the last time you "smelled a rat" in someone's argument. You sensed something was wrong, but just couldn't put your finger on it. Now that you know more about valid logic and fallacious reasoning, think back to that argument. What was the argument about? What claims, principles, or assumptions were included in it? Why do you think the argument was unsound? Were the claims supported and verified? Did the value premises pass the tests of adequacy discussed earlier in this chapter? Was that person's argument coherent, consistent, and valid? Was the other party guilty of any informal logical fallacies? Were you? Take some time now to rationally reflect. Jot down your thoughts in your philosophical journal. If you feel particularly creative, perhaps you could try to reconstruct the argument you had as a Platonic dialogue with you as Socrates and your friend as Euthyphro.*

inal position are exposed, the defender proceeds to argue for the new issue or position that is more supportable. In other words, attention is deflected from the original weak position to a new one, which is less open to negative criticism. A second stronger argument or position is used to justify a weaker and indefensible first one—slick, but sleazy!

## Guilt by Association Fallacy

This form of ill logic is used in adversarial situations in an attempt to discredit an opponent or that opponent's position. It draws attention to the opponent's alleged association with some group or an individual that has already been discredited. The attempt to discredit is not direct, as in *ad hominem* arguments, but is indirect. The guilt of the discredited individual or group is transferred onto the opponent.

Let's suppose, hypothetically, that a new Socialist Party of America has been formed and is running candidates in the next federal election. A friend of yours says he refuses to vote "socialist," on principle, and therefore he will not support the newly formed party. His reason is "Socialists almost sent England and France into bankruptcy." The unspoken claim is that, if elected here, they will bankrupt this country too. Apparently, for this voter, socialist mismanagement across the ocean is enough to convict socialists here of incompetence. They are found guilty prior to doing anything wrong. It is possible, of course, that a socialist government could mismanage a country like the United States, but some argue that the Democrats and Republicans have been doing so for years! But seriously, actions and policies of foreign socialist governments alone cannot serve as an adequate basis of judgment on domestic socialism. This socialism may be different in significant ways. The new socialists may have learned from the mistakes of their European counterparts. Perhaps contemporary North American socialism has evolved into something more akin to capitalism. Simply put, you cannot pin incompetence on American socialists because of what foreign socialists have done. To do so is to commit the **guilt by association fallacy.** Nonetheless, by using this diversionary tactic, fear can be created in the minds of unreflective voters, and it may work as a means of persuasion. Creating fear is not very rational, but against people lacking the skills of logical self-defense, it often works.

Now that we have covered a number of the most frequently used informal logical fallacies, practice your skill of identifying them in the exercise that follows.

In conclusion to this treatment of logic and philosophical argument, I invite you now to review some useful "Do's and Don'ts for Arguments Sake." They will help you to become more rational the next time you get involved in any sort of philosophical debate (see Table 3.3). Also, once you've finished this summary review, you may wish to complete the Meditative Moment exercise that follows the table for your personal journal. Doing so will underscore the personal and practical relevance of logical thinking in your everyday experience of life.

# PHILOSOPHERS IN ACTION

## Identifying the Fallacy

**IDENTIFY THE FALLACY** This exercise will give you an opportunity to apply your knowledge and understanding of fallacious reasoning. Practice here will help you to develop your skills of logical self-defense. Being able to identify fallacious reasoning will protect you against illogical attacks and irrational attempts to manipulate your thinking. Recognizing informal fallacies will also help you to minimize them in your own arguments.

**INSTRUCTIONS** Below are some examples of fallacious reasoning. Identify the fallacies by placing the appropriate letter next to each example. This exercise can be done individually or in groups. For classroom purposes, be prepared to provide explanations for each identification.

    A. *ad hominem* fallacy
    B. straw man fallacy
    C. circular reasoning/begging the question
    D. fallacy of two wrongs
    E. slippery slope fallacy
    F. fallacy of appealing to authority
    G. red herring fallacy
    H. fallacy of guilt by association

_____ 1. You shouldn't accept the city counselor's arguments in favor of legalized gambling. After all, he's a godless communist.

_____ 2. I can't believe you're thinking about sleeping with your boyfriend. It's obviously wrong. The Pope says so.

_____ 3. Two students were arguing about cars. The first student said, "I can prove to you that Fords are faster than Chevys. My cousin Bill owns a Ford, and he told me that he has beaten every Chevy that he has ever raced on the highway." The second student asked, "How do you know your cousin is telling you the truth." The first replied, "Someone who drives the fastest car wouldn't have to lie."

_____ 4. We cannot allow hashish to be legalized. If we do, then sooner or later everyone will become addicted to crack cocaine, and after that, the crime rate will surely rise.

_____ 5. It's perfectly all right to run red lights; everybody in town does it.

_____ 6. The business consultant recommended that we switch to voice mail for receiving and sending internal messages. She claims this change will make our operations more efficient. I can't believe this woman. She thinks every problem in the world has an electronic solution. Computers and telephones cannot improve the economy or morale at work. I think we should reject her recommendation.

_____ 7. You don't really believe that "joker" do you? Don't you know his uncle was caught selling illegal pornography? I wouldn't accept anything he says.

_____ 8. You say I'm not making sense. Give me a break. You're the one who failed the first logic exam.

**Answer Key**
1. A   2. F   3. C   4. E   5. D
6. B   7. H   8. G

**TABLE 3.3** Some Do's and Don'ts for Argument's Sake

| Don't | Do |
| --- | --- |
| Attack or intimidate | Adopt the proper attitude |
| Divert attention from the real issues | Remain rational and emotionally detached |
| Base arguments on emotional or psychological appeals | Stay objective |
| Build false or questionable claims into your argument | Listen to opposing viewpoints with openness |
| Use invalid logic | Analyze conflicting positions fairly and impartially |
| Use unjustifiable premises | Appraise factual claims |
| Make questionable assumptions | Evaluate major premises and assumptions |
| Confuse valid logic with truth | Examine the logical thinking behind particular conclusions |
| Take disagreements personally | Look for fallacious reasoning |
| Appeal to authorities unjustifiably | Appeal to higher-order values to justify your viewpoints |
| Attribute to others what they didn't say | |
| Make illegitimate associations | Distinguish between opinions and arguments |
| Contradict yourself | Stick to the issues |
| Change the subject when challenged | Use proper processes of inductive and deductive logic |
| Be inconsistent | Base your positions on sound arguments |
| Use faulty causal reasoning | Avoid diversion and intimidation by fallacious reasoning |
| Justify one wrongdoing with another | |

# STUDY GUIDE

## KEY TERMS

disagreement   127
rational disinterestedness   127
Socratic humility   128
opinion   139
grounds   139
argument   140
factual statements   140
value judgments   140
deductive logic   143
form   143
content   143
logical form   143
*modus ponens*(MP)   143
valid reasoning   143

antecedent   144
consequent   144
*modus tollens*   145
denying the consequent   145
denying the antecedent   145
syllogisms   145
affirming the inclusive
    disjunct   147
categorical syllogisms of class
    membership   149
practical syllogism   150
major premise   150
value premise   150
minor premise   150

factual premise   150
conclusion   150
inductive logic   151
argument by analogy   152
validity   153
truth   153
soundness   153
unsound argument   154
universalizability   155
higher-order principle test   155
new cases test   155
informal logical fallacies   156
*ad hominem* fallacy   156
straw man fallacy   157

circular reasoning   **157**
fallacy of begging the
  question   **157**
two wrongs fallacy   **158**

slippery slope fallacy   **158**
causal connection   **158**
fallacy of appealing to
  authority   **159**

red herring fallacy   **159**
guilt by association fallacy   **160**

## PROGRESS CHECK

**Instructions:** Fill in the blanks with the appropriate responses listed below.

groundless
form
rational disinterestedness
necessary
appealing to authority
straw man
premises
value

syllogisms
inductive generalization
factual
moral
*modus ponens*
inductive
content
two wrongs

sound
practical
nonmoral
arguments
logical fallacies
*modus tollens*
*ad hominem*

1. _____ statements make empirical claims, whereas _____ judgments make normative assertions.
2. There are two basic types of value judgment: _____ and _____ .
3. Everyday opinions, expressed without serious thought, tend to be _____ and little more than a statement of personal preference.
4. _____ involve a process of thought in which conclusions are derived from preceding premises.
5. If we remain objective and impartial in our disagreements with others, we display an attitude of _____ .
6. From the _____ of any particular argument, one can extract its logical _____ .
7. Arguments with the form "If p, then q; p; So, q" are given the label of _____ .
8. "If p, then q; not q; So, not p" is the form of a _____ argument.
9. _____ may be either hypothetical, disjunctive, practical, or categorical.
10. An argument that begins with a normative statement, includes a factual premise, and concludes with a value judgment is called a _____ syllogism.
11. _____ logic can only provide probability, not certainty.
12. When we make a(n) _____, we make a statement about all, some, or none of a class based on an empirical examination of only a part of the class.
13. Valid deductive arguments lead to _____ conclusions.
14. A(n) _____ argument is valid in form and contains true premises.
15. Value _____ can be tested using the role-exchange, new cases, and higher-order principle tests, as well as the consistency and universalizability test.
16. People who try to win arguments by resorting to diversion and intimidation tactics are guilty of using informal _____ .
17. Attacking the person, rather than criticizing the person's argument, is the definition of the _____ fallacy.
18. When we misrepresent someone's argument in order to reject what someone really did argue, we are guilty of committing the _____ fallacy.
19. Arguing that it's all right to commit a wrongdoing just because others are committing the same wrongdoing is to fall prey to the _____ fallacy.
20. Arguing that something is right or wrong / good or bad simply because the majority says so is evidence of the fallacy of _____ .

# SUMMARY OF MAJOR POINTS

1. *Are arguments beneficial?*
   Yes. They can open minds and contribute to social progress.

2. *What attitudes are useful for productive argument?*
   Rational disinterestedness, Socratic humility, openness, reduction of personal defensiveness, and willingness to change our position in view of counter evidence and justified criticism are all useful if we are to engage in productive argument.

3. *What are the differences between factual statements and value judgments?*
   Factual statements refer to what is or is not the case; value judgments make reference to what is good or bad, right or wrong, better or worse, obligatory or prohibited. The former are verified; the latter are justified.

4. *In what ways are opinions different from arguments?*
   Opinions are groundless. They express personal tastes, preferences, and beliefs without any basis in carefully reasoned thought. Arguments involve a process of rational thought whereby conclusions are derived from preceding premises. Arguments can be based on inductive or deductive logic.

5. *What are the general characteristics of deductive arguments?*
   They come in various forms (*modus tollens,* class syllogisms). They are either valid or invalid. They lead to necessary conclusions derived from preceding premises.

6. *How is the "form/content" distinction to be understood in the context of philosophical argument?*
   Underlying the content of any deductive argument is some kind of formal structure that is either valid or invalid.

7. *How do inductive and deductive logic differ?*
   Inductive logic leads to probable conclusions, whereas deductive logic leads to necessary conclusions. Inductive logic is better or worse; deductive logic is valid or invalid.

8. *What are some forms of deductive logic?*
   *Modus ponens, modus tollens,* hypothetical syllogisms, disjunctive syllogisms, syllogisms of class membership, and practical syllogisms are all forms of deductive logic.

9. *What are some forms of inductive logic?*
   They are arguments from past experience, arguments by analogy, and arguments by inductive generalization.

10. *In the context of logical argument, how are validity, truth, and soundness different?*
    Validity refers to the form of an argument. Truth refers to the premises and the conclusion. Soundness pertains to valid arguments having true premises leading to necessary conclusions.

11. *Do valid arguments always have to be accepted?*
    No. If a valid argument contains faulty or incorrect premises, then we do not have to accept the conclusion even though it follows logically.

12. *How can we test practical syllogisms?*
    Determine if the conclusion necessarily follows from preceding premises. Ask if the factual claims embedded in the syllogism are true; if not, reject the argument. Test the value premise of the syllogism to see if its starting point is acceptable. Arguments based on unacceptable value premises needn't be accepted.

13. *What is an informal logical fallacy?*
    An informal logical fallacy is an irrational rhetorical device designed to persuade through emotional and psychological appeals. Fallacies are used to divert attention, intimidate others, and thereby win arguments.

14. *What are some common fallacies?*
    Some common fallacies are the straw man, circular reasoning/begging the question, two wrongs, slippery slope, appealing to authority, red herring, guilt by association, and the *ad hominem.*

# SOURCE REFERENCES

**Barry, Vincent,** *Philosophy: A Text with Readings,* 2nd ed. (Belmont CA: Wadsworth Co., 1983).

**Cohen, Elliot D.,** *Making Value Judgments: Principles of Sound Reasoning* (Malabar, FL: Krieger, 1985).

**Coombs, Jerrold, Leroi Daniels, and Ian Wright,** "Introduction to Value Reasoning," *Prejudice: Teacher's Manual,* Value Reasoning Series (Toronto: The Ontario Institute for Studies in Education, 1978).

**Falikowski, Anthony,** *Moral Philosophy for Modern Life* (Scarborough, Canada: Prentice Hall/Allyn & Bacon, 1998).

**Johnson, R.H., and J.A Blair,** *Logical Self-Defense,* 2nd ed. (Toronto: McGraw-Hill Ryerson, 1983).

**Lawhead, William F.,** *The Voyage of Discovery: A History of Western Philosophy* (Belmont CA: Wadsworth, 1996).

**McDonald, Daniel,** *The Language of Argument,* 4th ed. (New York: Harper & Row, 1983).

**Rosenberg, Jay F.,** *The Practice of Philosophy: A Handbook for Beginners,* 2nd ed. (Upper Saddle River, NJ: Prentice Hall, 1984).

**Runkle, Gerald,** *Good Thinking: An Introduction to Logic,* 2nd ed. (New York: Holt, Rinehart and Winston, 1981).

**Russon, Lilly-Marlene, and Martin Curd,** *Principles of Reasoning* (New York: St. Martin's Press, 1989).

**Stewart, David, and H. Gene Blocker,** *Fundamentals of Philosophy,* 4th ed. (Upper Saddle River, NJ: Prentice Hall, 1996).

**Woodhouse, Mark,** *A Preface to Philosophy,* 5th ed. (Belmont CA: Wadsworth, 1994).

# PHILOSOPHY IN CYBERSPACE

**The Center for Critical Thinking**
www.criticalthinking.org
The center offers a collection of articles focused on the background and theory of critical thinking. It can help you to avoid irrationality and fallacious reasoning. The center offers an archive of a critical thinking e-mail discussion group, and information on critical seminars and in-service training.

**A Tutorial in Critical Reasoning**
http://commhum.mccneb.edu/argument/summary.htm
Visit this interactive website to learn more about the nature and structure of arguments.

**Association for Symbolic Logic**
www.aslonline.org/
This site provides an effective forum for the presentation, publication, and critical discussion of scholarly work in symbolic logic.

# ENDNOTES

1. The setting for the Euthyphro dialogue is set for us by John M. Cooper, ed., *Plato: Complete Works* (Indianapolis: Hackett Publishing, 1997).
2. Adapted from William F. Lawhead, *The Voyage of Discovery: A History of Western Philosophy* (Belmont, CA: Wadsworth, Publishing, Co., 1996), pp. 49–50.
3. See Mark Woodhouse, *A Preface to Philosophy,* 5th ed. (Belmont CA: Wadsworth, 1994), p. 63.
4. Ibid., p.6.
5. Much of the information for this section comes from R.H. Johnson and J.A. Blair *Logical Self-Defense* (Toronto: McGraw-Hill Ryerson, 1983).

# CHAPTER 4

# EPISTEMOLOGY, METAPHYSICS, AND GOD

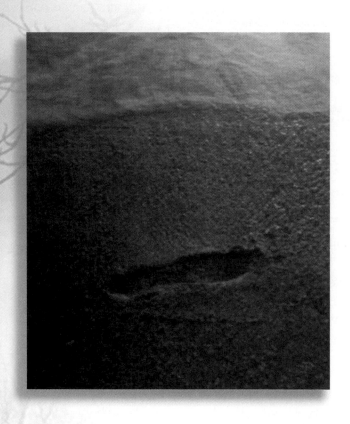

# CHAPTER OVERVIEW

**Take It Personally**

**KNOW THYSELF**
**My Philosophical Presuppositions about Knowledge and Reality**

**Preliminary Questions and Definitions**

**Plato's Metaphysical Epistemology**

PHILOSOPHICAL PROFILE
**PLATO**

    Divided Line Theory
    Theory of Forms
    Simile of the Sun

ORIGINAL SOURCEWORK
Plato, *Simile of the Sun*

    Allegory of the Cave

ORIGINAL SOURCEWORK
Plato, *Allegory of the Cave*

**Rationalism: René Descartes**

PHILOSOPHICAL PROFILE
**RENÉ DESCARTES**

PHILOSOPHICAL PROFILE
**OTHER CONTINENTAL RATIONALISTS**

    Historical Context
    The Quest for Certainty Using Methodological
    Doubt

ORIGINAL SOURCEWORK
Descartes, *First Meditation Concerning Things That Can Be Doubted*

    *Cogito Ergo Sum*—I Think, Therefore I Am

ORIGINAL SOURCEWORK
Descartes, *Second Meditation of the Nature of the Human Mind, and That It Is More Easily Known than the Body*

ORIGINAL SOURCEWORK
Descartes, *The Wax Example*

**British Empiricism: Locke, Berkeley, and Hume**
    Historical Background of Empiricism

PHILOSOPHICAL PROFILE
**JOHN LOCKE**

    John Locke
    Bishop George Berkeley

PHILOSOPHICAL PROFILE
**BISHOP GEORGE BERKELEY**

PHILOSOPHICAL PROFILE
**DAVID HUME**

    David Hume's Radical Skepticism

ORIGINAL SOURCEWORK
David Hume, *Skeptical Doubts Concerning the Operations of the Understanding*

ORIGINAL SOURCEWORK
Patricia Hill Collins, *An Afrocentric/Feminist Standpoint Challenges the Tradition of Positivism*

PHILOSOPHICAL PROFILE
**IMMANUEL KANT**

## Immanuel Kant's Synthesis of Rationalism and Empiricism

The Roles of Reason and Experience in Knowledge

The Copernican Revolution in Epistemology

*A Priori* Elements of Knowledge

Kantian versus Platonic Forms

The Categories of "Cause" and "Substance"

Types of Judgments

ORIGINAL SOURCEWORK
Immanuel Kant, *The Distinction between Analytic and Synthetic Judgments*

Metaphysics and the Regulative Function of Transcendental Ideas

ORIGINAL SOURCEWORK
Benjamin Whorf, *The Language of the Hopi Provides a Metaphysics Without Space and Time*

**PHILOSOPHICAL SEGUE**
**Proofs for the Existence of God**

PHILOSOPHICAL PROFILE
**ST. ANSELM**

## Anselm's Ontological Proof

## St. Thomas Aquinas's "Five Ways"—Proofs for the Existence of God

The First Way: Argument from Motion

The Second Way: Argument from Cause

The Third Way: Argument from Necessity

The Fourth Way: Argument from Perfection and Degree

The Fifth Way: Argument from Intelligent Design

PHILOSOPHICAL PROFILE
**ST. THOMAS AQUINAS**

ORIGINAL SOURCEWORK
St. Thomas Aquinas, *Whether God Exists*

**STUDY GUIDE**
Key Terms ■ Progress Check
Summary of Major Points ■ Source References
Philosophy in Cyberspace ■ Endnotes

# LEARNING OUTCOMES

*After successfully completing this chapter, you will be able to:*

Define epistemology and metaphysics, identifying fundamental questions raised by each.

Outline Plato's "Divided Line Theory of Knowledge," understanding its metaphysical underpinnings

Comprehend the Platonic concept of "goodness," using the simile of the sun

Give an account of the ascent from illusion to philosophical illumination in terms of Plato's "Allegory of the Cave"

Define rationalism and give the historical context out of which it emerged

Explain René Descartes's use of methodological doubt

State the importance of the "*Cogito*" in Descartes's philosophy

Outline the basic ideas of British empiricism with reference to John Locke, George Berkeley, and David Hume

Illustrate how Kant's epistemology represents a synthesis of rationalism and empiricism

Distinguish between Kantian and Platonic forms

Understand the various types of rational judgments and the special importance afforded to the "synthetic *a priori*"

Discuss the regulative function of the Kantian transcendental ideas of "self," "God," and "cosmos"

Outline the ontological, cosmological, and teleological proofs for the existence of God

# FOCUS QUESTIONS

1. Have you ever thought that you knew something for certain, only to find out later that you were wrong? What was that certain belief or idea? What was the basis for your initial certainty? What caused it to be called into question? Do you know anything for certain now? How do you know for sure that you know for sure?

2. How are epistemology and metaphysics related to each other?

3. What are some metaphysical worldviews implicit in the epistemological theories presented in this chapter?

4. What basic assumptions are built into rationalism and empiricism? What are Immanuel Kant's views on these assumptions?

5. What is meant by the suggestion that the human mind is either passive or active?

6. What proofs, if any, can be given for the existence of God?

Adam and Eve's desire to eat the forbidden fruit from the tree of knowledge led to their separation from God in the Garden of Eden. One could say that, in the beginning, there dawned on human consciousness an awareness of the connection between epistemology (knowledge) and metaphysics (God). That connection endures today and is the subject of this chapter.

## TAKE IT PERSONALLY

Our experience of philosophy began in Chapter 1 with a discussion of its nature and benefits, as well as with a brief outline of its historical periods and disciplinary subdivisions. Once we gained a general understanding of what philosophy was all about and why it was important, we proceeded in Chapter 2 to explore its "existential relevance" by comparing various life philosophies with our own, taking the opportunity to reevaluate our personal worldviews in light of these other alternatives, which, in some cases, have guided people for centuries. After situating ourselves philosophically, we went on in Chapter 3 to amass the logical tools required to do the serious work that philosophers do. This necessitated that we learn a few essentials, like distinguishing between factual statements and value judgments and also between thoughtless opinions and genuine philosophical arguments. We mastered some basic forms of inductive and deductive logic as well, being careful to distinguish among notions of validity, soundness, and truth. In addition, we spent some time studying a number of informal logical fallacies that are used as irrational rhetorical devices, not in the pursuit of wisdom, but for illegitimate purposes of persuasion, diversion and psychological attack.

Now that you know what philosophy is, where you stand with respect to your own personal philosophical worldview, and you have learned how to think critically and philosophically using proper methods of logic, you are finally prepared to engage in some heavy-duty philosophical deliberations pertaining to esoteric matters of epistemology, metaphysics, and God.

As we proceed through this section of the book, it might be interesting for you to reflect again on your personal philosophy of life. Discussions here on cause-and-effect relations and proofs given for the existence of God, for example, will have implications for everyone. Whether or not we are "condemned to be free" in an inherently meaningless and chaotic world, as Sartre claimed, or destined to be reunited with God depends on the nature of reality—a matter of ontology (the study of being) and metaphysics. This chapter will reinforce the point made in Chapter One that life philosophies are derivative of other primary branches of philosophical inquiry. As you go through this chapter, then, try to relate its content to your personal outlook on life—technically what's called your *Weltanschauung* (a German term). What do the philosophers say about reality, God, and knowledge that impacts on your own philosophical presuppositions?

As a way of prefacing my treatment of the important and overlapping concerns of epistemology and metaphysics, please allow me to take you back to my first geometry class in high school where, you could say, I "took it personally." My own first experience with philosophy may strike a resonant chord with some of you right here now.

In high school, I had the good fortune of being exposed to a very knowledgeable geometry teacher who appreciated the philosophical underpinnings of his discipline. I remember how, one day, he asked everyone in the class to imagine a point in space located just in front of him at the spot where his index finger met his thumb. Then, he directed us to imagine a second point in space using his other thumb and index finger. He proceeded to ask the class, "What is the shortest distance between these two imaginary points in space called?" Though somewhat hesitant, believing this was a trick question of sorts, most students were finally able to reply, "A straight line." "Correct," responded the teacher. This all seemed simple enough until the next somewhat mysterious question was posed. The teacher asked, "What was important to note in my earlier directions to you?" After some puzzlement, a student finally responded, "Imagine! You asked us to *imagine* two points in space." "Exactly," replied the teacher, "for in reality there are no such things as points in space. All we can do is represent them somehow, as located at our fingertips, or as two dots on the blackboard, for example." If this wasn't perplexing enough, my instructor then went on to claim that perfectly straight lines, like points in space, do not really exist either. He challenged us to draw the straightest line that we could freehand, then using a ruler, the side of a book, or anything else we could find. He said that no matter how straight the line appeared, in truth it was still imperfect. Although the naked eye might not be able to detect the tiny imperfections, one glance at our lines through a powerful microscope would reveal that they were not straight and smooth but jagged. I accepted his contention that the best we can produce are rough approximations of perfection. Also, familiar with the methods of my teacher, I knew this insight was just a preliminary set-up for a grander revelation of some sort . . . so I waited.

The teacher then drew a triangle on the board. He indicated that it contained one right angle and two equal sides (see Figure 4.1). He asked if anyone in the class knew the name of what he had drawn. A student shouted out, "A right-angled isosceles triangle!" Again, "Correct," was the reply. Judging by the tone of his voice, I knew we were approaching the climactic point of the lesson when he asked if anyone could figure out the length of "z," which we learned was called the hypotenuse. I think it was the same student who blurted out that the hypotenuse squared is equal to the sum of both equal sides squared. He was even able to express it mathematically, saying, "$Z^2 = X^2 + Y^2$." "Excellent," said the teacher. "But does anyone know what right-angled isosceles triangles and straight lines have in common?" On this one, everyone was stumped. After a lengthy pause, the teacher said that both are perfect geometric forms that do not actually exist in the real world; they are both theoretical entities grasped only by the mind. Furthermore, it was pointed out to us that the mathematical equation used to calculate the hypotenuse represented a necessary and undeniable truth. We couldn't say, for example, that $Z^3 = X^2 + Y^2$ or that $Y^2 = Z^3 + Y^3$—the statement in its original form was the only one which was absolutely true: true unconditionally for everyone and true for all time. Putting "two and two" together, so to speak, I came up with the realization that by means of a mathematical equation I had attained absolute and necessary truth about something that did not exist in the physical world. I had achieved certain knowledge of something that was not materially real. Things were beginning to get spooky!

**FIGURE 4.1**  How to find the hypotenuse of a right-angled isosceles triangle?

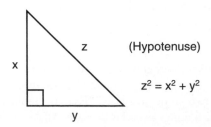

z    (Hypotenuse)

x

$z^2 = x^2 + y^2$

y

At the time, I didn't fully appreciate how I had been intellectually broadsided by some rather deep metaphysical and epistemological notions. It was only years later, through the study of philosophy, that I came to better understand those cryptic and puzzling questions of my geometry teacher. In what follows, you too will explore some of the mysteries of the mind that pertain to unchanging eternal verities concerning immaterial things. Before we begin to unravel these mysteries, however, we will define epistemology and metaphysics as well as list some of the fundamental questions that they both raise. Matters of God will be included in some of the theoretical discussions that follow. Indeed, several classical proofs for the existence of God are highlighted in this chapter's *Philosophical Segue* feature. Before getting to the main text, first complete the *Know Thyself* diagnostic. It will help you to identify more clearly your pre-reflective assumptions about knowledge and reality.

## KNOW THYSELF

### My Philosophical Presuppositions about Knowledge and Reality

**AIM** This diagnostic is designed to help you identify your pre-reflective assumptions about knowledge and reality.

**INSTRUCTIONS** Indicate your level of agreement or disagreement with each of the statements below using the scale provided. When finished, follow the scoring instructions and read about your metaphysical/epistemological outlook as encapsulated by one of the brief descriptions.

**Scoring Scale**
1 = strongly disagree
2 = disagree
3 = undecided (avoid, if possible)
4 = agree
5 = strongly agree

_____ 1. There exists a reality beyond the world of sensory experience.

_____ 2. All knowledge ultimately derives from our sensory experience of people, objects, and events.

_____ 3. Because the senses can sometimes be misleading, reason is the ultimate source of knowledge.

_____ 4. While not all knowledge is derived from experience, it begins with experience interacting with the faculty of human reason.

_____ 5. Behind the impermanence and transitoriness of life exists a timeless, spaceless, and changeless alternative reality.

_____ 6. With respect to what is true or false, I can doubt many things; but I cannot doubt that I exist as a thinking thing.

_____ 7. At birth, the human mind is like an empty blackboard, void of any knowledge or understanding.

_____ 8. Knowledge is the product of an active construction of the human mind assembling the data or sensible impressions of experience into meaningful objects and events.

_____ 9. The highest forms of knowledge are beyond logic and reason; they are attained only by immediate insight, pure thought, or by what might be called direct intellectual apprehension.

_____ 10. It is possible to prove the existence of God using the methods of reason alone.

_____ 11. Statements that are either not logically true, not true by definition, nor verifiable as true by observation and experiment are entirely meaningless statements.

_____ 12. In order to gain knowledge, we should not conform our minds to objects in the external world, but rather try to understand how external objects conform to the mind.

_____ 13. It is impossible for humans to have "certain" knowledge of that which is beyond space and time (e.g., God).

_____ 14. Whatever we know about the universe ultimately comes from our sensory-based experiences of it.

_____ 15. The concept of God must be an innate idea planted there by nature, since God has never been experienced by the senses.

_____ 16. It is possible to have absolute and certain knowledge of things that do not exist in the material world.

_____ 17. Perception and imagination can only yield opinion, whereas deductive reasoning and pure thought (i.e., direct intellectual apprehension) can provide knowledge.

_____ 18. Skeptical doubt is a good way of achieving rational certainty.

_____ 19. Complex and imaginary ideas ultimately find their source in sensory experience.

_____ 20. The reason we see things in the world in terms of cause-and-effect relationships is because our minds so organize our perceptions of reality.

## SCORING

Record the value you gave for each of the statements listed below. Add up each labeled column to discover your highest score. The column with the highest score points to your pre-reflective epistemological-metaphysical leanings.

| *Platonic Dualist* | *Cartesian Rationalist* | *Empiricist* | *Kantian Structuralist* |
|---|---|---|---|
| 1. | 3. | 2. | 4. |
| 5. | 6. | 7. | 8. |
| 9. | 10. | 11. | 12. |
| 16. | 15. | 14. | 13. |
| 17. | 18. | 19. | 20. |
| _____ | _____ | _____ | _____ |

Totals:

**Score Interpretation** This measure was designed to help you identify your pre-reflective assumptions about knowledge and reality. Not all epistemological (knowledge-related) and metaphysical perspectives are covered in this self-diagnostic, so the findings are only tentative. They need to be personally verified by you as we proceed through this chapter and later, as you continue your philosophical journey. It's quite possible, in fact, that your views will change after greater thought and reflection or after further readings in these areas of study. For now, let's review the results with a certain playfulness and intellectual curiosity.

*According to my highest score, my present views on reality and knowledge are most closely aligned with the:*

**Platonic Dualist** According to the Platonic Dualist, reality can be divided into two parts: the visible world of becoming and the intelligible world of being. The former yields opinion; the latter provides the highest forms of knowledge. Things in the physical world are merely imperfect approximations or copies of eternal spaceless and timeless forms. The highest knowledge is knowledge of "Goodness," achieved by a kind of immediate knowing or "direct intellectual apprehension." Lacking such apprehension, most unenlightened people confuse opinions about transitory things with knowledge of eternal verities.

**Cartesian Rationalist** The Cartesian Rationalist approaches questions of knowledge hoping to find certainty using the method of skeptical doubt. The senses are regarded as deceiving, so reason must be considered the ultimate source of truth. Conclusions about the nature of reality can be arrived at by means of logical deduction. Even the existence of God and the existence of the external world require rational justification. The one thing I can be absolutely sure of is that since I think, therefore I exist.

**Empiricist** The Empiricist argues that whatever knowledge is possible is ultimately derived from our sensory experience of the world. On this view, much of metaphysics—such as talk about God's existence or an afterlife—should be abandoned as "metaphysical rubbish." Any claims about such things cannot be verified as either true or false, and hence, it doesn't make any sense to debate them.

**Kantian Structuralist** According to the Kantian Structuralist, our experience of the world is a product of form and content. The mind brings to experience pure forms of sensory experience like space and time, by which all sensory impressions are structured. Human understanding makes judgments on the data of experience using intellectual forms like causality and object. Knowledge is therefore the result of an interaction between the rational subject and the sensible manifold of experience. Knowledge of super-sensible realities like God is impossible, for no sense impressions (content) can be provided for the mind to structure. Kantian theory represents a synthesis combining elements of both rationalism and empiricism.

# PRELIMINARY QUESTIONS AND DEFINITIONS

Now that you have some idea of your epistemological and metaphysical presuppositions, as identified by the preceding self-diagnostic, let us define our terms and proceed with some preliminary questions relevant to the subject matter of this chapter. We'll start with epistemology.

**Epistemology** is an impressive sounding term that comes from the Greek roots *episteme,* meaning "knowledge," and *logos,* meaning "the study of" or "the theory of." Hence, epistemology is an abbreviated way of saying the theory or study of knowledge. Under this rubric fall a number of fundamental questions and concerns. Epistemologists are particularly interested in the nature, sources, limitations, and validity of knowledge. Specifically, they ask questions such as the following:

What can we know? Where does our knowledge come from?
Can we know anything for sure, or is all truth relative?
Are there different kinds of knowledge?

What are the standards or criteria by which we can judge the reliability of knowledge claims?

What roles do experience and reason play in the formation of knowledge?

Are some things simply beyond human knowledge and comprehension?

What assumptions are embedded in the knowledge claims that we make?

**Metaphysics** is another term derived from the Greek, only this time from *meta,* meaning "after" or "beyond," and *physikos,* pertaining to "nature," or *physis,* referring to what is "physical" or "natural." Metaphysics can thus be conceptualized as a subdiscipline of philosophy that addresses issues taking us beyond nature and the realm of the physical. In one dictionary of philosophy, metaphysics is defined as:

The attempt to present a coherent picture of reality

The study of being

The study of the characteristics of the universe: existence, space, time, substance, identity, and causality

The study of ultimate reality

The study of a transcendental reality that is the cause or source of all existence

The critical examination of the underlying assumptions (presuppositions, basic beliefs) employed by our systems of knowledge in their claims about what is real.[1]

In light of these alternative definitions, metaphysicians ask questions like: "Is reality one or many?" "Can we be sure the world exists?" "Does God exist?" "Is the universe governed by laws of cause-and-effect, or is everything capricious and unpredictable?" "What do we mean by the notion of self?" To answer these and other metaphysical and epistemological questions, philosophers over the centuries have developed a number of identifiable theoretical perspectives associated either with particular thinkers or specific schools of thought. We cover several major ones for purposes of introduction. Plato's metaphysically based epistemology, René Descartes's rationalism, British empiricism, and Immanuel Kant's structural synthetic account, which combines elements of the preceding two. Coverage of these perspectives touches on many of the basic epistemological and metaphysical questions in a manageable and informative way. Let us begin with Plato.

> **When the mind's eye rests on objects illuminated by truth and reality, it understands and comprehends them, and functions intelligently; but when it turns to the twilight world of change and decay, it can only form opinions, its vision is confused and its beliefs shifting, and it seems to lack intelligence.**
>
> PLATO

## PLATO'S METAPHYSICAL EPISTEMOLOGY

In Plato's classic work, *The Republic,* we find not only a moral and social/political philosophy, but a metaphysics and supporting epistemology as well.[2] It is difficult, if not impossible, to discuss Plato's theory of knowledge in isolation from his metaphysical conception of reality because the two are so inextricably linked. In order to understand what he means by knowledge, we have to appreciate how he conceptualizes the relationships between permanence and change, appearance and reality, as well as the visible and the intelligible worlds. In our efforts to gain this appreciation, let us turn for a moment to two other ancient philosophers whose ideas place these relationships in bolder relief.

## PHILOSOPHICAL PROFILE

### Plato

**PLATO**

Plato lived from 427 to 347 B.C.E. He was born into a wealthy family that was both aristocratic and politically influential. His importance to intellectual history was underscored by Alfred North Whitehead, who once stated that all of western philosophy is but a series of footnotes on the work of Plato.

When Plato was 40, he founded the "Academy," an independent institution of learning which continued to exist for almost nine hundred years until the Roman Emperor Justinian closed it in 529 C.E. The Academy was a quiet retreat where teachers and students could meet to pursue knowledge. Students throughout Greece enrolled to partake in the adventure of learning and to experience personal growth toward wisdom. The Academy can be regarded as the precursor of today's modern university.

Plato himself studied under Socrates, once described by the Oracle at Delphi as the wisest man in Athens. Fifteen years after the tragic trial and death of Socrates, Plato began to write "dialogues" in which Socrates was the principal speaker. The dialogues explored moral, political, logical, religious, and cosmological topics. Though Socrates never actually recorded his ideas, we derive from the dialogues a profile of Socrates' personality and a statement of his doctrines which likely bear a very close resemblance to his actual philosophy and the historical figure himself. When reading Plato it is sometimes difficult, therefore, to determine what is attributable to Plato and what comes from Socrates. Some argue that the early works of Plato are more reflective of Socratic thinking, while the later works begin to reflect Plato's own philosophical investigations. Plato's most famous work is . . . *The Republic.* Other works by Plato include *The Apology, Crito, Phaedo,* and *Symposium.*

---

**Parmenides of Elea** (circa 500 B.C.E.) was a major influence on Plato. He was what is called in philosophical circles today a **monist,** meaning that for him, all of "what is" equals being. "What is" does not come in and out of being or change from being into non-being. The existence of nonexistence simply doesn't make any logical sense for him. Being is singular, eternal, and indivisible. It is immutable—the "unchanging one." Being is also perfect, complete, and whole. It does not move or transform itself in any way. When we witness apparent variety and change in the world, we are observing only appearances that are not ultimately real. Behind the apparent change is a stable permanent reality not apprehended by the senses. True being is recognized by reason alone.[3]

**Heraclitus of Ephesus** (circa 500 B.C.E.) believed something very much different from Parmenides. He maintained that "change alone is unchanging." Beneath the apparent permanence that accompanies our everyday perceptions and experiences of the world lies the hidden reality of continuous movement. Everything is always in a state of flux. Even the solid table or desk your book may be resting on right now is changing and moving about. Just think, the atoms and molecules that make it up are forever bouncing around, causing expansion and contraction in response to variations in temperature and humidity. The desk, as you see it now, is actually hurtling through space at thousands of miles per hour and will cease, in fact, to exist in centuries to come as it is currently in the process of breaking down and decomposing like garbage in a dump. To capture this continual state of change, Heraclitus used what has now become an often-cited aphorism. "*One cannot step twice into the same river for the water into which you first step has flowed on.*" Interestingly enough, this same insight is captured by Eastern Buddhist wisdom as well, which suggests that the "self" you were yesterday, five years ago, or the self you will become tomorrow is not the same self that you imagine yourself to be right now. The "self," like the river, is engaged in a continual process of change. Buddhists believe in the idea of ego-*im*permanence and claim that attach- ment to one's illusory identity reflects ignorance and selfish craving leading to suffering.

In a reconciliation of sorts between the worldviews presented by Heracli- tus and Parmenides, and also in efforts to respond to the relativism put forward by early sophist philosophers, Plato accepts both the ideas of permanence and impermanence and also the ideas of appearance and reality, seeing them not so much at odds with each other, but rather reflecting different levels of knowledge and states of being within one larger conceptual scheme. What is perceived by the senses, that which changes and is characterized by impermanence, belongs to Plato's metaphysical realm of "**becoming.**" What is intellectually grasped to be permanent and unchanging belongs, by contrast, to the intelligible realm of "**being.**"

As far as the world of becoming is concerned, for Plato it constitutes the visible world, the world about which we form opinions. The world of being, on the other hand, belongs to the intelligible world wherein human intelligence and understanding can provide eternal and unchanging knowledge. It is in the context of this framework, which integrates being and becoming, knowledge and opinion, as well as the visible and the intelligible worlds that Plato spells out his **divided line theory** of knowledge. As we go through this theory, you might find it helpful to refer to Figure 4.2 and Figure 4.3. The latter figure highlights different states of mind associated with the ascending levels of knowledge and different levels of reality.

## Divided Line Theory

First of all, imagine a vertical line divided into two unequal parts. Now divide the top and bottom parts unequally again in the same proportion. Label the di- viding lines A, B, C, and D starting at the top (see Figure 4.2). Having done this in your mind's eye, consider the segments as going from the lowest (D) to the highest (A). Furthermore, regard each level as having its own objects and its own method for knowing them.[4]

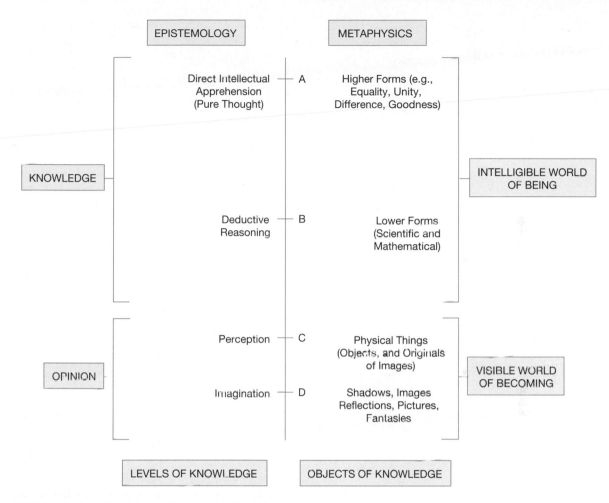

**FIGURE 4.2** An illustration of Plato's divided line theory.

The lowest level (D) is labeled **imagination.** It is at this level where mental activity is minimized, as is awareness of its objects. At the level of imagination, we carry illusions and hold opinions solely on the basis of appearances, unanalyzed impressions, uncritically inherited beliefs, and unevaluated emotions.[5] For instance, when you go to the movies, you "suspend judgment," as it were, allowing yourself to experience the combination of lights and sounds in a way that creates the illusion of reality, something which it clearly is not. We muse and sometimes worry when children cannot distinguish between fantasy and reality, yet we willingly fall prey to illusion ourselves when we pay the ticket price to go to the movies.

At the lowest level of the divided line we really don't have knowledge as such but rather unfounded **opinions.** Our experience of persons and objects is not direct but secondhand. A movie scene containing a basket of fruit is not the fruit

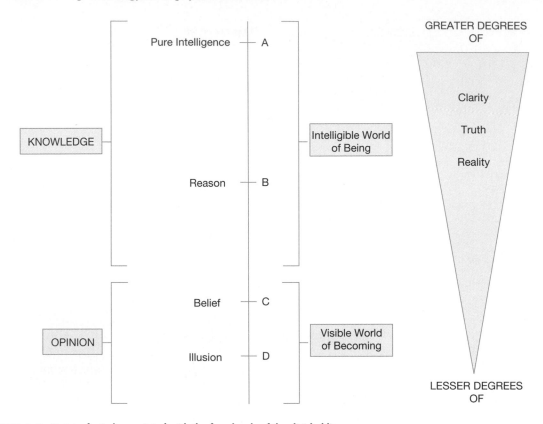

**FIGURE 4.3** States of mind associated with the four levels of the divided line.

itself, only a reflection or image of it. Seeing film footage of Bora Bora is not the same as being there. Don't we sometimes disparage people for their inferior knowledge of something because they just "read it in a book" or "saw it on television," but never directly experienced it themselves? We respect more those who have actually done it, seen it, or had contact with the things of which they claim to have knowledge. This takes us to the next level.

Proceeding upward to the next higher level lands us at **perception** (C). Unlike imagination—where we experience illusory images and fantasies or where we observe reflections, pictures, and shadows of things, here the objects of knowledge become the originals themselves. These original objects are physical and three-dimensional. They are things like cars, pets, trees, neighbors, fences, and so on. At the level of perception, classification and organization of objects can begin in a rudimentary way, but there is still no grasp of the abstract concept of the object(s) perceived. Being able to group red and green apples, for instance, is not the same as having a botanist's concept of "apple," which identifies the unchanging characteristics for each species of it.[6]

The second level from the bottom still belongs to the **visible world** of becoming. It constitutes the level of belief as captured by the saying, "Seeing is believing." Just so that we don't limit our understanding here to visual perception, perhaps we should also say hearing is believing, or more generally, that "experiencing is believing."

The level of perception is of most interest to the common sense mind—the mind of the "man-in-the-street." This type of person is wedded to what is perceived as concrete reality. Unfortunately, perception of objects in the physical world cannot give us true knowledge for a couple of reasons. First, what can be known by the senses belongs, for Plato, to the Heraclitian world of flux. At this level of reality, particular things are not stable. Whatever we know at the level of belief is always liable to change. As a consequence, we can never be entirely certain of our knowledge. All we know are appearances of things based on our perceptions; we know nothing of their true nature or essential qualities. We are limited to opinion. Second, sensory-based knowledge can never provide general, universal, unchanging, and abstract truth of the intelligible world. It can only give us specific "knowledge" of *this* particular pet or *that* particular house, and so on. And, as just stated, because all particulars are in flux, we can derive no certainty from our direct sensory observations of them. "Knowledge" at the level of perception is insecure.

As we move on to the second highest level along the divided line (B), we leave the realms of becoming and opinion and enter those of **being** and **knowledge,** both belonging to the **intelligible world.** At this level, knowledge is acquired through deductive reasoning. There is a movement away from belief in the concrete, changing, particular objects of perception and movement toward rational understanding and comprehension of abstract, unchanging universal concepts. Whereas at level (C) we have perception of this particular cat, dog or apple, at level (B), we gain an intellectual grasp of "catness," "dogness," and "appleness." We know something about these abstract concepts which allow us to label Fido a dog, Mittens a cat, or that MacIntosh an apple.

## Theory of Forms

Movement away from the visible world and toward the intelligible one takes us to Plato's **theory of forms.** In contrast to objects of perception in the visible world which are physical, those objects of the intelligible world at level (B) are abstract. Whereas perception focuses on concrete particulars, intellection and rational deduction focus on universal abstract concepts. The objects of perception found in the realm of becoming are in a constant process of Heraclitian flux; by contrast, the objects of the intellect at the level of being are unchanging, displaying a Paremenidian eternal immutability.[7] Those "concepts" of objects, as opposed to the objects themselves, Plato calls *forms*. Examples of these forms include mathematical and geometrical concepts such as circle and triangle, as well as concepts comprising our everyday vocabulary such as flower, rock, or leather.

According to Plato, the forms are not simply products of anyone's mind. They have an independent existence and are considered more real than things themselves. Unlike people, who are born and then die—who come in and out of existence—forms are eternal; they always remain. The concept or form "human" does not disappear with any particular person's death. Thus, we can perhaps think of forms as pure essences or abstract entities capturing the essential qualities of particular things.

Plato considers the forms to be perfect. Physical objects, which in some sense "partake in" or "belong to" forms themselves, are imperfect approximations of them. We saw how this could be so earlier with my geometry lesson about points in space, straight lines, and right-angled triangles. Remember, we can roughly approximate such things physically through drawings, representations, or constructions of some sort, but we can never achieve theoretical perfection no matter how hard we try. The best we can produce are imperfect "copies" of the forms of which they partake. In this context, we can say that knowledge of perfect forms in the intelligible world of being is superior to knowledge of imperfect physical objects in the visible world of becoming. Perfection trumps imperfection, immutability beats uncertain flux. And, just as original objects at level (C) make shadows and images of them possible at level (D), so too, forms at level (B) make it possible for us to know the actual world of things, along with the objects of mathematics, the sciences, and philosophy. Particular things are *real* only insofar as they measure up to, copy, or partake of the eternal reality and truth of their corresponding forms. Put another way, things are knowable in the visible world only insofar as we can name or identify them by a form, as members of a class of things that share the same form, the same set of defining qualities.[8] Without the form of the ideal birdhouse, for instance, we wouldn't be able to judge a particular one as a good or bad example. Without presupposing a concept of (perfect) justice, it would be impossible to justifiably criticize an action as unfair. The fact that we have never seen or experienced perfect justice in the material, physical world does not prevent us from charging that this person is unfair or that that act is unjust. We can know justice and fairness intellectually, even though we have never seen it experientially in the visible world.[9]

At level (B) on the divided line, we find lower forms of mathematics and science. Explaining Plato's position as to why knowledge of such forms at level (B) is still inferior, T.Z. Lavine writes:

> . . . the mathematician's knowledge has deficiencies. It is still tied to the visible world by its use of diagrams in the proofs of geometry, the well-known figures like angles, triangles, circles, parallelograms. A second limitation of knowledge at this level is that it does not examine or prove its own assumptions and thus remains hypothetical, or conditional, rather than being unconditional—based upon first principles which are proven to be true. A third limitation is that the various mathematical forms are uncoordinated, their relation to one another or to other forms is unexamined. Like mathematics, natural sciences have as their objects the forms with which these sciences are concerned, . . . the forms of air, water, animals, stars. And although the natural sciences, like mathematics, lie above the main division between knowledge and opinion, on the divided line of knowledge, and provide knowledge of the forms, both mathematics

and science are limited in three respects: (1) they rest upon unexamined first principles; (2) they are tied to instances, particulars, examples, from the visible world; and (3) they are piecemeal, fragmentary, since they fail to show the coordination of the forms which are their objects.[10]

At the uppermost level of knowledge (A), there is no need for perception, interpretation, or deductive reasoning, for the mind "directly apprehends" the higher forms. These higher forms are even more basic to thought than mathematical ones. Presupposed in every act of knowing are such fundamental ideas as equality, difference, sameness, unity, and diversity. For example, to "know" how a circle differs from a triangle, the concept of "difference" must first be grasped. Without an intellectual acquaintance with the form "difference," one could not perceive objects as separate and distinguishable from one another or make a judgment about how they are not alike.

## Simile of the Sun

Of all the higher forms, Plato considers **"Goodness"** or "The Good" as the absolute highest. It is given a privileged status because he claims goodness is what makes reality, truth, and the existence of everything else possible. Like all the other forms (higher and lower), it exists beyond the metaphysical level of becoming, residing at the highest reaches of being. To help us understand how The Good makes all else possible, Plato likens it to the sun. He asks, for instance, what is required for vision. Beyond objects to be seen and eyes to see them, what is still needed is a source of light. Without it, darkness descends and vision becomes impaired. However, with the illumination of the sun, figures stand out with vibrant clarity. So too, with the form Goodness. It is a form of intellectual illumination that makes objects knowable by the faculty of knowledge. Without it, reality could not exist. In the excerpt that follows, read Plato's *Simile of the Sun,* which gives pride of place to the form "Good."

### *Simile of the Sun*

**PLATO**

Yes, I said, but I must first come to an understanding with you, and remind you of what I have mentioned in the course of this discussion, and at many other times.
What?

The old story, that there is a many beautiful and a many good, and so of other things which we describe and define; to all of them 'many' is applied.
True, he said.

Plato, *The Republic,* trans. Benjamin Jowett, New York: P.F. Collier & Son, © 1901 The Colonial Press. Individual pages reflect content that is in the public domain.

And there is an absolute beauty and an absolute good, and of other things to which the term 'many' is applied there is an absolute; for they may be brought under a single idea, which is called the essence of each.

Very true.

The many, as we say, are seen but not known, and the ideas are known but not seen.

Exactly.

And what is the organ with which we see the visible things?

The sight, he said.

And with the hearing, I said, we hear, and with the other senses perceive the other objects of sense?

True.

But have you remarked that sight is by far the most costly and complex piece of workmanship which the artificer of the senses ever contrived?

No, I never have, he said.

Then reflect; has the ear or voice need of any third or additional nature in order that the one may be able to hear and the other to be heard?

Nothing of the sort.

No, indeed, I replied; and the same is true of most, if not all, the other senses—you would not say that any of them requires such an addition?

Certainly not.

But you see that without the addition of some other nature there is no seeing or being seen?

How do you mean?

Sight being, as I conceive, in the eyes, and he who has eyes wanting to see; colour being also present in them, still unless there be a third nature specially adapted to the purpose, the owner of the eyes will see nothing and the colours will be invisible.

Of what nature are you speaking?

Of that which you term light, I replied.

True, he said.

Noble, then, is the bond which links together sight and visibility, and great beyond other bonds by no small difference of nature; for light is their bond, and light is no ignoble thing?

Nay, he said, the reverse of ignoble.

And which, I said, of the gods in heaven would you say was the lord of this element? Whose is that light which makes the eye to see perfectly and the visible to appear?

You mean the sun, as you and all mankind say.

May not the relation of sight to this deity be described as follows?

How?

Neither sight nor the eye in which sight resides is the sun?

No.

Yet of all the organs of sense the eye is the most like the sun?

By far the most like.

And the power which the eye possesses is a sort of effluence which is dispensed from the sun?

Exactly.

Then the sun is not sight, but the author of sight who is recognised by sight.

True, he said.

And this is he whom I call the child of the good, whom the good begat in his own likeness, to be in the visible world, in relation to sight and the things of sight, what the good is in the intellectual world in relation to mind and the things of mind.

Will you be a little more explicit? he said.

Why, you know, I said, that the eyes, when a person directs them towards objects on which the light of day is no longer shining, but the moon and stars only, see dimly, and are nearly blind; they seem to have no clearness of vision in them?

Very true.

But when they are directed towards objects on which the sun shines, they see clearly and there is sight in them?

Certainly.

And the soul is like the eye: when resting upon that on which truth and being shine, the soul perceives and understands and is radiant with intelligence; but when turned towards the twilight of becoming and perishing, then she has opinion only, and goes blinking about, and is first of one opinion and then of another, and seems to have no intelligence?

Just so.

Now, that which imparts truth to the known and the power of knowing to the knower is what I would have you term the idea of good, and this you will deem to be the cause of science, and of truth in so far as the latter becomes the subject of knowledge; beautiful too, as are both truth and knowledge, you will be right in esteeming this other nature as more beautiful than either; and, as in the previous instance, light and sight may be truly said to be like the sun, and yet not to be the sun, so in this other sphere, science and truth may be deemed to be like the good, but not the good; the good has a place of honour yet higher.

What a wonder of beauty that must be, he said, which is the author of science and truth, and yet surpasses them in beauty; for you surely cannot mean to say that pleasure is the good?

God forbid, I replied; but may I ask you to consider the image in another point of view?

In what point of view?

You would say, would you not, that the sun is not only the author of visibility in all visible things, but of generation and nourishment and growth, though he himself is not generation?

Certainly.

In like manner the good may be said to be not only the author of knowledge to all things known, but of their being and essence, and yet the good is not essence, but far exceeds essence in dignity and power.

Glaucon said, with a ludicrous earnestness: By the light of heaven, how amazing!

Yes, I said, and the exaggeration may be set down to you; for you made me utter my fancies.

And pray continue to utter them; at any rate let us hear if there is anything more to be said about the similitude of the sun.

## DISCUSSION QUESTIONS FOR CRITIQUE AND ANALYSIS

1. Platonic forms are described as objects of intelligence, as opposed to objects of sensation. A flower in a garden, for example, is an object of sight, whereas "flower-ness" is an object grasped by the mind. In the case of flowers and other natural objects, this Platonic division of objects appears quite straightforward. However, what about things like computers and cell phones? Did eternal forms of such things exist before they were invented? How would we have to answer in order to be consistent with Plato's view as expressed by Socrates in this segment of *The Republic*? What criticism or concerns could be raised in light of Plato's position?

2. The claim is made that, "The good may be said to be the source not only of the intelligibility of the objects of knowledge, but also of their being and reality; yet it is not itself that reality, but is beyond it, and superior to it in dignity and power." In view of what you learned in Chapter Three, is this claim factual or normative (or logically self-evident)? Does it require empirical verification or rational justification? Does Plato (through Socrates) provide adequate support? How or why not?

## Allegory of the Cave

Plato uses the "**Allegory of the Cave**" to tell us more about the ascent from illusion to philosophical illumination and its associated difficulties. To better understand the correspondence between the Allegory of the Cave and the Divided Line Theory, let us draw the following parallels, which you can keep in mind while reading Plato (see Table 4.1).

**TABLE 4.1**   Allegorical Depiction of Knowledge Levels and States of Mind

| Level of Knowledge | Allegorical Depiction | State of Mind |
|---|---|---|
| Looking at the Sun = Philosophical enlightenment achieved by a vision or direct intellectual apprehension of the form Good | | |
| A (highest) | Looking at real things in the world outside the cave on the surface world | Intelligence |
| B | Those looking at shadows and reflections in the surface world and the ascent thereto | Reason |
| C | Those freed prisoners within the cave | Belief |
| D (lowest) | Prisoners, chained and facing the inner walls of the cave | Illusion |

## Allegory of the Cave

**PLATO**

And now, I said, let me show in a figure how far our nature is enlightened or unenlightened:—Behold! human beings living in an underground den, which has a mouth open towards the light and reaching all along the den; here they have been from their childhood, and have their legs and necks chained so that they cannot move, and can only see before them, being prevented by the chains from turning round their heads. Above and behind them a fire is blazing at a distance, and between the fire and the prisoners there is a raised way; and you will see, if you look, a low wall built along the way, like the screen which marionette players have in front of them, over which they show the puppets.

I see.

And do you see, I said, men passing along the wall carrying all sorts of vessels, and statues and figures of animals made of wood and stone and various materials, which appear over the wall? Some of them are talking, others silent.

You have shown me a strange image, and they are strange prisoners.

Like ourselves, I replied; and they see only their own shadows, or the shadows of one another, which the fire throws on the opposite wall of the cave?

True, he said; how could they see anything but the shadows if they were never allowed to move their heads?

And of the objects which are being carried in like manner they would only see the shadows?

Yes, he said.

And if they were able to converse with one another, would they not suppose that they were naming what was actually before them?

Very true.

And suppose further that the prison had an echo which came from the other side, would they not be sure to fancy when one of the passers-by spoke that the voice which they heard came from the passing shadow?

No question, he replied.

To them, I said, the truth would be literally nothing but the shadows of the images.

That is certain.

And now look again, and see what will naturally follow if the prisoners are released and disabused of their error. At first, when any of them is liberated and compelled suddenly to stand up and turn his neck round and walk and look towards the light, he will suffer sharp pains; the glare will distress him, and he will be unable to see the realities of which in his former state he had seen the shadows; and then conceive some one saying to him, that what he saw before was an illusion, but that now, when he is approaching nearer to being and his eye is turned towards more real existence, he has a clearer vision,—what will be his reply? And you may further imagine that his instructor is pointing to the objects as they pass and requiring him to name them,—will he not be perplexed? Will he not fancy that the shadows which he formerly saw are truer than the objects which are now shown to him?

Far truer.

And if he is compelled to look straight at the light, will he not have a pain in his eyes which will make him turn away to take refuge in the objects of vision which he can see, and which he will conceive to be in reality clearer than the things which are now being shown to him?

True, he said.

And suppose once more, that he is reluctantly dragged up a steep and rugged ascent, and held fast until he is forced into the presence of the sun himself, is he not likely to be pained and irritated? When he approaches the light his eyes will be dazzled, and he will not be able to see anything at all of what are now called realities.

Not all in a moment, he said.

He will require to grow accustomed to the sight of the upper world. And first he will see the shadows best, next the reflections of men and other objects in the water, and then the objects themselves; then he will gaze upon the light of the moon and the stars and the spangled heaven; and he will see the sky and the stars by night better than the sun or the light of the sun by day?

Certainly.

Last of all he will be able to see the sun, and not mere reflections of him in the water, but he will see him in his own proper place, and not in another; and he will contemplate him as he is.

Certainly.

He will then proceed to argue that this is he who gives the season and the years, and is the guardian of all that is in the visible world, and in a certain way the cause of all things which he and his fellows have been accustomed to behold?

Clearly, he said, he would first see the sun and then reason about him.

And when he remembered his old habitation, and the wisdom of the den and his fellow-prisoners, do you not suppose that he would felicitate himself on the change, and pity them?

Certainly, he would.

And if they were in the habit of conferring honours among themselves on those who were quickest to observe the passing shadows and to remark which of them went before, and which followed after, and which were together; and who were therefore best able to draw conclusions as to the future, do you think that he would care for such honours and glories, or envy the possessors of them? Would he not say with Homer,

'Better to be the poor servant of a poor master,'

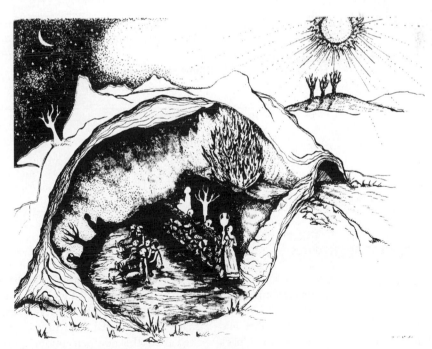

Drawing copyright © 1987 by Blocker. David Stewart and H. Gene Blocker, *Fundamentals of Philosophy* (4 ed.). Upper Saddle River, NJ: Prentice Hall, 1987, p.201.

and to endure anything, rather than think as they do and live after their manner?

Yes, he said, I think that he would rather suffer anything than entertain these false notions and live in this miserable manner.

Imagine once more, I said, such an one coming suddenly out of the sun to be replaced in his old situation; would he not be certain to have his eyes full of darkness?

To be sure, he said.

And if there were a contest, and he had to compete in measuring the shadows with the prisoners who had never moved out of the den, while his sight was still weak, and before his eyes had become steady (and the time which would be needed to acquire this new habit of sight might be very considerable) would he not be ridiculous? Men would say of him that up he went and down he came without his eyes; and that it was better not even to think of ascending; and if any one tried to loose another and lead him up to the light, let them only catch the offender, and they would put him to death.

No question, he said.

This entire allegory, I said, you may now append, dear Glaucon, to the previous argument; the prison-house is the world of sight, the light of the fire is the sun, and you will not misapprehend me if you interpret the journey upwards to be the ascent of the soul into the intellectual world according to my poor belief, which, at your desire, I have expressed—whether rightly or wrongly God knows. But, whether true or false, my opinion is that in the world of knowledge the idea of good appears last of all, and is seen only with an effort; and, when seen, is also inferred to be the universal author of all things beautiful and right, parent of light and of the lord of light in this visible world, and the immediate source of reason and truth in the intellectual; and that this is the power upon which he who would act rationally either in public or private life must have his eye fixed.

I agree, he said, as far as I am able to understand you.

## DISCUSSION QUESTIONS FOR CRITIQUE AND ANALYSIS

1. Plato distinguishes between ignorance and enlightenment using the "Allegory of the Cave." Do you find this allegorical treatment clarifying and persuasive or obscuring and questionable? Why?

2. In general, do you think allegorical arguments, arguments by analogy, or arguments based on metaphor and simile are effective? Or are they little more than dubious rhetorical devices, things that rational philosophers should be wary of? Discuss.

# PHILOSOPHERS IN ACTION

## Seeing Past Appearances

The Platonic notion that there exists an eternal and immutable reality behind the transitory and ever-changing world of appearances can be difficult to grasp. How can we penetrate apparent reality and break through to the other side? We have to go back to Plato for guidance on this, but we can still try to simulate the experience of what it must be like to envision a different and higher-order reality in an example of 3-D art. (See page 189.) Unfocus your eyes and hold the image about 12 inches from your face. Look and be patient. Sooner or later the three-dimensional image should reveal itself to you. If you become excited about this new perception, can you imagine what the philosophical illumination of ultimate goodness must be like! (Don't look now, but beneath the image you are told what is embedded in it.)

Lucasfilm Ltd. P.O. Box 2009, San Rafael, California 94912. © 1997 Lucasfilm Ltd. 3-D Art Created by Bohdan, 1996. (Can you see Yoda?)

# RATIONALISM: RENÉ DESCARTES

**Rationalism** is a term derived from the Latin *ratio*, meaning "reason." Variations of rationalism have emerged throughout the history of Western philosophy, but the movement itself has come to be most closely associated with thinkers such as **Baruch Spinoza** and **Gottfried Wilhelm Leibniz.** The most notable rationalist, however, is **René Descartes,** the seventeenth-century individual who is considered the father of modern philosophy. Given his historical importance and the influence he exerted on subsequent philosophical thinkers, we will focus on the work of Descartes as a way of gaining an introductory understanding of epistemological rationalism.

## Historical Context

René Descartes lived during a very exciting period in human history. Up until about the end of the sixteenth century, the medieval view of the world was dominant in Europe. It permeated many areas of life, including education. In fact, Descartes was immersed in this medieval worldview throughout his entire Jesuit schooling at the college in La Flèche (see Philosophical Profile). A number of questionable theological and philosophical beliefs had been perpetuated and justified on the basis of tradition and authority.[12] For instance, most ancient astronomers, *(continued on page 191)*

## PHILOSOPHICAL PROFILE

**RENÉ DESCARTES**

### René Descartes

René Descartes is one of the most significant figures of the Western rational tradition and is considered the father of modern philosophy. His work signaled the end of the medieval period, which was steeped in scholasticism—the movement that tried to integrate the natural wisdom of Greece, especially Aristotle with the supernatural elements of Christian revelation.

Descartes was born on March 31, 1596, in La Haye, Touraine, a former province of France. A devout Catholic throughout his life, he received his early instruction at the famous Jesuit College of La Flèche in Anjou from the intellectually formative ages of eight to eighteen.[11] He subsequently went on to study law at the University of Poitiers, graduating in 1616 but never actually practicing as a lawyer. With a sizable family fortune to support him and feeling somewhat restless, Descartes began a series of travels throughout Europe, joining different armies in the process in order that he might continue studying the "Book of the World." On November 10, 1619, he spent the day in deep philosophical reflection by a warm stove, shut in by the cold. That evening, as if in response to the profound thoughts of the day, he experienced three vivid dreams that provided him with a vision laying out his mission in life. Descartes had the revelation that he was to find the key to the mysteries of nature in a new philosophy based on mathematical reason. In gratitude for what he believed was divinely inspired direction, Descartes vowed to make a pilgrimage to the shrine of Our Lady of Loretto in Italy, which he later did.

For the next nine years after his visionary dreams, Descartes devoted himself to working out a method for unifying the sciences. He sold his inherited estates in France so that he could amass the financial resources necessary to live free from worries associated with having to earn a living. A life of leisure (often sleeping in until noon) enabled him to do his best intellectual work "without cares or passions to trouble me," as he said. Valuing his privacy and time, Descartes never made any social commitments that might interfere with his vow to advance knowledge in accordance with his divine calling. His only close emotional tie was with a daughter who was born out of wedlock and died at the age of five.[13]

At the age of 32, Descartes moved to Holland and lived there for 20 years, appreciating the intellectual and religious tolerance of the Dutch government. This tolerance offered Descartes peace of mind, for some of his writings were religiously threatening and, as a consequence, a danger to him personally.

In 1649, Descartes accepted an invitation, with some reluctance, to tutor Queen Christina of Sweden. Unfortunately, due to severe Swedish climate conditions and the rigorous early morning schedule imposed by the queen, he contracted pneumonia and died on February 11, 1650.

The best-known work by Descartes is *Discourse on Method and Meditations on the First Philosophy (in which the Existence of God and the Real Distinction between the Soul and the Body of Man are Demonstrated)*. Other notable works include *Principles of Philosophy, Passions of the Soul,* and *Rules for the Direction of the Mind.*

## PHILOSOPHICAL PROFILE

### Other Continental Rationalists

#### BARUCH (BENEDICT) SPINOZA

Baruch Spinoza was a Dutch rationalist philosopher born of Spanish-Portuguese-Jewish parentage in the city of Amsterdam on November 24, 1632. In his youth, he received a classical Jewish education but later became alienated from established Judaism, eventually being excommunicated and banished from his birthplace because of his unorthodox religious and philosophical views. Benedict is actually the Latin or Christian name equivalent of Baruch, which Spinoza adopted to express his independence from Jewish authorities. After being banished from Amsterdam, he became employed as an optical lens grinder, turning down a professorship at Heidelberg University, offered to him when his reputation as a thinker grew among prominent philosophers and scientists of the day.

**BARUCH (BENEDICT) SPINOZA**

Spinoza agreed with Galileo and Descartes that mathematics was the key to uncovering the structure of the universe, but unlike the latter, who wrote in essay style, Spinoza believed that philosophy should be conducted in an architectural manner, "starting with simple, foundational truths and from this foundation carefully building up the edifice of human knowledge, brick by brick, using the mortar of rigorous deductive logic." The architectural method is particularly evident in Spinoza's *Ethics*. Some other notable works by Spinoza include: *Principles of Cartesian Philosophy*, and *Short Treatise on God, Man and His Well-Being*. Spinoza died in 1677 after a long bout with tuberculosis aggravated by long-term exposure to glass dust.

#### GOTTFRIED WILHELM LEIBNIZ

Along with René Descartes and Benedict Spinoza, Leibniz is regarded as one of the three most significant continental rationalists. Born in Leipzig in 1646, he went on to study philosophy, mathematics, and jurisprudence, earning his doctorate in law at the age of 21. With respect to his highly technical thinking, Leibniz attempted to use the principles of theology and mathematics to work out his vision of a universal cosmic harmony in hopes of reconciling science and religion, mechanistic and teleological worldviews, as well as modern and ancient philosophy. Leibniz believed that the principles of logic and the methods of mathematics could provide the procedures for finding the truth about reality. Leibniz is credited with discovering infinitesimal calculus and the system of binary mathematics. Important works by Leibniz include: *New Essays in Human Thought, Monadology,* and *New System of Nature and the Interaction of Substances.* Leibniz died at the age of 70.

**GOTTFRIED WILHELM LEIBNIZ**

including Aristotle (a student of Plato), advanced a **geocentric view** of the universe, which was compatible with Christian church doctrine and divine revelation. In the geocentric view, the sun and planets revolve around the Earth. However, the sixteenth-century Polish astronomer **Mikolaj Kopernik** (1473–1543), Latinized as Nicholas Copernicus, presented a sun-centered, **heliocentric theory** that the Earth actually revolves on its own axis around the sun.[14] This "anti-religious" notion, contrary to the Biblical teachings of the church, gave rise to the so-called **Copernican Revolution** in human thought. Scientists who were supportive of Kopernik's heliocentric theory were excommunicated from the church; others were burned at the stake (Bruno, 1600; Vanini, 1620). In addition, Galileo—who, through the development of the telescope, observed the satellites of Jupiter, Saturn's rings, and the surface of the moon, and who supported the Copernican doctrine—was forced by the Inquisition to condemn it, to do penance, and to serve a life sentence of imprisonment at his home in Florence.

In spite of church opposition, modern science adopted the view that human reason had the power to know the truth of reality, a reality that was neither transcendent nor divine. For modern science, a philosophical worldview based on **medieval scholasticism** was no longer adequate. A new philosophy for the modern age was called for. Enter René Descartes.

The modern philosophical era begins with Descartes's revolutionary overthrow of all prior belief. Descartes breaks with the medieval world, including the authority of church-controlled scholastic philosophy. In such a philosophy, he finds no certainty. Of traditional philosophy he says, "It has been cultivated for many centuries by the most excellent minds and yet there is still no point in it which is not disputed and hence doubtful." On the subject of his own Jesuit education steeped in philosophical tradition, Descartes writes in his *Discourse on Method*:

> I was brought up from childhood on letters, and, because I had been led to believe that by this means one could acquire clear and positive knowledge of everything useful in life, I was extremely anxious to learn them. But, as soon as I had completed this whole course of study, at the end of which it is usual to be received into the ranks of the learned, I completely changed my opinion. For I was assailed by so many doubts and errors that the only profit I appeared to have drawn from trying to become educated, was progressively to have discovered my ignorance.

> *In our search for the direct road to truth, we should busy ourselves with no object about which we cannot attain a certitude equal to that of the demonstration of arithmetic and geometry.*
>
> DESCARTES

## The Quest for Certainty Using Methodological Doubt

Before Descartes, the methods of scholastic philosophy often involved comparing and contrasting the views of recognized authorities. However, weary of textbooks and learning procedures that merely rehashed the tired old ideas of Aristotle and the dogmas of scholasticism, and skeptical of their "truths," in view of the findings and developments of modern science, Descartes was determined to accept nothing as true until he himself, as an individual, had established solid grounds for believing it to be true. His iconoclastic, revolutionary overthrow of traditional belief was necessary if **certainty** was to be achieved and if he were to fulfill his visionary dream of establishing a universal science—one that would offer a unified set of principles from which he could deduce all answers to scientific questions. Descartes was very much impressed with Kopernik and Galileo, witnessing how the methods of mathematics could revolutionize the study of astronomy. For

Descartes, a mathematically precise method was the only reliable way to discover the truth about the universe.[15] Motivated by a new spirit of scientific inquiry, he adopted mathematical rigor in his reexamination of everything. In his *Rules for the Direction of the Mind,* Descartes spelled out two mental operations of mathematics by which true knowledge can be attained, namely **intuition** and **deduction.**[16] Self-evident principles are known intuitively and recognized as absolutely true by a faculty he calls the "Light of Nature." The rational mind cannot doubt them. To say that a straight line is the shortest distance between two points or that 7 + 5 = 12 is understood intuitively means that such statements are recognized by reason alone as necessary and certain.

As for deduction, Descartes means orderly, logical reasoning or inference making from solidly established, self-evident propositions, just as geometry is reasoned in strict order by a process of deduction from its self-evident axioms and postulates.[17] The idea behind establishing a proper method is to arrange all facts into a deductive logical structure. Descartes wanted to use intuition and deduction as building blocks to erect a system of philosophy as certain and imperishable as geometry.[18] His initial task, then, was to find a **self-evident principle** that could serve as the basis for his mathematical philosophy, for without it, no absolutely certain philosophy can be deduced.

## Method of Doubt

Ironically, the way Descartes set about to achieve certainty was to begin by doubting absolutely everything. Whatever would serve as the intuitively self-evident basis for the new Cartesian (from Descartes) **method of doubt** would have to meet certain conditions. The belief or principle or axiom would have to be impossible to doubt; its certainty would have to be ultimate and not dependent upon any other belief, and it would have to point to something actually existing if the existence of other things in the world were to be deduced from it.[19]

Practically speaking, it would be impossible for Descartes to doubt every single one of his inherited beliefs individually. For this reason, he examined them by groups or classes to see if he could discover one that was impossible to doubt—ultimately true and about something that certainly exists. Descartes chose to examine first those beliefs based on sense perceptions, concluding in the end that they were unreliable and therefore couldn't lead to certain knowledge. For example, things observed from far away look different up close. Straight sticks can look bent or broken when placed in a glass of water, and so on. Our sense perceptions may thus be subject to illusion. Furthermore, no matter how certain we are about our current sensory perceptions (for example, the fact that we're sitting in a chair or lying in a bed reading), it could also be that we are dreaming or having hallucinations. Dreams can seem so real sometimes that when awake we wonder if the events really occurred. How can I know with absolute certainty that whatever I see or hear or touch is not just part of some grand delusion or hallucinatory experience? I cannot, for I can always question what I experience. By this account, even the existence of the external world is cast into doubt, as I could be dreaming or imagining things.

> *"If a man will begin with certainties, he shall end in doubts. But if he will be content to begin with doubts, he shall end in certainties."*
>
> FRANCIS BACON

# PHILOSOPHERS IN ACTION

## When Science and Faith Conflict

The ideas of Kopernik and Galileo were considered by many of their time as anti-religious and a threat to religious authority. Martin Luther, leader of the Protestant Reformation, accused Kopernik of being a heretic in view of his heliocentric views, which allegedly contradicted the teachings of the Bible. To uphold faith in the Bible today, must we continue to believe that the sun revolves around the Earth? When faith and science conflict, must we always deny all empirical evidence contrary to belief? What happens, for example, in the context of sexual and biomedical ethics, if science discovers that homosexuality is genetically determined and not a matter of choice or conditioning? Many Christians point out that the Bible condemns homosexual acts as sinful. Is it sinful to express what could be your genetically determined nature? Could the Biblical view of homosexuality possibly be as misguided as the formerly accepted geocentric view of the universe? And what about findings in the field of paleontology? What must we think about dinosaur bones? Should we simply reject all evidence of them because they challenge one's cherished creationist belief system? What position should we take when science contradicts faith? What should be the basis for decision-making here? Discuss.

Martin Luther once described Copernicus as "that fool [who would] reverse the entire art of astronomy." Luther accepted the Ptolemaic conception of the universe which had the sun revolve around the earth—a conception that was consistent with Christian biblical belief. Copernicus's heliocentric perspective challenged the traditional Christian worldview. In this illustration taken from Martin Luther's Bible, we see God as the orderer of the Ptolemaic universe.

There might seem, at first glance, to be at least one sphere of knowledge whose principles and axioms are beyond skeptical doubt: namely, arithmetic and geometry. However, Descartes entertains the possibility—however improbable—that we have been deceived our entire lives by some evil genius or by some all-powerful malevolent being. We've been tricked all along, so to speak, to believe in *a priori* truths. Perhaps, he says, we have always been mistaken when we have added numbers together; and maybe we have always been wrong to conclude that a square is an enclosed figure containing four equal sides and four right angles. In raising such doubts, Descartes is not trying to be ridiculously difficult. His skepticism is designed to sweep away all uncertainty. If any belief can be doubted in the least, however remote the possibility that it is untrue, it must be rejected as quickly and as thoroughly as those beliefs that are patently and obviously false. Descartes is on the hunt for absolute certainty, not relative assurance. Let us now read Descartes in the original so that we might better appreciate his process of methodological doubt.

## ORIGINAL SOURCEWORK

## First Meditation Concerning Things that Can Be Doubted

### RENÉ DESCARTES

There is no novelty to me in the reflection that, from my earliest years, I have accepted many false opinions as true, and that what I have concluded from such badly assured premises could not but be highly doubtful and uncertain. From the time that I first recognized this fact, I have realized that if I wished to have any firm and constant knowledge in the sciences, I would have to undertake, once and for all, to set aside all the opinions which I had previously accepted among my beliefs and start again from the very beginning. . . .

I will therefore make a serious and unimpeded effort to destroy generally all my former opinions. In order to do this, however, it will not be necessary to show that they are all false, a task which I might never be able to complete; because, since reason already convinces me that I should abstain from the belief in things which are not entirely certain and indubitable no less carefully than from the belief in those which appear to me to be manifestly false, it will be enough to make me reject them all if I can find in each some ground for doubt. And for that it will not be necessary for me to examine each one in particular, which would be an infinite labor; but since the destruction of the foundation necessarily involves the collapse of all the rest of the edifice, I shall first attack the principles upon which all my former opinions were founded.

Everything which I have thus far accepted as entirely true (and assured) has been acquired from the senses or by means of the senses. But I have learned by experience that these senses sometimes mislead me, and it is prudent never to trust wholly those things which have once deceived us.

But it is possible that, even though the senses occasionally deceive us about things which are barely perceptible and very far away, there are many other things which we cannot reasonably doubt, even though we know them through the senses—as, for example, that I am here, seated by the fire, wearing a (winter) dressing gown, holding this paper in my hands, and other things of this nature. And how could I deny that these hands and this body are mine, unless I am to compare myself with certain lunatics whose brain is so troubled and befogged by the black vapors of the bile that they continually affirm that they are kings while they are paupers, that they are clothed in [gold and] purple while they are naked; or imagine (that their head is made of clay, or) that they are gourds, or that their body is glass? [But this is ridiculous;] such men are fools, and I would be no less insane than they if I followed their example.

Nevertheless, I must remember that I am a man, and that consequently I am accustomed to sleep and in my dreams to imagine the same things that lunatics imagine when awake, or sometimes things which are even less plausible. How many times has it occurred that (the quiet of) the night made me dream (of my usual habits:) that I was here, clothed (in a dressing gown), and sitting by the fire, although I was in fact lying undressed in bed! It seems apparent to me now, that I am not looking at this paper with my eyes closed, that this head that I shake is not drugged with sleep, that it is with design and deliberate intent that I stretch out this hand and perceive it. What happens in sleep seems not at all as clear and as distinct as all this. But I am speak-

*Discourse on Method and the Meditations,* René Descartes, translated by Lawrence J. Lafleur. © 1960. Reprinted by permission of Prentice Hall Inc., Upper Saddle River, NJ.

ing as though I never recall having been misled, while asleep, by similar illusions! When I consider these matters carefully, I realize so clearly that there are no conclusive indications by which waking life can be distinguished from sleep that I am quite astonished, and my bewilderment is such that it is almost able to convince me that I am sleeping.

So let us suppose now that we are asleep and that all these details, such as opening the eyes, shaking the head, extending the hands, and similar things, are merely illusions; and let us think that perhaps our hands and our whole body are not such as we see them. Nevertheless, . . . even if these types of things—namely, [a body,] eyes, head, hands, and other similar things—could be imaginary, nevertheless, we are bound to confess that there are some other still more simple and universal concepts which are true [and existent], from the mixture of which, neither more nor less than in the case of the mixture of real colors, all these images of things are formed in our minds, whether they are true [and real] or imaginary [and fantastic].

Of this class of entities is corporeal nature in general and its extension, including the shape of extended things, their quantity, or size and number, and also the place where they are, the time that measures their duration, and so forth. That is why we will perhaps not be reasoning badly if we conclude that physics, astronomy, medicine, and all the other sciences which follow from the consideration of composite entities are very dubious [and uncertain]; whereas arithmetic, geometry, and the other sciences of this nature, which treat only of very simple and general things without concerning themselves as to whether they occur in nature or not, contain some element of certainty and sureness. For whether I am awake or whether I am asleep, two and three together will always make the number five, and the square will never have more than four sides; and it does not seem possible that truths [(so clear and)] so apparent can ever be suspected of any falsity [or uncertainty].

Nevertheless, I have long held the belief that there is a God who can do anything, by whom I have been created and made what I am. But how can I be sure but that he has brought it to pass that there is no earth, no sky, no extended bodies, no shape, no size, no place, and that nevertheless I have the impressions of all these things [and cannot imagine that things might be other

than] as I now see them? And furthermore, just as I sometimes judge that others are mistaken about those things which they think they know best, how can I be sure but that [God has brought it about that] I am always mistaken when I add two and three or count the sides of a square, or when I judge of something else even easier, if I can imagine anything easier than that? . . .

I am at last constrained to admit that there is nothing in what I formerly believed to be true which I cannot somehow doubt, and this not for lack of thought and attention, but for weighty and well-considered reasons. Thus I find that, in the future, I should [withhold and suspend my judgment from these matters, and] guard myself no less carefully from believing them than I should from believing what is manifestly false if I wish to find any certain and assured knowledge [in the sciences].

I will therefore suppose that, not [a true] God, (who is very good and) who is the supreme source of truth, but a certain evil spirit, not less clever and deceitful than powerful, has bent all his efforts to deceiving me. I will suppose that the sky, the air, the earth, colors, shapes, sounds, and all other objective things [that we see] are nothing but illusions and dreams that he has used to trick my credulity. I will consider myself as having no hands, no eyes, no flesh, no blood, nor any senses, yet falsely believing that I have all these things. I will remain resolutely attached to this hypothesis; and if I cannot attain the knowledge of any truth by this method, at any rate [it is in my power to suspend my judgment. That is why] I shall take great care not to accept any falsity among my beliefs and shall prepare my mind so well for all the ruses of this great deceiver that, however powerful and artful he may be, he will never be able to mislead me in anything.

## DISCUSSION QUESTIONS FOR CRITIQUE AND ANALYSIS

1. In what does Descartes place most confidence, reason or experience? Why? Do you agree with his reasoning? Why or why not?

2. How did Descartes determine that the senses are deceiving? Was it the "*Cogito*" ("I Think") that established the deception, or just another sense experience that was different? Isn't Descartes's conclusion that the senses are deceiving really based on experience in the end?

## Cogito Ergo Sum—I Think, Therefore I Am

Doubting absolutely everything that he ever learned or took for granted before, Descartes appears to have placed himself in an epistemological bind as far as his quest for certainty is concerned. In some ways, he seems worse off now than before he began with his methodological doubt. However, in the darkness of skeptical obscurity, he finds rational illumination. Descartes discovers the intuitively self-evident truth upon which he can base subsequent epistemological deductions in line with his vision of a natural philosophy containing the precision of mathematics. Even if he is deceived in his experience by dreams, by hallucinations, and sensory illusions, or even by an all-powerful but evil being, the one thing that cannot be denied is that there is an "I" or "ego" that is being deceived. It is this same "I" that doubts and has doubted the existence of everything. Thus, even if we are confused about what we are, where we are, or the nature of reality that surrounds us, the one thing we cannot deny is that we are a thinking thing—a thing that doubts, understands, conceives, wills, rejects, imagines, and perceives. From the fact that "I think," one can conclude with certainty that "I exist." In the *Discourse on Method*, Descartes captures this insight with the Latin phrase *Cogito, ergo sum* (I think, therefore I am). Let us turn now to Descartes's "Second Meditation" to see more clearly how he arrives at the truth of the "*Cogito.*"

> **"*I am, I exist, is necessarily true each time that I pronounce it, or that I mentally conceive it.* "**
>
> DESCARTES, "SECOND MEDITATION"

## ORIGINAL SOURCEWORK

*Second Meditation of the Nature of the Human Mind, and That It Is More Easily Known than the Body*

### RENÉ DESCARTES

Yesterday's Meditation has filled my mind with so many doubts that it is no longer in my power to forget them. Nor do I yet see how I will be able to resolve them; I feel as though I were suddenly thrown into deep water, being so disconcerted that I can neither plant my feet on the bottom nor swim on the surface. I shall nevertheless make every effort to conform precisely to the plan commenced yesterday and put aside every belief in which I could imagine the least doubt, just as though I knew that it was absolutely false. And I shall continue in this manner until I have found something certain, or at least, if I can do nothing else, until I have learned with certainty that there is nothing certain in this world. Archimedes,

to move the earth from its orbit and place it in a new position, demanded nothing more than a fixed and immovable fulcrum; in a similar manner I shall have the right to entertain high hopes if I am fortunate enough to find a single truth which is certain and indubitable.

I suppose, accordingly, that everything that I see is false; I convince myself that nothing has ever existed of all that my deceitful memory recalls to me. I think that I have no senses; and I believe that body, shape, extension, motion, and location are merely inventions of my mind. What then could still be thought true? Perhaps nothing else, unless it is that there is nothing certain in the world.

---

*Discourse on Method and the Meditations,* René Descartes, translated by Lawrence J. Lafleur. © 1960. Reprinted by permission of Prentice Hall Inc., Upper Saddle River, NJ.

But how do I know that there is not some entity, of a different nature from what I have just judged uncertain, of which there cannot be the least doubt? Is there not some God or some other power who gives me these thoughts? But I need not think this to be true, for possibly I am able to produce them myself. Then, at the very least, am I not an entity myself? But I have already denied that I had any senses or any body. However, at this point I hesitate, for what follows from that? Am I so dependent upon the body and the senses that I could not exist without them? I have just convinced myself that nothing whatsoever existed in the world, that there was no sky, no earth, no minds, and no bodies; have I not thereby convinced myself that I did not exist? Not at all; without doubt I existed if I was convinced [or even if I thought anything]. Even though there may be a deceiver of some sort, very powerful and very tricky, who bends all his efforts to keep me perpetually deceived, there can be no slightest doubt that I exist, since he deceives me; and let him deceive me as much as he will, he can never make me be nothing as long as I think that I am something. Thus, after having thought well on this matter, and after examining all things with care, I must finally conclude and maintain that this proposition: *I am, I exist*, is necessarily true every time that I pronounce it or conceive it in my mind.

But I do not yet know sufficiently clearly what I am, I who am sure that I exist. So I must henceforth take very great care that I do not incautiously mistake some other thing for myself, and so make an error even in that knowledge which I maintain to be more certain and more evident than all other knowledge [that I previously had]. That is why I shall now consider once more what I thought myself to be before I began these last deliberations. Of my former opinions I shall reject all that are rendered even slightly doubtful by the arguments that I have just now offered, so that there will remain just that part alone which is entirely certain and indubitable.

What then have I previously believed myself to be? Clearly, I believed that I was a man. But what is a man? . . .

I shall rather pause here to consider the ideas which previously arose naturally and of themselves in my mind whenever I considered what I was. I thought of myself first as having a face, hands, arms, and all this mechanism composed of (bone and flesh and members), just as it appears in a corpse, and which I designated by the name

of "body." In addition, I thought of the fact that I consumed nourishment, that I walked, that I perceived and thought, and I ascribed all these actions to the soul. . . .

But I, what am I, on the basis of the present hypothesis that there is a certain spirit who is extremely powerful and, if I may dare to say so, malicious [and tricky], and who uses all his abilities and efforts in order to deceive me? Can I be sure that I possess the smallest fraction of all those characteristics which I have just now said belonged to the nature of body? I pause to consider this attentively. I pass and repass in review in my mind each one of all these things—it is not necessary to pause to take the time to list them—and I do not find any one of them which I can pronounce to be part of me. Is it characteristic of me to consume nourishment and to walk? But if it is true that I do not have a body, these also are nothing but figments of the imagination. To perceive? But once more, I cannot perceive without the body, except in the sense that I have thought I perceived various things during sleep, which I recognized upon waking not to have been really perceived. To think? Here I find the answer. Thought is an attribute that belongs to me; it alone is inseparable from my nature.

I am, I exist—that is certain; but for how long do I exist? For as long as I think; for it might perhaps happen, if I totally ceased thinking, that I would at the same time completely cease to be. I am now admitting nothing except what is necessarily true. I am therefore, to speak precisely, only a thinking being, that is to say, a mind, an understanding, or a reasoning being, which are terms whose meaning was previously unknown to me.

I am something real and really existing, but what thing am I? I have already given the answer: a thing which thinks. . . . A thinking being. What is a thinking being? It is a being which doubts, which understands, [which conceives,] which affirms, which denies, which wills, which rejects, which imagines also, and which perceives. It is certainly not a trivial matter if all these things belong to my nature. But why should they not belong to it? Am I not that same person who now doubts almost everything, who nevertheless understands [and conceives] certain things, who [is sure of and ] affirms the truth of this one thing alone, who denies all the others, who wills and desires to know more about them, who rejects error, who imagines many things, sometimes even against my will, and who also perceives many things, as through the medium of (the senses [or) the organs of the body]? Is there anything in all that which is not just as true as it is certain that I am and that I exist, even though I were always asleep and though the one who created me directed all his efforts to deluding me? And is there any one of these attributes which can be distinguished from my thinking or which can be said to be separable from my nature? For it is so obvious that it is I who doubt, understand, and desire, that nothing could be added to make it more evident. And I am also certainly the same one who imagines; for once more, even though it could happen that the things I imagine are not true, nevertheless this power of imagining cannot fail to be real, and it is part of my thinking. Finally I am the same being which perceives—that is, which observes certain objects as though by means of the sense organs, because I do really see light, hear noises, feel heat. Will it be said that these appearances are false and that I am sleeping? [Let it be so; yet at the very least] it is certain that it seems to me that I see light, hear noises, and feel heat. This much cannot be false, and it is this, properly considered, which in my nature is called perceiving, and that, again speaking precisely, is nothing else but thinking.

## DISCUSSION QUESTIONS FOR CRITIQUE AND ANALYSIS

1. How is Descartes's mind-body dualism established in the Second Meditation?

2. What role does the all-powerful but deceiving malevolent being play in Descartes's Meditation?

---

We see then, that the *Cogito* represents for Descartes the axiomatic and indubitable truth he needs and uses as the foundation for his new system of philosophy. It actually serves as a model for knowledge, providing the litmus test of "clear and distinct" ideas. Anything else that is as clear and distinct as his own existence as a thinking being would also have to be certain. Ah, but there's the rub! You see, in one respect the *Cogito* is empty. All we can know about is the existence of the thinking "I"; we do not know if there exists anything else in reality to think about. Remember, Descartes has already called into question the existence of the external world because perception of it is based on doubtful sensory experience. In fact, Descartes is not even sure that he himself does not pass in and out of existence, depending on whether he is thinking or not. Maybe he exists only while he thinks.

Using the **"clear and distinct" criterion** of truth, Descartes goes on in his meditations to establish beyond doubt that a God exists who would not deceive him. One of several arguments for the existence of God goes like this: (a) something cannot be derived from nothing—all effects (e.g., including ideas) are caused by something; (b) there is as much reality in the cause as there is in the effect; (c) the idea I have of God as a perfect and infinite being was caused by something; (d) since I am finite and imperfect, I could not be the cause of this idea; and (e) therefore God, understood as an infinite and perfect being, exists.[20] Descartes finds, then, within the certainty of the *Cogito* grounds for certainty in the belief that God does in fact exist. One can see clearly and distinctly that God must exist as a logical prerequisite for having the idea. In God's certain existence and infinite perfection, Descartes also finds certainty in the existence of the external world. A perfect God would not use deception and trick Descartes into believing that an outer reality exists when it does not. What does this mean? It means that not only does the *Cogito* exist, but so too does God and the physical material world. The existence of all three has been deduced by reason. Commenting on Descartes's rational procedures, one writer sums it up in the following fashion: "Descartes' doubting methodology is like the axiomatic method in logic and mathematics, in which a theorem whose truth initially seems likely but not *totally* certain [for example, the physical world exists] is demonstrated to be certain by deriving it from basic axioms by means of rules of inference. Descartes' 'axiom' is, in effect, 'I think, therefore I am,' and his 'rule of inference' is clear and distinct perception."[21]

On the subject of method, you should recall at this juncture that Descartes never appealed to the senses to discover the indubitable first truth on which to base his philosophy. His epistemological approach was purely rational and deductive. To demonstrate why reason, not sensory observation, is to be used as the method in the quest for certain knowledge, Descartes uses "the wax example." Descartes is willing to use information provided by the senses in order to understand the world, but only if we are able to judge this sensory-based information by the standards of rational insight.[22] This point emphasizes Descartes's contention that objects "are not known insofar as they are seen or touched, but only insofar as they are understood by thinking." It is by means of reason, not the senses, that we achieve genuine knowledge.

As you read "The Wax Example" below, note that it comes at a point in Descartes's meditations when he has not yet proved that anything else beyond himself exists. He uses the example as a kind of thought experiment, asking how and what we could possibly know about the wax if indeed it did exist. Of course, as you might expect by now, Descartes, the rationalist, concludes that it is only through use of the intellect that one can discover the true nature of material objects. If knowledge were derived from, or based exclusively on, the senses, then changes in the appearance of a ball of wax would force us to conclude that it was no longer the same ball that we started with—something clearly false. Reason enables us to understand the enduring real properties of the wax, which maintain its identity regardless of superficial changes to its sensory-based qualities and appearances. For Descartes, reason, not experience, is the ultimate source of knowledge about the world. The "I Think" must therefore be the foundation for his new mathematically precise system of philosophy.

## ORIGINAL SOURCEWORK

## *The Wax Example*

### RENÉ DESCARTES

Let us now consider the commonest things, which are commonly believed to be the most distinctly known and the easiest of all to know, namely, the bodies which we touch and see. I do not intend to speak of bodies in general, for general notions are usually somewhat more confused; let us rather consider one body in particular. Let us take, for example, this bit of wax which has just been taken from the hive. It has not yet completely lost the sweetness of the honey it contained; it still retains something of the odor of the flowers from which it was collected; its color, shape, and size are apparent; it is hard and cold; it can easily be touched; and, if you knock on it,

*Discourse on Method and the Meditations,* René Descartes, translated by Lawrence J. Lafleur. © 1960. Reprinted by permission of Prentice Hall Inc., Upper Saddle River, NJ.

it will give out some sound. Thus everything which can make a body distinctly known are found in this example.

But now while I am talking I bring it close to the fire. What remains of the taste evaporates; the odor vanishes; its color changes; its shape is lost; its size increases; it becomes liquid; it grows hot; one can hardly touch it; and although it is knocked upon, it will give out no sound. Does the same wax remain after this change? We must admit that it does; no one denies it, no one judges otherwise. What is it then in this bit of wax that we recognize with so much distinctness? Certainly it cannot be anything that I observed by means of the senses, since everything in the field of taste, smell, sight, touch, and hearing are changed, and since the same wax nevertheless remains.

The truth of the matter perhaps, as I now suspect, is that this wax was neither that sweetness of honey, nor that pleasant odor of flowers, nor that whiteness, nor that shape, nor that sound, but only a body which a little while ago appeared to my senses under these forms and which now makes itself felt under others. But what is it, to speak precisely, that I imagine when I conceive it in this fashion? Let us consider it attentively and, rejecting everything that does not belong to the wax, see what remains. Certainly nothing is left but something extended, flexible, and movable. But what is meant by flexible and movable? Does it consist in my picturing that this wax, being round, is capable of becoming square and of passing from the square into a triangular shape? Certainly not; it is not that, since I conceive it capable of undergoing an infinity of similar changes, and I could not compass this infinity in my imagination. Consequently this conception that I have of the wax is not achieved by the faculty of imagination.

Now what is this extension? Is it not also unknown? For it becomes greater in the melting wax, still greater when it is completely melted, and much greater again when the heat increases still more. And I would not conceive clearly and truthfully what wax was if I did not think that even this bit of wax is capable of receiving more variations in extension than I have ever imagined. We must therefore agree that I cannot even conceive what this bit of wax is by means of the imagination, and that there is nothing but my understanding alone which does conceive it. I say this bit of wax in particular, for as to wax in general, it is still more evident. But what is this bit of wax which cannot be comprehended except by the understanding, or by the mind? Certainly it is the

same as the one that I see, that I touch, that I imagine; and finally it is the same as I always believed it to be from the beginning. But what is here important to notice is that perception, or the action by which we perceive, is not a vision, a touch, nor an imagination, and has never been that, even though it formerly appeared so; but is solely an inspection by the mind, which can be imperfect and confused as it was formerly, or clear and distinct as it is at present, as I attend more or less to the things which are in it and of which it is composed.

Now I am truly astonished when I consider how weak my mind is and how apt I am to fall into error. For even though I consider all this in my mind without speaking, still words impede me, and I am nearly deceived by the terms of ordinary language. For we say that we see the same wax if it is present, and not that we judge that it is the same from the fact that it has the same color or shape. Thus I might be tempted to conclude that one knows the wax by means of eyesight, and not uniquely by the perception of the mind. So I may by chance look out of a window and notice some men passing in the street, at the sight of whom I do not fail to say that I see men, just as I say that I see wax; and nevertheless what do I see from this window except hats and cloaks which might cover ghosts, or automata which move only by springs? But I judge that they are men, and thus I comprehend, solely by the faculty of judgment which resides in my mind, that which I believed I saw with my eyes.

A person who attempts to improve his understanding beyond the ordinary ought to be ashamed to go out of his way to criticize the forms of speech used by ordinary men. I prefer to pass over this matter and to consider whether I understood that wax was more evidently and more perfectly when I first noticed it and when I thought I knew it by means of the external senses, or at the very least by common sense, as it is called, or the imaginative faculty; or whether I conceive it better at present, after more carefully examined what it is and how it can be known. Certainly it would be ridiculous to doubt the superiority of the latter method of knowing. For what was there in that first perception which was distinct and evident? What was there which might not occur similarly to the senses of the lowest of the animals? But when I distinguished the real wax from its superficial appearances, and when, just as though I had removed its garments, I consider it all naked, it is certain that although there might still be some error in my judgment, I could not conceive it in this fashion without a human mind.

And now what shall I say of the mind, that is to say, of myself? For so far I do not admit in myself anything other than the mind. Can it be that I, who seem to perceive this bit of wax so clearly and distinctly, do not know my own self, not only with much more truth and certainty, but also much more distinctly and evidently? For if I judge that the wax exists because I see it, certainly it follows much more evidently that I exist myself because I see it. For it might happen that what I see is not really wax; it might also happen that I do not even possess eyes to see anything; but it could not happen that, when I see, or what amounts to the same thing, when I think I see, I who think am not something. For a similar reason, if I judge that the wax exists because I touch it, the same conclusion follows once more, namely, that I am. And if I hold to this judgement because my imagination, or whatever other entity it might be, persuades me of it, I will still reach the same conclusion. And what I have said here about the wax can be applied to all other things which are external to me.

Furthermore, if the idea or knowledge of the wax seems clearer and more distinct to me after I have investigated it, not only by sight or touch, but also in many other ways, with how much more evidence, distinctness and clarity must it be admitted that I now know myself; since all the reasons which help me to know and conceive the nature of the wax, or of any other body whatsoever,

serve much better to show the nature of my mind! And we also find so many other things in the mind itself which can contribute to the clarification of its nature, that those which depend on the body, such as the ones I have just mentioned, hardly deserve to be taken into account.

And at last here I am, having insensibly returned to where I wished to be; for since it is at present manifest to me that even bodies are not properly known by the senses nor by the faculty of imagination, but by the understanding alone; and since they are not known in so far as they are seen or touched, but only in so far as they are understood by thinking, I see clearly that there is nothing easier for me to understand than my mind. But since it is almost impossible to rid oneself so soon of an opinion of long standing, it would be wise to stop a while at this point, in order that, by the length of my meditation, I may impress this new knowledge more deeply upon my memory.

## DISCUSSION QUESTIONS FOR CRITIQUE AND ANALYSIS

1. Do you think Descartes is on the right track when he tries to model philosophy after mathematics? Explain.

2. In the "Wax Example," Descartes concludes that bodies are not properly known by the senses but by the understanding alone. Is his argument in favor of this conclusion sound? Why or why not?

 # THINKING CAN BE DANGEROUS

It started out innocently enough. I began to think at parties now and then to loosen up. Inevitably though, one thought led to another, and soon I was more than just a social thinker. I began to think alone—"to relax," I told myself; but I knew it wasn't true. Thinking became more and more important to me, and finally, I was thinking all the time. I began to think on the job. I knew that thinking and employment don't mix, but I couldn't stop myself. I began to avoid friends at lunchtime so I could read Thoreau and Kafka. I would return to the office dizzied

and confused, asking, "What is it exactly we are doing here?" Things weren't going so great at home either. One evening I had turned off the TV and asked my wife about the meaning of life. She spend that night at her mother's. I soon had a reputation as a heavy thinker.

One day the boss called me in. He said, "Skippy, I like you, and it hurts me to say this, but your thinking has become a real problem. If you don't stop thinking on the job, you'll have to find another job." This gave me a lot to think about. I came home early after my conversation with the boss. "Honey," I confessed, "I've been thinking . . ."

"I know you've been thinking," she said, lower lip aquiver. "You think as much as college professors, and college professors don't make any money, so if you keep on thinking we won't have any money!"

"That's a faulty syllogism," I said impatiently, and she began to cry.

I had enough. "I'm going to the library," I snarled as I stomped out the door. I headed for the library, in the mood for some Nietzsche, with a PBS station on the radio. I roared into the parking lot and ran up to the big glass doors . . . they didn't open. The library was closed! To this

day, I believe that a Higher Power was looking out for me that night. As I sank to the ground clawing at the unfeeling glass, whimpering for Zarathustra, a poster caught my eye. "Friend, is heavy thinking ruining your life?" it asked. You probably recognize that line. It comes from the standard Thinker's Anonymous poster. Which is why I am what I am today: a recovering thinker. I never miss a TA meeting. At each meeting we watch a non-educational video; last week it was "Caddyshack." Then we share experiences about how we avoided thinking since the last meeting. I still have my job, and things are a lot better at home. Life just seemed . . . easier, somehow, as soon as I stopped thinking. Now that makes you think, doesn't it?

---

# BRITISH EMPIRICISM: LOCKE, BERKELEY, AND HUME

To help us understand **empiricism** and how it departs from rationalism as an approach to the study of knowledge, we will begin first by examining the etymological roots of the term itself. We will then look at the historical situation out of which the movement emerged; and finally, we will consider in brief outline the ideas of three of its major proponents: **John Locke, Bishop George Berkeley** and **David Hume.**

To begin with, empiricism is a technical philosophical term which has Greek roots. It comes from *empeiria*, meaning "experience," and from *empeirikos*, meaning "experiment" or "trial." Generally speaking, empiricists believe that knowledge is based on ideas that ultimately have as their source sense data or sensory experience. Those who would describe themselves as empirical researchers (for example, behavioral psychologists) base their conclusions on direct observations and on experimental trials.[23] Pure rational contemplation—the sort that might be done alone in a comfortable wing-back armchair—is not the preferred method of the empiricist. Of course, the empiricists are not totally unconcerned with, or oblivious to, the uses and advantages of deductive reason, just as rationalists appreciate the importance of sensory data to their own analyses. Though rationalism and empiricism are in some ways philosophically opposed to one another, "it does not follow that the rationalist is so committed to the deductive method that he discounts sense experience entirely, or that the empiricist is so committed to sense experience that he rejects the deductive method entirely. The difference between them is rather a question of emphasis: the more the sense aspect is stressed to the exclusion of the deductive, the more empirical the position is; the more the deductive aspect is stressed to the exclusion of sense, the more rationalist the position is. The position taken, therefore, is considered extreme or moderate depending on the degree of emphasis."[24] As we proceed in this outline of British empiricists, you can be the judge yourself as to how moderate or extreme each one is.

> *"What can give us more sure knowledge than our senses? How else can we distinguish between the true and the false?"*
>
> LUCRETIUS

Empiricism gained a strong foot-hold in the scientific and philosophical communities during the twentieth century. A group of thinkers advanced the philosophy of **logical positivism**—a radical empiricist position that maintains that statements have meaning only if they are analytically true—true by definition or verifiable at least in principle by experience. Because things like the existence of God, free will, or the human self cannot be empirically verified, and because they arguably lack the self-evidence of mathematical propositions, statements about them become, for logical positivists, meaningless and therefore not proper subjects of discussion for a greatly diminished field of philosophical activity.[25] For our purposes here, we will not conduct a further examination of logical positivism, but rather we will go back to explore its historical roots in classical British empiricism.

## Historical Background of Empiricism

Historians have described the years between 1650 and 1770 as the **"Age of Enlightenment,"** and it is during this period that the British empiricists lived and worked. Within this time frame, **Newtonian science** became firmly ensconced as the explanatory model of the physical universe. In his *Mathematical Principles of Natural Philosophy*, Newton was able to synthesize scattered bits of existing knowledge in astronomy and physics under a few simple principles.[26] For example, using the law of gravity, he could explain the motions of the planets and the Earth, as well as their satellites. He was also able to explain the moon's tidal effects and physical events like why apples fall from trees. In Newton's deterministic universe, the world is like a machine whose workings can be explained by mechanical laws of motion. The physical world operates in completely deterministic terms of cause-and-effect relationships.

Impressed by Newtonian physics and filled with optimistic self-confidence stemming from the rapid growth and vitality of the new emerging sciences, philosophers of the day looked to the methods of science in hopes that they could provide a better and more solid understanding of how we know. For the empiricists, if philosophy wished to describe the world, then it would have to base its descriptions on actual observations of the world itself, rather than simply on our ideas and unconfirmed thoughts about it.

It is interesting to note that both rationalists and empiricists claimed Newton for their own side.[27] From the rationalist's vantage point, what Newton did was construct a deductive system of mathematical reasoning from basic concepts like mass, energy, and the laws of motion. He used them to deduce an explanation of the entire physical universe. Of course, those in the empiricist's camp saw the situation quite differently. For them, what Newton did was begin with observations of facts and with the data of sensory experience aided by new scientific instruments. On the basis of his factual data derived from experience, he was able to construct a logical system out of the laws he discovered.[28] Was Newton a rationalist, empiricist, or something in between? For now, we'll leave the philosophical jury out to debate the issue as we move on to our first empiricist, John Locke. As we go through each of the British empiricists in

## PHILOSOPHICAL PROFILE

### John Locke

John Locke is one of a famous trio of philosophers that has come to be dubbed "The British Empiricists." An Englishman, he was born on August 28, 1632, in Wrington, Somerset, into a Puritan home emphasizing the virtues of temperance, simplicity, and aversion to display.[29] Locke received home instruction until 1646, at which time he entered Westminster School to study the classics, Hebrew, and Arabic. Once finished at Westminster, Locke went on to Oxford, earning his bachelor's and master's degrees. He eventually studied medicine but never did establish a general practice as a physician, even though in 1674 he did receive his medical degree. However, he did serve as a medical and political adviser to Lord Ashley, later to become the Earl of Shaftesbury. After accepting Locke's recommendation to drain an abscess on his liver, the Earl credited Locke with saving his life.[30] Through his affiliation with Ashley, Locke became involved in the civil service, met many significant politicians and scientists, and traveled to Holland and France. Locke's political interests are evidenced by the fact that he helped to draft a constitution for the American Carolinas in 1669.

**JOHN LOCKE**

Like Descartes, John Locke was critical of scholastic philosophy, and like him, he wanted to separate real knowledge from mere opinion. Locke was certainly familiar with the works of Descartes and very much influenced by him, though in the end, he had some significant epistemological disagreements with the Frenchman, taking an empirical, not rationalistic approach to the study of knowledge.

Today, John Locke is especially remembered not only for his epistemology but also for his political theorizing, which centered on the forming of a social contract and which attacked the notion of the divine right of kings and the nature of the state as conceived by the English philosopher Thomas Hobbes. Major works by Locke include *Two Treatises of Government* (1689), *An Essay Concerning Human Understanding* (1690), and *The Reasonableness of Christianity (1695)*. John Locke died in Oates, England, on October 28, 1704.

---

turn, you should begin to better appreciate the tension between reason and experience and the relative importance assigned to each.

## John Locke

John Locke is usually considered the founder of British empiricism. He was the first to launch a major attack against the continental rationalists. Specifically, he set out to remove the "metaphysical rubbish" from philosophical inquiry so that he might achieve his purpose, which was "to inquire into the original certainty and extent of human knowledge."[31] Like other philosophers before him (Plato,

> **"It is ambition enough to be employed as an under-laborer in clearing the ground a little and removing some of the rubbish that lies in the way of knowledge."**
>
> JOHN LOCKE

Descartes), Locke wanted to separate knowledge from mere opinion. Rather than examine knowledge claims directly, what he did instead was to probe into the source of the ideas we use in making them. Locke observed that scientists and metaphysicians alike made a practice of using words like space, time, cause, substance, self, and other descriptive terms such as hard, round, and white. If knowledge claims containing such terms and descriptors were to make any sense at all, they must all correspond to ideas located in the mind.[32] The first order of business, then, was *not* to investigate the "essence" of things—the nature of reality or other-worldly entities (a preoccupation with metaphysicians)—but to examine the source of our ideas of those things about which we make knowledge claims.

## Tabula Rasa

In answer to his own question as to the source of our ideas, Locke advances an essentially psychological thesis. He claims that when children are born into the world, their minds are like a blank slate or blank writing tablet—a **tabula rasa,** to use the Latin expression. There is nothing on that slate that is not put there by experience. At birth, we are ignorant of everything. Locke writes:

> Let us then suppose the mind to be as we say, white paper, void of all characters, without any ideas: How comes it to be furnished? Whence comes it by that vast store which the busy and boundless fancy of man has painted on it with an almost endless variety? Whence has it all the *materials* of reason and knowledge? To this I answer, in one word, from *experience*. In that all our knowledge is founded; and from that it ultimately derives itself.[33]

For Locke, there are actually two forms of experience. The one form is called **sensation,** and it is the type that provides ideas of the external world. The ideas we have of yellow, white, hot, cold, soft, hard, bitter, and sweet come from external objects and are conveyed to the mind. The second type of experience is called **reflection,** and it comes from "the perceptions of the operations of our own mind within us, as it is employed about the ideas it has got. . . ."[34] Included under reflection are perception, thinking, doubting, memory, imagination, believing, reasoning, knowing, and willing—all different acts of the mind. From such processes of mind, we receive distinct ideas as we do from bodies affecting our senses. This source of ideas is like an "internal sense"—the ideas it provides "being such only as the mind gets by reflecting on its own operations within itself."[35] When Locke says, then, that all knowledge is derived from experience, he is referring either to direct sensory experience or the result of the mind combing or reflecting on those experiences. The ideas we get through experience serve as the materials that are used by our mental faculties. To remember, we call up an idea; when we communicate, our intended meanings are conveyed by ideas; when we judge or discriminate, we compare ideas. Given its emphasis, Locke's philosophy is quite appropriately called "*the way of ideas.*"[36]

The ideas that furnish the mind may be either *simple* or *complex*. **Simple ideas** come from simple sensations like hard, cold, or sweet. **Complex ideas** like giraffe or navy can be broken down and analyzed into simple ones. Though imaginary ideas like unicorn or satyr may not at first glance seem to come from experience, upon further reflection it becomes clear that they are composed of simple ones originating in our experience, either in sensation or reflection. Add horn and wings to horse to produce the idea of unicorn; or combine the ideas of half, animal, and human to come up with the idea of satyr. Of course, ideas like horn, wings, animal, and human can all themselves be broken down further until we arrive at simple ideas.

## Criticisms of Innate Ideas

The notion of the mind as a *tabula rasa* is derivative of Locke's rejection of innate ideas and contains important epistemological implications that separate Locke the empiricist from rationalists like Descartes who came before. Though this point was not explicitly made in any great detail in the preceding section of this chapter, implicit in what was said is the fact that Descartes did abide by the notion of **innate ideas.** For him, all clear and distinct ideas are inborn. They are implanted in the mind by nature—a euphemism for God. Even the idea of God itself is innate. Remember, in order for an imperfect (human) being to have the idea of a perfect being (God), the perfect being must exist and must be the cause of that idea implanted in the imperfect being's mind. Imperfect humans cannot themselves generate ideas of perfection. They are placed there by an omniscient and omnipotent God. And just as the idea of God is innate, so too are the self-evident propositions of logic and mathematics and the clear and distinct ideas we have about things like "cause" and "substance." An infinite and perfect Cartesian God would never deceive us into believing a world exists when it doesn't, that things exist when they don't, or that $2 + 2 = 4$ when the sum is really 5.

In Chapter One (Book 1) of *An Essay Concerning Human Understanding*, Locke spells out his objections to the notion of innate ideas. He does not address Descartes directly, but writes of "men of innate principles" whose opinions he wishes to criticize.[37] His initial task is to prepare the empiricist foundations of knowledge by disposing of the theory of innate ideas. According to Locke, defenders of the thesis of innate ideas believe it holds true as evidenced by universal consent. They argue that there are universally agreed upon principles (both practical and speculative) to which all would agree. In response, Locke argues that even if it were true that all people could agree on certain truths, this in itself would still not prove their innateness. Rather than being inborn, the universal agreement surrounding "innate truths" could be demonstrated to result in different ways. This demonstration is not necessary, however, since there are no principles to which humankind gives its universal consent in the first place. He takes two of what could be considered widely accepted examples of so-called innate principles to illustrate his point. The first is, "Whatsoever is, is" and "It is impossible for the same thing to be and not to be." Locke quickly points out that young children and idiots are unable to understand these principles and therefore cannot give their assent to them. According to him, this observation alone is enough to destroy the universal consent notion of innate ideas. Even if we said that infants come to see innate ideas clearly and distinctly once older and sufficiently educated, this implies learning and hence, experience—Locke's point.

In further clarification of the *tabula rasa* concept, we can say that the mind, prior to experience, is blank. Experience is the ultimate source of all ideas in the mind and therefore the foundation of all thinking and knowledge.

## Primary and Secondary Qualities of Objects

If Locke's *tabula rasa* notion is correct, then, as suggested already, children start life with no innate knowledge and no knowledge of the material world. They enter a world of myriad sensations, one of virtually infinite sights and sounds, textures, tastes, and smells. Locke claims that from our simple sensations, we form simple ideas; whereas by using our capacity for reflecting on them, we combine our simple ideas into complex ones. Either way, all of our ideas ultimately have their origin in experience.

Now, the interesting epistemological question arises as to whether our ideas about the world actually correspond to it. Unlike Descartes, Locke does not use God to guarantee its existence and the connection between perception of clear and distinct ideas and reality. What Locke does do, however, is borrow a useful distinction made by Descartes in his "melting wax" example.[38] Recall that, for Descartes, even though every sensation produced by the wax changed during the time it was melted by the heat, we still were able to understand that it was the same piece of wax. While the color, scent, and solidity of the wax had been transformed, its essential characteristics remained the same. For Locke, our ability to recognize "sameness" in view of apparent transformation can be understood by making a distinction between primary and secondary qualities of material objects.

When faced with an object (for example, an apple), ideas of sensation are caused in us by the actions of the material objects on our sense organs. The idea or image that is caused, then, represents the object that caused it. Locke contends that some of the sensations we receive from objects really do resemble the object's qualities, though others do not. The sensations that do resemble the properties of material objects are called **primary qualities.** They include figure, solidity, extension, motion, and number.[39] Such qualities are "utterly inseparable from the body . . . and such as in all the alterations and changes it suffers . . . it constantly keeps. . . ."[40] By contrast, there are qualities that do not resemble "utterly inseparable" properties of material objects. They are described as **secondary qualities** and include color, taste, texture, odor, smell, and so forth. Locke writes: ". . . the ideas of primary qualities of bodies are resemblances of them, and their patterns do really exist in the bodies themselves, but the ideas produced in us by these secondary qualities have no resemblance of them at all."[41] To justify his claim that primary qualities are inseparable from material objects—from every particle of matter—he uses the following illustration:

> Take a grain of wheat, divide it into two parts; each part has still solidity, extension, figure and mobility: divide it again, and it retains still the same qualities; and so divide it on, till the parts become insensible; they must retain still each of them all those qualities. For division . . . can never take away either solidity, extension, figure, or mobility from any body, but only makes two or more distinct separate masses of matter, of that which was but one before . . .[42]

From this example, we see that, for Locke, the real primary qualities of objects are those that remain after repeated divisions. He argues that other apparent, secondary qualities of objects (for example, color) disappear as we divide them into smaller and more minute particles. This being the case, they cannot be the real qualities of objects. Thus, in similar fashion to Descartes, Locke maintains that the real properties of objects are unchanging and make reference to substance—the thing itself.[43] To support his point about how secondary qualities can change and hence cannot constitute the real qualities of objects, Locke writes:

> Had we senses acute enough to discern the minute particles of bodies, and the real constitution on which their sensible qualities depend, I doubt not but they would produce quite different ideas in us: and that which is now the yellow colour of gold, would then disappear, and instead of it we should see an admirable texture of parts, of a certain size and figure. This microscopes plainly discover to us; for what to our naked eyes produces a certain colour, is, by thus augmenting the acuteness of our senses, discovered to be quite a different thing.[44]

Now, if primary qualities of objects do not change and are inherent in them, then we can say that our ideas of primary qualities are copies of these qualities as they actually exist in the perceived objects.[45] Though the ideas are not the objects themselves, they are close enough to provide us with a correspondence between mind and external reality. On the other hand, since secondary qualities are not in the object, separable from it, and changed by division and magnification or distorted by the medium by which they make their way to the perceiving subject (such as increasing darkness, rose-colored glasses), they do not produce the same kind of reliable knowledge that primary qualities do.[46] By locating secondary qualities with the perceiver who is affected and primary qualities with the objects of experience, Locke thought he had created a mind-world connection that would be sufficiently solid to assure us that our ideas of the world do actually resemble the world as it really is. This he did using empirical means and without resorting to Descartes's non-deceiving deity and without worry about any evil spirit—presumably some of the "metaphysical rubbish" Locke was seeking to remove.

## Bishop George Berkeley

The next major British empiricist who follows on the heels of John Locke is Bishop George Berkeley. Berkeley was critical of Locke, providing a somewhat more radical perspective than his predecessor. Locke had bought into Descartes's notion of "substance," allowing for objects to exist independent of human perceivers in the external world. As we learned, primary qualities (solidity, figure, motion, extension, and number) were said to be inherent in objects, whereas secondary qualities (colors, textures, sounds, tastes) were thought to belong to the perceiver. Berkeley took issue with Locke here, contending that arguments used by Locke to prove that secondary qualities exist only in the mind of the perceiver apply likewise to primary qualities. To have knowledge of primary qualities

*" To be is to be perceived. "*
BERKELEY

## PHILOSOPHICAL PROFILE

**GEORGE BERKELEY**

### Bishop George Berkeley

George Berkeley was born on March 12, 1685, in Kilcrene, Ireland. Though not rich, his family possessed the financial resources to send him to the prestigious Kilkenny School and later to Trinity College, Dublin. It was there that Berkeley studied philosophy (focusing on Malebranche and Locke) in addition to Latin, Greek, French and Hebrew. Berkeley earned his bachelor's degree in 1704 and became a Fellow of Trinity College in 1707. In 1710 he was ordained a priest in the protestant church. In 1721, Berkeley was awarded a doctorate of divinity and lectured at Trinity.

Berkeley traveled extensively in Europe and spent a decade trying to found a university in Bermuda. He also spent some time in Newport, Rhode Island, trying to establish St. Paul's College. He returned to England in 1731 when the promised funding for the college failed to materialize. While in the colonies he was active in educational matters, visiting William and Mary College in Virginia and giving advice on the founding of Columbia University. Berkeley also became a benefactor of both Harvard and Yale. In remembrance of his involvement in early college education in America, Berkeley University in California was named after him. In addition to his travels and educational achievements, Berkeley spent 18 years overseeing an Irish diocese as the Bishop of Cloyne. He died in Oxford, England, in 1753. His most important philosophical works include: *Essay Towards a New Theory of Vision (1709), A Treatise Concerning the Principles of Human Knowledge* (1710), and *Three Dialogues between Hylas and Philonous* (1713).

is to have an idea of them in our minds. We do not know objects directly or in themselves, so to speak, but only indirectly through perception and the resulting ideas. Minds are aware of both primary and secondary qualities; objects are not. They both reside with the perceiver. Thus the "reliability" of primary qualities, which Locke used to prove that a world outside our minds exists, is called into question by Berkeley. Both belong to the perceiver and cannot prove that an external reality beyond the mind exists at all.

In further refutation of physical substance and the primary-secondary quality distinction, Berkeley argues that things can only correspond to things like themselves. This means that ideas can only correspond to other ideas; they cannot correspond to inert substance or unthinking matter. Berkeley writes:

> Some there are who make a distinction betwixt *primary* and *secondary* qualities: By the former, they mean extension, figure, mobility, rest, solidity or impenetrability, and number; by the latter they denote all other sensible qualities as colours, sounds, tastes, and so forth. The ideas we have of these last they acknowledge not to be resemblances of any things existing without the mind or unperceived

but they will have our ideas of the *primary* qualities to be patterns or image of things which exist without the mind, in an unthinking substance which they call Matter. By Matter, therefore, we are to understand an inert senseless substance, in which extension, figure, and motion do actually subsist. But it is evident, from what we have already shewn, that extension, figure, and motion are only ideas existing in the mind, and that an idea can be like nothing but another idea; and that consequently neither they nor their archetypes can exist in an unperceiving substance. Hence, it is plain that the very notion of what is called *Matter*, or *corporeal substance*, involves a contradiction in it.[47]

For Berkeley, another reason for rejecting the Lockean distinction between primary and secondary qualities is because, in truth, they cannot be separated even in the mind of the perceiver. Locke, the empiricist, was not very empirical, according to Berkeley, when he adopted the concept of **material substance.** The problem is that we can never have sensory experiences of material substances. Nobody actually experiences substance; one only experiences sensory qualities. For example, when you perceive a rose, you see it as a certain size and shape. You perceive the length of its stem, the size of its petals, the texture and color of the bloom, and you smell the fragrance it emits. What you can never perceive, however, is the so-called "substance" of the rose—presumably a colorless, odorless, texture-less figure of some sort. There is no perception of substance, only the experience of sensory qualities. Thus, physical substances exist only insofar as they are perceived. They cannot be known to have any existence other than in the qualities we perceive.[48] This is summed up by Berkeley in the expression "*To be is to be perceived*" (**Esse est Percipi**). In further rejection of the distinction between primary and secondary qualities, Berkeley writes:

They who assert that figure, motion, and the rest of the primary or original qualities do exist without the mind in unthinking substances, do at the same time acknowledge that colours, sounds, heat, cold, and such-like secondary qualities, do not; which they tell us are sensations, existing in the mind alone, that depend on and are occasioned by the different size, texture, and motion of the minute particles of matter. This they take for an undoubted truth, which they can demonstrate beyond all exception. Now, if it be certain that those *original* qualities are inseparably united with the other sensible qualities, and not, even in thought, capable of being abstracted from them, it plainly follows that they exist only in the mind. But I desire any one to reflect, and try whether he can, by an abstraction of thought, conceive the extension and motion of a body without all other sensible qualities. For my own part, I see evidently that it is not in my power to frame an idea of a body extended and moving but I must withal give it some colour or other sensible quality which is acknowledged to exist only in the mind. In short, extension, figure, and motion, abstracted from all other qualities, are inconceivable. Where therefore the other sensible qualities are, there must these be also, to wit, in the mind and nowhere else.[49]

Berkeley's notion that "to be is to be perceived" brings to mind a corollary, namely that "not to be perceived is not to be." This proposition reminds us of the riddle that so many philosophy graduates like to muse about: "If a tree falls in the middle of a forest and there is nobody around to hear it, does it make any sound?" To answer for Berkeley and to remain consistent with his logic, we would have to answer, "No." Sound is not in the tree or in the forest; rather it is in the perceiver. Without a perceiver, there can be no sound.[50]

A logical extension of the preceding point would seem to be that there is no reliability or permanence in physical reality. The world could be changing from one moment to the next depending on the presence or absence of a perceiver. Using the "tree in the forest" example again, if a perceiver is present, then the falling tree makes a sound. Without a perceiver, it doesn't make a sound; and if no perceiver is there to see the tree itself, it does not exist in the first place. Clearly, it would be impossible for a nonexistent tree to make a sound. By assigning both primary and secondary qualities to the mind of the perceiver, Berkeley rejects the mind-world connection Locke wishes to make.[51] In fact, by severing this connection, what Berkeley does, in effect, is cast doubt on the existence of the entire external world. If primary qualities, like secondary qualities, exist only in the mind, then inert matter or substance (that which we take as objects in the material world) may or may not actually exist. All we know for sure are the contents of our minds, which consist purely of ideas.

## God the Perpetual Perceiver

The idea that existence depends on perception places us in a very precarious and insecure position. What happens when we are asleep or when we fall unconscious? Does the world disappear, or does it remain intact when we are not functioning as perceiving subjects? To answer this question, Berkeley directs our attention to the apparent laws of nature manifested in the orderliness and steadiness of our perceptions. The good bishop then attributes the regularity of nature to its author, namely God. It is God, the **perpetual perceiver,** who makes sure that the world remains when we lose consciousness, sleep, or close our eyes. The fact that you are not at home, at your apartment, or at your college residence, for example, doesn't mean that your bed and stereo have suddenly disappeared. (Hopefully they haven't been stolen!) You can rest assured that their existence is guaranteed without your being present to perceive them. As well, don't worry that the workings of the world are about to go haywire, or that they will change from one moment to the next. Through God, we can trust in the uniformity of experience and in the dependability of scientific laws. But remember, when we observe orderliness and regularity, they manifest themselves in our mental perceptions and ideas, not in material substances or in physical objects located in the external world. The only "substances" that exist are mental: as finite minds in the case of human beings, and as an infinite mind in the case of God.[52]

## PHILOSOPHICAL PROFILE

### David Hume

**DAVID HUME**

David Hume was born in the year 1711 in Edinburgh, Scotland, into a Calvinist family of modest economic resources. Described as a "well-meanin' critter" by his mother, little did she know that her child would grow into a brilliant thinker whose skeptical ideas would devastate much of traditional epistemology and metaphysics.

Hume attended the University of Edinburgh for several years but left at the age of 16, without finishing his degree. He subsequently studied law, but eventually abandoned his legal studies as well, finding "insurmountable aversion to everything but the pursuits of philosophy and general learning." Law became "nauseous" to him. Hume confessed that achieving literary fame had become a ruling passion. In his early twenties, he traveled to France and wrote *A Treatise of Human Nature*—the book which presumably was to give him the celebrity he so much desired. Unfortunately for Hume, it did not garner the attention he had hoped for during his lifetime as it "fell dead-born from the press," to use his words. In efforts to salvage the book, which now is a philosophical classic, he rewrote and combined the first two parts of it in a more popular and lively fashion, entitling the new, shorter work *An Enquiry Concerning Human Understanding* (1748). In 1751, a revised version of the third part of the *Treatise* was published under the title *An Enquiry Concerning the Principles of Morals.* Surprisingly, perhaps, it was his six-volume *History of England* (1754–1762) that finally gave him the recognition he so craved. By 1763, his reputation as historian and man of letters preceded him. For a period in Paris, he led the life of a celebrity in leading social circles, hobnobbing with the likes of Voltaire and Jean-Jacques Rousseau.

In addition to fame, Hume wished to become a university professor. This dream was never to come true, however, as he failed to land a post at both Edinburgh and at the University of Glasgow. It was his deep-rooted skepticism and atheistic contempt for the prevailing religious beliefs of the day that probably prevented him from finding employment as an academic. Interestingly, and notwithstanding the hard edges of his skeptical criticism of traditional thought, Hume was a kind and gentle person admired by many. Friends called him St. David, and in remembrance of this fact, the street on which he lived is still called that today. Hume spent the last years of his life in Edinburgh, only now, in contrast to his modest beginnings, he lived a very opulent and contented lifestyle. David Hume died in 1776 from cancer at the age of 65. Other notable works by Hume include: *Essays Moral and Political* (1741–1742), *Political Discourses* (1752), and *Dialogues Concerning Natural Religion* (published posthumously in 1779). Hume's autobiography, *My Own Life* (1777), was edited by his friend and fellow Scottish philosopher, Adam Smith.

> *[It is] certain we cannot go beyond experience; and any hypothesis, that pretends to discover the ultimate original qualities of human nature, ought at first to be rejected as presumptuous and chimerical.*
>
> DAVID HUME

# David Hume's Radical Skepticism

In the epistemology of David Hume, we find the most hard-hitting application of empiricist principles. His thought forms a **radical skepticism** that has been described as a philosophical "wrecking-ball."[53] This instrument of mass theoretical destruction smashes to bits the pride emanating from the Age of Enlightenment and the scientific achievements of Newton. It reduces metaphysics to pretentious nonsense, shattering notions of God, mind, and the immaterial self to smithereens. Into the scrapheap of skepticism are also tossed ideas of physical substance and innate knowledge, which are all rendered epistemologically meaningless. In fact, Hume even goes so far as to question the philosophical validity of the most revered of all scientific concepts, namely that of *causality* itself, arguing that our use of it cannot be rationally justified either in scientific or in commonsense thinking. Like so many other philosophers before and after him, Hume upsets conventional thinking and forces us to re-examine our previously accepted beliefs about ourselves and the nature of reality. His writings confront us with several basic questions: "How do we know?" "What is the source of our knowledge?" and lastly, "What are its limits?" In the end, Hume concludes that we have no certain knowledge about the world but only beliefs that we feel are true.[54]

Hume's critique of conventional thinking about knowledge takes us back to Descartes and Plato, his rationalistic predecessors. Recall that, for them, reason offered a higher or superior level of knowledge, which could provide certainty. Plato had argued that this certainty resided in the metaphysical realm of *forms*, whereas Descartes said it could be found through the *Cogito's* recognition of clear and distinct ideas. For both, certain truth transcended physical, sensory experience. Such truth made metaphysics possible. Remember, too, that both Plato and Descartes conceptualized a lower or inferior type of knowledge. Bringing to mind Plato's divided line theory, recall that so-called knowledge of the sensible world—the world of experience that constantly changes—is really only opinion and illusion. Descartes was likewise skeptical of the senses, for they provided him no assurances that what he perceived in experience was reliable or indubitably true. The truth about the material world had to be rationally deduced. Descartes's "wax example" illustrated that whatever the wax was, it could not be determined by its sensory qualities alone, which changed with the application of heat. However, the mind could logically deduce the existence of "substance," which went beyond sensory experience. Prior to Hume, then, there had developed a longstanding tradition of belief in a kind of higher knowledge whose source was reason. Ultimately, the mind would allow us to know the truth about reality and serve as the basis for our metaphysical conception of the universe.

Hume's "wrecking ball" ends up destroying the traditional philosophical belief that there are two kinds of knowledge:—a higher one based on reason and a lower one based on experience. The idea that the *Cogito* can attain a superior kind of metaphysical understanding is, for him, nothing more than sophistry and lofty pretension. In fact, as you will learn, the mind (and self) is for Hume an illusion to which misguided rationalists and metaphysicians foolishly love to refer. For Hume, there is also a gulf between reason and the world; reason cannot speak with *a priori* authority about objects and events in experience. Despite the remarkable achievements of science in his day, Hume was disturbed by all the disagreements that seemed to pour from the scientific community. In the Introduction to *A Treatise of Human Nature,* he writes:

> Nor is there requir'd such profound knowledge to discover the present imperfect condition of the sciences, but even the rabble without doors may judge from the noise and clamour, which they hear, that all goes not well within. There is nothing which is not the subject of debate, and in which men of learning are not of contrary opinions. The most trivial question escapes not our controversy, and in the most momentous we are not able to give any certain decision. Disputes are multiplied, as if every thing was uncertain; and these disputes are managed with the greatest warmth, as if every thing was certain. Amidst all this bustle 'tis not reason, which carries the prize, but eloquence; and no man needs ever despair of gaining proselytes to the most extravagant hypothesis, who has art enough to represent it in any favourable colours. The victory is not gained by the men at arms, who manage the pike and the sword, but by the trumpeters, drummers, and musicians of the army.[55]

In efforts to establish the proper limits of knowledge and to get us back on a solid epistemological footing, Hume goes back to the beginning, as it were, and asks where our knowledge ultimately comes from. To discover the answer, Hume turns the study of human nature—in particular, human cognition. His rationale for doing so is given in the *Treatise:*

> 'Tis evident, that all the sciences have a relation, greater or less, to human nature; and that however wide any of them may seem to run from it, they still return back by one passage or another. Even *Mathematics, Natural Philosophy,* and *Natural Religion,* are in some measure dependent on the science of Man; since they lie under the cognizance of men, and are judged of by their powers and faculties. 'Tis impossible to tell what changes and improvements we might make in these sciences were we thoroughly acquainted with the extent and force of human understanding, and cou'd explain the nature of the ideas we employ, and of the operations we perform in our reasons.[56]

In short, the functioning of human understanding serves as the foundation for all knowledge—scientific and otherwise. By identifying the origins of our ideas, as well as the relations and operations among them, Hume initially set out to lay the foundations for all the sciences. As mentioned, however, the results of his efforts turned out to be quite different from his original plan.

## On the Origin of Ideas

**Impressions versus Ideas**    Hume begins his analysis of human understanding by examining the "perceptions of the mind," things that Locke and Descartes would label "ideas." Through a kind of rational introspective process, he discovers that "we may divide all the perceptions of the mind into two classes or

> *"The most lively thought is still inferior to the dullest sensation."*
>
> DAVID HUME

species, which are distinguished by their different degrees of force and vivacity."[57] Those perceptions containing the greatest force are called **impressions,** whereas those with lesser force and vivacity are dubbed **thoughts** or **ideas.** If, for example, you sustain a multiple fracture while trying to perform a gymnastics maneuver, the experience of pain would likely saturate your consciousness and envelop your entire being. No doubt, you would be "impressed" by the physical discomfort. On the other hand, if you remember months later, when all is healed and well, how your leg did hurt once upon a time, you are having a thought or idea about the incident. Clearly, recalling the break is less painful than actually experiencing it at the moment it occurred. The recollection of the fracture can be regarded as a **copy** of the original experience, but different from it in terms of liveliness and strength.

Impressions and ideas apply not only to physical sensations or sensory-based experiences, but also to all other perceptions of the mind, including sentiments and affections like anger and love. Remember, though, that experiencing anger in the moment is very different from thinking about a past outburst of it. Again, the former has greater force and vivacity. The latter may be emotionally upsetting as well, but not to the same degree. Hume writes: "When we reflect on our past sentiments and affections, our thought is a faithful mirror and copies its objects truly, but the colors which it employs are faint and dull in comparison of those in which our original perceptions were clothed."[58] Thus, the experience of anger constitutes an impression, but the thought of a previous outburst of anger is an idea. This partly explains the truth of the expression "Time heals"; over time, poignant and unpleasant feelings that are originally experienced seem to fade in the distance.

Important to note at this juncture is that there is a direct, one-to-one correspondence between impressions and ideas. All of our ideas are derived from our initial experiential impressions, no matter how bizarre or fantastic these ideas may seem. For example, Pegasus, the winged horse of Greek mythology, is not purely an invention of the imagination, completely devoid of any sensory impressions, for clearly, the idea of *horse* and the idea of *wings* ultimately come from impressions people have of such things. Hume uses the example of a golden mountain to make the same point. He contends that when we think of a golden mountain, all we really do is join two ideas, "gold" and "mountain," with which we were formerly acquainted. The mind did not create something in a rational vacuum independent of everything experiential. Hume says that the "creative power of the mind amounts to no more than the faculty of compounding, transposing, augmenting, or diminishing the materials afforded us by the senses and experience."[59]

## Rejection of Metaphysics

Hume's rather simple-sounding distinction between impressions and ideas contains powerful implications that may not be obvious at first glance. If all the ideas that furnish our minds have their origin in impressions, then those philosophers like Descartes and Locke, who talk about mental or physical substance, are engaged in some form of metaphysical nonsense, for there are no corresponding impressions of such hypothetical entities. Discussing "substance," then, is little more than fantasy or intellectual masturbation, pleasure-producing perhaps, but with no fruitful outcome.

Like Bishop Berkeley, Hume agreed that Locke's adoption of the idea of material substance, in which primary qualities allegedly inhere, was not justified when evaluated by empirical standards. However, for Hume, Berkeley's alternative solution to the problem of substance did not fare any better when judged by the same rigorous empirical criteria.[60] Berkeley argued that both primary and secondary qualities belong to the mind of the perceiver—neither one in external objects themselves. The problem for Hume is that the idea of a mind, self, or **mental substance** cannot be traced back to experience either. Consequently, it is a fiction as much as physical substance is. Whatever we refer to as the "self" is nothing more than a stream of consciousness. In Book One, Section VI of the *Treatise,* Hume has this to say about mind and personal identity:

> For my part, when I enter most intimately into what I call *myself,* I always stumble on some perception or other, of heat or cold, light or shade, love or hatred, pain or pleasure. I never can catch *myself* at any time without a perception, and never can observe any thing but the perception. When my perceptions are remov'd for any time, as by sound sleep; so long am I insensible of *myself,* and may truly be said not to exist. And were all my perceptions remov'd by death, and cou'd I neither think, nor feel, nor see, nor love, nor hate after the dissolution of my body, I shou'd be entirely annihilated, nor do I conceive what is farther requisite to make me a perfect non-entity. If any one upon serious unprejudic'd reflexion, thinks he has a different notion of *himself,* I must confess I can reason no longer with him. All I can allow him is, that he may be in the right as well as I, and that we are essentially different in this particular. He may perhaps perceive something simple and continu'd, which he calls *himself;* tho' I am certain there is no such principle in me. . . . But setting aside some metaphysicians of this kind, I may venture to affirm of the rest of mankind, that they are nothing but a bundle or collection of different perceptions, which succeed each other with an inconceivable rapidity, and are in a perpetual flux and movement. . . . The mind is a kind of theatre, where several perceptions successively make their appearance; pass, re-pass, glide away, and mingle in an infinite variety of postures and situations. There is properly no *simplicity* in it at one time, nor *identity* in different; whatever natural propension we may have to imagine that simplicity and identity. The comparison of the theatre must not mislead us. They are the successive perceptions only, that constitute the mind; nor have we the most distant notion of the place, where these senses are represented, or of the materials, of which it is compose'd.[61]

In further refutation of Berkeley, and specifically in reference to his notion of **God** as the "perpetual perceiver," Hume argues that since the "idea of God" has no basis in sense experience, it too is epistemologically meaningless. Because there is no impression to which it can correspond, the idea of God becomes as baseless as substance and self. Also, in view of the fact that all these concepts do not

> *"When we run over libraries, persuaded of these [empiricist] principles, what havoc must we make? If we take in our hand any volume of divinity or school metaphysics, for instance—let us ask, Does it contain any abstract reasoning concerning quantity or number? No. Does it contain any experimental reasoning concerning matter of fact and existence? No. Commit it then to the flames, for it can contain nothing but sophistry and illusion."*
>
> HUME

originate in sense experience, they can never direct us toward knowledge of the nature and character of reality. For this reason, Hume concludes that metaphysics should be abandoned. It provides no help whatsoever in understanding the world.

## Association of Ideas

> **" To me there appear to be only three principles of connection among ideas, namely, Resemblance, Contiguity in time or place, and Cause and Effect. "**
> DAVID HUME

The point has been well established by now that ideas are derivative of impressions. Even the creative powers of the mind "amount to no more than the faculty of compounding, transposing, augmenting, or diminishing the materials afforded us by the senses and experience."[62] In further analysis of ideas, Hume lays out the **laws of association.** He was influenced very much by other empiricists of the eighteenth century, who understood experience to be comprised of atomistic units in the same way that physicists saw particles in motion. Following the lead of Newton, who discovered the laws that govern physical particles, Hume saw the task of philosophy as setting out the laws governing mental particles (ideas). He found three patterns of association: **resemblance, contiguity,** and **cause and effect.** These patterns would explain for Hume the "bond of union" or "gentle force" that attracts one idea to another as a sort of "mental gravity."[63]

In the case of resemblance, think of how a caricature of a star like Dolly Parton brings to mind Dolly herself, the reason being that ideas that are similar tend to be associated with one another. The second law of association is captured by Hume with the example of an apartment dwelling. He says, "The mention of one apartment in a building naturally introduces an inquiry or discourse concerning the others."[64] Ideas that appear closely together in time or space are oftentimes connected in thought. This principle is called *contiguity.* Lastly, when one event follows another in regular fashion, we link them together using the principle of cause and effect. The experience of stepping on the gas peddle of a car in gear, for example, is associated with movement. The two events occur together so regularly that we associate them. The former "cause" leads to the latter "effect." If the car doesn't move when the gas peddle is pressed, we assume something is wrong. An empty gas tank may have "caused" the accelerator peddle not to perform as it should have and as we fully expected it to. In this case, one cause would override another, but cause is still present in our explanation of what occurred.

Hume makes the point that the "gentle force" accounting for these principles of association is not reason but **imagination.** The connections made by the imagination, however, are not **necessary** connections, as is the case in mathematics or deductive reasoning. For Hume, patterns of association emerge more from feeling or psychological impulse than from rationality. We want the universe to be orderly, so we associate events in understandable cause-and-effect relationships. However, Hume argues that this pattern resides in us and not in the events we observe.[65]

## Critique of Causality

Given that Sir Isaac Newton's scientific advancements were largely predicated on causal laws that could explain the movements of celestial bodies, ocean tides, and apples falling from trees, Hume's suggestion that causality is not found in nature but in our imaginations is very devastating. His critical analysis of causality does indeed serve again as a philosophical wrecking-ball, destroying the very foundations of science. If there is no causal order in the universe, then scientific cause-and-effect explanations are unjustified and ultimately wishful thinking.

Of all three laws concerning the association of ideas, cause and effect is the most important and powerful connection. Inevitably, when we reason about matters of fact, we use causal reasoning: "Why did John explode in class?" "*Because* he was embarrassed by the teacher's remarks." "Why did Mary apply to medical school?" "*Because* her parents pressured her into doing so." The conjunction "because" introduces the cause in answer to each question.

Our most important thinking concerning matters of fact is found in scientific reasoning, with its causal laws of nature. We ask questions like: "Why do avalanches occur?" "What causes cancer?" or "What makes leaves change color in autumn?" Recognizing the importance of cause-and-effect explanations to scientific inquiry, and commonsense understanding for that matter, Hume set out to analyze the concept of causation, assuming that it must be based on certain relations among objects.

For Hume, if one object or event is said to be the cause of another, there must be contiguity. That which is considered the cause must make spatio-temporal contact with its effect in some fashion. If a firecracker exploded in your hand and you immediately felt pain, the two events would be contiguous, and you would likely link them together. If you were at a fireworks display, however, and witnessed an exploding firecracker from a great distance, you would be unlikely to associate the distant explosion with the pain you coincidentally experienced in your hand at the same time. The two events would not be spatially contiguous.

Causality also involves **priority in time.** Causes come before, not after their effects. If, for instance, you take medication to fight a headache, and minutes later the pain goes away, you probably associate the pain reduction with the ingestion of medicine: taking medication (A) caused reduction of pain (B). Of course, contiguity can play a role here as well. You likely would not associate the disappearance of headache pain with the medication you took last week or last year. Causes are prior in time and contiguous with the events that result from them. Furthermore, you wouldn't claim that the soda pop you drank immediately *after* the headache went away caused it to do so. This wouldn't make any sense, for even though the two events were contiguous, the event of drinking soda followed the dissipation of pain; because it was not prior in time, we understand that it couldn't have been the cause.

A third element establishing cause-and-effect relationships between objects is **necessary connection.** Whatever the effect, it *must* follow from the cause, which is prior in time and contiguous with it. The need for necessary connection is assumed by many of us in our debates and semi-scientific conversations with friends and fellow students. Some claim, for instance, that "Smoking tobacco causes cancer," while others retort, "No it doesn't," pointing out that some people have smoked for decades and have never fallen prey to the disease. The objection here seems to be that smoking *does not necessarily* lead to cancer, as evidenced by cancer-free smokers. If one thing (cancer) does not necessarily follow from, or is not necessarily connected to another thing or activity (smoking), then no causal connection between them exists. As you probably are aware, medical researchers and tobacco companies are still at odds over whether smoking, in fact, causes cancer. In any event, if one object or event is the cause of another, then the latter must *always* result from the former. (It may be that smoking tobacco is just one of several multiple determinates causing cancer. It, alone, may not be sufficient as the sole causal factor.)

So far, all of this may appear intuitively clear to you, but Hume asks: *What is our idea of necessity, when we say that two objects are necessarily connected together?* His answer to this question certainly adds power and force to his wrecking-ball of radical skepticism. Hume precludes the possibility that reason is the source of this necessary connection, for all its ideas must ultimately be derived from impressions and hence, from experience. Secondly, causality is not found in objects themselves either. Hume says, "From the first appearance of an object we never can conjecture what effect will result from it . . . In reality, there is no part of matter that does ever, by its sensible qualities, discover any power or energy, or give us ground to imagine that it could produce anything, or be followed by any object, which we could determine its effect."[66] Look at a billiard ball, for example. Though you perceive size, shape and color, nowhere in it do you find *cause*. Causes do not exist in things. Even if, in this instance, you were to watch one billiard ball in motion make contact with another that falls into the corner pocket, you still don't have a sense impression of cause. Our idea of cause does not correspond to anything in experience. What does it look like?

Well then, if the idea of a necessary cause-and-effect relation is not produced by reason, not found in objects, not inherent in experience, and not based on sensory impressions, then we're still left wondering from where, exactly, it does come. In response to our bewilderment, Hume writes:

> It appears, then, that this idea of a necessary connection among events arises from a number of similar instances which occur, of the **constant conjunction** [my emphasis] of these events; nor can that idea ever be suggested by any one of these instances surveyed in all possible lights and positions. But there is nothing in a number of instances, different from every single instance, which is supposed to be exactly similar, except only that after a repetition of similar instances the mind is carried by *habit* [my emphasis], upon the appearance of one event, to expect its usual attendant and to believe that it will exist. This connection, therefore, which we *feel* in the mind, this customary transition of the imagination from one object to its usual attendant, is the sentiment or impression from which we form the idea of power or necessary connection. Nothing further is the case. Contemplate the subjects on all sides, you will never find any other origin of that idea.[67]

To illustrate and simplify Hume's remarks, let us go back to the billiard ball example. If you had no experience of billiard balls and knew nothing about their qualities, you would not be able to determine by reason alone if they exploded, melted, or were sweet and intended to be eaten. If you witnessed one ball hitting another on a billiard table and then a second one moved, you would regard these two events as *conjoined,* to used Hume's term. Only after repeated instances of watching the hitting of one billiard ball setting another in motion would you conclude that these two events are connected. Hume asks: "What alteration has happened to give rise to this idea of connection?" In answer to his own question, he replies: "Nothing but that he now *feels* these events to be *connected* in his *imagination,* and can readily foretell the existence of one from the appearance of the other."[68]

The implications of Hume's conclusion should not be underestimated here. The rigor of scientific inquiry has been seriously undermined. In place of verifiable scientific knowledge, we have only **feelings of compulsion,** that is, a "gentle force" or "mental gravity" that makes us feel that our ideas are connected by cause and effect. The astonishing claim is that scientific laws have their source in feelings, human expectations, and attitudes. They are based upon nothing but sense impressions, which are connected by psychological laws of association and by the feelings of compulsion they exert. There is no sense impression for cause or necessary connection itself. "But if the idea of necessary connection has no corresponding impression, then on Hume's empiricist principle: no impression, no idea—the idea of a necessary connection between causes and effects is worthless as knowledge and is meaningless, a fraud, nonsense."[69]

To the extent, then, that causal necessity is a subjective notion emanating from the laws of our own psychology, and to the degree it is not derived from rational self-evidence or from any empirical sense impressions, Hume's "wrecking-ball" appears to destroy the scientific foundations of causal necessity. For him, there are no objective cause-and-effect relationships between things for scientists to observe. All there is, is a subjective compulsion to relate things by the psychological laws of association. Causal necessity finds no source in our sense impressions but only in the laws of our own psychology.[70]

## "Hume's Fork" and Types of Reasoning

Hume's rejection of metaphysics and his insistence that we know nothing about the world apart from our sensory impressions of it severely restricts the range of legitimate philosophical inquiry. He divides the proper objects of human inquiry into two prongs or what has come to be known as **Hume's Fork.** They are objects showing: (a) the **relations of ideas,** and (b) those describing **matters of fact.** Propositions referring to the relations of ideas are those which belong to geometry, algebra, and arithmetic. Every affirmative statement that comes from these is "either intuitively or demonstratively certain." For example, *That the square of the hypotenuse is equal to the square of the two sides* is a proposition that expresses a relation between these figures. *That three times five is equal to the half of thirty* expresses a relation between these numbers."[71] Modern empiricists today generally call such propositions analytic.[72] **Analytic propositions** are self-evidently true or true by definition. They are known independently of experience and observation; nothing in experience can refute them, and nothing in experience is required to justify them. "Though there never were a circle or triangle in nature, the [analytic] truths demonstrated by Euclid [Euclidean geometry] would forever retain their certainty and evidence."[73] Modern empiricists describe what Hume calls propositions asserting relations of ideas as ***a priori* statements.** However, since analytic *a priori* statements are formal and abstract, they are empty of content, so to speak, telling us nothing of the world. What we gain in certainty, we lose in explanatory power to describe objects and events in experience.

The second prong of Hume's Fork refers to propositions describing matters of fact. As you can readily guess, such propositions tell us about the world. In contemporary philosophy, factual propositions are called **synthetic a posteriori.** Unlike analytic *a priori* statements referring to relations of ideas, they can be denied without contradiction. Hume writes: "The contrary of every matter of fact is still possible, because it can never imply a contradiction and is conceived by the mind with the same facility and distinctness as if ever so conformable to reality. *That the sun will not rise tomorrow* is no less intelligible a proposition and imples no more contradiction than the affirmation *that it will rise.* We should in vain, therefore, attempt to demonstrate its falsehood."[74]

Now, given that matters of fact are expressed in propositions derived from impressions and ideas, and also, given that no necessary causal relations can be derived from such impressions and ideas, there can be no certainty achieved in our knowledge claims about the world. Matters of fact are all based on cause-and-effect relations, which Hume has shown do not exist in the world but in the psychological association of ideas. Consequently, not only are metaphysics and science impossible, but so too is commonsense knowledge of everyday life, since it is based on causal reasoning. We have no basis for providing explanations or predicting events. We cannot with justifiability infer from events of yesterday what will happen today or tomorrow. And with this devastating conclusion, we may say that the job of Hume's wrecking-ball is complete. What we know for certain does not tell us about the world. What we "know" about the world is not certain. And, on top of all this, propositions that do not relate to matters of fact or relations of ideas are meaningless and not worth discussing (for example, the thesis that God exists). The radical skeptic has undermined metaphysics, science, and commonsense knowledge of the world. And with this realization, you may now be as badly shaken as Hume was when he wrote in the *Treatise:*

> The intense view of these manifold contradictions and imperfections in human reason has so wrought upon me and heated my brain that I am ready to reject all belief and reasoning and can look upon no opinion even as more probable than another. Where am I, or what? From what causes do I derive my existence and to what condition shall I return? I am confounded with all these questions and begin to fancy myself in the most deplorable condition imaginable, invironed in the deepest darkness and utterly deprived of the use of every member and faculty.[75]

On this somewhat depressing note concerning the limits of human knowledge, let us end this segment of the chapter on Hume by reading a selection from the skeptic himself. The passage, which comes from the *Inquiry,* is entitled "Skeptical Doubts Concerning the Operations of the Understanding." For a

**TABLE 4.2**   David Hume's Origins and Limits of Knowledge: A Summary

1. What we can possibly know must be limited to our impressions and corresponding ideas derived from experience. (Analytic propositions are empty of empirical content and cannot tell us about the world.)

2. We cannot know what causes these impressions and ideas. We have no basis for scientific knowledge, only associations of ideas through habit, psychological expectancy, and compulsion.

3. Metaphysics is impossible. There are no impressions corresponding to metaphysical concepts like God, the Platonic forms, mind, self, or the Cartesian *Cogito*.

4. We cannot predict future events on the basis of past experience (synthetic propositions can be denied without contradiction).

5. Common-sense knowledge of everyday events is impossible as it presupposes cause-and-effect relations.

contrasting perspective, read the second *Original Sourcework* entitled "An Afrocentric/Feminist Standpoint Challenges the Tradition of Positivism." It offers an alternative epistemology for assessing knowledge claims. Before reading both articles, you may wish to glance at Table 4.2 for a Humean summary of the origins and limits of knowledge.

## ORIGINAL SOURCEWORK

## *Skeptical Doubts Concerning the Operations of the Understanding*

### DAVID HUME

## PART I

All the objects of human reason or enquiry may naturally be divided into two kinds, to wit, Relations of Ideas, and Matters of Fact. Of the first kind are the sciences of Geometry, Algebra, and Arithmetic; and in short, every affirmation which is either intuitively or demonstratively certain. That the square of the hypothenuse is equal to the square of the two sides, is a proposition which expresses a relation between these figures. That three times five is equal to the half of thirty, expresses a relation between these numbers. Propositions of this kind are discoverable by the mere operation of thought, without

dependence on what is anywhere existent in the universe. Though there never were a circle or triangle in nature, the truths demonstrated by Euclid would for ever retain their certainty and evidence.

Matters of fact, which are the second objects of human reason, are not ascertained in the same manner; nor is our evidence of their truth, however great, of a like nature with the foregoing. The contrary of every matter of fact is still possible; because it can never imply a contradiction, and is conceived by the mind with the same facility and distinctness, as if ever so conformable to reality. That the sun will not rise to-morrow is no less intelligible a proposition, and implies no more contradiction than the affirmation, that it will rise. We should in vain, therefore, attempt to demonstrate its falsehood. Were it demonstratively false, it would imply a contradiction, and could never be distinctly conceived by the mind.

It may, therefore, be a subject worthy of curiosity, to enquire what is the nature of that evidence which assures us of any real existence and matter of fact, beyond the present testimony of our senses, or the records of our memory. This part of philosophy, it is observable, has been little cultivated, either by the ancients or moderns; and therefore our doubts and errors, in the prosecution of so important an enquiry, may be the more excusable; while we march through such difficult paths without any guide or direction. They may even prove useful, by exciting curiosity, and destroying that implicit faith and security, which is the bane of all reasoning and free enquiry. The discovery of defects in the common philosophy, if any such there be, will not, I presume, be a discouragement, but rather an incitement, as is usual, to attempt something more full and satisfactory than has yet been proposed to the public.

All reasonings concerning matter of fact seem to be founded on the relation of Cause and Effect. By means of that relation alone we can go beyond the evidence of our memory and senses. If you were to ask a man, why he believes any matter of fact, which is absent; for instance, that his friend is in the country, or in France; he would give you a reason; and this reason would be some other fact; as a letter received from him, or the knowledge of his former resolutions and promises. A man finding a watch or any other machine in a desert island, would conclude that there had once been men in that island. All our reasonings concerning fact are of the same nature. And here it is constantly supposed that there is a connexion between the present fact and that which is inferred from it. Were there nothing to bind them together, the inference would be entirely precarious. The hearing of an articulate voice and rational discourse in the dark assures us of the presence of some person: Why? because these are the effects of the human make and fabric, and closely connected with it. If we anatomize all the other reasonings of this nature, we shall find that they are founded on the relation of cause and effect, and that this relation is either near or remote, direct or collateral. Heat and light are collateral effects of fire, and the one effect may justly be inferred from the other.

If we would satisfy ourselves, therefore, concerning the nature of that evidence, which assures us of matters of fact, we must enquire how we arrive at the knowledge of cause and effect.

I shall venture to affirm, as a general proposition, which admits of no exception, that the knowledge of this relation is not, in any instance, attained by reasonings a priori; but arises entirely from experience, when we find that any particular objects are constantly conjoined with each other. Let an object be presented to a man of ever so strong natural reason and abilities; if that object be entirely new to him, he will not be able, by the most accurate examination of its sensible qualities, to discover any of its causes or effects. Adam, though his rational faculties be supposed, at the very first, entirely perfect, could not have inferred from the fluidity and transparency of water that it would suffocate him, or from the light and warmth of fire that it would consume him. No object ever discovers, by the qualities which appear to the senses, either the causes which produced it, or the effects which will arise from it; nor can our reason, unassisted by experience, ever draw any inference concerning real existence and matter of fact.

This proposition, that causes and effects are discoverable, not by reason but by experience, will readily be admitted with regard to such objects, as we remember to have once been altogether unknown to us; since we must be conscious of the utter inability, which we then lay under, of foretelling what would arise from them. Present two smooth pieces of marble to a man who has no tincture of natural philosophy; he will never discover that they will adhere together in such a manner as to require great force to separate them in a direct line, while they make so small a resistance to a lateral pressure. Such events, as bear little analogy to the common course of nature, are also readily confessed to be known only by experience; nor does any man imagine that the explosion of gunpowder, or the attraction of a load-stone, could ever be discovered by arguments a priori. In like manner, when an effect is supposed to depend upon an intricate machinery or secret structure of parts, we make no difficulty in attributing all our knowledge of it to experience. Who will assert that he can give the ultimate reason, why milk or bread is proper nourishment for a man, not for a lion or a tiger?

But the same truth may not appear, at first sight, to have the same evidence with regard to events, which have become familiar to us from our first appearance in the world, which bear a close analogy to the whole course of nature, and which are supposed to depend on the simple qualities of objects, without any secret structure of parts. We are apt to imagine that we could discover these effects by the mere operation of our reason, without experience. We fancy, that were we brought on a sudden into this world, we could at first have inferred that one Billiard-ball would communicate motion to another upon impulse; and that we needed not to have waited for the event, in order to pronounce with certainty concerning it. Such is the influence of custom, that, where it is strongest, it not only covers our natural ignorance, but even conceals itself, and seems not to take place, merely because it is found in the highest degree.

But to convince us that all the laws of nature, and all the operations of bodies without exception, are known only by experience, the following reflections may, perhaps, suffice. Were any object presented to us, and were we required to pronounce concerning the effect, which will result from it, without consulting past observation; after what manner, I beseech you, must the mind proceed in this operation? It must invent or imagine some event, which it ascribes to the object as its effect; and it is plain that this invention must be entirely arbitrary. The mind can never possibly find the effect in the supposed cause, by the most accurate scrutiny and examination. For the effect is totally different from the cause, and consequently can never be discovered in it. Motion in the second Billiard-ball is a quite distinct event from motion in the first; nor is there anything in the one to suggest the smallest hint of the other. A stone or piece of metal raised into the air, and left without any support, immediately falls: but to consider the matter a priori, is there anything we discover in this situation which can beget the idea of a downward, rather than an upward, or any other motion, in the stone or metal?

And as the first imagination or invention of a particular effect, in all natural operations, is arbitrary, where we consult not experience; so must we also esteem the supposed tie or connexion between the cause and effect, which binds them together, and renders it impossible that any other effect could result from the operation of that cause. When I see, for instance, a Billiard-ball moving in a straight line towards another; even suppose motion in the second ball should by accident be suggested to me, as the result of their contact or impulse; may I

not conceive, that a hundred different events might as well follow from that cause? May not both these balls remain at absolute rest? May not the first ball return in a straight line, or leap off from the second in any line or direction? All these suppositions are consistent and conceivable. Why then should we give the preference to one, which is no more consistent or conceivable than the rest? All our reasonings a priori will never be able to show us any foundation for this preference.

In a word, then, every effect is a distinct event from its cause. It could not, therefore, be discovered in the cause, and the first invention or conception of it, a priori, must be entirely arbitrary. And even after it is suggested, the conjunction of it with the cause must appear equally arbitrary; since there are always many other effects, which, to reason, must seem fully as consistent and natural. In vain, therefore, should we pretend to determine any single event, or infer any cause or effect, without the assistance of observation and experience.

Hence we may discover the reason why no philosopher, who is rational and modest, has ever pretended to assign the ultimate cause of any natural operation, or to show distinctly the action of that power, which produces any single effect in the universe. It is confessed, that the utmost effort of human reason is to reduce the principles, productive of natural phenomena, to a greater simplicity, and to resolve the many particular effects into a few general causes, by means of reasonings from analogy, experience, and observation. But as to the causes of these general causes, we should in vain attempt their discovery; nor shall we ever be able to satisfy ourselves, by any particular explication of them. These ultimate springs and principles are totally shut up from human curiosity and enquiry. Elasticity, gravity, cohesion of parts, communication of motion by impulse; these are probably the ultimate causes and principles which we shall ever discover in nature; and we may esteem ourselves sufficiently happy, if, by accurate enquiry and reasoning, we can trace up the particular phenomena to, or near to, these general principles. The most perfect philosophy of the natural kind only staves off our ignorance a little longer: as perhaps the most perfect philosophy of the moral or metaphysical kind serves only to discover larger portions of it. Thus the observation of human blindness and weakness is the result of all philosophy, and meets us at every turn, in spite of our endeavours to elude or avoid it.

Nor is geometry, when taken into the assistance of natural philosophy, ever able to remedy this defect, or lead us into the knowledge of ultimate causes, by all that accuracy of reasoning for which it is so justly celebrated. Every part of mixed mathematics proceeds upon the supposition that certain laws are established by nature in her operations; and abstract reasonings are employed, either to assist experience in the discovery of these laws, or to determine their influence in particular instances, where it depends upon any precise degree of distance and quantity. Thus, it is a law of motion, discovered by experience, that the moment or force of any body in motion is in the compound ratio or proportion of its solid contents and its velocity; and consequently, that a small force may remove the greatest obstacle or raise the greatest weight, if, by any contrivance or machinery, we can increase the velocity of that force, so as to make it an overmatch for its antagonist. Geometry assists us in the application of this law, by giving us the just dimensions of all the parts and figures which can enter into any species of machine; but still the discovery of the law itself is owing merely to experience, and all the abstract reasonings in the world could never lead us one step towards the knowledge of it. When we reason a priori, and consider merely any object or cause, as it appears to the mind, independent of all observation, it never could suggest to us the notion of any distinct object, such as its effect; much less, show us the inseparable and inviolable connexion between them. A man must be very sagacious who could discover by reasoning that crystal is the effect of heat, and ice of cold, without being previously acquainted with the operation of these qualities.

## DISCUSSION QUESTIONS FOR CRITIQUE AND ANALYSIS

1. How does Hume distinguish between "relations of ideas" and "matters of fact"? Do very young children intuitively understand and accept the "truths" of arithmetic, algebra, and geometry? If not, do you think Hume is correct when he concludes that propositions reflecting relations of ideas are "discoverable by the mere operation of thought, without dependence on what is anywhere existent in the universe"? Explain.

2. Do you believe that cause-and-effect relations are a product of human imagination or embedded externally in the physical world? Give reasons for your answer, paying attention to the formal structure of the argument you construct.

---

## ORIGINAL SOURCEWORK

*An Afrocentric/Feminist Standpoint Challenges the Tradition of Positivism*

### PATRICIA HILL COLLINS

**Patricia Hill Collins** (1948–  ) is a sociologist whose research on the experiences of African-American women calls into question its tradition of positivism and the empirical philosophy on which it's based.

---

Positivist approaches aim to create scientific descriptions of reality by producing objective generalizations.

Because researchers have widely differing values, experiences, and emotions, genuine science is thought to be unattainable unless all human characteristics except rationality are eliminated from the research process. By following strict methodological rules, scientists aim to distance themselves from the values, vested interests, and emotions generated by their class, race, sex, or unique situation. By decontextualizing themselves, they

Source: Patricia Hill Collins, *Black Feminist Thought.* © 1990, 1999. Reproduced by permission of Taylor & Francis, Inc., Routledge, Inc. (http://www.routledge-ny.com).

allegedly become detached observers and manipulators of nature. Moreover, this researcher decontextualiztion is paralleled by comparable efforts to remove the objects of study from their contexts. The result of this entire process is often the separation of information from meaning.

Several requirements typify positivist methodological approaches. First, research methods generally require a distancing of the researcher from her or his "object" of study by defining the researcher as a "subject" with full human subjectivity and by objectifying the "object" of study. A second requirement is the absence of emotions from the research process. Third, ethics and values are deemed inappropriate in the research process, either as the reason for scientific inquiry or as part of the research process itself. Finally, adversarial debates, whether written or oral, become the preferred method of ascertaining truth: the arguments that can withstand the greatest assault and survive intact become the strongest truths.

Such criteria ask African-American women to objectify ourselves, devalue our emotional life, displace our motivations for furthering knowledge about Black women, and confront in an adversarial relationship those with more social, economic, and professional power. It therefore seems unlikely that Black women would use a positivist epistemological stance in rearticulating a Black women's standpoint. Black women are more likely to choose an alternative epistemology for assessing knowledge claims, one using different standards that are consistent with Black women's criteria for substantiated knowledge and with our criteria for methodological adequacy. If such an epistemology exists, what are its contours? . . .

Because Black women have access to both the Afrocentric and the feminist standpoints, an alternative epistemology used to rearticulate a Black women's standpoint should reflect elements of both traditions . . . While an Afrocentric feminist epistemology reflects elements of epistemologies used by African-Americans and women as groups, it also paradoxically demonstrates features that may be unique to Black women. On certain dimensions Black women may most closely resemble Black men; on others, white women; and on still others Black women may stand apart from both groups. Black women's both/and conceptual orientation, the act of being simultaneously a member of a group and yet standing apart

from it, forms an integral part of Black women's consciousness. . . .

Rather than emphasizing how a Black women's standpoint and its accompanying epistemology are different from those in Afrocentric and feminist analysis, I use Black women's experiences to examine points of contact between the two. Viewing an Afrocentric feminist epistemology in this way challenges additive analyses of oppression claiming that Black women have a more accurate view of oppression than do other groups. Such approaches suggest that oppression can be quantified and compared and that adding layers of oppression produces a potentially clearer standpoint. One implication of standpoint approaches is that the more subordinated the group, the purer the vision of the oppressed group. This is an outcome of the origins of standpoint approaches in Marxist social theory, itself an analysis of social structure rooted in Western either/or dichotomous thinking. Ironically, by quantifying and ranking human oppressions, standpoint theorists invoke criteria for methodological adequacy characteristic of positivism. Although it is tempting to claim that Black women are more oppressed than everyone else and therefore have the best standpoint from which to understand the mechanisms, processes, and effects of oppression, this simply may not be the case. . . .

For most African-American women those individuals who have lived through the experiences about which they claim to be experts are more believable and credible than those who have merely read or thought about such experiences. Thus concrete experience as a criterion for credibility frequently is invoked by Black women when making knowledge claims. For instance, Hannah Nelson describes the importance personal experience has for her: "Our speech is most directly personal, and every black person assumes that every other black person has a right to a personal opinion. In speaking of grave matters, your personal experience is considered very good evidence. With us, distant statistics are certainly not as important as the actual experience of a sober person." Similarly, Ruth Shays uses her concrete experiences to challenge the idea that formal education is the only route to knowledge: "I am the kind of person who doesn't have a lot of education, but both my mother and my father had good common sense. Now, I think that's all you need. I might not know how to use thirty-four words where three would do, but that does not mean that I don't know what I'm talking about. . . . I know what I'm talking about because I'm talking about myself. I'm talking about what I've lived through." Implicit in Ms. Shays's self-assessment is a critique of the type of knowlege that obscures the truth, the "thirty-four words" that cover up a truth that can be expressed in three.

Even after substantial mastery of white masculinist epistemologies, many Black women scholars invoke our own concrete experiences and those of other African-American women in selecting topics for investigation and methodologies used. . . .

Experience as a criterion of meaning with practical images as its symbolic vehicle is a fundamental epistemological tenet in African-American thought systems . . . In valuing the concrete, African-American women invoke not only an Afrocentric tradition but a women's tradition as well. . . .

"Dialogue implies talk between two subjects, not the speech of subject and object. It is a humanizing speech, one that challenges and resists domination," as-serts Bell Hooks. For Black women new knowledge claims are rarely worked out in isolation from other individuals and are usually developed through dialogues with other members of a community. A primary epistemological assumption underlying the use of dialogue in assessing knowledge claims is that connectedness rather than separation is an essential component of the knowledge validation process. . . . Not to be confused with adversarial debate, the use of dialogue has deep roots in an African-based oral tradition and in African-American culture.

## DISCUSSION QUESTIONS FOR CRITIQUE AND ANALYSIS

1. According to Patricia Hill Collins, what is the problem with positivist approaches to describing and understanding reality?

2. How is an "Afrocentric feminist epistemology" different from other, more traditional approaches to the study of knowledge?

## PHILOSOPHICAL PROFILE

**IMMANUEL KANT**

### Immanuel Kant

Immanuel Kant was born on April 22, 1724, in the East Prussian town of Königsberg (present day Kaliningrad), situated near the southeastern shore of the Baltic Sea between Poland and Lithuania. Immanuel was the fourth of nine children, only five of whom survived to adulthood.[76] His parents were pietist Lutherans who belonged to the lower middle class. Throughout his life, Kant always maintained an honest respect for religion and a deep moral sense, though he eventually abandoned the puritanical pietism that had been a dominating influence in his family. Immanuel Kant's life could hardly be described as eventful and is now famous for its routine. He was very much a creature of habit, having a fixed hour for all of his daily activities, whether it was waking, drinking coffee, eating lunch, or going for a stroll. It has been said that people could set their clocks by Kant's afternoon walks at half past three. Each day he would put on his grey coat and, with bamboo cane in hand, would walk down Lime Tree Avenue, now called "Philosopher's Walk" in honor of Kant. Though Kant had a goodly number of friends and associates, he never married, and in contrast to many of his contemporaries, who were filled with the spirit of travel, he never ventured more than about 40 miles in any direction of Königsberg. This lack of travel apparently did not affect his wandering intellectual genius, however. For more than a dozen years, Kant lectured as a *Privatdozent* at what was then known as Albertus University in Königsberg in subjects as varied as mathematics, logic, geography, history, and philosophy. He also worked as a family tutor before finally being appointed professor of philosophy at his alma mater in 1770. Apparently Kant had a reputation as an excellent lecturer, full of wit and good nature. He must have been a late bloomer, as his first important book was not published until he was 57 years old, a fact which doesn't go entirely unnoticed among aging and frustrated academics today!

Immanuel Kant is considered by many contemporary philosophers as the greatest thinker since Plato and Aristotle. His influence is still strongly felt not only in epistemological circles, but in fields as diverse as cognitive psychology, moral education, ethics, and social/political philosophy. Kant is best known for the following books: *Critique of Pure Reason* (1781), *Prolegomena to Any Future Metaphysics (1783), Foundations of the Metaphysics of Morals (1785), and Critique of Judgment (1790).* Immanuel Kant died on February 12, 1804.

# IMMANUEL KANT'S SYNTHESIS OF RATIONALISM AND EMPIRICISM

> *"There can be no doubt that all our knowledge begins with experience. . . . But though all our knowledge begins with experience, it does not follow that it all arises out of experience."*
> IMMANUEL KANT

As a university student, Immanuel Kant was educated in a tradition steeped in philosophical rationalism. However, he eventually became critical of the rationalist's use of reason or pure intellect as a basis for making claims about God and the essences of mind and matter. He argued that rationalist philosophers could not possibly know what they claimed to know about such things, since direct knowledge of a mind-independent reality goes beyond the capacity of the human intellect to comprehend.[77] Like the empiricists Locke and Hume, Kant wished to prescribe certain limits to human understanding. On the subject of Hume, it is worth noting that it was not until the middle of his academic career that Kant actually became familiar with Hume's empiricist philosophy. Kant said that reading Hume awakened him from his "dogmatic slumbers." This awakening caused Kant to become disillusioned with the philosophy of his youth. From his new enlightened position, Kant concluded that rationalists had failed to critically assess the powers of human reason before engaging in their grand speculations.[78] This is not to suggest that Kant uncritically accepted all the ideas of Hume and the other empiricists. He certainly took issue with many empiricist assumptions and with Humean skepticism in particular. As we proceed through this section, you will come to better appreciate how Kant was influenced by both empiricists and rationalists, and how he combined ideas from both in the development of his own synthetic epistemology.

As a way of rounding out this discussion, we'll also bring Plato back into view. Of course, Plato revered rationality in the quest for knowledge and placed great faith in the powers of the mind to achieve an intellectual acquaintance of the eternal and immutable truths found in the supernatural realm of forms. We'll soon see what Kant had to say about this.

## The Roles of Reason and Experience in Knowledge

Kant's synthesis of rationalism and empiricism can be better understood by initially looking at how each perspective we have discussed viewed **reason** and **experience.** Take Descartes, for example, the preeminent rationalist. Recall how he used the technique of methodological doubt to arrive at the conclusion that the ultimate foundation of knowledge had to be the *Cogito*, or *I Think*. All sensory-based experience could be doubted as illusory, as an evil deception or a dream perhaps. What could not be doubted was that Descartes existed as a thinking thing. Using self-conscious rationality as a basis of certainty, Descartes proceeded to deduce logically the existence of God and later the existence of the external, physical world. In his "wax example," we learned how Descartes tried to deduce the notion of "substance" through rational abstraction, that is, by eliminating the changing, sensory-based qualities of the wax to arrive at its essential nature. For Descartes, reason ruled supreme. Truths were to be logically derived from rationally established axioms.

Empiricists like Locke and Hume, differed with Descartes, arguing that the source of all knowledge is found in experience. For Locke the mind was a "*tabula rasa*"—blank slate upon which objects in experience imprinted themselves. Hume, as well, posited that all mental ideas, even fantastic ones like unicorns and satyrs, ultimately had their source in experience, especially in sensory-based impressions. Furthermore, unlike Descartes, who took the *Cogito* as self-evidently certain, Hume argued that the "I," "self," or Cartesian *Cogito* represent nothing more than a steady stream of consciousness. Impressions simply come and go. Now, whether the self is conceptualized as nothing more than a random series of fleeting images as in Hume's "theater of the mind," or as Locke's *tabula rasa*, in both instances experience becomes the ultimate source of whatever knowledge is possible.

Immanuel Kant's synthesis of rationalism and empiricism allows for both reason and experience to play a role in the formation of knowledge. Kant accepts the Humean notion that sensory impressions come from experience. He calls them **matter, content,** or **sensible intuitions.**[79] However, for Kant, there is a second element to knowledge, which comes from the mind itself. According to Kant, the human mind is not a passive entity like a *tabula rasa*. It does not merely receive and record what comes to it from the external world through the senses. Rather, for Kant, the mind is *active*, providing the *forms* into which the contents of experience are poured, shaped and arranged. In other words, we are not just stimulus receptors registering externally derived impressions. We actively construct and make sense of the outer world, bringing to our encounter with objects mental forms, which make experience possible in the first place. Reality as we know it is, therefore, not completely external and independent of ourselves. We actually *do something* to incoming sensory information to produce our experience of the world. This process is instantaneous and pre-reflective, and consequently, we are not usually aware that it is happening when it does. In efforts to momentarily slow down this unconscious process of reality construction, involving the assimilation of sense data into perceptual and cognitive forms furnished by the understanding (mind), look at Figure 4.4. What do you see in Box A? Do you see a triangle? If so, your mind actively linked the three dots

A
B

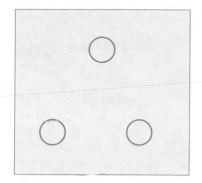
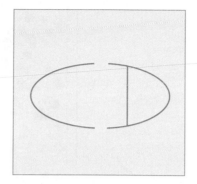

**FIGURE 4.4**

together. Perhaps you saw the "therefore" symbol used in logic and mathematics. In either case, sensory input provided the raw data, or content, of this perception, while your mind provided the forms of understanding that allowed you to give unity to it and make sense of three otherwise unrelated dots.

Now look at Box B. What do you see there? Perhaps you see the letters C and D. If so, ask yourself what they mean. What judgment can you make about what you see? If you come from a computer background, the letters may mean "change directory." If you know something about fashion, they may stand for the designer label Christian Dior. If you are a music enthusiast, they could mean "compact disc." However, if you just saw the movie Roxanne, you might conclude that CD refers to the nickname of the firechief Steve Martin plays in the film. The point is that however Box B is perceived and understood depends on how it fits into the structural forms provided by your mind. (By the way, many of my students do not see the letters CD at all, but rather a shoe print.)[80]

Just in case you are still having trouble understanding how random content is structured by the mind, look now at Figure 4.5 (on page 232). There you have four more frames, only this time, they are a little more complex. What do you see in each frame? (Don't read on until you look for a while at each one.)

As you looked at the frames, did you notice how your *mind's eye* kept trying to arrange and rearrange the shapes in each one to "fit" some idea or concept of what it might be? The perceptual mechanisms of your mind spontaneously tried to assimilate the sensory data (content) of the various frames into pre-existing mental or cognitive forms derived from the understanding. Perhaps you were readily able to see objects in each frame. If so, the process was spontaneous and automatic. As a result, you might not have appreciated the cognitive process that made the experience possible. If you haven't been able to see anything, let me give you categories that you can use in each frame to make sense of it. In Frame A, look for a person on a bicycle. In Frame B, look for a teapot. In Frame C, look for three shoes, and in Frame D, look for a water faucet. Now that you have been given the forms, I suspect you will begin to mentally arrange the sensory impressions to see what is there.[81]

> **❝ . . . no form of knowledge, not even perceptual knowledge, constitutes a simple copy of reality, because it always includes a process of assimilation to previous structures. ❞**
> JEAN PIAGET, A KANTIAN PSYCHOLOGIST

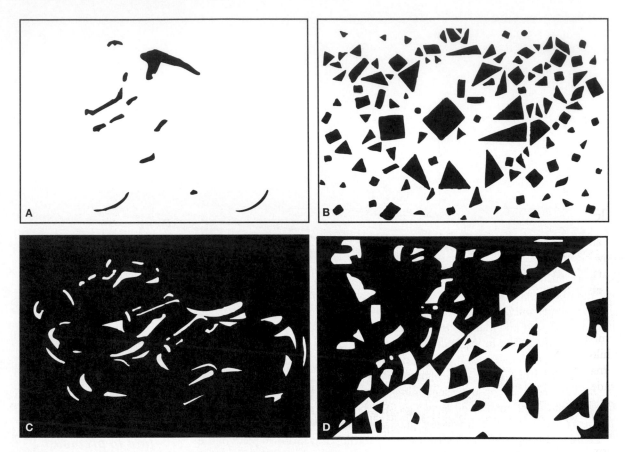

**FIGURE 4.5** Anthony Falikowski, *Mastering Human Relations*, 3/e, Toronto: Prentice Hall, 2002, p. 234. © 2002 Pearson Education Canada Inc., Toronto, Ontario.

Notice the significant activity involved in the experience of seeing the various objects. Perception was not a passive recording but an **active construction**—Kant's point illustrated. However, had you lived in a culture where running tap water did not exist, where faucets were unheard of, where there were no such things as bicycles, where tea was unknown, and where people walked barefoot, it would have been impossible for you to see the objects in the manifold of sensory data presented to you. You had to *bring something to the experience* itself. Without your contribution of mental concepts, the content of experience would never have formed identifiable objects. As Kant says in the "Introduction" to the *Critique of Pure Reason:*

There can be no doubt that all our knowledge begins with experience. For how should our faculty of knowledge be awakened into action did not objects affecting our senses partly of themselves produce representations, partly arouse the activity of our understanding to compare these representations, and, by combining or separating them, work up the raw material of the sensible impressions into that knowledge of objects which is entitled experience? In the order of time, therefore, we have no knowledge antecedent to experience and with experience all our knowledge begins.

But though all our knowledge begins with experience, it does not follow that it all arises out of experience. For it may well be that even our empirical knowledge is made up of what our own faculty of knowledge (sensible impressions serving merely as the occasion) supplies from itself. If our faculty of knowledge makes any such addition, it may be that we are not in a position to distinguish it from the raw material, until with long practice of attention we have become skilled in separating it.[82]

## The Copernican Revolution in Epistemology

In an earlier reference to Mikolaj Kopernik, the Polish astronomer, we learned how humanity's worldview was changed when he presented the thesis that the Earth revolved around the sun on its own axis and not the other way around. In effect, Kopernik stripped the Earth of its "God-given" status and position as the center of the universe, transforming it into just one planet among others. Understandably, this led to an upheaval in human and scientific thought. In a similar fashion, Kantian epistemology represents a Copernican revolution in philosophical thinking. Before Kant, attention was generally focused on the external world. Knowledge meant knowledge of objects or things *out there*. Human understanding had to conform to its objects, which possessed primary and secondary qualities (Locke), or which produced sensory impressions on which mental ideas were ultimately based (Hume). In a Copernican fashion, Kant reverses all of this, asking us to consider the possibility that the mind does not conform to objects but that objects must conform to the mind. Kant writes:

> Hitherto it has been assumed that all our knowledge must conform to objects. But all attempts to extend our knowledge of objects by establishing something in regard to them *a priori*, by means of concepts, have, on this assumption, ended in failure. We must therefore make trial whether we may not have more success in the tasks of metaphysics if we suppose that objects must conform to our knowledge. This would agree better with what is desired, namely, that it should be possible to have knowledge of objects *a priori*, determining something in regard to them prior to their being given. We should then be proceeding precisely on the lines of Copernicus' primary hypothesis (Bxvi).[83]

In the activity we just completed, involving the structuring of sense data by conceptual forms, we observed first-hand how our minds play an active role in determining experience. When we see objects (shoes, faucets) as objects of knowledge, sense data from experience must be arranged and ordered to conform to the structural forms imposed on them by the mind.

The new Kantian way of conceptualizing knowledge constitutes an important turn in philosophy—a turn away from seeing the external world as something possessing an independent nature and a turn toward the inner

*"Mind is the law-giver to Nature."*

KANT

> *"Thoughts without content are empty, intuitions without concepts are blind."*
>
> KANT

workings, activities, and powers of the mind. For Kant, the mind's structure holds an important key to what we experience and what we can know. With the external world stripped of its independent status, the object of knowledge becomes always, and in some degree, the creation or construction of the subject. Whatever is experienced or known results in large part as a product of the mind itself, in interaction with sense data. Objects must conform to the concepts by which the mind understands things.[84] Remember, however, that the mind alone, without external sensations, has nothing to structure, and hence, without sensory intuitions, the rational understanding cannot do the job. Capturing the *interactive* nature of reason and experience in a nutshell, Kant writes: "Without sensibility no object would be given to us, without understanding no object would be thought. Thoughts without content are empty, intuitions [sense data] without concepts are blind."[85] Reason and experience are thus both necessary in the formation of knowledge.

## A Priori Elements of Knowledge

The perceptual activity involving the faucet and teapot (see Figure 4.5) was helpful with respect to understanding how form and content relate to one another and how the mind interacts with sense data to make experience possible. What could have been a little misleading in my illustration, however, were the concepts to be applied, since they were all empirical—that is, derived from a particular cultural experience. The point was even made that if you were born and raised in a society that had no concept of shoes, running water, tea, or two-wheeled transportation (and assuming you had never been exposed to them before), it would have been impossible for you to have seen such objects in each frame. Granted this, I suppose the empiricist could argue that such concepts are clearly learned through experience, and thus, even if forms do indeed give structure to the content of sensory impressions, the forms are still ultimately empirically derived.

In further clarification of Kant, I should emphatically point out that the forms that concern him are not empirical but **a priori.** Describing the Kantian forms as *a priori* means they are not derived from experience or learned from it; they are prior to it in the sense of being logically presupposed in it. The Kantian *a priori* categories (forms of intuition and understanding) are universal and necessary. They form the structure of the mind, of any consciousness. Without the *a priori* forms of experience, there could be no knowledge, nor even any experience itself. This requires some explanation.

In a section of the *Critique of Pure Reason* entitled "The Transcendental Aesthetic," Kant introduces the *a priori* concepts of **space** and **time.** He calls them **forms of intuition.** Let us take space first. For Kant, space is one of the mind's forms that serves to arrange sensations. Note that it is not itself a sensation. There is no sense impression of space. We do not actually experience space itself, though we experience objects that are spatially structured within it. Kant says, "By means of outer sense, a property of our mind, we represent to ourselves objects as outside us, and all without exception in space."[86] It is in space that objects take on shape, magnitude, and relations to one another (that is, closer or farther apart). Three-dimensional objects take up space and are experienced in space. Thus, without the category of space already being embedded in the experience of any particular object, the experience of that object would be impossible. Try to remember any experience you've had of a tree or chair or other object that does not occupy space. You cannot. Space is the form of outer sense structuring the experience of all objects external to us.

Whereas space is the form of outer sense, *time* is the form of inner sense. Kant says, "Time cannot be outwardly intuited any more than space can be intuited as something in us."[87] The fact that objects appear permanent or at least appear to endure from one moment to the next, and the fact that we can represent to ourselves a number of things existing simultaneously or successively (one after the other) presupposes the *a priori* concept of time. An object is either here now or it is not; an object can come before or after or at the same time. The object in front of us at this moment in time remains the same object in the next moment. We do not experience a new world of ever-changing objects every instant of our lives. To borrow a phrase from cognitive-developmental psychology, we perceive "object permanence" through time.[88]

Like space, time is a *pure form of sensible intuition* necessarily underlying all our sensory experiences of objects. Objects that appear to us must do so in time. As Kant points out, "Appearances may, one and all, vanish; but time (as the universal condition of their possibility) cannot itself be removed."[89] This being said, it becomes clear that for Kant all our knowledge and experience of objects stemming from sensibility must be organized and arranged by the *a priori* forms of space and time.

Of course, sensations and the forms of intuition do not, in themselves, afford us actual knowledge of objects. If cognitive (mental) functioning involved only the mechanisms of perception, we would have spatially and temporally ordered sensations but not knowledge itself. In addition to the **faculty of sensibility** from which we get space and time, Kant also formulated a **faculty of understanding,** which houses an entire set of other categories allowing us to connect experiences and make judgments about them. Kant writes: ". . . there are two stems of human knowledge, namely *sensibility* and *understanding*, which perhaps spring from a common, but to us unknown, root. Through the former, objects are given to us; through the latter, they are thought."[90]

In his examination of the kinds of judgments we can make about objects (found in the "Transcendental Deduction" of the *Critique*), Kant discovers that there are twelve kinds and believes it is possible to logically deduce the categories (*a priori* concepts) required to make them. The twelve categories fall under four headings: quantity, quality, relation, and modality. A chart containing all the *a priori* categories of the understanding, as well as those belonging to sensibility, is included in Figure 4.6 (on page 236).

A complete and detailed coverage of the Kantian *a priori* categories of the understanding would take us far beyond the introductory purposes of this text. What we can do, however, is focus on the specific categories of *substance* and *cause* to better appreciate Kant's disagreements with the empiricists—and Hume in particular. But before we do so, allow me to make a clarifying point by bringing Plato back into the discussion for a moment.

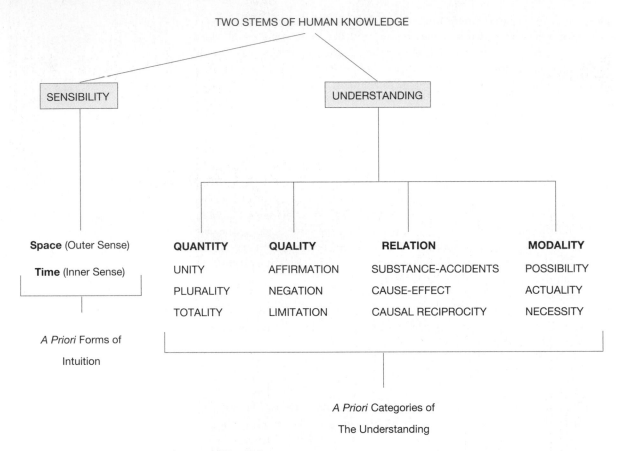

**FIGURE 4.6** Kantian *a priori* elements of knowledge.

## Kantian versus Platonic Forms

Earlier in this chapter, we learned about Plato's Divided Line Theory of Knowledge and his conceptualization of a realm of forms. Plato argued that forms or ideas in this realm have an independent ontological status apart from all individual minds. They represent the ultimate structures of reality that the world of flux copies. As we learned, any particular object participates in its form, which is perfect and ideal. Actual objects themselves are merely transitory and imperfect approximations of what is ultimately real. They belong to the visible world of becoming. By contrast, Kantian forms are not structures of metaphysical reality but structures of human consciousness. They constitute the ordering principles of the mind, which combine with sensations to make experience possible. Unlike Plato, who grants forms their own realm within which to reside, Kant gives them only epistemological significance. He does not imbue them with any special metaphysical or ontological status in the way Plato does. It is important, therefore, for you to distinguish between Kantian and Platonic forms and not to confuse them for purposes of your own understanding of epistemology.

# The Categories of "Cause" and "Substance"

While objects are given to us in sensibility through the forms of intuition, space, and time, we make judgments about them in the understanding, presupposing *a priori* categories like "causality" and "substance." David Hume allowed for no coherent notion of substance, since all ideas must have their origin in impressions. Because there is no impression corresponding to substance, any discussion of it becomes for him pure fantasy. Hume also pointed out that there is no sense impression of causality. Causes do not exist in objects or substance either. For Hume, when we assign cause-and-effect relationships, the human mind is really falling prey to habit or custom. After witnessing two separate and isolated events occur contiguously and one always before the other, we erroneously conclude that a "necessary causal connection" exists. A "gentle force" makes us "feel" that the objects are connected by cause and effect. Causal necessity is not a feature of the world but a subjective construct emanating from an habitual association of ideas.

As for Kant, he would agree that there are no impressions, sensory or otherwise, that correspond to substance and causality, yet he does not give in to Humean skepticism. This is not to suggest that Kant believes that substance, for instance, is some kind of property or quality inherent in objects, as Locke and Descartes argued. For Kant, substance constitutes an *a priori* category of the understanding by means of which the mind selectively groups sensations from the manifold of experience and unifies them into meaningful and coherent units we recognize as objects. For example, the category of substance is presupposed when we combine the sensations of salty, greasy, crunchy, and yellowy-white into the empirical concept of "potato chip." Thus, the *a priori* category of substance is not derived from experience but logically presupposed in it. Without substance, the experience of objects, as objects, would be impossible. Had the category of substance been absent, we couldn't have experienced the potato chip as a potato chip.

Kant's thinking on causality is similar to that on substance. He would admit that there is no sense impression that corresponds to causality, and to this extent, he would agree with Hume. Furthermore, remember that, for Hume, causality is not somehow embedded in reality as an ontological or metaphysical fact. Again, Kant would agree here. However, Kant disagrees with Hume, who argued that our belief in causality comes merely from custom and mental habit or from the observation of consistent conjunction. Hume used this claim to reject the scientific idea of necessary (causal) connection and also to reject the scientific notion of inductive inference. What happened yesterday or many times before cannot guarantee what will happen today or tomorrow. Of course, it is precisely upon causality and inductive inference that science is built. Hume's rejection of their legitimacy thus constitutes a skeptical attack on the very foundations of scientific knowledge.

As a challenge to Humean skepticism, Kant claims that we do, in fact, have knowledge about causality, necessary connections, and universally true propositions. For example, we know with certainty that $7 + 5 = 12$ in every instance where it occurs. We also know that heavy objects cannot float in space under normal gravitational conditions, that they must always fall to the ground necessarily. We know this without having seen every heavy object fall. Furthermore, we say with confidence things like "Every change must have a cause" and we say this though we have not learned it from experience.

In Kantian epistemology, we recognize cause-and-effect relationships in the world of experience because of the way in which our brains are wired to perceive objects given to us in sensible intuition. The experiences we have are structured and organized through the cognitive filter of causality. Like the other forms of sensibility and categories of the understanding, causality is logically prior to experience and it is what makes experience possible. Seeing "causal connections" is not something that results only as a product of repeated pairings in experience; these perceived connections presuppose the concept of causality in the first place.

For Kant, then, experience will always have a universal and necessary structure. Forms of intuition (space and time) and categories of the understanding (causality and substance) guarantee that we are not presented with a mere random display of meaningless sensory impressions giving rise to a buzzing, booming, confusion. When we open our eyes, we consistently see objects that appear external to ourselves and are in some relation to one another. Our minds take impressions from the sensible manifold, unify them, and organize them into objects within a three-dimensional representation of space. Instead of seeing a flat, two-dimensional blur, we see substantial things "out there." The upshot of the Kantian *a priori* categories of thought is that they provide us with knowledge about objects in experience that is both universal and necessary. Since the forms of intuition and the categories of understanding come into play on the occasion of experience but are not derived from it, they can be described as *a priori*, pure of anything empirical. In short, there can be certain knowledge that is not based entirely on sense impressions or ideas stemming from our experience of objects.

## Types of Judgments

In our earlier discussion of "Hume's Fork," we learned that, for Hume, objects of human inquiry fall under one of two types: those that demonstrate the relations of ideas and those that describe matters of fact. Knowledge claims based on relations of ideas (for examples, mathematical statements) could provide us with certainty, Hume said, but unfortunately they could not tell us anything about the world. On the other hand, propositions stating matters of fact could describe the world, but unfortunately they had to remain uncertain, since they are all based on inductive inference and causal thinking, and we know that, for Hume, no certainty can be found there.[91]

For Kant, knowledge claims always come in the form of judgments in which something is affirmed or denied. A judgment is a mental operation whereby we connect a **subject** and a **predicate.** The predicate functions to qualify the subject in some fashion. For instance, "This rose is beautiful." is a judgment in which our mind is able to see a connection between a subject (rose) and a predicate (beautiful). As Kant demonstrates, subjects and predicates can be related to each other in a variety of ways to form different types of judgments: **analytic,**

**synthetic,** *a priori* and *a posteriori*. These types of judgments can also be combined to produce **analytic** *a priori,* **synthetic** *a priori,* and **synthetic** *a posteriori.* Analytic *a posteriori* judgments cannot exist, for the two elements (analytic and *a posteriori*) are logically contradictory with each other. You will understand why in a moment. See Figure 4.7 for a classification of Kantian judgments.

With analytic judgments we find that the predicate is already contained in the concept of the subject. To repeat an often-used example: "Triangles are enclosed three-sided figures containing three angles." In this instance, the predicate is implicit in the subject. By triangle we mean "enclosed three-sided figure containing three angles." Thus, the predicate offers us no new knowledge about the subject. Another example is: "All bodies are extended." It must be analytic, for the idea of extension is already contained in the idea of body. A major feature of analytic judgments is that we find necessary truth in them simply because of the logical relations between subjects and predicates. Any denial of an analytic judgment represents a logical contradiction.

By contrast to analytic judgments, synthetic judgments do not have their predicates contained in their subjects. In a synthetic judgment, the predicate adds something new to the subject. "The bookshelf is tall" is an example of a synthetic judgment because it joins or "synthesizes" two entirely independent

**FIGURE 4.7**   **A table of Kantian judgments.**

| | Analytic | Synthetic |
|---|---|---|
| A Priori | Analytic *A Priori* | Synthetic *A Priori* |
| A Posteriori | Analytic *A Posteriori* (logically Incoherent) | Synthetic *A Posteriori* |

concepts. The concept of "bookshelf" does not contain the concept of "tall" and vice versa. Bookshelves can be short, while not everything that is tall is necessarily a bookshelf.

Kant also distinguishes between *a priori* **judgments** and *a posteriori* **judgments.** All analytic judgments are *a priori.* They are marked by necessity and strict universality. Their meaning and validation do *not* depend on experience since they are completely independent of it. Nothing in experience is required to prove them; nothing in experience could falsify them. The best examples of *a priori* judgments are found in mathematics. The empirical fact that one raindrop plus one raindrop equals one larger raindrop cannot threaten the truth of the mathematical statement that one plus one equals two.

While analytic statements are all *a priori,* synthetic judgments are frequently *a posteriori.* To say that a statement or judgment is *a posteriori* is to say that is based on observation and experience, or at least that its truth is verifiable by such things. "Mary achieved the highest grade on the last philosophy test" is an example of a synthetic a posteriori statement. The concept of "highest grade" is not necessarily included in the idea or concept of Mary. Whether or not she actually got the highest grade can be established by comparing student scores in the class. It's possible, of course, that we made a mistake in our conclusion. Perhaps another student actually scored the highest. Empirical means are required to determine the truth or falsity of our claim. We could deny that Mary scored the highest without contradicting ourselves. Thus, we find in synthetic *a posteriori* statements no logical necessity. Again, note that since the predicate (highest grade) is not necessarily contained in the subject (Mary), we can understand how this proposition is synthetic as well as *a posteriori.*

As far as analytic *a posteriori* judgments are concerned, there are none. An analytic *a posteriori* judgment is a contradiction in terms. Something cannot be *a priori*—universally necessary and independent of experience—while at the same time being contingent or conditional and based on observation and experience. This just doesn't make sense. Hence, the matrix in Figure 4.6 depicting Kant's classification of judgments, does not come out as neatly as one might like.

A controversial issue worth noting in Kant's classification pertains to synthetic *a priori* judgments. It was just said that synthetic judgments, like those about tall bookshelves, are often based on experience; but if this is so, how can they also be *a priori,* not contingent on experience? Kant argues that in fields like mathematics, physics, and ethics, we actually do make judgments that are both synthetic and *a priori.* For instance, the mathematical statement that "7 + 5 = 12" must be *a priori* in view of the fact that it reflects necessity and universality. The sum cannot be otherwise. Seven plus five must always and unconditionally equal twelve. To suggest otherwise is to deny the truth. Furthermore, Kant claims that this *a priori* statement is indeed synthetic, not analytic, arguing that 12 cannot be derived by a mere analysis of the numbers 7 and 5. An operation of the mind synthesizes the two numbers to arrive at 12. It is on this point that the controversy rests.

Another example of a synthetic *a priori* judgment can be taken from scientific reasoning. The proposition that "*All events have a cause.*" is *a priori* since it is based on the categorical concept of causality, which is logically prior to all experience. We don't say that some or most events have a cause, based on our experience or on most people's experience, but that *all* events necessarily and universally have a cause. Such knowledge is not contingent and therefore, not *a posteriori*. In addition, since we find that the concept of "cause" is not logically presupposed by the concept of "event" or "all events," the judgment proves to be synthetic, combining two separate notions. What we have in this case, then, is a synthetic *a priori* judgment that gives us necessary and certain knowledge of the world.

Still another example of a synthetic *a priori* judgment comes from geometry. Take the proposition: "A straight line is the shortest distance between two points." In this proposition, the concept of "straight" is a qualitative notion that does not contain within itself the quantitative notion of "shortest" or "shortest distance." Nonetheless, we know with absolute certainty that this statement will always be necessarily true. We do not have to experiment or measure every straight line in the world to find out for sure. We know it *a priori*.[92]

In view of what's been said so far, it would appear that Kant has rescued us from Humean skepticism. By means of his Copernican revolution, wherein objects were made to conform to the human mind, *a priori* elements of sensibility and understanding were uncovered. The categories of the mind and forms of intuition were used to illustrate how reason and experience combine in the construction of objects and in the formation of knowledge as expressed in the various types of judgments. Since, for Kant, all human minds are structured in the same way, we can conclude that within the bounds of human experience, it is possible to attain knowledge that is both universal and necessary.

Before we move on, let us now look at an excerpt from Immanuel Kant's "Introduction" of *The Critique of Pure Reason*. The selection addresses the notion that there exist different types of judgments, such as the ones already discussed.

## ORIGINAL SOURCEWORK

## *The Distinction between Analytic and Synthetic Judgments*

### IMMANUEL KANT

In all judgments in which the relation of a subject to the predicate is thought (I take into consideration affirmative judgments only, the subsequent application to negative judgments being easily made), this relation is possible in two different ways. Either the predicate B belongs to the subject A, as something which is (covertly) contained in this concept A; or B lies outside the concept A, although it does indeed stand in connection with it. In the one case I entitle the judgment analytic, in the other synthetic. Analytic judgments (affirmative) are therefore those in which the connection of the predicate with the subject is thought through identity; those in which this connection is thought without identity should be entitled synthetic. The former, as adding nothing through the predicate to the concept of the subject, but merely breaking it up into those constituent concepts that have all along been thought in it, although confusedly, can also be entitled analytic. The latter, on the other

Immanuel Kant, (tr.) Norman Kemp Smith, *Critique of Pure Reason*, New York: St. Martin's: Press, 1929, pp. 48–55.

hand, add to the concept of the subject a predicate which has not been in any wise thought in it, and which no analysis could possibly extract from it; and they may therefore be entitled analytic. If I say, for instance, "All bodies are extended," this is an analytic judgment. For I do not require to go beyond the concept which I connect with "body" in order to find extension as bound up with it. To meet with this predicate, I have merely to analyse the concept, that is, to become conscious to myself of the manifold which I always think in that concept. The judgment is therefore analytic. But when I say, "All bodies are heavy," the predicate is something quite different from anything that I think in the mere concept of body in general; and the addition of such a predicate therefore yields a synthetic judgment.

Judgments of experience, as such, are one and all synthetic. For it would be absurd to found an analytic judgment on experience. Since, in framing the judgment, I must not go outside my concept, there is no need to appeal to the testimony of experience in its support. That a body is extended is a proposition that holds *a priori* and is not empirical. For, before appealing to experience, I have already in the concept of body all the conditions required for my judgment. I have only to extract from it, in accordance with the principle of contradiction, the required predicate, and in so doing can at the same time become conscious of the necessity of the judgment—and that is what experience could never have taught me. On the other hand, though I do not include in the concept of a body in general the predicate "weight," nonetheless this concept indicates an object of experience through one of its parts, and I can add to that part other parts of this same experience, as in this way belonging together with the concept. From the start I can apprehend the concept of body analytically through the characters of extension, impenetrability, figure, etc., all of which are thought in the concept. Now, however, looking back on the experience from which I have derived this concept of body, and finding weight to be invariably connected with the above characters, I attach it as a predicate to the concept; and in doing so I attach it synthetically, and am therefore extending my knowledge. The possibility of the synthesis of the predicate "weight" with the concept of "body" thus rests upon experience. While the one concept is not contained in the other, they yet belong to one another, though only contingently, as parts of a whole,

namely, of an experience which is itself a synthetic combination of intuitions.

But in *a priori* synthetic judgments this help is entirely lacking: [I do not here have the advantage of looking around in the field of experience.] Upon what, then, am I to rely, when I seek to go beyond the concept A, and to know that another concept B is connected with it? Through what is the synthesis made possible? Let us take the proposition, "Everything which happens has its cause." In the concept of "something which happens," I do indeed think an existence which is preceded by a time, etc., and from this concept analytic judgments may be obtained. But the concept of a "cause" lies entirely outside the other concept, and signifies something different from "that which happens," and is not therefore in any way contained in this latter representation. How come I then to predicate of that which happens something quite different, and to apprehend that the concept of cause, though not contained in it, yet belongs, and indeed necessarily belongs, to it? What is here the unknown = X which gives support to the understanding when it believes that it can discover outside the concept A a predicate B foreign to this concept, which it yet at the same time considers to be connected with it? It cannot be experience, because the suggested principle has connected the second representation with the first, not only with greater universality, but also with the character of necessity, and therefore completely *a priori* and on the basis of mere concepts. Upon such synthetic, that is, ampliative principles, all our *a priori* speculative knowledge must ultimately rest; analytic judgments are very important, and indeed necessary, but only for obtaining that clearness in the concepts which is requisite for such a sure and wide synthesis as will lead to a genuinely new addition to all previous knowledge.

# IN ALL THEORETICAL SCIENCES OF REASON SYNTHETIC *A PRIORI* JUDGMENTS ARE CONTAINED AS PRINCIPLES

1. *All mathematical judgments, without exception are synthetic.* This fact, though incontestably certain and in its consequences very important, has hitherto escaped the notice of those who are engaged in the analysis of human reason, and is, indeed, directly opposed to all their conjec-

tures. For as it was found that all mathematical inferences proceed in accordance with the principle of contradiction (which the nature of all apodeictic certainly requires), it was supposed that the fundamental propositions of the science can themselves be known to be true through that principle. This is an erroneous view. For though a synthetic proposition can indeed be discerned in accordance with the principle of contradiction, this can only be if another synthetic proposition is presupposed, and if it can then be apprehended as following from this other proposition; it can never be so discerned in and by itself.

First of all, it has to be noted that mathematical propositions, strictly so called, are always judgments *a priori*, not empirical; because they carry with them necessity, which cannot be derived from experience. If this be demurred to, I am willing to limit my statement to *pure* mathematics, the very concept of which implies that it does not contain empirical, but only pure *a priori* knowledge.

We might, indeed, at first suppose that the proposition $7 + 5 = 12$ is a merely analytic proposition, and follows by the principle of contradiction from the concept of a sum of 7 and 5. But if we look more closely we find that the concept of the sum of 7 and 5 contains nothing save the union of the two numbers into one, and in this no thought is being taken as to what that single number may be which combines both. The concept of 12 is by no means already thought in merely thinking this union of 7 and 5; and I may analyze my concept of such a possible sum as long as I please, still I shall never find the 12 in it. We have to go outside these concepts, and call in the aid of the intuition which corresponds to one of them, our five fingers, for instance, or, as Segner does in his *Arithmetic*, adding to the concept of 7, unit by unit, the five given in intuition. For starting with the number 7, and for the concept of 5 calling in the aid of the fingers of my hand as intuition, I now add one by one to the number 7 the units which I previously took together to form the number 5, and with the aid of that figure [the hand] see the number 12 come into being. That 5 should be added to 7, I have indeed already thought in the concept of a sum $= 7 + 5$, but not that this sum is equivalent to the number 12. Arithmetical propositions are therefore always synthetic. This is still more evident if we take larger numbers. For it is then obvious that, however we might turn and twist our concepts, we could never, by the mere analysis of

them, and without the aid of intuition, discover what [the number is that] is the sum.

Just as little is any fundamental proposition of pure geometry analytic. That the straight line between two points is the shortest, is a synthetic proposition. For my concept of *straight* contains nothing of quantity, but only of quality. The concept of the shortest is wholly an addition, and cannot be derived, through any process of analysis, from the concept of the straight line. Intuition, therefore, must here be called in; only by its aid is the synthesis possible. What here causes us commonly to believe that the predicate of such apodeictic judgements is already contained in our concept, and that the judgment is therefore analytic, is merely the ambiguous character of the terms used. We are required to join in thought a certain predicate to a given concept, and this necessity is inherent in the concepts themselves. But the question is not what we *ought* to join in thought to the given concept, but what we *actually* think in it, even if only obscurely; and it is then manifest that, while the predicate is indeed attached necessarily to the concept, it is so in virtue of an intuition which must be added to the concept, not as thought in the concept itself.

Some few fundamental propositions, presupposed by the geometrician, are, indeed, really analytic, and rest on the principle of contradiction. But, as identical propositions, they serve only as links in the chain of method and not as principles; for instance, $a = a$; the whole is equal to itself; or $(a + b) > a$, that is, the whole is greater than its part. And even these propositions, though they are valid according to pure concepts, are only admitted in mathematics because they can be exhibited in intuition.

2. *Natural science (physics) contains a priori synthetic judgments as principles.* I need cite only two such judgments: that in all changes of the material world the quantity of matter remains unchanged; and that in all communication of motion, action and reaction must always be equal. Both propositions, it is evident, are not only necessary, and therefore in their origin *a priori*, but also synthetic. For in the concept of matter I do not think its permanence, but only its presence in the space which it occupies. I go outside and beyond the concept of matter, joining to it *a priori* in thought something which I have not thought *in* it. The proposition is not, therefore, analytic, but synthetic, and yet is thought *a priori*; and so likewise are the other propositions of the pure part of natural science.

3. *Metaphysics*, even if we look upon it as having hith-erto failed in all its endeavours, is yet, owing to the nature of human reason, a quite indispensable science, and *ought to contain a priori synthetic knowledge.* For its business is not merely to analyze concepts which we make for our-selves *a priori* of things, and thereby to clarify them ana-lytically, but to extend our *a priori* knowledge. And for this purpose we must employ principles which add to the given concept something that was not contained in it, and through *a priori* synthetic judgments venture out so far that experience is quite unable to follow us, as, for instance, in the proposition, that the world must have a first begin-ning, and such like. Thus metaphysics consists, at least *in intention*, entirely of *a priori* synthetic propositions.

### DISCUSSION QUESTIONS FOR CRITIQUE AND ANALYSIS

1. How do Kant's views on *causality* and *causal judg-ments* differ from David Hume's? Which position do you favor? Why?

2. Given that very young children do not intuitively recognize *a priori* mathematical statements as certainly and necessarily true, are they really *a priori?* Can we be sure that they are pure, devoid of anything empirical? Why?

---

## "CHICKEN METAPHYSICS"

Here is some philosophical humor in response to the age-old question: "Why did the chicken cross the road?"

| | |
|---|---|
| **PLATO** | To escape the darkness of the cave and enter the realm of forms. |
| **DESCARTES** | To get a clear and distinct idea of what was on the other side. |
| **LOCKE** | It was a complex idea based on the simpler notions of "road," "cross," and "chicken." |
| **BERKELEY** | If the chicken crossed the road but nobody was there to perceive the act, then did it really get to the other side? |
| **HUME** | Out of custom and habit. |
| **KANT** | It was a purely constructive rational act performed out of *a priori* necessity. |

---

> **6 6 *There will always be metaphysics in the world, and what is more, in every-one, especially in every thinking man.* 9 9**
>
> KANT

## Metaphysics and the Regulative Function of Transcendental Ideas

### *Noumena* versus *Phenomena*

At this point in our discussion, it should be clear how Kant made efforts to undo the damage done by the Humean wrecking-ball of skepticism. By means of the synthetic *a priori*, Kant tried to illustrate how it is possible to make mean-ingful statements about the world. Also, by concluding that experience will al-ways display universal and necessary *a priori* structure, he believed that he had established the foundations required for scientific knowledge.

However, it should be clearly noted that Kant does assign limits to knowl-edge by drawing a distinction between **noumena** and **phenomena**. Remember that, for Kant, knowledge is comprised of two components: the sense data provided by the sensible manifold and the categories of the mind. The implication of this dual contribution is that we cannot know reality as it actually is, but only as it is organized by the human understanding. The world as we experience it can be called "phenomenal reality" and the things and events within it *phenomena*. By contrast, *noumenal* reality is a reality independent of our perceptions. *Noumena* are "**things-in-themselves**" that have not been structured by the mind's *a priori* categories. *Noumena*, whatever they are, ultimately cannot be known, for in the cognitive activity of imposing order, the mind transforms things-in-themselves into something that is comprehensible to it. All we can know, then, is what appears to us in experience; we cannot know things as they are in themselves. Ultimate reality, or any transcendental reality of pure essences is beyond our grasp. *Take that, Plato!*

## Pure Reason as the Source of Transcendental Ideas

We find in the *Critique* that Kant posits the existence of a third faculty besides sensibility and understanding, namely **reason** or **pure reason,** as it is called. Reason is a higher faculty than understanding, in the same way that understanding is a higher faculty than sensibility. By means of its categories, the understanding provides rules for the systematizing and arranging of sensible intuitions. Similarly, through what Kant calls **transcendental ideas,** reason seeks to provide principles for a type of higher-level ordering of concepts and judgments produced by the understanding.[93] The faculty of reason is also what makes logic and syllogistic inference possible.[94]

The transcendental ideas just referred to cannot be used to increase our scientific knowledge of objects. Nor can they give us special knowledge of things-in-themselves and supersensible realities. For Kant, because all genuine knowledge is the product of an interaction between sensibility and understanding, *noumenal* realities, imperceptible substances, and so on,—to the extent they exist at all—fall beyond the scope of human knowledge. For this reason, Kant regards traditional speculative metaphysics as illusory. Describing the features of deities or the essence of things is beyond the human capacity to know. What is beyond experience is beyond human knowledge. Nonetheless, Kant does allow for certain revised metaphysical notions to constitute part of his thinking.

In Kant's view, the impulse to metaphysics is an inescapable impulse in the human mind.[95] The problem with this natural instinct toward metaphysical speculation is that the faculty of pure reason tends sometimes to fly beyond experience and to illegitimately draw conclusions about the *noumenal* realm that only lead to paradoxes and illusions. Nonetheless, for Kant, the faculty of reason generates several transcendental ideas that properly perform positive **regulative function,** even though they do not expand our knowledge. These regulative ideas include the notions of *self,* the *cosmos,* and *God.* See Figure 4.8, The Kantian Faculties.

### SELF

Logically presupposed in any experience of the world or in any knowledge of objects is the knower or **self** who experiences. The reference here is not to an **empirical self,** defined by some particular individual's physical and psycho-

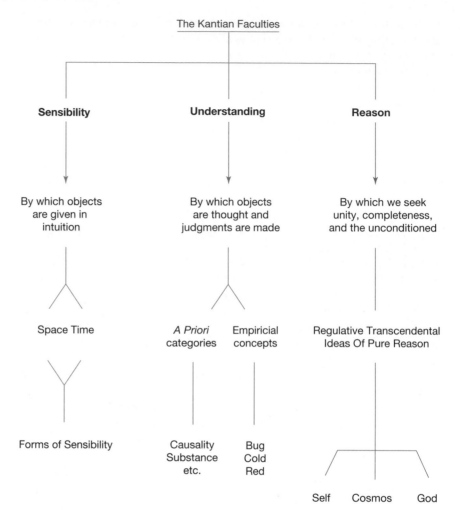

**FIGURE 4.8** The Kantian faculties.

logical characteristics, but to the **"I Think"** which accompanies anyone's thoughts and mental representations. This "I Think" or **logical self** is labeled by Kant as the **transcendental unity of apperception.** Given its transcendental nature, we do not experience this self directly. It is logically implied in view of the fact that our actual experience displays a coherence and unity.[96] For example, we speak of thoughts or memories as belonging to me or being "mine." It has to be the same self that senses the objects, remembers them, and imposes upon them forms of space and time, as well as categories like causality. If there were not this transcendental unity of apperception (to apprehend = to perceive or take cognizance of), then the sensible manifold could never be combined into a structured and organized whole. Sensible intuitions would be scattered and not cohere as objects. All temporal sequence would be lost in experience. Like the *a priori* categories of thought, the transcendental "I" is void of content. All we can say about it is that it is "an expression of the necessary unity of consciousness, a unity that manifests itself in the fact that all that is said, thought, and represented must necessarily always be able to be combined with an "I." To speak about pure apperception or the pure "I" is not to speak about an act, a process, or a thing but about the fundamental logical condition of having concepts like judgment, assertion, and consciousness.[97] Pure reason's generation of the transcendental "I" thus serves a useful regulative function by synthesizing experience on a grander scale than the faculty of understanding alone would allow. The many judgments made by the understanding are unified by the "I Think." Always remember, though, that the "I" is not a concept somehow related to ego-identity. Rather, it is a transcendental or logically necessary idea without empirical content.

## COSMOS

A second regulative idea produced by pure reason is the notion of **cosmos.** It refers to the totality of all phenomena. By means of it, reason attempts to create a synthesis of the many events in experience by forming the concept of the world. Putting it another way, the idea of cosmos takes us from considering experiences singly to considering experience as a whole—that is, as the collective unity or absolute totality of all possible experience. When you ponder life, ask why things happen, or wonder about your place in the universe—what your role and significance might be—you are posing cosmological questions and implicitly attempting to form a metaphysical cosmology. Of course, when you do so, you may allow yourself to take reason beyond its proper limits, as Kant charges philosophers have done before. In the *Critique*, Kant tries to show how reason becomes entangled by a number of inconsistencies when it proceeds to draw conclusions about ultimate (*noumenal*) realities, beyond the realm of human experience. He labels these inconsistencies **antinomies** and attributes each side of the apparent logical inconsistencies to either rationalism or empiricism. Kant points out that it is possible to argue, in an equally cogent fashion, for opposing metaphysical claims about the universe that clearly contradict each other. For example, one could argue equally well for the thesis that: (a) *The world had a beginning in time and is limited in space;* and (b) *The world had no beginning and is infinite in time and space.* The rational cogency of each contradictory position illustrates for Kant that reasoning about such topics leads to metaphysical nonsense, and that reason has overstepped its proper boundaries of application.[98] Whatever the cosmos is, it cannot be experienced as a phenomenon, nor can it be made an object of knowledge. Metaphysical talk about the specific nature of the cosmos is therefore illusory. Like the transcendental idea of the self or "I," *cosmos* serves an overarching regulative and unifying function that brings separate experiences together. *Cosmos* itself is without empirical content.

## GOD

**God** is the third concept produced by pure reason, and like *self* and *cosmos,* it too is without empirical content. Like them, as well, it performs a regulative function serving to give completeness and finality. According to Kant, the idea of God is not an arbitrary invention, but for any being that reasons, it is an absolutely unavoidable concept.[99] For any determinate thing that there is in experience, reason asks

*Philosophy is often regarded as a dangerous subject of study. For some, it constitutes a subversive activity that undermines the very foundations of tradition, authority, and religious belief. Now that you have become familiar with several epistemological and metaphysical perspectives, do you feel more or less confident about your most cherished beliefs? Why? Do you think that philosophy is, in fact, dangerous and subversive? Or do you think it can be liberating and enlightening? Reflect on this dilemma and record your thoughts in your philosophical journal.*

the question, "What is it?" Determinate things are experienced as displaying some properties and not others. To clarify, any specific thing is determinate if "given every possible property together with its *contradictory opposite*, one out of each pair of such opposites belongs to the thing."[100] Take, for example, the common egg you might have for breakfast. It is either white or it is not. It is either living or it is not alive. It is either fragile or not fragile, and so on. In fact, the list about what "determines" what an egg is could go on virtually forever. In view of the fact that our egg is a real egg, we are led to the conclusion that the sum total of all the egg's possible properties cannot be imaginary. There must be, we reason, a being of some sort that makes all these possibilities possible. We have not made them possible ourselves. This being—the foundation for the determinate nature of all things—we call God.[101]

Given that the idea of God is produced by reason without the aid of sensible intuitions, it cannot provide us knowledge of what God is, understood as a *noumenal* reality or thing-in-itself. By refusing to overstep the boundaries of human knowledge in order to make dogmatic and illusory claims about the nature of God, Kant does not advance atheism but leaves room for faith.[102] The God which transcends human knowledge becomes an object of faith.

The *Original Sourcework* that follows brings to mind our possible Western ethnocentrism on metaphysical matters insofar as the observation is made that the Hopi natives of America apparently do not "construct reality" using Kantian *a priori* forms of space and time. Benjamin Whorf, an American linguist and cognitive scientist, has found, for instance, that the Hopi have no counterparts in their language to temporal notions of past, present, and future. The implications for Kantian epistemology could be enormous!

After reading this article, you may also wish to read the extended *Philosophical Segue* entitled "Proofs for the Existence of God." While Kant regarded God as the "foundation for the determinate nature of all things," others have seen Him as the "first cause," the "unmoved mover," and "governor or grand designer of the universe." It goes without saying, perhaps, that whether or not there is a God and a good justification for believing in a supreme being will have very important implications for your philosophical worldview.

## ORIGINAL SOURCEWORK

## *The Language of the Hopi Provides a Metaphysics Without Space and Time*

**BENJAMIN WHORF**

I find it gratuitous to assume that a Hopi knows only the Hopi language and the cultural ideas of his own society has the same notions, often supposed to be intuitions, of time and space that we have, and that are generally assumed to be universal. In particular, he has no general notion or intuition of time as a smooth flowing continuum in which everything in the universe proceeds at an equal rate, out of a future, through a present, into a past; or, in which, to reverse the picture, the observer is being carried in the stream of duration continuously away from a past and into a future.

After long and careful study and analysis, the Hopi language is seen to contain no words, grammatical forms, constructions or expressions that refer directly to what we call "time," or to past, present, or future, or to enduring or lasting, or to motion as kinematic rather than dynamic (i.e. as a continuous translation in space and time rather than as an exhibition of dynamic effort in a certain process), or that even refer to space in such a way as to exclude that element of extension or existence that we call time, and so by implication leave a residue that could be referred to as time. Hence, the Hopi language contains no reference to "time," either explicit or implicit.

At the same time, the Hopi language is capable of accounting for and describing correctly, in a pragmatic or operational sense, all observable phenomena of the universe. Hence, I find it gratuitous to assume that Hopi thinking contains any such notion as the supposed intuitively felt flowing of time, or that the intuition of a Hopi gives him this as one of its data. Just as it is possible to have any number of geometries other than the Euclidean which give an equally perfect account of space configurations, so it is possible to have descriptions of the universe, all equally valid, that do not contain our familiar contrasts of time and space. The relativity viewpoint of modern physics is one such view, conceived in mathematical terms, and the Hopi *Weltanschauung* is another and quite different one, nonmathematical and linguistic.

Thus, the Hopi language and culture conceals a METAPHYSICS, such as our so-called naive view of space and time does, or as the relativity theory does; yet it is a different metaphysics from either. In order to describe the structure of the universe according to the Hopi, it is necessary to attempt—insofar as it is possible—to make explicit this metaphysics, properly describable only in the Hopi language, by means of an approximation expressed in our own language, somewhat inadequately it is true, yet by availing ourselves of such concepts as we have worked up into relative consonance with the system underlying the Hopi view of the universe.

In this Hopi view, time disappears and space is altered, so that it is no longer the homogeneous and instantaneous timeless space of our supposed intuition or of classical Newtonian mechanics. At the same time, new concepts and abstractions flow into the picture, taking up the task of describing the universe. . . .

The objective or manifested comprises all that is or has been accessible to the senses, the historical physical universe, in fact, with no attempt to distinguish between present and past, but excluding everything that we call future. The subjective or manifesting comprises all that we call future, BUT NOT MERELY THIS; it includes equally and indistinguishably all that we call mental—everything that appears or exists in the mind, or, as the Hopi would prefer to say, in the HEART, not only the heart of man, but the heart of animals, plants, and things, and behind and within all the forms and appearances of nature in the heart of nature, and by an implication and extension which has been felt by more than one anthropologist, yet would hardly ever be spoken of by a Hopi himself, so charged is the idea with religious and magical awesomeness, in the very heart of the Cosmos, itself. The subjective realm (subjective from our viewpoint, but intensely real and quivering with life, power, and potency to the Hopi) embraces not only our FUTURE, much of which the Hopi regards as more or less predestined in essence if not in exact form, but also all mentality, intellection, and emotion, the essence and typical form of which is the striving of purposeful desire, intelligent in character, toward manifestation—a manifestation which is much resisted and delayed, but in some form or other is inevitable. It is the realm of expectancy, of desire and purpose, of vitalizing life, of efficient causes, of thought thinking itself out from an inner realm (the Hopian HEART) into manifestation. It is in a dynamic state, yet not a state of motion—it is not advancing toward us out of a future, but ALREADY WITH us in vital and mental form, and its dynamism is at work in the field of eventuating or manifesting, that is, evolving without motion from the subjective by degrees to a result which is the objective. In translating into English, the Hopi will say that these entities in process of causation "will come" or that they—the Hopi— "will come to" them, but, in their own language, there are no verbs corresponding to our "come" and "go" that mean simple and abstract motion, our purely kinematic concept. The words in this case translated "come" refer to the process of eventuating without calling it motion—they are "eventuates to here" (*pew'i*) or "eventuates from it" (*angqo*) or "arrived" (*pitu*, pl. *oki*) which refers only to the terminal manifestation, the actual arrival at a given point, not to any motion preceding it.

## DISCUSSION QUESTIONS FOR CRITIQUE AND ANALYSIS

1. What in Benjamin Whorf's studies of the Hopi natives of America challenges Kantian epistemology and metaphysics? Do his findings successfully refute any Kantian claims? If so, which ones? If not, why not?

2. What is the relationship between language, reality, and experience? If there are no verbal equivalents in the Hopi language for "time," for example, does that mean that no temporal sequence is experienced? Is it possible to experience reality in an ever-present "now," without some intuitive understanding of "before," "concurrently," and "after"? How or why?

# PHILOSOPHICAL SEGUE

## Proofs for the Existence of God

Very much hinges, personally and philosophically, on the existence or non-existence of God. If there is such a thing as a Creator-God, as conceived by Judaism, Christianity, and Islam, then it makes sense to talk about a spiritual soul, an afterlife, and a reality beyond that of the physical world. If, on the other hand, there is no God in heaven, then perhaps moral concepts of right and wrong must be reinterpreted. (For a discussion of these questions, see the section pertaining to Friedrich Nietzsche's moral philosophy in the chapter on ethics). Maybe what has given us spiritual direction and meaning in the past is completely misguided or only a symptom of psychological neurosis? Further, if there is no God, then what happens to political and legal systems based on "natural law"—a perspective that presupposes that God establishes order in the moral universe in the same way that He establishes the laws of nature in the physical universe? Appreciating how important the metaphysical issue of God is for all of us, let us now examine several proofs for His existence provided by St. Anselm and St. Thomas Aquinas. Given what you now know about valid reasoning, try to philosophically evaluate the arguments that are presented.

# PHILOSOPHICAL PROFILE

**ST. ANSELM**

## St. Anselm

St. Anselm was a Christian philosopher, theologian, and church leader who attempted to prove the existence of God by the use of reason. His now-famous **ontological argument** is still debated today, centuries after its initial statement, and so qualifies Anselm to be called one of philosophy's intellectual immortals. His ideas live on though he passed away many hundreds of years ago.

Sources: "Saint Anselm" by Thomas Williams, *Stanford Encyclopedia of Philosophy;* also "St. Anselm" in the *Catholic Encyclopedia,* on the World Wide Web.

Anselm was born of a noble family in 1033 in Aosta, a Burgundian town in the Italian Alps on the frontier with Lombardy. Though we have little information about his early life, we do know that he rejected the political career for which his father had prepared him. He apparently left home at the age of 23 upon the death of his mother and feeling rebellious toward his father. For several years, he wandered about Burgundy and France and eventually ended up in Normandy in 1059. It was there that Anselm's interest was captured by the Benedictine abbey at Bec, whose reputable school was directed by Lanfranc, the abbey's prior (a monk next in dignity to an abbot). Lanfranc was a famous scholar and teacher under whose leadership the school at Bec had become an important center of learning, especially for dialectics. (Dialectics is that branch of logic that teaches the rules and modes of reasoning.) In 1060, Anselm entered the abbey as a novice, and as a result of his great intellect and obvious spiritual gifts, he was elected to succeed Lanfranc as prior when the latter was appointed abbot of Caen in 1063. When Herluin, the founder and first abbot of Bec died, Anselm was elected abbot in 1098.

Though busy with teaching, administration, and extensive correspondence as an adviser and consultant to dignitaries, Anselm still managed to further the reputation of Bec as an important intellectual center by writing several philosophical and theological works, including the *Monologion*, a soliloquy in which, reflecting on the influence of St. Augustine, he wrote of God as the highest being and investigated God's attributes (1076). In the *Proslogion* (discourse or allocution), (1077–1078), we find the original statement of the ontological argument. Anselm also wrote four philosophical dialogues: *De grammatico, De veritate, De libertate arbitrii* (1080–1085), and *De casu diaboli* (1085–1090).

Anselm continued to follow his master Lanfranc when, in 1093, he was installed Archbishop of Cantebury. Then King, William Rufus, kept the position vacant so that he could plunder the archiepiscopal revenues. William was hostile toward the Church with the intent to impose royal authority over ecclesiastical affairs. To demonstrate this power, William did not allow Anselm to return when he visited Rome in 1097 without the King's permission. After William was killed in 1100, Henry I, his successor, invited Anselm to return to his see (i.e., diocese). However, Henry was much like William insofar as he wanted to maintain royal jurisdiction over the Church and soon Anselm found himself exiled again from 1103 to 1107. Nevertheless, as Archbishop of Cantebury, he continued to write. Works before and during exile and works following his installation include: *Epistola de Incarnatione Verbi* (1092–1094), *Cur Deus Homa* (1094–1098), *De conceptu virginali* (1099–1101), *De processione Spiritus Sancti* (1102), *Epistola de sacrificio azymi et fermentati* (1106–1107), *De sacramentis ecclesiae* (1106–1107), and *De concordia* (1107–1108). At the age of 76, after having been a simple monk for 3 years, prior for 15, abbot for 15, and archbishop for 16, Anselm died on April 21, 1109. He was canonized a saint by the Catholic Church in 1494 and named a Doctor of the Church in 1720.

# ANSELM'S ONTOLOGICAL PROOF

*The fool has said in his heart, "There is no God."*

PSALM 14:1

*I do not seek to understand that I may believe; no, I believe so that I may understand.*

ST. ANSELM

For centuries, human beings have wrestled with the question: Does God exist? For some of us, this question only takes on a special urgency on our deathbed or when facing the very real possibility of death. Philosophers and non-philosophers alike have recognized the importance of arriving at an answer to this fundamental question for, as I mentioned earlier, so much hinges on it. In the 11th century C.E., St. Anselm tried to provide a proof for the existence of God by formulating what has come to be known as the *ontological argument*. The argument, found in Anselm's *Proslogion*, was branded with the descriptive label of "ontological" by one of its critics, Immanuel Kant, in the eighteenth century.[103] (The term *ontological* comes from the Greek word for "being.") Anselm's argument does not begin empirically from facts about the world but goes directly from the idea of God to a conclusion about His actual existence (or being). Anselm's proof addresses the skeptical disbelief of the atheist. He tries to demonstrate on purely logical grounds that such disbelief is unjustified and irrational. Referring to Psalm 14:1, he tells us that, "The fool has said in his heart, 'There is no God.'" Anselm's proof is a response to the psalmist's fool and an effort to convince the disbeliever that he is wrong. For philosophical beginners, Anselm's argument may at first glance appear overly subtle and complex, but in truth, is rather simple. His ontological proof, as found in Chapter 2 of the *Proslogion*, may be summarized as follows:

1. Contained within my understanding is some notion or idea of God.
2. God can be understood as "something-than-which-nothing-greater-can-be-thought."
3. Even the psalmist's "fool" understands what is meant by the concept or idea of God when he hears it.
4. Something (or any being) is greater if it exists in reality than if it exists only in the understanding.
5. If God (the greatest conceivable Being), "something-than-which-nothing-greater-can-be-thought," exists only in the understanding, then it is possible for a greater being to be conceived, that is, one that also exists in reality.
6. However, premise 5 must be contradictory, for it allows us to conceive a greater being than the greatest conceivable being. (Anselm's assumption here is that actually existing in reality is "greater than" existing only in the understanding.)
7. So, if I have an idea of the greatest conceivable being, such a being must exist both in my understanding and in reality.
8. Given premise 7, God must therefore exist in reality.[104]

In Chapter 3 of the *Proslogion*, Anselm offers a slightly different version of his proof for the existence of God. Among philosophers, there is some uncertainty as to whether this version is, in fact, a completely different argument, or whether it serves only as an elaboration of the first argument, which has already been summarized. Not wishing to embroil you in the debate at this point, let's just say that it reads something like the negative flip-side of the first proof. In brief, Anselm asks us to accept again the notion that we have an idea of God, and that this idea is of the greatest conceivable being or "something-than-which-nothing-greater-can-be-thought." Now for the flip-side: A being whose *non*existence is impossible must be greater than a being whose nonexistence is possible. However, if the greatest possible being's nonexistence is rationally conceivable, then the greatest possible being is not the greatest possible being. Clearly, this is a contradiction. The nonexistence of the greatest possible being cannot make any rational sense. Therefore, God must necessarily exist.[105]

## ST. THOMAS AQUINAS'S "FIVE WAYS"— PROOFS FOR THE EXISTENCE OF GOD

*The divine rights of grace do not abolish the human rights of natural reason.*

THOMAS AQUINAS

To better appreciate Aquinas's five ways for proving the existence of God, it is helpful to begin by learning some historical context.[106] Before and during Aquinas's lifetime, the complete works of Aristotle, the Greek philosopher, became available to Christian scholars. Aristotle's works were very persuasive and systematic, notwithstanding the fact that some of his teachings appeared to contradict church doctrine. For instance, Aristotle's view of the world as eternal and uncreated opposed Christianity's notion of a Creator-God. Furthermore, a number of ideas and assumptions embedded in neo-Platonic philosophy had already influenced the minds of Christian thinkers for so long that, by contrast, Aristotle's empirical and naturalistic leanings appeared dangerously alien. No doubt influenced by his mentor Albert the Great, Aquinas tried, like him, to apply Aristotelian insights to the Christian tradition. Aquinas believed that Platonic Christianity, with its concentrated focus on the eternal and its otherworldly notion of the spiritual realm, was ill-equipped to keep pace with the social changes and scientific achievements of the day. As one writer put it: "By merging Aristotle with Christian theology, Aquinas thought he could gain a perspective on our human involvements in culture, science, politics, and bodily existence that would be philosophically rigorous and theologically adequate."[107] For Aquinas, a proper integration of Aristotle could allow Christianity to hold on to the notions of a transcendent God, a spiritual realm, and an afterlife, but still address our daily earthly concerns in more rationally acceptable ways.

In his attempted reconciliation between Christianity and Aristotelianism, Aquinas carefully discriminated between what "natural reason" can do from what must be learned from scripture. He certainly had respect for philosophers, who were lovers of wisdom, but he felt that they lacked the fullness of wisdom as revealed only in Christ. Unlike St. Augustine (and Protestant reformers to come in later centuries), however, who felt that the natural light of reason is distorted in sinful, unbelieving minds, Aquinas maintained that sinful minds may obscure the truth, but that on its own, human reason can do much. He held that spiritual revelation builds upon reason but does not destroy it.[108] As Aquinas says: "The truth of the Christian faith . . . surpasses the capacity of reason, nevertheless that truth that the human reason is naturally endowed to know can not be opposed to the truth of the Christian faith."[109] In this statement, Aquinas would have us separate theology from philosophy, believing that the former supplements, but appreciates, the value of the latter. Theology provides knowledge through faith and revelation, whereas philosophy provides knowledge through the natural powers of reason available to all.

The distinction between theology and philosophy led Aquinas to divide the field of human knowledge into two areas. In the first, truths are given in revelation and known in faith. In the second, truths are revealed in nature and known by reasoning through experience. But revelation can sometimes overlap philosophical knowledge; the same "truth" can be grasped either by faith *or* by reason. For example, the existence of God or the presence of a soul can be revealed by faith or proven using rational means. Where faith and reason overlap like this, we have *natural theology*. In this region of inquiry, philosophy and theology cannot contradict one another because both reveal those truths which ultimately originate in the Source of All Truth.[110] It is here that reason serves as the loyal servant of faith. Aquinas's depiction of the relationship between philosophy (reason) and theology (faith) is captured in Figure 4.9.

In the well-known *Summa Theologica*, we find a brilliant example of Aquinas's method of natural theology using what is now known as the "scholastic" form of presentation.[111] Essentially, it comprises the following steps:

1. First, the question at issue is stated.
2. Second, objections are listed (standard answers to the question, which are considered incorrect).
3. The third step begins with, "On the contrary . . ." At this step of the reasoning process, an answer to the question is provided—one that contradicts the previous answers but supports his own views.
4. The fourth step begins with, "I answer that . . ." Here Aquinas develops his own position and provides arguments to defend it.
5. The last step details the separate replies to each of the objections originally offered against his own position.

In the *Summa Theologica*, Aquinas rejects Anselm's ontological argument for God's existence. He does not accept Anselm's idea that the proposition "God exists" is self-evident. Clearly, if it were, then all people would believe this as an *a priori* truth, but this is not the case. Furthermore, Aquinas doesn't think we can know God's nature through reason, for such truths must be revealed by the "light of faith," not human intelligence. As Frederick Copleston puts it: ". . . the intellect has no *a priori* knowledge of God's nature. In other words, owing

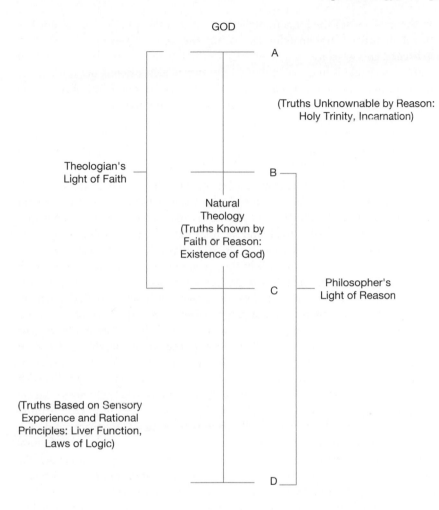

GOD

A

(Truths Unknowable by Reason:
Holy Trinity, Incarnation)

Theologian's
Light of Faith

B

Natural
Theology
(Truths Known by
Faith or Reason:
Existence of God)

C

Philosopher's
Light of Reason

(Truths Based on Sensory
Experience and Rational
Principles: Liver Function,
Laws of Logic)

D

THE WORLD

*Line Key*     A to B = Truths Known Only by Revelation and Faith

B to C = Truths Permitting Overlap between Revelation
(Faith) and Philosophical Knowledge (Reason)

C to D = Truths Belonging to Sensory Observation and Logic
That Cannot Be Known by Divine Revelation

*Natural Theology* =     A Branch of Philosophical Inquiry Seeking to
Prove Conclusions about God Based on Natural
Reason and Experience

**FIGURE 4.9** Truths captured by faith and reason.

to the weakness of the human intellect, we cannot discern *a priori* the positive possibility of the supremely perfect Being, the Being the essence of which is existence, and we come to a knowledge of the fact that such a being exists not through an analysis or consideration of the idea of such a Being, but through arguments from its effects, *a posteriori.*"[112] Let us now look at Aquinas's five ways for proving the existence of God using logical argumentation.

## The First Way: Argument from Motion

A quick look around reveals the indisputable fact that things in the world are constantly in motion. Think of motion here not only in terms of movement from one location to another, but also in terms of change or transformation from one (potential) state to another (actual) state. A rack of billiard balls may be sitting stationary one moment on a pool table, only to be dispersed in all directions when hit by the cue ball in the opening break. Marshmallows, which are potentially hot, can become actually hot when toasted over a campfire; what was cool, white, and spongy becomes hot, toasty, and gooey. In both cases, however, neither the billiard balls nor the marshmallows can move or transform themselves. In fact, nothing in nature can move itself. Thus, for an object to be in motion, it must have a mover. In the case of the pool table, the rack is set in motion only after being hit by a cue ball directed at it. The cue ball, once motionless itself, is set into motion after being struck by a cue stick. And that stick was without motion until someone picked it up and took a shot, causing the tip of the cue stick to strike the cue ball. The player in this case was initially set into motion at conception, or what we describe as the time of "quickening" during pregnancy, when the baby's first movements can be detected. This kind of causal explanation is intuitively obvious, but it indirectly poses the problem of *infinite regress.* Couldn't we go back forever, finding a cause for every preceding cause? The problem with infinite regress is that we cannot account for the fact that objects are actually in motion now. "If each thing that moves is in turn moved by something that itself moves, which in turn requires a cause of motion that itself moves, then there will nowhere be a first mover, and hence no motion at all. But there is motion."[113] The conclusion that follows is that there must be a first mover that is not itself moved. "First Mover" is another way of saying "God."

## The Second Way: Argument from Cause

Even though Aquinas's first argument from motion may be understandable, you might still remain unconvinced about the existence of God. What, after all, could account for the very existence of things like marshmallows and cue balls in the first place? To answer this question, Aquinas offered a second *cosmological argument* built on the Aristotelian concept of efficient cause.[114] In essence, it states that because it is impossible for natural things to be the complete and sufficient sources of their own existence, there must be an *uncaused cause* capable of imparting existence to all other things. Let's see why. To begin with, I could not be the source of my own existence. For that to be the case, I would have had to exist before I existed, and this is logically absurd. Your biological parents existed and they conceived you. In like fashion, your parents had their own biological parents—your grandparents—who, in turn, had their own parents, namely, your great grandparents. This argument from cause appears at first glance to be liable to infinite regress, just as with the first argument from motion. If everything that exists requires a cause for its own existence, a cause which itself was brought into existence as an effect by a more distant "caused cause," then at no time would there be a first cause, and hence, nothing in existence at all, since nothing in nature can be the cause of itself. Yet the fact is that people and things do exist. The conclusion follows, therefore, that there must be an Uncaused Cause—a Cause that is the complete and sufficient source of its own existence, a Cause that imparts existence to all else. That Uncaused Cause is God. Without God, no effect would have ever occurred, so nothing in the natural world would exist today.

## The Third Way: Argument from Necessity

Aquinas's third argument for the existence of God begins with the distinction between possibility and contingency. Contingent things in the world have no necessity to their existence; they might or might not exist at any particular point in time. What is true about contingent things is that they will eventually cease to exist. My cat Carl or your dog Fido do not exist out of necessity. There was a time before they existed, and a time will unfortunately come in the future when they will cease to exist again. The important point to note about possible or contingent things in nature is that it is impossible for them to *always* exist. Now, if it is possible for everything not to exist, then at one time there could have been nothing at all in existence. But if there was a time when nothing was in existence, then nothing could have begun to exist, and nothing would exist, since that which does not exist only begins to exist by something else already existing. Again, a brief look around confirms the fact that things actually do exist in the world. Hence, there must exist a *necessary* being, one that must always have existed and will never cease to exist. This Necessary Being causes all possible things to come into existence and caused the first thing to exist at a time when nothing else existed. This Necessary Being must be the cause of itself, requiring no other cause outside of itself. This being is God.

## The Fourth Way: Argument from Perfection and Degree

Aquinas's fourth way presents us with a problem concerning its classification. This argument from perfection and degree, sometimes called the *henological argument*, is often treated as a different type from the first three ways (all so-called *cosmological arguments*) and the fifth way (a *teleological argument*). Part of the confusion, perhaps is that, "In his 'fourth way,' Aquinas combines the form of cosmological argument with some of the ideas from the ontological argument."[115] Let's not worry too much here about classification, but simply recognize that it is a type of hybrid which, like the Fifth Way, makes efforts to personalize God, taking us beyond a very impersonal concept of God as an "Unmoved Mover" or "Uncaused Cause" which was established by the first Three Ways.

The fourth way begins with the observation that the things we experience in the world do not all have the same value. We find some things that are better, truer, or more noble than others. When we make comparative evaluations about "these things that are better than those things that are worse," we implicitly assume that there is "something which exemplifies those characteristics to a superlative degree."[116] To underscore the point, Aquinas argues that things possessing degrees of goodness, truth, nobility, and so on, depend on a superlative for their very being. Without the superlative or perfect exemplar, the imperfect approximations could not exist. In other words, if there were not in existence a superlative degree of goodness, then the existence of any lesser degree of goodness would be impossible and inexplicable. The notion here sounds very Platonic and is reminiscent of Plato's Divided Line Theory, which separates being and becoming. Remember how, for him, physical objects are lesser, imperfect approximations of the supernatural (timeless/spaceless) forms they reflect or in which they participate. One could say their transitory, imperfect existence derives from, or is contingent upon, perfect forms of Being. For Aquinas, in order for lower degrees of anything to exist, the maximum must also really exist. "The maximum is what explains the fact that we observe all these degrees of goodness in things: It is their cause. This maximum 'best of all things,' Aquinas says, 'we call God.'"[117]

## The Fifth Way: Argument from Intelligent Design

Beginning again empirically with the observation of earthly realities, Aquinas notices that the natural world displays order, purpose, and design. For example, in the northern hemisphere, birds migrate south for the winter and return northward for the summer, thereby ensuring their survival. The seasons always change in predictable sequence, so that frigid winters do not immediately follow springtimes by skipping summers and autumns. Boulders fall down mountainsides; they do not float upwards into the sky. That the natural world displays order is what makes it possible for us to do physics and to quantify scientific laws. "Things happen for a reason," as we often say. Given that order and natural design imply purpose, plan, or conscious intent, and given that inanimate objects lack both consciousness and intentionality, it follows logically for Aquinas that there must be a grand Designer or Master Intelligence governing the world. As Aquinas himself says in the fifth proof: "Now whatever lacks intelligence cannot move towards an end, unless it be directed by some being endowed with knowledge and intelligence; as the arrow is shot to its mark by the archer. Therefore, some intelligent being exists by whom all natural things are directed to their end; and this being we call God."[118] Falling boulders do not determine their own movement and direction, nor does the Earth establish its own seasons. Inanimate, unconscious entities cannot act intentionally with purpose or design in mind. This is why there must be a God.

# PHILOSOPHICAL PROFILE

## St. Thomas Aquinas

**THOMAS AQUINAS**

Thomas Aquinas is recognized today as one of the greatest philosopher theologians within the Roman Catholic tradition. He was born the youngest son
to Teodora and Landulph, Count of Aquino, in the castle of Rocca Secca about
half-way between Naples and Rome. Thomas's parents planned to groom their
beloved son for a career of service in the church. Their ambitions were not entirely honorable, however. They hoped he would climb to a position of ecclesiastical authority, thereby achieving political influence and wealth.
Unfortunately for Thomas's parents, things did not turn out as they planned.

By the age of five, Thomas began his elementary studies under the Benedictine monks at nearby Monte Cassino. It was there that he received his basic
religious instruction, while developing his academic skills and good study habits.
The Benedictines were well-known for their modest lifestyles, which involved
much physical labor and spiritual discipline.

In about the year 1236, Thomas was sent to the Imperial University of
Naples, where he studied the liberal arts. The Abbot of Monte Cassino wrote
to Thomas's father that a boy with such talents should not be left in obscurity
and so should move on. This was perhaps not surprising, since a holy hermit
had made a prediction to Teodora before the birth of her son that his learning
and sanctity would be so great that no one would ever be found to equal him.[119]
While at the University of Naples, Thomas befriended a number of Dominican monks whose order was dedicated to education and preaching to common
folk. Members of the Dominican order were also obliged to take vows of poverty,
chastity, and obedience. Obviously influenced by his newfound friends, Thomas
entered the Order of St. Dominic sometime between 1240 and 1243.

It was a bit surprising, perhaps, that such a noble young man should join
a mendicant (begging) order and don the garb of a poor Dominican friar. Obviously, Thomas's decision was not in line with his parents' aspirations for him.
After learning about Thomas's decision to become a Dominican, his mother,
Teodora, rushed to Naples to visit her son. The Dominicans feared that she
would take him away, so they sent him to Rome, en route to his ultimate destination of Paris or Cologne. Thomas's brothers, who were soldiers serving
under Emperor Frederick, captured Thomas near Aquapendente and confined
him for nearly two years in the fortress of San Giovanni at Rocca Secca. His
family endeavored by various means—possibly even using a temptress, as one
story goes—to destroy his vocation, but to no avail. Eventually, his family became convinced of Thomas's commitment and finally released him.

Once freed, Thomas went to Cologne, where he studied for a number of
years with Albert the Great (Albertus Magnus), whose major contribution to
the Church was the realization of the need to ground Christian faith in philosophy and science. Thomas was very much influenced by Albert's breadth of
knowledge, his familiarity with Christian, Muslim, and Jewish writers, and his
efforts to make Aristotle accessible by paraphrasing many of his works. In the

end, Thomas went far beyond his teacher's efforts by building a rational theology of his own.

In 1245, Albert was sent to Paris, and Thomas accompanied him as a student. Both returned in 1248, when Albert was appointed regent of the new *Studium Generale*, where Thomas was to teach under him. In 1250 Thomas entered the priesthood and began to preach the Word of God in Germany, France, and Italy. In 1251 or 1252, Thomas was sent back to Paris by the master general of the order to fill the office of Bachelor (subregent) in the Dominican *Studium*. This appointment launched his public career, attracting the attention of both students and professors alike. At the University of Paris, Thomas earned the degree of Doctor in Theology in October 1257.

On a personal note, it might be mentioned that, given his heavy-set frame, quiet and humble rural manners, and inclination to slow response in class, Thomas earned the nickname "the Dumb Ox," soon after his arrival as a student in Paris. However, when Albert heard of Thomas's brilliant defense of a difficult thesis, he explained: "We call this young man a dumb ox, but his bellowing in doctrine will one day resound throughout the world."

Thomas Aquinas was a prolific writer, having produced more than 60 works in a lifespan of less than 50 years. His works may be classified as either philosophical, theological, scriptural, or apologetic, though these categories may not always hold up under closer scrutiny. Two of his better-known major works are a multivolumed series entitled the *Summa Theologica* (Summary of Theology) and *Summa Contra Gentiles* (Summary on the Truth of the Catholic Faith against the Gentiles). On December 6, 1273, the prolific Thomas laid down his pen for good and wrote nothing more. While saying Mass, Thomas experienced a mystical revelation of God, subsequent to which he concluded, "All that I have written seems to me like straw compared to what has now been revealed to me." Consequently, the *Summa Theologica* was never finished, having been completed only as far as the nineteenth question of the third part.

In 1274, Thomas set out on foot from Italy for Lyons, France, to attend a general council meeting invoked by Pope Gregory X. Unfortunately, Thomas's health failed, and he fell to the ground near Terracina. He received care there until the end by the Cistercian monks of *Fossa Nuova*, dying on March 7, 1274. In 1323, less than 50 years after his death, Thomas Aquinas was canonized a saint. In 1879, Pope Leo XIII recommended that Thomism—that is, the philosophy of Thomas Aquinas—become the model for Catholic thought. His rational, metaphysical basis for Christian theology remains the dominant intellectual influence of the Church today.

Sources: "St. Thomas Aquinas" in the *Catholic Encyclopedia* on the world wide web (www.newadvent.org); Vernon J. Bourke, "Thomas Aquinas," *The Encyclopedia of Philosophy*, Vol. 8, (New York: Macmillan, 1967), pp. 105–116; William Lawhead, *The Voyage of Discovery* (Belmont, CA.: Wadsworth, 1996), pp. 182–98; Douglas Soccio, *Archetypes of Wisdom*, 4th ed. (Belmont, CA.: Wadsworth, 2001), pp. 238–42; and Robert Paul Wolff, *About Philosophy*, 7th ed. (Upper Saddle River, NJ: Prentice Hall, 1998).

To conclude this chapter, let us now turn to "Whether God Exists." written by Thomas Aquinas. Remember to pay attention to the scholastic form of presentation.

## *Whether God Exists?*

ST. THOMAS AQUINAS

**Objection 1.** It seems that *God* does not exist; because if one of two contraries be infinite, the other would be altogether destroyed. But the word "God" means that He is infinite goodness. If, therefore, *God* existed, there would be no evil discoverable; but there is evil in the world. Therefore *God* does not exist.

**Objection 2.** Further, it is superfluous to suppose that what can be accounted for by a few principles has been produced by many. But it seems that everything we see in the world can be accounted for by other principles, supposing *God* did not exist. For all natural things can be reduced to one principle which is nature; and all voluntary things can be reduced to one principle which is human reason, or will. Therefore there is no need to suppose *God's existence.*

**On the contrary,** it is said in the person of *God*: "I am Who am." (Exodus 3:14)

**I answer that,** The *existence of God* can be proved in five ways.

The first and more manifest way is the argument from motion. It is certain, and evident to our senses, that in the world some things are in motion. Now whatever is in motion is put in motion by another, for nothing can be in motion except it is in potentiality to that towards which it is in motion; whereas a thing moves inasmuch as it is in act. For motion is nothing else than the reduction of something from potentiality to actuality. But nothing can be reduced from potentiality to actuality, except by something in a state of actuality. Thus that which is actually hot, as fire, makes wood, which is potentially hot, to be actually hot, and thereby moves and changes it. Now it is not possible that the same thing should be at once in actuality and potentiality in the same respect,

but only in different respects. For what is actually hot cannot simultaneously be potentially hot; but it is simultaneously potentially cold. It is therefore impossible that in the same respect and in the same way a thing should be both mover and moved, i.e. that it should move itself. Therefore, whatever is in motion must be put in motion by another. If that by which it is put in motion be itself put in motion, then this also must needs be put in motion by another, and that by another again. But this cannot go on to infinity, because then there would be no first mover, and, consequently, no other mover, seeing that subsequent movers move only inasmuch as they are put in motion by the first mover, as the staff moves only because it is put in motion by the hand. Therefore it is necessary to arrive at a first mover, put in motion by no other, and this everyone understands to be *God.*

The second way is from the nature of the efficient cause. In the world of sense we find there is an order of efficient causes. There is no case known (neither is it, indeed, possible) in which a thing is found to be the efficient cause of itself; for so it would be prior to itself, which is impossible. Now in efficient causes it is not possible to go on to infinity, because in all efficient causes following in order, the first is the cause of the intermediate cause, and the intermediate is the cause of the ultimate cause, whether the intermediate cause be several, or only one. Now to take away the cause is to take away the effect. Therefore, if there be no first cause among efficient causes, there will be no ultimate, nor any intermediate cause. But if in efficient causes it is possible to go on to infinity, there will be no first efficient cause, neither will there be an ultimate effect, nor any intermediate efficient causes; all of which is plainly false.

Thomas Aquinas, *The Summa Theologica,* translated by the Fathers of the English Dominican Province, originally published in 1911; A reproduction was published by Thomas More Publishing in 1947.

Therefore it is necessary to admit a first efficient cause, to which everyone gives the name of *God*.

The third way is taken from possibility and necessity, and runs thus. We find in nature things that are possible to be and not to be, since they are found to be generated, and to corrupt, and consequently, they are possible to be and not to be. But it is impossible for these always to exist, for that which is possible not to be at some time is not. Therefore, if everything is possible not to be, then at one time there could have been nothing in existence. Now if this were true, even now there would be nothing in existence, because that which does not exist only begins to exist by something already existing. Therefore, if at one time nothing was in existence, it would have been impossible for anything to have begun to exist; and thus even now nothing would be in existence—which is absurd. Therefore, not all beings are merely possible, but there must exist something the existence of which is necessary. But every necessary thing either has its necessity caused by another, or not. Now it is impossible to go on to infinity in necessary things which have their necessity caused by another, as has been already proved in regard to efficient causes. Therefore we cannot but postulate the existence of some being having of itself its own necessity, and not receiving it from another, but rather causing in others their necessity. This all men speak of as *God*.

The fourth way is taken from the gradation to be found in things. Among beings there are some more and some less good, true, noble and the like. But "more" and "less" are predicated of different things, according as they resemble in their different ways something which is the maximum, as a thing is said to be hotter according as it more nearly resembles that which is hottest; so that there is something which is truest, something best, something noblest and, consequently, something which is uttermost being; for those things that are greatest in truth are greatest in being, as it is written in Metaph. ii. Now the maximum in any genus is the cause of all in that genus; as fire, which is the maximum heat, is the cause of all hot things. Therefore there must also be something which is to all beings the cause of their being, goodness, and every other perfection; and this we call *God*.

The fifth way is taken from the governance of the world. We see that things which lack intelligence, such as natural bodies, act for an end, and this is evident from their acting always, or nearly always, in the same way, so as to obtain the best result. Hence it is plain that not fortuitously, but designedly, do they achieve their end. Now whatever lacks intelligence cannot move towards an end, unless it be directed by some being endowed with knowledge and intelligence; as the arrow is shot to its mark by the archer. Therefore some intelligent being exists by whom all natural things are directed to their end; and this being we call *God*.

**Reply to Objection 1.** As *Augustine* says (Enchiridion xi): "Since *God* is the *highest good,* He would not allow any evil to exist in His works, unless His omnipotence and goodness were such as to bring good even out of evil." This is part of the infinite goodness of *God,* that He should allow evil to exist, and out of it produce good.

**Reply to Objection 2.** Since nature works for a determinate end under the direction of a higher agent, whatever is done by nature must needs be traced back to *God,* as to its first cause. So also whatever is done voluntarily must also be traced back to some higher cause other than human reason or will, since these can change or fail; for all things that are changeable and capable of defect must be traced back to an immovable and self-necessary first principle, as was shown in the body of the Article.

## DISCUSSION QUESTIONS FOR CRITIQUE AND ANALYSIS

1. As you read this selection by Thomas Aquinas, compare it to Plato's dialogue *Euthyphro* and Descartes's *Meditations*. Which style of doing philosophy do you prefer? Why? What are the advantages and disadvantages of each approach to philosophical argumentation? Discuss.

2. What weaknesses, if any, can you find in Aquinas's five arguments for the existence of God? Critically examine his claims and logical inferences. Do you see any problems? Explain.

3. Has Aquinas convinced you that God must exist? Why or why not?

# STUDY GUIDE

## KEY TERMS   (Arranged by Philosopher)

### *Plato*

| | | |
|---|---|---|
| epistemology   **175** | divided line theory   **178** | knowledge   **181** |
| metaphysics   **176** | imagination   **178** | theory of forms   **181** |
| Parmenides of Elea   **177** | opinions   **179** | intelligible world   **181** |
| monist   **177** | perception   **180** | Simile of the Sun   **183** |
| Heraclitus of Ephesus   **177** | visible world   **181** | Goodness   **183** |
| becoming   **178** | being   **181** | Allegory of the Cave   **185** |

### *René Descartes*

| | | |
|---|---|---|
| rationalism   **189** | heliocentric theory   **192** | deduction   **193** |
| Baruch Spinoza   **189** | Copernican revolution   **192** | self-evident principle   **193** |
| Gottfried Wilhelm Leibniz   **189** | medieval scholasticism   **192** | method of doubt   **193** |
| geocentric view   **191** | certainty   **192** | *cogito, ergo sum*   **197** |
| Mikolaj Kopernik   **191** | intuition   **193** | clear and distinct criterion   **199** |

### *John Locke*

| | | |
|---|---|---|
| empiricism   **203** | Newtonian science   **204** | complex ideas   **206** |
| Bishop George Berkeley   **203** | *tabula rasa*   **206** | innate ideas   **207** |
| David Hume   **203** | sensation   **206** | primary qualities   **208** |
| logical positivism   **204** | reflection   **206** | secondary qualities   **208** |
| age of enlightenment   **204** | simple ideas   **206** | |

### *George Berkeley*

| | | |
|---|---|---|
| material substance   **210** | *esse est percipi*   **210** | perpetual perceiver   **212** |

### *David Hume*

| | | |
|---|---|---|
| radical skepticism   **214** | resemblance   **218** | Hume's Fork   **221** |
| impressions   **215** | contiguity   **218** | relations of ideas   **221** |
| thoughts   **216** | cause and effect   **218** | matters of fact   **221** |
| ideas   **216** | imagination   **218** | analytic propositions   **221** |
| copy   **216** | priority in time   **219** | *a priori* statements   **222** |
| mental substance   **217** | necessary connection   **219** | synthetic a posteriori   **222** |
| God   **217** | constant conjunction   **220** | |
| laws of association   **218** | feelings of compulsion   **221** | |

### *Immanuel Kant*

| | | |
|---|---|---|
| reason   **230** | sensible intuitions   **230** | time   **234** |
| experience   **230** | active construction   **232** | forms of sensible intuition   **234** |
| matter   **230** | *a priori*   **234** | faculty of sensibility   **234** |
| content   **230** | space   **234** | faculty of understanding   **234** |

analytic *a priori* judgments   **238**
synthetic *a priori* judgments   **239**
synthetic *a posteriori* judgments   **239**
*a priori* judgments   **240**
*a posteriori* judgments   **240**
*noumena*   **244**
*phenomena*   **244**

things-in-themselves   **245**
(pure) reason   **245**
transcendental ideas   **245**
regulative function   **245**
self   **245**
empirical self   **245**
"I Think"   **246**

logical self   **246**
transcendental unity of
   apperception   **246**
cosmos   **247**
God   **247**
antinomies   **247**
ontological argument   **249**

# PROGRESS CHECK

**Instructions:** Fill in the blanks with the appropriate responses listed below.

| | | |
|---|---|---|
| Bishop Berkeley | rationalist | simple ideas |
| becoming | perceiver | secondary qualities |
| goodness | impressions | opinion |
| deduction | self | Copernican revolution |
| wax example | wrecking-ball | God |
| *tabula rasa* | allegory of the cave | thoughts |
| sensibility | John Locke | causality |
| *cogito ergo sum* | being | categories |
| complex idea | methodological doubt | synthesis |
| metaphysics | pure reason | innate ideas |
| primary qualities | epistemology | active construction |

1. The term meaning the theory or study of knowledge is _____ .

2. The branch of philosophy that studies ultimate and transcendent reality is called _____ .

3. What changes and is characterized by impermanence belongs to Plato's metaphysical realm of _____ .

4. According to Plato's Divided Line Theory, perception and imagination belong to the level of knowledge called _____ .

5. The lower and higher forms belong to the intelligible world of _____ .

6. The highest Platonic form compared to the illumination of the sun is _____ .

7. The _____ captures the fact that most of us confuse transitory appearances with ultimate reality.

8. The most significant _____ of the seventeenth century is René Descartes.

9. The _____ replaced the geocentric view of the world with the heliocentric theory, which states that the Earth revolves around the sun, not vice versa.

10. For Descartes, knowledge is to be achieved through the combined mental operations of intuition and _____ .

11. Descartes discovered the self-evident principle upon which to base his philosophy using a process of _____ .

12. The intuitive first principle that Descartes uses to deduce all other epistemological conclusions can be stated as _____ .

13. Descartes's _____ proves to him that the senses cannot provide the certainty he seeks.

14. _____ wished to clear the "metaphysical rubbish" from philosophical inquiry.

15. The _____ notion of the mind presents it as passive and receptive.

16. According to John Locke, a _____ like unicorn can be built upon _____ stemming from sensory experience.

17. Locke rejects the notion of _____ .

18. For Locke, _____ are found in the object, whereas _____ are located in the subject perceiving them.

19. This philosopher coined the phrase: "To be is to be perceived." _____.

20. What guarantees the existence of the world while we sleep or fall unconscious is _____, the "perpetual perceiver."

21. Unlike John Locke, who agreed with Descartes that primary qualities belong to the object, Bishop Berkeley locates them in the _____.

22. David Hume's radical skepticism has been described as a _____.

23. For Hume, those perceptions of the mind with the greatest force and vivacity are called _____, while those with lesser force and vivacity are called _____ or ideas.

24. According to Hume, what we call the _____ is nothing more than a steady stream of consciousness.

25. In Humean epistemology, there is no sense impression that corresponds to _____; we arrive at the notion from habit and the perception of constant conjunction.

26. Kant's epistemology can be seen as a _____ between rationalism and empiricism.

27. For Kant, knowledge of experience is not a passive recording, but an _____.

28. Space and time are *a priori* forms of _____ or intuition.

29. The understanding allows us to make judgments about objects through *a priori* _____ of thought.

30. The transcendental ideas of self, cosmos, and God serve a regulative function and are generated by _____.

## SUMMARY OF MAJOR POINTS

1. What are the definitions of epistemology and metaphysics?
   * *Epistemology:* The theory of knowledge or the study of its origins, nature, and justification.
   * *Metaphysics:* The field of philosophy addressing itself to issues beyond nature and the realm of the physical; the study of being, the universe, ultimate reality; the critical examination of the underlying assumptions employed by our system of knowledge.

2. What is Plato's metaphysical conception of the universe?
   * The universe containing objects of knowledge is divided into the intelligible world of being and the visible world of becoming.
   * Lower and higher forms belong to the world of being; physical things and their shadows or reflections belong to the visible world of becoming.
   * Knowledge is found in the intelligible world; opinion is located in the visible world.

3. What are the four levels of knowledge discussed in Plato's Divided Line Theory?
   * Imagination, perception, deductive reasoning, and direct intellectual apprehension

4. How does Plato conceptualize the forms?
   * The forms are perfect, eternal, and immutable. Objects in actual experience partake in the forms; the forms are "more real" than the things we perceive. Physical objects are merely rough approximations of the forms; forms have an independent ontological status beyond any individual mind.

5. Of what significance is the "Simile of the Sun?"
   * Plato uses the simile to capture the nature of Goodness—the highest of all the forms. The sun is used to illustrate how Goodness is absolutely essential to our experience of reality and our understanding of all things.

6. How is the Allegory of the Cave used?
   * Plato uses it to describe the ascent from illusion to philosophical illumination. The cave dwellers erroneously take the shadows in the cave as ultimate reality, whereas those who escape the darkness of the cave to gaze at the sun represent the "*illuminati*," or philosopher kings.

7. What is Descartes's method of doubt? For what is it used?
   * The French rationalist René Descartes used the method of doubt as a way to achieve certainty. By establishing a first principle that was ultimately

certain, Descartes's intention was to deduce other conclusions about reality.

8. What became Descartes's first principle of certainty?
   * *"Cogito, ergo sum"* (I think, therefore I am) became Descartes's self-evident foundation for all future deductions.

9. In what ways is Descartes's Wax Example important to rationalistic philosophy?
   * The Wax Example illustrates how knowledge cannot ultimately be based on sensory experience.

10. Who was John Locke? What was his philosophical mission?
    * John Locke is considered the founder of British empiricism. He launched an attack against the continental rationalists with the aim of removing the "metaphysical rubbish" from philosophical inquiry.

11. How did Locke conceive of the human mind?
    * The human mind is a *tabula rasa* (blank slate); it is passive and receptive. The mind is furnished by experience. All ideas (simple and complex) are derived from experience.

12. How does Locke conceptualize the subject-object relation?
    * Primary qualities (such as solidity) are found in objects; secondary qualities (such as color) are found in the subjects.

13. In what ways does Berkeley's epistemology differ from Locke's?
    * For Berkeley, both primary and secondary qualities are found in the subject. To be is to be perceived: Mental ideas can only correspond to like things, not to physical objects. Berkeley's epistemology calls into question the mind-world connection that Locke sought to establish.

14. Can the continued existence of the world be guaranteed if we fall asleep or are unconscious, since we are no longer aware and awake to perceive it?
    * According to Berkeley, the answer is yes. God, the "perpetual perceiver," continues to perceive when we stop.

15. How is David Hume's theory the equivalent of a philosophical wrecking-ball?
    * Hume's thought forms a radical skepticism; it smashes to bits causal scientific explanation; it reduces metaphysics to pretentious nonsense; "God" and "self" are reduced to illusions.

16. From where do ideas originate according to Hume?
    * All ideas are derived from our initial experiential impressions. Even ideas of fantasy (for example unicorns) are ultimately combinations of sensory-based impressions.

17. In what ways can ideas be associated for Hume?
    * Patterns of association include resemblance, contiguity, and cause and effect.

18. What are the essential features of so-called "causes"?
    * *Contiguity:* spatially or temporally close
    * *Priority in time:* causes precede effects
    * *Necessary connection:* effects are always preceded by the same thing or event if it is to be considered the cause.

19. What is Hume's view of causality?
    * The perception of causality is an act of the imagination. Causes are not found in objects, but from a perception of constant conjunction and the development of habit and custom. We feel (by gentle force) that one thing will lead to another as we have always seen. There is no sense impression of "necessary connection."

20. What is "Hume's Fork?"
    * Epistemological statements either refer to "relations of ideas" or "matters of fact"—the two prongs of the "fork." Anything in between, (any statement that does not fit into one of these categories) is meaningless.

21. In general terms, how could one describe Kant's epistemology?
    * It could be described as a synthesis of rationalism and empiricism. It is certainly a response to Humean skepticism.

22. How does Kant conceptualize knowledge?
    * Knowledge is an active construction. It results as the product of an interaction between reason and experience. From experience, sense data are given; from reason, forms of sensibility and understanding are imposed.

**23.** To what does the *Copernican revolution* of Kantian philosophy refer?
  - Instead of having the mind conform to objects of knowledge, Kant turned things around and had objects conform to the mind.

**24.** What are the *a priori* elements of knowledge?
  - *A priori* forms of sensibility include space and time. *A priori* categories of understanding include causality and substance, etc. Whatever is *a priori* is "pure"—empty of all empirical content and derivation.

**25.** How are Kantian and Platonic forms different?
  - Platonic forms are metaphysical realities (more real than actual objects); they have an independent ontological status. Kantian forms originate in the human faculties; they are not located "somewhere out there," but in the mind of the knower.

**26.** What is Kant's response to Hume?
  - Kant agrees with Hume that no impressions directly correspond to causality and substance, for example. For Kant, however, a concept like *substance* is already logically presupposed in experience. Without the concept already assumed, we could not perceive objects as objects. Causal connections are also made logically possible by being presupposed in our perceptions; they are not derived from them, as Hume would say, through the experience of "constant conjunction." For Kant, certain and reliable knowledge is possible when limited to human experience, given its universal and necessary structure, as defined by the *a priori* forms and categories of understanding.

**27.** What metaphysical ideas does Kant discuss? What is their origin? How do they function?
  - *God, self,* and *cosmos* are three metaphysical ideas covered by Kant in the context of the distinction between *noumena* and *phenomena.* These three so-called "transcendental ideas" find their origin in the faculty of pure reason. These transcendental ideas serve a regulative function giving unity and completeness to our experience.

## SOURCE REFERENCES

**Angeles, Peter A.,** *The HarperCollins Dictionary of Philosophy* (New York: HarperPerennial, 1992).

**Berkeley, George,** *Berkeley's Philosophical Writings,* David Armstrong, ed. (New York: Collier Books, 1965).

**Chappell, Vere,** ed., *The Cambridge Companion to Locke* (Cambridge: Cambridge University Press, 1994).

**Copleston, Frederick,** "Modern Philosophy: The British Philosophers," *A History of Philosophy,* Vol. 5, Part 1 (Garden City, NY: Image Books, 1994), chaps. 4–7.

———, "Berkeley to Hume," *A History of Philosophy,* Vol. 5, Part 2.

**Descartes, René,** *Discourse on Method and The Meditations,* trans. F.E. Sutcliffe (Harmondsworth, England: Penguin Books, 1974).

**Dicker, Georges,** *Hume's Epistemology and Metaphysics* (London: Routledge, 1998).

**Falikowski, Anthony,** *Piaget's Kantianism and the Critique of Pure Knowledge;* Master's Thesis, University of Toronto, 1979.

**Gardner, Sebastian,** *Kant and The Critique of Pure Reason* (London: Routledge, 1999).

**Hakim, Albert,** *Historical Introduction to Philosophy* (New York: MacMillan, 1987).

**Hartnack, Justus,** trans. M. Holmes Hartshorne, *Kant's Theory of Knowledge* (New York: An Original Harbinger Book, 1967).

**Hume, David,** *An Inquiry Concerning Human Understanding,* Charles W. Hendel, ed. (Upper Saddle River, NJ: Prentice Hall 1955).

———, *A Treatise of Human Nature,* L.A. Selby-Bigge, ed. (Oxford: Clarendon Press, 1975).

**Kant, Immanuel,** *Critique of Pure Reason,* trans. Norman Kemp Smith (New York: St. Martin's Press, 1965).

———, *Prolegomena to Any Future Metaphysics,* trans. Gary Hatfield, (New York: Cambridge University Press, 1997).

**Korner, S.,** *Kant,* (Baltimore, MD: Penguin Books, 1974).

**Lavine, T.Z.,** *From Socrates to Sartre: The Philosophic Quest* (New York: Bantam Books, 1989).

**Lawhead, William,** *A History of Western Philosophy* (Belmont, CA.: Wadsworth, 1996), chaps. 15, 19, 20, 21, 22.

**Melchert, Norman,** *The Great Conversation: A Historical Introduction to Philosophy,* 3rd ed. (Mountain View, CA: Mayfield, 1999).

**Mitchell, Helen Buss,** *Roots of Wisdom: Speaking the Language of Philosophy* (Belmond CA.: Wadsworth, 1996).

**Moore, Brooke Noel, and Kenneth Bruder,** *Philosophy: The Power of Ideas,* 3rd ed., (Mountain View, CA.: Mayfield, 1996).

**Plato,** *The Republic,* trans. Desmond Lee, Harmondsworth, England: Penguin Books, 1974).

**Rée, Jonathan,** *Descartes* (London: Allen Lane, 1974).

**Scott-Kakures, Dion, Susan Casagnetto, Hugh Benson, William Taschek, and Paul Hurley,** *History of Philosophy* (New York: Harper-Collins, 1993).

**Soccio, Douglas,** *Archetypes of Wisdom: An Introduction to Philosophy,* 3rd ed. (Belmont, CA.: Wadsworth, 1998).

**Stewart, David, and H. Gene Blocker,** *Fundamentals of Philosophy,* 4th ed. (Upper Saddle River, NJ: Prentice Hall, 1996).

**Stumpf, Samuel Enoch,** *Philosophy: History and Problems,* 5th ed., (New York: McGraw-Hill, 1994).

**Wolff, Robert Paul,** *About Philosophy,* 7th ed. (Upper Saddle River, NJ: Prentice Hall, 1998).

**Zweig, Arnulf,** ed., *The Essential Kant* (New York: Mentor Book, 1970).

## PHILOSOPHY IN CYBERSPACE

**The Epistemology Page**
http://pantheon.yale.edu/~47/e-page.htm
A philosophy professor at Yale University presents resources dealing with epistemology. Find anthologies, graduate programs and publications.

**Metaphysics Resources on the Internet**
http://www.uno.edu/~phil/metalinks.htm
Produced by the University of New Orleans, this website enables you to access many resources relevant to the study of metaphysics.

## ENDNOTES

1. Peter A. Angeles, *The HarperCollins Dictionary of Philosophy* (New York: HarperPerennial, 1992), pp. 184–185.
2. See sections numbered 507-521 in *Plato: The Republic,* 2nd ed., trans. Desmond Lee (Hammondsworth, England: Penguin Books, 1974).
3. See Douglas Soccio, *Archetypes of Wisdom: An Introduction to Philosophy,* 3rd ed. (Belmont, CA: Wadsworth, 1998), pp. 38–39.
4. This clarification is provided by T.Z. Lavine, *From Socrates to Sartre: The Philosophic Quest* (New York: Bantam Books, 1984), p. 32.
5. Soccio, *Archetypes of Wisdom,* p. 131.
6. Lavine, *From Socrates to Sartre.*
7. Ibid., p. 36.
8. Ibid., p. 38.
9. Lavine, *From Socrates to Sartre,* p. 38.
10. Ibid., p. 40.
11. Jonathan Ree, *Descartes* (London: Allen Lane, 1974), p. 17.
12. William F. Lawhead., *The Voyage of Discovery: A History of Western Philosophy* (Belmont CA.: Wadsworth 1996), p. 243.
13. Ree, *Descartes,* p. 17.
14. Lavine, *From Socrates to Sartre,* p. 84.
15. Soccio, *Archetypes of Wisdom,* p. 293.
16. A point undersored by Lavine, *From Socrates to Sartre,* p. 94.
17. Ibid., p. 94.
18. Ibid.
19. These conditions are nicely summed up by Lavine, ibid., p. 95.
20. This summation of Descartes's causal argument for God's existence is borrowed from Lawhead, *Voyage of Discovery,* p. 249.
21. Noel Moore Brooke and Kenneth Bruder, *Philosophy: The Power of Ideas,* 3rd ed. (Mountainview, CA.: Mayfield, 1996), p. 82.
22. David Stewart and H. Gene Blocker, *Fundamentals of Philosophy,* 4th ed. (Upper Saddle River, NJ: Prentice Hall, 1996), p. 218.
23. Albert Hakim, *Historical Introduction to Philosophy* (New York: Macmillan, 1987), p. 338.
24. Ibid., p. 338.
25. Helen Buss Mitchell, *Roots of Wisdom: Speaking the Language of Philosophy* (Belmont, CA: Wadsworth, 1996).
26. Lavine, *From Socrates to Sartre,* p. 135.
27. Ibid.
28. Ibid.
29. James Gordon Clapp, "Locke John" article in *The Encyclopedia of Philosophy,* Vol. 4 (New York: Macmillan Publishing Co., Inc, and the Free Press, 1967), p. 487.
30. Vere Chappell, *The Cambridge Companion to Locke* (Cambridge: Cambridge University Press 1994), p. 9.
31. John Locke, "Introduction", *An Essay Concerning Human Understanding,* Vol. I (New York: Dover Publications, 1959 [original publication 1894]), p. 26. Collated and annotated by Alexander Campbell Fraser.
32. A point stressed by Robert Paul Wolff, *About Philosophy,* 7th ed. (Upper Saddle River, NJ: Prentice Hall, 1998).
33. Locke, *An Essay,* Vol II, pp. 121–22.
34. Ibid., p. 123.
35. Ibid., p. 124.
36. Dion Scott-Kakures, Susan Castagnetto, Hugh Benson, William Taschek, and Paul Hurley, *History of Philosophy* (New York: Harper-Perennial, 1993), p. 167.
37. Locke, *An Essay,* Vol I, annotated footnote 1, p. 37.
38. Mitchell, *Roots of Wisdom,* p. 237.
39. Locke, *An Essay,* Vol II, p. 170.
40. Ibid., p. 169.
41. Ibid., p. 173.
42. Ibid., p. 170.
43. Scott-Kakures et al., *History of Philisophy,* p. 171.
44. Locke, *An Essay,* Vol II, p. xxiii.
45. Mitchell, *Roots of Wisdom,* p. 237. Mitchell does an excellent job of simply describing the development of empiricism and the ideas of various empirical philosophers. I have made numerous references to her work in this section.
46. Ibid., p. 237.
47. George Berkeley, "Of the Principles of Human Knowledge," section 9 in David M. Armstrong, ed., *Berkeley's Philosophical Writings* (New York: Collier Books, Division of Macmillan, 1965), p. 64.

48. Lavine, *From Socrates to Sartre*, p. 143.

49. Berkeley, *Philisophical Writings*, section 10, p. 64.

50. This example is borrowed from Mitchell, *Roots of Wisdom*, p. 240.

51. Ibid., p. 279.

52. Lavine, *From Socrates to Sartre*, p. 144.

53. Lawhead, *The Voyage*, p.332; also see Mitchell, *Roots of Wisdom*, p. 242.

54. Lavine, *From Socrates to Sartre*, p. 151.

55. David Hume, *A Treatise of Human Nature*, L.A. Selby-Biggc, ed. (Oxford: Clarendon Press, 1975 [first edition, 1888]).

56. Ibid., "Introduction," p. xv.

57. David Hume, *An Inquiry Concerning Human Understanding*, Charles W. Hendel, ed. (Upper Saddle River, NJ: Prentice Hall, 1960), pp. 26–27.

58. Ibid.,p. 26.

59. Ibid., p. 27.

60. Lawhead, *The Voyage*, p. 331.

61. Hume, *A Treatise of Human Nature*, pp. 252–53

62. Hume, *Inquiry*, p. 27.

63. Lawhead, *The Voyage*, p. 328.

64. Hume, *Inquiry*, p. 29.

65. See Mitchell, *Roots of Wisdom*, p. 243, for a discussion of this point.

66. Hume, *Inquiry*, p. 75.

67. Ibid., p. 86.

68. Ibid., p. 86.

69. Lavine, *From Socrates to Sartre*, p. 163.

70. Ibid., p. 164.

71. Hume, *Inquiry*, p. 40.

72. Copleston, *A History of Philosophy*, Vol.5, *Berkeley to Hume*, (Garden City, NY: Image Books 1959).

73. Copleston, *A History*, p. 81.

74. Hume, *Inquiry*, p. 40.

75. From Hume's *Treatise*, quoted in Lavine, *From Socrates to Sartre*, pp. 168–69.

76. Gary Hatfield, ed., "Introduction" to Kant's *Prolegomena to Any Future Metaphysics*, (New York: Cambridge University Press, 1997).

77. Ibid., p.ix.

78. Lavine, *From Socrates to Sartre*, pp. 193–98.

79. By *intuition*, Kant does not mean special insight or any kind of sixth sense. When something is given in intuition, it becomes the object of the mind's direct awareness.

80. This illustrative example is taken from Anthony Falikowski, *Mastering Human Relations* (Scarborough, Ontario: Prentice Hall, Allyn and Bacon Canada, 1999), chap. 7.

81. Ibid., pp. 232–33.

82. Immanuel Kant, *Critique of Pure Reason*, (trans.) Norman Kemp Smith (New York: St. Martin's Press, 1965), pp. 41–42.

83. Ibid., p. 22.

84. For a further discussion of the Kantian "turn" in philosophy, see Lavine, *From Socrates to Sartre*, pp. 196–98.

85. Kant, *Critique*, p. 93.

86. Ibid., p. 67.

87. Ibid., p. 68.

88. For a discussion of Kantian categories in a psychological cognitive-developmental context, see Anthony Falikowski, *Piaget's Kantianism and the Critique of Pure Knowledge*, Master's Thesis, University of Toronto, 1979.

89. Kant, *Critique*, p. 75.

90. Ibid., pp. 61–62.

91. See Hume, *Inquiry*, pp. 49–50.

92. The examples used here were drawn from Samuel Enoch Stumpf, *Philosophy: History and Problems*, 4th ed. (New York: McGraw-Hill, 1994), pp. 303–6.

93. John Kemp, *The Philosophy of Kant* (London: Oxford University Press, 1968), p. 38.

94. Ibid., p. 40.

95. Frederick Copleston, *A History of Philosophy*, Vol.6, *Kant* (Garden City, NY: Image Books, 1960), p. 72.

96. Stumpf, *Philosophy*, p. 310.

97. Justus Hartnack, (trans.) M. Holmes Hartshorne, *Kant's Theory of Knowledge* (New York: Original Harbinger Book, 1967), p. 55.

98. Lawhead, *The Voyage*, p. 353.

99. This point was underscored by Norman Melchert *The Great Conversation: A Historical Introduction to Philosophy*, 3rd ed. (Mountain View, CA: Mayfield, 1999), p. 455.

100. Ibid., p. 455.

101. The example of the egg is borrowed from Melchert, *The Great Conversation*, pp. 455–56.

102. See "Preface" to Kant's *Critique of Pure Reason*, 2nd ed., p. 29.

103. Melchert, *The Great Conversation*, p. 270.

104. This summary is an adaptation of Lawhead, *The Voyage*, pp. 172–73.

105. Ibid.

106. Lawhead, *The Voyage*, pp. 185–86.

107. Ibid., p. 184.

108. Melchert, *The Great Conversation*, p. 275.

109. Thomas Aquinas, quoted in Norman Melchert, *The Great Conversation*, ibid. p. 275.

110. See Lawhead, *The Voyage*, p.185 for a discussion of this.

111. Melchert, *The Great Conversation*, p. 274.

112. Frederick Copleston, *A History of Philosophy*, Vol.2, *Medieval Philosophy: From Augustine to Duns Scotus* (New York: Image Books, 1993), p. 338.

113. Robert Paul Wolff, *About Philosophy*, 7th ed. (Upper Saddle River, NJ: Prentice Hall, 1998), p. 275.

114. Soccio, *Archetypes*, p. 247. An "efficient cause" is the "triggering" action or motion that begins the thing.

115. Robert C. Solomon, *Introductory Philosophy: A Text with Integrated Readings*, 7th ed. (Fort Worth: Harcourt College Publishers, 2001), p. 143.

116. Melchert, *The Great Conversation*, p. 283.

117. Ibid., p. 283.

118. St. Thomas Aquinas, *Summa Theologica*, rev. ed. (Fathers of the Dominican Province, 1920) Question 3, Article 3.

119. *Catholic Encyclopedia* on the World Wide Web (http://www.newadvent.org)

# CHAPTER 5

# ETHICS AND MORAL DECISION MAKING

# CHAPTER OVERVIEW

**Take It Personally**

KNOW THYSELF
**The Ethical Perspective Indicator**

**Character Ethics: Plato**
> Plato's Teleology
> Vision of the Soul
> Moral Balance and Plato's Functional
>     Explanation of Morality

KNOW THYSELF
**Platonic Character Type Index (PCTI)**

> Plato's Character Types

ORIGINAL SOURCEWORK
Plato, *Virtue and Justice in the Individual and in the State*

PHILOSOPHICAL PROFILE
**JEREMY BENTHAM**

**Utilitarian Ethics: Jeremy Bentham**
> The Problem of Pleasure
> Is-Ought Fallacy
> Theory of Sanctions
> The Hedonic Calculus

ORIGINAL SOURCEWORK
Bentham, *An Introduction to the Principles of Morals and Legislation*

**Deontological Ethics: Immanuel Kant**
> The Rational Basis of Morality
> Concept of the Good Will
> Notion of Duty
> Moral Duties to Oneself and to Others

> Maxims and Moral Behavior
> Kantian Formalism and the Categorical
>     Imperative
> Hypothetical versus Categorical Imperatives
> Autonomy versus Heteronomy of the Will

ORIGINAL SOURCEWORK
Kant, "Preface," *The Foundations of the Metaphysics of Morals*

**Feminine Ethics: Carol Gilligan and Nel Noddings**
> Male Bias in Moral Research

PHILOSOPHICAL PROFILE
**CAROL GILLIGAN**

> Gilligan's Morality of Care

PHILOSOPHICAL PROFILE
**NEL NODDINGS**

> Nel Noddings and Feminine Ethics
> Romanticizing Rationality: Reasons to Reject
>     Principled Morality
> Relation as Ontologically Basic
> Brief Outline of Noddings's Care-Based Ethic

ORIGINAL SOURCEWORK
Nel Noddings, "Introduction," *Caring: A Feminine Approach to Ethics and Moral Education*

PHILOSOPHICAL PROFILE
**FRIEDRICH WILHELM NIETZSCHE**

**Existentialist Ethics: Friedrich Wilhelm Nietzsche**
> God Is Dead

**ORIGINAL SOURCEWORK**
Nietzsche, *The Gay Science*

Will to Power
Master versus Slave Morality
Traditional (Herd) Morality and the Revaluation
of All Values
The Superman/Übermensch

**PHILOSOPHICAL PROFILE**
**AYN RAND**

**Objectivist Ethics: Ayn Rand**
Ethical Egoism
Objectivist Ethics
Altruism Is Inhumane
Values and Virtue
Rational Selfishness

**ORIGINAL SOURCEWORK**
Ayn Rand, *The Objectivist Ethics*

**PHILOSOPHICAL SEGUE:**
**Religion and Ethics: Islamic, Hindu, and Christian Perspectives**

Islamic Ethics

**ORIGINAL SOURCEWORK**
Riffat Hassan, *Islamic View of Human Rights*

Hindu Ethics

**ORIGINAL SOURCEWORK**
A.K. Malhotra, *Transcreation of the Bhagavad Gita*

Christian Ethics

**ORIGINAL SOURCEWORK**
Brian Berry, *Roman Catholic Ethics:
Three Approaches*

**STUDY GUIDE**
Key Terms ■ Progress Check
Summary of Major Points ■ Source References
Philosophy in Cyberspace ■ Endnotes

# LEARNING OUTCOMES

*After successfully completing this chapter, you will be able to:*

Explain the teleological nature of Plato's ethics in terms of his tripartite division of the soul

Offer a functional explanation of morality

Outline each of Plato's character types

Distinguish between psychological and ethical egoism

Show how sanctions are involved in moral action

Apply the criteria of Jeremy Bentham's hedonic calculus to a practical decision

Give Immanuel Kant's justification for why reason should be the basis of morality

Explain how moral duty relates to rational principle

Offer insight into self-referring and other-referring duties

Elucidate the relationship between moral maxims and formal principles

Distinguish between moral and nonmoral imperatives

Appreciate the importance of personal autonomy in the context of morality

Outline the feminine ethics of Carol Gilligan and Nel Noddings as alternatives to rational-based morality

Explain the meaning and relevance of the Nietzschean notion that "God is dead"

Elucidate how and why the will to power serves as the basis of Nietzsche's (existentialist) morality

Distinguish among master, slave, and herd moralities

Define what is meant by the concept of "übermensch" (superman)

Offer reasons why Ayn Rand rejects collectivist ethics and prefers a morality of ethical egoism

Provide Rand's explanation for why rational selfishness is acceptable

# FOCUS QUESTIONS

1. On what kinds of things have philosophers tried to base morality? To what have they given priority?

2. What is the place of the "I," or the individual, or the "ego-self" in the various approaches to morality?

3. What are the advantages and disadvantages of purely rational and nonrational ethical viewpoints?

4. Does gender make a difference to moral theorizing? If so, how?

5. What relevance do notions of freedom, autonomy, and liberation have for the moralists discussed here?

6. Are equality and altruism necessarily good from all moral perspectives? Why or why not?

7. What are some of the most provocative and challenging ideas presented in this chapter?

# TAKE IT PERSONALLY

Of all the subdisciplines of philosophy outlined in Chapter 1, the study of ethics is perhaps the most strikingly relevant and practical, especially given that so much of our life is awash in morality. For example, after the terrorist attack on the World Trade Center in New York City on September 11, 2001, some screamed for blood vengeance, others for compassion, and still others for forgiveness and understanding. There were those who wanted criminal prosecution, while many advocated full-scale war. When events like those of "9/11" occur, people are stunned into a new ethical awareness, frequently characterized by confusion and moral self-doubt. Questions are asked: "What *should* we do?" "What is the *right* response?" "How could anyone morally *justify* such actions?" "Does America really *deserve* this?" Not only in such extreme cases as terrorist attack, but also with respect to world events in general, a moral response is demanded from all of us as well. In plain view of poverty, hunger, the inequitable treatment of minorities, and global injustice, for example, we may choose to accept responsibility and take action, or we may do nothing by ignoring the problem, defensively rationalizing our noninvolvement or blaming the victims who suffer. One should note, however, that even choosing not to respond by hiding behind a veil of noncommitment is itself a moral response needing justification.

> **"The hottest places in hell are reserved for those who, in times of great moral crisis, maintain their neutrality."**
> DANTE

We're reminded here of Dante's claim concerning what God allegedly has in store for those who remain neutral in times of great moral crisis (read the adjacent quotation). If even neutrality is an ethical position that has consequences and requires justification, then it would appear that there is, in fact, no escaping moral responsibility. Life cannot be lived in a moral vacuum. To make use of a metaphor borrowed from Chapter 3, let's say we can either stay afloat in our philosophical lifeboats by making repairs to our damaged and leaking moral planks, or we can break apart and capsize in a whirlpool of moral indecision. Morality is not something that should be left unattended, for our own safe travels through life depend upon it.

Given that morality is unavoidable and so important, the question arises as to why so many people still try to sidestep it. Part of the reason, perhaps, is because of morality's serious, difficult, and sometimes overwhelming nature. Morality often deals with the "big issues" of life, things like war, capital punishment, and euthanasia—favorite topics covered in many applied ethics textbooks. Because most of us are not in the military, on death row, or dying from terminal illness, however, these enormously important moral issues and others like them can sometimes appear like distant hypothetical concerns, things we needn't worry about while commuting to school in rush hour traffic or stocking the shelves at our place of part-time employment. Notwithstanding this, let me suggest that morality is not all "out there," nor is it always "too huge" to be handled by us as individuals. A great deal of morality is an *inside job*. One could even argue that morality is part of human consciousness, that who we are as persons is a reflection of our morality. Indeed, the originator of psychoanalysis, Sigmund Freud, observed this himself when developing his concept of the *superego*.

According to Freud, the psychodynamics of the personality cannot be properly understood without appreciating the roles payed by moral conscience and our ego-ideals. The internalization of moral standards—stemming from parental, religious, and educational influences, for example—helps to define for us what is acceptable and nonacceptable behavior. Violation of these standards is what leads to guilt feelings, moral anxiety, and in extreme cases, to what Freud diagnosed as "neurosis." When, for instance, biological instincts like aggression and sexuality, arising out of the Freudian *id*, seek expression, superego moral prohibitions may dictate that we leave those instincts unexpressed, as this would constitute some sort of violation against societal norms or personal standards of morality. Consequently, the ego structure of the personality is left either to sublimate those instincts in socially acceptable ways, displace them onto less morally objectionable objects, deny that they exist, or repress them in the unconscious. When what the biological id desires is deemed by the superego (moral conscience) to be morally wrong, it becomes the rational ego's task to diffuse the tension between those two opposing psychic structures. Without a proper resolution to the moral conflict involved, we are left with a disturbed and conflicted mind. The Freudian depiction of moral conflict is, in fact, predated by the Christian *New Testament*. The conflict here is placed in the context of the *flesh* (id) opposing the *spirit* (moral conscience). It is written: *"For the flesh lusteth against the Spirit and the Spirit against the flesh: and these are contrary the one to the other: so that ye cannot do the things that ye would"* (St. Paul to the Galatians, 5:17).

Though many of the biologically deterministic and sexual components of Freudian theory are considered highly controversial in light of contemporary psychological research, the notion that moral conscience can lead to mental disturbance is one insight most of us can intuitively grasp and hence, more easily accept. The psychological torment that a conflicted moral conscience can cause is brilliantly illustrated by Shakespeare's *Hamlet*. The basic moral dilemma that Hamlet faces is whether he should accept stoically the events that affect his life or take action against them. You may recall that Hamlet's uncle kills his father and then marries his mother. Hamlet feels compelled to avenge his father's death, but to do so requires an act of murder. Hamlet's moral indecision gives rise to his famous soliloquy in Act 3, Scene 1, beginning with the words *"To be, or not to be, that is the question:/ Whether 'tis nobler in the mind to suffer the slings and arrows of outrageous fortune,/ Or to take arms against a sea of troubles/ And by opposing end them."*

For a slightly less "dramatic" illustration, suppose you were taught as a youngster to value honesty, loyalty, and friendship, but you are now troubled because you have been subpoenaed to testify in court against your best buddy, who has been charged with a crime you know he did, in fact, commit. If you're honest and tell the truth, you'll probably lose a friend who'll resent you for sending him to jail. If you stand by your friend out of loyalty and lie to the authorities, you're committing the crime of purgery—an immoral act. This difficult situation can obviously cause indecision and a lot of worry, guilt, fear, and other forms of mental disturbance. Being able to decide what is the morally right thing to do certainly does have real-life practical value; your psychological well-being may depend upon it.

On this note, I'm reminded of the time when a former student of mine raised his hand in class. He was obviously very agitated and upset. We had been discussing the ethics of abortion that day when he suddenly blurted out: "C'mon Tony, you've been studying this ethics stuff for years. You're the expert. Let's stop all of this arguing. It's driving me crazy. Just tell me, will you, is abortion right or wrong?" Thinking back to this painful experience of my student, I cannot help but become a little disturbed myself by the mental torment he was suffering. He was apparently experiencing considerable anxiety in his efforts to make the correct moral value judgment on the controversial issue of abortion. He knew that abortion was a serious matter and that it was important for him to take the right moral position on it; yet he was uncertain about how to decide for himself. He wanted me to decide for him. Like this student, you too may experience mental anguish when making important ethical decisions. Values must be championed, people must be confronted, principles must be defended, and sometimes difficult or unpleasant actions must be carried out. When there is much uncertainty or diversity of opinion, psychological tension can result. Moral doubt can be a significant source of stress in modern life.

In desperate efforts to cope with the moral suffering of the mind, some individuals like my tormented student look to experts and gurus for answers. By placing their faith in the judgment of others, people try to relieve themselves of the burden of having to decide for themselves. By granting moral authority to an ethics professor, a cult leader, a politician, or a military officer, some people attempt to escape from the personal responsibility of making moral decisions as independent agents. If any wrongdoing or bad judgment arises as a result of someone else's decision, the moral authorities are to blame, not the would-be moral escape artists. It is possible, then, that in some cases, deferring to moral authority is little more than a veiled attempt to get off the moral hook of life. Perhaps the most obvious example of this was found in the war crimes trials that followed World War II. At that time, a number of senior German officers pleaded innocent to war crimes charges on the grounds that they were "just obeying orders" from the Führer. In their minds, they were not responsible. World opinion seems to suggest otherwise.

Another psychological strategy to relieve morally induced mental stress is to quit thinking and simply conclude that all values are a matter of personal preference. Once this stance is adopted, there is no real need to agonize over moral matters. After all, no one person has the right to make a value judgment on the actions or character of another. As the saying goes, "different strokes for different folks." People just have different feelings and opinions about what is morally acceptable in any situation or given set of circumstances.

Although this relativistic position is one that some might wish to defend, and though it offers a degree of psychological solace, it is fraught with difficulties. If, for example, everybody is right and nobody is wrong because rightness and wrongness are relative to the person, culture, or generation, then opposite and conflicting moral positions could both be right at the same time—a proposition that does not make very much logical sense. Furthermore, if there is no objective way to decide matters of right and wrong or good and bad, then there would be no ethical basis for criticizing social policies or for improving society. We'd even be forced to concede that from the "terrorists' perspective," the attack in New York was justified, and further, we would have no *objective* basis for concluding otherwise. So too, in cases like slavery, child abuse, or discrimination against women, we would have to accept them on the grounds that, morally speaking, it is all a matter of personal opinion and how people feel at the time.

If we are not to abandon morality in our lives and the possibility of social progress, if we do not wish to wash our hands of moral responsibility or to escape from it by becoming mindless followers and sheep, we must look for adequate ways to make moral decisions for ourselves. Fortunately for us, a great many thinkers have grappled for centuries with the problems of ethical decision making. We need not bow down and worship these thinkers; nor do we have to accept unconditionally all of what they say to us. This would be mindless following again. As thoughtful and mature adults, now equipped with some of the basics of logic useful for critical analysis, what we can do is begin to consider intelligently the insights the thinkers have to offer and evaluate their moral philosophies from a rational, objective perspective. We can decide which ideas have worth, which ones need alteration, and which ones must be rejected altogether. We can do all this if we choose to be free and independent thinkers ourselves, and if we assume at the outset that when it comes to moral matters, debate is meaningful and there are better and worse decisions to be made.

With this assumption in mind, we move into the realm of moral theory. Of course, in an introductory text such as this, it would be impossible to cover all of the significant ethical thinkers from ancient times to the present. What is manageable is a brief sampling, so to speak, of different and widely varying ethical perspectives presented by major figures in the field. The sampling can help you to appreciate the complexity of moral thought, as well as its many useful insights for responsible and enlightened living. It can also serve as an invitation for you to continue your ethical explorations independently beyond the boundaries of what is presented here.

In what follows, you will be exposed to ancient and modern thinkers, to male and female theorists, to rational and nonrational approaches, as well as to atheistic, Christian, Eastern, and Middle Eastern religious ethical perspectives. The objective here is to present moral philosophy in a way that is respectful of diverse viewpoints and gender differences. To do otherwise might be considered unethical. (For anyone especially interested in Eastern views, flip back to the discussion on Buddhism in Chapter 2, Philosophies of Life. In that discussion, a moral prescription for living is offered by Siddhartha Gautama.)

Our moral trek in this chapter will start off with Plato's virtue-based character ethics. This ancient Greek perspective will facilitate self-reflection and consideration of the type of person we would like to become. Next, we will turn to Jeremy Bentham, a representative of British utilitarianism. Bentham would help us very much with our moral decision making by providing us with a "hedonic calculus"—a tool we can use to arrive at our moral conclusions in a spirit of scientific objectivity. Immanuel Kant also tries to provide us with a solid and secure foundation for ethical choice by presenting us with the "categorical imperative"—what he believes to be a purely rational, universally prescriptive principle we can use to derive all other moral maxims and ethical rules of conduct. In stark contrast to Kant, we then move on to consider the work of two contemporary American women—Nel Noddings and Carol Gilligan. They offer us modern feminine alternatives to rationally based and (allegedly) historically male-biased approaches like Kant's and its derivatives. After the discussion on feminine morality, we will then enter the dangerous territory of another European, namely Friedrich Wilhelm Nietzsche. Nietzsche explodes our complacency based on moral tradition and authority. He advocates a moral perspective that transcends rationality and what he regards as dishonesty cloaked in a mantel of altruism and community-mindedness. Like Nel Noddings and Carol Gilligan, Nietzsche also rejects reason as the basis of morality; however, unlike them, who appeal to care and the human affective response, he makes the "will to power" the foundation of his ethical thinking. The influence of Nietzsche on modern thought will become evident as we study Ayn Rand, a native-born Russian, who later became a U.S. citizen. Rand argues for ethical egoism, maintaining that the "virtue of selfishness" has been misunderstood by collectivist thinkers and their sympathizers. Finally, by means of another *Philosophical Segue,* we will briefly examine religious ethics—specifically, Islamic ethics, Hindu duty-based morality as presented in the *Bhagavad Gita,* and Christian ethics as interpreted from a modern-day Roman Catholic perspective.

But before we begin our study of moral theories, I invite you, as has become custom by now, to engage in a bit of self-examination by completing the *Know Thyself* diagnostic that follows. It will help you to identify your ethical assumptions and presuppositions before we start covering some others. Without fully appreciating it, perhaps, you have already internalized some sort of moral perspective. Now is the time to make it explicit to yourself and to become clearer on exactly what it is that you value in life. Knowing what your values are is a logical prerequisite for appraising their justifiability and worth.

# KNOW THYSELF

## The Ethical Perspective Indicator

**AIM** The purpose of this measure is to enable you to identify your moral assumptions and presuppositions by finding which moral perspective covered in this chapter most closely resembles your own.

**INSTRUCTIONS** Each moral statement that follows reflects a particular moral perspective. Your task is to indicate your level of agreement or disagreement with each one using the scale provided.

1 = strongly disagree
2 = disagree somewhat
3 = undecided
4 = agree somewhat
5 = strongly agree

## STATEMENTS

_____ 1. Morality is largely about character and finding psychological balance.

_____ 2. Morality should be based on happiness and the desire for pleasure.

_____ 3. Human reason should serve as the basis of morality.

_____ 4. Morality should be understood in terms of care and maintaining human relationships rather than in terms of rights, principles, duties, and the pursuit of personal happiness.

_____ 5. Morality cannot have a religious basis, for there is no creator-God.

_____ 6. Morality that does not further individual self-interest is dangerous and nonsensical.

_____ 7. A moral person is one whose personality functions with integrity.

_____ 8. Humans are biologically determined to seek pleasure and avoid pain. Hence, actions that maximize pleasure or reduce pain are good.

_____ 9. Morality is basically about duty—doing your duty for the sake of duty.

_____ 10. Moral decisions must be made by individuals in context. It is misguided to think that general principles of morality can be applied unconditionally across situations.

_____ 11. Morality should affirm and celebrate self-will.

_____ 12. Altruistic morality uses guilt to coerce people into doing for others, when they would really rather do things to benefit themselves personally.

_____ 13. People become morally corrupt when their appetites and desires seize control of their lives.

_____ 14. No actions are inherently right or wrong in themselves. Whether an action is right or wrong depends on its consequences.

_____ 15. A person is moral when he or she is motivated to do the right thing for the right reason.

_____ 16. Philosophers throughout history appear to have romanticized rationality, giving it far too much importance.

_____ 17. Traditional religious moralities are nihilistic, condemning those values and instincts that belong to "natural man."

_____ 18. The value of life is ultimately the ground for any rational morality; that which furthers life is good, that which threatens it is evil.

_____ 19. Morality is largely about the virtues of courage, temperance, and wisdom.

_____ 20. When making moral decisions, it's best to engage in a kind of cost-benefit analysis. Those actions producing the greatest benefits relative to cost should be preferred.

_____ 21. When people do the right thing (their moral duty) for the wrong reason (exclusively for self-interest), their action does not belong to the moral domain.

_____ 22. Exceptions to purely rational principles of morality are almost always inevitable, making them less sound than they appear at first.

_____ 23. Some forms of morality are dishonest, serving only the interests of the weak and fearful.

_____ 24. Productive work is the central _purpose_ of a rational man's life, the central value that integrates and determines the hierarchy of all his other values. Reason is the source, the precondition of his productive work—pride is the result.

_____ 25. The faculty of reason should harness both appetite and passion in the human character.

_____ 26. Punishment should be used only as a practical deterrent, not for retribution or revenge.

_____ 27. Moral duties—whether to ourselves or others—are unconditional and prescriptive for all.

_____ 28. Principles and duties should sometimes be overridden in order to maintain caring relationships.

_____ 29. People are not equal. Some characters are higher or more noble than others.

_____ 30. Altruism transforms people into sacrificial animals (those giving of themselves) and profiteers-of-sacrifice (those gladly accepting the sacrificial offerings).

_____ 31. People do wrong not because they are inherently evil, but because they are ignorant.

_____ 32. It's possible to make moral judgments in a spirit of scientific objectivity using mathematical-like calculations.

_____ 33. In order for a principle to be considered morally justifiable, it must be rationally consistent and universally applicable regardless of person, place, or time.

_____ 34. It's not dour obligation that moves us to moral action, but joy and desire to exercise the virtue of goodness by fulfilling ourselves in the other.

_____ 35. The best way to live is to see yourself as an artist and life as a work of art. You're the artistic creator, free and unbridled, painting the masterpiece in any way you choose.

_____ 36. In order for morality to work and make any sense, there must be something in it for me.

**Scoring Instructions** Record your answers next to the numbers listed in the columns below. Compare the totals. The highest total suggests that your current values, ideals, and moral beliefs are most consistent with the particular ethical theory identified by the label. You may be a character moralist, a utilitarian, deontologist, feminine moralist, existential atheist, or objectivist. Read the descriptions for each type of moralist.

| *Character Moralist* | *Utilitarian* | *Deontologist* |
|---|---|---|
| 1. | 2. | 3. |
| 7. | 8. | 9. |
| 13. | 14. | 15. |
| 19. | 20. | 21. |
| 25. | 26. | 27. |
| 31. | 32. | 33. |
| _____ Total | _____ Total | _____ Total |

| *Feminine Moralist* | *Existential Atheist* | *Objectivist* |
|---|---|---|
| 4. | 5. | 6. |
| 10. | 11. | 12. |
| 16. | 17. | 18. |
| 22. | 23. | 24. |
| 28. | 29. | 30. |
| 34. | 35. | 36. |
| _____ Total | _____ Total | _____ Total |

# INTERPRETATION OF RESULTS

**Character Moralist:** Those adopting this perspective see morality largely in terms of character development. They ask with Plato, "What sort of person should I strive to become?" and "What constitutes the good life?" Perhaps another way of putting it is: "How should I live?" (with emphasis on the "I"). Character moralists fitting the Platonic mold seek to balance various elements of what he calls the "soul," or human character structure, but appreciate the special importance of *reason* when it comes to harnessing one's appetites and unruly passions. Platonic character moralists see the highest level of moral development in the "philosopher king," one who displays virtues like temperance, wisdom, and courage. Misguided lives result from character imbalances arising from ignorance.

**Utilitarian:** The utilitarian moralist bases ethical decision making on the principle of utility. The morally right thing to do in any situation is that which maximizes people's benefit or happiness. Thus, the consequences of actions determine their moral worth. No actions are necessarily right or wrong in themselves. The moral value of actions can be determined by a kind of cost-benefit analysis known as the *hedonic calculus.* Actions producing the greatest net value of utility are those we're obligated to perform. The only thing good in itself is utility (pleasure, happiness, personal advantage); the only thing bad in itself is pain or other forms of disutility. On this account, the ends justify the means.

**Deontologist:** The (Kantian) deontologist is a rational, principled, duty-based moralist. The right thing to do is your duty, for the sake of duty alone. Dutiful acts are regarded as intentional human behaviors based on rules or maxims that can be derived from them. Actions that can be morally justified are those whose underlying maxims are logically consistent, universally prescriptive, unconditional, impartial, and rationally objective. Formal principles of rational thought serve, therefore, as the criteria determining whether actions are moral or morally justified. The thrust here is to act in accordance with rational, duty-based principles, not to maximize utility or promote happiness. Here, the ends do *not* justify the means. Morality is *not* about promoting human happiness; it's about acting on your obligations. The highest obligation is the categorical imperative: *"Act only according to that maxim by which you can at the same time will that it should become a universal law."*

**Feminine Moralist:** Feminine ethicists take issue with the whole notion of a purely rational, principle-based morality, arguing that exceptions to rules are inevitable and that strict and unyielding adherence to principles often undermines the very human relationships they are intended to strengthen and protect. For the feminist, morality should be based on care and the human affective response. The emphasis of morality should foster interdependence and responsibility for others, not the exertion of self-interest or the defense of individual rights (though these are important as well). For the feminist, emotional detachment is not a virtue but an unrecognized bias resulting from a history of males idolizing reason. It is not the rational subject (Descartes's *Cogito*) that is fundamental; rather "relation" is ontologically basic. Morality doesn't arise from the *a priori* structure of reason (Kant), but rather from the interpersonal dynamic of persons in relation.

**Existential Atheist:** The existential atheism covered in this chapter, namely Friedrich Nietzsche's, begins with the premise that there is no creator-God. Furthermore, morality is not somehow embedded in nature, to be discovered by the rational mind. Human beings do not need redemption, as they are not born stained with original sin. Human beings are ultimately free and self-determining. By exercising their instinctual will to power, they become legislators of morality themselves. The ideal for Nietzschean moralists is to live as nobles (those able to master themselves), overcome obstacles, and unhesitatingly display strength, courage, and pride. By sublimating the power of passion into creative acts of self-will, individuals can become "supermen," making life an aesthetic phenomenon.

**Objectivist:** The objectivist also is an atheist opposed to any sort of mysticism and blind faith, but equally against emotionalism and subjective preference serving as the basis of any justified morality. The objectivist bases morality on the notion of "rational selfishness." Moralities that require self-sacrifice to benefit the group, state, or collectivity are ultimately destructive. Forcing altruism upon people and making others the necessary beneficiaries of actions if they would be considered moral is inhumane. "Life is an end in itself, so every living human being is an end in himself, not the means to the ends or the welfare of others—and, therefore . . . man must live for his own sake, neither sacrificing himself to others nor sacrificing others to himself. To live for his own sake means that the achievement of his own happiness is man's highest moral purpose."

# CHARACTER ETHICS: PLATO

As we enter the moral domain, let us take what guidance we can from the immortal wisdom of Plato. In his writings, Plato addressed perennial questions like, "What constitutes the good life?" and "What sort of person should I endeavor to become?" To answer such questions, Plato paid particular attention to the soul. He believed that, like the body, the soul could enjoy health or could suffer from dysfunction. If the soul is to become and to remain healthy, then, for Plato, a certain harmonious balance of psychic elements must be established within the self. Physical, emotional, and intellectual components of the personality must be coordinated to work smoothly together. A smoothly functioning psyche constitutes a healthy, well-ordered soul, whereas an imbalanced psyche makes for a disordered one. The insight that we gain from this thinking is that if one wishes to live a life of virtue, then certain inner adjustments may be required. Morality is, as we suggested earlier, an "inside job." To understand precisely what is meant by this suggestion, it is necessary to examine Plato's notion of teleology and how it fits into his concept of the soul.

> *"Character is fate."*
> HERACLITUS

## Plato's Teleology

According to Plato's doctrine of **teleology,** everything in the universe has a proper function to perform within a harmonious hierarchy of purposes. This means that the development of anything follows from the fulfillment of the purpose for which it was designed. For us to evaluate something as good or bad, we must, therefore, examine and appraise it in light of its proper function. Does it perform well what it was designed to do? Take a pen, for example. A pen performs well if it writes smoothly and without blotting. This is what a pen is designed to do. Given the function of a pen, we should not expect it to perform well as an eating utensil or as a weapon of self-defense. It would be inappropriate to describe a pen as bad simply because eating with it is too difficult or defending oneself with it is not very effective. Our evaluation of a pen's good or bad performance depends on its designated purpose.

As for humans, we too have a function. In view of Plato's teleological explanation of morality, we live the morally good life insofar as we perform our distinctively human function well. Being less efficient than a robot on a factory assembly line, for instance, does not make us bad or morally deficient. We are not designed by nature to be mindless machines. What we are designed to do and how we are supposed to function, according to Plato, can best be understood by turning to his explanation of the structure and workings of the human soul.

## Vision of the Soul

Plato conceptualizes human nature in terms of a three-part division of the soul.[1] When reading about soul, try not to invest it with any religious significance. Understand that it is a metaphor to explain the main motives or impulses to action. For Plato, the **soul** is the principle of life and movement. Since the bodily self is inanimate, it must be moved by something and, for Plato, that something is the soul. While Plato's discussion of the soul is not intended as a scientific analysis of the mind, seeing the soul metaphorically as something akin to psyche, self, or personality structure is helpful for analytical purposes.

Plato's soul is made up of appetite, spirit, and reason, each aiming at different things. Take appetite first. **Appetite,** or **desire** as it is sometimes called, seeks to satisfy our biological instinctive urges. It looks after the physical side of our lives. There is an element in all of us that functions to achieve physical pleasure, release from pain, and material-want satisfaction. We all wish to eat, drink, sleep, act upon our sexual urges, minimize pain, experience pleasure, acquire a certain number of possessions, and live comfortably. When we diet, date, shop, or workout, for example, we are being driven by appetite—the physical side of our selves.

The second structural element of the human soul is **spirit,** that which drives us toward action. Sometimes referred to as **passion,** it includes our self-assertive tendencies. Spirit targets glory, honor, reputation, and the establishment of a good name. It also provides the impetus or force behind all ambitious pursuits, competitive struggles, and feelings of moral outrage and indignation. It is also the seat of human enterprise and pugnacity. As the emotional element of the psyche, spirit manifests itself in our need to love and be loved. It is present when we wish to make an impression, to be accepted and admired by others, or when we work hard to be liked.

**Reason** is the third element of the soul, representing what might be called the intellect. Reason can be described as the faculty that calculates, measures, and decides. It seeks knowledge and understanding, affording us insight and the ability to anticipate the future with foresight. By means of reason we are able to think and to make up our minds before we act. We can weigh options, compare alternatives, suppress dangerous urges, and make reasonable choices. Whenever we are curious, trying to make sense of things, or whenever we display an inquiring mind in our search for meaning, reason is that which moves us.

## Moral Balance and Plato's Functional Explanation of Morality

Having outlined the parts of the soul, let us go back to Plato's **functional explanation of morality.** Remember that, for Plato, anything is good to the extent that it performs its function well. So the question now becomes: How is the human soul supposed to work?

In answer to this, Plato suggests that the soul that is functioning properly is doing so in a kind of harmonious **moral balance.** When the faculty of reason governs both appetite and spirit—that is, our physical desires as well as our passions and emotions—then an orderly and well-balanced moral character results. Thus, people who are living the morally good life maintain a rational, biological, and emotional equilibrium with reason in charge.

Control of inner harmony by reason is not easy to achieve. We all experience turmoil and psychological conflict. It is as if there are warring factions within the mind that cause tension and upheaval. This internal conflict is not abnormal or psychopathological; it is part of the human condition. Inner struggle is part of life.

To help us better appreciate this struggle, Plato describes it metaphorically, using the illustrative example of a charioteer with two horses in reign. The charioteer symbolizes the faculty of reason; the horses represent appetite and spirit. One horse (appetite) "needs no touch of the whip, but is guided by word and admonition only." The other horse (spirit) is unruly, "the mate of insolence and pride . . . hardly yielding to whip and spur." While the charioteer (reason) has a clear vision of the destination and the good horse is on track, the bad horse "plunges and runs away, giving all manner of trouble to his companion and charioteer."[2]

In the scenario presented to us by Plato, we have two horses pulling in different directions, while a charioteer watches his commands go unheeded. The charioteer's job is to guide and control the horses. What is clear is that the chariot cannot go anywhere unless the driver can work together with the two horses and bring them under control. So too with life. Just as both horses are necessary to achieve the charioteer's goal, appetite and spirit are indispensable to reason. Reason identifies the goal, harnessing the power of appetite and spirit as it proceeds toward its chosen destination. Appetite and spirit cannot be disposed of, since they are essential to the well-ordered functioning of the human soul.

When reason is in control and the soul is functioning in a harmonious balance, we can say that it is functioning as it should. For Plato, fulfillment of our function as human beings is equivalent to the attainment of **moral virtue.** When we are unhappy or when we have lost our sense of well-being, disharmony of the soul is the problem. If the "wild horses" of passion and desire are running rampant in our lives, then we fall into disorder manifesting itself in ignorance. We begin to confuse **appearance** with **reality.** We mistake apparent goods for real goods. We pursue things we think will make us happy when, in fact, they will not. We make wrong choices and do wrong things out of false knowledge. As poor misguided souls, we fall prey to moral evil and corruption. Only by allowing reason to regain control of our lives can we enjoy peace of mind, inner harmony, and lasting happiness. Reason can offer us true knowledge of what is ultimately good, and only reason can properly guide us in what we should do

> *"Zeal without knowledge is a runaway horse."*
> PROVERB

## PHILOSOPHERS IN ACTION

Think about the last time you let your appetites, feelings, or passions "run wild." What were the immediate consequences and longer term results? Do you agree with Plato that reason should rule our lives? Why or why not?

with our lives. It is reason that yields the knowledge necessary for moral virtue; ignorance can produce only evil and misdirection.

At this point, you're invited to consider the questions asked in the Philosophers in Action feature on page 284. Once done, you are also welcome to complete The Platonic Character Type Index, which will help you to identify your character dispositions at this time in your life.

# KNOW THYSELF

## Platonic Character Type Index (PCTI)

The PCTI is an informal self-analytical tool that can help you begin identifying which part of your psyche or "soul" is dominant in your life at this time. Knowledge of this fact can help you to understand better the internal workings of your "Platonic character type." Such information can also suggest paths for future character development and healthy personality maintenance. Your results are not intended to be scientifically valid, but rather suggestive. (I am not sure the soul lends itself very well to empirical, scientific investigation!) The accuracy of the results ultimately will be determined by your own rational self-analysis or, should I say, "philosophical psychoanalysis."

# INSTRUCTIONS

Next to each phrase below, indicate how reflective of you the item, action or activity is. Unless absolutely necessary, try to avoid 3 as your answer. Answering 3 too often will not likely reveal any character preferences.

1 = not reflective of me at all
2 = hardly reflective of me
3 = moderately reflective of me
4 = very reflective of me
5 = exactly reflective of me

How accurate would it be to say that you

_____ 1. seek truth

_____ 2. wish to become famous

_____ 3. want to make large sums of money

_____ 4. enjoy being carefree

_____ 5. experience pleasure through artificial or chemical means

_____ 6. trust thinking more than sensory perception

_____ 7. are competitive

_____ 8. wish strongly to live a materially comfortable lifestyle

_____ 9. avoid restrictions and restraints

_____ 10. look out for number one

_____ 11. pursue knowledge (as opposed to data or information)

_____ 12. have difficulty dealing with subordinates (those lower in rank)

_____ 13. do not waste time on activities that have little financial payoff

_____ 14. treat all wants as equal

_____ 15. do what you want regardless of the consequences for other people

_____ 16. control your physical urges and biological appetites

_____ 17. want to be liked by others

_____ 18. value being economical

_____ 19. live in the moment and for the moment

_____ 20. deceive people to get what you want

_____ 21. do what is right, putting aside personal feelings and wants

_____ 22. value achievement (fame) over money

_____ 23. avoid financial disaster

_____ 24. enjoy equally all the pleasures of life

_____ 25. fall prey to manias or compulsions

_____ 26. like intellectual thought

_____ 27. try to look successful to others

_____ 28. seize opportunities to better yourself economically

_____ 29. take life a day at a time

_____ 30. tell people whatever is necessary to get what you want

_____ 31. display temperance (moderation)

_____ 32. assume an attitude of superiority

_____ 33. work hard to ensure the basic necessities of life

_____ 34. do what feels good

_____ 35. take by force, if necessary

_____ 36. regulate personal habits

_____ 37. enjoy exhibitions of courage and strength

_____ 38. live consistently with the principle: Money first, then morality

_____ 39. frequently change your mind about what you want

_____ 40. display addictive behavior

**Scoring**   Next to each of the question numbers below, fill in your response. Add the total scores for each column and then plot them on your PCTI. See the example for help on how to do this.

| *PK* | *Tim* | *O* | *D* | *T* |
|------|-------|-----|-----|-----|
| 1 | 2 | 3 | 4 | 5 |
| 6 | 7 | 8 | 9 | 10 |
| 11 | 12 | 13 | 14 | 15 |
| 16 | 17 | 18 | 19 | 20 |
| 21 | 22 | 23 | 24 | 25 |
| 26 | 27 | 28 | 29 | 30 |
| 31 | 32 | 33 | 34 | 35 |
| 36 | 37 | 38 | 39 | 40 |
| _____ | _____ | _____ | _____ | _____ |

Totals

PK  = Philosopher King/Ruler   _____

Tim = Timarchic Character   _____

O   = Oligarchic Character   _____

D   = Democratic Character   _____

T   = Tyrannical Character   _____

**Interpretation**   To learn what your results mean, refer to the abbreviated descriptions that follow. More information on each character type is found in the main text (pp. 288–296). Note that you probably have a mixture of different character elements making up your personality. It is unlikely that anyone is purely one type. Nonetheless, the character type with the highest score may be most reflective of what you are like as an individual right now. Your responsibility is to decide for yourself. After reading the descriptions of the character types, you may be favorably impressed or you may feel the need to change as a result. The moral decision is yours!

Example:

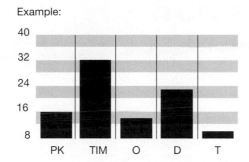

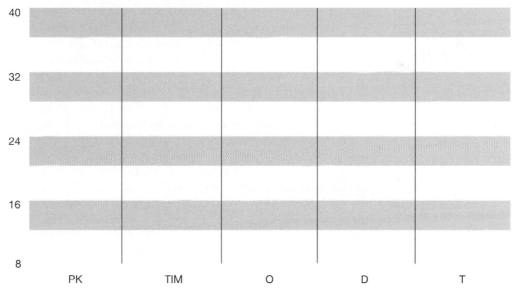

**FIGURE 5.1** Platonic Character Type Bar Graph Index

**Timarchic Character**   Driven by spirit, energetic, competitive, self-assertive, can also be insecure, jealous, vain and self-inflating, fearful of falling behind

**Democratic Character**   Versatile, easy-going, treats all passions and desires equally, but is frequently aimless, without principle, torn apart inside

**Philosopher King/Ruler**   Enlightened, internally balanced, morally virtuous, i.e., temperate, courageous, wise, just, ruled by reason, careful to distinguish between appearance and reality

**Oligarchic Character**   Driven by appetite, frugal, hardworking, materialistic and oftentimes money-hungry, dissatisfied, internally disturbed, dirty and wretched opportunist

**Tyrannical Character**   Possessed by master passion, criminal personality, totally undisciplined, least self-sufficient, anxiety ridden

Source: Anthony Falikowski, *Moral Philosophy for Modern Life,* Scarborough, Prentice Hall Canada, 1998, pp. 23–27.

# PLATO'S CHARACTER TYPES

In *The Republic*, differently functioning "souls" are described using Plato's notion of **character types.** The ideal character is exemplified by the philosopher king or ruler. Corrupt, imperfect types arc given these labels: timarchic, oligarchic, democratic and tyrannical. You will note that all of these types have political-sounding categorizations. The reason for this, according to Plato, is that in each kind of societal structure there is a corresponding individual who is admired within it, so that in an oligarchy, for instance, the values and attributes of the oligarchic character are praised. Likewise, in a timarchic society, the qualities you find in the timarchic person would be extolled as virtues. Understand, however, that not every individual in a particular society necessarily displays the corresponding character type. Oligarchs can be found in democracies, virtuous people can be found in tyrannies, and so on. The point is that individuals give rise to societies that, in turn, praise the qualities possessed by those individuals.

> **"Know thyself."**
> THE ORACLE AT DELPHI

An interesting parallel between individuals and societies can also be seen by looking at the class system proposed by Plato for the *just society*—the system that functions in harmonious balance. In the ideal or just society, there would emerge three classes of people corresponding to the three parts of the soul. Each class would serve different, but complementary, roles. First, there would be those whose lives would be driven primarily by the appetites. These would be the craftsmen, artisans, and traders. In modern times, we might see these people as the producers, workers, consumers, and business class. Second, there would be the auxiliaries (a subdivision of guardians), motivated in their lives mostly by spirit. They would serve to protect and preserve internal order under the guidance of rulers. Examples of this class in today's world would include the police, militia, and civil servants. Third, individuals would be selected from the auxiliaries to become the most highly trained and educated members of an elite guardian class, namely the philosopher kings/rulers. Membership in any class would not be determined by birth or inheritance; rather, children would be moved from class to class according to merit and capability. Only those who passed the most rigorous tests and who would be best suited to work for the good of the community would become philosopher rulers. In the just society, the lower classes would not gain undue influence, or else internal anarchy would result, just as it does in the world when appetite or spirit overrule reason. Reason must rule, as must those whose lives are governed by reason, not by greed (appetite) or self-assertion (spirit).

Let us now look at the character of the philosopher king and examine in more detail the corrupt character types located at lower levels of society. Though the notion than an elite class should govern society may not be popular today, Plato argued that ". . . the human race will not be free of evils until either the stock of those who rightly and truly follow philosophy acquire political authority, or the class who have power in the cities be led by some dispensation of providence to become real philosophers." To paraphrase, rulers must become philosophers or philosophers must become rulers if we are to establish the ideal social system. Just as reason must rule the soul, so too must philosophers rule the social order if the just society is ever to become a reality. (For a further discussion of this and related points, see Chapter 6, "Plato's Political Theory.") At this point, you might also wish to refer to the *Original Sourcework* by Plato dealing with justice in both the individual and society.

ORIGINAL SOURCEWORK

## Virtue and Justice in the Individual and in the State

**PLATO**

And so, after much tossing, we have reached land, and are fairly agreed that the same principles which exist in the State exist also in the individual, and that they are three in number.

Exactly.

Must we not then infer that the individual is wise in the same way, and in virtue of the same quality which makes the State wise?

Certainly.

Also that the same quality which constitutes courage in the State constitutes courage in the individual, and that both the State and the individual bear the same relation to all the other virtues?

Assuredly.

And the individual will be acknowledged by us to be just in the same way in which the State is just?

That follows, of course.

We cannot but remember that the justice of the State consisted in each of the three classes doing the work of its own class?

We are not very likely to have forgotten, he said.

We must recollect that the individual in whom the several qualities of his nature do their own work will be just, and will do his own work?

Yes, he said, we must remember that too.

And ought not the rational principle, which is wise, and has the care of the whole soul, to rule, and the passionate or spirited principle to the subject and ally?

Certainly.

And, as we were saying, the united influence of music and gymnastic will bring them into accord, nerving and sustaining the reason with noble words and lessons, and moderating and soothing and civilizing the wildness of passion by harmony and rhythm?

Quite true, he said.

And these two, thus nurtured and educated, and having learned truly to know their own functions, will rule over the concupiscent, which in each of us is the largest part of the soul and by nature most insatiable of gain; over this they will keep guard, lest, waxing great and strong with the fullness of bodily pleasures, as they are termed, the concupiscent soul, no longer confined to her own sphere, should attempt to enslave and rule those who are not her natural-born subjects, and overturn the whole life of man?

Very true, he said.

Both together will they not be the best defenders of the whole soul and the whole body against attacks from without; the one counselling, and the other fighting under his leader, and courageously executing his commands and counsels?

True.

And he is to be deemed courageous whose spirit retains in pleasure and in pain the commands of reason about what he ought or ought not to fear?

Right, he replied.

And him we call wise who has in him that little part which rules, and which proclaims these commands; that part too being supposed to have a knowledge of what is for the interest of each of the three parts and of the whole?

Assuredly.

Plato, *The Republic*, trans. Benjamin Jowett, New York: P.F. COLLIER & SON
© 1901 The Colonial Press, section (441c–445b)

And would you not say that he is temperate who has these same elements in friendly harmony, in whom the one ruling principle of reason, and the two subject ones of spirit and desire are equally agreed that reason ought to rule, and do not rebel?

Certainly, he said, that is the true account of temperance whether in the State or individual.

And surely, I said, we have explained again and again how and by virtue of what quality a man will be just.

That is very certain.

And is justice dimmer in the individual, and is her form different, or is she the same which we found her to be in the State?

There is no difference in my opinion, he said.

Because, if any doubt is still lingering in our minds, a few commonplace instances will satisfy us of the truth of what I am saying.

What sort of instances do you mean?

If the case is put to us, must we not admit that the just State, or the man who is trained in the principles of such a State, will be less likely than the unjust to make away with a deposit of gold or silver? Would any one deny this?

No one, he replied.

Will the just man or citizen ever be guilty of sacrilege or theft, or treachery either to his friends or to his country?

Never.

Neither will he ever break faith where there have been oaths or agreements?

Impossible.

No one will be less likely to commit adultery, or to dishonour his father and mother, or to fail in his religious duties?

No one.

And the reason is that each part of him is doing its own business, whether in ruling or being ruled?

Exactly so.

Are you satisfied then that the quality which makes such men and such states is justice, or do you hope to discover some other?

Not I, indeed.

Then our dream has been realized; and the suspicion which we entertained at the beginning of our work of construction, that some divine power must have conducted us to a primary form of justice, has now been verified?

Yes, certainly.

And the division of labour which required the carpenter and the shoemaker and the rest of the citizens to be doing each his own business, and not another's, was a shadow of justice, and for that reason it was of use?

Clearly.

But in reality justice was such as we were describing, being concerned however, not with the outward man, but with the inward, which is the true self and concernment of man: for the just man does not permit the several elements within him to interfere with one another, or any of them to do the work of others,—he sets in order his own inner life, and is his own master and his own law, and at peace with himself; and when he has bound together the three principles within him, which may be compared to the higher, lower, and middle notes of the scale, and the intermediate intervals—when he has bound all these together, and is no longer many, but has become one entirely temperate and perfectly adjusted nature, then he proceeds to act, if he has to act, whether in a matter of property, or in the treatment of the body, or in some affair of politics or private business; always thinking and calling that which preserves and co-operates with this harmonious condition, just and good action, and the knowledge which presides over it, wisdom, and that which at any time impairs this condition, he will call unjust action, and the opinion which presides over it ignorance.

You have said the exact truth, Socrates.

Very good; and if we were to affirm that we had discovered the just man and the just State, and the nature of justice in each of them, we should not be telling a falsehood?

Most certainly not.

May we say so, then?

Let us say so.

And now, I said, injustice has to be considered.

Clearly.

Must not injustice be a strife which arises among the three principles—a meddlesomeness, and interference, and rising up of a part of the soul against the whole, an assertion of unlawful authority, which is made by a rebellious subject against a true of whom he is the natural vassal—what is all this confusion and delusion but injustice, and intemperance and cowardice and ignorance, and every form of vice?

Exactly so.

And if the nature of justice and injustice be known, then the meaning of acting unjustly and being unjust, or again, of acting justly, will also be perfectly clear?

What do you mean? he said.

Why, I said, they are like disease and health; being in the soul just what disease and health are in the body.

How so? he said.

Why, I said, that which is healthy causes health, and that which is unhealthy causes disease.

Yes.

And just actions cause justice, and unjust actions cause injustice?

That is certain.

And the creation of health is the institution of a natural order and government of one by another in the parts of the body; and the creation of disease is the production of a state of things at variance with this natural order?

True.

And is not the creation of justice the institution of a natural order and government of one by another in the parts of the soul, and the creation of injustice the production of a state of things at variance with the natural order?

Exactly so, he said.

Then virtue is the health and beauty and well-being of the soul, and vice the disease and weakness and deformity of the same?

True.

And do not good practices lead to virtue, and evil practices to vice?

Assuredly.

Still our old question of the comparative advantage of justice and injustice has not been answered: Which is the more profitable, to be just and act justly and practice virtue, whether seen or unseen of gods and men, or to be unjust and act unjustly, if only unpunished and unreformed?

In my judgement, Socrates, the question has now become ridiculous. We know that, when the bodily constitution is gone, life is no longer endurable, though pampered with all kinds of meats and drinks, and having all wealth and all power, and shall we be told that when the very essence of the vital principle is undermined and corrupted, life is still worth having to a man, if only he be allowed to do whatever he likes with the single exception that he is not to acquire justice and virtue, or to escape from injustice and vice; assuming them both to be such as we have described?

Yes, I said, the question is, as you say, ridiculous.

## DISCUSSION QUESTIONS FOR CRITIQUE AND ANALYSIS

1. What do you think of Plato's use of descriptive terms? An individual might be "brave," but can a "state" be brave as well? Further, while it makes sense to talk about a "just" society, what could it possibly mean to say that someone's character is "just?" Discuss.

2. When Plato claims that classes in society parallel the three parts of the soul, what sort of claim is he making: *a priori*, empirical, prescriptive, or normative? Does he provide sufficient support or justification for his claim? Why or why not?

# PHILOSOPHERS IN ACTION

What do you think about having a class system in society? Is our society presently governed by philosopher kings/rulers? What has been the result? Should the leaders in our society come from an intellectually and morally elite ruling class? Why or why not? If you object to a class system, is your honest objection to rule by an elite based on a hidden fear that you may not qualify to govern? If commitment to justice and truth does not make the philosopher king fit to rule, then what makes anyone a good social leader?

## Philosopher Kings/Rulers

According to Plato, the just society is a form of **aristocracy.** In an aristocracy, **philosopher kings** who belong to the *guardian class* become the rulers. (Note that no gender discrimination is intended by the use of the label "kings." Qualified women also would be selected to serve as rulers in Plato's ideal government.)

Philosopher kings (or rulers) are morally virtuous individuals. They are temperate, allowing no physical appetites or material desires to enslave them. Virtuous souls regulate their appetites by reason. Philosophers also exhibit the virtue of courage—a passion that supports reason in its judgments and decisions to act. Plato says, "He is deemed courageous whose spirit retains in pleasure and in pain the commands of reason about what he ought or ought not to fear. . . ."

The morally virtuous person is also wise, knowing what is best for each part of the soul. The wise person "has in him that little part which rules, and which proclaims these commands [of reason]; that part too being supposed to have a knowledge of what is for the interest of each of the three parts of the whole . . . " In addition, philosopher rulers are just. With respect to character, remember that *just* means balanced and *functioning harmoniously.* In the just character of the philosopher king, reason, emotion, and physical nature work well together, with reason in charge, of course. It is the faculty of reason that prevents inner rebellion and disorder of the soul. It establishes an internal constitution based on peaceful coexistence.

Besides being truly virtuous, another distinguishing characteristic about philosopher kings is that they have special knowledge. By an elaborate process of education, philosopher kings learn how to distinguish between appearance and reality. They learn how to acquaint themselves intellectually with the eternal and immutable **realm of forms.** The "forms," so called, can be known only by reason and, according to Plato, are more real than the transitory things that we see, hear, taste, touch, and feel. Sensory experience can yield only imperfect approximations of the ideal forms. For example, it is rational acquaintance with the form "justice" that allows us to describe any act as fair or unfair, just or unjust. Even though we have never seen complete fairness or universal justice in the world, we still know what it is. Reason offers us perfect knowledge in an imperfect world. It shows us what the eyes have not seen. (To learn more about the perfect forms found in the realm of being, see the section on Plato in Chapter 4, "Epistemology, Metaphysics, and God.")

Those who fall prey to the imperfect false knowledge offered by the senses, and those who become morally sidetracked by physical appetites and emotions, end up living disordered lives of unhappy ignorance. Philosopher rulers make no such mistake. They are not lured away from truth and moral goodness by misleading appearances, by the "drone's honey" or the "power monger's prestige and influence." Philosopher kings appreciate how such things can only end in disillusioned moral bankruptcy. Philosopher kings are enlightened souls who are not entrapped by fantasies and temptations but are guided on the right path by the light of true moral goodness.

Now, before you foolishly bow down in humble worship of your philosophy teacher, understand that being a philosopher king today has nothing to do with occupation, but it has everything to do with character and disposition. A philosophy professor may teach all the right things, but for selfish and vainglorious motives to which he or she will not admit. Joe or Jill Average, on the other hand, may display many, or all, of the philosopher king's virtues without ever teaching the subject itself. Be aware, then, that anybody, even the student sitting beside you in class, could be a "closet philosopher." Maybe it is time for you to come out of the "king's closet" yourself and continue your character training as one of society's future guardians? Will you accept the call?

## Timarchic Character

The dominant part of the soul that drives the **timarchic character** is spirit. People with timarchic characters are distinguished, in large part, by their energy, competitiveness, and the urge to dominate. For example, do you know anyone whose life seems to be based on "oneupmanship?" Does that person try to better you at no matter what? Do all of your accomplishments pale in comparison to that other individual—at least in his or her estimation? Is whatever you do unfavorably compared or belittled by your timarchic friend's (alleged) superior performance? In short, does it seem that being with this person is like being engulfed in a continual struggle, an athletic contest, or a battle of wills? If so, then you can appreciate what this character type brings to the table of life.

Timarchic characters are self-assertive individuals, liking to be "out there" and trying to make an impression on other people. No matter how favorable the impression made or how successful the person is, they still retain a nagging insecurity. Reputations must be maintained; people must continue to be impressed; nobody else must be allowed to dominate, control, or look better. Life at the top of the ladder of success is very precarious. Once at the top, there is only one way to go—down—down in the estimation of others and, hence, down in one's own estimation. The ambitious pride characterizing timarchic persons can thus create only a very thin veneer of confidence. Below the surface, these people fear that they will fall behind, lose, be humiliated and embarrassed, or that approval from others will be withdrawn at any time. These fears will manifest themselves in jealousy, as timarchic persons begrudge the successes of others.

The pitfalls of the timarchic character can be observed in the misguided athlete. Investing years of one's life in hopes of winning an Olympic gold medal in the shot-put event, for example, may leave a person wasted and could result in financial ruin. Finishing twelfth after years of self-financed training—out of the medals and out of the record books, with no fame, no endorsements, and possibly no perceived future—could also leave the person embittered and insecure. Failed efforts at vainglorious pursuits are not always pretty to witness. With or without success, the timarchic character is destined to a life of underlying fears, jealousies, and insecurities. Ignorant of the fact that vanity and self-inflation cannot ultimately lead to a tranquil and balanced soul, timarchic characters will never achieve true and lasting happiness. At best, they will achieve only a cheap and transitory semblance of it.

**❝ . . . and the higher the prestige of wealth and the wealthy, the lower that of goodness and good men will be. ❞**

PLATO

## Oligarchic Character

In a society where wealth dominates and the wealthy are in control (arguably, our own), the qualities of the **oligarchic character** are revered. In the oligarch, we discover a character transformation from the ambitious, competitive type of person to money-loving business person. Suggesting that our own society is a form of oligarchy is arguably a fairly accurate assessment. After all, is it not true that many people in North American society judge the worth of an individual by what that person owns? "How much are they worth?" we ask. Is it not a widespread belief that you are "somebody" because you own many expensive things and having a lot of cash makes you a V.I.P. (a very important person)? When people say they want to "better" themselves, is it not the case that they usually mean acquire more wealth and material possessions?

Of course, not everybody in contemporary society displays an oligarchic character. Those who do are simply the ones who are recognized and rewarded. They are the ones on the cover of *Fortune* magazine or featured in the *Financial Post* or *Wall Street Journal.* Wherever they are found, the oligarchs' main objective in life is to make money. In the oligarchic character, appetite rules and dominates the rest of the soul by a desire for riches. When reason is called upon, it is called upon only in the service of making more money. Spirit, by contrast, is "forbidden to admire or value anything but wealth and whatever leads to it."

Plato's oligarch is frugal, economical, and hardworking, wasting as little as possible on nonessentials. Hard effort is spent on trying to satisfy only necessary wants. Unnecessary want and desires, which do not function to accumulate greater wealth, are regarded as pointless and therefore, repressed. A stingy oligarch today might not want to spend all that hard-earned money on a flashy new automobile, for instance, as it is little more than a depreciating asset—a bad financial investment.

The character imperfections of the oligarch are, perhaps, most plainly evident in the huckster, pedlar, or hawker on late-night television infomercials. Plato says the oligarch possesses a squalid (dirty and wretched) character "always on the make and putting something by" others. The person who can "sell snow to an Eskimo," get you to buy more than you wanted, or persuade you to purchase what you really do not need, is the one who becomes rich, famous, and admired.

In the oligarch, there is a dramatic movement from ambition to avarice. For the oligarch, there is no advantage to having a good name and a moral reputation if there are no financial rewards. Because money and profit are the basic driving forces behind the oligarchic character, the person will be dishonest when able. The only deterrent is fear of punishment; there is certainly no moral conviction or taming of desire by reason.

Plato described oligarchs as having dual personalities. They usually manage to maintain a certain degree of respectability as, on the whole, better desires master the worse. Nonetheless, good and bad desires engage in a battle for dominance within the psyche of the oligarch. The unfortunate result is that oligarchic individuals are never really at peace within themselves. When the worse desires are subdued, the oligarch manages "a certain degree of respectability, but comes nowhere near the real goodness of an integrated and balanced character."[3]

Finally, though some degree of social respectability can be achieved by oligarchs, they will usually make little significant contribution to public life where money and profit may have to be sacrificed. An oligarch might ask, "Why be a politician when there is so little financial reward?" Did you know that the lowest paid hockey player in the National Hockey League has a greater "market value" and earns more money than the prime minister of Canada, the leader of thirty million people? Oligarchs would probably say, "Rightly so!" When it comes to the worth of a man or woman, oligarchs would most likely let the market decide. Given the thinking of oligarchs, their achievements and ambitions in public life are not likely to amount to much, but then again, they are also not likely to sustain large financial losses in pursuing vain ambitions of power or political glory.

## Democratic Character

In contrast to the oligarchic character who distinguishes between necessary and unnecessary desires, the **democratic character** does not. All desires and appetites are treated equally. Democrats are charming but aimless individuals, spending as much money, time, and effort on necessary desires as on unnecessary ones. For the democratic personality, no pleasure is underprivileged; each gets its fair share of encouragement. This type of character lives from day to day, indulging in any momentary pleasure that presents itself. The pleasures are varied. About the oligarch, Plato writes:

> . . . he lives from day to day, indulging the pleasure of the moment. One day it's wine, women and song, the next water to drink and a strict diet; one day it's hard physical training, the next indolence and careless ease, and then a period of philosophic study. Often he takes to politics and keeps jumping to his feet and saying or doing whatever comes into his head. Sometimes all his ambitions and efforts are military, sometimes they are all directed to success in business. There's no order or restraint in his life, and he reckons his way of living is pleasant, free and happy, and sticks to it through thick and thin.[4]

People displaying a democratic character are versatile because they lack principles. The problem is that if people do not live a rational, principled life, then diverse and incompatible pleasures, appetites, and passions can pull them in different directions at the same time. Their personalities are, consequently, not integrated and functioning harmoniously. Individuals with a democratic character become torn apart inside. As Plato says, there is no order or restraint, but rather, disorder and lack of control. Persons obsessively pursuing different and sometimes conflicting pleasures cannot avoid becoming disorganized and fragmented. Their lives exhibit a definite lack of rational coherence and direction. Democrats are like children in a candy store. They are excited but torn apart inside because they want everything in the store at the same time, and this is impossible.

Plato speculates about how the democratic character is formed. He believes that children raised in a strict oligarchic household, where unnecessary pleasures have been denied, eventually are lured by those outside the family who do enjoy them. A basic diet, for instance, becomes insufficient or unsatisfactory, and their desire grows for luxurious, exotic food. Simple tastes are replaced by sophisticated, extravagant ones. Unnecessary desires, immediate pleasures, and extravagant tastes eventually transform the oligarchic person into a democratic character. Plato writes:

> Let's go back to the question how the democratic man originates from the oligarchic. This generally happens, I think, as follows.
> How?
> When a young man, brought up in the narrow economical way we have described, gets a taste of the drones' honey and gets into brutal company, where he can be provided with every variety and refinement of pleasure, with the result that his internal oligarchy starts turning into a democracy.[5]

## Tyrannical Character

According to Plato, the **tyrannical character** is the worst, being the most unhappy and undesirable. The tyrant personifies the criminal personality. People with a tyrannical character suffer from a kind of mania. "Maniacs" possess one master passion that controls all other idle desires. This master passion becomes so powerful that it runs wild, causing madness in the individual. The object of this passion may be sex, alcohol, or drugs, for example. In the tyrannical personality's pursuit of pure pleasure, no shame or guilt is experienced as all discipline is swept away and usurped by madness. Tyrannical people are thus the least self-sufficient of all individuals. Their satisfaction depends entirely on external things and objects of maniacal desire. Tyrants are full of anxiety and constantly trying to fulfill their unrelenting appetite for more. Tyrants will do anything and everything to satisfy themselves, even if they must perform terrible deeds and become hated in the process. Tyrants' lives are lawless and disgusting. Though all of us have aggressive, bestial, and erotic urges—evidenced especially in dreams—most of us are able to control them; the tyrant, however, cannot. If and when tyrants have spent all of their money indulging their master passion, they will start borrowing to satisfy it. When they are no longer able to borrow, they may proceed to rob, commit fraud, or engage in acts of violence. Tyrannical characters become thieves, pick-pockets, kidnappers, church robbers, and murderers to satisfy their manias. From this fact alone, it should be clear why tyrants are the most morally corrupt of all the character types.

## PHILOSOPHERS IN ACTION

Pick out a well-known historical figure or notorious individual from contemporary society. The person could be an actor, sports celebrity, villain, businessperson, literary figure, or fictional character from any book, movie, or television show. Examine and appraise that person's actions, intentions, and motivations. What Platonic character type does that individual display? Give support for your answer.

## PHILOSOPHICAL PROFILE

### Jeremy Bentham

Jeremy Bentham was born in London in 1748. As a child, he was intellectually precocious. By the age of 4 Bentham was already studying Latin grammar and, at age of 12, he enrolled at Queen's College, Oxford. In 1763 Bentham earned a Bachelor of Arts degree and thereupon began legal studies at Lincoln's Inn. In that same year, he returned to Oxford for what turned out to be one of the most decisive experiences of his intellectual life. Bentham attended a number of lectures on law given by Sir William Blackstone. Blackstone presented his legal theory based on "natural rights." Regarding this theory as little more than rhetorical nonsense, Bentham began setting the stage for the development of his own utilitarian conception of law, justice, and society. Bentham earned his Master of Arts degree in 1766 and then proceeded to London. Having never really developed a fondness for the legal profession, he decided against becoming a practicing lawyer. Instead, he embarked on a literary career, the basic object of which was to bring order and moral defensibility into what he perceived as the deplorable state of the law and the social realities it made possible in his day. Jeremy Bentham can thus be regarded as a social reformer. He undertook the task of trying to modernize British political and social institutions. There is little doubt that it was due at least in part to his influence that an historical landmark was established, the Reform Bill of 1832, which transformed the nature of British politics. The control of Britain's parliament was taken away from the landed aristocracy and placed into the hands of the urban bourgeoisie.

**JEREMY BENTHAM**

On a personal note, Jeremy Bentham was the godfather of John Stuart Mill, son of James Mill, a friend and colleague. John Stuart Mill later became the godfather of Bertrand Russell, a famous English philosopher who led the fight for nuclear disarmament in the 1960s. Starting with Bentham, an interesting philosophical lineage begins to evolve that has had political activism as an essential element.

# UTILITARIAN ETHICS: JEREMY BENTHAM

In the world of moral philosophy, when the subject of **utilitarianism** is raised, the name Jeremy Bentham is one of the first to come to mind. For many, his name is virtually synonymous with this ethical theory. It should be noted, however, that Bentham was not the sole inventor of this theoretical perspective. Elements of utilitarianism are found in the writings of people such as Thomas Hobbes and John Locke. Bentham's significant contribution comes from his efforts to connect and apply its basic principles to the problems of his time. He sought to provides nineteenth-century English society with philosophical foundations for moral thought and practical social reform. Bentham believed that ethical questions could be answered in a spirit of **scientific**

> **"Nature has placed mankind under the governance of two sovereign masters, pain and pleasure. It is for them alone to point out what we ought to do, as well as to determine what we shall do. "**
> JEREMY BENTHAM

**objectivity.** He rejected such things as tradition, aristocratic privilege, and religious faith as legitimate bases for moral evaluation. He believed that such things too easily serve the interests of the dominant ruling classes and that they lead to the continued mistreatment of the poor and disenfranchised. Rather than appeal to religious, political, or cultural authorities, Bentham chose to adopt a much more commonsense empirical approach to the improvement of society. He argued that people's actions and those of governments could, and should, be evaluated according to their practical consequences of how much good they produce. For Bentham, no action is necessarily right or wrong in itself. The ethical value of anything is determined by its real-life results. Utilitarianism is, therefore, a form of **consequentialism.** It is the effect of an action that establishes its moral worth.

In his most famous work, *An Introduction to the Principles of Morals and Legislation* (1789), Bentham outlines his objective basis for morality. He calls it the **principle of utility.** Bentham writes:

> By the principle of utility is meant that principle which approves of every action whatsoever, according to the tendency which it appears to have to augment or diminish the happiness of the party whose interest is in question: or, what is the same thing in other words, to promote or to oppose that happiness. I say of every action whatsoever; and therefore not only of every action of a private individual, but of every measure of government.[6]

The term "utility" is one you might not use in everyday conversation. Think of it as the same thing as *benefit, advantage, pleasure, happiness,* and *goodness.* Whatever prevents mischief, pain, evil, suffering or unhappiness also has utility or utilitarian value for Bentham.

## The Problem of Pleasure

Bentham's utilitarianism is based on a premise of **psychological egoism,** which states that it is human nature for us to seek pleasure and to avoid pain. To quote Bentham: "Nature has placed mankind under the governance of two sovereign masters, pain and pleasure. It is for them alone to point out what we ought to do, as well as to determine what we shall do."[7] This, in itself, is not problematic. If this were all Bentham were saying, then he would be making nothing other than a psychological claim about human behavior that we could try to verify empirically. To assert that humans are motivated by a self-interested pursuit of pleasure would simply make Bentham a psychological egoist. Bentham, however, goes further and becomes an ethical egoist as well. He argues that because it *is* in our nature to seek pleasure, that is what we morally *ought* to do. For him, pleasure becomes a value that we ought to pursue and a standard against which to judge all actions and activities. In making a connection between "moral or ethical oughts" and "pleasure," Bentham is suggesting that right and wrong or good and bad cannot be properly be understood in any other way. The right or good thing to do is to seek pleasure, for it is only pleasure and the avoidance of pain that give actions any real value. Conversely, the wrong or bad thing to do is to reduce or minimize the amount of pleasure experienced. It is also wrong to promote pain, misery, and suffering.

## Is-Ought Fallacy

Bentham's leap from psychological egoism to **ethical egoism** might make good intuitive sense to you. From a purely logical perspective, however, it falls prey to what, in logic, is called the "**is-ought fallacy.**" When this fallacy is committed, the reasoner tries unjustifiably to derive a moral "ought" from an "is" of experience. To illustrate, just because it *is* true that people lie, kill, cheat, and steal, we cannot conclude solely on that basis that they *should* or *ought* to do so, for obvious reasons. In fact, even if we suggested that people are inherently evil by nature (the biological equivalent of original sin), we probably still would not accept evil behavior on the grounds that we are so constituted. More likely, we would say that the right thing to do is to suppress our (natural) aggressive, bestial, and dishonest inclinations. The "is" is that in fact which "ought" to be repressed or somehow extinguished. As we can see, then, arguing from what is true to what ought to be is clearly a problematic and debatable step.

   Bentham did not deal at length with the is-ought problem inherent in his utilitarianism. What he did was to suggest that all other moral theories were either vague and inconsistent or else reducible to pleasure and the principle of utility in the end. Furthermore, providing no substantial defense or justification of the principle of utility as the basis of morality, he simply concluded that "that which is used to prove everything else, cannot itself be proved: a chain of proofs must have their commencement somewhere. To give such proof is as impossible as it is needless."

## PHILOSOPHERS IN ACTION

Do you think Bentham's acceptance of pleasure (utility) as a standard of morality is justified? Why or why not? Would it be wise to accept an "unnatural" morality, one that requires us to work against our natural urges and inclinations? What would Bentham say? Discuss.

## The Theory of Sanctions

If, as Bentham claims, psychological egoism is what motivates people to behave as they do, then what is preventing them from doing anything they want at any time they want, even if this entails violating others? For Bentham, the answer is found in the notion of **sanctions.** Think of a sanction as a source of pleasure and pain that acts to give binding force to any law or rule of conduct. Sanctions can also be seen as rewards and punishments or as causal and determining factors influencing our behavior. According to Bentham, we, as individuals, respond egoistically to sanctions, trying to maximize our pleasure and minimize our pain. We generally avoid behaving in ways that lead to pain and other negative sanctions, preferring instead to act in ways that lead to pleasure, happiness, personal benefit, or satisfaction. Sanctions govern what we do, perhaps more than we sometimes realize.

Sanctions come in a variety of types. *Physical sanctions* are not administered by any human or divine source. They are what bind us to the laws of nature. For example, you cannot jump off the Empire State building or off a mountain peak in Washington State without suffering the consequences. The law of gravity in this case will produce "grave" consequences for you—no pun intended. Because we recognize the physical sanctions associated with certain kinds of dangerous acts like these, virtually all of us refrain from them.

*Moral sanctions* arise in our informal relationships with others. If you have ever experienced peer-group pressure, you can probably appreciate the power, influence, and control that public opinion can have. To spare ourselves mental pain or embarrassment and loneliness, we often go along with the crowd and conform to the expectations of others. Other people actually contribute to the governance of our behavior in ways of which we are not always consciously aware. For instance, if your friends start avoiding you because you constantly lie to them, you may be dissuaded from continuing the practice. The underlying fear of ostracism is often enough to prompt a change in behavior.

In addition to physical and moral sanctions, our behavior can also be regulated by *religious sanctions,* that is, if we believe in a rewarding and punishing supreme being, as in the Islamic-Judeo-Christian tradition. People may do what is right according to their religion, church, or holy book in hope of entering the gates of heaven or because they fear the hell-fire of eternal damnation. Religious sanctions affecting the afterlife can impact on behavior in the here and now.

Finally, Bentham writes of *political sanctions.* These sanctions are issued formally by judges and magistrates on behalf of the state. Punishments issuing from the state (province, county, municipality, federal court) include things like fines, penalties, and jail terms. Fear of such punishment is what deters people from breaking the law and violating the rights of other citizens. On a positive note, things like peace and good order, which result from abiding by the law, are what people find rewarding. Such things create the conditions most conducive to our pursuit of pleasure.

Of all sanctions, Bentham was most interested in the political type. As a reformer, he wished to change the laws of English society in such a fashion that the general welfare would be promoted by each individual pursuing his or her own advantage. Political sanctions embodied by the rewards and punishments issued by a carefully crafted legal system would promote the greatest happiness for the greatest number. Thus, for Bentham, laws should serve utilitarian ideals.

Laws are not necessarily right or wrong in themselves, but they are acceptable only to the extent that they further human happiness.

## The Hedonic Calculus

To help individuals as well as lawmakers and legislators decide what ought to be done in any given set of circumstances, Bentham developed what has come to be known as the **hedonic calculus.** As the term suggests, the hedonic calculus involves the calculation of pleasure or hedonistic consequences. Remember that Bentham wanted to conduct moral inquiry in a spirit of scientific objectivity. By using the hedonic calculus to determine the pleasures and pains produced by any particular action or policy, he thought we could decide empirically on what is the right or good thing to do. The hedonic calculus might be more understandable if you see it as a kind of "cost-benefit" analysis. In moral and ethical decision making, Bentham recommends that the bottom line should be the maximization of pleasure and the minimization or elimination of pain. Actions producing the greatest happiness for the individual or group concerned are actions we morally ought to perform.

The hedonic calculus gives us seven criteria by which to measure the pleasure and pain produced by any particular action:

1. **Intensity:**      Ask how strong the pleasure or emotional satisfaction is.
2. **Duration:**      Ask how long the pleasure will last. Will it be short-lived or long-lasting?
3. **Certainty:**      Ask how likely or unlikely it is that pleasure will actually result. What is the probability of the result?
4. **Propinquity:**      Ask how soon the pleasure will occur. How near are the consequences?
5. **Fecundity:**      Ask how likely it is that the action will produce more pleasure in the future. Will the good/pain produced create more good/pain down the road?
6. **Purity:**      Ask if there will be any pain accompanying the action (some pleasurable acts are accompanied by painful elements). Is there some bad you have to take with the good?
7. **Extent:**      Ask how many other people will be affected by the considered action.

When making a moral or ethical decision, what Bentham suggests you do is attach numerical values to each of the elements listed above. You can use any scale you like. For our purposes, let us use a scale ranging from $-100$ to $+100$. Negative values indicate pain, positive values indicate pleasure. Thus, $-100$ means high pain, $-50$ means moderate pain, and $-10$ means low pain. Similarly, $+100$ stands for high pleasure, $+50$ stands for moderate pleasure, and $+10$ stands for low pleasure. Once the scale is determined, you then perform a pain-pleasure calculation of alternative courses of action. (There is an actual sequence of calculation discussed by Bentham in the *Principles of Morals and Legislation,* see Chapter VI.)

Suppose you have to decide between doing *A* and not-doing *A*. Which should you choose from a utilitarian perspective? First, look at *A* in regard to its intensity, duration, and other elements of the hedonic calculus. How much pleasure and how much pain is produced? On balance, is there more pleasure or more pain? Now, consider not-doing *A*. Again, calculate the quantities of pain and pleasure, using the criteria of the hedonic calculus. Once the calculations are done for each alternative action—doing *A* versus not doing *A*—compare them. The alternative action producing the most pleasure is the morally preferable one. If both alternatives produce a net balance of pain, then the alternative producing the least pain is to be preferred.

I should add here that if the implications of the considered action go beyond the individual to include others, then Bentham recommends that we repeat the hedonic calculus taking their interests into account. What is the net balance of pleasure and pain for others if alternative *A* is performed? What are the hedonic consequences for them if *A* is not performed? Take note that Bentham was interested not only in maximizing the happiness of the individual but also in maximizing the happiness of the broader community. Thus, if our actions impact on others, then we must account for them in our hedonic calculation.

At this point, I might add that Bentham was not unrealistic. For him, "It is not to be expected that this [hedonic calculation] process should be strictly pursued previously to every moral judgment, or to every legislative or judicial operation."[8] To do a formal hedonic calculation every time we were about to act would be highly impractical. Yet according to Bentham, each of us goes through some semblance of this process on a commonsense intuitive level, only we may do it so quickly that we are virtually unconscious that we have done it. We may not wittingly go through all of the criteria outlined by Bentham, but in general terms, we probably go through some kind of weighing and balancing process, considering the pros and cons before we act.

The hedonic calculus can be made more understandable by working out an actual example. Let us say that you are back in high school and that you are thinking about going on to college or university in a distant city. The school you have in mind has the best program in your chosen field, and for years you have longed to attend it. The problem is that you have become involved in a serious relationship with someone who prefers that you stay in your hometown and find employment at the local manufacturing plant. You two have discussed the possibility of marriage, though no firm commitments have been made either way. Your dilemma involves choosing between: (A) staying at home to work and continuing to develop your personal relationship with your special someone; and (B) going away to school and pusuing your career and academic dreams. What is the best thing to do? Let us find out using the hedonic calculus. Note that a complete calculation would entail not only a consideration of your interests but also a consideration of the interests of the other party involved. For brevity's sake, we will do a partial calculation based only on your interests. The values given to each part of the decision would likely vary in real life from person to person. I will take the liberty here of reading your mind and feeling your emotions.

# A HEDONIC CALCULATION

*Alternative A—Stay at Home and Work
in the Local Plant*

1. *Intensity:* If I choose to stay at home, (−50) I will probably experience intense feelings of disappointment. I may also become regretful and may possibly resent how another person has frustrated the pursuit of my personal dream. Some of the resentment and anger I feel will be diminished by the loving feelings I have for my boyfriend/girlfriend and by the love I feel for my family.

2. *Duration:* Any acute feelings of anger (−25) and resentment are likely to subside in a relatively short period of time. Nagging doubts, however, may remain for years, causing unpleasantness and insecurity. Time may heal, but the emotional scars may remain.

3. *Certainty:* Who knows? What people (−10) want often changes. I might change my mind about working at the plant. It is possible that I will learn to like it there, though I really believe I will not.

4. *Propinquity:* The frustration and disap- (−50) pointment will result fairly soon. It is now July and classes start in September. The mental pain is not that far down the road.

5. *Fecundity:* If I stay at home, I can (+100) save myself a lot of money. Mom and Dad will not accept rent from me, so I will be able to save almost everything I earn. I also will not have to pay ridiculously high tuition fees that I cannot afford. I will be able to invest the money I earn in the stock market. I do not think I could ever recoup what I would lose in wages, residence, and tuition by going to college or university.

6. *Purity:* Sure, there will be financial (−25) gains if I stay at home, but I will experience considerable pain due to possible missed opportunities. There will be things I never learn and people I never meet because I opt for the financially preferable course of action.

7. *Extent:* Other people will be af- (+100) fected by my decision. Mom and Dad do not value formal education, so they would prefer that I stay home. My boyfriend/girlfriend also prefers that I stay home. I get the feeling that people in the neighborhood would also like me to stay. They say they would miss me if I went away.

*Utilitarian Value of Alternative A*

|  | Utility | Disutility |
|---|---|---|
| Intensity |  | −50 |
| Duration |  | −25 |
| Certainty |  | −10 |
| Propinquity |  | −50 |
| Fecundity | +100 |  |
| Purity |  | −25 |
| Extent | +100 |  |
|  | +200 | −160 |

*Result:* Alternative A would produce +40 net units of pleasure

### Alternative B—Go Away to School

1. *Intensity:*  If I choose to go away to school, the excitement will be wonderful. I will be enthusiastic, energized, and optimistic about going to a new place, meeting new people, and learning new things. (+75)

2. *Duration:*  I know my positive feelings will tend to subside in time. Reality hits during exams. I am likely to miss my family and special loved one. I know I can sometimes easily become bored. Nonetheless, I think the experience will be great and I will like it. (+25)

3. *Certainty:*  Well, if I go, I am pretty certain of having fun and enjoying myself. I have been accepted both at the school and at the residence, so I know that there are no practical obstacles preventing me from going. I guess it is possible my roommate and I will be incompatible, but I will hope for the best. (+75)

4. *Propinquity:*  The good times will start soon. We are just weeks away from homecoming, pub-crawls, intermural sports—you name it. If I choose to go to school, I will not have to wait long to enjoy myself. (+75)

5. *Fecundity:*  I know that by going to school, I am going to cultivate my mind and possibly open up new horizons I never dreamt of before. I do not know of anyone who has ever been hurt by knowledge and understanding. On the downside, I do stand to lose a lot of money over the next four years. Getting a job at the plant would have paid well, and I could have invested my earnings. No doubt about it, I will lose in the immediate future, but I hope to make it up over my lifetime. (+25)

6. *Purity:*  I know that going off to school is not all fun and games, at least if I want to pass. Studying is hard and so are exams. You cannot party when you are doing an all-nighter mastering Plato. Furthermore, I am likely to encounter professors and courses I do not really like. I guess school has its good and bad sides, just like everything else. (+10)

7. *Extent:*  I know the people around me will be sorry to see me go. They will be saddened and possibly lonely. I hope my boyfriend/girlfriend does not take my decision (−50)

personally. I do not mean to hurt, but I cannot help but think that hurt feelings will be created anyway.

### Utilitarian Value of Alternative B

|  | Utility | Disutility |
|---|---|---|
| Intensity | +75 | |
| Duration | +25 | |
| Certainty | +75 | |
| Propinquity | +75 | |
| Fecundity | +25 | |
| Purity | +10 | |
| Extent | | −50 |
| | +285 | −50 |

*Alternative B would produce +235 units of pleasure.*

### Comparing Alternatives

| | A<br>Staying at Home | B<br>Going to School |
|---|---|---|
| Intensity | −50 | +75 |
| Duration | −25 | +25 |
| Certainty | −10 | +75 |
| Propinquity | −50 | +75 |
| Fecundity | +100 | +25 |
| Purity | −25 | +10 |
| Extent | +100 | −50 |
| | +40 units | +235 units |

*Findings:* Alternative B produces greater pleasure than Alternative A.

*Conclusion:* Alternative B is the right thing to do.

# PHILOSOPHERS IN ACTION

This exercise can be done individually or in small groups. Your task will be to perform a hedonic calculation for the following situation. Imagine that you are on the student council and that you are away at a convention. At the convention, you meet another student delegate from across the country. After a few drinks and some pleasant conversation, you are propositioned and invited to that person's hotel room for an "overnight stay." You hesitate because you are engaged to be married. What should you do? Decide, using Bentham's hedonic calculus.

*For further discussion:* What problems, if any, did you discover doing your hedonic calculation? Assuming you are the student in the situation above, would you want *your* fiancé/fiancée to be a utilitarian? Why or why not?

Before we move on to the next ethical perspective by the philosopher Immanuel Kant, let us continue our treatment of Bentham for a moment with a brief sampling from his original work entitled *An Introduction to the Principles of Morals and Legislation.*

ORIGINAL SOURCEWORK

*An Introduction to the Principles of Morals and Legislation*

JEREMY BENTHAM

# OF THE PRINCIPLE OF UTILITY

I.  Nature has placed mankind under the governance of two sovereign masters, pain and pleasure. It is for them alone to point out what we ought to do, as well as to determine what we shall do. On the one hand the standard of right and wrong, on the other the chain of causes and effects, are fastened to their throne. They govern us in all we do, in all we say, in all we think: every effort we can make to throw off our subjection, will serve but to demonstrate and confirm it. In words a man may pretend to abjure their empire: but in reality he will remain subject to it all the while. The principle of utility recognises this subjection, and assumes it for the foundation of that system, the object of which is to rear the fabric of felicity by the hands of reason and of law. Systems which attempt to question it, deal in sounds instead of sense, in caprice instead of reason, in darkness instead of light.

But enough of metaphor and declamation: it is not by such means that moral science is to be improved.

II.  The principle of utility is the foundation of the present work: it will be proper therefore at the outset to give an explicit and determinate account of what is meant by it. By the principle of utility is meant that principle which approves or disapproves of every action whatsoever, according to the tendency which it appears to have to augment or diminish the happiness of the party whose interest is in question: or, what is the same thing in other words, to promote or to oppose that happiness. I say of every action whatsoever; and therefore not, only of every action of a private individual, but of every measure of government.

III.  By utility is meant that property in any object, whereby it tends to produce benefit, advantage, pleasure, good, or happiness, (all this in the present case comes to the same thing) or (what comes again to the same thing) to prevent the happening of mischief, pain, evil, or unhappiness to the party whose interest is considered: if that party be the community in general, then the happiness of the community: if a particular individual, then the happiness of that individual.

IV.  The interest of the community is one of the most general expressions that can occur in the phraseology of morals: no wonder that the meaning of it is often lost. When it has meaning, it is this. The community is a fictitious body, composed of the individual persons who are considered as constituting as it were its members. The interest of the community then is, what?—the sum of the interests of the several members who compose it.

V.  It is in vain to talk of the interest of the community, without understanding what is the interest of the individual. A thing is said to promote the interest, or to be for the interest, of an individual, when it tends to add to the sum total of his pleasures: or, what comes to the same thing, to diminish the sum total of his pains.

VI.  An action then may be said to be conformable to the principle of utility, or, for shortness sake, to utility, (meaning with respect to the community at large) when the tendency it has to augment the happiness of the community is greater than any it has to diminish it.

VII.  A measure of government (which is but a particular kind of action, performed by a particular person or persons) may be said to be conformable to or dictated by the principle of utility, when in like manner the tendency which it has to augment the happiness of the community is greater than any which it has to diminish it.

VIII.  When an action, or in particular a measure of government, is supposed by a man to be conformable to the principle of utility, it may be convenient, for the purposes of discourse, to imagine a kind of law or dictate, called a law or dictate of utility: and to speak of the action in question, as being conformable to such law or dictate.

IX.  A man may be said to be a partizan of the principle of utility, when the approbation or disapprobation he annexes to any action, or to any measure, is determined

Jeremy Bentham, *An Introduction to the Principles of Morals and Legislation*, Oxford: Oxford University Press, 1823.

by and proportioned to the tendency which he conceives it to have to augment or to diminish the happiness of the community: or in other words, to its conformity or unconformity to the laws or dictates of utility.

X.  Of an action that is conformable to the principle of utility one may always say either that it is one that ought to be done, or at least that it is not one that ought not to be done. One may say also, that it is right it should be done; at least that it is not wrong it should be done: that it is a right action; at least that it is not a wrong action. When thus interpreted, the words ought, and right and wrong, and others of that stamp, have a meaning: when otherwise, they have none.

XI.  Has the rectitude of this principle been ever formally contested? It should seem that it had, by those who have not known what they have been meaning. Is it susceptible of any direct proof? It should seem not: for that which is used to prove every thing else, cannot itself be proved: a chain of proofs must have their commencement somewhere. To give such proof is as impossible as it is needless.

XII.  Not that there is or ever has been that human creature breathing, however stupid or perverse, who has not on many, perhaps on most occasions of his life, deferred to it. By the natural constitution of the human frame, on most occasions of their lives men in general embrace this principle, without thinking of it: if not for the ordering of their own actions, yet for the trying of their own actions, as well as of those of other men. There have been, at the same time, not many, perhaps, even of the most intelligent, who have been disposed to embrace it purely and without reserve. There are even few who have not taken some occasion or other to quarrel with it, either on account of their not understanding always how to apply it, or on account of some prejudice or other which they were afraid to examine into, or could not bear to part with. For such is the stuff that man is made of: in principle and in practice, in a right track and in a wrong one, the rarest of all human qualities is consistency.

XIII.  When a man attempts to combat the principle of utility, it is with reasons drawn, without his being aware of it, from that very principle itself. His arguments, if they prove anything, prove not that the principle is wrong, but that, according to the applications he supposes to be made of it, it is misapplied. Is it possible for a man to move the earth? Yes; but he must first find out another earth to stand upon.

XIV.  To disprove the propriety of it by arguments is impossible; but, from the causes that have been mentioned, or from some confused or partial view of it, a man may happen to be disposed not to relish it. Where this is the case, if he thinks the settling of his opinions on such a subject worth the trouble, let him take the following steps, and at length, he may come to reconcile himself to it.

1.  Let him settle with himself, whether he would wish to discard this principle altogether; if so, let him consider what it is that all his reasonings (in matters of politics especially) can amount to?

2.  If he would, let him settle with himself, whether he would judge and act without any principle, or whether there is any other he would judge and act by?

3.  If there be, let him examine and satisfy himself whether the principle he thinks he has found is really any separate intelligible principle; or whether it be not a mere principle in words, a kind of phrase, which at bottom expresses neither more nor less than the mere averment of his own unfounded sentiments; that is, what in another person he might be apt to call caprice?

4.  If he is inclined to think that his own approbation or disapprobation, annexed to the idea of an act, without any regard to its consequences, is a sufficient foundation for him to judge and act upon, let him ask himself whether his sentiment is to be a standard of right and wrong, with respect to every other man, or whether every man's sentiment has the same privilege of being a standard to itself?

5.  In the first case, let him ask himself whether his principle is not despotical, and hostile to all the rest of human race?

6.  In the second case, whether it is not anarchial, and whether at this rate there are not as many different standards of right and wrong as there are men? and whether even to the same man, the same thing, which is right today, may not (without the least change in its nature) be wrong tomorrow? and whether the same thing is not right and wrong in the same place at the same time? and in either case, whether all argument is not at an end? and whether, when two men have said, 'I like this,' and 'I don't like it,' they can (upon such a principle) have anything more to say?

7. If he should have said to himself, No: for that the sentiment which he proposes as a standard must be grounded on reflection, let him say on what particulars the reflection is to turn? if on particulars having relation to the utility of the act, then let him say whether this is not deserting his own principle, and borrowing assistance from that very one in opposition to which he sets it up: or if not on those particulars, on what other particulars?

8. If he should be for compounding the matter, and adopting his own principle in part, and the principle of utility in part, let him say how far he will adopt it?

9. When he has settled with himself where he will stop, then let him ask himself how he justifies to himself the adopting it so far? and why he will not adopt it any farther?

10. Admitting any other principle than the principle of utility to be a right principle, a principle that it is right for a man to pursue; admitting (what is not true) that the word right can have a meaning without reference to utility, let him say whether there is any such thing as a motive that a man can have to pursue the dictates of it: if there is, let him say what that motive is, and how it is to be distinguished from those which enforce the dictates of utility: if not, then lastly let him say what it is this other principle can be good for?

## DISCUSSION QUESTIONS FOR CRITIQUE AND ANALYSIS

1. What sort of claim does Bentham make when he says: "Nature has put mankind under the governance of two sovereign masters, pain and pleasure. It is for them alone to point out what we ought to do, as well as to determine what we shall do." Should we accept this claim? Why or why not?

2. Bentham suggests that critics of the principle of utility unwittingly presuppose it in their criticisms of it. Is Bentham able to convince you that this is true? Why or why not?

---

# DEONTOLOGICAL ETHICS: IMMANUEL KANT

*"Two things fill the mind with ever new and increasing admiration and awe . . . the starry heavens above and the moral law within."*

IMMANUEL KANT

So far in our treatment of ethical theories, we have learned how thinkers throughout the ages have sought the philosophical foundations of morality in different places and in different things. Recall, for example, how Bentham argued that the morality of particular actions could be established by reference to their consequences. For him, an action was good to the extent that it produced pleasure, bad to the extent that it caused pain. As a consequentialist, Bentham would say that the moral worth of a particular action can be evaluated by its results. As for Plato, remember how he too sought the basis of morality in his philosophical investigations. He eventually located moral goodness in a transcendent realm of forms—something timeless and spaceless, known not by the senses, but only through intellectual acquaintance. As we turn now to Immanuel Kant's **deontological ethics,** we will see how he tries as well to provide morality with a solid and secure foundation of rationality.

## The Rational Basis of Morality

To start with, you should note that Kant is not an **ethical relativist,** meaning that he does not regard morality as merely a matter of personal opinion or subjective preference; nor does he think that morality is completely dependent on cultural, historical, or societal factors. Although it is undeniably true that people are different and often choose to differ with one another on moral matters, that fact alone does not, for him, make everybody right and nobody wrong. Kant would admit it is also certainly true that cultural practices vary throughout the world, and that different values are held in higher or lower esteem depending on the society, group, or nation involved. Moreover, it cannot be denied that social values undergo changes and transformations over time. Compare today's attitudes toward sexuality, for example, with those of the 1950s or Queen Victoria's era.

In recognition of human diversity and that what people actually do, say, experience, believe, think, feel, and value vary, Kant concludes that no **moral certainty** can be found there. If morality is to make any sense, and if it is to be considered valid and binding for all, then moral certainty must be found somewhere apart from the transitory and diverse world of everyday experience. For Kant, it is to be found in the structure of reason itself. The ultimate basis of morality must be purely rational, or *a priori,* not in any way derived from experience or dependent upon it. For example, rational moralists would, no doubt, condemn the torturing of innocent children, regardless of whether anybody actually engages in this practice and whether any society condones it. The moral judgment in this instance is not derived from experience or observation of people's behavior. Such knowledge is *a priori* and independent of what people actually do. For Kant, it is up to the human sciences (anthropology, psychology, sociology) to inform us about human behavior and the differences among people; it is philosophy's task to use reason to help us determine what is right and wrong. In support of Kant, one could argue that despite the apparent diversity easily observable among people throughout the world, the faculty of reason is one common and universal element shared by all individuals and by all of humanity more generally. Explaining why reason must be the basis of morality, Kant writes:

> Is it not of the utmost necessity to construct a pure moral philosophy which is completely freed from everything which may be only empirical thus belong to anthropology? That there must be such a philosophy is self-evident from the common idea of duty and moral laws. Everyone must admit that a law, if it is to hold morally, i.e., as a ground of obligation, must imply absolute necessity; he must admit that the command, "Thou shalt not lie" does not apply to men only, as if other rational beings had no need to observe it. The same is true for all other moral laws properly so called. He must concede that the ground of obligation here must not be sought in the nature of man or in the circumstances in which he is placed, but sought *a priori* solely in the concepts of pure reason, and that every other precept which rests on principles of mere existence, even a precept which is in certain respects universal, so far as it leans in the least on empirical grounds (perhaps only in regard to the motive involved), be called a practical rule but never a moral law.[9]

## Concept of the Good Will

In the "First Section" of the *Foundations of the Metaphysics of Morals,* Kant picks up on the idea that moral goodness is not something external or psychological. He recognizes that talents of the mind (intelligence,

## PHILOSOPHERS IN ACTION

In efforts to appreciate moral diversity, try to identify any norms, values, and beliefs that conflict with one another. Such things could be personal, social, political, religious, and so on. Once you have identified these different and conflicting values, think about the idea that not one of them is better or worse than any of the others. Do you agree? Would you necessarily be biased, chauvinistic, or discriminatory if you suggested that some values, beliefs, or norms were better than others? Does tolerance of moral diversity mean that you are obligated to accept everyone's values no matter what? If you would be willing to criticize any value or norm as unacceptable, what would be the basis of your moral disagreement?

*For further discussion*: Is there something that makes people reluctant to criticize the values, behaviors, or lifestyle choices of others? If so, what? Do we have any social responsibility to ensure that people make the right choices in their lives? Explain.

judgment, wit), qualities of temperament (courage, resoluteness, perseverance), and gifts of fortune (power, riches, honor, contentment), which contribute to happiness, may in many respects be good and desirable.[10] He underscores, however, the fact that such things are not unconditionally good. Power, for instance, could lead to pride and arrogance if not corrected by reason and good will. The cool courage of a villain is not morally praiseworthy in itself, and the actions following from such a virtue are more likely to cause harm than lead to ethically acceptable behavior. **The good will** is, according to Kant, good even if it is prevented from achieving its end. The goodness of the good will is to be established solely by virtue of its willing. The motive to do the right thing for the right reason is enough to make the good will good. Kant says, "The good will is not good because of what it effects or accomplishes or because of its adequacy to achieve some proposed end; it is good only because of its willing, i.e., it is good of itself."[11] In view of this, people who are motivated and make efforts to do the right thing, but fail in their attempts, can still be seen to be acting morally. By contrast, people who somehow manage to achieve their ends or enjoy uninterrupted happiness in life, but without the influence of good will motivating their behavior, are not, in Kant's opinion, even worthy to be happy. Right things can be done for the wrong reasons. Good things like pleasure and happiness can result from moral injustices—a fact that calls into question the value of such things. This is why only a good will is unconditionally good.

When exercising good will, what you must do is bring forward all the means in your power to do your **duty** (the right thing). Individuals are morally good or behave in a morally good fashion when they are motivated by the desire to do their duty, simply for the sake of duty alone. The morally virtuous person is not concerned with maximizing people's happiness or cultivating moderation in their lifestyle, but with doing what is required by *practical reason* (reason in its applications to morality). The moral quality of an act is, therefore, established by the rational principle to which the good will consciously assents.

## Notion of Duty

Kant gives us some insight into what he means by "duty," a basic building block of his ethical thinking. For Kant, "Duty is the necessity of an action executed from respect for [moral] law."[12] He goes on to say, "An action performed from duty does not have its moral worth in the purpose which is to be achieved through it but in the **maxim** [rule of conduct] by which it is determined."[13] We will examine the formal characteristics of moral maxims in a moment, but first let us look at a couple of important distinctions made by Kant.

## In Accordance with Duty, But Not for Duty's Sake

Kant observes that while some actions accord with duty, they are not performed for the sake of duty. In other words, people can act consistently with what duty requires, but still not act for the sake of duty or in recognition of the moral law. For example, maybe you have stopped yourself from stealing in the past, not because of any rational choice to do your ethical duty, but because you feared getting caught and going to jail. If so, then doing the right thing out of fear or self-interest did not give your action any moral worth. Actions performed in accordance with duty but not for duty's sake do not belong to the moral domain. It's not that they are immoral; they are just not relevant to morality, having no moral status. For Kant, this example of stealing would be an instance of **prudence,** not morality. Doing what is in your self-interest because of self-interest alone is nonmoral behavior. In *Foundations of the Metaphysics of Morals,* Kant offers his own illustration to support the point that not all actions in accordance with moral duty possess moral worth. He uses a business example.

> It is in fact in accordance with duty that a dealer should not overcharge an inexperienced customer, and wherever there is much business the prudent merchant does not do so, having a fixed price for everyone, so that a child may buy of him as cheaply as any other. Thus, the customer is honestly served. But this is far from sufficient to justify the belief that the merchant has behaved in this way from duty and principle or honesty. His own advantage required this behavior, but it cannot be assumed that over and above that he had a direct inclination to the purchaser and that, out of love, as it were, he gave none an advantage in price over another. Therefore, the action was done neither from duty nor from direct inclination, but only for a selfish purpose.[14]

In this example, the merchant did the "right" thing out of prudence, not morality. Again, it is not that the reason was wrong; it simply was not moral. It is worth noting, then, that actions can be *moral* (belonging to morality), *nonmoral* (not belonging to the moral domain), and *immoral* (wrong, bad or unjustifiable). To argue, as Kant does, that the merchant has acted prudently (for his own advantage) is not to condemn him, nor is it to praise him morally.

## In Accordance with Duty, But Out of Inclination

To further clarify the nature of (moral) duty, Kant also distinguishes between actions performed out of **inclination** and those performed out of a recognition of duty. He argues that only the latter are genuinely moral. Suppose, for example, that you are the kind of person who is generally predisposed by temperament to act kindly toward others. You simply like being nice to people. In fact, being nice to others is "what comes naturally" to you. If this were so, Kant would say that, as nice as you are, there is still no moral worth to your actions. It is not that you are morally corrupt or that you are doing anything wrong; it is just that the naturally inclined actions you perform have no moral worth.

If this seems counterintuitive, it will help to look at another example of action by inclination. Suppose a husband and wife are completely in love with one another, and they both have no inclination to cheat on each other (that is, each one is inclined to be faithful); should we praise the marital fidelity? From a Kantian perspective, the principle of fidelity is good (because it conforms to the moral law), but the husband or wife who is faithful in this case is not acting in a morally praiseworthy fashion. There was no action performed for the sake of duty. Had either person's inclinations been different (for example, had the husband or wife been tempted), he or she might have cheated. Doing what you feel like doing without thought or recognition of ethical duty gives your action no moral worth. The *motive* behind the action determines its moral status. Distinguishing between inclination and duty, using kindness as an example, Kant writes:

> To be kind where one can is duty, and there are, moreover, many persons so sympathetically constituted that without any motive of vanity or selfishness they find an inner satisfaction in spreading joy, and rejoice in the contentment of others which they have made possible. But I say that, however dutiful and amiable it may be, that kind of action has no true moral worth.[15]

## In Accordance with Duty, for the Sake of Duty

Well, if morality is not about natural inclination or prudence, then we are left needing further clarification. For Kant, a morally acceptable action must not only accord with duty (be consistent with it) but it must also be performed by the agent for the sake of duty. The individual must recognize what should be done and do it for that reason alone. "Duty for duty's sake" is another way of putting it. Even if doing the morally right thing is not something we are inclined to do at the moment, or if the right action does not appear to produce the best consequences, duty may dictate that we do it nonetheless. To illustrate the moral priority of duty over inclination, Kant asks us to imagine a person whose life has been entirely clouded by sorrow. This person is miserable, and all sympathetic feelings toward others have been extinguished. The person still possesses the means to help others and to improve their situations, but his deadened sensibility leaves him untouched by their unfortunate plight. Now, as Kant suggests, if this individual, who is wallowing in self-pity and has no desire or inclination to help others, tears himself away from his own preoccupations to assist another distressed person because of a recognition of duty, then his action assumes moral worth. The individual does what should be done, not out of natural inclination, but for the sake of duty. You could say, then, that a test of moral character is to discover whether one is strong enough to follow duty in spite of one's inclination not to do so.

## Moral Duties to Oneself and to Others

In *Lectures on Ethics* Kant points out that moral duties include not only those obligations we have toward others, but also those we have toward ourselves.[16] In other words, Kant allows for both personal and social dimensions of morality. This is not to suggest that personal morality is private and subjective, or that duties to oneself are somehow conditional and not applicable to others. For Kant, there are duties that we all have toward ourselves and duties that we all have toward other people. Although it goes almost without saying that morality involves relations and duties to others, Kant contends that individual morality should not be an afterthought or be considered an appendix to ethical inquiry. Too often moral discussions are restricted to social matters and interpersonal conflict. Kant insists, however, that "our duties towards ourselves are of primary importance and should have pride of place."[17] Arguing that we can expect nothing from a person who dishonors his own person, he maintains that "a prior condition of our **duties to others** is our **duty to ourselves;** we can fulfill the former only insofar as we first fulfill the latter."[18] To illustrate and support his point, Kant asks us to consider drunkards. Such people may do no harm to others, and provided their physical constitutions are strong, they may not even harm themselves. Nonetheless, Kant claims that drunkards become, for us, objects of moral contempt. Such individuals degrade themselves and damage their personal dignity. They lose their inner worth as moral subjects. Kant writes:

> Only if our worth as human beings is intact can we perform our other duties; for it is the foundation stone of all other duties. A man who has destroyed and cast away his personality, has no intrinsic worth, and can no longer perform any manner of duty.[19]

In *Lectures on Ethics,* Kant enumerates and explains a number of self-regarding and other-regarding duties. In reference to the former, we have duties of proper self-respect, self-mastery, duties concerning the body, and duties concerning how we occupy ourselves in work and in play. In reference to the latter, we have duties to show respect for persons and to honor their inherent worth and dignity as human beings.

> *"Suicide is not an abomination because God has forbidden it; it is forbidden by God because it is abominable."*
>
> IMMANUEL KANT

## Maxims and Moral Behavior

According to Kant, anytime you act voluntarily, you operate under some kind of maxim, rule, or directive. For instance, if in situation A, you choose to do B, then you are acting on the maxim "In situation A, do B." This kind of thinking is what has led some people to describe humans as "rule-governed" animals. Unlike lower-level organisms, which are mostly reactive to external stimuli or responsive to instinctual impulses and other determining factors, we, as humans, can act freely and rationally on the basis of self-generated rules or laws or conduct. If this seems a bit vague, imagine yourself lying to your course instructor about the reasons why you missed an ethics term test. You might say that you were ill, when, in fact, you slept in because you were up very late the night before partying with friends. In this case, the personal maxim or rule of conduct underlying your behavior could be expressed something like this: "When in trouble, lie your way out of it" or "If caught doing something wrong, then lie" or "Lie to get what you want."

To say maxims underlie our behaviors does not mean to suggest that we always abide by them. For example, on most occasions when you are caught doing something wrong, you might "fess up"; however, at other times, you might lie, like the student in the preceding illustration. You should also note that people are not always or usually aware of the maxims that they use to govern their behavior. Implicit maxims are most likely to come to people's attention and to be made explicit when they are asked to justify their behaviors to others or when conscience forces them to justify their actions to themselves. Aware of them or not, maxims are embedded in our actions and in the way we behave.

## Kantian Formalism and the Categorical Imperative

In efforts to determine which maxims of behavior are distinctively moral and morally acceptable and which are not, Kant formulated **the categorical imperative.** This moral imperative can be expressed in a number of different ways, but the best-known formulation is the following: "Act only according to that maxim by which you can at the same time will that it should become a universal law."[20] According to this formulation, a moral maxim is one that can, without contradiction, be willed to be a rule of conduct for everyone. The categorical imperative implies that the essence of morality lies in acting on the basis of an impersonal principle that is *valid for every person,* including oneself. As morality has a rational foundation for Kant, he believes that one must be able to *universalize* maxims of conduct in a logically consistent fashion if those maxims are to be binding on all rational beings. Maxims that cannot be universalized consistently are not moral or morally prescriptive. For example, the maxim "Never help others, but always be helped by them" could not be accepted as a valid moral rule of conduct because of its logical implications. It does not make sense even to talk about accepting help from others if the maxim were universalized and acted upon, because nobody would ever try to help others, and thus there would be no help to be accepted. From this illustration, we see how the categorical imperative's formal requirement of universal consistency allows us to evaluate the moral acceptability of particular maxims and rules of conduct. The categorical imperative can serve as a test of morality or an ultimate standard for moral evaluation.

A second formulation of the categorical imperative draws attention to its social implications. It states: "Act so that you treat humanity, whether in your own person or in that of another, always as an end and never as a means only."[21] According to this statement of the categorical imperative, we should show respect for all human beings *unconditionally* and avoid exploiting anyone. When we exploit others and disrespect them in this way, we treat them merely as objects or means to our own ends. We fail to see others as beings whose existence has absolute worth in itself. In Kant's view, the dignity and worth of any human being are not conditional on any empirical factors. Just as you would not wish to be used against your will and exploited by others so they could attain their ends, so too is it wrong for you to use people against their will and to exploit them or treat them only as objects or merely as a means to gain your own ends.

Implicit in what was just stated is the formal requirement of *reversibility*. This concept holds that a maxim or rule of conduct is morally unacceptable if the individual acting on it would not wish to be the person most disadvantaged or most adversely affected by its application. If one approves of a maxim, one must approve of it both from the perspective of the one who benefits and from the one most negatively affected. An act must be acceptable *objectively*, regardless of whether the individual is at the giving or the receiving end of an action. If, for instance, a person chooses to approve of stealing in his or her own case, then that person must be willing to become victimized by theft if the corresponding maxim is to be deemed acceptable. Presumably, nobody wishes to be robbed and, therefore, no rational moral thinker would accept such a maxim.

The formal criteria of *universality, consistency,* and *reversibility* point to the idea that moral maxims must also display *impartiality;* that is, the rightness or wrongness of actions and the moral adequacy of their underlying maxims must have nothing to do with *who* happens to be in a favored or disadvantaged position regarding the actions. Certain acts are right or wrong in themselves, regardless of whose interests are served and regardless of the favorable or unfavorable consequences to oneself or anyone else for that matter. The categorical imperative is an abstract principle that requires that empirical content particulars be removed as much as possible from the ethical appraisal and justification process. Because morality must have a purely rational *a priori* basis, particulars of content referring to specific persons, places, times, interests, desires, inclinations, and so forth must be removed when the moral acceptability of maxims is being determined. Recall that, for Kant, morality cannot have an empirical or anthropological basis, for this would not provide him with the solid and secure ethical foundation that he seeks. Only reason can provide the *certainty* and *necessity* required for a universal, binding morality.

Another formal (content free) element contained in the categorical imperative is the notion of *prescriptivity*. One cannot simply opt out of morality if one chooses, for the requirements of morality are unconditionally binding on all rational beings. One cannot justifiably argue that morality applies to everyone else "but me," or that everyone else should always tell the truth "but me." Ethically speaking, you cannot make yourself the exception to the rule. To do so is to use two standards of morality, one for others and one for yourself. If this practice of making personal exceptions were universalized, then nobody would be required to adhere to the moral law, and any objective morality would become impossible. You cannot, therefore, be freed of moral obligation simply because you do not feel like living up to the moral law or because making an exception in your case is likely to further your own interests or promote greater happiness within yourself. Distinctively moral maxims and ethical principles of conduct apply to everyone unconditionally, whether people like them or not.

## PHILOSOPHERS IN ACTION

Morality can be based on a number of things: faith, authority, tradition, and feelings. What do you think of Kant's cornerstone of morality, the categorical imperative? Does it provide you with a solid and stable foundation upon which to build your moral life? Why or why not? Do you have another cornerstone? If so, which one? Why is your foundational cornerstone preferable to Kant's?

## Hypothetical versus Categorical Imperatives

In everyday language, we often use words like "should," "have to," and "must," but it is not clearly the case that we always mean to suggest moral obligations are associated with them. Saying to someone "You ought to . . ." may be intended simply as a bit of personal advice, not as a universal ethical prescription. Saying to yourself, "I must . . ." or "I have to . . ." or "I should . . ." may involve some trivial action that does not call forth any moral considerations. Recognizing this, Kant, in the *Foundations of the Metaphysics of Morals*, made a distinction between **categorical and hypothetical imperatives.** He wrote:

> All imperatives command either hypothetically or categorically . . .
> If the action [commanded by an imperative] is good only as a means to something else, the imperative is hypothetical; but if it is thought of as good in itself, and hence as necessary in a will which of itself conforms to reason as the principle of this will, the imperative is categorical.[22]

As we have previously learned about categorical imperatives, they imply universal necessity and prescriptivity. They are purely rational and *a priori*. Hypothetical imperatives, by contrast, are *conditional* and *particular* (specific) and, therefore, lack the formal properties of distinctively moral commands. They cannot be universalized and prescribed unconditionally. On the subject of hypothetical imperatives, Kant speaks of **technical imperatives,** or rules of skill, that require us to do certain things if we want to achieve specific ends. For instance, if you wish to properly install an interlocking patio that will not shift with changing weather conditions, you must prepare the base with appropriate amounts of gravel and sand. Of course, you do not have to do this if you prefer to build a wooden deck or to lay sod.

Kant also draws our attention to **prudential imperatives,** another type of conditional command. Here is an example: "If you wish to make a favorable impression on people, then you should do certain things (for example, laugh at their humorless jokes)." Again, you have no moral duty to make favorable impressions, so you have no ethical obligations to do those things that will accomplish that end. It could be that you are highly introverted, prefer to be alone, and do not care what others think of you. Given that prudential and technical imperatives command us only under certain conditions, they are hypothetical, not moral and categorical.

## Autonomy versus Heteronomy of the Will

In closing this discussion of Kantian ethics, a brief mention should be made of the role played by **autonomy** in morality, for without personal autonomy, morality becomes an impossibility. When people act morally, they act freely or willfully out of respect or reverence for the moral law. They willingly obey the moral law for the sake of the moral law alone. To go back to a point made earlier, moral agents do their duty for duty's sake, not because of external incentives or coercive influence. When outside determining forces are not present, then we can speak of autonomy of the will. **Heteronomy of the will,** by contrast, is evident when the will obeys laws, rules, or injunctions from any other source besides reason. Obeying the law because you fear incarceration or doing your duty only under threat of physical force does not reflect autonomous moral action. Rather, it is more like protecting your hindside. Somehow, I do not think this is what the venerable Kant intended to include in his conception of a universal morality!

Finally, when as autonomous and rational moral agents, we base our actions on universally valid laws that we have laid down for ourselves, we participate in something Kant calls the **realm of ends**—a kind of ideal moral universe in which we respect the intrinsic worth and dignity of all persons. In this kingdom, we never treat people solely as means to our ends, but as ends in themselves. Of course, to some extent, we all use one another. For instance, you may use your neighbor's teenager as a babysitter for your child, or your neighbors may use your son or daughter as help to cut their grass. This is not what Kant is talking about. In many practical ways, we all use one another in cooperative living. It is when we violate others, abuse or mistreat them, or use them merely as a means to achieve our own ends that we dishonor their dignity as persons.

Before we move on, let us now take a few moments to read an excerpt from Kant's *Foundations of the Metaphysics of Morals*. In it, Kant explains why the basis of morality must be found in the structure of reason itself.

## ORIGINAL SOURCEWORK

# *Fundamental Principles of the Metaphysics of Morals*

**IMMANUEL KANT**

## PREFACE

Ancient Greek philosophy was divided into three sciences: physics, ethics, and logic. This division is perfectly suitable to the nature of the thing; and the only improvement that can be made in it is to add the principle on which it is based, so that we may both satisfy ourselves of its completeness, and also be able to determine correctly the necessary subdivisions.

All rational knowledge is either material or formal: the former considers some object, the latter is concerned only with the form of the understanding and of the reason itself, and with the universal laws of thought in general without distinction of its objects. Formal philosophy is called logic. Material philosophy, however, has to do with determinate objects and the laws to which they are subject, is again twofold; for these laws are either laws of nature or of freedom. The science of the former is physics, that of the latter, ethics; they are also called natural philosophy and moral philosophy respectively.

Logic cannot have any empirical part; that is, a part in which the universal and necessary laws of thought should rest on grounds taken from experience; otherwise it would not be logic, i.e., a canon for the understanding or the reason, valid for all thought, and capable of demonstration. Natural and moral philosophy, on the contrary, can each have their empirical part, since the former has to determine the laws of nature as an object of experience; the latter the laws of the human will, so far as it is affected by nature: the former, however, being

laws according to which everything does happen; the latter, laws according to which everything ought to happen. Ethics, however, must also consider the conditions under which what ought to happen frequently does not.

We may call all philosophy empirical, so far as it is based on grounds of experience: on the other hand, that which delivers its doctrines from a priori principles alone we may call pure philosophy. When the latter is merely formal it is logic; if it is restricted to definite objects of the understanding it is metaphysic.

In this way there arises the idea of a twofold metaphysic—a metaphysic of nature and a metaphysic of morals. Physics will thus have an empirical and also a rational part. It is the same with Ethics; but here the empirical part might have the special name of practical anthropology, the name morality being appropriated to the rational part.

All trades, arts, and handiworks have gained by division of labour, namely, when, instead of one man doing everything, each confines himself to a certain kind of work distinct from others in the treatment it requires, so as to be able to perform it with greater facility and in the greatest perfection. Where the different kinds of work are not distinguished and divided, where everyone is a jack-of-all-trades, there manufactures remain still in the greatest barbarism. It might deserve to be considered whether pure philosophy in all its parts does not require a man specially devoted to it, and whether it would not be better for the whole business of science if those who, to please the tastes of the public, are wont to blend the

*Source*: T.K. Abbott, *Kant's Theory of Ethics*, 1879, translated by Thomas Kingsmill Abbott; publisher unknown, found at website; http://www.knuten.liu.se/~bjoch509/works/kant/princ_morals.txt.
*Note*: Abbott's book combines *Fundamental Principles of the Metaphysics of Morals* with *Critique of Practical Reason*.

rational and empirical elements together, mixed in all sorts of proportions unknown to themselves, and who call themselves independent thinkers, giving the name of minute philosophers to those who apply themselves to the rational part only—if these, I say, were warned not to carry on two employments together which differ widely in the treatment they demand, for each of which perhaps a special talent is required, and the combination of which in one person only produces bunglers. But I only ask here whether the nature of science does not require that we should always carefully separate the empirical from the rational part, and prefix to Physics proper (or empirical physics) a metaphysic of nature, and to practical anthropology a metaphysic of morals, which must be carefully cleared of everything empirical, so that we may know how much can be accomplished by pure reason in both cases, and from what sources it draws this its a priori teaching, and that whether the latter inquiry is conducted by all moralists (whose name is legion), or only by some who feel a calling thereto.

As my concern here is with moral philosophy, I limit the question suggested to this: Whether it is not of the utmost necessity to construct a pure moral philosophy which is completely freed from everything which may be only empirical and which belongs to anthropology? for that such a philosophy must be possible is evident from the common idea of duty and of the moral laws. Everyone must admit that if a law is to have moral force, i.e., to be the basis of an obligation, it must carry with it absolute necessity; that, for example, the precept, "Thou shalt not lie," is not valid for men alone, as if other rational beings had no need to observe it; and so with all the other moral laws properly so called; that, therefore, the basis of obligation must not be sought in the nature of man, or in the circumstances in the world in which he is placed, but a priori simply in the conception of pure reason; and although any other precept which is founded on principles of mere experience may be in certain respects universal, yet in as far as it rests even in the least degree on an empirical basis, perhaps only as to a motive, such a precept, while it may be a practical rule, can never be called a moral law.

Thus not only are moral laws with their principles essentially distinguished from every other kind of practical knowledge in which there is anything empirical, but all moral philosophy rests wholly on its pure part. When applied to man, it does not borrow the least thing from the knowledge of man himself (anthropology), but gives laws a priori to him as a rational being. No doubt these laws require a judgement sharpened by experience, in order on the one hand to distinguish in what cases they are applicable, and on the other to procure for them access to the will of the man and effectual influence on conduct; since man is acted on by so many inclinations that, though capable of the idea of a practical pure reason, he is not so easily able to make it effective in concreto in his life.

A metaphysic of morals is therefore indispensably necessary, not merely for speculative reasons, in order to investigate the sources of the practical principles which are to be found a priori in our reason, but also because morals themselves are liable to all sorts of corruption, as long as we are without that clue and supreme canon by which to estimate them correctly. For in order that an action should be morally good, it is not enough that it conform to the moral law, but it must also be done for the sake of the law, otherwise that conformity is only very contingent and uncertain; since a principle which is not moral, although it may now and then produce actions conformable to the law, will also often produce actions which contradict it. Now it is only a pure philosophy that we can look for the moral law in its purity and genuineness (and, in a practical matter, this is of the utmost consequence): we must, therefore, begin with pure philosophy (metaphysic), and without it there cannot be any moral philosophy at all. That which mingles these pure principles with the empirical does not deserve the name of philosophy (for what distinguishes philosophy from common rational knowledge is that it treats in separate sciences what the latter only comprehends confusedly); much less does it deserve that of moral philosophy, since by this confusion it even spoils the purity of morals themselves, and counteracts its own end.

## DISCUSSION QUESTIONS FOR CRITIQUE AND ANALYSIS

1. Why does "moral duty" imply absolute necessity for Kant?

2. What does Kant mean by the notion of a "pure philosophy?"

# FEMININE ETHICS: CAROL GILLIGAN AND NEL NODDINGS

## Male Bias in Moral Research

*Masculine and feminine values, together and in balance yield complementary benefits that enrich life. When either overwhelms the other, neither is life giving. In our society—deprived of soul and therefore of a conscious understanding of the feminine—we've been looking at the feminine through the wrong lens, the lens of masculine understanding. However, just as masculine values were never intended to be evaluated through a feminine perspective, feminine values can't be understood from a masculine viewpoint.*

KATHLEEN HURLEY
AND THEODORE DOBSON

Regrettably, a survey of historical writings in philosophy generally, and in ethics more particularly, reveals a serious underrepresentation of women. One can speculate about all of the sociopolitical factors accounting for this conspicuous absence of half the human race in the history of ethical-philosophical thought; but whatever conclusions are reached, we should not be quick to dismiss feminine insights into morality just because they have not been well represented in the past. Indeed, women like Carol Gilligan and Nel Noddings are two contemporary researchers who have delved deeply into issues of morality and have offered us fresh new insights challenging traditional male-oriented ethical viewpoints. Gilligan, for instance, has argued that there has been an inherent **psychological bias** contained in the assumptions underlying a lot of the research done on moral reasoning development—a bias that devalues the feminine perspective and considers it less developed and less adequate as compared to forms of ethical thinking preferred by males and more likely to be exhibited by them.[23] Nel Noddings alleges, as well, that the male-dominated philosophical community has been guilty of its own **ethical bias** insofar as it has concentrated its study of morality largely on moral rationality, in contrast to basing it on emotion or the human affective response.[24] The problem with this, in her estimation, is that a rational male presentation of ethics gives it a mathematical appearance, as if it were governed by the same kind of logical necessity characteristic of geometry—but not so for her, as you will soon learn. An ethic like Kant's, for example, which is characterized by rational consistency, detachment, objectivity, and the universal prescriptive application of principles, is an ethic guided by the masculine spirit.

There is another alternative capturing the feminine spirit, she claims, one which is a more natural approach to morality. It is rooted in *care,* or what can be called the *receptive rationality of caring.* **Feminine ethics** is at least worth consideration, in Noddings's estimation, as rational principle-based thinking is fraught with danger. History reveals only too well how atrocities and acts of violence are often committed in the name of principle. We'll examine Noddings's feminine view of ethics shortly, but before we do, let us revisit the idea of male bias inherent in developmental theories of morality. By locating points of bias, the contrasts with feminine interpretations can be better understood. Though a prolonged historical absence of women in moral theorizing should have been a clue for modern ethicists that "something was up," so to speak, it was in the field of developmental psychology and moral education that allegations of male bias in ethics were perhaps most loudly voiced. Let us see how and why by examining the findings and moral research of Lawrence Kohlberg.

In his now-classic studies of **moral reasoning development,** Harvard researcher Lawrence Kohlberg claimed to have discovered the universal sequence of moral development for all human beings.[25] This sequence was based on moral reasoning abilities and was said to involve three basic levels of moral progression, each consisting of two substages, making for six stages in all. Kohlberg labeled these levels *preconventional, conventional,* and *postconventional.* At preconventional Level One, children are responsive to cultural rules and labels of good and bad, right and wrong. These labels are interpreted either in terms of their physical-hedonistic consequences (punishment, reward, exchange of favor) or in terms of the physical power of those who state the rules and apply the label.

Stage One of this level is called the "Punishment and Obedience Orientation." At this stage, avoiding punishment and adhering unquestioningly to power are valued in their own right—not because one is cognizant of any underlying moral order. Might makes right, as it were, as those with power and authority dictate what is and is not acceptable. At Stage Two—"The Instrumental-Relativist Orientation"—right actions are those which instrumentally satisfy one's own needs and occasionally the needs of others. Human relations are viewed as marketplace exchanges. Moral reciprocity at this stage can be translated as, "I'll scratch your back if you scratch mine." Fairness and equal sharing are present but are always interpreted in a physical or pragmatic way. Reciprocity, here, has nothing to do with loyalty, gratitude, or justice.

At the conventional level, perceptions of morality change, as does thinking about it. What becomes important are the expectations of one's family, group, or nation. These are valued in their own right, regardless of immediate, obvious consequences. Individuals at the conventional level of morality conform to personal expectations and the requirements of maintaining social order. They act out of loyalty to it, actively supporting and justifying the order and identifying with the persons or group involved in it. At Stage Three, what Kohlberg calls "The Interpersonal Concordance of 'Good Boy-Nice Girl' Orientation," good behavior is that which helps others and is approved by them. People's actions are judged by the intentions behind them. The idea that "the person meant well" becomes important for the first time. At Stage Three, one is able to earn approval by being "nice." As we move to Stage Four, "The Law and Order Orientation," the focus turns to fixed rules, authority, and the preservation of the social order. The right thing to do is one's duty. This shows respect for authority and maintaining the social order for its own sake. The law must be obeyed for *a law is a law, is a law!*

At the postconventional level of morality, we find clear efforts to define moral values and ethical principles that have validity and application apart from the authority of the groups or persons holding these principles and distinct from the moral agent's own identification with these persons and groups. Postconventional morality is therefore the most autonomous of all three levels. Like the others, it contains two substages. We discover at Stage Five, "The Social-Contract Legalistic Orientation," that there are utilitarian overtones. What is right is defined with respect to generally agreed upon individual rights and in terms of standards that have been critically examined, evaluated, and agreed upon by the whole society—not just some subgroup within it. At this stage, people emphasize the legal point of view but accept the possibility that the law might have to be changed in view of rational considerations of social utility (in contrast to strictly upholding the law in terms of Stage Four law and order, where a law is a law, is a law. Here, free and contractual agreement becomes the binding element of obligation. Kohlberg sees Stage Five morality as the "official" morality of the U.S. government and Constitution.

Finally, at Stage Six, "The Universal Ethical Principle Orientation," what is right is established in accordance with self-chosen ethical principles—ones appealing to logical comprehensiveness, universality, and consistency. Principles at Stage Six are formal and abstract. Examples would include the Golden Rule and Kant's categorical imperative. As two writers put it: "At heart, these are universal principles of justice, of the reciprocity and equality of the human rights, and of respect for the dignity of human beings as individual persons."[26]

In the context of the transition from one stage or level to the next, Kohlberg argues on the basis of empirical study that movement is invariant and sequential, and furthermore, that it is culturally universal. In stage development, people are cognitively attracted to reasoning one step above their own. Movement is effected when psychological disequilibrium is created; that is, when individuals discover that their current thinking is somehow inadequate to deal with the moral problem at issue. Finally, it should be noted that moral thinking progresses and gains in adequacy by becoming less concrete and morally abstract. At the preconventional level, moral goodness is determined by tangible and physical consequences; at the conventional level, by group wishes and the maintenance of social order for its own sake; and lastly, at the postconventional level, by adherence to abstract universal principles of justice, which transcend any individual or group. The postconventional level represents, for Kohlberg, the most adequate, developed, and ethically sound form of moral reasoning. As mentioned, Kohlberg's Stage Six morality sits squarely in line with Kant's categorical imperative.[27] For Kohlberg, Stage Six principled morality is superior by virtue of its being the preferred choice of rational self-interested persons finding themselves in what John Rawls describes as the original position.[28]

## PHILOSOPHICAL PROFILE

### Carol Gilligan

Carol Gilligan, the 1997 recipient of the Heinz Award in the Human Condition, is currently the first chair of Gender Studies in the Graduate School of Education at Harvard University. Although she is technically an empirical psychological researcher, her theorizing and findings have had significant implications for thinkers in the fields of moral and political philosophy. In her work, Gilligan criticizes long-held assumptions about moral development, specifically those contained in the cognitive-developmental theories of Piaget and Kohlberg. In her estimation, they are based on rational, universalistic assumptions that contain a male bias and devalue the caring relational nature of feminine moral experience, relegating women's moral thinking to a position of inferior and less adequate moral reasoning development. Her critical rebuttals to Piaget and Kohlberg constitute, in effect, a critique of formalistic Kantian-Rawlsian morality to which their developmental

theories are closely aligned. Gilligan calls into question the ultimate authority of reason as the basis of morality and because of this, is relevant to philosophical inquiry.

In response to Kohlberg's findings and conclusions, Gilligan points out
that his original research was limited to an all-male sample of subjects. For
15 years, Kohlberg studied the development of moral judgment by following
the same group of 75 boys at three-year intervals from early adolescence through
young adulthood. The boys/men were presented with **hypothetical moral
dilemmas** like the one about Heinz that follows, and then their responses to
related questions were recorded. It was on the basis of these male responses to
hypothetical dilemmas that Kohlberg initially formulated his theory of moral
development.

## HEINZ'S DILEMMA

In Europe, a woman was near death from a special kind of cancer.
There was one drug that the doctors thought might save her. It was
a form of radium that a druggist in the same town had recently discovered. The drug was expensive to make, but the druggist was
charging ten times what the drug cost him to make. He paid $200
for the radium and charged $2000 for a small dose of the drug. The
sick woman's husband, Heinz, went to everyone he knew to borrow
the money, but he could only get together about $1000, which is half
of what it cost. He told the druggist that his wife was dying and
asked him to sell it cheaper or let him pay later. The druggist said,
"No, I discovered the drug and I'm going to make money from it."
So Heinz got desperate and broke into the man's store to steal the
drug for his wife. Should the husband have done that? Why?[29]

Gilligan takes exception to the fact that Kohlberg's initial research sample
was all-male and, furthermore, that the dilemmas addressed were all hypothetical, and hence abstract and artificial. Understandably, it's problematic to make
universalistic generalizations about all people when you leave out one-half of the
human race—a fact Gilligan strongly underscores. Secondly, the dilemmas that
were addressed by research subjects were "canned," or prepared in advance without any input from those responding to them. Moral problems were presented,
not constructed by the subjects themselves. This is important for Gilligan, since
she claims, on the basis of her own research, that women tend to view morality
more personally and concretely than impersonally and abstractly—the ideal for
Kohlberg. Women also tend, in their ethical experience, to operate more naturally from a feminine position of moral care and relationship and less from a masculine position of rational morality and impersonal justice, with which
adjudications of interpersonal conflicts work most easily. Just like Kohlberg,
who failed to acknowledge the serious nature of his gender bias in his original
studies, so too have some moral thinkers failed to appreciate the inherent bias
of a purely formal, rationalistic ethic. Critics like Gilligan would be inclined to

say that strict adherence to rational principles of morality is a choice, not a non-negotiable feature of moral discourse or morality's nature.

In fairness to masculine moralists, however, let me add that existential philosophers, such as Søren Kierkegaard, have also discussed the limitations of a purely rational, objective morality. He explains that a mode of existence based on a faith in God transcends reason and the ethical rules and obligations issuing from it. Accepting reason as a basis of (moral) life or taking an irrational leap of faith that allows God to direct one's life is a matter of will and commitment, not pure logical deduction. Though obviously not a "feminine thinker" himself, Kierkegaard does draw our attention to the problematic nature of rational ethics. He argues that there are relevant considerations, like faith, will, and commitment, that lie beyond the scope of a purely rational and objective morality—Gilligan's point, though made differently. On this note, one should be reminded that Gilligan conceptualizes the differences between masculine and feminine morality more by theme than by gender itself.[30] Although it is empirically true that more women tend to operate from a perspective of feminine morality, nothing prevents them from displaying masculine moral preferences.[31] Likewise, men can function morally from both perspectives as well, only they tend to prefer a more detached rational objectivity, often presupposing that it is more adequate or superior in some fashion.

This is true, in fact, for Kohlberg. Women, who often do not "reach" Stage Six in his conceptual framework because of their own conceptions and presuppositions about morality, come out as less developed and less mature in their moral reasoning abilities. What Gilligan would describe as a feminine **morality of care** and relation fits into Kohlberg's scheme at the conventional level—a less adequate form of moral thinking as compared with the more autonomous, impersonal, and detached forms of morality found at Stages Five and Six of the postconventional level. Given that Kohlberg's research methodology was seriously flawed from the outset, and that his own presuppositions about morality used in the construction of hypothetical moral dilemmas, are open to serious question, Gilligan argues that Kohlberg's studies of morality fail to do justice to women's moral experience. Women are not less developed morally, as some of the empirical studies might suggest; rather, for Gilligan, there has been a failure by theorists to produce models of human growth that acknowledge and respect male-female differences. The universal and prescriptive paradigm of Kantian morality, supported by Kohlberg's cognitive-developmental studies, is arguably not more adequate or more justified—just more male.

## Gilligan's Morality of Care

The different voice of morality to which Gilligan would have us listen could have its roots in individual **identity formation**. Gilligan cites the research of Nancy Chodorow to explain how men and women come to experience and conceptualize morality differently. As Gilligan says, female identity formation occurs in a context of ongoing relationships. Mothers have a tendency to experience their daughters as more alike and as extensions of themselves. Correspondingly, daughters, in their self-identifications as females, experience themselves as

> **❝** . . . the logic underlying an ethic of care is a psychological logic of relationship, which contrasts with the formal logic of fairness that informs the justice approach. **❞**
>
> CAROL GILLIGAN

similar to their mothers. Thus, the experience of attachment is fused with the process of identity formation. By contrast, as boys come to define themselves as masculine, they separate their mothers from themselves and thereby curtail their primary love object and sense of empathetic tie. Chodorow concludes that male development entails a "more emphatic individuation and a more defensive firming of experienced ego boundaries." The ultimate result of this that "girls emerge from this period with a basis for 'empathy' built into their primary definition of self in a way that boys do not." Furthermore, "Girls emerge with a stronger basis for experiencing another's needs or feelings as [their] own."[32] They experience themselves as less differentiated than boys and as more continuous with, and related to, others. Given the differences between boys' and girls' psychological attachments and individuation patterns, male gender identity is threatened by **intimacy,** while female gender identity is threatened by **separation.** In this context, it becomes more easily understandable how rational detachment becomes a virtue of a masculine moral perspective, whereas relation and care become hallmarks of feminine morality. Commenting on Kohlberg and the historical male bias in moral theorizing, Gilligan writes:

> The quality of embeddedness in social interaction and personal relationships that characterizes women's lives in contrast to men's, however, becomes not only a descriptive difference but also a developmental liability when the milestones of childhood and adolescent development in the psychological literature are markers of increasing separation. Women's failure to separate then becomes by definition a failure to develop.[33]

Of course, Gilligan sees nothing wrong with women's experience of morality, but does point to serious flaws in models of morality (like Kohlberg's) that fail to capture it properly. A feminine morality of relational care is only less developed and less adequate when viewed through the lens of masculine values and male identity formation.

The voice of feminine morality is, for Gilligan, perhaps best heard in women's construction of the abortion dilemma. Talk about abortion by women frequently uses the language of selfishness and responsibility, defining the basic moral problem as one of obligation to exercise care and avoid hurt. As Gilligan points out, the infliction of hurt is considered selfish and immoral insofar as it reflects unconcern. By contrast, the expression of care is regarded as the fulfillment of moral responsibility. For Gilligan, the repeated use by women of the words "selfish" and "responsible" when talking about choice and moral conflict directs us toward a different understanding of moral development and a moral orientation quite apart from the one Kohlberg structured.

In her own developmental research, Gilligan did not present subjects with abstract, hypothetical dilemmas for resolution. Instead, she asked people: (1) how they defined moral problems themselves; and (2) what experiences they construed as moral conflicts in their lives. Her sample of 29 women, ages 15 to 33 years, were drawn from an "abortion decision study," which looked at the relation between experience and thought and the role of conflict in development. The women in the study were initially interviewed in the first trimester of their

> **" . . . *as long as the categories by which development is assessed are derived from research on men, divergence from the masculine standard can be seen only as a failure of development. As a result, the thinking of women is often classified with that of children.* "**
> CAROL GILLIGAN

pregnancies, at a time when they were contemplating having abortions. Most of the women were interviewed again at the end of year following their choice. Complete interview data were available for 24 of them.

In a second "rights and responsibility" study, a sample of males and females were matched for age, intelligence, education, occupation, and social class at nine points across the life cycle. Data were collected on conceptions of self and morality, experiences of moral conflict and choice, and judgments on hypothetical moral dilemmas. Gilligan's findings from her studies suggest we should broaden our understanding of human (moral) development. Women apparently tend to display perspectives different from men when it comes to: (1) images of humankind, (2) the human condition, (3) human development, and (4) what is of value in life. In brief, moral development for women involves a progressive change in the understanding of responsibility and relationships. For men, or at least for Kohlberg, morality, seen as justice, ties development to the logic of equality and reciprocity.

In her book *In a Different Voice: Psychological Theory and Women's Development,* Gilligan spells out for us the development sequence for the ethics of care. At Stage One, the individual is most concerned with caring for herself to ensure survival. In time, this life position and the judgments flowing from it come to be criticized as selfish. A transitional phase emerges whereby a new understanding of connection between oneself and others is articulated. Here, at Stage Two, good is essentially equated with caring for others. A type of maternal morality develops that seeks to ensure care for the dependent and unequal. Stage Two eventually opens the door to the next transitional phase. When only others are allowed to be the recipients of the woman's care—when she cannot care for herself without being selfish—this exclusion of herself gives rise to problems in relationships and thereby creates disequilibrium. At the third and final stage of development, care is understood not in a dichotomous fashion (caring only for me or only for others) but as an interconnection between oneself *and* others. This third stage highlights the dynamics of relationships and causes a reduction in the tension between selfishness and responsibility. As Gilligan puts it:

> Care becomes the self-chosen principle of a judgment that remains psychological in its concern with relationships and response but becomes universal in its condemnation of exploitation and hurt. Thus a progressively more adequate understanding of the psychology of human relationships—an increasing differentiation of self and other and a growing comprehension of the dynamics of social interaction—informs the development of an ethic of care. This ethic, which reflects a cumulative knowledge of human relationships, evolves around a central insight, that self and other are interdependent.[34]

Clearly, we see, that Gilligan's feminine morality of care, characterized by interdependence and responsibility for others, stands in stark contrast to the Kantian-Rawlsian-Kohlbergian model of masculine morality, defined by autonomy, impartiality, and rational self-interest. As philosophers, we might ask: "Is one moral perspective necessarily better or more adequate than the other?" "Should an ethic of care overrule an ethic of justice?" or "Are both perspectives limited viewpoints of something perhaps much broader in scope?" Maybe we need to reason more with care, and care more about reason?

## PHILOSOPHICAL PROFILE

### Nel Noddings

Nel Noddings is currently Lee L. Jacks Professor of Child Education at Stanford University. After completing her Bachelor of Arts degree at Montclair State College, she went on to do her M.A. at Rutgers and her Ph.D. in Educational Philosophy and Theory at Stanford University (1973). Having worked at all levels of education, she now teaches introductory classes in educational philosophy, the philosophical and educational thought of John Dewey, moral education, as well as contemporary social and ethical philosophy. In addition to *Caring: A Feminine Approach to Ethics and Moral Education,* she has produced numerous other publications, including more than 125 articles. She has served as past president for the Philosophy of Education Society and the John Dewey Society. Noddings has also been the recipient of many awards and distinctions, including the Medal for Distinguished Service given by the Teacher's College of Columbia University.

**NEL NODDINGS**

## Nel Noddings and Feminine Ethics

In her book *Caring: A Feminine Approach to Ethics and Moral Education,* Nel Noddings presents an ethic of care that bears a noticeable resemblance to Carol Gilligan's. Noddings develops certain notions further than Gilligan does, however, while she disagrees with her on others. For instance, Noddings works out in detail the implications of ethical interdependence for individual character—Gilligan does not. Furthermore, in contrast to Gilligan, who appears to allow for both justice and care in a fully mature ethic, Noddings presents her own ethic of care as a distinct alternative to principled ethics.[35]

Like Gilligan, Noddings accepts the notion that there are at least two basic approaches to morality, which tend to be either more masculine or more feminine in approach. **Masculine ethics** presents itself as principled and emotionally detached. In male ethics, moral conclusions are derived from general ethical principles in a logically consistent fashion. There is an effort to proceed rationally without emotional influence. Objectivity and detachment require that feelings be left out of moral deliberations, since they are regarded as contaminating variables.

## Romanticizing Rationality: Reasons to Reject Principled Morality

Cautioning us not to romanticize rationality by holding it in unconditional positive regard, Noddings draws our attention to some of the limitations inherent in a purely rational, principled approach. She alleges that such a morality is ambiguous and unstable. Whenever you have a principle, exceptions are almost

> *"Indeed, one who attempts to ignore or to climb above the human affect at the heart of ethicality may well be guilty of romantic rationalism."*
>
> NEL NODDINGS

> *"The heart has reasons that reason does not know."*
>
> BLAISE PASCAL

always implied. The general principle "Never kill," for instance, could easily be followed by "except in self-defense" or "except in defense of an innocent other" and so on. General principles of conduct are not as solid and reassuring as some would like to think. Another drawback to principled morality is that principles can often separate people and alienate them from one another. Have you ever stubbornly refused to budge *on principle?* Have you ever terminated a relationship for the same reason? Have principles ever pushed you farther away from others, instead of bringing you closer to them? If so, then you can appreciate how principled thought and action could be counterproductive as far as bringing people together and having them live harmoniously together are concerned. As Noddings expresses it: "We may become dangerously self-righteous when we perceive ourselves as holding a precious principle not held by the other. The other may then be devalued and treated 'differently.' Our ethic of caring will not permit this to happen."[36]

Noddings's rejection of principled morality leads her to reject the rational concept of **universalizability.** From our coverage of Immanuel Kant's formalistic theory, you may remember that, for him, any maxim or principle of behavior had to be universalizable, or universally prescriptive, in order for it to belong to morality and to be morally justifiable. Maxims or principles of conduct that could not be universally prescribed were deemed to be either nonmoral or not morally justifiable. Thus, if under condition *X,* you are morally required to do *A,* then under sufficiently similar conditions, I too am required to do *A,* along with everyone else. The moral obligation applies to everybody universally and unconditionally. This line of moral thinking is rejected by Noddings because it allegedly fails to recognize and preserve the uniqueness of human encounters. Because of the highly personal, idiosyncratic, and subjective experience of those involved in particular ethical relations, conditions are seldom "sufficiently similar" for anyone to declare what we must do in our situation or what anyone else should do in their situation. For Noddings, the universalizability criterion doesn't work, as principles of moral conduct simply cannot be properly universalized. Efforts to abstract them from concrete situations cause us to lose sight of the unique features and personal variables that give rise to the moral question or dilemma in the first place. In other words, though two situations may appear somewhat similar from a detached observer's perspective, they are likely not sufficiently similar when viewed from within the situation. Consequently, the detached application of a universal principle from one situation to another is not appropriate.

Given Noddings's rejection of the universalizability criterion and her criticism of principled morality, it is interesting to refer back for a moment to Lawrence Kohlberg's theory of moral development. Remember that, for him, the most highly developed and most adequate morality is the one that is the most rational, abstract, and universal. That which is concrete or person-specific is less developed and less mature, labeled as conventional or preconventional. However, insofar as Noddings's criticisms and rejections are justified, it behooves us to reexamine the assumptions underlying a rational, principle-based masculine morality. As Noddings says: "Women can and do give reasons for their acts, but the reasons often point to feelings, needs, impressions, and a sense of personal ideal rather than to universal principles and their application. We shall see that, as a result of this 'odd' approach, women have often been judged inferior to men in the moral domain."[37] The point here is that women who operate from the vantage point of feminine ethics do not proceed deductively from principles superimposed on situations. In response to Kohlberg's dilemmas, women would seek to fill out those hypothetical situations in a "defensible move toward concretization."[38]

In the case of administering punishment, say, for one who is guilty of committing a crime, the traditional masculine approach asks about the principle under which this case falls, so that it may be applied. The feminine approach, by contrast, asks us to consider the feelings involved and the personal history of the wrongdoer. When the situation is concretized by such things as feelings and personal histories, what is appropriate punishment or what is the appropriate resolution to the conflict may change. For Noddings, there is no virtue in abstraction, where thinking can occur in a logical vacuum, apart from the complicating factors of particular persons, places, and circumstances.[39] These "complicating factors" are what make the moral situation real. The move toward logical abstraction, which admittedly unclutters the complexity of any moral dilemma, in the end undermines itself with artificiality and the prospect of destroying interpersonal relationships—the very thing morality is meant to preserve and protect.

## Relation as Ontologically Basic

In articulating her conception of morality, Noddings clearly does not begin with reasoning or with the Cartesian *Cogito* (the I Think). Furthermore, in contrast to John Rawls, who conceptualizes the moral agent as rational, self-interested, autonomous, and independent of others, Noddings takes **relation** as ontologically basic and the *caring relation* as ethically basic. To be human is to be in relation to others. We do not stand alone, isolated and apart from others, either psychologically or existentially. Human existence is relational. Morality comes not from the *a priori* structure of reason itself (à la Kant), but rather from the interpersonal human dynamic of persons in relation. It is affect and connection that should serve as the basis of morality, not reasoning. Of course, in her book, Noddings spells out the details of her care-based ethic, and for a fuller appreciation of what's at issue here, I invite you to read it. For our purposes here, I'll just mention a few of the general features characterizing this moral perspective.

## Brief Outline of Noddings's Care-Based Ethic

Noddings takes the caring relation as ontologically basic. There is the **one caring** and the **one cared for** to use her terminology. The conception of morality Noddings has in mind could be described as an ethic of virtue. It establishes an ethical ideal of what it means to be the one caring for others. This virtue involves reaching out to others and growing in response to others. Interpreting morality as persons in relation means that it is not an emotionally sterile conception of rationally self-interested individuals seeking to further their own interests and cooperating only when it is mutually advantageous. Ethical caring emerges from **natural caring**—a condition toward which we long and strive. In our infancies, we begin to develop memories of caring and being cared for. The resulting caring attitude provides the motivation to be moral, and because it is so basic and natural, it is universally accessible. The relation of natural caring represents moral goodness. When we remain in a concrete caring relation and enhance the ideal of ourselves as ones caring, we do the morally good thing. Everything hinges on the nature and strength of this ideal. There are no rational absolutes to guide us. This does not mean, for Noddings, that morality disintegrates into relativity, however, since the natural caring attitude supporting ethical caring is a universal phenomenon. Universality, understood as a foundational basis of morality, is not rational but relational for Noddings. Obligation is therefore not a matter of acting in ways consistent with abstract-formal principles (regardless of who's involved) but in response to commitments and to the maintenance of relationships. Noddings writes: "The source of my obligation is the value I place on the relatedness of caring. This value itself arises as a product of actual caring and being cared-for and my reflection on the goodness of these concrete caring situations."[40] In short, the ethical ideal of maintaining the caring relation should, for Noddings, be placed above principle as a guide to moral action. In this, we find a basic difference between Noddings's feminine ethic and the masculine ethic represented by thinkers like Kohlberg, Kant, and Rawls.

The last point to be made here refers to the basic human affect grounding morality. Unlike suffering existentialists, who recognize their unique subjectivity as aloneness in the world and who consequentially experience anguish, Noddings considers joy as the fundamental human emotion rooted in relation. She states that it is our recognition of, and longing for, relatedness that forms the foundation of the feminine ethic. "[T]he joy that accompanies fulfillment of our caring enhances our commitment to the ethical ideal that sustains us as one-caring."[41] It's not dour obligation that moves us to moral action, then, nor capricious subjectivity, but rather the joy and desire to exercise the virtue of goodness by fulfilling ourselves in the other. Responsiveness and receptivity are key, not detachment or cold rational aloofness. In this moral attitude, or psychological posture, we find a fundamental difference between masculine and feminine orientations to ethics. And in the discussion of this difference, we discover many fresh new insights that challenge the male-dominated historical assumptions about morality.

Let us now turn to an excerpt from Noddings's writings to continue our exposure to original philosophical sourceworks.

## *Caring: A Feminine Approach to Ethics and Moral Education*

### NEL NODDINGS

# INTRODUCTION

Ethics, the philosophical study of morality, has concentrated for the most part on moral reasoning. Much current work, for example, focuses on the status of moral predicates and, in education, the dominant model presents a hierarchical picture of moral reasoning. This emphasis gives ethics a contemporary, mathematical appearance, but it also moves discussion beyond the sphere of actual human activity and the feeling that pervades such activity. Even though careful philosophers have recognized the difference between "pure" or logical reason and "practical" or moral reason, ethical argumentation has frequently proceeded as if it were governed by the logical necessity characteristic of geometry. It has concentrated on the establishment of principles and that which can be logically derived from them. One might say that ethics has been discussed largely in the language of the father: in principles and propositions, in terms such as justification, fairness, justice. The mother's voice has been silent. Human caring and the memory of caring and being cared for, which I shall argue form the foundation of ethical response, have not received attention except as outcomes of ethical behavior. One is tempted to say that ethics has so far been guided by Logos, the masculine spirit, whereas the more natural and, perhaps, stronger approach would be through Eros, the feminine spirit. I hesitate to give way to this temptation, in part because the terms carry with them a Jungian baggage that I am unwilling to claim in its totality. In one sense, "Eros" does capture the flavor and spirit of what I am attempting here; the notion of psychic relatedness lies at the heart of the ethic I shall propose. In another sense, however, even "Eros" is masculine in its roots and fails to capture the receptive rationality of caring that is characteristic of the feminine approach.

When we look clear-eyed at the world today, we see it wracked with fighting, killing, vandalism, and psychic pain of all sorts. One of the saddest features of this picture of violence is that the deeds are so often done in the name of principle. When we establish a principle forbidding killing, we also establish principles describing the exceptions to the first principle. Supposing, then, that we are moral (we are principled, are we not?), we may tear into others whose beliefs or behaviors differ from ours with the promise of ultimate vindication.

This approach through law and principle is not, I suggest, the approach of the mother. It is the approach of the detached one, of the father. The view to be expressed here is a feminine view. This does not imply that all women will accept it or that men will reject it; indeed, there is no reason why men should not embrace it. It is feminine in the deep classical sense—rooted in receptivity, relatedness, and responsiveness. It does not imply either that logic is to be discarded or that logic is alien to women. It represents an alternative to present views, one that begins with the moral attitude or longing for goodness and not with moral reasoning. It may indeed be the case that such an approach is more typical of women than of men, but this is an empirical question I shall not attempt to answer.

It seems to me that the view I shall try to present would be badly distorted if it were presented in what I have referred to as the "language of the father." Several theorists in education—among them, William Pinar, Madeleine Grumet, Dwayne Huebner, Elliot Eisner—have suggested that our pictures of the world are unduly cramped and narrowed by reliance on a restricted domain of language. Pinar and Grumet, in particular, have looked at this problem in the context of gender studies. I agree with their assessment. But we must realize, also, that one writing on philosophical/educational problems may be handicapped and even rejected in the attempt

Nel Noddings, *Caring: A Feminine Approach to Ethics and Moral Education.* Berkeley: University of California Press 1984, pp. 1–6.

to bring a new voice to an old domain, particularly when entrance to that domain is gained by uttering the appropriate passwords. Whatever language is chosen, it must not be used as a cloak for sloppy thinking; that much is certain. This part of what I am doing, then, is not without risk.

Women, in general, face a similar problem when they enter the practical domain of moral action. They enter the domain through a different door, so to speak. It is not the case, certainly, that women cannot arrange principles hierarchically and derive conclusions logically. It is more likely that we see this process as peripheral to, or even alien to, many problems of moral action. Faced with a hypothetical moral dilemma, women often ask for more information. We want to know more, I think, in order to form a picture more nearly resembling real moral situations. Ideally, we need to talk to the participants, to see their eyes and facial expressions, to receive what they are feeling. Moral decisions are, after all, made in real situations; they are qualitatively different from the solution of geometry problems. Women can and do give reasons for their acts, but the reasons often point to feelings, needs, impressions, and a sense of personal ideal rather than to universal principles and their application. We shall see that, as a result of this "odd" approach, women have often been judged inferior to men in the moral domain.

Because I am entering the domain through a linguistic back door of sorts, much of what I say cannot be labeled "empirical" or "logical." (Some of it, of course, can be so labeled.) Well, what is it then? It is language that attempts to capture what Wittgenstein advised we "must pass over in silence." But if our language is extended to the expressive—and, after all, it is beautifully capable of such extension—perhaps we can say something in the realm of ethical feeling, and that something may at least achieve the status of conceptual aid or tool if not that of conceptual truth. We may present a coherent and enlightening picture without *proving* anything and, indeed, without claiming to present or to seek moral *knowledge* or moral *truth*. The hand that steadied us as we learned to ride our first bicycle did not provide propositional knowledge, but it guided and supported us all the same, and we finished up "knowing how."

This is an essay in practical ethics from the feminine view. It is very different from the utilitarian practical ethics of, say, Peter Singer. While both of us would treat animals kindly and sensitively, for example, we give very different reasons for our consideration. I must resist his charge that we are guilty of "speciesism" in our failure to accord rights to animals, because I shall locate the very wellspring of ethical behavior in human affective response. Throughout our discussion of ethicality we shall remain in touch with the affect that gives rise to it. This does not mean that our discussion will bog down in sentiment, but it is necessary to give appropriate attention and credit to the affective foundation of existence. Indeed, one who attempts to ignore or to climb above the human affect at the heart of ethicality may well be guilty of romantic rationalism. What is recommended in such a framework simply cannot be broadly applied in the actual world.

I shall begin with a discussion of caring. What does it mean to care and to be cared for? The analysis will occupy us at length, since relation will be taken as ontologically basic and the caring relation as ethically basic. For our purposes, "relation" may be thought of as a set of ordered pairs generated by some rule that describes the affect—or subjective experience—of the members.

In order to establish a firm conceptual foundation that will be free of equivocation, I have given names to the two parties of the relation: the first member is the "one-caring" and the second is the "cared-for." Regular readers of "existentialist" literature will recognize the need for such terminology—bothersome as it is. One may recall Sartre's use of for-itself and in-itself, Heidegger's being-in-the-world, and Buber's I-Thou and I-It. There are at least two good reasons for invoking this mechanism. First, it allows us to speak about our basic entities without explaining the entire conceptual apparatus repeatedly; second, it prevents us from smuggling in meanings through the use of synonyms. Hence, even though hyphenated entities offend the stylist, they represent in this case an attempt to achieve both economy and rigor. Another matter of style in connection with "one-caring" and "cared-for" should be mentioned here. In order to maintain balance and avoid confusion, I have consistently associated the generic "one-caring" with the universal feminine, "she," and "cared-for" with the masculine, "he." Clearly, however, when actual persons are substituted for "one-caring" and "cared-for" in the basic relation, they may be both male, both female, female-male, or male-female. Taking *relation* as ontologically basic simply means that we recognize human encounter and affective response as a basic fact of human existence. As we examine what it means to care and to be cared for, we shall see that both parties contribute to the relation; my caring must be somehow completed in the other if the relation is to be described as caring.

This suggests that the ethic to be developed is one of reciprocity, but our view of reciprocity will be different from that of "contract" theorists such as Plato and John Rawls. What the cared-for gives to the caring relation is not a promise to behave as the one-caring does, nor is it a form of "consideration." The problem of reciprocity will be, possibly, the most important problem we shall discuss, and facets of the problem will appear in a spiral design throughout the book. When we see what it is that the cared for contributes to the relation, we shall find it possible to separate human infants from nonhuman animals (a great problem for those who insist on some form of rationality in those we should treat ethically), and we shall do this without recourse to notions of God or some other external source of "sanctity" in human life.

The focus of our attention will be upon how to meet the other morally. Ethical caring, the relation in which we do meet the other morally, will be described as arising out of natural caring—that relation in which we respond as one-caring out of love or natural inclination. The relation of natural caring will be identified as the human condition that we, consciously or unconsciously, perceive as "good." It is that condition toward which we long and strive, and it is our longing for caring—to be in that special relation—that provides the motivation for us to be moral. We want to be *moral* in order to remain in the caring relation and to enhance the ideal of ourselves as one-caring.

It is this ethical ideal, this realistic picture of ourselves as one-caring, that guides us as we strive to meet the other morally. Everything depends upon the nature and strength of this ideal, for we shall not have absolute principles to guide us. Indeed, I shall reject ethics of principle as ambiguous and unstable. Wherever there is a principle, there is implied its exception and, too often, principles function to separate us from each other. We may become dangerously self-righteous when we perceive ourselves as holding a precious principle not held by the other. The other may then be devalued and treated "differently." Our ethic of caring will not permit this to happen. We recognize that in fear, anger, or hatred we will treat the other differently, but this treatment is never conducted ethically. Hence, when we must use violence or strategies on the other, we are already diminished ethically. Our efforts must, then, be directed to the maintenance of conditions that will permit caring to flourish. Along with the rejection of principles and rules as the major guide to ethical behavior, I shall also reject the notion of universalizability. Many of those writing and thinking about ethics insist that any ethical judgment—by virtue of its *being* an ethical judgment—must be universalizable; that is, it must be the case that, if under conditions X you are required to do A, then under sufficiently similar conditions, I too am required to do A. I shall reject this emphatically. First, my attention is not on judgment and not on the particular acts we perform but on how we meet the other morally. Second, in recognition of the feminine approach to meeting the other morally—our insistence on caring for the other—I shall want to preserve the uniqueness of human encounters. Since so much depends on the subjective experience of those involved in ethical encounters, conditions are rarely "sufficiently similar" for me to declare that you must do what I must do. There is, however, a fundamental universality in our ethic, as there must be to escape relativism. The caring attitude, that attitude which expresses our earliest memories of being cared for and our growing store of memories of both caring and being cared for, is universally accessible. Since caring and the commitment to sustain it form the universal heart of the ethic, we must establish a convincing and comprehensive picture of caring at the outset.

## DISCUSSION QUESTIONS FOR CRITIQUE AND ANALYSIS

1. What problems with masculine morality does Noddings identify? Give your reasons for agreeing or disagreeing.

2. What does Noddings mean when she says that "relation" is ontologically basic? How is it relevant to her conception of morality?

# PHILOSOPHERS IN ACTION

Developmental theory would appear to force us as philosophers to revisit the idea that "the more rational and objective, the better." Could it be that a large part of Western rational philosophy is little more than a manifestation of male psychology? Discuss.

## PHILOSOPHICAL PROFILE

**FRIEDRICH WILHELM NIETZSCHE**

### Friedrich Wilhelm Nietzsche

A brief excursion through the philosophy section of any major North American bookstore is likely to reveal a disproportionate number of books written by a particular author, namely, Friedrich Wilhelm Nietzsche. Though not recognized as such for almost his entire lifetime, Nietzsche has now come to be celebrated as a *philosophical superstar* of sorts—one of the most provocative and influential thinkers of the nineteenth century. Serious philosophers and lay people alike have responded intellectually and in a deeply emotional fashion to his bombastic style and disturbing allegations regarding the moral corruption of religious and conventional moralists. Agree or disagree with Nietzsche's philosophy, there can be little doubt that exposure to it leaves one changed forever. Though the term *existentialism* was not yet coined at the time of his writing, Nietzsche certainly belongs in the existentialist camp, given his methods and preoccupations.

Nietzsche was born on October 15, 1844, in Prussian Saxony. Given that he was born on the birthday of the reigning king of Prussia, and also given that his father was a great admirer of the monarch, young Nietzsche was named Friedrich Wilhelm in his honor.

Friedrich was raised in a family with a long religious tradition. His father and both grandfathers were Lutheran ministers, and for the first five and a half years of his life he was raised in a parsonage. In 1849, Nietzsche's father passed away. This left him to be raised by his mother, sister, grandmother, and two aunts in Naumburg. From 1854 to 1858, young "Fritz" studied at the local gymnasium before moving on to a celebrated boarding school at Pforta (1858–1864). After completing his studies there, he distinguished himself at the Universities of Bonn and Leipzig, where he studied classical philology (the study of languages in connection with the whole moral and intellectual tradition of the peoples using them). Although religiously devout in his younger years—examples of his devotional poetry exist—Nietzsche became acquainted with the work of Arthur Schopenhauer and eventually departed from his earlier piety. By his early twenties, he had espoused a hard-hitting atheism, which was later to rock the very foundations of traditional religion itself. A brilliant scholar, he was appointed at the age of 25 as professor of classical philology at the University of Basel, even before he had earned his doctorate. Unfortunately, chronic ill health with symptoms of nausea, bad eyesight, and migraine headaches led him to retire from his academic post in 1879. He spent much of his time after that traveling from one resort to another throughout Switzerland and Italy in efforts to regain his health.

From 1880 to 1890, Nietzsche published the books for which he is best known. They include: *The Gay Science* (1882); *Thus Spoke Zarathustra* (1883–1885); *Beyond Good and Evil* (1886); *On the Genealogy of Morals* (1887); *Twilight of the Idols* and *The Antichrist* (both in 1889).

In January 1889, Nietzsche collapsed in the street while protecting a horse from being beaten by its owner. Tragically, for the remaining years of his life, he was physically disabled and pathetically insane. After failed efforts to treat him in clinical settings, he was taken home and cared for by his mother and later by his sister. Nearing the end of his life, when his writings were receiving a great deal of notice, he was unfortunately not lucid enough to enjoy his celebrity. Nietzsche died on August 25, 1900.

As a parting footnote, it is ironic that some have regarded Nietzsche as the prototypical Nazi. His notions of the *übermensch* (loosely translated as the "superman" or "overman") and master morality have strangely been linked in the minds of some to Hitler's notions of the master race, and it may indeed be that some Nazi propagandists, including Nietzsche's sister, twisted his ideas for their own purposes. In fact, however, Nietzsche lived by a romanticized myth, namely that he was descended from Polish nobility—though the truth of this is highly unlikely. In a letter to Georg Brandes, he writes: "My ancestors were Polish noblemen (Nietzky); the type seems to have been well preserved despite three generations of German mothers." R.J. Hollingdale, a commentator on Nietzsche, suggests that Nietzsche did not so much wish to be thought of as aristocratic as to be thought of as Polish. He believes Nietzsche's propagation of the legend was part of his campaign against (a decadent) Germany. It's ironic, then, that a proud (albeit mistaken) self-professed Slav should be seen as the prototypical Nazi. Slavs were considered one of Hitler's inferior races.

# EXISTENTIALIST ETHICS: FRIEDRICH WILHELM NIETZSCHE

> **"I am no man, I am dynamite."**
> NIETZSCHE

In the history of philosophy, perhaps no other thinker explodes our moral complacency as much as Friedrich Wilhelm Nietzsche does. He is truly a disturber of the peace, our peace of mind. With his bombastic writing style and iconoclastic outpourings, he strikes terror in the hearts of the religiously devout and fear in the minds of conventional thinkers and traditionalists who unquestioningly accept their ancestors' ethical prescriptions about how life ought to be lived. Be forewarned, young inquisitor, that our explorations here will require you to travel over some rocky and dangerous terrain. Along the way, you may suffer a number of psychospiritual bumps and bruises, if not deep lacerations of the psyche severing you from some of your most cherished beliefs. This part of our exploratory journey into ethics is not for the faint of heart. It is for bold, courageous individuals who are not afraid to affirm life and take responsibility for themselves. Proceed with caution, then. The future of your life is at stake here! (How's that for some Nietzschean bombast?)

## God Is Dead

Many moralists throughout history have sought direction and solace in a belief in God. If there exists a God, then all is secure. God, understood as the grand architect of the universe, establishes order, structure, and predictability. As our creator, God determines human nature, defining who we are and prescribing the purpose for which we were born. For those belonging to the **Judeo-Christian tradition,** for instance, the task of life is to do God's will and obey His commandments. Although it is difficult sometimes to abide by the rules, at least there are rules for personal moral guidance. In a world created by God, "essence precedes existence," to use existentialist phraseology (see Chapter 2: Philosophies of Life). We do not have the freedom to determine our natures, but we do have the freedom of choice to realize our God-given potentialities as His servants. We cannot determine the future, only respond to it with humble acceptance of God's will. What we don't understand or what makes no apparent sense is simply beyond human comprehension. As the saying goes: God works in mysterious ways. Who are we to judge? In a world created by God, morality is objective, absolute, and universally binding. All that happens, happens for the best as part of the divine plan. In this we find safety and moral certainty.

In *The Gay Science,* Nietzsche became a prophet for the twentieth century. He predicted with some accuracy that with the growing secularism in European society, a new psychological and cultural phenomenon was about to take place in which people would no longer find relevance in the notion of God. Notwithstanding the fact that theism has played a significant part in the development of Western civilization, he boldly proclaimed that the age of belief was over. In his typically bombastic and dramatic way, Nietzsche made his proclamation through the ravings of a madman entering a town square. In *The Gay Science,* we find the following excerpt.

## ORIGINAL SOURCEWORK

### *The Gay Science*

#### FRIEDRICH WILHELM NIETZSCHE

*The madman.*—Have you not heard of that madman who lit a lantern in the bright morning hours, ran to the market place, and cried incessantly: "I seek God! I seek God!"—As many of those who did not believe in God were standing around just then, he provoked much laughter. Has he got lost? asked one. Did he lose his way like a child? asked another. Or is he hiding? Is he afraid of us? Has he gone on a voyage? emigrated?—Thus they yelled and laughed.

Friedrich Nietzsche, *The Gay Science,* trans. Walter Kaufmann, New York: Vintage Books, 1974, pp. 181–182.

The madman jumped into their midst and pierced them with his eyes. "Whither is God?" he cried; "I will tell you. *We have killed him*—you and I. All of us are his murderers. But how did we do this? How could we drink up the sea? Who gave us the sponge to wipe away the entire horizon? What were we doing when we unchained this earth from its sun? Whither is it moving now? Whither are we moving? Away from all suns? Are we not plunging continually? Backward, sideward, forward, in all directions? Is there still any up or down? Are we not straying as through an infinite nothing? Do we not feel the breath of empty space? Has it not become colder? Is not night continually closing in on us? Do we not need to light lanterns in the morning? Do we hear nothing as yet of the noise of the gravediggers who are burying God? Do we smell nothing as yet of the divine decomposition? Gods, too, decompose. God is dead. God remains dead. And we have killed him.

"How shall we comfort ourselves, the murderers of all murderers? What was holiest and mightiest of all that the world has yet owned has bled to death under our knives: who will wipe this blood off us? What water is there for us to clean ourselves? What festivals of atonement, what sacred games shall we have to invent? Is not the greatness of this deed too great for us? Must we ourselves not become gods simply to appear worthy of it? There has never been a greater deed; and whoever is born after us—for the sake of this deed he will belong to a higher history than all history hitherto."

Here the madman fell silent and looked again at his listeners; and they, too, were silent and stared at him in astonishment. At last he threw his lantern on the ground, and it broke into pieces and went out. "I have come too early," he said then: "my time is not yet. This tremendous event is still on its way, still wandering; it has not yet reached the ears of men. Lightning and thunder require time; the light of the stars requires time; deeds, though done, still require time to be seen and heard. This deed is still more distant from them than the most distant stars—*and yet they have done it themselves.*"

It has been related further that on the same day the madman forced his way into several churches and there struck up his *requiem aeternam deo.* Led out and called to account, he is said always to have replied nothing but: "What after all are these churches now if they are not the tombs and sepulchers of God?"

## DISCUSSION QUESTIONS FOR CRITIQUE AND ANALYSIS

1. What allegation does Nietzsche's madman make? Does it make any sense? Is it justified? Why?

2. What is suggested by the madman's statement that, "I have come too early"? Do you agree? Why or why not?

---

Rather than get depressed about the death of God or worry that the world is going to hell in a handbasket, we should celebrate, according to Nietzsche. We are no longer bound by supernatural superstitions and invented moral restraints; nor need we any longer be prisoners chained by projections of our own fears onto a man-made idol called God. We are free, free at last! In celebration of the death of God, Nietzsche writes:

> Indeed, we philosophers and 'free spirits' feel, when we hear the news that 'the old god is dead,' as if a new dawn shone on us; our heart overflows with gratitude, amazement, premonition, expectation. At long last the horizon appears free to us again, even if it should not be bright; at long last our ships may venture out again, venture out to face any danger; all the daring of the lover of knowledge is permitted again; the sea, *our* sea, lies open again; perhaps there has never yet been such an 'open sea.'[42]

Although, personally, you may resist the notion that God is dead, or, perhaps be terrorized by such a proposition, for Nietzsche, "His death" should be viewed in a positive light. Since God and religion are both hostile to life, the destruction of a belief in God makes it possible for man's creative energies to develop fully. We no longer have to hate our "sinful" natures or discount the value or our flesh and blood lives. No longer must we engage in purgative, pious rituals and humiliating confessions of self-loathing. No more need we direct our gaze toward some unreal supernatural realm formed by our desperate imaginations. Rather than dream of other nonexistent worlds, we can live in this one. Instead of feebly hoping that a phantom God will tell us what to do, we can take the place of God as legislators ourselves, creating our own values. Oh, glory to man!

> *"That lambs dislike great birds of prey does not seem strange: only it gives no ground for reproaching these birds of prey for bearing off little lambs."*
>
> NIETZSCHE

## Will to Power

If belief in God should not properly serve as the basis of morality, then the question arises: What should become the moral foundation for life? Nietzsche has a life-affirming answer for us: the **will to power.** For Nietzsche, the will to power is a fundamental psychological force. At first glance, it may seem that Nietzsche is advancing some kind of Darwinian universe governed by the principle of survival of the fittest. In truth, Nietzsche does agree with Charles Darwin that nature is a brutal arena of struggle and war. However, in contrast to Darwin, Nietzsche does not regard survival as the absolute end. Some people will, in fact, risk their self-preservation in order to expand their power. People often do dangerous things at great risk to achieve dominance or position. As human beings, we continually press onward, trying to exceed limits and constraints to achieve. Seldom are we content with where we are, incessantly striving to go beyond what we have achieved and to become more than we have become.[43] When you are tired and completely exhausted as a rock climber, for instance, but drag yourself up to the next plateau before mounting upward again to reach the summit, the will to power is what drives you. When you study all night in order to get the highest grade needed to win the scholarship, the will to power is active again. Freed from religious fears of vanity, selfishness, and the sin of pride (metaphysical inventions), you can now self-assertively attempt to climb your mountains, win your prizes, and realize your ambitions without unnatural guilt induced by otherworldly sources. You are free to make of yourself what you will. "Let *Thy* will be done" now means, "Let *my* will be done!"

The will to power aims not at mere survival, but at a particular way of surviving or being in the world. As we can see ourselves from everyday experience, many people do not wish to live a paltry existence. Simply trying to survive or just get by is not enough. They exhibit a strong will to overcome obstacles and make something of themselves. Here, the goal of power is manifested by **self-overcoming** and **self-mastery.** People everywhere seek to overcome their fears and rise above their limitations. They strive constantly to get beyond themselves and to achieve some sort of distinction. The will to power may sometimes emerge in tyrannical rulers who wish to dominate others. However, it should be noted that domination here is really instrumental—a means to an end. Ultimately, the goal is to increase power and to gain mastery over oneself. Striving for power, then, is not necessarily military, political, or economic, though it can be. In expressing the will to power, we seek to create ourselves by surmounting those obstacles that would block our self-realization. In the will to power, we find the instinctual urge to express our freedom. When we express that freedom in the act of self-creation, we build a monument to our own glory. We become masters in our own home. We perfect ourselves and thereby distinguish ourselves by our very uniqueness as human beings. Even when the saint engages in rituals of fasting and meditation, the true goal is self-transcendence, achieving an ecstatic experience of the holy beyond oneself. When the artist fights against poverty and criticism to impose his vision upon reality, again the will to power is at work.[44] Or when the engineer constructs a dam and diverts the surging river in a direction of her own bidding, we witness yet another manifestation of this same will. In short, the will to power is natural and life-affirming. As the vital life force, it should, and must, be the basis of any honest morality. Not all moralities are "honest," as you will soon learn.

## Master versus Slave Morality

Nietzsche asserts that the will to power manifests itself in two basic ethical orientations, which he labels **master morality** and **slave morality.** These moralities are displayed by individuals and more generally by societies. Nietzsche makes the point that they are not necessarily mutually exclusive. Within any given individual or cultural group, there can be admixtures of both moralities, resulting, however, in confusion and misunderstanding.

Regardless of the extent to which we exhibit master and slave moralities—either individually in our personal lives or collectively as a society—we all nonetheless possess the drive to overcome and perfect ourselves. This is what the will to power impels us to do. What Nietzsche claims is that not all people are equal with respect to their strength of will. Not all of us can gain power over ourselves to become creators of our own values. Those of us who do and are able to chart our own course and determine our own values live by a master morality. By contrast, those of us who lack the strength to stand alone must satisfy our will to power in another fashion. For instance, we may obey and follow the dictates of a powerful commander. It is possible to find strength in numbers and obedience to authority.

Though the labels "master morality" and "slave morality" might quickly predispose you to regard one as better than the other, Nietzsche tries to establish the value of each by examining its origins, including the political and psychological conditions under which the moral value orientation was devised.[45] It is here where we enter murky waters, however. In his book *On the Genealogy of Morals,* we find the subtitle *A Polemic.* This raises the question of whether Nietzsche's moral genealogy (study of the line of development) should be taken as an actual historical explanation, or whether it is his way of clarifying and justifying his own conception of human excellence and the moral significance of the moralities that either enhance or diminish it. Peter Berkowitz writes:

> Inasmuch as Nietzsche reduces the whole complex and multifarious moral past of mankind to two competing moralities, it is

closer to the truth to say that in practice his genealogy is painted in black and white. Nor is Nietzsche's genealogy meticulous. Inasmuch as he names no names, dates no events, and shows scant concern for details, variations, and anomalies, it would be more accurate to call his genealogy inspired guesswork, suggestive speculation, or a likely tale. And Nietzsche's genealogy, strikingly devoid of empirical evidence or scholarly apparatus, is anything but patiently documentary.[46]

Given what Berkowitz says, it may be that Nietzsche is a lousy historian, but we should not, as a consequence, summarily reject his views. Berkowitz goes on to say:

While he plainly intends the *Genealogy* to at least roughly approximate the actual unfolding of history, in execution his genealogy constitutes the creation of an illustrative myth or poem. . . . Nietzsche poeticizes history the better to bring out the truth about the origins and thereby the nature, of our moral prejudices.[47]

One thing we can say for Nietzsche, his two basic moralities do have at least loose historical ties to actual master-slave relationships—particularly to the Romans and early Christians, as well as to the Ancient Egyptians and the Jews. For Nietzsche, emerging out of such historical master-slave relations were essentially two ideal types of personality. We will look at these two personality types in a moment. For now, it should be stressed that one needn't literally be a "slave" to live a slave-like existence. Nineteenth-century Europe was anything but a slave society, yet Nietzsche regarded its morality as very slavish, something that needed reevaluation. On the other hand, one could live in a highly conventional slave-like conformist society and yet rise above it as a master, noble type. I suppose it could be said that while the origins of master and slave moralities are historical and sociopolitical, their expressions are psychological, reflecting the values and qualities of character within the individual. Let us examine, then, the features that typify both master and slave moralists.

Master moralists are psychologically powerful, strong-willed individuals. They affirm life, equating "good" with that which leads to self-fulfillment and the exercise of personal power. Master moralists are **nobles,** displaying strength, courage, and pride. They are truly people of higher caliber. Noble types do not live their lives constantly looking over their shoulders in fear and insecurity. They are never at the mercy of the approval of others. What we describe as "peer group pressure" would be lost on noble types. The only self-referring value judgments they accept are the ones that they themselves pass on their own person. Nobles are not interested in conforming to social conventions, fitting in, or finding solace in metaphysical revelations. They regard themselves as creators and moral legislators, determiners of their own values.

Noble types worship power in all of its forms and venues of expression, be it in the arts, politics, philosophy, or war. They show reverence for all that is severe and hard. They like to conquer obstacles and distinguish themselves. Thus, whatever restricts growth and accomplishment is bad; so too is anything born of weakness and timidity. Nobles value toughness and rigor.

Though these values and attitudes of the nobles might make them sound a bit cruel or harsh, this is not necessarily so. Nobles can be kind and helpful to the unfortunate, but never out of pity or utilitarian consideration. When nobles help the unfortunate, they do so out of a feeling of generosity of spirit and strength, not pitying empathy.

What is refreshing about noble types is their **psychological honesty.** They express the will to power openly, without deception, excuse, or guilt. Morality, for them, is an exercise in self-glorification. Noble types are often feared because they do not veil their self-assertive tendencies. Nobles are explorers, inventors, and experimenters; their courage and audacity serve to remind the weak exactly how pathetic they really are. What the nobles detest and consider bad are those things which are vulgar and base, plebeian, common, banal, petty, cowardly, timid, or humble. Such things diminish us; they do not glorify and uplift us. Interesting, isn't it, how many of us take pride in being the "average Joe." The desire to be "normal" is anything but praiseworthy for Nietzsche's master moralists.

In the slave moralist we find a very different kind of individual. Slave moralists, like master moralists, are driven by the will to power, but they are hesitant to express this instinct directly. They do so in a dishonest fashion, through what one commentator describes as a "sour grapes" morality.[48] By condemning the virtues and attributes of the master moralist (noble traits beyond their reach), slave moralists can feel better about their own weaknesses and inadequacies. In view of this, slave moralists see life in terms of **reaction** and **negation,** as opposed to noble affirmation. They resent the excellence, achievement, unbridled individuality, and power that the master moralists so freely and easily express. Out of their **resentment,** slave moralists negate what is truly great and make it sound evil. Slave moralists thus do not express an authentic self-generated morality, but one created as a reaction against the values of the powerful—those whom they fear. In other words, the slave moralist first develops a conception of what is negative or evil and then constructs a framework of morality to support it. It is saturated with suspicion, fear, and resentment, but not much that is positive and life-affirming.

According to Nietzsche's historical or genealogical account, variations of slave morality took root among the oppressed peoples of the world. These oppressed people constituted the lowest elements of society. The oppressed were the abused and uncertain. They were the exploited and the enslaved. Nietzsche describes the early Christians and Jews as two social groups living by a slave morality. He also contends that more modern derivations of Judeo-Christian morality, found in democratic and socialist societies, are also slave-like. It was when the Roman emperor Constantine converted to Christianity that the slave moralists really began to take control. Outnumbered by the slaves and outmaneuvered by their skillful dishonesty, the strong came to accept slave morality. They started to feel guilty about their own power and excellence. Apology and shamefulness replaced willful self-assertion. Unfortunately Western civilization (Europe in particular) accepted the grotesque notion of equality. The values of the mediocre were glorified over the achievement and creative power of the individual. A negative psychic attitude was developed toward the most natural drives of man. Slave morality compounded its moral degeneracy by its inconsistency. The weak ganged together in order to grab the very power they condemned as evil in the master moralist. Their unannounced and surreptitious purpose was to render the nobles harmless so they would no longer constitute a threat to their paltry lives. The slaves would be in control.

What the slave moralists value and consider good, therefore, are those qualities that enable sufferers to endure their life situation. For the weak and powerless, character traits such as patience and humility, submissiveness, friendliness, and compassion are applauded. It is good to resign oneself to a difficult life and to pity others who, like yourself, suffer. In very general terms, "good" is defined in a utilitarian fashion; it is that which is most beneficial to the group or society as a whole. What you notice in the slave moralist is a lack of vitality and a seeking for ease and contentment. Needless to say, perhaps, but such a life is pathetic according to Nietzsche. It stinks of mediocrity, dishonesty, and self-denial. Slave morality is not life-affirming, but life-denying. On the subject of Christian-slave morality, Nietzsche writes: "I regard Christianity as the most fatal and seductive lie that has ever existed—as the greatest and most impious lie. . . . "[49] Disgusted that the morality of paltry people has been made the measure of all things, he thought that subjecting Europe to the morality produced by a small group of wretched Jesus-followers constituted "the most repugnant kind of degeneracy that civilization has ever brought into existence."[50] (I guess you've noticed by now that Nietzsche has no penchant for understatement!)

## Traditional (Herd) Morality and the Revaluation of All Values

Clearly, Nietzsche regards slave morality as degenerate in its negativity, dishonesty, inconsistency, and reactivity. And, of course, as just mentioned, he regards Christianity as the prime example of this degeneracy. There is yet another form of inferior morality, which may appear slave-like on the surface, but which contains several subtle differences that Nietzsche does not always clearly explain, and which some analysts have overlooked and confused.[51] This other inferior type can be called **traditional, customary,** or **herd morality.** According to this moral perspective, one is moral to the extent one acts in accordance with custom where custom is the traditional way of behaving. Tradition becomes the higher moral authority we must obey if we are to do the right thing. One can obey tradition as mindlessly as one can obey God or the Pope. The point is that following the prescriptions and demands of tradition requires that we give up our rationality and individual autonomy. Traditional morality suppresses thinking and requires people to surrender their power and freedom for the sake of the collective herd. There is a "payoff" for individuals, of course, or else they likely would not conform to the dictates of traditional authority. The weak can protect themselves from the strong and thereby achieve power. On the flip side, there is a cost associated with mindless conformity to the herd. As Nietzsche puts it: "All community makes somehow, somewhere, sometime—common."[52] Traditional herd morality does not enrich or advance humankind. Those belonging to the communal group will be of average strength and vitality, average confidence and courage, average health, and so on.

> “*The man of faith, the believer is necessarily a small type of man. Hence 'freedom of spirit,' i.e., unbelief as an instinct, is a precondition of greatness.*”
>
> NIETZSCHE, *THE WILL TO POWER*

In contrast to slave morality, which is reactive to the master moralists, traditional (herd) morality is not. It is produced in conditions of contentment, not resentment; its principle function is not revenge or control, but to maintain the life of the herd. Thus, herd moralists simply wish to preserve their situation, whereas slave moralists wish to change theirs.

Another feature of herd morality is expressed by its mediocrity. It opposes all rankings of people (higher versus lower). It makes efforts to produce a type of person as close as possible to the herd average. Since the herd is quite content, it has a positive orientation toward life, not like the slaves who are negative and bitter toward the nobles.

## PHILOSOPHERS IN ACTION

Is educational excellence possible in a value system that treats all students as equals? When your professor teaches to the "class average," is human greatness achieved? How should students be ranked, if at all? How should teaching methods be varied to suit the ranks, if at all? Are your responses to these questions reflective of your basic moral beliefs? Are you a master, slave, or herd moralist? In view of Nietzsche's hierarchical ordering of moralities, how would he describe you? How would you respond to Nietzsche?

## Evaluating Values

Because, for Nietzsche, all value orientations are products of human beings, their ultimate worth can and should be determined by the characteristics of their producers. A system of moral values produced by the strong and healthy is thus better than the value system produced by the weak and ailing.[53] We cannot evaluate moral actions in themselves or examine the logical features of moral language to determine right from wrong. The underlying rationale and justification for any morality must be based on the producers of that morality and cannot be properly and fully understood in isolation from them. Embedded in Nietzsche's thinking is also an extension to the idea just mentioned, namely that those moralities which serve to produce stronger and healthier types are better than those which produce weaker and sicklier types. A system of morality that, by design, produces moral degenerates is not as good as one that produces moral heroes.

Another criterion Nietzsche uses to evaluate moralities is tied to the notion of human freedom. Systems of value that are generated in conditions of **autonomy** are preferable to systems generated in situations of constraint.[54] In other words, those moralities which are conducive to autonomous and creative self-expression are better than those which call for limits and self-repression.

When it comes to evaluating systems of morality, Nietzsche would have us first look at its origins and producers, at its intended and actual function, as well as at its ability to respect and enhance individual autonomy.

In light of these evaluative criteria, Nietzsche concluded that we must reject traditional morality in the name of honesty. In the same way that Christianity was a revaluation of all the values of antiquity, so now the dominant traditional morality of the day must be rejected and refigured in favor of humankind's original and deepest nature. If we engage in a critical, historical analysis of modern man's ideals, we will find that so-called "moral truth," as we understand it now, is really a perversion. Nietzsche "showed that what modern man called 'good' was not at all virtuous, that his so-called truth was disguised selfishness and weakness, and that his religion was a skillful creation of psychological weapons with which moral pigmies domesticated natural giants." Once the disguise is removed from modern morality, Nietzsche thought, the true values will emerge.[55] They will be based on the internal will to power, one that uses and exploits the environment for its own pleasure and satisfaction. By overcoming or going beyond traditional values we, as humans, can fully express the will to power and thereby realize ourselves.

Furthermore, Nietzsche would have us go beyond blind observance to tradition since no set of ready-made rules can be used to apply in every situation. The suggestion is *not* that we become totally selfish and self-centered and that we no longer do for others. However, what we must do in our revaluation is get beyond the view that unegoistic and selfless actions are morally good. The fact is that egoism and selfishness are not only unavoidable aspects of human nature, but that their presence is necessary if we would achieve our best.[56] Nietzsche would have us integrate all aspects of our human nature. This would be life-affirming. Christianity, by contrast, is life-denying insofar as it deprecates the body, condemns instinctual impulse, passion, the free and untrammeled exercise of the mind, aesthetic values, and so on.[57] And not only that, Christian morality is motivated by fear, which is based on a consciousness of weakness.

## The Superman/Übermensch

Readers of Nietzsche are sometimes inclined to think that his philosophy subjects us to a gloomy **nihilism.** At first glance, it might appear that life in the Nietzschean universe is meaninglessness and without value. After all, for him, God is dead, no objective morality exists, slave morality lacks honesty and integrity, and traditional herd morality is a collective cop-out for a pig's life of contentment.

Interestingly enough, for Nietzsche, slave moralities are themselves nihilistic. As mentioned, Christianity, for example, is life-denying. According to Christian belief, we are born stained with original sin. We are corrupt or damaged at birth. We need to die to the flesh in order to be reborn in the spirit. We must suffer on earth in order to enjoy our rewards in heaven. Our natural cravings and desires are sinful. We must be redeemed and saved from ourselves. We must never display self-will, for this is pride, and we are taught by religionists that "pride cometh before the fall." We simply cannot be human without guilt, fear, and shame. We are told that while we live in this world, we should not be of this world. For Nietzsche, all of this clearly points to nihilism. The promise of spiritual salvation by the "preachers of doom" is really an attack on the values of life. For Nietzsche, Christian slave morality is, in fact, nihilistic, but his is not. I'm sure he would think he has done the world a great favor by annihilating the nihilism of Christianity.

Nietzsche does indeed provide us with an ideal for humanity—the image of the **Übermensch** (translated into English as **superman** or **overman**). One should not confuse the Nietzschean superman with any television figure or comic book character; the term *superman* does not refer to any bulked-up superhero sold as an action figure in toy stores. The superman is not any particular individual but a type of person. The superman is not produced through biological evolution or any process of eugenics. He is not a tyrant either, one who has a maniacal need to dominate. The superman, for Nietzsche, constitutes a "union of spiritual superiority with well-being and an excess of strength."[58] The kind of person Nietzsche has in mind here would combine "the Roman Caesar with Christ's Soul" (see *The Will to Power,* aphorism 983). To put it another way, the superman represents the highest level of development and expression of physical, intellectual, and emotional strength.[59] Nothing would be forbidden to the superman except what interferes with the will to power.

Of course, the superman will be rare. It is only when superior types muster the courage to revalue all values and respond with freedom to their internal will to power that the next stage of human development can be reached. Nietzsche was impressed by the Greek poet Homer and his accounts of **Apollo** and **Dionysus.** He used these figures as symbols in order to capture two powerful elements in human nature and to illustrate how they could be combined as a balanced unity in the superman or superior individual. This harmony could help us, in turn, to understand how life could be lived as an **aesthetic phenomenon.** Dionysus symbolizes the power of passion. He represents the dynamic stream of life, which knows no restraining barriers. The Dionysian element in us is that which defies all limitations. It is potentially dangerous, serving as the reservoir for the negative, dark, and destructive powers of the soul. We express the Dionysian mood most obviously when boundaries of separation between us and the world are broken down, and as we lapse into drunken frenzies or immerse ourselves in feelings of abandonment in music.[60] Without controls, the Dionysian element would turn us into savage beasts, disgusting individuals capable of great cruelty and voluptuousness.

Fortunately, there is a rational Apollonian element in us as well. Apollo serves as the symbol representing the power to control and restrain the dynamic forces of life. The Apollonian dimension can harness destructive energies and sublimate or transform them into creative acts. Dionysus captures the instinctual drives that are tamed and harnessed by Apollo to produce controlled individual characters.

It should be emphasized that the Dionysian element is not intrinsically evil or diseased. It is not something we wish to get rid of. It is detrimental only when unharnessed and uncontrolled. Without it, life would lack vital energy. The Dionysian element serves as the stimulus for achievement, self-overcoming, and artistic expression in whatever form it might take. What some may describe as the "beast within" is not to be purged or destroyed, but transmuted into an aesthetic phenomenon, a work of art.

Nietzsche's aesthetic ideal or aesthetic mode of existence is concerned more with "style" than with content. What is important is fitting one's traits into "an artistic plan, until each thing appears as art and reason, and even the weakness charms the eye."[61] You might wish to think of your "self" as a personal creation—a masterpiece you are in the process of creating throughout your entire lifetime. You could choose to think of your life as a story, in which the objective is to mold your life's events into a coherent narrative within which you assume the identity that you've created for yourself. The aim here is *not* to realize your essence or pre-given potential, but to blend everything that you have done, are doing, and will do in the future into a perfectly coherent whole. The task, for Nietzsche, is to fully embrace one's existence and to affirm all that one is.[62] This is how you follow Nietzsche's injunction to "Become who you are." This is the meaning of your life and this is what you must do.

## PHILOSOPHICAL PROFILE

**AYN RAND**

### Ayn Rand

Ayn Rand, *née* Alissa Rosenbaum, was born on February 2, 1905, in St. Petersburg, Russia. A graduate of the University of Leningrad, she studied history and worked as a museum guide. After graduating, Rand entered the State Institute for Cinema Arts and began to study English. In 1926, she arrived in New York City, later to become a citizen of the United States. After a brief stay with relatives in Chicago, Rand moved to Hollywood, where she worked for the famous Cecil B. DeMille as a movie extra and script reader. Rand eventually went on to write a couple of Broadway plays and several movie scripts of her own, in addition to her best-known novels, *The Fountainhead* and *Atlas Shrugged*.

From the age of 40, Rand's career began to move in a different direction, as she started to see herself more as a philosopher, embodying many of her philosophical ideas in the thoughts, words, and deeds of her fictional characters. For the last 25 years of her life, she abandoned fiction altogether, deciding to dedicate herself to the advancement of her own philosophy, which she entitled "Objectivism." In the process, Rand became one of America's most respected, and arguably most reviled, thinkers from the late 1950s to the middle 1970s. Whether admired or despised, there can be little doubt she had an impact on modern thought. It could be argued that she enjoyed perhaps the largest and most loyal following of any living philosopher of the modern Western world.[63] The Ayn Rand Institute still exists today and serves as the center for the advancement of Objectivism, Ayn Rand's individualistic philosophy of reason, egoism, and laissez-faire capitalism. Nonfictional philosophical works by Rand include: *The Virtue of Selfishness: A New Concept of Egoism, For the New Intellectual, Introduction to Objectivist Epistemology,* and *Capitalism: The Unknown Ideal.* Rand died in 1982.

# OBJECTIVIST ETHICS: AYN RAND

## Ethical Egoism

Over the years, I've noticed that many students have displayed a wide array of negative emotions, ranging from mild insecurity to aggressive outrage, whenever matters of morality are discussed in class. The best I can surmise is that, for a few at least, the whole notion of morality appears to be something unpleasant, involving a lot of self-denial, guilt, and fear. Others seem to see it as a system of arbitrary prescriptions and prohibitions—a bunch of "Thou shalts" and "Thou shalt nots" imposed by often-distrusted authorities. From this perspective, morality is all about deference to others, personal sacrifice, the threat of sanctions, and psychological regret. Regarded in this way, morality is thought to bring more pain than pleasure, more abstinence than self-gratification. Presumably, nothing personally advantageous can come of it, so morality is "bad news," so to speak. For this reason, some students try to defensively avoid discussions of morality; others treat them with bored indifference; while still others summarily dismiss them as matters of personal opinion. Of course, there are always those dogmatic individuals who think they know what is absolutely right and wrong and don't hesitate to remind us.

In efforts to respond to those who have turned away from moral discourse because they perceive morality as some kind of disturbing threat or violation of personal liberty, we will now briefly examine the moral theory developed by Ayn Rand (Ayn rhymes with mine), which can be described as a form of **ethical egoism.** On the subject of morality, Ayn Rand takes seriously the question: "What's in it for me?" In her estimation, a morality that does not further the interests of the individual is dangerous and nonsensical. In the development of what she calls **objectivist ethics,** Rand argues that morality must be consistent with one's rational self-interest. In fact, she proudly advocates and extols the virtues of what she calls **rational selfishness.** She strongly rejects **collectivist thinking,** which requires that individuals sacrifice their personal interests for the benefit of the group, society, state, or anyone else for that matter. Any collectivist **ethic of altruism** that necessitates this is, for Rand, ultimately destructive. To understand her position better, let us now consider Rand's egoistic theory of ethical objectivism.

## Objectivist Ethics

In a collection of essays brought together in a short book polemically entitled *The Virtue of Selfishness,* Rand spells out her highly individualistic theory of morality.[64] She begins in the Introduction by challenging our conventional understanding of the term "**selfishness**" itself. As she points out, most of us equate the idea of selfishness with evil. To be selfish is to be some kind of ruthless brute who coldly steps on people whenever necessary to achieve his or her own ends. Such a person displays little or no care for others and pursues nothing but immediate gratification of mindless whims and momentary desires. Selfish people simply do what they want—all others be damned. The selfish person is assumed to be morally contemptible, a callous and self-centered creature. No wonder few aspire to become selfish, while still fewer openly admit to being so.

According to Rand, however, our failure to properly understand selfishness has led to the arrested moral development of humankind.[65] Selfishness should *not* lead us to the conclusion that an action is right simply because one has chosen it. Self-interest cannot be determined by random whim and blind desire. It must be discovered and achieved by the guidance of rational principles. Selfishness, rightly understood, "does not tell us whether concern with one's own interests is good or evil; nor does it tell us what constitutes man's actual interests. It is the task of [rational] ethics to answer such questions."[66]

## Altruism Is Inhumane

Rand asserts that the ethics of altruism, which makes others the beneficiaries of our moral action, requires us to accept two inhumane tenets: the first is that any concern with one's own interests is evil, regardless of what they might be; the second is that to act or engage in any activities that further one's own interests is to make one an evil brute. From Rand's perspective, altruism requires you to renounce your own "selfish" interests for the sake of your neighbor's. If you do things for others at your own expense, that's good. If you do things for yourself, to benefit only yourself, that's bad. "Thus, the **beneficiary** of an action is the only criterion of moral value—and so long as that beneficiary is anybody other than oneself, anything goes."[67]

Rand finds the implications of making the beneficiary of an action the only criterion of moral value grotesque and absurd. For example, businesspeople and bank robbers can now be lumped together as immoral crooks, since they both seek wealth for their own "selfish" benefit. A young man who gives up his career in order to support his parents and never rises beyond the rank of grocery clerk is regarded as morally superior to the young man who endures an excruciating struggle and achieves his personal ambition. (He did it for himself, after all.) A dictator is regarded as moral, since the unspeakable atrocities he committed were intended to benefit "the people, not himself."[68] The point is that adherence to the "beneficiary criterion of morality" teaches individuals that morality is their enemy. They can only lose from it. There is no prospect of gain. Dutifully sacrificing for others and hoping that others will dutifully sacrifice for oneself breeds mutual resentment, not pleasure or happiness. As Rand puts it, the pursuit of values becomes, "like an exchange of unwanted, unchosen Christmas presents, which neither [one] is morally permitted to buy for himself."[69]

Another problem with altruistic ethics is that it does not recognize self-respecting, self-supporting persons—individuals who determine their own lives by sacrificing neither themselves nor others. Altruism transforms people into sacrificial animals (those giving of themselves) and profiteers-on-sacrifice (those gladly accepting the sacrificial offerings). People are thereby turned into victims and parasites. For Rand, this view of human beings allows for no acceptable concept of justice, nor any possibility of benevolent coexistence among them. It breeds only cynicism and guilt. People become cynical because they neither practice nor accept altruistic morality. They experience guilt because they don't dare to reject it. Try defending the proposition that you should place your own self-interests before everyone else's and see what reaction you get. Even if you believe this proposition, you defend it at your own peril against the "collectivist herd" waiting for your sacrificial offering!

Rejecting the "other-as beneficiary" criterion, Rand argues that the basis of morality, as well as the justification of particular ethical actions and decisions, must come from **human nature** and the function of morality in human life:

> The Objectivist ethics holds that the actor must always be the beneficiary of his action and that man must act for his own *rational* self-interest. But his right to do so is derived from his nature as man and from the function of moral values in the context of a rational, objectively demonstrated and validated code of moral principles which define and determine his actual self-interest. It is not a license "to do as he pleases" and it is not applicable to the altruist's image of a "selfish" brute nor to any man motivated by irrational emotions, feelings, urges, wishes or whims.[70]

The questions of what is morally right and who should benefit from moral action are, for Rand, actually secondary ones. She would have us ask initially, "*Do we even need a morality?*" For her, the answer to this primary question serves as the precondition for any system of ethics we might try to justify or prescribe for others. As she says, "The first question is not: What particular code of values should man accept? The first question is: Does man need values at all—and why?"[71] In answer to her own question, Rand posits that we need a new code of values to save civilization. The history of ethics reveals, for her, that it has fallen prey to mysticism and subjective bias. Objectivist ethics' goal, therefore, is to give values a basis other than faith, intuition, taste, feeling, urge, wish, and personal whim. This is what morality has been based on in the past, and we need only look at the disastrous effects it has produced to be horrified. Rand asserts that, historically speaking, philosophers have simply taken ethics as a given, never concerning themselves with its metaphysical cause or objective validation. Past efforts to break the monopoly of mysticism (religion, the Church) in the field of ethics by justifying morality on social grounds merely resulted in a substitution of **society** for God. Instead of acting morally in accordance with the will of God, the neomystics, as Rand calls them, prescribed that we act for the good of society. There are allegedly two problems with this maneuver. First, Rand argues that there is "no such entity as 'society,' since society is only a number of individual men." In other words, the notion of society is a questionable abstraction. Secondly, in a society, the mob is allowed to pursue any whims (or any atrocities) it desires, while dissenting individuals are ethically required to spend their lives in service to those who claim to be the spokespersons for the collective good or for the "gang" who would have their way. The result of this subjugation of the individual to the gang, society, group, or collective is an irrational ethic—one based on feelings, tastes, wishes, and whims of others. Emotional commitment becomes the basis of such a social morality, representing nothing other than a subjective choice or personal preference.

Accepting **personal whim** as the basis of morality creates a conflict. The battle inevitably rages over whose whim should be accepted: the individual's, one's own, society's, the dictator's or God's? Skeptical, Rand does not accept **mysticism** (God, religion, or blind faith), **neomysticism** (the primacy of society and the collective), **emotionalism** (capricious feelings), or **subjective preference** (personal whim) as the foundation of her moral thinking. Rather, she begins with an analysis of values and asks why we need them. She does not consider the concept of values in isolation, however. The idea of values relates necessarily to the questions: "Of value to *whom*?" and "Of value for *what*?" If something has value, then it is presupposed that there is a valuing agent able to achieve that value (or goal) in face of alternatives. If there is no one to choose, or if there are no alternatives to choose from, then no goals or values are possible.

The most fundamental alternative for humankind involves the choice between existence or nonexistence. All other choices are contingent on this one. Such a choice can apply only to conscious living organisms, not to inanimate things like rocks. Furthermore, if the life choice were not an issue—if we were immortal, indestructible robots, unaffected by anything—we would not have any values. If we could not be changed, damaged, injured, or destroyed, if nothing we did threatened or secured our survival, then we would never have anything to lose or gain. Nothing would serve or threaten our welfare; nothing could further or frustrate our interests since we would be immune to all outside influence. As indestructible robots, valuing would become irrelevant since nothing would be of any consequence.

The truth is, however, that we are not indestructible robots but real live conscious beings. Some things are in our interest and other things are not. To quote Rand, "It is only the concept of 'Life' that makes the concept of 'Value' possible. It is only to a living entity that things can be good or evil."[72] For her, **life** is a process of self-sustaining and self-generating action. It is life that gives humanity goals. It is also life that serves as the ultimate value to which all lesser goals are the means. All these lesser goals are to be evaluated in terms of the human organism's life. That which furthers life is good; that which threatens it is evil. Value is therefore derivative of life. One cannot meaningfully discuss the concept of value outside the context of life. One does not live to value, but values to live. We make value judgments in order to secure our survival. Continued existence is the purpose of valuing.

The premise that any concept of value must be based on life has enormous implications. When it comes to survival, much is determined by **nature,** by the kind of entities we are as human beings. If we don't eat, we die. If we jump off a cliff, we threaten our continued existence. This is not a matter of opinion, faith, majority rule, intuition, or subjective preference; it is merely a fact. Thus, value judgments can be validated by reference to the facts of reality. "The fact that a living entity *is*, determines what it *ought* to do."[73] In one fell swoop, then, Rand believes she has dismissed the logical problem of deriving a moral "ought" from an "is" of experience.[74] Reality serves as the basis of (moral) value judgment. The foundation of morality need not have a mystical, social, or emotional foundation. Nature decides what is necessary for survival.

Of course, newborn children do not enter the world with innate knowledge of what has survival value. The genetically determined pleasure-pain mechanism of the body does, however, initially serve to protect the organism's life. Pleasure becomes the signal that the organism is pursuing the right course of action. Unfortunately, some children are born with a rare disease that renders them unable to experience pain. These children do not usually survive for long. They possess no warning signals letting them know that they are suffering physically or doing things that hurt them. Avoiding pain and injury is not only "right," if we are to survive; it is necessitated by our very natures—Rand's point.

As conscious beings, reason becomes through the development of consciousness our tool for distinguishing between what is ultimately pleasurable or painful, life-sustaining or life-threatening. We need not always touch the hot stove to know that it is hot and dangerous. Through the use of cognitive function, we can store past experiences in memory, anticipate, calculate, and conceptualize in ways which keep us out of harm's way and on the road to happiness and pleasure. Since the conscious mind, or rationality, is part of our core human nature and the basic means to our survival, Rand concludes "that which is proper to the life of a rational being is the good; that which negates, opposes or destroys it is the evil."[75]

## Values and Virtue

In "The Objectivist Ethics," Rand distinguishes between **value** and **virtue:** "Value is that which one acts to gain and/or keep—*virtue* is the act by which one gains and/or keeps it."[76] According to her, there are three values which, when taken together, constitute the means to, and realization of, one's ultimate value, namely life. They are: (1) **reason,** (2) **purpose** and (3) **self-esteem.** The virtues that correspond to these values are in order: **rationality, productivity** and **pride.** The virtue of rationality is expressed by one's acceptance of reason as the only source of knowledge and guide to action. Rational virtue involves a total commitment to full, conscious awareness and to the maintenance of complete mental focus on all matters and all choices in all of one's waking hours. Rational people do not allow their minds to become unfocused. This would constitute a suspension of consciousness, a form of irrationality rejecting our very means of survival as human beings. To be unfocused is to be anti-rational, and therefore anti-mind and anti-life.

To be committed to rationality also means that all of one's values, goals, and desires must be validated by logical thought processes. One must never engage in mystical or metaphysical speculation, placing anything above one's perception of reality. To be rational is to accept responsibility for forming one's own judgments and living by the work of one's own mind. The rationally self-interested person should never sacrifice his or her own convictions simply to conform to the opinions of others or to satisfy *their* (selfish) desires.

Productive work is the process by which man's mind supports and sustains life. By practicing the virtue of productiveness, we adjust our natural physical background to suit us, unlike lower-level organisms who must adapt to environmental circumstances. Productive work elicits the highest qualities of man's character—creativity, ambition, self-assertiveness, and dedication—to "reshaping the earth in the image of his values." Productive work encompasses the most complete and purposeful use of the mind.

The third virtue discussed by Rand is pride. For her, it is roughly equivalent to moral ambitiousness. Pride is something one earns by working toward one's own moral perfection, which is done by refusing to accept any code of irrational virtues impossible to practice and by practicing the virtues one knows to be rational. The virtue of pride, stemming from the value of self-esteem, means that we should never accept unearned guilt, never earn any guilt, or if we've earned it, do what is required to correct matters. The person of pride does what he or she can to overcome character flaws and by never putting any concern, wish, fear, or mood of moment above one's own self-esteem. The virtue of pride also requires that we refuse to accept the role of sacrificial animal. We are obliged to reject any philosophy, doctrine, or religion that preaches self-denial as a virtuous moral duty. This last point is nicely capped off by Rand with the following statement:

> The basic *social* principle of the Objectivist ethics is that just as life is an end in itself, so every living human being is an end in himself, not the means to the ends or the welfare of others—and, therefore, that man must live for his own sake, neither sacrificing himself to others nor sacrificing others to himself. *To live for his own sake means that the achievement of his own happiness is man's highest moral purpose.*[77]

## Rational Selfishness

Happiness, then, is not some kind of abstract principle that one applies to situations or uses for guidance when trying to make correct moral value judgments. "Life" is the irreducible primary, and it is in support of life that rational value judgments can be made. If one were to make happiness the standard of morality, then whatever made one happy would be right. One's emotional whims would end up as the basis of action, and since whims vary from person to person, no rationality or objectivity could be found with them. Rand contends, therefore, that happiness should be seen as the *purpose* of ethics, but not the *standard.* "The task of ethics is to define man's proper code of values and thus to give him the means of achieving happiness."[78]

Defining her proper code of values as *rational selfishness,* Rand underscores the fact that this does not involve sacrificing others for one's own benefit. It is not in one's rational self-interest to injure, enslave, rob, or murder others. In fact, for her, rational interests do not clash: "There is no conflict of interests among men who do not desire the unearned, who do not make sacrifices nor accept them, who deal with one another as *traders,* giving value for value."[79]

According to Rand, **traders** are people who earn what they get and refuse to take the undeserved. Traders deal with each others as equals; there are no slaves and masters in a world of rational selfishness. Traders deal with others in terms of a free and uncoerced exchange. In this exchange, both parties benefit

**"The principle of trade is the only rational ethical principle for all human relationships, personal and social, private and public, spiritual and material. It is the principle of justice."**

AYN RAND

in their own independent judgment. Traders do not expect something for nothing, nor do they expect to be paid for their failures and defaults. Only achievement is to be rewarded. Furthermore, traders do not place the burden of their failures upon others; neither will they accept a life of bondage because of others' failures.

The notion of people as traders extends beyond impersonal business relationships. Love, friendship, and admiration, for instance, constitute a kind of "spiritual payment" one gives in exchange for the selfish pleasure one derives from the virtues and companionship of another. Traders do not seek love for their weaknesses, only for their strengths and virtues. Traders also do not give their love to others because of their flaws and weaknesses, but because of the virtuous gifts those others have to offer.

Finally, in her essay "The Objectivist Ethics," Rand makes the point that only on the basis of rational selfishness can we live together in a free, prosperous, and benevolent society. In a rational society of human beings, knowledge can be gained, stored, and traded from one individual to another or from one generation to another. Fair trade and cooperation "allows all men who take part in it to achieve a greater knowledge, skill and productive return than they could achieve if each had to produce everything he needs, as on a desert island or on a self-sustaining farm."[80] Rational selfishness is against initiating any form of physical force. It is only justified in self-defense as a retaliation against someone wishing to make one a victim. Rand puts this in the context of self-defense. If one kills in order to rob a victim, the holdup man seeks to gain value or wealth and to grow riches. If the targeted victim kills in self-defense, that person gains nothing from the holdup assassin. The underlying principle of rational selfishness is this: "No man may obtain any values from others by resorting to physical force."[81]

Regarding moral agents as free and equal traders prohibited from using physical force or violence allows Rand to couple her ethical theory quite easily with *laissez-faire* **capitalism.** In her estimation, the only moral purpose of government is to protect human rights—to protect people's lives, liberty, their property, and their right to pursue individual happiness. In all this, rights are highly significant, if not of paramount importance. As Rand says, "Without property rights, no other rights are possible."[82] In "The Objectivist Ethics," she does not spell out in any detail her sociopolitical theory of objectivism. As she points out, that is discussed in her novel *Atlas Shrugged.* What she does say in this essay is that every political system must be based on, and derived from, a theory of ethics, and that Objectivist ethics is that theory which best supports American capitalism—something that is continually under attack from varying sources. For readers who are interested in the history and the psychological causes of the philosopher's treason against capitalism, I recommend you read the title essay of Rand's book *For the New Intellectual.* Rather than discuss that work here, I invite you to read the following excerpt from it. But first, let's finish off with one of Rand's concluding statements in that work:

> It is philosophy that sets men's goals and determines their course;
> it is only philosophy that can save them now. Today, the world is
> facing a choice: if civilization is to survive, it is the altruistic moral-
> ity that men have to reject.[83]

## The Objectivist Ethics

### AYN RAND

Since I am to speak on the Objectivist Ethics, I shall begin by quoting its best representative—John Galt, in *Atlas Shrugged:*

"Through centuries of scourges and disasters, brought about by your code of morality, you have cried that your code had been broken, that the scourges were punishment for breaking it, that men were too weak and too selfish to spill all the blood it required. You damned man, you damned existence, you damned this earth, but never dared to question your code. . . . You went on crying that your code was noble, but human nature was not good enough to practice it. And no one rose to ask the question: Good?—by what standard?

"You wanted to know John Galt's identity. I am the man who has asked that question.

"Yes, this *is* an age of moral crisis. . . . Your moral code has reached its climax, the blind alley at the end of its course. And if you wish to go on living, what you now need is not to *return* to morality . . . but to *discover* it."

What is morality, or ethics? It is a code of values to guide man's choices and actions—the choices and actions that determine the purpose and the course of his life, Ethics, as a science, deals with discovering and defining such a code.

The first question that has to be answered, as a precondition of any attempt to define, to judge or to accept any specific system of ethics, is: *Why* does man need a code of values?

Let me stress this. The first question is not: What particular code of values should man accept? The first question is: Does man need values at all—and why?

Is the concept of *values,* "good or evil" an arbitrary human invention, unrelated to, underived from and unsupported by any facts of reality—or is it based on a *metaphysical* fact, on an unalterable condition of man's existence? (I use the word "metaphysical" to mean: that which pertains to reality, to the nature of things, to ex-

istence.) Does an arbitrary human convention, a mere custom, decree that man must guide his actions by a set of principles—or is there a fact of reality that demands it? Is ethics the province of *whims:* of personal emotions, social edicts and mystic revelations—or is it the province of *reason?* Is ethics a subjective luxury—or an *objective* necessity?

In the sorry record of the history of mankind's ethics—with a few rare, and unsuccessful, exceptions—moralists have regarded ethics as the province of whims, that is: of the irrational. Some of them did so explicitly, by intention—others implicitly, by default. A "whim" is a desire experienced by a person who does not know and does not care to discover its cause.

No philosopher has given a rational, objectively demonstrable, scientific answer to the question of *why man* needs a code of values. So long as that question remained unanswered, no rational, scientific, *objective* code of ethics could be discovered or defined. The greatest of all philosophers, Aristotle, did not regard ethics as an exact science; he based his ethical system on observations of what the noble and wise men of his time chose to do, leaving unanswered the questions of: *why* they chose to do it and *why* he evaluated them as noble and wise.

Most philosophers took the existence of ethics for granted, as the given, as a historical fact and were not concerned with discovering its metaphysical cause or objective validation. Many of them attempted to break the traditional monopoly of mysticism in the field of ethics and, allegedly, to define a rational, scientific, non-religious morality. But their attempts consisted of accepting the ethical doctrines of the mystics and of trying to justify them on *social* grounds, merely substituting *society* for *God.*

The avowed mystics held the arbitrary, unaccountable "will of God" as the standard of the good and as the validation of their ethics. The neomystics replaced it

Source: *The Virtue of Selfishness: A New Concept of Egoism,* New York: Signet 1963; New York: New American Library, 1964.

with "the good of society," thus collapsing into the circularity of a definition such as "the standard of the good is that which is good for society." This meant, in logic—and, today, in worldwide practice—that "society" stands above any principles of ethics, since *it* is the source, standard and criterion of ethics, since "the good" is whatever *it* wills, whatever *it* happens to assert as its own welfare and pleasure. This meant that "society" may do anything it pleases, since "the good" is whatever it chooses to do because it chooses to do it. And—since there is no such entity as "society," since society is only a number of individual men—this meant that *some* men (the majority or any gang that claims to be its spokesman) are ethically entitled to pursue any whims (or any atrocities) they desire to pursue, while *other* men are ethically obliged to spend their lives in the service of that gang's desires.

This could hardly be called rational, yet most philosophers have now decided to declare that reason has failed, that ethics is outside the power of reason, that no rational ethics can ever be defined, and that in the field of ethics—in the choice of his values, of his actions, of his pursuits, of his life's goals  man must be guided by something other than reason. By what? Faith—instinct—intuition—revelation—feeling—taste—urge—wish—*whim*. Today, as in the past, most philosophers agree that the ultimate standard of ethics is *whim* (they call it "arbitrary postulate" or "subjective choice" or "emotional commitment")—and the battle is only over the question of *whose* whim: one's own or society's or the dictator's or God's. Whatever else they may disagree about, today's moralists agree that ethics is a *subjective* issue and that the three things barred from its field are: reason—mind—reality.

If you wonder why the world is now collapsing to a lower and ever lower rung of hell, *this* is the reason.

If you want to save civilization, it is *this* premise of modern ethics—and of all ethical history—that you must challenge.

To challenge the basic premise of any discipline, one must begin at the beginning. In ethics, one must begin by asking: What are *values*? Why does man need them?

"Value" is that which one acts to gain and/or keep. The concept "value" is not a primary; it presupposes an answer to the question: of value to *whom* and for *what*? It presupposes an entity capable of acting to achieve a goal in the face of an alternative. Where no alternative exists, no goals and no values are possible?

I quote from Galt's speech: "There is only one fundamental alternative in the universe: existence or non-existence—and it pertains to a single class of entities: to living organisms. The existence of inanimate matter is unconditional, the existence of life is not: it depends on a specific course of action. Matter is indestructible, it changes its forms, but it cannot cease to exist. It is only a living organism that faces a constant alternative: the issue of life or death. Life is a process of self-sustaining and self-generated action. If an organism fails in that action, it dies; its chemical elements remain, but its life goes out of existence. It is only the concept of 'Life' that makes the concept of 'Value' possible. It is only to a living entity that things can be good or evil."

To make this point fully clear, try to imagine an immortal, indestructible robot, an entity which moves and acts, but which cannot be affected by anything, which cannot be changed in any respect, which cannot be damaged, injured or destroyed. Such an entity would not be able to have any values; it would have nothing to gain or to lose; it could not regard anything as *for* or *against* it, as serving or threatening its welfare, as fulfilling or frustrating its interests. It could have no interests and no goals.

Only a *living* entity can have goals or can originate them. And it is only a living organism that has the capacity for self-generated, goal-directed action. On the *physical* level, the functions of all living organisms, from the simplest to the most complex—from the nutritive function in the single cell of an amoeba to the blood circulation in the body of a man—are actions generated by the organism itself and directed to a single goal: the maintenance of the organism's *life*.

An organism's life depends on two factors: the material or fuel which it needs from the outside, from its physical background, and the action of its own body, the action of using that fuel *properly*. What standard determines what is *proper* in this context? The standard is the organism's life, or: that which is required for the organism's survival.

No choice is open to an organism in this issue: that which is required for its survival is determined by its *nature*, by the kind of entity it *is*. Many variations, many forms of adaptation to its background are possible to an organism, including the possibility of existing for a while in a crippled, disabled or diseased condition, but the fundamental alternative of its existence remains the same: if an organism fails in the basic functions required by its nature—if an amoeba's protoplasm stops assimilating food, or if a man's heart stops beating—the organism dies. In a fundamental sense, stillness is the antithesis of life. Life can be kept in existence only by a constant process of self-sustaining action. The goal of that action, the ultimate *value* which, to be kept, must be gained through its every moment, is the organism's *life*.

An *ultimate* value is that final goal or end to which all lesser goals are the means—and it sets the standard by which all lesser goals are *evaluated*. An organism's life is its *standard of value:* that which furthers its life is the *good,* that which threatens it is the *evil.*

Without an ultimate goal or end, there can be no lesser goals or means: a series of means going off into an infinite progression toward a nonexistent end is a metaphysical and epistemological impossibility. It is only an ultimate goal, an *end in itself,* that makes the existence of values possible. Metaphysicially, *life* is the only phenomenon that is an end in itself: a value gained and kept by a constant process of action. Epistemologically, the concept of "value" is genetically dependent upon and derived from the antecedent concept of "life." To speak of "value" as apart from "life" is worse than a contradiction in terms. "It is only the concept of 'Life' that makes the concept of 'Value' possible."

In answer to those philosophers who claim that no relation can be established between ultimate ends or values and the facts of reality, let me stress that the fact that living entities exist and function necessitates the existence of values and of an ultimate value which for any given living entity is its own life. Thus the validation of value judgments is to be achieved by reference to the facts of reality. The fact that a living entity *is,* determines what it *ought* to do. So much for the issue of the relation between "*is*" and "*ought*."

## DISCUSSION QUESTIONS FOR CRITIQUE AND ANALYSIS

1. What is Ayn Rand's foundation for ethics? Is it reasonable and justified? Why?

2. Is Rand guilty of bad reasoning by committing the is-ought fallacy? Why or why not? What would Rand argue?

## PHILOSOPHICAL SEGUE

### Religion and Ethics: Islamic, Hindu, and Christian Perspectives

For many people in the world today, ethical questions pertain not only to matters of character, duty, fairness, or the protection and preservation of a well-ordered society, but also to considerations of the divine, an afterlife, or one's position within the cosmological order of things. For the religious, ethical conduct and decision making are not always seen purely in terms of rational considerations; nor are they necessarily viewed exclusively in terms of hedonic, utilitarian outcomes. The fact is that for many individuals, morality and religion are often conceived as tightly interwoven, with one sewn right into the fabric of the other. Take the Christian moralist, for example; not only is murder morally wrong for that person, but the moral prohibition against taking innocent human life is sanctioned by God. God's will, as revealed by the Ten Commandments, proscribes murder by stating, "Thou shalt not kill." In this case, Divinity provides the ultimate foundation for the Christian's system of ethical conduct. In the section that follows, we will begin to better appreciate the links between religion and morality by briefly examining Eastern, Middle Eastern, and Western perspectives. In each case, we'll start with a brief introduction and then move on to a reading pertinent to the ethical perspective under consideration.

## ISLAMIC ETHICS

Islam is one of the youngest of the world's major religions, belonging to a family of monotheistic faiths including Judaism and Christianity. Followers of Islam, called Muslims, can be found in the Middle East, Africa, and Asia. In addition, substantial increases in Muslim populations have been recorded during the last quarter-century in the Americas, Europe, and Australia. In view of this proliferation, it's somewhat amazing to think how little about Islam is actually known in the West, especially given that it is one of the fastest growing religions, boasting of one billion adherents, or one-sixth of the world's population. Indeed, you might be surprised to learn that three to four million Muslims now make the United States their home—a number slightly higher than the current Jewish population. A study of American culture reveals that Islam has certainly had an impact on the lives of Americans in all walks of life, be they social activists, rappers, politicians, artists, athletes, academics, or just plain folk.

Islam began as a religion over 1400 years ago when a man named Muhammad, sitting in a cave just outside of Mecca, was struck by a brilliant flash of light and commanded by God (whom Muslims refer to as Allah) to "Read." This became the first word of a twenty-three-year revelation received from the divine Creator, but largely delivered by the archangel Gabriel. Other sources of inspiration were dreams, instantaneous heart-felt revelations, and a kind of inner-voice dictation. Muhammad's initial instruction from Allah to "read" is the source from which we get the name of the Qur'an. Qur'an literally means the "reading" or "recital." Because he was, in fact, illiterate, the Qur'an was given orally to Muhammad, who would then ask other people to write down the verses he dictated to them. In the end, the Qur'an became an inspired holy book consisting of 114 chapters called *Surahs,* covering a wide variety of moral, spiritual, and social topics. Muslims believe that the ultimate arrangement of all the chapters and verses of the Qur'an came under the direction of the archangel Gabriel.

From the vantage point of the practicing Muslim, morality is ultimately dependent on Allah—the absolute sovereign. The supreme good is considered to be faith in the one God and submission to Him. *Islam* actually means "submission" in Arabic. By showing obedience to Allah and by possessing faith in the truth of the Qur'an, Muslims discover not only a religion, but also a way of life or philosophy of living that can be referred to on a daily basis. Islam provides answers to existential, moral, and metaphysical questions like: Why are we here?" "Who is God?" "What sort of life should a person lead?" "What happens to us after we die?" In its answers to these questions, Islam provides a program for opening the heart, developing the mind, and cultivating spiritual strength. For devotees to Islam, a daily regimen of prayer, supplication (humble petition), and good works constitute a strong commitment to faith and help Muslims live in harmony with others and the world around them.

The moral norms and assumptions characterizing Islamic belief and action find their inspiration in two foundational sources. Not too surprisingly, the first one is scriptural—embodying the message revealed by Allah to the Prophet Muhammad. The second source of inspiration is the exemplification of the Qur'an's message in the model of the Prophet's words and deeds. This recorded testament of Muhammed's life is called the *Sunnah*. One writer says: "Muslims regard the Quran [sic] as the ultimate closure in a series of revelations to humankind from God, and the *Sunnah* as the historical projection of a divinely inspired and guided human life in the person of the Prophet Muhammad, who is also believed to be the last in a series of Messengers from God [following Moses and Jesus]."[84] In the same way, then, that Jesus became the moral model for Christians, so too Muhammad became the model for hundreds of millions of Muslims throughout the world.

In addition to the similarities regarding moral modeling, Islam resembles Christianity in still another way. Just as we find different sects or denominations with Christianity (see the section on Christian ethics in this *Segue* feature on Religion and Ethics), so too do we find divisions within the Islamic community. The Sunnis comprise approximately 85 percent of the world's Muslim population, while the Shi'as make up most of the rest. A Sunni follows the tradition and example of the Prophet and his companions. For a Sunni, any righteous Muslim can be elected to the position of *Caliph*, or chief civil and religious ruler. Shi'as contend, however, that there is no need for elections, since birthright provides enough legitimacy to rule. For Shi'as, only a descendent of the Prophet Muhammad has the right to assume religious authority.

Within the Islamic tradition, we also find *Sufis*, possibly the most well-known Muslims in the Western world. Sufis, or those belonging to Sufiism, do not actually constitute a separate sect or division, *per se*. There are Sunni and Shi'a Sufis who all place a very esoteric, spiritual emphasis on the practice of Islam. They make efforts to experience faith at a deep heartfelt level in order to achieve a state of inner ecstacy. Concerned about Islam's digression from the Prophet's example of frugality and self-denial and worried about Islam's movement toward opulence and pageantry, the Sufis began to renounce the world and to live simple lives. In fact, the name "Sufi" is derived from the Arabic word for wool, the preferred cloth for these humble believers who shunned silk and other fineries. As well as following the Qur'an and the *Hadiths* (those sayings, actions, or things to which Muhammad gave silent approval and which formed the basis of the Sunnah), members of Sufiism also place great value on the teachings of their great Sufi masters. These teachings consist of poems and wisdom stories possessing important hidden meanings. Sufi practices for achieving enlightenment include chanting in praise of Allah, fasting and meditation in remote natural places, prolonged prayer at night, and pilgrimages to the shrines of past Sufi masters known as saints. One Sufi master, Jalaluddin Rumi, has become a famed Sufi poet appreciated today by Sufis and non-Sufis alike. Here's a sample of his efforts to bring ecstasy and joy into the experience of faith: "What God said to the rose and caused it to laugh in full-blown beauty, He said to my heart and made it a hundred times more beautiful"(*The Mathnawi*, Vol. 111, Couplet 4129).

So much more needs to be said about Islam in order to fully understand and appreciate its ethical underpinnings, but unfortunately, practical time and space limitations will not allow for a fuller treatment of this important world religion here. What we can do, however, is read the following short excerpt from Riffat Hassan's article "Islamic View of Human Rights." Hassan is a feminist Muslim thinker born in Pakistan, educated in England, and now working at the University of Louisville in the United States. The goal in her article is to distinguish between the actual Islamic code of ethics embodied by the Qur'an and the prevalent stereotypes and distortions of Islamic belief held by many and perpetuated sometimes by the media. While some of her interpretations of Islamic teachings may not be accepted by all followers of the faith, she backs up her claims with references to holy scripture.

## ORIGINAL SOURCEWORK

*Islamic View of Human Rights*

**RIFFAT HASSAN**

It is profoundly ironic that stereotypes identify Islam with war and militancy, whereas the very term *islām* is derived from a root, one of whose basic meanings is "peace." Not only is the idea of peace of pivotal significance in the theological worldview of Islam, it also permeates the daily lives of Muslims. Each time two Muslims greet each other, they say *salam alaikum*, "peace be on you," and *alaikum assalum*, "peace be on you (too)." The regularity and fervor with which this greeting is exchanged shows that it is not a mechanical reiteration of words that have little or no meaning but a religious ritual of great importance. The ideal of being at peace with oneself, one's fellow human beings, the world of nature, and God, is deeply cherished by Muslims in general. But if that is the case, why is there such manifest lack of peace, and so much talk of violence, in the present-day world of Islam? In order to answer this question it is necessary to understand what "peace" means according to the perspective of "normative" Islam.

Many, including some who are committed to the ideal of peacemaking, tend, unfortunately, to define peace negatively, as "absence of war" (just as some tend to define "health" as "absence of sickness"). But, in quranic terms, peace is much more than mere absence of war. It is a positive state of safety or security in which one is free from anxiety or fear. It is this state that characterizes both *islām*, self-surrender to God, and *imān* true faith in God, and reference is made to it, directly or in-

directly, on every page of the Qur'an through the many derivatives of the roots "s-l-m" and "a-m-n" from which *islām* and *imān* are derived, respectively. Peace is an integral part not only of the terms used for a believer, "muslim" (i.e., one who professes *islām*) and *mo'min* (i.e, one who possesses *imān*), but also of God's names *As-Salām* and *Al-Mo'min* mentioned in the Qur'an:

> He is Allāh, beside whom there is no God; the King, the Holy, the Author of Peace [As-Salām], the Granter of Security [Al-Mo'min], Guardian over all, the Mighty, the Supreme, the Possessor of greatness [Surah 59.23].

As pointed out by G. A. Parwez, *As-Salām* is the Being who is the source of peace and concord and who assures peaceful existence to all beings. *Al-Mo'min* is the Being who shelters and protects all and bestows peace in every sphere of life.

That God "invites" humanity to *dār as-salām* (i.e., the abode of peace) is stated by the Qur'an (Surah 10.25), which also promises the reward of peace to those who live in accordance with God's will:

> God guides such as follow His pleasure into the ways of peace, and brings them out of darkness into light by His will, and guides them to the right path [Surah 5.16]

---

Gail M. Presbey, Kursten J. Struhl and Richard E. Olsen, *The Philosophical Quest: A Cross-Cultural Reader*, Boston: McGraw-Hill Higher Education, 1995, pp. 417–419.

In other words, peace on earth (which is a precondition of peace in heaven) is the result of living in accordance with God's will and pleasure. Here it is important to note that Islam conceives of God as *Rabb Al-'Alamīn:* Creator and Sustainer of all the peoples and universes, whose purpose in creating (as stated in Surah 51.56) is that all creatures should engage in God's *'ibādat*. This term, which is commonly understood as "worship," in fact has a much broader meaning and refers to "doing what God approves." In Islam "doing what God approves" is not conceived in terms of seeking salvation from the burden of original sin through belief in redemption or a redeemer (none of these ideas/concepts being present in the Qur'ān) or through renunciation of the world (monasticism not being required by God, according to the Qur'ān). Rather, it is conceived in terms of the fulfillment of *Haquq Allāh* (rights of God) and *Haquq al-'ibād* (rights of God's servants—namely, human beings). The Qur'ān considers the two kinds of "rights" to be inseparable as indicated by the constant conjunction of *salāt* (signifying remembrance of, and devotion to, God) and *zakāt* (signifying the sharing of one's possessions with those in need). In fact, as Surah 107 shows, the Qur'ān is severe in its criticism of those who offer their prayers to God but are deficient in performing acts of kindness to those in need:

Hast thou ever considered [the kind of person] who
　　gives the lie to all moral law?
Behold, it is this [kind of person] who thrusts the orphan
　　away,
and feels no urge to feed the needy.
Woe, then, unto those praying ones whose hearts from
　　their prayers are remote—

those who want only to be seen and praised,
and, withal, deny all assistance [to their fellows].

In quranic terms, then, peace is obtained in any human society when human beings, conscious of their duty to God, fulfill their duty to other human beings. In fulfilling this duty they honor what I call the "human rights" of others. These rights are those that all human beings *ought* to possess because they are rooted so deeply in our humanness that their denial or violation is tantamount to negation or degradation of that which makes us human. These rights came into existence when we did; they were created, as we were, by God in order that our human potential could be actualized. These rights not only provide us with an opportunity to develop all our inner resources, but they also hold before us a vision of what God would like us to be: what God wants us to strive for and live for and die for. Rights given by God are rights that ought to be exercised, because everything that God does is for "a just purpose" (Surah 15.85; 16.3; 44.39; 45.22; 46.3). Among these rights, there are some that have an important, perhaps even a crucial, bearing on whether or not a society can realize the ideal of peace: hence a brief account of them follows.

## DISCUSSION QUESTIONS FOR CRITIQUE AND ANALYSIS

1. What is the author's intention in this reading?

2. To which ethical perspective is Islamic morality most closely related: utilitarianism, ethical egoism, existentialism, natural law theory or Greek virtue ethics? Explain.

# HINDU ETHICS

Hinduism is one of the world's major religions, reflecting the beliefs and values of an estimated 700 million people. Originating in India sometime around 1500 B.C.E., it continues to be the dominant religious influence for most of that country's inhabitants today. Because of Indian migration patterns in the past, a significant Hindu presence can also be felt in East and South Africa, Southeast Asia, the East Indies, and England.

A simple and uncomplicated description of Hinduism is very difficult owing to its rich diversity and ancient roots. Not only has Hinduism influenced many other religious traditions during its lengthy, unbroken history, but it too has tended to assimilate elements from other traditions that cannot always be easily integrated and, at times, may even be irreconcilable. In fact, it's been suggested that Hinduism is not something unitary or monolithic, but merely a convenient Western term for the many diverse ideas and practices found in India. As one commentator put it: "There is no single Hindu religion or Hindu philosophy, but rather a variety of ways of understanding and relating to the world that are blended from a stock of widely held ideas, some more ancient than others."[85] The interesting diversity within Hinduism is perhaps best captured by a study of its major sacred texts, which include the *Vedas,* the *Upanishads,* the *Bhagavad-Gita,* and the *Vedanta.* The contemporary Hindu commentator S. Abhayananda tries to help Westerners understand these texts better by classifying the *Vedas* as something akin to the "Old Testament," while referring to the *Upanishads* and the *Bhagavad-Gita* as the "New Testament." As for the *Vedanta,* what it means is "the end of the *Veda.*" The *Vedanta* was originally intended to signify the collection of writings called the *Upanishads,* which were written nearly three thousand years ago by some anonymous Indian sages and appended to earlier *Vedas* as their final portion. Given that the word *Veda* means "knowledge" or "wisdom," the *Vedanta* is therefore regarded by many as the "end of knowledge" or "the ultimate wisdom." One should understand, however, that *Vedanta,* as used today, refers not only to the *Upanishads,* but also includes an entire corpus of writings that explains, elaborates, and makes commentary on the Upanishadic teachings from their conception to the present. The *Vedanta* is equivalent to what is sometimes called "the perennial philosophy," that universal knowledge of unity possessed by all the mystics and sages throughout history. It is the final philosophy discovered time and again by seekers of Truth in every age.[86]

Notwithstanding that the *Vedanta* represents some sort of culmination of Hindu wisdom, the *Bhagavad-Gita* provides us arguably with the clearest and most direct treatment of the "ethics of duty"—something you may wish to revisit by reading the section on Immanuel Kant earlier in this chapter. The *Bhagavad-Gita* is the most translated book after the Bible, composed around the fourth century B.C.E. in India. Scholars have said that in order to appreciate the Hindu mind, one must understand the essence of the *Gita.* This little book contains philosophical, religious, and moral relevance. It first discusses human nature and the nature of the world, then it depicts human spirit, the cosmic form of God, and mystical experience. And, as mentioned, it also has moral relevance, providing us with a succinct system of duty ethics.[87] The *Gita,* in itself, is a relatively short poem that was originally passed down through time by oral tradition. Eventually, it found its way into a much larger Hindu epic poem called the *Mahabharata,* the longest in the world. In the *Gita,* we find a struggle between the forces of good and evil. Good is represented by the Pandavas and evil by the Kauravas. The Pandavas and Kauravas are related royal families torn apart by conflict due to a rivalry over choosing an heir-apparent to the throne.

As we read in the *Gita,* Arjunas arrives on the scene of an immanent battle, instructing his charioteer Krishna to bring their chariot between the two conflicting families. Arjuna is a member of the Pandavas family, while Krishna is actually an avatar, or incarnation of God, who advises Arjuna on the battlefield. Arjuna is caught on the horns of an ethical dilemma. On the one hand, he is moved by the sight of his friends and relatives. He has a personal duty to protect family and relatives from physical harm. On the other hand, he is a member of the warrior caste and therefore, it is his duty to safeguard the kingdom from internal and external dangers—in this case, the evil Kauravas. Arjuna becomes besieged by doubt and indecision as a result of this dilemma. He challenges the morality of war by raising the following questions: Why is he fighting this war? What will be gained? What is the goal of victory? Is killing moral? And is war ever justified?

In response to Arjuna's moral indecision, Krishna offers a number of arguments to explain to Arjuna how he is justified in going to war. Arjuna is not convinced by Krishna's logic, so when reasoning doesn't work, Krishna reveals himself to be God, who is creator of the universe and all human beings. He tells Arjuna that his assigned task on this earth is to eradicate the evil represented by the Kaurava brothers. In the end, Arjuna is ready to fight the war as directed by Krishna. Arjuna learns that as long as wars are not fought for personal gain or power, but for a justifiable cause, the mind will not be clouded, allowing the soul to find peace. Krishna teaches Arjuna that doing one's Godly ordained duty is the way to true spiritual happiness. Other pleasures pass and eventually end in despair. Arjuna needn't worry too much about killing others, for this involves extinguishing other empirical selves, which are limited and transitory anyway. The transcendental self that Krishna says makes all human beings identical cannot be hurt.

The dialogue between Krishna and Arjuna actually takes place over eighteen chapters wherein the complete religio-philosophical system of Hinduism is laid out. We limit ourselves here to the first chapter: Arjuna's Moral Dilemma. Later, in what is not included, Krishna informs Arjuna that there are two paths to salvation, depending on the kind of person one is. The wise take the path of knowledge, whereas the path of action is for "doers," as it were. Because nobody ever achieves perfection through inaction or renunciation, and because Arjuna is a man of action, he should fight the war.

Turn now to Malhotra's modernized *Transcreation of the Bhagavad-Gita*.[88] A reading of this text should give you some insight into the Hindu mind.

---

## ORIGINAL SOURCEWORK

*Transcreation of the Bhagavad Gita*

**A.K. MALHOTRA**

## ARJUNA'S MORAL DILEMMA PRINCIPAL CHARACTERS

**ARJUNA**   One of the Pandava princes. He is the great warrior who questions the reasons for fighting the war. His name means "silver white."

**BHIMA**   One of the Pandava princes and brother of Arjuna. His name means "enormous" or "dreadful."

---

Source: Ashok Kumar Malhotra, *Transcreation of the Bhagavad Gita*, Library of Liberal Arts, Prentice Hall, Upper Saddle River, NJ 07458, 1999, pp. x, 1–4.

| BHISHMA | He is the grand uncle of the Pandavas. He has reluctantly chosen to fight the war. His name means "fearsome" or "shocking." |
|---|---|
| DHRITARASHTRA | The blind king whose children (the Kauravas) and nephews (the Pandavas) have gathered together to fight the war. His name means "he who controls the kingdom." |
| DURYODHANA | Chief of the Kaurava princes. His name means "dirty fighter." |
| DRONA | The great teacher who taught both the Kauravas and the Pandavas the art of war. |
| KRISHNA | The god-incarnate. Also, Arjuna's charioteer, who offers a metaphysical discourse which constitutes the text of the *Bhagavad Gita*. |
| KAURAVAS | The 100 sons of the blind king Dhritarashtra. They represent the forces of evil. |
| PANDAVAS | The five Pandava brothers: Yudhisthira, Bhima, Arjuna, Nakula, and Sahdeva. They represent the forces of good. |
| SANJAYA | He is the minister of King Dhristarashtra. Sanjaya is given the divine sight by the sage Vyasa, through which he describes the battle to the blind king. |

## SUMMARY

The armies of Kauravas and Pandavas have assembled to fight a war. The blind king Dhritarashtra asks his minister, Sanjaya, to describe the battle and the dialogue between Arjuna, the Pandava warrior, and Krishna, the God incarnate, who is Arjuna's charioteer. Arjuna's chariot is brought between the two armies and he sees brothers, cousins, and relatives on both sides. He becomes unsure of fighting this war: to do his caste duty, he must fight his relatives; but to do his family duty, he must not kill them. He undergoes an ethical dilemma and refuses to fight.

## TEXT

*Dhritarashtra asked Sanjaya:*

Tell me about my children and Pandava's children, who have assembled in the field of righteousness to fight a battle.

*Sanjaya replied:*

After scrutinizing the army of the Pandavas, Duryodhana came closer to his teacher, Drona, and said:

"Behold the Pandavas' huge army arranged by the intelligent son of Drupada.

In *their* army there are great archers like Arjuna, Bhima, Yayudhana, Virata, and the mighty charioteer Drupada.

Dhrishtaketu, Cekitana, and the mighty king of Varanasi; Purujit, Kuntibhoja, and Saibya, who are the best among men.

The performer of great deeds, Yudhamanyu, the bold Uttamauja, Abhimanyu, and Draupadi's sons, are all great charioteers.

O Drona, great among the brahmins! Now I will tell you the names of *our* mighty soldiers and commanders.

Your revered self, Bhishma, Karna, the victorious Kripa, Ashvatthama, Vikarna, and the son of Somadatta.

Not only are they skilled in weaponry and in the art of warfare, but they are also ready to sacrifice their lives for me.

Bhishma is the defender of our limitless and undefeatable army, whereas Bhima is the defender of the limited and defeatable army of the Pandavas."

Then Duryodhana commanded his army, "All of you take your posts and cautiously safeguard our commander-in-chief Bhishma."

To make Duryodhana happy, Bhishma blew his mighty conch hard, like a lion's roar.

The conches, kettledrums, horns, and tabors resounded together producing a horrifying sound.

While sitting in their chariot with white horses, Krishna and Arjuna of the other army blew their godly conches.

Krishna blew *pancajanya* (acquired from a demon), Arjuna, *devadatta* (bestowed by the gods), and Bhima, *paundra* (powerful conch).

King Yudhisthira, the son of Kunti, blew *anantavijaya* (eternal victory), while Nukula and Sahdeva blew *sughosa* (sweet tone) and *manipuspaka* (jewel flower).

The skillful archer, the king of Varanasi, the mighty charioteer-fighter Shikhandin, Dhrishtadyumna, Virata, and the undefeatable Satyaki.

The King Drupada, Draupadi's five sons, and the strong-armed Abhimanyu, blew their conches one by one.

The thunderous sound of the conches shook the earth, the sky, and the confidence of Dhritarashtra's army.

*Sanjaya continued his explanation:*

Just when the battle was about to start and Dhritarashtra's children were ready to fight, Arjuna picked up his bow and turned to Krishna.

Arjuna said, "Bring my chariot in between the two armies!

I wish to see the ones who are desirous of this war.

I want to look at all of those who are supporting the misguided Duryodhana."

As directed by Arjuna, Krishna brought the shining chariot in the middle of the two armies.

Glancing directly toward Bhishma, Drona, and the powerful kings, Krishna said, "Arjuna, look at the Kauravas with your own eyes."

Arjuna saw his uncles, grandfathers, teachers, brothers, sons, grandsons, and friends in the two armies.

Seeing his fathers-in-laws, friends, and relatives assembled for war, Arjuna was overcome with great compassion and said to Krishna:

"On seeing my relatives who are desirous of fighting this war, my limbs have become numb, my throat has turned dry, my body is trembling, and my hair is standing on end.

My skin is burning, my mind is confused, I can't stand up straight, and the mighty bow is falling out of my sweaty hands.

I see unholy omens. This fight seems illogical and unnecessary. Nothing good will come out of killing my own relatives.

Glory, happiness, or victory are no use to me. I do not desire a kingdom, pleasures, or life.

Those who seek a kingdom, pleasures, and enjoyments are assembled here to fight a battle for which they have put their lives and property at stake.

There are teachers, fathers, sons, grandfathers, maternal uncles, fathers-in-laws, grandsons, brothers-in-laws, and other relatives all fighting against each other.

The kingdom of the earth and the *three worlds* is not worth killing them. I would rather let them take my life instead.

What is the benefit of killing the sons of Dhritarashtra? By slaughtering our ignoble kin, we can only accumulate sin.

For this reason, I shall not kill my relatives. It is below me to kill my kinsmen because there is no happiness in this kind of act.

Blinded by greed, these people do not see any sin in the destruction of their own clan or in the hatred of their friends.

Those of us who have the clarity of mind to discern right from wrong ought to stay away from the destruction of our family.

With the destruction of the family, the ancient traditions would perish, and when tradition is destroyed lawlessness will increase.

With the growth of lawlessness, the women of the family will be corrupted; and if they go astray, the caste system will get mixed up.

The mixing of castes sounds a death knell for all families because therein respect for the ancestors is lost.

Through their wrongdoings, the corrupters of the family would create caste confusion and thus both the caste duties and the traditional laws of the family would be destroyed.

O Krishna, it is common knowledge that when family tradition disappears, the relatives secure their place in hell.

I was ready to kill my own relatives and covet the kingdom, and through that, I was going to perform a terrible deed.

If the sons of Dhritarashtra, armed with weapons, kill me while I am unarmed and unresisting in the field of battle, I will happily find my salvation."

Overwhelmed by grief, Arjuna placed aside his bow and arrows and sat down in the chariot.

## DISCUSSION QUESTIONS FOR CRITIQUE AND ANALYSIS

1. What precisely is the moral dilemma that Arjuna faces? Explain in detail.

2. What advice would Jesus or Muhammad give Arjuna? Justify your position.

# CHRISTIAN ETHICS

Christianity is one of the world's major religions and is found in every continent of the globe, claiming an estimated total membership of 1.7 billion people. Understood as a tradition of belief, Christianity does not constitute a systematic philosophy like you find in Platonism or in Aristotle's thinking. In contrast to Platonism (discussed in Chapter 4) which starts off with a number of philosophical concepts and principles and then seeks by means of them to construct a comprehensive understanding of the universe, Christianity begins with certain significant revelatory historical events and, on that basis, draws conclusions concerning the ultimate nature and structure of reality. In the testimonies of the Biblical prophets and apostles, we do not find grand theoretical formulations of doctrine, nor abstract metaphysical speculations, but rather, descriptions of intense religious experience.

Given the magnitude and geographic breadth of Christianity, it is perhaps not surprising that different sects and denominations have arisen within it. There are really too many to mention individually here, but most Christians could be said to belong either to the Roman Catholic Church, the Eastern Orthodox Church, or one of the Protestant denominations, such as the Episcopalian Church or the Southern Baptist Convention. Notwithstanding all of their differences with respect to ritual, practice, and doctrinal emphasis, a number of core Christian beliefs can still be identified: the reality of God, the divine creation of the universe, the Holy Trinity, human sinfulness, divine incarnation in the person of Jesus, Christ's reconciliation of man to God through his death and resurrection, the founding of the Christian church, the continuing operation of the Spirit within it, the eventual end to human history, and the fulfillment of God's purpose for his creations.

These core beliefs and central teachings of the Christian church provide its adherents with moral guidance for the time that they live on this earth. Central to this guidance is the person of Jesus Christ. Christians are instructed that His example should be followed and that Christ's teachings about life and fellowship should serve as the basis of all human relations. The ethical message of Jesus is succinctly captured when he responds to the Pharisee who asks what is the greatest commandment in [Jewish/moral] law. Jesus replies: "You shall love the Lord your God with all your heart, and with all your soul, and with all your mind./ This is the great and foremost commandment./ And a second is like it, 'You shall love your neighbor as yourself.'/ On these two commandments depend the whole Law and the Prophets" (Matthew 22: 36–40). With respect to the second commandment, a variation of it is often referred to as the Golden Rule: "Do unto others as you would have others do unto you."

As simple and straightforward as Jesus's words might seem to you, real life experience reveals that application of these commandments does not produce a uniformity of moral, social, and political behavior. This can be easily illustrated, for example, by the fact that some Christians regard the drinking of alcoholic beverages as sinful, while others do not. Some churches may countenance divorce, whereas others will allow no other to "put asunder what God has joined together" in holy matrimony, only with very rare exceptions and under very extraordinary circumstances. Whatever the contemporary moral issue, Christians can be found

on the far right and on the far left, as well as in the middle. There are strict conservatives, moderates, and liberal interpreters of Christ's message. Some take the message of the Bible as literally true and historically accurate, while others regard the truth of the Bible as allegorical and interpretive in nature. Nonetheless, it is still reasonable to speak generally of a "Christian way of life" informed by the call to service and discipleship. Morally speaking, several basic commitments that all Christians would likely accept involve the following: the inherent worth of every person, who is created in the likeness of God; and the sanctity of life and the imperative to strive for justice in a fallen world. Living according to this ethic of love under conditions of existence continues to be difficult, however. Never has there been a "golden age" of universal agreement in which it was otherwise.

On this note, we find a convenient segue for drawing our attention to the article that follows. In it, Brian Berry appreciates the diversity of approach and emphasis within the Christian church. In fact, he observes that even within one major tradition, Roman Catholicism, there is a plurality of approaches to ethical thinking, which can potentially give rise to chaos and confusion. Berry contends that the future of Roman Catholic moral theology (that is, Christian ethics) lies in the dialogue that must occur among these existing approaches, each of which has its basis in the thought of St. Thomas Aquinas (see Chapter 4, where Aquinas is discussed). In the following article, Berry outlines these approaches and thereby gives us a better appreciation of Christian morality viewed from three contrasting Roman Catholic perspectives. As you read this article, compare it with what you've already learned about Immanuel Kant, Thomas Aquinas, and Plato. Get a sense of how philosophers of one epoch can influence the thinking and lives of those at a later time.[89]

## ORIGINAL SOURCEWORK

## *Roman Catholic Ethics: Three Approaches*

### BRIAN BERRY

One of the evident features of contemporary reflection on ethical issues by Roman Catholic theologians is its plurality. Moral theologians today write about a range of concrete moral issues, such as homosexuality, physician-assisted suicide, and affirmative action. They also specialize in a variety of subdisciplines within moral theology, including sexual ethics, bioethics, social ethics, and environmental ethics. But, most importantly, they approach their reflection from within a variety of moral systems or schools of ethical thought, which have different perspectives on what ethics is and how it should proceed. All of this leads to not only an overwhelming amount of data, but a confusing cacophony of diverse moral positions within the one the community of faith. Some even suggest that it has left the discipline of moral theology in a state of "disarray."

This article attempts to bring some order to the seeming chaos that exists in Roman Catholic moral theology today. I suggest that developments in the discipline since the Second Vatican Council can be grouped under three main approaches to ethical reflection, what I describe as deontology, revisionism, and virtue ethics.

Brian Berry, "Roman Catholic Ethics: Three Approaches," in Catholic Practice, the E-Magazine of Pastoralink. www.liguori.org/pastoralink.htm

Each of these approaches has distinct views about what ought to be the subject matter of ethics and its method of moral deliberation. In what follows, I will outline the main features of these three approaches using the thought of representative theologians, showing how their theories shape the position they take on the issue of abortion, a complex moral problem that is of special concern to the Roman Catholic community.

## DEONTOLOGY

One of the main approaches to Roman Catholic moral theology since Vatican II is "deontology." This approach places strong emphasis on human actions. It seeks to evaluate human behavior by asking, "What is my duty?" and appeals to moral laws, norms, principles, and rules that are then applied to particular situations. According to deontological ethics, a behavior is moral if the act in itself is right and it is done with the right motive or intention. The consequences of the act are irrelevant for evaluating its moral status.

A key representative of the deontological approach to Roman Catholic ethics is Germain Grisez. Taking the formal principle "do good and avoid evil" as his starting point, Grisez argues that knowledge of the good is "self-evident" to human beings. By this he means that human beings, on the basis of their experience of desiring those things towards which all persons are naturally inclined, can know that certain human goods are "basic" or desirable in and of themselves. Grisez identifies eight such basic human goods: life, play, aesthetic experience, speculative knowledge, integrity, practical reasonableness, friendship, and religion. No one of these is more important than any other, and the ideal of integral human fulfillment means the enjoyment of all eight of these basic goods.

How are individual actions to be evaluated from a deontological perspective? Grisez argues that a human action is moral only if it is aimed in some way at securing one or more of the basic human goods. We cannot aim at all eight of the basic goods at all times, but we must act in a way which remains open to those basic goods that we do not actively pursue in any given action. A behavior which aims at one basic good, while arbitrarily slighting another, is immoral to the extent that it turns from a basic good without adequate reason.

This last point is especially important for Grisez. He interprets it to mean that some kinds of actions are never morally permissible. In other words, certain human behaviors are "intrinsically evil," that is, always and everywhere wrong, regardless of the circumstances. Specifically, he insists that any kind of action that involves a direct attack on a basic human good, for example, direct homicide, deliberate contraception, or lying, can never be morally justified.

What are the implications of this interpretation for evaluating the morality of abortion?

Grisez insists that direct abortion is always wrong, since it involves a direct attack on the basic good of human life. However, under certain circumstances, indirect abortion can be morally justified. An abortion is indirect if a good effect is intended, for example, saving the life of the mother, and the bad effect, namely, the killing of the fetus, is not. Classic cases of indirect abortion are those performed in cases of an ectopic pregnancy or cancerous uterus, providing these are done before late second trimester. These are referred to as indirect abortions because the intention is not to kill the innocent life of the fetus, but to remove the pathological condition that will otherwise kill both the mother and the fetus.

While the deontological approach to ethics has traditionally been more typical of Protestant theologians, it exercised a considerable influence on Roman Catholic ethics in the twentieth century, particularly before the Second Vatican Council. The deontological approach of Grisez in particular has also shaped the moral teaching of Pope John Paul II, especially his recent encyclical, Veritatis Splendor.

## REVISIONISM

A second main approach to Roman Catholic ethics since the Council is "revisionism" or "proportionalism." Like deontology, this approach places great emphasis on human actions. However, it seeks to evaluate human behavior not deontologically but teleologically by asking "What is my goal?" Viewing the ultimate goal or end of human life as union with God, it then tries to determine which actions are most conducive to achieving the values and goods that will lead to this ultimate end.

Revisionism, while working within the above framework, has a deeper appreciation of the range of goods and evils that might result from a given action than more traditional teleological approaches tended to acknowledge. Like the deontological approach, it considers the act in itself as well as the intention, but it also takes account of the likely consequences of an action on the human relationships that are involved. It then asks, "Which alternative course of action would not intend wrong and would result in a proportionately greater amount of good over evil?"

A major figure representing the revisionist approach to Roman Catholic ethics is Richard McCormick. McCormick accepts much of Grisez's analysis of basic human goods, and agrees that an action that aims at one basic good, while arbitrarily slighting another without adequate reason, is immoral. Where he differs from Grisez, however, are in his claims that there are no "intrinsically evil" acts, and that directly turning against a basic human good is not always morally wrong. McCormick insists that a direct attack on a basic human good is only a "premoral"—rather than a moral—evil if there is a proportionate reason for doing the act. "Premoral" evil here refers to the inconvenience, limitations, and harm that are inevitably a part of all human efforts to do good, since human beings are historical, social and live in a sinful world.

When is there a proportionate reason for doing an action that contains premoral evil? McCormick explains that a "proportionate reason" exists when (a) there is a value at stake at least equal to the value being sacrificed; (b) there is no less harmful way of protecting the value at present; and (c) the manner of protecting it under the circumstances will not actually undermine it. Admittedly, determining whether such conditions exist is a difficult one. It means weighing the likely consequences of an action, but also asking if it would be good if everyone in similar circumstances did this, asking whether one is operating out of cultural bias, paying attention to the wisdom of past experience embodied in moral norms, consulting broadly to avoid personal bias, and allowing the full force of one's religious beliefs to be brought to bear on one's judgment. A correct judgment that a proportionate reason exists would mean that the good intended by a given action outweighs the evil results, and that forming the act would be morally permissible.

What are the implications of this approach for evaluating the morality of abortion?

In a lecture he gave nearly ten years ago, entitled "Abortion: A Middle Ground," McCormick argued that, while there is a moral presumption against abortion since it involves the killing of human life, abortion to save the life of the mother is morally acceptable. By this he would have meant not only that indirect abortions are permissible, such as in cases of an ectopic pregnancy or cancerous uterus, but that direct abortions are sometimes morally justified. In other of his writings, he has suggested that a proportionate reason for abortion may exist in the case of a mother whose life is threatened by pregnancy because she has a bad heart, or in the case of anencephalic fetus.

# VIRTUE ETHICS

A third major approach to Roman Catholic ethics since the Council is "virtue ethics." Unlike deontology and revisionism, this approach does not focus on human actions, but on being a certain kind of person. In fact, virtue ethics criticizes deontology and revisionism for focusing on actions and neglecting the importance of moral character. It argues that morality is as much about who we are as about what we do. Who we are extends into what we do and do not do, and what we do and do not do shapes the kind of persons we become.

At the same time, virtue ethics is similar to revisionism inasmuch as it seeks to evaluate moral character teleologically by asking, "What is my goal?" Viewing the ultimate goal or end of human life as union with God, it attempts to determine which virtues ought to be cultivated, both by individuals and communities, to achieve this ultimate end. "Virtues" refer to habits or practiced patterns of doing good and living life well, as opposed to "vices" or habits of doing evil and living life badly. Virtues traditionally have been "theological," such as faith, hope, and love, as well as "moral," such as prudence, justice, temperance, and fortitude.

A major representative of the "virtue ethics" approach in Roman Catholicism today is James Keenan. Keenan argues that the focus of ethics should not be on acts, but on who we are, who we are to become, and how we are to get there. The specific tasks of virtue ethics are to help us understand ourselves as the people we are, to set goals for the type of people we ought to become, and to suggest what are the significant steps we should take to achieve these ends. In other words, for Keenan, the virtues inform us both about who we are to be and about what we are to do. And like revisionism, Keenan sees human relationships as the context within which the moral life is practiced and evaluated.

What implications does this approach have for evaluating the morality of abortion?

Rather than examining the question of whether abortion is ever morally licit, Keenan criticizes aspects of American culture that have led to us having the most liberal abortion policy in the developed world. Rather than pitting the rights of the woman against those of the fetus, and leaving the woman to make her own private decision, Keenan advocates that we rediscover a concern for the common good, address ourselves to why so many pregnancies in our society are unwanted, and ask how we are the way we are and how can we become better. At present, we seem incapable as a society of making ourselves into the kind of people we would or could want to become in our relationships with the unborn.

In this article, I have outlined three main approaches to ethics that typify the thought of Roman Catholic moral theologians writing today. The moral systems of deontology and revisionism are primarily interested in the moral evaluation of particular human actions, the deontologists arguing that only indirect attacks on a basic human good may be justified, the revisionists insisting that even direct attacks may be permissible if there is a proportionate reason. Virtue ethics, however, is more interested in the moral character of persons, inviting us to focus on the good habits we need to cultivate if we are to live a genuinely moral life.

The future of Roman Catholic moral theology, it seems to me, lies in the dialogue between these three existing approaches, each of which have their basis in the thought of Thomas Aquinas. Deontology and revisionism have some specific moral guidance to offer those concerned with such "big-life" moral dilemmas as whether or not to have or provide an abortion, and do so with varying degrees of appreciation of the regrettable and often tragic dimension of much of human existence. At the same time, virtue ethics gives much needed attention to the commonplace, to such things as bettering one's relationships, doing one's job better, taking better care of one's health, and becoming more conscious of one's neighbor, all with a view to helping people become the best persons they can be.

## DISCUSSION QUESTIONS FOR CRITIQUE AND ANALYSIS

1. Would Immanuel Kant agree completely with the deontological approach to Roman Catholic moral theology? Why?

2. What are the similarities and differences between Christian virtue ethics and Plato's moral philosophy?

3. Which approach to Christian (Catholic) moral theology is most adequate? Why?

# STUDY GUIDE

## KEY TERMS   (Listed in order of occurrence for each ethical perspective)

### Character Ethics

teleology  282
soul  283
appetite  283
desire  283
spirit  283
passion  283
reason  283

functional explanation of morality  283
moral balance  283
moral virtue  284
appearance  284
reality  284
character types  288
aristocracy  292

philosopher king  292
guardian class  292
realm of forms  292
timarchic character  293
oligarchic character  294
democratic character  295
tyrannical character  296

### Utilitarian Ethics

utilitarianism  297
scientific objectivity  297
consequentialism  298

principle of utility  298
psychological egoism  298
ethical egoism  299

is-ought fallacy  299
sanctions  300
hedonic calculus  301

## Deontological Ethics

deontological ethics   **308**
ethical relativist   **308**
moral certainty   **309**
*a priori*   **309**
the good will   **310**
duty   **310**
maxim   **311**

prudence   **311**
inclination   **312**
duties to others   **313**
duties to ourselves   **313**
the categorical imperative   **314**
categorical and hypothetical
     imperatives   **316**

technical imperatives   **317**
prudential imperatives   **317**
autonomy   **317**
heteronomy of the will   **317**
realm of ends   **317**

## Feminine Ethics

psychological bias   **320**
ethical bias   **320**
feminine ethics   **320**
moral reasoning
     development   **320**

hypothetical moral
     dilemmas   **323**
morality of care   **324**
identity formation   **324**
intimacy   **325**
separation   **325**

masculine ethics   **327**
universalizability   **328**
relation   **329**
one caring   **329**
one cared for   **329**
natural caring   **330**

## Existentialist Ethics

Judeo-Christian tradition   **336**
will to power   **338**
self-overcoming   **338**
self-mastery   **338**
master morality   **339**
slave morality   **339**
nobles   **340**

psychological honesty   **341**
reaction   **341**
negation   **341**
resentment   **341**
traditional/customary/herd
     morality   **342**
autonomy   **343**

nihilism   **344**
*Übermensch*/superman/
     overman   **345**
Apollo   **345**
Dionysus   **345**
aesthetic phenomenon   **345**

## Ethical Egoism

ethical egoism   **347**
objectivist ethics   **347**
rational selfishness   **347**
collectivist thinking   **347**
ethic of altruism   **347**
selfishness   **347**
beneficiary   **348**
human nature   **349**
society   **349**

personal whim   **350**
mysticism   **350**
neomysticism   **350**
emotionalism   **350**
subjective preference   **350**
life   **350**
nature   **350**
value   **351**
virtue   **351**

reason   **351**
purpose   **351**
self-esteem   **351**
rationality   **351**
productivity   **351**
pride   **351**
traders   **352**
*laissez-faire* capitalism   **353**

## PROGRESS CHECK

**Instructions:** Fill in the blanks with the appropriate responses listed below.

philosopher kings/rulers
utility
is-ought
relation
God
maxims

teleology
care
destructive
objectivist ethics
categorical imperative
character

rationality
ethical bias
superman/*übermensch*
sanction
hypothetical
similar

will to power
rational
postconventional
revaluation

traders
soul
democratic characters
ethical egoism

slave morality
nature
good will
hedonic calculus

1. According to the doctrine of _____, everything in the universe has a proper function to perform within a harmonious hierarchy of purposes.
2. For Plato, the _____ is comprised of appetite, spirit and reason.
3. The timarchic, oligarchic, democratic, and tyrannical are all corrupt _____ types.
4. The _____ should govern society since they are not corrupted by greed and vanity.
5. _____ are flexible and versatile, but suffer because they lack stable principles by which to govern their lives.
6. The concept of _____ serves as the basis of Bentham's moral theory.
7. For Bentham, _____ has placed humankind under the control of two sovereign masters —pain and pleasure.
8. A _____ is a source of pleasure or pain that serves to give binding force to any law or rule of conduct.
9. From the utilitarian perspective, moral decisions can be made in a spirit of scientific objectivity using the _____.
10. One commits the _____ fallacy when one concludes that we should do something because of the fact that it's simply the way things are.
11. According to Immanuel Kant, morality must have a _____ basis.
12. For Kant, the only thing which is unconditionally good is the _____.
13. From the vantage point of deontological ethics, our moral duties are based on _____ of behavior which can be prescribed universally.
14. The _____ states that we should never use people solely as a means to an end, but always respect them as ends in themselves.
15. _____ imperatives are not moral because they have conditions attached.
16. According to feminist thinkers such as Gilligan and Noddings, there has been gender-based _____ in

moral thinking throughout the ages and in contemporary moral development research.
17. According to Lawrence Kohlberg, the highest form of moral reasoning development is captured by _____ thinking, which is characterized by it impartial, detached, and rational features.
18. Carol Gilligan contends that women interpret morality more from the perspective of _____, whereas men are more likely to view moral situations from the vantage point of impersonal justice.
19. Nel Noddings believes that a male-dominated field of philosophical inquiry has tended to romanticize _____, failing at the same time to recognize its dangers and limitations.
20. Two situations are seldom, if ever sufficiently _____ in morally relevant respects to allow for proper blanket application of impersonal, abstract principles.
21. For Noddings, human _____ is ontologically basic, not the isolated individual or Cartesian *Cogito* (the I Think).
22. It was Nietzsche who declared that "_____ is dead."
23. According to Nietzsche, morality should not be based on reason, tradition, or authority, but rather on the _____.
24. Nietzsche argues that Christianity and Judaism are examples of _____.
25. The _____ lives by master morality.
26. Traditional morality requires _____ for master morality to emerge.
27. Ayn Rand promotes a moral perspective based on _____.
28. Rand believes that an ethic of altruism based on collectivist thinking is ultimately _____ and inhumane.
29. From the vantage point of _____, rational self-interest or "rational selfishness" should serve as the basis of morality.
30. According to Ayn Rand, persons in moral relation to each other should be regarded as _____.

# SUMMARY OF MAJOR POINTS

1. What ethical perspectives are dealt with in this chapter?
   - Plato's character ethics; Jeremy Bentham's utilitarian ethics; Immanuel Kant's deontological ethics, Gilligan and Noddings's feminine ethics; Nietzsche's existentialist ethics, and Ayn Rand's ethical egoism.

2. From the vantage point of Plato's theory, how are characters corrupted?
   - Ideally, reason should be the controlling faculty of the soul. When appetite or passion assume control, then either timarchic, oligarchic, deomocratic, or tyrannical character types result. All are corrupt and inferior relative to the philosopher king, who is ruled by reason.

3. What tool does Jeremy Bentham provide to help us make moral decisions in a spirit of scientific objectivity?
   - Bentham offers us the "hedonic calculus" based on the principle of utility to facilitate moral decision making.

4. What is the foundational principle of Kant's deontological ethics? How is ethical theory formalistic?
   - The categorical imperative serves as the basis of Kantian ethics. Moral duty can be expressed in maxims or rules of conduct adhering to the following formalistic criteria: they must be rational, *a priori*, impersonal, universalizable, prescriptive, unconditional, reversible, impartial, objective, and logically consistent.

5. How do gender considerations impact on traditional moral theories?
   - Carol Gilligan and Nel Noddings have identified male bias in traditional theories of morality. Male perspectives tend to romanticize rationality and inappropriately abstract from concrete human relationships within which moral concerns arise. Matters of care, relation, and the human affective response can either enrich limited male perspectives or replace them altogether.

6. What are some of the most provocative challenges to traditional morality raised by Friedrich Nietzsche?
   - Nietzsche rejects God as a basis for morality, for "God is dead." A life-affirming morality must be based on the will to power, not equality or altruism or self-denial. There are higher and lower forms of morality, the latter being inferior and meant for slavish, mediocre types. People are not equal by virtue of the quantum of power they possess; some are weak-willed, others are strong. Religious morality is dishonest and a veiled attempt to grab the power religionists themselves condemn in master moralists. Religious morality is nihilistic, that is, life-denying, anti-human. We should adopt the aesthetic form of life, not the life of reason or religious piety.

7. On what should morality be based according to Ayn Rand? Why?
   - Morality should properly be based on rational self-interest or "rational selfishness," not on mysticism, emotionalism, or subjective preference. Any collectivist ethic of altruism is ultimately destructive and inhumane. A morality of rational selfishness conforms to human nature. "Life" is that which makes the concept of value possible.

# SOURCE REFERENCES

(*Listed by philosopher, moral theory or approach*)

### PLATO
**Copleston, Frederick,** *A History of Philosophy*, Vol. 1 (New York: Image Books, 1993).

**Falikowski, Anthony,** *Moral Philosophy for Modern Life* (Scarborough: Prentice Hall/Allyn & Bacon, Canada, 1998).

**Plato,** *The Republic of Plato*, 2nd ed., trans. Allan Bloom, (New York: Basic Books, 1968).

———, *The Republic*, 2nd ed., trans. Desmond Lee (Middlesex, England: Penguin Books, 1976).

Stumpf, Samuel Enoch, *Socrates to Sartre: A History of Philosophy*, 5th ed. (Toronto: McGraw Hill, 1993).

Wolff, R.P., *About Philosophy*, 7th ed. (Upper Saddle NJ: Prentice Hall, 1998).

## BENTHAM
Ayer, A.J. "The Principle of Utility," in *Philosophical Essays*, ed. A.J. Ayer (New York: St. Martin's Press, 1955).

Bentham, Jeremy, "An Introduction to the Principles of Morals and Legislation" in *The English Philosophers from Bacon to Mill*, ed. E.A. Burtt (New York: Modern Library, 1939).

Falikowski, Anthony, *Moral Philosophy for Modern Life* (Scarborough: Prentice Hall/Allyn & Bacon, Canada, 1998).

Narveson, Jan, *Morality and Utility* (Baltimore: Johns Hopkins University Press, 1967).

Runckle, Gerald, *Ethics: An Examination of Contemporary Moral Problems* (New York: Holt, Rinehart and Winston, 1982).

Smart, J.J., *Outline of a Utilitarian System of Ethics* (London: Cambridge University Press, 1961).

## KANT
Copleston, Frederick, *A History of Philosophy*, Vol.6, (Garden City NY: Image Books, 1960).

Hospers, John, *Human Conduct: Problems of Ethics* (New York: Harcourt Brace Jovanovich, 1972).

Kant, Immanuel, *Foundations of the Metaphysics of Morals*, trans. L. W. Beck (Indianapolis, IN: Bobbs-Merrill, The Library of Liberal Arts, 1959).

———*Lectures on Ethics*, trans. Louis Infield (Indianapolis: Hackett Publishing, 1963).

———*The Metaphysical Principles of Virtue*, trans. James Ellington (Indianapolis: Bobbs-Merrill, The Library of Liberal Arts, 1964).

Kemp, John, *The Philosophy of Kant* (London: Oxford University Press, 1968).

Korner, S., *Kant* (Harmondsworth, Middlesex: Penguin Books, 1955).

Ross, W.D., *Kant's Ethical Theory* (New York: Oxford University Press, 1954).

Singer, Marcus, "The Categorical Imperative" in *Moral Philosophy: An Introduction*, ed. Jack Glickman (New York: St. Martin's Press, 1976).

## FEMININE ETHICS
Cochrane D.B., C.M. Hamm, and A.C. Kazepides, *The Domain of Moral Education* (New York: Paulist Press, 1979).

Duska, Ronald, and Mariellen Whelan, *Moral Development: A Guide to Piaget and Kohlberg* (New York: Paulist Press, 1975).

Falikowski, Anthony, *Moral and Values Education: A Philosophical Appraisal*; Doctoral Dissertation, University of Toronto, 1984.

Gilligan, Carol, *In A Different Voice: Psychological Theory and Women's Development* (Cambridge: Harvard University Press, 1982).

Kohlberg, Lawrence, *Essays on Moral Development*, Vol. I, *The Philosophy of Moral Development* (San Francisco: Harper & Row, 1981).

Mischel, Theodore, *Cognitive Development and Epistemology* (New York: Academic Press, 1971), pp. 151–235.

Nodding, Nel, *Caring: A Feminine Approach to Ethics and Moral Education* (Berkeley: University of California Press, 1986).

Rawls, John, *A Theory of Justice* (Cambridge: Harvard University Press, 1971).

## NIETZSCHE
Berkowitz, Peter, *Nietzsche: The Ethics of an Immoralist* (Cambridge: Harvard University Press, 1966).

Copleston, Frederick, *A History of Philosophy*, Vol.III (New York: Image Books, 1994), pp. 390–420.

Guignon, Charles, and Derk Pereboom, eds., *Existentialism: Basic Writings* (Indianapolis: Hackett Publishing 1995), pp. 85–173.

Lawhead, William, *The Voyage of Discovery: A History of Western Philosophy* (Belmont CA: Wadsworth 1996), pp. 433–49.

Nietzsche, Friedrich, *The Birth of Tragedy and The Case of Wagner*, trans. Walter Kaufmann (New York: Vintage Books) 1967.

———*On the Genealogy of Morals*, trans. Walter Kaufmann and R.J. Hollingdale, and *Ecco Homo*, ed. Walter Kaufmann (New York: Vintage Books, 1967).

———*The Will to Power*, trans. Walter Kaufmann and R.J. Hollingdale (New York: Vintage Books, 1968).

———*Twilight of the Idols: The Antichrist*, trans. R.J. Hollingdale (Baltimore: Penguin Books 1968).

———*Thus Spoke Zarathustra*, trans. R.J. Hollingdale (Baltimore: Penguin Books, 1972).

———*The Gay Science*, trans. Walter Kaufmann (New York: Vintage Books, 1974).

———*Beyond Good and Evil*, trans. R.J. Hollingdale (New York: Penguin Putnam, 1990).

Oaklander, Nathan, ed., *Existentialist Philosophy: An Introduction* (Upper Saddle River, NJ: Prentice Hall, 1996), pp. 75–143.

Sleinis, E.E., *Nietzsche's Revaluation of Values: A Study in Strategies* (Urbana: University of Illinois Press, 1994), pp. 56–92

Stumpf, Samuel E., *Philosophy: History and Problems* 5th ed., (New York: McGraw 1993), pp. 19–30.

## AYN RAND
Baker, James T., *Ayn Rand* (Boston: Twayne Publishers, 1987).

Baier, Kurt, "Egoism," in *A Companion to Ethics*, Peter Singer, ed. (Oxford: Blackwell Publishers, 1997), pp. 197–204.

Feinberg, Joel, "Psychological Egoism," in *Ethics: History, Theory and Contemporary Issues*, eds. Steven M. Cahn and Peter Markie (New York: Oxford University Press, 1998) pp. 557–65

Peikoff, Leonard, *Objectivism: The Philosophy of Ayn Rand* (New York: Meridian, 1993).

**Rand, Ayn,** *The Virtue of Selfishness: A New Concept of Egoism* (New York: Signet, 1961).

———*For the New Intellectual: The Philosophy of Ayn Rand* (New York: Signet, 1963).

———*Atlas Shrugged* (New York: Random House, 1957).

———*We the Living* (New York: Macmillan, 1936).

———*Anthem* (New York: Signet, 1961).

# PHILOSOPHY IN CYBERSPACE

### Centre for Applied Ethics
http://www.ethics.ubc.ca/resources/dec-mkg/
The Centre for Applied Ethics at the University of British Columbia aims to bring moral philosophy into the public domain by advancing research in applied ethics, supporting courses with a significant ethical component, and acting as a community resource.

### Institute for Global Ethics
http://www.globalethics.org/
The Institute for Global Ethics promotes ethical behavior in individuals, institutions and nations through research, public discourse, and practical action.

### Association for Practical and Professional Ethics
http://php.indiana.edu/~appel/home.html
The Association for Practical and Professional Ethics is committed to encouraging high quality interdisciplinary scholarship and teaching in practical and professional ethics by educators and practitioners who appreciate the theoretical and practical aspects of their subjects.

# ENDNOTES

1. See Plato, *The Republic,* Part Five, Book Four, 2nd ed., trans. Desmond Lee, pp. 206–22.
2. Plato, quoted in Samuel H. Stumpf, *Philosophy: History and Problems,* 5th ed. (New York: McGraw-Hill, 1993), p. 63.
3. Plato, *The Republic,* p. 373.
4. Ibid., p. 381.
5. Ibid., p. 378.
6. Jeremy Bentham, *An Introduction to the Principles of Morals and Legislation,* in *The English Philosophers from Bacon to Mill,* ed. by E.A. Burtt (New York: Modern Library, 1939), p. 792.
7. Bentham, *An Introduction,* p. 791.
8. Ibid., p. 804.
9. Immanuel Kant, *Foundations of the Metaphysics of Morals,* trans. Lewis White Beck (Indianapolis; IN: Bobbs-Merrill Library of Liberal Arts, 1959), p. 5.
10. Ibid., p. 9.
11. Ibid., p. 10.
12. Ibid., p. 16.
13. Ibid.
14. Ibid., pp. 13–14.
15. Ibid., p. 14.
16. See Immanuel Kant, *Lectures on Ethics,* trans. Louis Infield (Indianapolis, IN: Hackett Publishing, 1963).
17. Ibid., pp. 117–118.
18. Ibid., p. 118.
19. Ibid., p. 121.
20. Kant, *Foundations of the Metaphysics of Morals,* p. 39.
21. Ibid., p. 47.
22. Ibid., p. 31.
23. Carol Gilligan, *In a Different Voice: Psychological Theory and Women's Development* (Cambridge: Harvard University Press), 1982.
24. Nel Noddings, *Caring: A Feminine Approach to Ethics and Moral Education* (Berkeley: University of California Press, 1986).
25. See Lawrence Kohlberg, "From Is to Ought: How to Commit the Naturalistic Fallacy and Get Away with it in the Study of Moral Development," in Theodore Mischel, ed., *Cognitive Development and Epistemology* (New York: Academic Press, 1971), pp.151–235. Also see Kohlberg, *Essays on Moral Development,* Vol.1, *The Philosophy of Moral Development* (San Francisco: Harper & Row, Publishers, 1981).
26. Ronald Duska and Mariellen Whelan, *Moral Development: A Guide to Piaget and Kohlberg* (New York: Paulist Press, 1975). Provides an easily understood description of Kohlberg's theory, which I have used in my own summary here.
27. For further discussion see, for example, Anthony Falikowski, *Moral and Values Education: A Philosophical Appraisal,* Doctoral Thesis, University of Toronto, 1984; also Brian Crittenden, "The Limitations of Morality as Justice in Kohlberg's Theory" in D.B. Cochrane, C.M. Hamm, and A.C. Kazepides, *The Domain of Moral Education* (New York: Paulist Press, 1979). Also see John Rawls, *A Theory of Justice* (Cambridge: Harvard University Press, 1971).
28. In the "original position," conflicting parties are placed behind a "veil of ignorance," which prevents them from knowing what is in their personal self-interest. Without such knowledge, the parties must formulate, in advance, mutually acceptable principles they could use to adjudicate conflicts when they arise in the future. Since no personal reference can be made to favor any party, the resulting principles turn out to be formal and abstract.
29. Heinz Dilemma from A. Colby, L. Kohlberg, J. Gibbs and M. Lieberman, (1983, p. 77) "A longitudinal study of moral judgment." *Monographs of the Society for Research in Child Development,* 48(1–2, Serial No. 200)

30. Carol Gilligan, *In a Different Voice,* p. 2
31. This appears to be well illustrated by the work of Ayn Rand, also covered in this chapter.
32. Gilligan, *In a Different Voice,* p. 8.
33. Ibid., pp. 8–9.
34. Ibid., p. 74.
35. For a discussion of this point, see Claudia Cord, *Hypatia* 5, no.1 (Spring 1990): p.101. Gilligan's views on the relation between justice and care may have evolved or may simply be ambiguous.
36. Noddings, *Caring,* p. 5.
37. Ibid.
38. Ibid., p. 36.
39. Ibid., p. 37.
40. Ibid., p. 84.
41. Ibid., p. 6.
42. Friedrich Nietzsche, *The Gay Science* (trans.) Walter Kaufmann (New York: Vintage Books, 1974), p. 279.
43. A point emphasized in Charles Guignon and Derk Pereboom, eds., *Existentialism: Basic Writings,* (Indianapolis, IN: Hackett Publishing 1995), pp. 103–6.
44. These examples are borrowed from William F. Lawhead, *The Voyage of Discovery: A History of Western Philosophy* (Belmont: Wadsworth Publishing, 1996), p. 441.
45. Peter Berkowitz, *Nietzsche: The Ethics of an Immoralist* (Cambridge: Harvard University Press, 1995), p. 67.
46. Ibid., pp. 68–69.
47. Ibid., p. 70
48. Lawhead, *Voyage of Discovery,* p. 443.
49. Nietzsche, quoted in Stumpf, *Philosophy: History and Problems,* p. 427.
50. Ibid.
51. Nathan Oaklander regards traditional morality as one form of slave morality. He writes: "Nietzsche's attack on Christianity parallels his criticisms of traditional morality, and it is easy to see why. Both are examples of slave morality and both, according to Nietzsche, are the result of certain 'errors of reason.'" See *Existentialist Philosophy: An Introduction,* 2nd ed. (Upper Saddle River NJ: Prentice Hall, 1996, p.89.) E.E. Sleinis points out that Nietzsche accepts that there are many moralities, and his thinking is dominated by "three types—the master morality, the slave morality, and the herd morality." In his footnote to this point, Sleinis writes: "Slave morality and herd morality are not always clearly distinguished by Nietzsche, but his discussions imply that there are important differences." See Sleinis, *Nietzsche's Revaluation of Values: A Study in Strategies* (Urbana: University of Illinois Press, 1994) p. 214.
52. Nietzsche, Beyond Good and Evil, p. 284.
53. Sleinis, *Neitzsche's Revaluation,* p. 63.
54. Ibid., p. 64.
55. Stumpf, Philosophy p. 105.
56. Oaklander, *Existentialist Philosophy,* p.89; the quotations that follow this footnote are also taken from Oaklander.
57. Frederick Copleston, *A History of Philosophy,* Vol. VII (New York: Image Books, 1994), pp. 390–420.
58. Nietzsche, *The Will to Power,* trans. Walter Kaufmann and R.J. Hollingdale (New York: Vintage Books, 1968), p. 478.
59. Stumpf, *Philisophy.*
60. Ibid., p. 109.
61. Charles Guignon, and Derk Pereboom, eds. *Existentialism: Basic Writings* (Indianapolis: Hackett Publishing, 1995), p. 103.
62. Ibid., p. 104.
63. James T. Baker, *Ayn Rand* (Boston: Twyne Publishing, 1987).
64. See Rand's essay entitled "The Objectivist Ethics," pp. 13–35.
65. Ayn Rand, *The Virtue of Selfishness* (New York: New American Library, 1964), p. vii.
66. Ibid.
67. Ibid., p. viii.
68. Ibid.
69. Ibid.
70. Ibid., p. x
71. Ibid., p. 13.
72. Ibid., pp. 16–17.
73. Ibid., p. 17.
74. This is normally regarded as fallacious reasoning.
75. Rand, *The Virtue of Selfishness,* p. 23.
76. Ibid., p. 25.
77. Ibid., p. 27.
78. Ibid., pp. 29–30.
79. Ibid., p. 31.
80. Ibid., p. 32.
81. Ibid., p. 33.
82. Ibid.
83. Ibid., p. 35.
84. Azim Nanji, "Islamic Ethics" in Peter Singer (ed.) *A Companion to Ethics* (Oxford: Blackwell Publishers, 1993) pp. 106–117.
85. Mel Thompson, *Eastern Philosophy* (Chicago, IL: Teach Yourself Books, 1999), p. 7.
86. S.Abhayananda, *The Wisdom of Vedanta* (Olympia, WA: Atma Books, 1994), p. 5.
87. Ashok Kumar Malhotra, *Transcreation of the Bhagavad-Gita* (Upper Saddle River, NJ: Prentice Hall, 1999).
88. This discussion of Arjuna's dilemma is adapted from Ashok Kumar Malhotra, *Transcreation of the Bhagavad-Gita* (Upper Saddle River, NJ: Prentice Hall, 1999), pp. viii–ix.
89. John Hick, "Christianity," *The Encyclopedia of Philosophy,* Vol. 2. (New York: MacMillan and Free Press, 1972), pp. 104–8; Jaroslav Pelikan, "Christianity," *Microsoft Encarta Encyclopedia,* 1993–1997; J. Francis Stafford, "Foundational Norms for Christian Ethics.") (http://www.Catholic.net/rec/periodicals/faith/0708-96/article/.html)

# POLITICAL PHILOSOPHY

# CHAPTER OVERVIEW

**Take It Personally**

**KNOW THYSELF**
**My Political Outlook**

**Political Philosophy versus Politics and Political Science**

**Plato's Republic**

The Individual and the State
Plato's Class System
Imperfect Societies
Women, Marriage, and the Family

**ORIGINAL SOURCEWORK**
Plato, *The Nature of Woman*

**Social Contract Theorists: Hobbes and Locke**

**PHILOSOPHICAL PROFILE**
**THOMAS HOBBES**

**Thomas Hobbes**

State of Nature
Laws of Nature
The Commonwealth—Hobbes's *Leviathan*
The Social Contract
Conditions on the Sovereign

**ORIGINAL SOURCEWORK:**
Hobbes, *Of the Causes, Generation, and Definition of a Commonwealth*

**John Locke**

Locke's State of Nature and Natural Law
Property Rights

Political Society and Government
Social Compact
Limits on Government
Divisions of Power
The Dissolution of Government

**ORIGINAL SOURCEWORK**
John Locke, *Of the Ends of Political Society and Government*

**PHILOSOPHICAL PROFILE**
**KARL MARX**

**Karl Marx**

Marx's Metaphysics and Dialectical Materialism
Class Conflict
Alienation as a Byproduct of Capitalism
Idolatry/Fetishism of Commodities
Division of Labor
After Capitalism

**ORIGINAL SOURCEWORK**
Karl Marx, *Economic and Philosophical Manuscripts*

**STUDY GUIDE**
Key Terms ■ Progress Check
Summary of Major Points ■ Source References
Philosophy in Cyberspace ■ Endnotes

## LEARNING OUTCOMES

*After successfully completing this chapter, you will be able to*

Define the field of political philosophy, distinguishing it from politics and political science

Outline Plato's *Republic* and its class system, relating each class to a corresponding element of the soul

Describe the flaws inherent in various types of imperfect societies, according to Plato

Present in summary fashion Hobbes's grim state of nature and the commonwealth Leviathan proposed to deal with it

Compare Locke's understanding of natural law and the state of nature with Hobbes's understanding

Elucidate the importance Locke gives to property rights in any constitutional structure formed by a social compact

Enumerate the limits John Locke places on government

Discuss Marx's metaphysics, the influences upon his thought, and the notion of dialectical materialism

Appreciate how capitalistic modes of production foster alienation, idolatry, and oppression

## FOCUS QUESTIONS

1. How are Plato's views of the state different from social contractarians and modern-day libertarians?

2. In what ways can societies be corrupted or flawed according to the philosophers studied? What is your response?

3. How does Plato view the role of women in society?

4. What are the theoretical similarities and differences between Hobbes and Locke, both of whom are social contractarians?

# TAKE IT PERSONALLY

In a society like ours, preoccupied with economic prosperity, leisure, entertainment, and fun, political philosophy is not likely to be on the minds of most people much of the time. Sure, there are social and political activists who address a particular issue or promote a particular cause, but etiquette continues to dictate that we never discuss politics—or religion for that matter—in polite company. Such topics evoke strong feelings that inevitably give rise to conflict. Presumably, it is better to discuss last night's game or a new recipe, for example, than to debate something as serious as health care reform, the morality of capitalism, or the philosophical basis of democracy. Such esoteric issues are usually considered far too serious as topics of conversation and, hence, terminally boring for fun-seekers and adrenalin junkies scampering off to the nearest amusement park for a thrill. For others, even to suggest the possibility that our political system is flawed or that other forms of government have advantages over our own could constitute an act of subversion, especially during wartime. To criticize the American way of life can be regarded as unpatriotic. Of course, a national pastime can be made of presidential scandals and acts of corruption by government officials. Think of the Lewinsky-Clinton affair, for example. In such cases, public interest may not be genuinely philosophical, however, but rather salacious and puerile—something you would expect from immature, gossiping schoolchildren.

In this chapter, we will not enter the minefield of politics; that is, we will not engage in partisan debates on local, national, or international issues. We will leave that to the politicians hoping to win the next election. We also have no intent here of performing any kind of character assassination or challenging the patriotism of those who hold dissenting views. These tasks can be completed, for better or worse, by campaign spin doctors and military apologists. Instead, what we will do is focus on historically important political theorists and their philosophies, examining their underlying assumptions about human nature, morality, and the ideal system of social organization.

To personalize the relevance of political philosophy, it might be useful to think back for a moment to what the existentialists told us about human existence in Chapter 2. Remember how, according to them, we all find ourselves simply thrown into the world at birth. We could add to this the fact that we tend to be unreflective at early ages, merely responding in spontaneous ways to objects, people, and events. Sadly, one could argue, a sizable number of individuals choose to remain largely unreflective throughout their entire lives, living inauthentically, as the existentialists would say, by mindlessly accepting the social order into which they were born with little question. Indeed, for some thoughtless ethnocentric people, the status quo of society may even take on the appearance of being "natural," unquestionably the best, or as God planned it. In this chapter, we'll have the opportunity to think about political matters and the socioeconomic structures into which we have been born and by which we have been raised and educated. If psychology is the study of the obvious, as some have suggested, then perhaps political philosophy might be seen, in part at least, as an inquiry into what seems obvious—or what is accepted when it comes to things like government, social organization, individual rights, and the role of the state.

Though it's apparent, for example, that governments do, in fact, exist, have you ever wondered *why* we need governments in the first place? Anarchists and paramilitary groups are often suspicious of governments and have even taken up arms to protect themselves against what they regard as coercive state powers. For example, the Oklahoma bombing by Timothy McVeigh and the postal service anthrax-related deaths across the nation following the events of September 11, 2001, point to the fact that some citizens, even within the United States, have chosen to wage war against the federal government. You and I, by contrast, might just sit idly by accepting governmental authority with relative complacency. Are the anarchists and revolutionary paramilitary groups crazy, or are *we* hopelessly naive and unsuspecting? Is government simply bad in itself, a necessary evil or something to be minimized? Could it be, on the other hand, that government should be seen as a good and noble protector of the people, whose involvement is to be encouraged? Isn't it government that makes the good life for all of its citizens possible? Wouldn't life be horribly insecure without government protection and control?

If you're interested in the answers to such questions, then reading about Thomas Hobbes's *Leviathan,* John Locke's *Social Contract,* and Plato's utopian *Republic,* should prove helpful. They all provide alternative visions of how societies should properly organize themselves. The treatment of Karl Marx's theory of dialectical materialism should also give you pause to reconsider the moral and philosophical merits of American liberal democracy as it functions today in the context of an emerging global market economy. Before we get down to work, however, let us first identify your personal sociopolitical values and presuppositions by completing the *Know Thyself* diagnostic that follows.

# KNOW THYSELF

## My Political Outlook

**AIM** In this self-diagnostic, you'll begin to identify some of your political values, ideals, and beliefs, however clear or unclear they are at this time. As with the other measures found in this text, the results obtained are not intended to be scientific or conclusive in any way but only suggestive, affording you an opportunity to reflect on your political outlook on life. Of course, reading and thinking about this chapter may change some of your views, but at least with this diagnostic, you'll have a basis for comparative analysis and evaluation.

**INSTRUCTIONS** Indicate your level of agreement or disagreement with each of the following statements using this scale:

1 = strongly disagree
2 = disagree
3 = undecided (avoid, if possible)
4 = agree
5 = strongly agree

_____ 1. Not everybody is suited to govern, so not everybody should have the opportunity.

_____ 2. It is naive to think that altruism is a natural emotion and that humans are, by nature, social animals.

_____ 3. God has created natural laws governing not only the physical universe but the moral universe as well.

_____ 4. Societies develop and progress as a product of class struggle.

_____ 5. Democracies are flawed because the "ignorant masses" are too easily swayed by demagogues (unprincipled orators pandering to the prejudices of the population).

_____ 6. Human beings are primarily motivated by egoistic desires to survive and experience pleasure.

_____ 7. Reason can be used to discern God's natural laws of morality, which then can serve as the basis of a democratic society.

_____ 8. There are no God-created natural laws of morality in the universe. The material interests of the dominant ruling classes ultimately determine right and wrong, good and evil, and social values in general.

_____ 9. The state is not a necessary evil, but rather an institution enabling individuals to realize themselves and live the good life.

_____ 10. In the original state of nature, where no governments ruled, the human condition was a condition of warring enemies, involving distrust, fear, and competition for resources.

_____ 11. The right to own property is a "natural right" basic to a democratic society.

_____ 12. The highly mechanized and technologically sophisticated modes of production we find in a capitalistic economy cause alienation at work as well as among members of society.

_____ 13. In an orderly society, people should know their place and not interfere with the responsibilities of others.

_____ 14. Without the state, there is no morality, only chaos, disorder, and opposition.

_____ 15. Government authority should not be absolute. It too should be subject to the rule of law.

_____ 16. A society should be based on the following principle: "We should take from each according to his ability and give to each according to his need."

_____ 17. Not everyone has the ability to be a good leader; the business of politics should be left to a class of experts who possess the skills, training, and aptitude for it.

_____ 18. The best way to protect ourselves and preserve the public order is by everyone relinquishing their rights to the state and allowing state control. Multiple wills are thereby transformed into a single will representing the best interests of all the citizens.

_____ 19. Governments cannot be imposed; they must arise from consent, either tacit or direct.

_____ 20. A market economy degrades human beings by forcing people to "sell themselves" in order to procure employment and feed their families.

_____ 21. The people least equipped to govern society are those belonging to the business class.

_____ 22. The sovereign body of the state should not be challenged, for then we return to a condition of chaos and disunity.

_____ 23. Governments established by public consent should be subject to majority rule.

_____ 24. The technology we create as a convenience often becomes our master, dictating what we must know and do in order to survive.

_____ 25. Corrupt societies produce corrupt individuals who are praised for exhibiting the vices and faults of that society.

_____ 26. The state should be seen as the protector of its citizens.

_____ 27. Citizens have the right to dissolve governments if they begin to exert power in capricious and tyrannical ways.

_____ 28. Laws of social evolution point to the day when a classless society witll eventually emerge, one in which the exploited and their exploiters no longer exist as enemies, for all will be free and equal, working toward the common good of the state.

## SCORING

The statements you just responded to are listed numerically below. Next to each number, write down the value you gave it indicating your level of agreement or disagreement. Then add the totals separately.

| *Plato's Aristocracy* | *Hobbes' Commonwealth* | *Locke's Consensual Democracy* |
|---|---|---|
| 1. | 2. | 3. |
| 5. | 6. | 7. |
| 9. | 10. | 11. |
| 13. | 14. | 15. |
| 17. | 18. | 19. |
| 21. | 22. | 23. |
| 25. | 26. | 27. |
| Total: | Total: | Total: |

*Marx's Communism*

4.

8.

12.

16.

20.

24.

28.

Total:

**Interpretation of Results:**  The column with the highest score suggests that your political philosophy at this time is most in line with that perspective. The various philosophies in the diagnostic are described briefly below.

My political philosophy is most consistent with: _____ (highest score)

# DESCRIPTIONS OF POLITICAL PHILOSOPHIES

**Plato's Aristocracy:**  Plato believes in "rule by the best." Democracy as we know it in North America, where one person gets one vote, is abandoned in favor of an expert aristocratic elite of guardians who have been properly trained and have proven themselves worthy of political authority. Social harmony is maintained by members of each social class accepting their roles and functioning at their best in those roles. This form of government is based on *meritocracy.* One must earn the right to govern through appropriate character education. Among the guardian elite, women are treated as equals and share in all responsibilities.

**Hobbes's Commonwealth:**  Hobbes assumes that the state of nature is a state of war amongst men who are essentially desirous of the same things. To have peace and order, people are required in the commonwealth to give up their rights to the great "Leviathan"—a coercive power compelling individuals to live by their covenant or social contract. This strong sanctioning body is like a Mortal God. The Leviathan (sovereign power or assembly of men) is not really divine, but rather a human creation brought into existence to enable individuals achieve their egoistic goals. The deal is to receive individual protection by everyone forfeiting their rights to the Leviathan.

**Locke's Consensual Democracy:**  This political system is based on "natural law," which sets limits on the individual exercise of human freedom. It dictates, for example, that no one ought to harm the life, liberty, or possessions of another. Natural law, created by God, endows all individuals with rights to self-preservation, self-defense, and personal liberty. The most important of all rights in Locke's political system are property rights, as they precede society and because the primary function of government is to protect them. By establishing government, disputes can be adjudicated by impartial judges who can mete out punishments for wrongdoing when necessary. The government is a servant of the people. By operating according to principles of natural law, it provides a strong philosophical foundation for individualism. Governments assume their authority by consent of all the people and accept decisions by democratic rule.

**Marx's Communism:**  This political philosophy reflects an atheistic materialism. The communistic state represents a classless society and is the final stage of a long evolutionary history of social class struggle between oppressor and oppressed. The moral basis of communism can be so expressed as: "From each according to his ability; to each according to his needs." In a classless communistic state, market forces and competition (like those in capitalism) are largely absent, with the consequence that workers enjoy greater dignity. Because wealth cannot become concentrated in the hands of the rich minority, greater numbers of people can enjoy the fruits of their productivity. Also, because the "dog-eat-dog" world of the competitive marketplace is abolished, people can also learn to cooperate, work for the good of the state, and feel less alienated toward their neighbors who, in a capitalist system, are their competitive adversaries.

# POLITICAL PHILOSOPHY VERSUS POLITICS AND POLITICAL SCIENCE

If we wish to make sense of **political philosophy,** then maybe we ought to be precise in our terminology, noting that it is not equivalent to **politics.** The term *politics* is usually used in the context of elections and political campaigns. However, it has also come to be negatively associated with self-serving egos, arm-twisting, name-calling, back-room deals, deceptive half-truths, distorted statistics, lobby groups, questionable campaign contributions, broken promises, stonewalling, and filibustering. Little wonder, then, that politics has been given such a bad name and that so many avoid it like the plague. Politics sometimes appears to operate from a perversely partisan logic of power, not from a more morally acceptable logic of impartial reason. Perhaps if our politicians were swayed less by the desire for control and more by the force of honest rationality, a greater degree of integrity could enter into the political arena, and we could get on with the nation's business.

As dirty as the business of politics can sometimes be, politicians generally hold, implicitly at least, theoretical views that coalesce to form more or less coherent political philosophies and ideological perspectives. In other words, politics takes place against a backdrop of political theory. When unarmed Chinese students are confronted by tanks in Tiananmen Square, when the National Guard shoots protesting students at Kent State University, when free-trade agreements result in a greater degree of economic globalization, or when nation-states try to protect their cultural industries from foreign domination, certain philosophical visions of nationhood, legitimate government authority, and individual rights give rise to those actions.

Of course, it is not necessarily the case that politicians, protestors, or even voters fully understand their own political presuppositions. Though people often self-identify as liberal or conservative, Democratic or Republican, Marxist or monarchist, they do not always appreciate the implications of such identifications. Individuals sometimes adopt political views because of family loyalties, social conditioning, indoctrination, peer-group pressure, or because of other nonrational considerations. In short, we do not always understand the philosophies that support differing political outlooks and their derivative policies, which are passed into legislation and sanctioned by law. If, then, we wish to become more responsible and enlightened citizens, able to provide good reasons for the stands we take on particular sociopolitical issues, it would behoove us to gain a better appreciation of some differing political theories and their philosophical underpinnings. People are not really politically free to choose until they have alternative options to choose from; and to the extent that true freedom necessitates intelligent and informed choice, an understanding of political theory would seem to be indispensable. This points again to the practical value of philosophy, which helps us to develop this understanding.

So far in our efforts to grasp the nature of political philosophy, we have distinguished it from politics. Remember, political philosophy forms the *theoretical basis* for political action. Another distinction needs to be made for purposes of clarity, that between political philosophy and **political science.** Though the two are related in some ways, they are certainly different. It has been said that: "Political science is a comparative study of the forms and functions of power systems, whereas political philosophy directs much of its attention to the basic assumptions about human nature, reality, and value that are claimed to justify the patterns and practices by which human beings govern themselves and exert authority over one another."[1] Political science, as a study of various types of governments and social organizations, is essentially descriptive and empirical. It explains to us how past and existing social structures function. Political science is a type of factual inquiry regarding the structure and workings of political institutions, such as the state and its constitutive parts: the legislative, executive, and judicial. More recently, influenced by psychology and sociology, political scientists have started to focus on the political behaviors of individuals and groups in their investigations.[2]

By contrast to political science, political philosophy tends to be normative, prescribing actions, making value judgments, offering justifications, and putting forward suggestions for how society "ought" to be structured and regulated. With its focus on normative considerations, political philosophy is often categorized as a branch of **axiology**—that division of philosophical inquiry dealing with matters of value. Indeed, political philosophy's preoccupation with values sometimes makes it difficult to distinguish it from ethical inquiry. It could be argued that politics is continuous with morality and that many of our political duties and obligations are tantamount to our moral duties and obligations.[3] The individual's civil rights as a member of society are often defended, for example, by reference to the individual's moral rights as a human being. In such instances, the overlap between ethics and political philosophy is undeniable. Notwithstanding their similarities, however, political philosophy and ethics do diverge from each other at certain points. In general terms, morality is more concerned with relations between particular individuals and with matters of personal conscience, whereas political philosophy is more concerned with social institutions and with large and impersonal groups. Morality also directs its attention to the cultivation of virtue and character development, which no doubt have indirect implications for the good of society but are not the main focus of political theory.

On this last note, it might be worth adding here that political philosophy and political theory are sometimes used synonymously in the same way that ethics and morality are. We can speak of classical political theories and modern political theories as representing different philosophical ideas and approaches. Classical theories tend to offer advice and prescriptions for achieving an ideal or utopian society. Modern theories, on the other hand, tend to approach the subject matter of political philosophy from a more conceptual-analytical viewpoint in efforts to clarify the meaning of the advice given in classical theories for the purpose of rendering more intelligible the concepts and terms we use in political discussions. A political philosopher adopting an analytical approach would ask questions like: "What is meant by the phrase 'universal human rights' as it appears in the Charter of the United Nations?" or "What is the correct analysis of the word 'state'?"[4] By analyzing technical terms and concepts such as "the state" and "universal human rights," political philosophy separates itself as a specialized discipline that cannot be reduced entirely to ethics or to the empirical social sciences.

In a final effort here to grasp the nature and scope of political philosophy, it might be helpful to enumerate some of the basic questions that theorists in the field have posed. Historically speaking, political philosophers have been preoccupied with definitions of justice, as well as with the attitudes and arrangements that ought to create and perpetuate it.[5] They have also discussed a variety of ideas concerning the organization of human beings into collectivities. A sampling of basic questions asked by political philosophers include the following:

1. What is the ultimate justification for the existence of any form of government?

2. What should be the proper limits of government over the members of society?
3. Why should anyone obey the law?
4. Why should anyone pay taxes?
5. How do we harmonize governmental authority with human rights and individual freedoms?
6. Under what conditions is it legitimate to replace those who currently rule?
7. Should we allow political power to be concentrated in the hands of a few leaders, or should it be widely distributed among the members of society at large?
8. Should politicians vote according to personal conscience or represent the wishes of their constituents?

Now that we have a better idea of what political philosophy is all about, let us turn to several historically important representatives in the field, starting with Plato.

## PLATO'S REPUBLIC

In Plato's, *The Republic,* we find not only an epistemology, metaphysics, and theory of character ethics, as we have already learned, but also an example of a classical political theory offering us a vision of the ideal, utopian society. This vision was developed against a backdrop of small but numerous Greek city-states that all had their own autonomous governments. History reveals that these states were in constant warfare with each other, and also that most suffered from a great deal of internal strife.[6] The result was that life for the average citizen was precarious indeed. In view of this situation, Plato's aim was to create the blueprint for a society that would be able to achieve its objectives, defend itself against its external enemies, and free itself from defects giving rise to internal disturbances. The general question was posed: "What would the ideal society be like if it were brought into existence?[7] Note that Plato was not engaged in political science. He was not interested in the empirical study of actual states, but rather, his aim was to present a vision of what states "should" be like, even if they were not as he envisioned. Plato's hypothetical Republic represents the ideal pattern to which every state ought to conform itself, in so far that it can. So much the worse for states that fall short of his expressed ideal.[8]

In what follows, we will examine more closely the particulars of Plato's utopian blueprint. Suffice it to say at this juncture that the ideal society constitutes a type of **aristocracy,** a term derived from the Greek roots, *ariston* and *krato,* suggesting "rule by the best."[9] This presentation of Plato's utopian ideal will surely give us occasion to reflect upon our own political presuppositions and perhaps reason to modify or even reject them altogether. Just as David Hume awoke Kant from his dogmatic slumbers, maybe Plato (and those who follow) will awaken us to our many accepted, but unexamined, political beliefs regarding justice, autonomy, the rights of individuals, and their proper place in the state. Pardon any discomfort that might ensue. Waking from one's sleep is not usually a pleasant affair, but necessary for rational enlightened living.

The possibility of a rude awakening arises because Plato had only contempt for democracy, as he knew it in his time, and quite possibly, he would heap scorn on contemporary forms of it, which allow the general masses, including those who are ignorant and unwise, selfish and greedy, as well as those who are vain and undisciplined, to seize the reigns of power. Also, in democracies, the "ignorant masses" can be too easily manipulated by demagogues. In contrast to our modern liberal-democratic state, one in which we allow one person one vote, Plato would prefer governance by an expert elite.

## The Individual and the State

As we begin our trek into this, the first decade of the new millennium, it would appear that **individualism** still reigns supreme in North American society. Certainly, group work and team building are collective activities emphasized in contemporary learning and business environments, but usually for instrumental purposes. One learns to function cooperatively in groups and to become a team player within the corporation, for example, for personal advancement and individual gain. Groups are good because of what they get you; they are not necessarily good in themselves. Indeed, even in government, efforts are continuously made to reduce the influence of politicians and legislators in the daily affairs of private citizens. "Reduce government!" and "Too much government regulation!" have become rallying calls for libertarians and hard-core individualists. One example of attempts to keep government out of the private lives of individuals is captured in a statement made by former Canadian prime minister Pierre Elliot Trudeau in the context of decriminalizing homosexuality. He asserted that *"The state has no business in the bedrooms of the nation."* From the individualistic perspective, the less government intervention and control in the lives of private citizens, the better. What is sought is greater independence and liberty for all. As we learned in our earlier coverage of Ayn Rand (see Chapter 5), sacrificing the rights and interests of the individual to the welfare of the state or to any collectivity within it smacks of communism or totalitarian repression—presumably evil things without justification.

Now, as far as Plato is concerned, the "state," so called, is neither inherently evil nor obstructionist with respect to the attainment of individual goals. State control is not something that must unquestionably be reduced, minimized, and dispensed with whenever possible, though our prevailing value system would seem to lead us confidently to this conclusion. Of course, the city-state ideal Plato refers to in his writings would be small. One could imagine that it would be a little like smalltown America where people know their neighbors. The state governance Plato had in mind would certainly not resemble the Politburo in Russia or the multilayered impersonal bureaucracy in Washington, D.C., which oversees millions.

In defense of the state and its proper jurisdiction, Plato offers the observation that human beings, as individuals, are not entirely self-sufficient. The reason societies formed in the first place was to establish systems of cooperation that

> *We are bound to admit that the elements and traits that belong to the state must also exist in the individuals who compose it. There is nowhere else for them to come from.*
> — PLATO

would enable members to achieve the necessities of life that would be more difficult, if not sometimes impossible, to obtain alone. In large part, the state arose to serve the economic interests of its citizens. Thus, the state is not evil but potentially very good, satisfying the natural desires of human beings. In fact, for Plato, who regards human beings as social animals, "the good life" cannot be lived apart from active participation in state affairs. The **city-state or** *polis* (to use the Greek equivalent) provides the natural setting for the life of any individual. Since we all have a natural desire to live in communities, cities and their governments are just as natural as human beings are. The good life for the individual is possible only within the good state.[10]

In *The Republic,* Plato explains how the good state is supposed to operate if it is to function properly. His depiction of the properly functioning ideal society interestingly combines principles of psychology and political science, which are considered essentially the same.[11] For Plato, the **soul** of the individual—what we would call today the psyche, self, or personality—is actually a miniature version of the structure of society. The *polis* or Greek city-state is like man "writ large against the sky."[12] In *The Republic,* Plato actually believes we can more easily gain insight into the workings of the human soul by examining society first; after all, it is larger and hence easier to see. Conveniently for us, we have already studied the structure and workings of the soul in our earlier moral discussion on Plato in Chapter 5.

The parallels between the individual and the state, as well as the similarities between psychology and political science, can be observed in the correspondence between the three elements of the soul and the three types or classes of people within society Plato identifies. Just as each part of the soul has its proper target objects and specific role to play in the harmonious functioning of the individual's psyche, so too does each kind of person have his or her special job to perform within society. For Plato, the ideal state is built around a **division of labor.** We find differences in aptitude in people, making different people good at different things. Thus, it is most beneficial for all that individuals concentrate on developing their particular talents. If we all do what we're good at, then we all win in the end. A society that nurtures the development of individual aptitudes by means of its laws and regulations promotes a pattern of natural growth. Just as there can be an organic harmonious balance within the individual soul, so too can such a balance exist within the state, displayed by a harmonious hierarchy of purposes among its citizens.

So far, you might be inclined to side with Plato regarding his conception of the ideal state. After all, who would complain about a state designed to help you develop your natural gifts? Sounds pretty good, doesn't it? Before you get too excited, however, recall what Plato said about the soul in the context of morality and character development. For him, the soul is comprised of three elements: appetite, spirit, and reason. Also, remember that not all parts of the soul were to have equal influence on the functioning of the personality. Appetite and spirit were seen as "wild horses" to be reigned in by the controlling faculty of reason. With authority handed over to reason, "psychological equality" did not exist in the personality. Similarly, for Plato, the harmoniously balanced or most functional state is not based on any notion of "democratic equality." The business of politics should be left to a class of experts who possess the skills, training, and aptitude for it. Not everyone has the ability to be a good leader, and hence, not just anybody should be given the right to assume leadership positions in society. This notion appears to be in direct opposition to the American ideal that, in principle, any person should be able to run for public office and even become the president of the United States. Of course, this would not be so in Plato's aristocracy. How could the esteemed Plato put forward a conception that is so counterintuitive, even hostile, to the cherished values embodied in a democratic system of government such as ours?

Essentially, Plato defends his position by analogy. He argues that just as we should yield to the advice of medical experts when we are concerned about the health of the body, so too, when we are concerned about the health of the state, we should seek out the advice of experts possessing the necessary wisdom to govern properly. The masses simply lack the knowledge and intelligence needed for proper governance. Just imagine how silly, even dangerous, it would be when seriously ill to ask every stranger you met on the street for advice on how to treat your ailment. Surely you wouldn't take a democratic vote among the clueless mob to diagnose your condition or establish the preferred course of treatment. Yet when it comes to the problems of the body politic affecting the health of the state, we proudly seek the advice of the ignorant masses through such vehicles as elections, referenda, and town hall meetings. Plato asks why it is that:

> When we Athenians are met together in the assembly, and the matter in hand relates to building, the builders are summoned as advisers; when the question is one of ship-building, then the shiprights . . . But when the question is an affair of state, then everybody is free to have a say—carpenter, tinker, cobbler, merchant, sea captain, rich and poor, high and low—anyone who likes gets up, and no one reproaches him, as in the former case, with not having learned . . . and yet giving advice.[13]

## Plato's Class System

Given that people possess different aptitudes, not all people are the same, intellectually and morally speaking. While it is true that we all share the same basic elements of the soul and are alike in this respect, we nonetheless find that these elements, taken individually, exert varying degrees of influence or psychological force in different individuals. This fact gives rise to three different classes in society. For each class a particular element of the soul is dominant. This dominating element motivates members of its corresponding class to value certain types of objects and to display particular kinds of virtues that make them best suited to perform specific kinds of social function (see Table 6.1).

### Artisans

Driven primarily by the psychological faculty of appetite are the **artisans** or what we might call today the **business class.** Under this generic heading, we can include merchants and shopkeepers. We can also put workers, traders, and

**TABLE 6.1**

| Parts of the Soul | Classes in Society |
|---|---|
| Appetite | Artisans/Business Class |
| Spirit | Auxiliaries/Soldier Class |
| Reason | Philosopher Kings/Rulers |

farm producers under this category, as well as those "born to shop," namely those we would describe as consumers. Members of this class value wealth, materialism, and appetite satisfaction. Even though this class is regarded as inferior and subordinate to the guardians, it enjoys the most freedom and physical comforts. People in this class are allowed to pursue their material dreams as long as they live within the boundaries of the law and as long as unacceptable poverty does not develop as a result of an overconcentration of wealth in the hands of too few people. The job of the business class is to generate trade, commerce, and other economic activities, providing the material necessities of the community.

Though this lower class is placed under the authority and direction of others, understand that it is not exploited in the same way that the proletariat is by the bourgeoisie in the Marxist interpretation of economic history (see the section on Marx later in this chapter).[14] Furthermore, members of the business class are permitted to marry whomever they wish and to raise their own children—rights not afforded the other two classes.[15] Using the prevailing values of contemporary North American society as a standard, some might suggest, that those in this "lowest class" are the ones best off. (If you agree, perhaps you deserve to belong to it!)

Virtue is manifested in this class through obedience, moderation, and **self-discipline.** Appetites within the individual are to be controlled and kept temperate. Socially, the artisans are to display self-discipline by showing due obedience to those who govern and those who carry out the orders of the highest ruling class. In fact, "self-discipline stretches across the whole scale [of classes]. It produces a harmony between its strongest and weakest and middle elements . . . And so we are quite justified in regarding self-discipline as this unanimity in which there is a natural concordance between higher and lower about which of them is to rule in state and individual."[16]

## Auxiliaries

In the ideal society Plato envisions, not only is it necessary to produce the material necessities of life, but also to maintain internal order and defense against external enemies. These tasks are allotted to the **auxiliaries,** who comprise the professional soldier class and police, as well as those we would call in today's world government officials, federal agents, and state administrators—civil servants in general. Auxiliaries are actually a subordinate subgroup of a larger **guardian class,** which includes the **philosopher rulers**—those ultimately charged with the authority and control over the city-state. Auxiliaries have more in common with this aristocratic ruling class than with the workers, merchants, and artisans below them. In fact, the commonalities are so great, that one might be tempted to conclude that Plato's three classes are really only two, one of which is further subdivided.[17] These commonalities are quite apparent in view of the fact that both philosopher rulers and auxiliaries live a life of austere simplicity. Because Plato believed that material possessions constituted the major temptation leading people to sacrifice the public good for personal gain, he required that both auxiliaries and philosopher rulers possess no private property beyond the barest essentials. Guardians (both auxiliaries and philosopher rulers) were to live and eat communally. Guardians were not allowed to own their own homes or live independently in their own quarters. Basically, they lived like soldiers in a camp. Guardians were even forbidden to handle gold and silver, being taught that "heavenly" gold and silver had been infused into their very beings by the gods and that it would be "wicked to pollute the heavenly gold [and silver] in their possession by mixing it with earthly [gold and silver], for theirs is without impurity."[18] This "noble act of deception" (sometimes translated as "noble lie" or "magnificent myth") on the part of the rulers was to be propagated like a folkloric tale in order to build commitment to one's designated societal function and to maintain social order.[19]

In contrast to the appetite-driven business class, infused by mother earth with bronze, "silver-injected" auxiliaries are motivated by the **spirit** element of the soul. In defense of the state and in the maintenance of its internal order, they must exhibit **courage,** the distinguishing virtue of this class. Of course, courage is required if one is to perform one's duty, because such responsibility can oftentimes be dangerous or aversive in some fashion. Yet the auxiliaries somehow must manage to muster the requisite "intestinal fortitude" if they are to achieve the honor that accompanies the dutiful protection of the state and the implementation of the philosopher rulers' decisions.

## Philosopher Kings/Rulers

As mentioned, the third class envisioned by Plato in his utopian Republic is constituted by an elite subgroup of guardians known as the philosopher kings or rulers (We will use "rulers" to avoid any suggestion of gender bias). This gold class represents the highest social echelon charged with the responsibility of establishing laws and policies within society. The philosopher rulers are not voted into office, but rather earn the right to govern as an aristocracy after a long period of training and moral character development. The philosopher rulers are truly wise, enlightened leaders, possessing a higher kind of knowledge that comes only from an intellectual acquaintance with true Goodness, which ultimately resides in a supersensible, timeless, spaceless *realm of forms.* Rulers having this special knowledge are able to exercise the virtue of *wisdom,* knowing what is best for all the classes. Because they have demonstrated through tests of moral character that they are not corrupted by greed (appetite) and vanity (spirit), they become the best fit to rule, and so they should. They are the ones who always place care of the state above their own interests. More accurately, they identify the interests of the state *as* their own. Historical experience tells us what happens when corrupt and morally inferior people are allowed to assume power. Think of Russia's Joseph Stalin, for instance, who during the 1930s, in the so-called "harvest of despair," killed an estimated seven to twelve million Ukrainians through systematic starvation. Maybe Plato was correct when he concluded that rulers must become philosophers or that philosophers must become rulers if the ideal society is ever to be established.

So far in our discussion of the ideal state, we have learned that its class members display the virtues of moderation, courage, and wisdom. In this vein, we should recognize that the utopian republic is also characterized by the virtue of **justice.** The "just state" is one wherein everyone attends to his or her own business without interfering with anyone else's. People know their station in life and perform their function to the best of their ability. It would be presumptuous and misguided, for example, for artisans to think their wealth and business savvy qualified them to govern as guardians. In the just state, they are required to exhibit obedience to authority, namely the auxiliaries and ultimately to the philosopher rulers above them. When all the citizens of the state exhibit self-discipline and do what they are qualified to do, keeping their noses out of other people's business, so to speak, then harmony results in the state as it does in the soul when there is a stable balance and governance by reason (see Table 6.2). As Plato puts it:

> . . . justice is keeping what is properly one's own and doing one's own job. . . . Interference by the three classes with each other's jobs, and interchange of jobs between them, therefore, does the greatest harm to our state, and we are entirely justified in calling it the worst of evils. . . . So that is what injustice is. And conversely, when each of our three classes (businessmen, auxiliaries, and guardians) does its own job and minds its own business, that, by contrast, is justice and makes our state just.[20]

## Imperfect Societies

In *The Republic,* Plato discusses various forms of **imperfect societies,** which directly parallel the corrupt character types described in Chapter 5. They include the **timocracy,** the **oligarchic state,** the **democracy,** and the **tyrannical society.**[21] Along with his descriptions of various character types and explanations of their gradual descent into maniacal immorality, Plato also provides a corresponding outline of how societies can progressively degenerate from a utopian aristocracy (Plato's Republic) to the worst state of all, that is, tyranny. On his account, which is likely not to be taken as an accurate historical depiction, democracies mirror the democratic character; oligarchies reflect the oligarchic type, and so on. And just as imperfect character types are ruled by something other than reason, so too imperfect societies are governed by classes driven by spirit and appetite. In all of the degenerate societies identified by Plato, philosophers lose their place as controlling guardians of the state. Classes best suited to obey and produce goods take on inappropriate roles that they are not properly qualified to play. Values of relatively lesser importance become highly esteemed, while virtue and true goodness are dethroned and subordinated in status. The

**TABLE 6.2**   Social Classes, Their Functions, and Values Corresponding to Each Part of the Soul

| Dominant Part of the Soul | Social Class | Valued Objects | Societal Functions |
|---|---|---|---|
| Appetite | *Artisans/ Businessclass:* Includes merchants, manufacturers, producers, traders, consumers<br><br>*Symbolic Metal:* Bronze<br><br>*Virtue:* Moderation, obedience and self-discipline | Wealth, appetite satisfaction, material aquisition, property | Generate economic activity, provide the material and economic necessities of the community |
| Spirit | Auxiliaries: Soldierclass, government officials, civil servants administrators, federal agents<br><br>*Symbolic Metal:* Silver<br><br>*Virtue:* Courage | Community service, honor, duty, competition | Soldiering, protection of state interests, assist rulers and enforce their decisions |
| Reason | Philosopher Kings/Rulers: Elite sub-class of guardians<br><br>*Symbolic Metal:* Gold<br><br>*Virtue:* Wisdom | Enlightened understanding of true goodness, aquaintance with the forms | Establish laws and policies within society; govern as aristocracy |

harmonious balance of the healthy functioning aristocracy is disturbed, as divisions and conflicts are allowed to arise between rich and poor; the internal security and protection of the state are jeopardized; individuals start interfering with the proper functioning of others; principles of order and good taste are trampled under foot, a disregard for laws and disrespect for authority emerges; and as social relations become inverted—with subjects acting as rulers and rulers acting as subjects—excessive freedom erupts, leading to anarchy and eventually to tyranny—the worst form of unjust state that can exist.

Plato's prescription to end all of this injustice is, of course, to establish an aristocracy where carefully trained and selected philosophers become rulers. Only in such a hierarchal meritocracy can we find enlightened leadership providing order, stability, and proper direction (see Table 6.3). The devolution from

**TABLE 6.3** States and Their Corresponding Character Types

| States | Social Features | Corresponding Character Types | Psychological Profiles |
|---|---|---|---|
| Aristocracy (Ideal State) | Governed by guardian elite<br>Hierarchical meritocracy<br>Division of labor<br>Harmoniously functioning | Philosopher ruler | Virtuous: Wise, courageous, disciplined, just, Enlightened<br>Dedicated to state's welfare |
| Timocracy | Military aristocracy<br>Devoted to war<br>Overvaluation of physical<br>Population enslaved<br>Internal strife | Timarchic | Ambitious, energetic, athletic<br>Egoistic, self-assertive, insecure, conflicted, spirit driven |
| Oligarchy | Wealthy in control<br>Poor despised<br>Drone class of criminals emerges<br>Rampant crime | Oligarchic | Money-hungry, hard-working, squalid character<br>No moral conviction, appetite-driven |
| Democracy | Equality or political opportunity<br>Few restraints<br>Lawlessness<br>Anarchic form of society<br>Wide variety of pleasures | Democratic | Versatile, pleasure-loving<br>Poor judgment, unprincipled<br>Confused necessary & unnecessary desires |
| Tyranny (Worst State) | Growth of oppression<br>Tyrants grasp reins of power<br>Poverty<br>Violence against internal opposition | Tyrannical | Criminal type, maniac, ruled by master passion (i.e., lust)<br>Violent, despot without restraint. |

the utopian ideal in the Republic to the worst of all states, the tyranny, is described by Frederick Copleston:

> In the eighth and ninth Books of *The Republic* Plato develops a sort of philosophy of history. The perfect State is the aristocratic State; but when the two higher classes combine to divide the property of the other citizens and reduce them practically to slavery, aristocracy turns into timocracy, which represents the preponderance of the spirited element. Next the love of wealth grows, until timocracy turns into oligarchy, political power coming to depend on property qualifications. A poverty-stricken class is thus developed under the oligarchs, and in the end the poor expel the rich and establish

democracy. But the extravagant love of liberty, which is characteristic of democracy, leads by way of reaction to tyranny. At first the
champion of the common people obtains a bodyguard under spe-
cious pretenses; he then throws off pretense, executes a *coup d'état*
and turns into a tyrant. Just as the philosopher, in whom reason
rules, is the happiest of men, so the aristocratic State is the best and
happiest of States; and just as the tyrannical despot, the slave of
ambition and passion, is the worst and most unhappy of men, so is
the State ruled by the tyrant the worst and most unhappy of States.[22]

## Women, Marriage, and Family in the Republic

Discussions of women in contemporary society often raise issues of discrimination, gender bias, inequality, and political oppression. Indeed, it goes without
saying that women have generally not been treated equally or with complete
respect throughout human history. These days, fair-minded people of both sexes
have certainly applauded the writings and past efforts of political activists such
as Simone de Beauvoir, Germain Greer, Gloria Steinem, Nellie McClung, and
countless others who, in the second half of the twentieth century, helped to raise
our collective consciousness regarding the treatment of women in society. In
view of centuries-old female discrimination and the relatively recent emergence
of the women's movement in the West, it is interesting to note that Plato was
arguably an ancient **feminist** of sorts. For Plato, guardian women, at least, were
not to remain *barefoot and pregnant in the kitchen,* to use a colloquial expression.
Their role was not simply to stay at home and mind the baby. While Plato did
recognize that men and women are not exactly alike, especially where reproduction is concerned, he did not regard these biological differences as relevant
when it comes to playing leadership roles in society.

In recognition of women's intellectual and moral equality, they were to be
given the same education as men. Like males, females were to receive instruction
in music, gymnastics, military discipline, astronomy, mathematics, and so forth.
As with males, the best of the females, who passed the same moral tests of character and intellectual bars of admission, would be further trained as guardians of
the state. The best of the best, of course, would then be selected as elite philosopher rulers. The remaining ones would become part of the auxiliary class. Plato's
Republic thus allows for women to be admitted to all social pursuits, even war.
Both men and women share the same natural capacities for guardianship, and
where physical strength is an issue, women are simply to be given a lighter load.

Women in contemporary society are often torn apart inside trying to achieve
a balance between the responsibilities of work and family, or between career and
spousal commitments. In Plato's Republic, women in leadership roles are liberated, as Plato makes it possible for them to be relieved of their parental and
marital obligations. Guardian women (both auxiliary and philosopher ruler)
are, like men, not allowed to have families and normal marriage relations. Such
things were restricted to the artisan class. Because Plato is most interested in the
governing elite and the establishment of a just state ruled by them, the role of
women within the artisan class is not discussed in any detail. Much is missing,

and for this, Plato has been criticized. From some of Plato's writings, one can speculate that artisan women are not given an equally "fair deal" in society like their guardian counterparts. Be that as it may, regarding the guardians, about whom Plato says most, he felt it was necessary to get rid of distracting loyalties, self-interests, and affectional ties associated with the family system. He wanted focus to be on service to the community. Instead of couple arrangements and nuclear families, then, the guardians would constitute, and belong to, one large extended family—the guardian herd.

To ensure that guardians were not side-tracked by long-term love relations and by contaminating family loyalties, men and women were allowed multiple mating opportunities. Be clear, however, that this was no system of "free love." Contrived lotteries, run by the philosopher rulers, rigged things so that only the bravest and the best of the guardians would be allowed to have intercourse and conceive, and only during scheduled marriage festivals. Plato believed that the offspring of the best and the bravest would most likely produce the desirable traits of their guardian parents. What Plato had in mind was a systematic program of **eugenics,** bearing great similarity to animal breeding. Plato recognized, or course, that breeding practices cannot always guarantee the best progeny. Thus, children not suited to belong to the guardian class would be dispersed among the artisans and raised by them. Conversely, those children "born of the bronze," who displayed the virtues and qualities of the gold, would be elevated to the guardian classes for proper training and education. Class placement was therefore not a birthright, since in Plato's **meritocracy** one was required to earn one' position in society. With marriage abolished for the guardians and with state-run nurseries charged with the responsibility of raising guardian-produced children, women rulers and auxiliaries were thus given freedom and access to the same leadership opportunities as men—something that no doubt would be considered today a victory for feminists. Read the Original Sourcework below to see exactly what Plato says about women in *The Republic.*

## ORIGINAL SOURCEWORK

### *The Nature of Woman*

**PLATO**

First, then, whether the question is to be put in jest or in earnest, let us come to an understanding about the nature of woman: Is she capable of sharing either wholly or partially in the actions of men, or not at all? And is the art of war one of those arts in which she can or can not share? That will be the best way of commencing the enquiry, and will probably lead to the fairest conclusion.

That will be much the best way.

Shall we take the other side first and begin by arguing against ourselves; in this manner the adversary's position will not be undefended.

Why not? he said.

Then let us put a speech into the mouths of our opponents. They will say: "Socrates and Glaucon, no adversary need convict you, for you yourselves, at the first foundation of the State, admitted the principle that

*Source:* Plato, *The Republic,* trans. Benjamin Jowett, New York: P.F. Collier & Son © 1901, The Colonial Press, section 453a–457a.

everybody was to do the one work suited to his own nature." And certainly, if I am not mistaken, such an admission was made by us. "And do not the natures of men and women differ very much indeed?" And we shall reply: Of course they do. Then we shall be asked, "Whether the tasks assigned to men and to women should not be different, and such as are agreeable to their different natures?" Certainly they should. "But if so, have you not fallen into a serious inconsistency in saying that men and women, whose natures are so entirely different, ought to perform the same actions?"—What defence will you make for us, my good Sir, against any one who offers these objections?

That is not an easy question to answer when asked suddenly; and I shall and I do beg of you to draw out the case on our side.

These are the objections, Glaucon, and there are many others of a like kind, which I foresaw long ago; they made me afraid and reluctant to take in hand any law about the possession and nurture of women and children.

By Zeus, he said, the problem to be solved is anything but easy.

Why yes, I said, but the fact is that when a man is out of his depth, whether he has fallen into a little swimming bath or into mid-ocean, he has to swim all the same.

Very true.

And must not we swim and try to reach the shore: we will hope that Arion's dolphin or some other miraculous help may save us?

I suppose so, he said.

Well then, let us see if any way of escape can be found. We acknowledged—did we not? that different natures ought to have different pursuits, and that men's and women's natures are different. And now what are we saying?—that different natures ought to have the same pursuits,—this is the inconsistency which is charged upon us.

Precisely.

Verily, Glaucon, I said, glorious is the power of the art of contradiction!

Why do you say so?

Because I think that many a man falls into the practice against his will. When he thinks that he is reasoning he is really disputing, just because he cannot define and divide, and so know that of which he is speaking; and he will pursue a merely verbal opposition in the spirit of contention and not of fair discussion.

Yes, he replied, such is very often the case; but what has that to do with us and our argument?

A great deal; for there is certainly a danger of our getting unintentionally into a verbal opposition.

In what way?

Why, we valiantly and pugnaciously insist upon the verbal truth, that different natures ought to have different pursuits, but we never considered at all what was the meaning of sameness or difference of nature, or why we distinguished them when we assigned different pursuits to different natures and the same to the same natures.

Why, no, he said, that was never considered by us.

I said: Suppose that by way of illustration we were to ask the question whether there is not an opposition in nature between bald men and hairy men; and if this is admitted by us, then, if bald men are cobblers, we should forbid the hairy men to be cobblers, and conversely?

That would be a jest, he said.

Yes, I said, a jest; and why? because we never meant when we constructed the State, that the opposition of natures should extend to every difference, but only to those differences which affected the pursuit in which the individual is engaged; we should have argued, for example, that a physician and one who is in mind a physician may be said to have the same nature.

True.

Whereas the physician and the carpenter have different natures?

Certainly.

And if, I said, the male and female sex appear to differ in their fitness for any art or pursuit, we should say that such pursuit or art ought to be assigned to one or the other of them; but if the difference consists only in women bearing and men begetting children, this does not amount to a proof that a woman differs from a man in respect of the sort of education she should receive; and we shall therefore continue to maintain that our guardians and their wives ought to have the same pursuits.

Very true, he said.

Next, we shall ask our opponent how, in reference to any of the pursuits or arts of civic life, the nature of a woman differs from that of a man?

That will be quite fair.

And perhaps he, like yourself, will reply that to give a sufficient answer on the instant is not easy; but after a little reflection there is no difficulty.

Yes, perhaps.

Suppose then that we invite him to accompany us in the argument, and then we may hope to show him that there is nothing peculiar in the constitution of women which would affect them in the administration of the State.

By all means.

Let us say to him: Come now, and we will ask you a question:—when you spoke of a nature gifted or not gifted in any respect, did you mean to say that one man will acquire a thing easily, another with difficulty; a little learning will lead the one to discover a great deal; whereas the other, after much study and application, no sooner learns than he forgets; or again, did you mean, that the one has a body which is a good servant to his mind, while the body of the other is a hindrance to him?—would not these be the sort of differences which distinguish the man gifted by nature from the one who is ungifted?

No one will deny that.

And can you mention any pursuit of mankind in which the male sex has not all these gifts and qualities in a higher degree than the female? Need I waste time in speaking of the art of weaving, and the management of pancakes and preserves, in which womankind does really appear to be great, and in which for her to be beaten by a man is of all things the most absurd?

You are quite right, he replied, in maintaining the general inferiority of the female sex: although many women are in many things superior to many men, yet on the whole what you say is true.

And if so, my friend, I said, there is no special faculty of administration in a state which a woman has because she is a woman, or which a man has by virtue of his sex, but the gifts of nature are alike diffused in both; all the pursuits of men are the pursuits of women also, but in all of them a woman is inferior to a man.

Very true.

Then are we to impose all our enactments on men and none of them on women?

That will never do.

One woman has a gift of healing, another not; one is a musician, and another has no music in her nature?

Very true.

And one woman has a turn for gymnastic and military exercises, and another is unwarlike and hates gymnastics?

Certainly.

And one woman is a philosopher, and another is an enemy of philosophy; one has spirit, and another is without spirit?

That is also true.

Then one woman will have the temper of a guardian, and another not. Was not the selection of the male guardians determined by differences of this sort?

Yes.

Men and women alike possess the qualities which make a guardian; they differ only in their comparative strength or weakness.

Obviously.

And those women who have such qualities are to be selected as the companions and colleagues of men who have similar qualities and whom they resemble in capacity and in character?

Very true.

And ought not the same natures to have the same pursuits?

They ought.

Then, as we were saying before, there is nothing unnatural in assigning music and gymnastic to the wives of the guardians—to that point we come round again.

Certainly not.

The law which we then enacted was agreeable to nature, and therefore not an impossibility or mere aspiration; and the contrary practice, which prevails at present, is in reality a violation of nature.

That appears to be true.

We had to consider, first, whether our proposals were possible, and secondly whether they were the most beneficial?

Yes.

And the possibility has been acknowledged?

Yes.

The very great benefit has next to be established?

Quite so.

You will admit that the same education which makes a man a good guardian will make a woman a good guardian; for their original nature is the same?

Yes.

I should like to ask you a question.

What is it?

Would you say that all men are equal in excellence, or is one man better than another?

The latter.

And in the commonwealth which we were founding do you conceive the guardians who have been brought up on our model system to be more perfect men, or the cobblers whose education has been cobbling?

What a ridiculous question!

You have answered me, I replied: Well, and may we not further say that our guardians are the best of our citizens?

By far the best.

And will not their wives be the best women?

Yes, by far the best.

And can there be anything better for the interests of the State than that the men and women of a State should be as good as possible?

There can be nothing better.

And this is what the arts of music and gymnastic, when present in such manner as we have described, will accomplish?

Certainly.

Then we have made an enactment not only possible but in the highest degree beneficial to the State?

True.

Then let the wives of our guardians strip, for their virtue will be their robe, and let them share in the toils of war and the defence of their country; only in the distribution of labours the lighter are to be assigned to the women, who are the weaker natures, but in other respects their duties are to be the same. And as for the man who laughs at naked women exercising their bodies from the best of motives, in his laughter he is plucking

"A fruit of unripe wisdom,"

and he himself is ignorant of what he is laughing at, or what he is about;—for that is, and ever will be, the best of sayings, *That the useful is the noble and the hurtful is the base.*

Very true.

## DISCUSSION QUESTIONS FOR CRITIQUE AND ANALYSIS

1. When it comes to the role of women in society, specifically in the context of war, does Socrates contradict himself, in fact, as some of his opponents might suggest? Why or why not? Do you agree with Socrates or take issue with him?

2. What is the general structure or form of Socrates's argument? See if you can summarize it in outline form or explain it diagrammatically.

# SOCIAL CONTRACT THEORISTS: HOBBES AND LOCKE

Having now considered how Plato would have organized his ideal Greek city-state, let us now leap centuries forward to learn about **social contract theory** and its conception of society. "Social contract theory" does not actually refer to the work of a singular theorist or to some sort of singular approach, but is a label assigned to a group of political thinkers whose ideas overlap one another. Social contract theorists give primacy of place to the individual in discussions of the state. The collectivity, however conceived, represents the product of an agreement, covenant, or contract among the individuals who constitute it. By means of a social contract, individuals are brought together in society to form some sort of formal governmental structure upon which they can all agree. The particular parties who contract in society can differ. Sometimes contracts are made between individuals, sometimes between individuals and governments (or sovereign powers), or sometimes between a body of individuals acting as a fictitious person (*persona ficta*) and either a sovereign leader or a member of that body.[23] However contracts are established, we generally find that individual rights are recognized and that consent is used as the basis for the formation of government. Let us now turn to the first social contractarian to be discussed in this chapter, namely, Thomas Hobbes. He is often regarded as the founder of the social contract tradition. Later, we will examine the work of John Locke.

## PHILOSOPHICAL PROFILE

**THOMAS HOBBES**

### Thomas Hobbes

Thomas Hobbes was born prematurely on April 5, 1588, during a period of international turbulence and family turmoil. Legend, if not truth, has it that his early arrival was induced by his mother's anxiety about the threatening invasion by an approaching Spanish armada. This belief led Hobbes to conclude about himself that: "Fear and I were born twins." On the family front, things were not any more secure. Hobbes's father was a quarrelsome and uneducated vicar of Westport, near Malmesbury, Wiltshire, England. Not only did his unruly father destroy his career by engaging in fisticuffs with another clergyman in front of his own church door; he then fled to London, abandoning his family altogether.[24] Rescued financially by a wealthy relative, Hobbes was lucky enough to receive a good education in spite of his family's unfortunate plight. He eventually earned a Bachelor's degree at Oxford University's Magdalen Hall.

While at Oxford, Hobbes received a traditional Scholastic education, consisting mainly of studies in logic and the philosophy of Aristotle. Though he developed a number of serious disagreements with Aristotelian philosophy, he must have been influenced by Aristotle to some extent, since he was the first major political theorist since Aristotle to separate politics from theology, lending greater weight to the adage that "Our enemies help define us."

After graduating from Oxford, Hobbes accepted an appointment as tutor to the son of William Cavendish, the first Earl of Devonshire. This began a lifelong relationship with three generations of the Cavendish clan as tutor, scholar, and companion.[25] As a wonderful result of his long-term affiliation with the wealthy Cavendishes, Hobbes was given many opportunities to travel and to meet some of the most prominent figures of the day, including Sir Francis Bacon and Galileo in Italy. It is not known for sure, but Hobbes may have even met René Descartes in Paris, France. He certainly travelled in Cartesian circles, establishing friendships with both critics and admirers of this intellectual revolutionary.[26]

In 1640, Hobbes was forced to leave England and seek refuge in France because of his support for the monarchy. He lived during an unsettled time in English history highlighted by civil war between defenders of the throne and the antiroyalists. After an eleven-year period of self-imposed exile for prudential reasons, Hobbes ironically had to escape back to England when he found himself in danger of assassination by his political foes. Hobbes discovered upon his return home that his writings were considered subversive. In 1662, he was ordered by threat of imprisonment to refrain from publishing any further works on social and political matters. Hobbes died in Hardwick, Derbyshire, in 1679 at the ripe old age of 91. He is probably best known for his book *Leviathan*. Other lesser known works include *The Elements of Law, Natural and Political,* and *A Short Tract on First Principles.* Hobbes's initial publication was actually a translation of Thucidides's *History of the Peloponnesian War.* In his youth, the melancholy Hobbes was nicknamed "the Crow." As his namesake might suggest, this political bird presents us with a dark and ominous conception of human nature and a vision of political organization founded upon fear of death.

# THOMAS HOBBES
## State of Nature

Thomas Hobbes's political philosophy differs significantly from his historical predecessors, Plato and Aristotle. Living through a period of civil war in England, during which time his own security was threatened, and witnessing the brutality of the Thirty Years' War on the European continent (1618–1648), Hobbes certainly did not share the Greek duo's idealism. He considered it unrealistic to assume that people are naturally capable of virtue and wisdom.[27] Hobbes would take issue with Aristotle's contention, for example, that humans are, by nature, social animals. He believed that without social conditioning, we have no genetically innate, built-in affinity or sympathy for other members of our own species. Altruism is therefore not a natural emotion. We are simply driven by our egoistic desires to survive and gain pleasure, and nothing guarantees any sort of harmony between the motives of one person and another.[28] One could ask if slaves and barbarian serfs gladly and without struggle gave up their own desires to serve the needs of the Aristotelian middle class. Would you? Furthermore, is it reasonable to believe that Plato's artisan class would take orders from above and happily perform their inferior functions in service to the Republic's greater good? I'll let you be the judge of that.

According to Hobbes, all human beings are equal by nature with respect to their bodily and mental capacities. He does not suggest that all people possess exactly the same level of physical strength or quickness of mind; rather, he points out that individuals who are deficient or weaker in one respect can make up for this in other ways. For example, those who are physically weak can overcome the physically strong by craft, cunning, or by conspiracy.

The **natural equality** among human beings gives all persons equal hope of achieving their life goals. The problem with this **state of nature,** however, wherein everybody is more or less equal and desirous of the same things, is that competition and mistrust of others grow. Add to this the fact that individuals want others to value them as much as they value themselves, and that individuals preoccupied with their own self-worth are quick to resent every slight and all signs of contempt, and what arises is a condition of war. Hobbes writes (in old English):

> Hereby it is manifest that during the time men live without a common Power to keep them all in awe, they are in that condition which is called Warre; and such a Warre, as is of every man, against every man.[29]

Commenting on the reasons for conflict among humans, he states:

> So that in the nature of man, we find three principall causes of quarrell. First, Competition; Secondly, Diffidence [mistrust]; Thirdly, Glory. The first maketh men invade for Gain; the second, for Safety; and the third, for Reputation. The first use Violence to make themselves Masters of other mens persons, wives, children and cattell; the second, to defend them; the third, for trifles, as a word, a smile, a different opinion, and any other signe of undervalue, either direct in their Persons, or by reflexion in their Kindred, their Friends, their Nation, their Profession, or their Name.[30]

By positing that the human condition is a condition of warring enemies, Hobbes is not suggesting that everyone around the world is currently, or was during his time, engaged in armed conflict. The natural state of war is a hypothetical condition in which civilization and all its benefits are absent; it is not a historical condition, though Hobbes does remark that the state of nature did exist in many places like America, where "savages" [his word] "live at this day in that brutish manner." For all others, the state of nature is a characterization resulting from a thought experiment, imagining what things would be like without organized society and sanctioned law.

In the natural state of war, there are no moral distinctions between right and wrong, good or bad. There is no justice or injustice, only chaos, disorder, and opposition. Of course, today we have governments, constitutions, and ruling bodies supported by law; however, if the veneer of civilization were suddenly stripped of such things, we would revert back to the warring condition Hobbes describes as the state of nature.[31] This does not necessarily imply that war would break out immediately and everywhere, or nonstop for all eternity. For Hobbes, the nature of war consists not just in actual fighting, but in the known disposition to fight during all the time there is no assurance of peace.[32] Explaining this by analogy to weather, he writes (in old English again):

> For Warre, consisteth not in Battell onely, or the act of fighting; but in a tract of time, wherein the Will to contend is sufficiently known: and therefore the notion of *Time*, is to be considered in the nature of Warre; as it is in the nature of Weather. For as the nature of Foule weather, lyeth not in a showre or two of rain; but in an inclination thereto of many dayes together; so the nature of War (sic, Old English), consisteth not in actuall fighting: but in the known disposition thereto, during all the time there is no assurance to the contrary.[33]

In the state of nature, there is no place for industry or hard work, since the fruits of one's labors are always at risk of invasion or destruction by others. Living in continual fear and danger of violent death, much of what we take to be included in our conception of a civilized society becomes impossible or at least seriously threatened—things like culture, travel (navigation), construction, the pursuit of knowledge, literature, the arts, and so on. "The life of man [becomes] solitary, poore, nasty, brutish, and short."[34]

Hobbes arrives at the conclusion that life in the natural state is characterized by competitive struggle, fear, and distrust through a deductive process based on a consideration of man's passions and natural inclinations. He also provides examples from everyday experience, drawing our attention, for example, to the fact that people going on trips (in his day) arm themselves for protection. When going to sleep at night, they lock the doors. Even when at home, they lock their valuables away, knowing that there are laws and armed officers to protect them and prosecute those who would harm them or violate them in any way. Rhetorically, Hobbes asks, aren't such protective measures and security officers in truth accusations? Addressing the individual who takes precautions against his fellow men, Hobbes writes:

> . . . what opinion he has of his fellow subjects, when he rides armed, of his fellow Citizens when he locks his dores; and of his children, and servants, when he locks his chests. Does he not there as much accuse mankind by his actions, as I do by my words?[35]

## PHILOSOPHERS IN ACTION

What specific claims does Hobbes make about human behavior? Are these claims empirical or normative (see Chapter 3)? From what you have learned about reasoning, do you think he provides sufficient proof or justification? In your philosophical opinion, what, if anything, could, or should, Hobbes do to further support his claims? Discuss with classmates.

## Laws of Nature

In the preceding section, we learned how Hobbes arrived at his conception of a natural state of war from a deduction based on the nature of man and his passions. Note, too, that in the state of nature, no desires or passions could be considered right or wrong in themselves, as there is no objective morality. And where there is no objective morality, no law, there is no injustice. The only "**right of nature**," so-called by Hobbes, that we all share is the freedom to use our power in any way we wish for purposes of self-preservation, even if this entails attack on another's body. In a lawless condition of natural equality, where everyone has the right to anything and everything that one desires, there can be no security for anybody. Fortunately, the same natural passions that lead to war can also lead to

> ❝*Where there is no common Power, there is no Law, where no Law, no Injustice. Force and Fraud are in warre the two Cardinal vertues.*❞
>
> HOBBES

peace. According to Hobbes, fear of death, a desire to acquire and hold on to things as are necessary to "commodious" (comfortable and convenient) living, and hope of achieving such things through personal effort are passions that incline us to seek peace. What reason dictates we do to get us out of a condition of war and into a position of personal security, Hobbes calls a **law of nature.** Think of a law of nature as a kind of duty emanating from egoistic prudence. All people strive for security and self-preservation. They are not merely creatures of instinct and blind impulse, genetically determined to behave in this way or that. There is something one might refer to *as rational self-preservation*. The laws of nature state the conditions of this rational self-preservation.[36] On this note, Hobbes says: "A Law of Nature (*Lex Naturalis*) is a Precept, or generall Rule, found out by Reason, by which a man is forbidden to do, that, which is destructive of his life, or taketh away the means of preserving the same; and to omit, that, by which he thinketh it may be best preserved."[37]

In *Leviathan*, Hobbes actually enumerates nineteen laws of nature in all. We will restrict ourselves here to the three most important ones. The first precept, or natural law of reason, is stated so: "That every man, ought to endeavour Peace, as farre as he has hope of obtaining it; and when he cannot obtain it, that he may seek, and use, all helps, and advantages of Warre."[38] The first part of this precept tells us to seek peace and follow it; the second part underscores our natural right to defend ourselves by all means possible.

From the first fundamental law of nature follows the second, which ensures our survival. It prescribes: "That a man be willing, when others are so too, as farreforth, as for Peace, and defence of himselfe he shall think it necessary, to lay down this right to all things; and be contented with so much liberty against other men, as he would allow other men against himselfe."[39] Expressed in more contemporary English: We should give up our individual rights to take by force whatever we want, provided that everyone else does too in order to preserve the peace. Like the first law of nature, this one also constitutes an **egoistic rule of prudence**—something like a "selfish golden rule."[40] By denying our rights to ourselves (on the condition that others do too), we are not being altruistic or self-sacrificial; we are doing what is in our own best interest.

Closely related to the second precept is the third law of nature, namely: "That men performe their Covenants made: without which, Covenants are in vain, and but Empty words; and the Right of all men to all things remaining, we are still in the condition of Warre."[41] To establish a covenant, contract, or deal, if you will, but not live by the terms of it, is to accomplish nothing and to secure nothing. We go back to where we started—in a condition where every man is enemy to every other man.

## The Commonwealth — Hobbes's *Leviathan*

On the assumption that human beings are vain and greedy egoists, who are likely to violate each other when it is in their self-interest to do so; Hobbes concludes that ". . . there must be some coërcive Power, to compel men equally to the performance of their Covenants, by the terrour of some punishment, greater than the benefit they expect by the breach of their Covenant. . . ."[42] In other

The Frontispiece of *Leviathan* displays an all-powerful sovereign with long hair, twisted moustache, and pointed beard like a Stuart king. The crown signifies his sovereign power.

words, there must be some sort of strong sanctioning body which, by threat of severe retribution, forces people to live by their promises and agreements with others. For Hobbes, the only way for people to ensure that covenants are not broken is: "to conferre all their power and strength upon one Man, or upon one Assembly of men, that may reduce all their Wills, by plurality of voices, unto one Will. . . ." This 'Man' or 'assembly of men' Hobbes calls the "great **Leviathan**" (meaning something large and formidable; or a sea monster of immense size). He even refers to it as that "*Mortall God*, to which wee owe under the *Immortal God*, our peace and defence."[43]

The sovereign power of the Leviathan is based on people's fear. Leviathan is necessary, for the only way to transform multiple wills into a single will is to agree that the sovereign's will and judgment represent the will and judgment of all the citizens.[44] No attempt is made by Hobbes to derive the legitimacy of sovereign power either from theological or metaphysical principles.[45] Though a royalist himself (see Philosophical Profile), he does not give kings or queens any divine right to govern. Governments are not instituted by God. Rather, they are purely human creations brought into existence in order to enable individuals to achieve their egoistic goals. The covenant among individuals could, in principle, establish any one of a variety of governmental structures besides a monarchy, including, say, a democracy or aristocracy.[46] Whatever form of governance the Leviathan assumes, self-interest will lie at the basis of it.

## The Social Contract

The ability of the Leviathan or sovereign body to secure the safety, security, and peace of all its citizens depends on a **social contract.** This contract should not be taken literally as an historical artifact, as in an actual document signed by lawyers representing warring enemies; rather, it is a notion that stipulates what is ultimately required by the laws of nature that direct us toward peaceful coexistence. In order to survive peacefully, we must implicitly, or explicitly, all agree to transfer our rights to one ruler or assembly. The agreement could be expressed something like so:

> I Authorize and give up my Right of Governing my selfe, to this Man, or to this Assembly of men, on this condition, that thou give up thy Right to him, and Authorise all his Actions in like manner.[47]

When the multitude of citizens is so united in one person or governing body, we have what Hobbes calls a "Common-Wealth." The **commonwealth** (to use the contemporary spelling) is instituted for a very specific purpose, namely, for the peaceful security of those who are a party to the social covenant.[48] Its purpose is therefore utilitarian. Hobbes firmly believed that if one centralized authority in the person of the sovereign, then the evil Hobbes dreaded—namely, civil war—could be avoided.

Whatever form it takes (monarchy, democracy), the sovereign body has to be indivisible and absolute. If one tried to divide or limit sovereignty, one would risk anarchy. Furthermore, limiting sovereignty would be illogical, since it would then create opposing and warring parties—something over which the sovereign was to have absolute authority. Absolutism thus becomes a logical consequence of government by consent.

The subjects belonging to a commonwealth cannot change the form of government or repudiate the authority of the sovereign, as this would only serve to return isolated individuals to a disunited and chaotic multitude. The sovereignty of the great Leviathan must be inalienable. No sovereign can justly be executed or punished in any way by his subjects. If the sovereign is guilty of iniquitous actions, then the matter becomes one between the sovereign and God, not between the citizens and the sovereign. Though the sovereign is created by the contract, the ruling body is not party to it.

## Conditions on the Sovereign

There are some conditions that can be placed on the sovereign in the commonwealth notwithstanding his absolute authority. Subjects are absolved of their duty to obey the sovereign if: (1) he relinquishes his sovereignty; (2) if the commonwealth is torn apart internally and the sovereign no longer has effective power, at which time the subjects go back to the state of nature requiring a new sovereign; and finally, (3) if the sovereign is conquered in war, and surrenders to the victor, then the citizens become subjects to the latter.[49]

## Of the Causes, Generation, and Definition of a Commonwealth

### THOMAS HOBBES

The final cause, end, or design of men, who naturally love liberty and dominion over others, in the introduction of that restraint upon themselves in which we see them live in commonwealths is the foresight of their own preservation, and of a more contented life thereby—that is to say, of getting themselves out from that miserable condition of war which is necessarily consequent, as has been shown (Chapter XIII), to the natural passions of men when there is no visible power to keep them in awe and tie them by fear of punishment to the performance of their covenants and observation of those laws of nature set down in the fourteenth and fifteenth chapters.

For the laws of nature—as *justice, equity, modesty, mercy,* and, in sum, *doing to others as we would be done to*—of themselves, without the terror of some power to cause them to be observed, are contrary to our natural passions, that carry us to partiality, pride, revenge, and the like. And covenants without the sword are but words, and of no strength to secure a man at all. Therefore, notwithstanding the laws of nature (which everyone has then kept when he has the will to keep them, when he can do it safely), if there be no power erected, or not great enough for our security, every man will—and may lawfully—rely on his own strength and art for caution against all other men. And in all places where men have lived by small families, to rob and spoil one another has been a trade, and so far from being reputed against the law of nature that the greater spoils they gained, the

greater was their honor; and men observed no other laws therein but the laws of honor—that is, to abstain from cruelty, leaving to men their lives and instruments of husbandry. And as small families did then, so now do cities and kingdoms, which are but greater families, for their own security enlarge their dominions upon all pretenses of danger and fear of invasion or assistance that may be given to invaders, and endeavor as much as they can to subdue or weaken their neighbors by open force and secret arts, for want of other caution, justly; and are remembered for it in after ages with honor.

Nor is it the joining together of a small number of men that gives them this security, because in small numbers small additions on the one side or the other make the advantage of strength so great as is sufficient to carry the victory, and therefore gives encouragement to an invasion. The multitude sufficient to confide in for our security is not determined by any certain number but by comparison with the enemy we fear, and is then sufficient when the odds of the enemy is not of so visible and conspicuous moment to determine the event of war as to move him to attempt.

And be there never so great a multitude, yet if their actions be directed according to their particular judgments and particular appetites, they can expect thereby no defense nor protection, neither against a common enemy nor against the injuries of one another. For being distracted in opinions concerning the best use and application of their strength, they do not help but hinder

*Source:* Thomas Hobbes, *Leviathan.* Originally published in 1651. Library of Liberal Arts, Prentice-Hall, Inc. A Simon & Schuster Company, Englewood Cliffs, New Jersey 07632. The first edition of Thomas Hobbes's *Leviathan* was published in 1651 by A. Crooke, London. The original *Leviathan* was also published by Sir William Noleworth, (ed.), *The English Works of Thomas Hobbes,* 11 volumes, London, 1839–45.

one another, and reduce their strength by mutual oppo- sition to nothing; whereby they are easily not only sub- dued by a very few that agree together, but also, when there is no common enemy, they make war upon each other for their particular interest. For if we could suppose a great multitude of men to consent in the observation of justice and other laws of nature without a common power to keep them all in awe, we might as well suppose all mankind to do the same; and then there neither would be, nor need to be, any civil government or com- monwealth at all, because there would be peace without subjection.

Nor is it enough for the security which men desire should last all the time of their life that they be gov- erned and directed by one judgment for a limited time, as in one battle or one war. For though they obtain a victory by their unanimous endeavor against a foreign enemy, yet afterwards, when either they have no com- mon enemy or he that by one part is held for an enemy is by another part held for a friend, they must needs, by the difference of their interests, dissolve and fall again into a war among themselves.

It is true that certain living creatures, as bees and ants, live sociably one with another—which are therefore by Aristotle numbered among political creatures—and yet have no other direction than their particular judg- ments and appetites, nor speech whereby one of them can signify to another what he thinks expedient for the common benefit; and therefore some man may perhaps desire to know why mankind cannot do the same. To which I answer:

First, that men are continually in competition for honor and dignity, which these creatures are not; and consequently among men there arises on that ground envy and hatred and finally war, but among these not so.

Secondly, that among these creatures the common good differs not from the private; and being by nature inclined to their private, they procure thereby the com- mon benefit. But man, whose joy consists in comparing himself with other men, can relish nothing but what is eminent.

Thirdly, that these creatures—having not, as man, the use of reason—do not see nor think they see any fault in the administration of their common business; whereas among men there are very many that think themselves wiser and abler to govern the public better than the rest, and these strive to reform and innovate,

one this way, another that way, and thereby bring it into distraction and civil war.

Fourthly, that these creatures, though they have some use of voice in making known to one another their desires and other affections, yet they want that art of words by which some men can represent to others that which is good in the likeness of evil, and evil in the like- ness of good, and augment or diminish the apparent greatness of good and evil, discontenting men and trou- bling their peace at their pleasure.

Fifthly, irrational creatures cannot distinguish be- tween *injury* and *damage,* and therefore, as long as they be at ease, they are not offended with their fellows; whereas man is then most troublesome when he is most at ease, for then it is that he loves to show his wisdom and control the actions of them that govern the commonwealth.

Lastly, the agreement of these creatures is natural, that of men is by covenant only, which is artificial; and therefore it is no wonder if there be somewhat else re- quired besides covenant to make their agreement con- stant and lasting, which is a common power to keep them in awe and to direct their actions to the common benefit.

The only way to erect such a common power as may be able to defend them from the invasion of foreigners and the injuries of one another, and thereby to secure them in such sort as that by their own industry and by the fruits of the earth they may nourish themselves and live contentedly, is to confer all their power and strength upon one man, or upon one assembly of men that may reduce all their wills, by plurality of voices, unto one will; which is as much as to say, to appoint one man or as- sembly of men to bear their person, and everyone to own and acknowledge himself to be author of whatsoever he that so bears their person shall act or cause to be acted in those things which concern the common peace and safety, and therein to submit their wills every one to his will, and their judgments to his judgment. This is more than consent or concord; it is a real unity of them all in one and the same person, made by covenant of every man with every man, in such manner as if every man should say to every man, *I authorize and give up my right of governing myself to this man, or to this assembly of men, on this condition, that you give up your right to him and authorize all his actions in like manner.* This done, the multitude so united in one person is called a COM-

MONWEALTH, in Latin CIVITAS. This is the generation of that great LEVIATHAN (or rather, to speak more reverently, of that *mortal god*) to which we owe, under the *immortal God,* our peace and defense. For by this authority, given him by every particular man in the commonwealth, he has the use of so much power and strength conferred on him that, by terror thereof, he is enabled to form the wills of them all to peace at home and mutual aid against their enemies abroad. And in him consists the essence of the commonwealth, which, to define it, is *one person, of whose acts a great multitude, by mutual covenants one with another, have made themselves every one the author, to the end he may use the strength and means of them all as he shall think expedient for their peace and common defense.* And he that carries this person is called SOVEREIGN and said to have *sovereign power;* and everyone besides, his SUBJECT.

The attaining to this sovereign power is by two ways. One, by natural force, as when a man makes his children to submit themselves and their children to his government, as being able to destroy them if they refuse, or by war subdues his enemies to his will, giving them their lives on that condition. The other is when men agree among themselves to submit to some man or assembly of men voluntarily, on confidence to be protected by him against all others. This latter may be called a political commonwealth, or commonwealth by *institution,* and the former a commonwealth by *acquisition.* And first I shall speak of a commonwealth by institution.

## DISCUSSION QUESTIONS FOR CRITIQUE AND ANALYSIS

1. How does Hobbes conceptualize human nature? Does he give adequate support or evidence for his claims? Explain and illustrate.

2. How does Hobbes envision the state of nature without government? Given what he says, what does he propose and why? Provide reasons for your agreement or disagreement with his views and recommendations.

# JOHN LOCKE

John Locke (see his Philosophical Profile in Chapter 4) is a political philosopher whose ideas have been interwoven into the very fabric of American society. We could describe him as one of the theoretical architects of democracy in the Western world.[50] He certainly exerted a profound influence on the formation of the political philosophies underlying the American and French republics. His thinking is said to have served as a main source of the ideas supporting the American Revolution of 1776. The observation has been made that a good deal of the language contained in the **Declaration of Independence** and the later **American Constitution** was taken liberally from Locke's *Second Treatise of Government.* (Locke's *First Treatise* was an attack on divine right monarchy, while his second was written in opposition to Hobbesian absolutism, though Hobbes was never mentioned explicitly.[51]) Some have even accused Thomas Jefferson of copying the *Second Treatise.* Though such an allegation may be somewhat extravagant, there are indeed some interesting similarities of expression between Locke and Jefferson that are worth noting.[52] What is certain is that Locke's writings provide an impressive framework for refining our democratic and political ideas relating to concepts of property, individual rights, and the ultimate sovereignty of the citizen population.

Like Thomas Hobbes, Locke belongs to the social contract/natural law tradition of political thought, and like Hobbes as well, he allows a central role to be played by considerations of self-preservation. Despite these broad similarities,

> *"The end of government is the good of mankind."*
> JOHN LOCKE

however, there are profound differences between these two men that need to be explained. Perhaps the best place to start is with how each conceptualizes the state of nature.

## Locke's State of Nature and the Natural Law

Hobbes presented us with a rather grim picture of life before the establishment of sovereign-controlled society. Recall how the natural state, for Hobbes, was a state of war in which every person was at war with every other person. Motivated by competitiveness, mistrust, and egoistic pride, humans were portrayed as nasty, antisocial brutes who are both greedy and selfish. In the Hobbesian state of nature, there is no objective morality or altruistic tendencies. The only "natural" right anyone has is freedom based on power—more specifically, the right to do anything necessary for survival—and we are all equal in this. There is certainly no goodness or justice as understood in the usual sense. Clearly, the Hobbesian state of nature is not a very hospitable setting. We fear death and we fear each other.

Like Hobbes, John Locke also bases his political philosophy on an interpretation of human nature, but he comes to radically different conclusions about it. He says, ". . . we must consider what state all men are naturally in, and that is a state of perfect freedom to order their actions and dispose of their possessions and persons as they think fit, within the bounds of the law of nature, without asking leave or depending upon the will of any other man."[53] The key phrase in the preceding statement is "within the bounds of the law of nature." In the state of nature, humans have freedom but not license to do absolutely anything they wish. Locke says: "The **state of nature** has a law of nature to govern it, which obliges every one; and reason, which is that law, teaches all mankind who will but consult it that, being all equal and independent, no one ought to harm another in his life, health, liberty or possessions; . . . "[54] This **natural law,** like human beings, is "the workmanship of one omnipotent and infinitely wise Maker"—namely God. Thus, even prior to organized society, people can distinguish between right and wrong by reference to the moral law. **God** created human beings as rational creatures, acquainting them with the law of nature which enjoins them to be helpful and well-disposed toward one another. Given that we are all free and equal, then, and cognizant of the fact that freedom is not tantamount to license, the natural law would have us seek peace and the preservation of all humankind, not just our own personal gain and survival. In contrast to Hobbes, for whom natural law meant the law of power, force, and fraud, for Locke it means a universally obligatory moral law promulgated by human reason as it "reflects on God and His rights, on man's relation to God and on the fundamental equality of all men as rational creatures."[55] Viewing natural law in this way, Locke grants human beings **natural rights** independently of any state and its legislation. All individuals have the right to self-preservation, self-defense, and personal liberty.[56]

From here, we can see that Locke's state of nature is pre-political, but not pre-social. Individuals living together are guided by the law of nature by which their rights and responsibilities are determined. There is a significant amount of peace, good will, and mutual assistance, quite unlike Hobbes's natural state of enmity, malice, violence, and mutual destruction. Capturing the pre-political condition of humankind, Locke writes: "Men living together according to reason, without a common superior on earth with authority to judge between them, is properly the state of nature."[57] Even with an earthly superior, however, remember that human rationality can be counted upon to produce a fair amount of order and stability, for human nature being what it is, we are so inclined to want such things.

Of course, human beings are not perfect. The relatively peaceful state of nature can become like a state of war whenever anyone threatens the self-preservation of another. Threats can be direct or indirect. Direct threats endanger the life or person of another; indirect threats represent an attack on the person's property. Locke regards attacks upon an individual's property as essentially an attack upon the individual, the reason being that property is necessary to preserve life. Also, by virtue of mingling their labors with things and objects, such things and objects belong to the person and become part of him or her. Therefore, to attack a person's property is the same thing as declaring an intention to do with the person what one pleases, including the taking of that person's life.[58] If you've ever been the victim of robbery or vandalism, then you probably know intimately the experience of feeling violated. The act of theft or destruction of your property is like an attack on yourself. We take up the business of property rights in more detail in the next section. For the moment, the point should be stressed that in the event of any transgressions against one's person or property, "every man has a **right to punish** the offender and be executioner of the law of nature."[59] Natural law requires that retribution be proportionate to the transgression, governed by calm reason and conscience, and serve only for purposes of reparation and restraint, "for these two are the only reasons why one man may lawfully do harm to another."[60]

## Property Rights

So far, we have identified a number of rights stemming from natural law: the right to self-preservation, the right to personal liberty, and the right to punish those who violate the law of nature. It is important to repeat that the rights we have are not bestowed upon us by some sort of societal authority; rather, they follow from an objective rule and measure emanating from God and discernable by human reason.[61] The law of nature, which gives rise to natural rights, provides a test or criterion by which political institutions and behaviors can be limited and judged.[62] Of all the rights embedded in natural law, Locke pays most attention to **property rights.** In his coverage of them in the *Second Treatise,* we find again some very substantial differences between himself and his predecessor Hobbes. For Hobbes, before society exists, there is no "thine or mine." Individuals own what they take by force; they have no natural or earned entitlements. To quote Hobbes: ". . . every man has a Right to everything; even to one anothers [sic] body."[63] At first glance, it might appear by his use of terminology that at least one pre-societal right does exist, namely, the "right to every thing." However, if we all have a right to everything, including the bodies of others, then in effect we own nothing. If what we have can be forcefully taken by others without moral repercussions, and if it is not inherently "wrong" to steal what is not yours because you have the power to take what you want, then the whole notion of property rights flies in the face of anyone who holds a conventional understanding of ownership. According to Hobbes, individuals own what they can hold by force. They have no inherent or natural "right" to anything that others have a duty to respect. "Property," as such, is a creation of society, and rights to it must be sanctioned by sovereign authority.

Locke, on the other hand, regarded property as a natural right that precedes society and is not created by it. In fact, Locke regards the protection of property or one's property rights as the primary function of government. He states: "The great and chief end, therefore, of man's uniting into commonwealths and putting themselves under government is the preservation of their property."[64]

By "property," Locke means people's "lives, liberties, and estates."[65] He says: "By property I must be understood here, as in other places, to mean that property which men have in their persons as well as goods."[66] The notion of property rights is closely tied, for Locke, to the **right of self-preservation.** Just as individuals have the right (and correlative duty) to self-preservation, so too do they have a right to those things which are necessary for it. Locke's assumption is that God has given the earth to humankind, and all that is contained within it is for their support and well-being. Furthermore, reason reveals that, though the earth was not originally partitioned off with property fences, and objects did not have the stamp of possession upon them, it is consistent with God's will that there should be private property. The reference here is not only with respect to the fruits of the earth and the things upon it, but also with respect to the earth itself.[67] Given that the earth was not created with boundaries demarcating what is "thine or mine," the question arises as to what constitutes the primary title to private property? Simply, what makes something "mine"?

Locke would concede that initially, in the state of nature, the earth and all its fruits are common to all. To use the metaphor of fruits literally, let us say that there is an apple tree in a distant field. The tree belongs to no one; nor does its bountiful fruit. However, if someone took the time and trouble to pick a basket of apples from the tree, the fruit would suddenly belong to the individual. How so? According to Locke, there is "property" in an individual's labor: "I own my work" or "My work is mine." When I perform an action upon a thing or object, in this case by picking apples from a tree, I mix my labor with those fruits, making them objects of my possession. Similarly, shells and stones at the seaside are there for everyone's pleasure and interest, but once I gather some and place them in my collection, they belong to me. I have labored over these natural curiosities, giving me property rights over them.

Limits accompany natural property rights. The right to land acquisition is not unbounded. With respect to land, Locke says: "As much land as a man tills, plants, improves, cultivates, and can use the product of, so much is his property. He by his labor does, as it were, enclose it from the common."[68] Individuals are entitled to as much property as they can use without spoilage. Taking more than necessary or more than one can work with is wrong. Also, any appropriations of property that would leave others "without enough and as good" would be similarly unacceptable.

# Political Society and Government

If all human beings are born free and equal, endowed with natural rights and subordinate to nobody, then the question arises as to why anybody would allow themselves to be subjected to the control of any other power. As alluded to earlier, the primary reason is for the preservation of property. In the state of nature, there is no sanctioning body or public law that has been established and promulgated as a measure of right and wrong. There is no formal procedure to identify rights violations or to settle interpersonal property disputes. Furthermore, "though the law of nature be plain and intelligible to all rational creatures, yet men, being biased by their interest as well as ignorant for want of studying it, are not apt to allow of it as a law binding on them in the application of it to their particular cases."[69] In short, the civil law does not exist in nature, and the natural law that does exist is either unknown, ignored, or twisted in one's favor. Given this, it is to one's advantage to establish a **political society** so that impartial judges can be installed in positions of authority. Judges can be responsible for resolving disputes in a rational and disinterested fashion. To use Locke's descriptive term, judges can be "indifferent." The problem with allowing individuals in the state of nature to be both judge and executioner of the natural law is that "passion and revenge is very apt to carry them too far and with too much heat," especially when prosecuting others guilty of offense. Partiality toward oneself, on the other hand, as well as "negligence and unconcernedness" are likely to make one remiss in prosecuting cases of wrongdoing involving other people's rights. Simply, people tend to decide in their own favor and neglect the interests of others. Impartial and disinterested judges can remedy this, as they are in the best position to reasonably adjudicate conflicts and issue punishments.

Locke describes the partial and negligent tendencies inherent in people's efforts to punish wrongdoers as "inconveniences." He writes the following about human beings in the natural state:

> The inconveniences that they are therein exposed to by the irregular and uncertain exercise of the power every man has of punishing the transgressions of others make them take sanctuary under the established laws of government and therein seek the preservation of their property. It is this makes them so willingly give up every one his single power of punishing, to be exercised by such alone as shall be appointed to it amongst them; and by such rules as the community, or those authorized by them to that purpose, shall agree on. And in this we have the original right of both the legislative and executive power, as well as of the governments and societies themselves.[70]

By entering a civil society, human beings do not transfer all of their natural rights to any judge or sovereign body. Morality continues to precede civil society, and civil society can still be judged in terms of morality. By entering into society, individuals give up only the power of punishment to an **executive** whom they appoint. This is very different from Hobbes, whose absolute monarchy required all rights (power) to be given up to the monarch so that the sovereign could govern by decree. For Locke, the rule of law—not force—becomes the basis of society. Without law, a government becomes tyrannical, operating arbitrarily by whim and caprice much like Hobbes's brutish egoist. Locke's political society, by contrast, must create laws consistent with the law of nature and enforce them for the good of all. The ultimate end of law making and law enforcement is the "peace, safety, and public good of the people."

Understanding civil society in this way, the government is entrusted with the welfare of its citizens and serves only a **fiduciary role.** Its authority is not unconditional or absolute. The government is a servant to the people, not the other way around. Individuals do not work for the benefit of the state; the state works for the benefit of citizens. Indeed, Locke's conception of civil society and his reformulation of natural law provides us with a strong philosophical foundation for **individualism.** Precepts issuing from the law of nature, which buttress civil society, are concerned mostly with individual rights, rather than with individual responsibilities to society.[71] It would appear, then, that many of the seeds of contemporary individualism were sewn by John Locke generations ago.

## Social Compact

It has been said that in order to protect their property rights, to establish nondiscriminatory public laws, to have "indifferent" judges, and also to be protected by a power that can enforce the law by executing the sentences of judges, human beings are led into a commonwealth through the formation of a political society. Specifically, for Locke, this is done through the creation of a **social compact.**

Locke's social compact uses **consent** as its rational foundation. Since all individuals are free, equal, and independent in the state of nature, nobody can be subjected to the political power of another without his or her permission. Such permission or consent must, of course, be freely given without coercion of any kind. Individuals who do not wish to belong to civil society are permitted to go elsewhere or to remain in the state of nature. In Locke's day, it was no doubt easier to find unsettled territories and wilderness lands where one could actually live independently in relative isolation. However, immigration laws, national boundaries, increases in world population, state-owned lands, and other such factors create restraints that would obviously make "free-range" living in the state of nature much more problematic today. In any case, for those who participate in a Lockean civil society, the choice to do so must be unanimous. The contract or agreement here is not between the sovereign state or ruling monarch and the individual citizens, but rather, among the citizens themselves.

The issue of consent raises a historical problem. Did a state of nature ever actually exist, and was a social compact ever entered into in the creation of political society? In answer, Locke says yes. Regarding the state of nature, he cites Josephus Acosta, who reported that in many parts of America, for example, there was no government at all, presumably leaving it in a state of nature. (No doubt native North Americans would take issue with this claim.) Also, he names Rome and Venice as two places where, "by the uniting together of several men free and independent of one another, amongst whom there was no natural superiority or subjection," a political society was formed.[72] Though these and other examples used by Locke may represent questionable facts contributing to some shoddy history, Locke appears unconcerned. Actual historical documentation of social contracts being signed or agreed to are difficult, if not impossible, to locate since:

> Government is everywhere antecedent to records, and letters seldom come in amongst a people till a long continuation of civil society has, by other more necessary arts, provided for their safety, ease, and plenty; and then they begin to look after the history of their founders and search into their original, where they have outlived the memory of it; for it is with commonwealths as with particular persons—they are commonly ignorant of their own births and infancies; and if they know anything of their original, they are beholden for it to the accidental records others have kept of it. An those that we have of the beginning of any politics in the world, excepting that of the Jews, where God himself immediately interposed, and which favors not at all paternal dominion, are all either plain instances of such a beginning as I have mentioned, or at least have manifest footsteps of it.[73]

Even if we grant Locke the historical proposition that individuals were once in the state of nature and entered into a social compact to form society, we could still ask whether any individual today must abide by its terms, since that individual was not present at the time of the original agreement. From Locke's perspective, there are two types of consent. The first is direct; the second is tacit. We give **tacit consent** to the social compact which preceded us by enjoying all the privileges of citizenship; that is, by owning and exchanging property, relying on the police and the courts for protection, and so on. When we accept the benefits of civil society, we tacitly give consent to our participation, which entails certain responsibilities of citizenship. And like other citizens, we give up certain things (the right to punish violators of the law of nature). The fact that we stay in a particular country or state, when we could just as easily leave, confirms our consent.[74]

## Limits on Government

Whether our consent is direct and overt or tacit and implied, we do not, of course, automatically agree to just any law or any decision of the state. There are certain limitations. The laws which are made and enforced must confirm those inalienable rights that people have by virtue of nature—underscoring again the fact that morality precedes civil government, that natural law overrides civil law.

Consent, as Locke understands it, also involves acceptance of **majority rule.** He writes:

> And thus every man, by consenting with others to make one body politic under one government, puts himself under an obligation to every one of that society to submit to the determination of the majority and to be concluded by it; or else this original compact, whereby he with others incorporates into one society, would signify nothing, and be no compact, if he be left free and under no other ties than he was in before in the state of nature.[75]

The myriad daily decisions taken by an established civic community cannot depend upon unanimity or consensus. Such a requirement would be highly impractical. Though the social compact must be agreed to unanimously, Locke was reasonable enough to assume that the majority would rule once the social compact became a "done deal," to use a contemporary expression. This is not to suggest that minorities could be abused by the tyranny of the majority, or that the majority could pass any and all legislation at will. Laws would still have to be properly promulgated and applied equally to all groups and classes. The government would not be able to raise taxes without the consent of the people or their deputies. Still further, the kind of democratic government based on majority rule that Locke has in mind could not simply delegate its legislative powers to others.[76] Compare all of this with Hobbes.

For Hobbes, the sovereign power is absolute. Whatever the monarch or governing assembly dictates goes. The authority of the legislative body cannot be questioned on moral grounds, since that body creates justice and goodness by its own proclamations. Allowing the Leviathan to be attacked places us all back in what Hobbes described as the condition of war. Presumably, either the Leviathan has absolute power, or we are all back to anarchy.

As for Locke, while he regards the legislative government as the "supreme" body, he does not accept Hobbes's idea that it is "absolute"—unquestionable in its authority. The point was made earlier that, for Locke, the legislative is entrusted by the citizen population to govern in favor of its own interests, giving the legislative power only a fiduciary role. As a result, "there remains still in the people a supreme power to remove or alter the legislative when they find the legislative act contrary to the trust reposed in them." One writer suggests that government, on this account, is like a "glorified secretary," entrusted to do those things we find inconvenient or impossible to do ourselves.[77]

## Divisions of Power

To ensure that the state does not assume greater power than justified, and that it does not violate its own laws with impunity, Locke envisioned a system of checks and balances involving different levels of government, each wielding its own power. He labelled them the legislative, executive, and federative. Intuitively, we can probably all appreciate how it would be undesirable for lawmakers to be responsible for executing the laws they create for us. Locke says: "they may exempt themselves from obedience to the laws they make, and suit the law, both in its making and execution, to their own private advantage, and thereby come to have a distinct interest from the rest of the community contrary to the end of society and government; . . ."[78] Locke concludes, therefore, that the executive branch of government should be distinct from the legislative. The executive does not have the authority to make laws like the legislative branch, but it has judicial powers to make sure the laws are followed. The executive and legislative branches of government function more or less in the same fashion as they do in the United States government. The third branch, envisioned by Locke, called the federative, was given the power to make war and peace, alliances, and treaties with other nations, and to conduct, "all the transactions with all persons and communities without [outside of] the commonwealth."[79]

In the *Second Treatise,* Locke addresses the notion of **prerogative power** and how it may be given to the executive when the legislative is not in session.

Worried about too much executive control, Locke underscores the fact that it has no authority of its own and cannot claim the right of obedience except when it is enforcing the law of society. Members of the executive can be removed from office if the legislative or the people believe that they have violated the limits of power assigned to them.[80] With the legislative branch of government making sure the executive does not go too far in executing its dictates, and with the executive branch ensuring that the legislative live according to the laws of the state, we can see a clear example of how government power is regulated by a system of checks and balances.

## The Dissolution of Government

Governments are not absolute and eternal entities. They can be dissolved from "within" or "without." In the latter case, that is, "dissolution from without," the cause is generally war. Putting it quite graphically, Locke writes: ". . . conquerors' swords often cut up governments by the roots and mangle societies to pieces, separating the subdued or scattered multitude from the protection of and dependence on that society which ought to have preserved them from violence."[81] "Dissolution from within" can occur from rebellion against authority, for example, when the citizenry is subjected to the arbitrary caprice of tyrannical power. Let's say, for instance, a prince in a constitutional monarchy changes the methods of elections or alters the legislative branch without the people's consent and in violation of their trust. Let's assume further that this tyrant then goes on to claim dominion over people's lives, liberties, and property. In such a case, overthrow of the government would be justified.[82] Unlike Hobbes, Locke allows government rule to be questioned and, if necessary, replaced without assuming that the dissolution of governmental authority necessarily leads us back to a state of chaos and jungle warfare. Society and government are not synonomous for Locke. While it is true that when societies are dissolved, governments must necessarily disappear, the converse is not so; governments can be dissolved, leaving societies with the task of establishing new governmental structures.

As a way of concluding this discussion of Locke, let us now read an excerpt from *The Second Treatise of Government* to gain an even greater exposure to some of philosophy's greatest writings.

---

### ORIGINAL SOURCEWORK

## *Of the Ends of Political Society and Government*

### JOHN LOCKE

*Sec. 123.* If man in the state of nature be so free, as has been said; if he be absolute lord of his own person and possessions, equal to the greatest, and subject to nobody, why will he part with his freedom, why will he give up this empire, and subject himself to the dominion and control of any other power? To which it is obvious to

---

*Source:* John Locke, *Two Treatises on Government*, Chapter IX. Published in London. MDCL XXXVIIII.

answer, that though in the state of nature he hath such a right, yet the enjoyment of it is very uncertain, and constantly exposed to the invasion of others: for all being kings as much as he, every man his equal, and the greater part no strict observers of equity and justice, the enjoyment of the property he has in this state is very unsafe, very unsecure. This makes him willing to quit a condition, which, however free, is full of fears and continual dangers: and it is not without reason, that he seeks out, and is willing to join in society with others, who are already united, or have a mind to unite, for the mutual preservation of their lives, liberties and estates, which I call by the general name, property.

*Sec. 124.* The great and chief end, therefore, of men's uniting into commonwealths, and putting themselves under government, is the preservation of their property. To which in the state of nature there are many things wanting. First, there wants an established, settled, known law, received and allowed by common consent to be the standard of right and wrong, and the common measure to decide all controversies between them: for though the law of nature be plain and intelligible to all rational creatures; yet men being biassed by their interest, as well as ignorant for want of study of it, are not apt to allow of it as a law binding to them in the application of it to their particular cases.

*Sec. 125.* Secondly, In the state of nature there wants a known and indifferent judge, with authority to determine all differences according to the established law: for every one in that state being both judge and executioner of the law of nature, men being partial to themselves, passion and revenge is very apt to carry them too far, and with too much heat, in their own cases; as well as negligence, and unconcernedness, to make them too remiss in other men's.

*Sec. 126.* Thirdly, In the state of nature there often wants power to back and support the sentence when right, and to give it due execution, They who by any injustice offended, will seldom fail, where they are able, by force to make good their injustice; such resistance many times makes the punishment dangerous, and frequently destructive, to those who attempt it.

*Sec. 127.* Thus mankind, notwithstanding all the privileges of the state of nature, being but in an ill condition, while they remain in it, are quickly driven into society. Hence it comes to pass, that we seldom find any number of men live any time together in this state. The inconveniencies that they are therein exposed to, by the irregular and uncertain exercise of the power every man has of punishing the transgressions of others, make them take sanctuary under the established laws of government, and therein seek the preservation of their property. It is this makes them so willingly give up every one his single power of punishing, to be exercised by such alone, as shall be appointed to it amongst them; and by such rules as the community, or those authorized by them to that purpose, shall agree on. And in this we have the original right and rise of both the legislative and executive power, as well as of the governments and societies themselves.

*Sec. 128.* For in the state of nature, to omit the liberty he has of innocent delights, a man has two powers.

The first is to do whatsoever he thinks fit for the preservation of himself, and others within the permission of the law of nature: by which law, common to them all, he and all the rest of mankind are one community, make up one society, distinct from all other creatures. And were it not for the corruption and viciousness of degenerate men, there would be no need of any other; no necessity that men should separate from this great and natural community, and by positive agreements combine into smaller and divided associations.

The other power a man has in the state of nature, is the power to punish the crimes committed against that law. Both these he gives up, when he joins in a private, if I may so call it, or particular politic society, and incorporates into any common-wealth, separate from the rest of mankind.

*Sec. 129.* The first power, viz. of doing whatsoever he thought for the preservation of himself, and the rest of mankind, he gives up to be regulated by laws made by the society, so far forth as the preservation of himself, and the rest of that society shall require; which laws of the society in many things confine the liberty he had by the law of nature.

*Sec. 130.* Secondly, The power of punishing he wholly gives up, and engages his natural force, (which he might before employ in the execution of the law of nature, by his own single authority, as he thought fit) to assist the executive power of the society, as the law thereof shall require: for being now in a new state, wherein he is to enjoy many conveniencies, from the labour, assistance, and society of others in the same community, as well as protection from its whole strength; he is to part also with as much of his natural liberty, in providing for himself, as the good, prosperity, and safety of the society shall require; which is not only necessary, but just, since the other members of the society do the like.

*Sec. 131.* But though men, when they enter into society, give up the equality, liberty, and executive power they had in the state of nature, into the hands of the society, to be so far disposed of by the legislative, as the good of the society shall require; yet it being only with an intention in every one the better to preserve himself, his liberty and property; (for no rational creature can be supposed to change his condition with an intention to be worse) the power of the society, or legislative constituted by them, can never be supposed to extend farther, than the common good; but is obliged to secure every one's property, by providing against those three defects above mentioned, that made the state of nature so unsafe and uneasy. And so whoever has the legislative or supreme power of any common-wealth, is bound to govern by established standing laws, promulgated and known to the people, and not by extemporary decrees; by indifferent and upright judges, who are to decide controversies by those laws; and to employ the force of the community at home, only in the execution of such laws, or abroad to prevent or redress foreign injuries, and secure the community from inroads and invasion. And all this to be directed to no other end, but the peace, safety, and public good of the people.

## DISCUSSION QUESTIONS FOR CRITIQUE AND ANALYSIS

1. Locke and Hobbes offer different visions of government. How do they compare?

2. What values, interests, or rights are most fundamental for Locke? Do you agree with the importance allotted to them? Why or why not?

## PHILOSOPHICAL PROFILE

### Karl Marx

Karl Marx was born on May 5, 1818, in Trier, a small Prussian town in what is now part of Germany. A descendant of a long line of rabbis, he was the oldest son and the second child in a family of eight. His father was a middle-class lawyer who, for the sake of professional expediency, changed his name from Levi to Marx. When Karl was six, his father also converted to Lutheranism in order to avoid any anti-Semitic complications that might have interfered with retaining his legal position in the Prussian civil service. New laws were passed preventing Jews from occupying governmental positions. What might have turned out to be religiously confusing for the young Marx (who, incidentally, was baptized a Christian) became inconsequential in one respect, since he eventually became a rabid atheist in his later life, declaring that religion was nothing more than a stupefying opium for the masses.

**KARL MARX**

Marx began his first year of university education in 1835 at Bonn, where he studied law. His days there were limited but not entirely uneventful. On one occasion he was arrested for drunkenness, and on another, he sustained a wound from dueling which left him with a lasting scar.[83] Displeased with events at Bonn, Marx's father sent Karl to continue his studies more seriously at the University of Berlin. There, the young Marx turned his attention away from his previous legal studies and toward philosophy and history. He became familiar with the work of the great Georg Wilhelm Hegel (1770–1831) and associated himself with one particular branch of Hegelianism known as the "Young Hegelians" or "Hegelians of the Left." In 1841, Marx submitted his dissertation and received his doctorate from the University of Jena, though he never studied there formally. The dissertation was entitled "On the Difference Between the Democritean and Epicurean Philosophies of Nature."

While becoming a university professor after graduation seemed to be the obvious option for Marx, that option abruptly became unavailable as the Prussian Ministry of Education condemned the Left Hegelians with whom Marx had become associated. Given that he was also a militant atheist whose professed credo was "Criticism of religion is the foundation of all criticism," his reputation made an academic career impossible.[84] Unlike his father, who once gave a mild speech for social reform and then recanted when the Prussian authorities showed up at his doorstep, Karl was not one to back down or compromise morally for personal advantage. Summarizing Marx's personality, the German-American statesman Carl Schurz wrote:

> I have never seen a man whose bearing was so provoking and intolerable. To no opinion, which differed from his, he accorded the honor of even a condescending consideration. Everyone who contradicted him he treated with abject contempt; every argument that he did not like he answered either with biting scorn at the unfathomable ignorance that had prompted it, or with opprobrious aspersions upon the motives of him who had advanced it.[85]

For an alternative portrayal of Marx's personality, Erich Fromm claims that Marx was a highly productive individual with a great capacity for love and friendship, judging by his relationship with Engels and members of his family. His apparent arrogance purportedly stemmed from his inability to tolerate sham, deception, and dishonest rationalization.[86]

In retrospect, it would appear that Karl Marx's exclusion from academia was just a prelude to the turbulent times that were still to come in his life. After drifting for about a year following his graduation, Marx entered the field of journalism and became the editor of a liberal newspaper in Cologne entitled the *Rheinische Zeitung*. After moving the paper politically to the left, he resigned in a futile effort to forestall its eventual banning in 1843. In that same year, he and Jenny Westphalen—the daughter of neighbor Baron von Westphalen who had befriended Marx in his youth—were married and despite opposition from both sides of the family, they moved to Paris, France.

During his stay in Paris, Marx encountered a number of important radical intellectuals including the poet Heinrich Heine, the anarchist Mikhail Bakunin, as well as the socialist Pierre-Joseph Proudhon. Of all his new acquaintances, the most significant for Marx was another German, Friedrich Engels.[87] Together they formed one of the most important literary partnerships in western intellectual history.[88] While in Paris, Marx sketched out his *Economic and Philosophic Manuscripts of 1844*, containing an insightfully original view of human society that integrated elements of French socialism, English economics, and German philosophy. In Paris Marx continued his struggle against Prussian aristocracy and began what was to become his lifelong exile.

In 1845, Marx and Engels collaborated on a book of social criticism entitled *The Holy Family*. In the same year, Marx was forced to leave Paris at the behest of the French government. Banished again, he settled in Brussels, where he became affiliated with a working-men's association (The League of the Just), which was in the midst of reestablishing itself as the Communist Party. Marx and Engels were given the task of producing a written statement of the party's purpose and principles. The result was a little book to become the gospel for millions around the world: *Manifesto of the Communist Party* (referred to more simply as *The Communist Manifesto*). The book was actually published in London in 1848, just a few weeks before the first of a number of European revolutions that took place at that time. Unfortunately for Marx, in the midst of the upheaval of 1848, the Belgian authorities expelled him from Brussels, even though the *Manifesto* likely played no part in contributing to any uprisings.

After going back first to Paris, Marx then returned to Cologne, where a democratic government had been erected. He edited the *Neue Rheinische Zeitung* during a brief abortive experiment in parliamentary democracy. Once things crumbled, Marx was arrested, tried for sedition, acquitted, and then expelled in 1849. Again in exile, he lived the rest of his life in London, England, supported financially by Friedrich Engels and later by some inheritance money. Marx never did have a full-time, regular job as such, but interestingly, did earn an income as a journalist writing articles for the *New York Tribune* in the United States, certainly not a hotbed of communism. Most of the time, however, he spent in the British Museum, gathering research material for his monumental historical analysis of capitalism, *Das Kapital* (1867), only the first volume of which he was ever to publish. (Engels put together Volumes 2 and 3 from posthumous papers.) Marx's only political activity during this period in England was personal involvement in the International Working Men's Association. It was formed in 1864 and then scuttled by Marx in 1872 after prolonged internal conflict, principally between himself and Bakunin.

Marx leaves us today with quite a legacy. His life was dedicated to political revolution and to the passionate quest for a synthetic view of history and culture.[89] No truly educated person can ignore the ideas and influence of this intellectual immortal. In closing, it could be said that Marx did not enjoy an easy life. Apart from repeated banishments forcing him from country to country, Marx suffered from poverty, chronic illness, and the early deaths of three of his children (three daughters survived). He also suffered from obscurity and intellectual isolation, surely stinging conditions for a genius who so moved the world. Marx's wife, Jenny, died in 1882 and so did Karl in the following year. At the burial site in Highgate Cemetery, his lifelong friend, Friedrich Engels, began Marx's eulogy with the following words: "On the 14th day of March, at a quarter to three in the afternoon, the greatest living thinker ceased to think."[90]

# KARL MARX

Though dead for over a century, the mere mention of Karl Marx is still able to conjure up a number of different and frightening images in the minds of people acquainted with his work. Many Christians, for example, regard this atheist as the embodiment of the anti-Christ, a threat to all that is good and holy

> **"The philosophers have only interpreted the world in various ways: the point is to change it."**
>
> KARL MARX

in the world. If this seems like a bit of an exaggeration, then perhaps we should be reminded of how former President Ronald Regan described the Marxist-Leninist-based Soviet Union, before its collapse, namely, as the "evil empire." Marxism and the communistic system of government that glorified it were identified during the Cold War period (1950–1991) as threats to American security. Communism had to be stamped out for love of God and country. On this note, I can remember, for example, when former Canadian prime minister Pierre Elliot Trudeau was not allowed into the United States for a time for fear that he was a socialist who had communist ties around the world (Trudeau once visited Fidel Castro in Cuba.). A 1960s rock-and-roll song entitled "Share the Land" by The Guess Who was also banned on many U.S. radio stations due to its "subversive" collectivist insinuations. Combine these facts with the political "witch hunts" carried out during the Joseph McCarthy era (1950–1954), when efforts were made to investigate supposedly subversive communist activities in the United States, and you can well appreciate how anything Marxist had been demonized. Fears escalated as by the end of 1950, the Chinese communists had seized power in China, the Soviet Union had developed the atomic bomb, and North Korea had invaded South Korea. As a result, the United States was hit with a wave of anticommunist hysteria.

With respect to Cold War sentiments, Erich Fromm wrote the following in 1961:

> The world is torn today between two rival ideologies—that of "Marxism" and that of "Capitalism." While in the United States "Socialism" [read Marxism-Communism] is a word on the Devil's tongue and not one that recommends itself, the opposite is true in the rest of the world. Not only do Russia and China use the term "socialism" to make their systems attractive, but most Asian and African countries are deeply attracted to the ideas of Marxist socialism. To them socialism and Marxism are appealing not only because of the economic achievements of Russia and China, but because of the spiritual elements of justice, equality and universality which are inherent in Marxist socialism (rooted in the Western spiritual tradition).[91]

With the dissolution of the Soviet Union, the Cold War fizzled out, and closer ties with communist nations like China and North Korea are now being made. (News reports today inform me that Coca-Cola has just established itself in North Korea as I write this passage. Given history, this is quite a remarkable development.) Nevertheless, an objective analysis of Karl Marx's ideas is still made difficult by a Cold War hangover, or at least by an implicit identification people still make between Marx and the oppressive political regimes of self-professed communist states. Opposing the political actions taken by so-called communist countries under the banner of Marxism is not the same, however, as opposing Marx himself. On this note, Fromm writes:

> I am convinced that only if we understand the real meaning of Marxist thought, and hence can differentiate it from Russian and Chinese pseudo-Marxism, will we be able to understand the realities of the

present-day world and be prepared to deal realistically and constructively with their challenge. I hope [to] . . . contribute not only to a greater understanding of Marx's humanist philosophy, but also . . . to diminish the irrational and paranoid attitude that sees in Marx a devil and in socialism a realm of the devil.[92]

Put simply, "Marxism" as practiced is not "Marxism" as Karl Marx envisioned it. In fact, Marx once declared that he was not a Marxist himself. I suspect this statement is somehow related to his reactions regarding what people were doing with his ideas. In any case, neither Stalinist oppression, Maoist conformity, nor any other type of military dictatorship embodies the basic principles of Marxist thought. To condemn Marx for others' perversions of his ideas is clearly irrational. In fact, Marx never intended to profess any political ideology at all. He believed that his work was scientific, in the sense that he was uncovering the structural dynamics underlying social-historical change. The predicted communist revolution was not an ideal but a developmental necessity. Marx was not setting himself up as a hero but rather a historian doing political science. In the Preface to the first edition of *Das Kapital*, he writes: ". . . it is the ultimate aim of this work to lay bare the economic law of motion of modern society." He thought that a scientific understanding of human nature and the physical universe could solve the most significant of our social problems.[93]

If there is any group that rightfully should be terrorized by Marxist thought, perhaps it should be philosophers themselves. Indeed, Marx could be dubbed the "anti-philosopher." Karl Marx reviled philosophy as a symptom of social malaise that would disappear once the inevitable communist revolution placed society on a healthier foundation.[94] After the revolution, philosophy would become unnecessary, as men and women would be brought back to the study of "the real world." The "idealistic phantoms" of reason, justice, and liberty that philosophers consoled themselves with in a sick society would finally be exorcized, as the study of real world would become to philosophy "what sexual love is to masturbation." Traditionally, philosophers have often taken for granted the notion that intellectual ideas are the causes of historically significant changes in the social order. By contrast, Marx maintained that, "it is not the consciousness of men that determines their being but . . . their social being that determines their consciousness."[95] For Marx, gone is the belief that philosophers can objectively stand back in a detached fashion to rationally discuss eternal forms, natural laws, human essences, and the like. Rational objectivity and its fruits are themselves the products of social conditioning whose determining influences are manifest in historical circumstances and the society's prevailing mode of production. Philosophy, for Marx, is thus stripped of its independent, exalted status as the queen of all the sciences. It is seen merely as the product of social forces. In view of this, it is not surprising that Marx is sometimes regarded as the father of sociology and not the champion of philosophical inquiry. The irony of all this is that since Marx's death, his anti-philosophy, and the theory of historical/dialectical materialism on which it is based, has blossomed into a veritable philosophical doctrine itself. The anti-philosopher has become a prime subject of philosophical study.

> **"Religion is the sigh of the oppressed creature, the heart of a heartless world, just as it is the spirit of spiritless conditions. It is the opium of the people. "**
>
> KARL MARX

# Marx's Metaphysics and Dialectical Materialism

Underlying Marx's political thought is a metaphysics which he borrowed from **Hegel,** but then modified under the influence of Ludwig Feuerbach. According to the Hegelian worldview, known as **absolute idealism,** "the real is the rational and the rational is the real." Contained in this rather cryptic statement is the notion that reality displays the characteristics of mind. It reflects Absolute Mind or Spirit, what some have argued is just a euphemism for God. This Absolute Mind reveals itself in all areas of human experience and knowledge, from history and politics, to art, religion, and philosophy.[96] God, who is total reality and truth, reveals Himself to our limited minds in every aspect of life. The task of metaphysics for Hegel thus becomes one of showing the diversity of components comprising reality, their limits, and their interconnections in a unified whole. Explaining this, T.Z. Lavine writes:

> Absolute mind, Hegel says, is the one single reality which reveals itself to us in the concepts of all the areas of human experience. Different aspects of this reality are revealed in different areas of human experience. This single reality manifests itself to us in ordinary experience, in logic and natural science, in psychology, politics and history, in painting, poetry, and architecture, and in religion and philosophy. We understand physics and art and psychology by means of the concepts used in each of these fields. Each of these areas of reality yields a true view of reality, but each yields only a partial, limited, and incomplete view. Physics for example, reveals one important aspect of reality, but it is only one aspect, it is not the whole of reality. . . . The task of metaphysics, of a theory of all reality, is to identify all of the dimensions or aspects of reality, all of the ways in which reality in its great variety and complexity, is grasped by our concepts and to show the limits of each dimension of reality and how they are interconnected.
>
> This is the meaning of reality for Hegel—that reality is the whole truth, grasped by our rational concepts. Reality is the absolute truth, it is the totality and synthesis of all partial and limited truth. Reality, properly understood, is the totality of truth of absolute mind. The breathtaking vision of absolute, total reality is linked to the method by which it is known. This is the famous method of dialectic to which we now turn.[97]

Like other nineteenth-century philosophers, Hegel was seeking "the Philosopher's Stone" in some form of universal wisdom.[98] But unlike his predecessors who were baffled by the ephemeral nature of things—apparently the stone was a little too slippery to hold on to—Hegel made "change" the core concept of his world-system. Change, for him, resulted as a product of conflicting ideas. The process of change can be explained in the following fashion. First of all, an idea (captured, say, by a principle) presents itself as the *thesis*. This idea is then challenged by its opposite, called the *antithesis*. Neither side wins in the conflict, for out of the tension between them emerges the *synthesis*— a combination of both. In time, this synthesized idea becomes its own thesis, to be challenged again by a new antithesis. Out of this second conflict emerges a second synthesis, only to be challenged by still another antithesis, and so on and on. Hegel believed that this **dialectical process** of thesis-antithesis-synthesis moves ever forward, gradually revealing **Absolute Mind** or Spirit (as it is sometimes translated). Eventually this dialectic would reach its term, and the ideal would be achieved. At first, Hegel thought the dialectical ideal of history had been reached with Napoleon. Later he believed it had been discovered in the Prussian state, which presumably represented the perfect society.[99] This dialectical process is captured graphically in Figure 6.1.

From Hegel, Marx borrowed the notion of dialectic to explain historical evolution and change, but influenced by Ludwig Feuerbach, he concluded that the source of conflict was in the material world itself. Ideas spring from conflict; they do not in themselves cause it. Commenting on the influence of Feuerbach on Marx, Douglas Soccio writes:

> Marx's admiration for Hegel was altered by an article called "Theses on the Hegelian Philosophy" by Ludwig Feuerbach (1804–1872). Feuerbach was a materialist who challenged Hegel's notion that the driving force behind historical eras was their *zeitgeist,* or unique spirit, the *spirit of the age.* Feuerbach argued that any given era was the accumulation of the actual, concrete material conditions of the time—not some abstract "spirit of the age." So important were material conditions, according to Feuerbach, that they controlled not just the way people behave, but how they think and what they believe. Different material conditions result in what we think of as different cultural eras. After reading Feuerbach, Marx retained Hegel's belief in the dialectics of history, and a single reality, but concluded that reality was material, not spiritual.[100]

For Marx, the only demonstrable reality became matter, not some fuzzy conception of history as Absolute Mind revealing itself in an interplay of ideas.

**FIGURE 6.1** Hegel's dialectic of ideas.

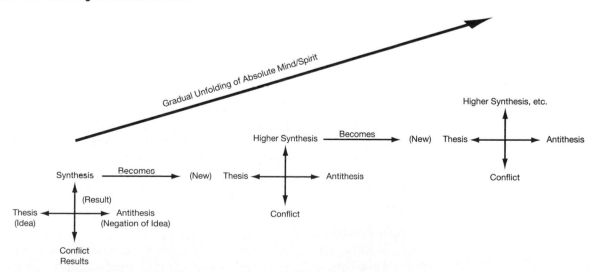

Marx found Hegelianism standing on its head, so to speak, and he intended to put it right side up. He argued that any meaningful thought-system must first start with real, existing individuals and with the actual concrete conditions in which they live, not with abstract ideas. By giving primacy to matter over mind, and by injecting Hegelianism with a good dose of concrete reality, Marx's **dialectical materialism** (sometimes called historical materialism) was introduced into the world. In *The German Ideology,* Marx wrote:

> In direct contrast to German philosophy [esp. Hegel] which descends from heaven to earth, here we ascend from earth to heaven. . . . We set out from real, active men, and on the basis of their real-life process we demonstrate the development of the ideological reflexes and echoes of this life process.[101]

## Class Conflict

While in Paris, Marx encountered Comte de Saint-Simon (1760–1825), another radical thinker who concluded that economic conditions determine history.[102] Specifically, he argued that historical change is the product of **class conflict.** Those who control the means of production are in a never-ending struggle with those who do not. Accepting this insight, and integrating it with Feuerbach's materialism as well as Hegel's dialectic, Marx produced his own unique theory of historical development. Class conflict, which was used to explain historical change, was given an economic, material foundation and interpreted in the context of a Hegelian dialectical framework. The importance of class conflict to historical progression is addressed by Marx and Engels, who wrote the following in *The Communist Manifesto:*

> The history of all hitherto existing society is the history of class struggles. . . . Freeman and slave, patrician and plebeian, lord and serf, guild-master and journeyman, in a word, oppressor and oppressed, stood in constant opposition to one another, carried on an uninterrupted, now hidden, now open fight, a fight that each time ended, either in a revolutionary re-constitution of society at large, or in the common ruin of the contending classes.[103]

In the Marxist account, history in essence is the ongoing result of constant tensions or struggles arising between dominant and subordinate classes, between upper classes of rulers and lower classes of those who are controlled and exploited. Marx's point is that conflicts between the classes are essentially economic, and that out of the class-conflict struggle between different and opposing economic interests there emerge brand new economic structures.[104]

The five stages of historical development or **"epochs of history"** identified by Marx and Engels as having structurally different modes of economic production, are:

1. Primitive/communal
2. Slave
3. Feudal

4. Capitalist
5. Socialist/communist

Details of Marx's explanation for how the actual historical process unfolds was very sketchy for epochs prior to feudalism and the emergence of capitalism. He postulated that there must have been a first epoch of history in which the mode of production was a primitive type of communism, without division of labor and without exploiters and the exploited. Presumably, all succeeding epochs display the economic laws of motion characterizing dialectical materialism. Summarizing how economic factors influence the historical dialectic (after the primitive/communal phase), Scott-Kakures et al. write:

> Division of labor among segments of the populace manifests itself as division into classes, historically, into minority propertied classes that oppress and majority propertyless classes that are oppressed. The oppressor classes control the forces of production, including the products of the labor of the oppressed majority. The nature of that oppressive control manifests itself as the form of property in existence at a given time. The history of the development of ever more sophisticated productive forces is thus a history of class struggle between the minority oppressors and the majority oppressed. These class relations are simply the productive relations that have been generated by the productive forces at a given time. Whether the oppressor and the oppressed are citizens and slaves, aristocracy and serfs, or the bourgeoisie and the proletariat, the productive relations have ever taken the form of minority oppressor classes and majority oppressed locked in struggle for the control of the materials and products of production.[105]

They go on to say:

> When a set of productive relations has become outmoded, that is, has lagged behind the development of productive forces, it has historically been overthrown in revolution. But the new productive relations that have resulted from such revolutions have until now merely instituted a new oppressor class in place of the old. For instance, with the dramatic changes in productive forces brought about by the industrial revolution and expansion of trade, the modern bourgeoisie has (largely) overthrown the aristocracy. Yet for Marx, this was merely another case of a new oppressor class (the bourgeoisie), better suited to the new productive forces, replacing the old oppressor class (the aristocracy).[106]

According to Marx then, from an initial situation where people lived cooperatively together, a slave economy was born due to the need for more labor, arising from increasingly sophisticated tools and techniques of production. In the slave economy, skills and techniques continued to improve along with the greater accumulation of information. The result was that people began to gather around towns, making possible the emergence of craft guilds. Craft guilds, in turn, made specialization possible. Fewer people were required to work at meeting basic agricultural needs, thereby allowing craftsmen the opportunity to further develop their expert talents. With this economic development, slaves needed more freedom than they had earlier been given, and labor needed to become even more concentrated. In response to these needs, the feudal system arose. In this economic arrangement, the lords owned the land, while the serfs leased portions of it, giving in lease payment most of what they produced. Feudal society represented a period of semi-freedom—a time when the majority of the population resided in semi-rural or small, but growing towns.

As craft guilds further refined their specialized manufacturing techniques, increasing numbers and varieties of goods became available. The growing demand for these goods increased trade and barter, paving the way for **capitalism.** The capitalistic epoch represented for Marx a higher synthesis of slave and feudal economies.[107] With trade and barter, money became increasingly important, as did the need for financial brokers. Once steam-powered manufacturing techniques came into use, feudalism was doomed because of its inefficiency and inability to satisfy the wants of an emerging capitalist middle class.

The industrial age gave birth to great centers that provided the power and transportation services necessary for mass production. Goods became less expensive, their numbers and varieties continued to grow, while the demand for them accelerated. The consequence of all this activity was that a new class of middlemen (speculators, entrepreneurs) who neither owned the means of production, nor produced anything themselves, grew in power. They worked at investing and acquiring greater and greater sums of capital. Marx predicted in his day that the inequalities in wealth between the **bourgeois** capitalists (speculators and those owning the modes of production) and the **proletarian** workers would continue to increase. The rich (thesis element in society) would get richer, and the poor (antithesis element in society) would get poorer. The bourgeois capitalists would earn their money on the backs of a larger exploited proletarian class. Eventually, discontent would become so deep and widespread that workers would rise up in violent revolution. On this, Marx writes in *The Communist Manifesto:* "What the bourgeoisie, therefore, produces, above all, is its own grave-diggers. Its fall and the victory of the proletariat are equally inevitable."

The final synthesis of historical development culminating in **communism** would require the abolition of private property. Basic needs would be met, enabling all people to live a dignified, meaningful life. Rather than trying to outdo one another in the competitive marketplace jungle, people would live harmoniously, actively engaged in creative, satisfying work that would benefit not only themselves, but also the rest of society. Since all classes would be abolished, so too would all class conflict.

Once capitalism became an obsolete and defunct economic system, a stage of transition would actually be required before reaching the end of the dialectical process. The transitional state would require the "dictatorship of the proletariat"— a necessarily unhappy time when the proletariat would use their political power to stamp out the last vestiges of capitalism. A socialist intermediary state would arise wherein the state would take over the means of production. Eventually, the socialist phase would give way to the final stage of communism wherein the people would control political decision making as well as the economic life of the country.[108] This would constitute a utopian ideal based on the moral dictum: "Each should give according to his ability and receive only according to his needs."

## PHILOSOPHERS IN ACTION

Marx predicted that as the rich get richer and the poor get poorer in a capitalistic society, the proletariat (poor) would eventually overthrow the political system in violent revolution, ushering in the new communist state. Do you think his predication has, or will ever, come true? Explain and illustrate why? What factors make, or made, the revolution more or less likely to occur?

## Alienation as a Byproduct of Capitalism

Before leaving Marxist theory, it is important to clear up a serious misunderstanding often associated with it. Many people believe Marx's central criticism of capitalism pertains to the injustice in the distribution of wealth within society. Surely Marx did object to the growing disparities in income between rich and poor, and insisted that they would only precipitate what, for him, was the inevitable communist revolution. Nonetheless, the problem with capitalism goes far deeper than the size of one's paycheck. Marx says: "An enforced *increase in wages* . . . would be nothing more than a *better remuneration of slaves,* and would not restore, either to the worker or to the work, their human significance and worth."[109]

Especially in the *Economic and Philosophical Manuscripts,* but in other places as well, Marx addresses the problem of alienated labor and how it is a direct result of the capitalist mode of production. He says that the capitalist system degrades workers, alienates them, and reduces them to saleable commodities in the workplace. Generally speaking, **alienation** is a feeling of separation, difference, or estrangement. When people feel alienated, they do not experience themselves as freely and actively engaged in the world. There is a "dis-connect" or "dis-engagement," creating a perception that one is not comfortably immersed in reality, but that objects and people in it stand over and against oneself. Such perceptions and feelings are not necessary. For Marx, they are the products of a capitalist system. For a vivid illustration of how the assembly line, as a capitalist mode of production, can be humanly degrading and thereby alienating, read the newspaper article entitled "GM Suspends Worker for Going to Bathroom."

## GM SUSPENDS WORKER FOR GOING TO BATHROOM
### Foreman Orders Ailing Man to Stay at His Post On Line

BY TONY VAN ALPHEN, Business Reporter

General Motors of Canada Ltd. suspended a worker last week because he left his work station to go to the bathroom.

Greg Taylor, a veteran assembler at GM's Number 2 car plant in Oshawa, lost more than $800 in net pay when he decided to answer nature's call instead of following a direct order to remain on the production line.

"I simply had to go but they (management) kept ordering me to stay," Taylor said yesterday. "They never showed me any dignity. Obviously none of them believed I had a condition."

Taylor, 39, suffers from irritable bowel syndrome, which sometimes forces frequent trips to the bathroom.

His union, the Canadian Auto Workers, has filed a grievance to recover the five days of lost pay.

"The whole situation is appalling," said Doug Sanders, a union committee man at the plant.

"I think it's very unjust that people are not allowed to go to the bathroom. GM is more concerned about efficiency than letting people go wee-wee."

Stew Low, GM's director of public relations, said the company would not discuss details of the incident because it is a private matter between an employee and management.

"There is a formalized grievance process to ensure both sides have a fair hearing on the issue," Low said.

Under company rules, employees must provide documentation of physical conditions that may warrant special accommodation in the workplace. Taylor said he didn't think the rule applied to his situation.

He said that when he showed his foreman an intestinal relaxant he uses to help control his problem, the foreman said he needed a doctor's note to justify leaving his work station frequently for bathroom trips.

The next day, on June 7—before he had a chance to see his doctor—Taylor said he felt a serious urge to go to the bathroom. He sought a relief employee to continue his work of bolting engines to chassis.

His work team leader arrived but the foreman insisted Taylor stay on the job. Taylor refused and walked off to the bathroom.

Taylor, who has worked for GM for 15 years, said the foreman asked him repeatedly if he understood the order.

"I told him, 'I don't understand and excuse me, I'm going to the bathroom,'" Taylor said.

GM, the country's biggest auto maker, put Taylor on notice for refusing a job order and leaving his work area.

*Source:* Reprinted with permission—The Toronto Star Syndicate, From the *Toronto Star,* Wed. June 21, 2000, Section E, page 3.

As someone who once worked on a factory assembly line myself, I recall only too clearly how this mode of production regulated my biological functions, including when I ate and slept. Hungry or not, I was forced to eat lunch from 12:00 to 12:30 p.m. Need it or not, my rest breaks were at 9:30 a.m. and 2:15 p.m. If I was moved to the night shift, without my consent I might add, then I had to sleep unnaturally during the daylight hours. If I was overheated and perspiring profusely in a poorly ventilated work space during the summer months, I was given salt tablets, as the factory owners and executives on the other side of the plant wall enjoyed air-conditioned comfort, while their cooling units spewed forth hot air exhaust onto the shop floor, and the assembly line workers begged for permission to get a drink of water before break. If replacement workers were not available for the particular work station to be momentarily vacated, then permission was usually denied by the production foreman. The "line" simply could not be stopped. It was not as if I, or anyone else for that matter, had a job that nobody else could do. My moronic task was simply to affix the lid of an air conditioner with screws. Every 30 seconds or so, another air conditioner confronted me like an unwanted enemy, sucking the enthusiasm and lifeblood from my body. I grew to hate air conditioners, and like other long-time employees, dubbed "lifers," I was sometimes tempted to sabotage the line so that the relentless thing would finally stop and give everyone a rest. I couldn't even afford to buy one of the units I produced with my own hands—only "rich" people could, not a poor student like me. Talk about feeling alienated from the fruits of my labors! In view of my own experience, it is perhaps easier to understand what Marx meant when he wrote:

> Within the capitalist system all methods for raising the social productiveness of labor are brought about at the cost of the individual laborer; all means for the development of production transform themselves into means of domination over, and exploitation of, the producer; they mutilate the laborer into a fragment of a man, degrade him to the level of an appendage of a machine, destroy every remnant of charm in his work and turn it into a hated toil; they estrange from him the intellectual potentialities of the labor process in the same proportion as science is incorporated in it as an independent power.[110]

In response to Marx, one might argue that working conditions are improving all the time, making his comments much less relevant today. One might also say the greater wealth afforded a much larger middle class no longer makes alienation the problem it once was. Witness all the sport utility vehicles on the highways, expensive clothes, summer and winter vacation packages, electronic gadgets and so on. None of this affluence points to an exploited proletariat, dominated and oppressed by the industrial factory owner. Maybe it is only the blue-collar industrial working class that needs liberation. In response to such a suggestion, Erich Fromm answers for Karl Marx:

> If anything, the clerk, the salesman, the executive, are even more alienated today than the skilled manual worker. The latter's functioning still depends on the expression of certain personal qualities like skill, reliability, etc., and he is not forced to sell his "personality,"

his smile, his opinions in the bargain; the symbol manipulators are hired not only for their skill, but for all those personality qualities which make them "attractive personality packages," easy to handle and manipulate. They are true "organization men"—more so than the skilled laborer—their idol being the corporation.[111]

In short, just because one enjoys greater wealth or wears a white collar instead of a blue one at work does not mean that one is any less alienated under a capitalist system. Selling your smile or your dignity as a "symbol manipulator" (image consultant, advertiser) is no less demeaning than being forced to sell your muscle power as an appendage to a machine in order to survive and earn a living for yourself and your family.

## Idolatry/Fetishism of Commodities

Marx claims that people can be alienated from a number of things—from nature, themselves, from what he calls their "species-being," and from other people. All of these forms of alienation are associated with economic forces embodied in the predominant societal mode of production. As already stated, Marx contends that capitalism greatly contributes to alienation. It does so by giving rise to a kind of **idolatry** or **fetishism of commodities** whereby lifeless material things are endowed with power over the living subjects who should be their master. For example, we talk about the "almighty dollar" when we make money our god. Also, take the computer. Once thought to be a convenient "calculator" or a rapid "information processor" that would make our collective lives easier and more efficient, this technological device now lords it over us. How much pressure is placed on you, or any prospective employee, to become "computer literate?" How disadvantaged are you in the job market without computer skills? Clearly, in today's world, many doors of opportunity are closed to people who cannot make use of computer technology. The servant has become the master, dictating what we must know and be able to do if we wish to work and feed ourselves.

This idolatry or fetishism of commodities also exhibits itself in capitalistic consumerism. For instance, we often attribute human qualities to man-made objects, describing vehicles as sexy and compressed carbon crystals (diamonds) as loving symbols of engagement, without which commitment is questioned. How many times have you felt frustrated, insecure, or inadequate because you could not afford to buy some status symbol or article of clothing that would make you feel good, enhance your self-esteem, or place you higher up in the social pecking order? Remember what the image consultants tell us: "Clothes make the man." or "You never get a second chance to make a first impression." Believing that in an Armani suit you are a somebody, but that in a polyester garment you amount to nothing and nobody, do you feel ennobled by your vain pursuit of a particular cut of cloth or designer label? Have Armani, Hilfiger or Gucci become your gods? How do you relate to the "haves" as one of the "have-nots"? How do you think the "haves" perceive you? Are you brought closer, in more intimate relations, or alienated further by envy, jealousy, and egoistic pride? If capitalistic consumerism makes people so happy, then why are you so sad?

# Division of Labor

From increasing knowledge and more sophisticated techniques of production characterizing the various historical epochs emerged the information-based technological age of today. Throughout this historical development, we have witnessed ever increasing specialization in the workplace. This tendency toward specialization, which was clearly present in Marx's time, can be said to require a **division of labor,** another contributing factor to alienation. To help you understand in plain terms what is meant by this, let us go back to simpler days before computerized robotics, assembly lines, global markets, world exports, and electronic information highways. As someone in the primitive communal epoch, you hunted and gathered in the morning, built huts in the afternoon, made and worked with tools in the early evening, and spent time together with other members of the community in ritualistic celebration at night. You did many different things and played many different roles (hunter, builder, storyteller, protector). Things were done in community with a common purpose—the most obvious of which was survival. Relations were close and interests were common.

Now, let us fast-forward to the feudal era. Imagine yourself as a cobbler centuries ago, living in a small village where everybody knew of your reputation for making fine sandals. You took great pride in going to neighbors' farms to purchase the finest hides you could find, magically treating the leathers in your patented way. You creatively designed your sandals and then painstakingly cut out the patterns before you stitched them up. You enjoyed the expert workmanship you put into the sandal and felt a sense of pride as you stamped your initials into the sole. You also took pleasure greeting prospective buyers of your footwear, talking to them about their families and future plans. In this quaint recreation of the past, you can begin to appreciate how the cobbler was very active and certainly in control of his life, attached to the products of his labor and the creative process that went into the fabrication of the sandal. There was no foreman or factory owner dictating the pace, stifling the cobbler's creativity for mass market consumption, or requiring quotas of production.

Suggesting that the alienation of work in capitalistic modes of production is much greater than during earlier times, when production was by **handicraft** and **manufacture** (making articles from raw material), Marx says:

> In handicrafts and manufacture, the workman makes use of a tool; in the factory the machine makes use of him. There the movement of the instrument of labor proceeded from him; here it is the movement of the machines that he must follow. In manufacture, the workmen are parts of a living mechanism; in the factory we have a lifeless mechanism, independent of the workman, who become its mere living appendage.[112]

He says further:

> This fact simply implies that the object produced by labor, its product, now stands opposed to it as an *alien being,* as a *power independent* of the producer. The product of labor is labor which has been

embodied in an object and turned into a physical thing; this product is an objectification of labor. The performance of work is an objectification. The performance of work appears in the sphere of political economy as a vitiation [faulty rendering] of the worker, objectification as a loss and as servitude to the object and appropriation as *alienation*. . . . So much does the performance of work appear as vitiation that the worker is vitiated to the point of starvation. So much does objectification appear as loss of the object that the worker is deprived of the most essential things, not only of life but also of work. Labor itself becomes an object which he can acquire only by the greatest effort and with unpredictable interruptions. So much does the appropriation of the object appear as alienation that the more objects the worker produces the fewer he can possess and the more he falls under the domination of his product, of capital.[113]

We learn from the quotation above that in the capitalist economy, products of labor (belonging to the employer) become alien objects. Labor, in fact, itself becomes a commodity. The more the worker produces, the less he or she is worth. The individual, as a person, is transformed into "cheap labor," earning a wage that is less than the worth of the products produced. The **surplus value** constituting the profit can then be used for further investment. The worker is left to pray that markets do not evaporate and that sales continue for fear of lay-off or plant-closures. In a capitalistic market economy, the future is in the hands of uncontrollable market forces and subject to the whims of factory owners, shareholders, and corporate presidents. If company profits can be maximized by shutting down operations in a particular location, they usually are without much concern about the displaced and unemployed workers. That's business, after all. Don't take it personally!

It doesn't take much insight or intelligence to grasp how doing mindless, repetitive work in an insecure market environment, which could cost workers their jobs at any moment, undermines human dignity. Workers are robbed of their freedom and the opportunity for creative self-fulfilment. They are prevented from expressing their own nature or "species-being" as they are enslaved by uncontrollable economic forces. They are alienated from the objects of their labor and placed in competitive struggles with other people against whom they compete for scarce jobs. Marx says: "A direct consequence of the alienation of man from the product of his labor, from his life activity and from his species life is that *man is alienated* from other *men*. When man confronts himself he also confronts *other* men. What is true of man's relationship to his work, to the product of his work and to himself, is also true of his relationship to other men, to their labor and to the objects of their labor."[114] In such a dreadfully alienated state, "The worker therefore feels himself at home only during his leisure time, whereas at work he feels homeless. His work is not voluntary but imposed, *forced labor*. It is not the satisfaction of a need, but only a *means* for satisfying other needs. Its alien character is clearly shown by the fact that as soon as there is no physical or other compulsion it is avoided like the plague.[115] One could argue that as testimony to the truth of Marx's insight here, a person only needs to point to the abundance of diversion and escape that we've created. We spend millions, if not billions, on sports and entertainment, all with the painful subconscious realization that we have to go to work tomorrow morning!

What Marx might describe as the alienating moral bankruptcy of capitalism is exquisitely captured by the film *American Beauty*. In it, we find an exploration of alienation in the character of Lester Burnham (played by Kevin Spacey), a middle-aged man "trapped in a marriage that he no longer takes any pleasure in, father of a daughter who seems to hate him, and worker at a job that he finds totally boring and morally compromising, and from which he expects to be removed for the sake of efficiency."[116] *American Beauty* masterfully portrays the emptiness of the American Dream. Though Burnham has achieved the good life by capitalistic standards—a well paying job, attractive wife, intelligent daughter, and fine home in the suburbs—he's trapped in a world of sham and inauthenticity. His wife, who so desperately clings to appearances and "idols" of success, is so alienated from herself that she cannot experience genuine feelings any longer. In one attempt to reconnect emotionally and passionately with his wife, Carolyn (played by Annette Bening), Lester fails because she cannot release her vain and neurotic attention to her home's appearance long enough to be swept up by the tide of emotion that is about to pour over her. As film reviewer Thomas Wartenberg observes: "Once it has staked out the alienation of the American male as its subject . . . *American Beauty* seems eager to contain the possibility that there is something rotten at the core of the American Dream. Faced with the possibility that Burnham's discovery of the emptiness of his own life will lead to a more general condemnation of America's lust for more, the film proposes an aesthetic stance to life as the solution to Burnham's *angst*."[117] This "solution" reflects the inevitable **dehumanization of capitalism** according to Marx. On the subject of retreating to the "aesthetic stance of life," Marx writes:

> We arrive at the result that man (the worker) feels himself to be freely active only in his animal functions—eating, drinking and procreating, or at most also in his dwelling and in personal adornment—while in his human functions he is reduced to an animal. The animal becomes human and the human becomes animal.
>
> Eating, drinking and procreating are of course also genuine human functions. But abstractly considered, apart from the environment of other human activities, and turned into final and sole ends, they are animal functions.[118]

*Reflect on those political ideas you found most interesting in this chapter. Which ones caused you to stop and question your values? Why?*

## After Capitalism

Time and space limitations do not allow me to discuss in any great detail Marx's socialist-communist utopia, which will follow after the fall of capitalism. Briefly, what can be said is that the basic mode of production within society will not be competitive, but cooperative and by association. Production will be brought under the control of workers in a rational and unalienated way. Socialism will provide a system that allows for the actualizing of human potentiality at its best, by overcoming alienation. A socialist-communist state will create the conditions necessary for living in a truly free, active, rational, and independent fashion. It will aim at the destruction of idols and at the satisfaction of the true needs of mankind, not the gratification of synthetic, artificially produced needs created by capitalistic hucksters. Who "really" needs satellite TV, for example, and why should anyone be made to feel deprived because they don't have it? For Marx, a system like capitalism, hell-bent on producing artificial needs, is necessarily destined to produce a class of disenfranchised, alienated individuals.

By way of concluding this section on Marx, let us gain first-hand exposure to his ideas through an excerpt from Marx's *Economic and Philosophical Manuscripts*, which deals with the alienation of labor. In this translation, alienated labor is often called estranged labor. Whenever estranged is used, one could read alienated.

## ORIGINAL SOURCEWORK

*Economic and Philosophical Manuscripts*

**KARL MARX**

What constitutes the alienation of labor?

Firstly, the fact that labor is external to the worker—*i.e.,* does not belong to his essential being; that he, therefore, does not confirm himself in his work, but denies himself, feels miserable and not happy, does not develop free mental and physical energy, but mortifies his flesh and ruins his mind. Hence, the worker feels himself only when he is not working; when he is working, he does not feel himself. He is at home when he is not working, and not at home when he is working. His labor is, therefore, not voluntary but forced, it is *forced labor.* It is, therefore, not the satisfaction of a need but a mere *means* to satisfy needs outside itself. Its alien character is clearly demonstrated by the fact that as soon as no physical or other compulsion exists, it is shunned like the plague. External labor, labor in which man alienates himself, is a labor of self-sacrifice, of mortification. Finally, the external character of labor for the worker is demonstrated by the fact that it belongs not to him but to another, and that in it he belongs not to himself but to another. Just as in religion the spontaneous activity of the human imagination, the human brain, and the human heart, detaches itself from the individual and reappears as the alien activity of a god or of a devil, so the activity of the worker is not his own spontaneous activity. It belongs to another, it is a loss of his self.

The result is that man (the worker) feels that he is acting freely only in his animal functions—eating, drinking, and procreating, or at most in his dwelling and adornment—while in his human functions, he is nothing more than animal.

It is true that eating, drinking, and procreating, etc., are also genuine human functions. However, when abstracted from other aspects of human activity, and turned into final and exclusive ends, they are animal.

We have considered the act of estrangement of practical human activity, of labor, from two aspects: **(1)** the relationship of the worker to the product of labor as an alien object that has power over him. The relationship is, at the same time, the relationship to the sensuous external world, to natural objects, as an alien world confronting him, in hostile opposition. **(2)** The relationship of labor to the *act of production* within labor. This relationship is the relationship of the worker to his own activity as something which is alien and does not belong to him, activity as passivity [Leiden], power as impotence, procreation as emasculation, the worker's own physical and mental energy, his personal life—for

*Source:* Karl Marx, "First Manuscript: Estranged Labor," in Sections XXIII and XXIV *Economic and Philosophical Manuscripts,* available on-line through the Marxist Internet Archive. Web address is http://www. marxists.org/admin/intro/main.htm, *The Economic and Philosophical Manuscripts* of 1884 were first published in 1932 in the Marx-Engels collected works, vol. 3. The Publisher was Martin Milligian of Progress Publishers.

what is life but activity?—as an activity directed against himself, which is independent of him and does not belong to him. Self-estrangement, as compared with the estrangement of the object [Sache] mentioned above.

We now have to derive a third feature of estranged labor from the two we have already examined.

Man is a species-being, not only because he practically and theoretically makes the species—both his own and those of other things—his object, but also—and this is simply another way of saying the same thing—because he looks upon himself as the present, living species, because he looks upon himself as a universal and therefore free being.

Species-life, both for man and for animals, consists physically in the fact that man, like animals, lives from inorganic nature; and because man is more universal than animals, so too is the area of inorganic nature from which he lives more universal. Just as plants, animals, stones, air, light, etc., theoretically form a part of human consciousness partly as objects of science and partly as objects of art—his spiritual inorganic nature, his spiritual means of life, which he must first prepare before he can enjoy and digest them—so, too, in practice they form a part of human life and human activity. In a physical sense, man lives only from these natural products, whether in the form of nourishment, heating, clothing, shelter, etc. The universality of man manifests itself in practice in that universality which makes the whole of nature his inorganic body, (1) as a direct means of life and (2) as the matter, the object, and the tool of his life activity. Nature is man's inorganic body—that is to say, nature insofar as it is not the human body. Man lives from nature—*i.e.,* nature is his body—and he must maintain a continuing dialogue with it if he is not to die. To say that man's physical and mental life is linked to nature simply means that nature is linked to itself, for man is a part of nature.

Estranged labor not only (1) estranges nature from man and (2) estranges man from himself, from his own function, from his vital activity; because of this, it also estranges man from his species. It turns his species-life into a means for his individual life. Firstly, it estranges species-life and individual life, and, secondly, it turns the latter, in its abstract form, into the purpose of the former, also in its abstract and estranged form.

For in the first place labor, life activity, productive life itself, appears to man only as a means for the satisfaction of a need, the need to preserve physical existence.

But productive life is species-life. It is life-producing life. The whole character of a species, its species-character, resides in the nature of its life activity, and free conscious activity constitutes the species-character of man. Life appears only as a means of life.

The animal is immediately one with its life activity. It is not distinct from that activity; it is that activity. Man makes his life activity itself an object of his will and consciousness. He has conscious life activity. It is not a determination with which he directly merges. Conscious life activity directly distinguishes man from animal life activity. Only because of that is he a species-being. Or, rather, he is a conscious being—*i.e.,* his own life is an object for him, only because he is a species-being. Only because of that is his activity free activity. Estranged labor reverses the relationship so that man, just because he is a conscious being, makes his life activity, his being [Wesen], a mere means for his existence.

The practical creation of an *objective world,* the fashioning of inorganic nature, is proof that man is a conscious species-being—*i.e.,* a being which treats the species as its own essential being or itself as a species-being. It is true that animals also produce. They build nests and dwelling, like the bee, the beaver, the ant, etc. But they produce only their own immediate needs or those of their young; they produce only when immediate physical need compels them to do so, while man produces even when he is free from physical need and truly produces only in freedom from such need; they produce only themselves, while man reproduces the whole of nature; their products belong immediately to their physical bodies, while man freely confronts his own product. Animals produce only according to the standards and needs of the species to which they belong, while man is capable of producing according to the standards of every species and of applying to each object its inherent standard; hence, man also produces in accordance with the laws of beauty.

It is, therefore, in his fashioning of the objective that man really proves himself to be a species-being. Such production is his active species-life. Through it, nature appears as *his* work and his reality. The object of labor is, therefore, the objectification of the species-life of man: for man produces himself not only intellectually, in his consciousness, but actively and actually, and he can therefore contemplate himself in a world he himself has created. In tearing away the object of his production from man, estranged labor therefore tears away from him his species-life, his true species-objectivity, and transforms his advantage over animals into the disadvantage that his inorganic body, nature, is taken from him.

In the same way as estranged labor reduces spontaneous and free activity to a means, it makes man's species-life a means of his physical existence.

Consciousness, which man has from his species, is transformed through estrangement so that species-life becomes a means for him.

(3) Estranged labor, therefore, turns man's species-being—both nature and his intellectual species-power—into a being alien to him and a means of his individual existence. It estranges man from his own body, from nature as it exists outside him, from his spiritual essence [Wesen], his human existence.

(4) An immediate consequence of man's estrangement from the product of his labor, his life activity, his species-being, is the estrangement of man from man. When man confronts himself, he also confronts other men. What is true of man's relationship to his labor, to the product of his labor, and to himself, is also true of his relationship to other men, and to the labor and the object of the labor of other men.

In general, the proposition that man is estranged from his species-being means that each man is estranged from the others and that all are estranged from man's essence.

Man's estrangement, like all relationships of man to himself, is realized and expressed only in man's relationship to other men.

In the relationship of estranged labor, each man therefore regards the other in accordance with the standard and the situation in which he as a worker finds himself.

## DISCUSSION QUESTIONS FOR CRITIQUE AND ANALYSIS

1. How could the advocate of free-market economics answer the charge that corporate capitalism is alienating and disenfranchising? How would you evaluate this answer? Why?

2. How do you think Marx would respond to Ayn Rand (Chapter 5), who extols the virtue of selfishness in capitalism? Who is right? Why?

# STUDY GUIDE

## KEY TERMS (arranged by philosophy in order of appearance)

political philosophy   383
politics   383

political science   384
axiology   385

### *Plato*

aristocracy   386
individualism   387
city-state (*polis*)   388
soul   388
division of labor   388
artisans (business class)   389
self-discipline   390

auxiliaries   390
guardian class   390
philosopher rulers   390
spirit   391
courage   391
justice   392
imperfect societies   392

timocracy   392
oligarchic state   392
democracy   392
tyrannical society   392
feminist   395
eugenics   396
meritocracy   396

### *Hobbes*

social contract theory   399
natural equality   401
state of nature   401

right of nature   403
law of nature   404
egoistic rule of prudence   404

*Leviathan*   405
social contract   406
commonwealth   406

### John Locke

Declaration of Independence   **409**
American Constitution   **409**
*Second Treatise of Government*   **409**
state of nature   **410**
natural law   **410**
God   **410**
natural rights   **410**

right to punish   **411**
property rights   **411**
right of self-preservation   **412**
political society   **413**
executive   **413**
fiduciary role   **414**
individualism   **414**

social compact   **414**
consent   **414**
tacit consent   **415**
majority rule   **415**
prerogative power   **416**

### Karl Marx

Hegel   **424**
absolute idealism   **424**
dialectical process   **425**
Absolute Mind   **425**
dialectical materialism   **426**
class conflict   **426**
epochs of history   **426**

capitalism   **428**
bourgeois   **428**
proletarian   **428**
communism   **428**
alienation   **429**
idolatry   **432**
fetishism of commodities   **432**

division of labor   **433**
handicraft   **433**
manufacture   **433**
surplus value   **434**
dehumanization of capitalism   **435**

## PROGRESS CHECK

**Instructions:** Fill in the blanks with the appropriate responses listed below.

*polis*
altruism
*Leviathan*
tyranny
labor
class conflicts
consent
aristocracy
divisions
war

axiology
inconveniences
commonwealth
objective morality
epochs of history
politics
idolatry
alienation
philosopher rulers
John Locke

property
artisans
God
Cold War
rights
Hegel
division of labor
fiduciary role
women

1. Political philosophy is not the same thing as _____ or political science.
2. Political philosophy, as a subdiscipline of philosophy, is often classified as a branch of _____ (the study of values).
3. For Plato, the ideal society was a form of _____.
4. The Greek term for city-state is _____.
5. Those responsible in Plato's Republic for looking after the material needs of society are called the _____.
6. Those ultimately responsible for the state's governance are called the _____.
7. According to Plato, the worst form of government is the _____.
8. _____ are treated as equals in the philosopher ruler and auxiliary classes.
9. According to Thomas Hobbes _____ is not natural to human beings.
10. Hobbes argues that during the time human beings are without the sovereign authority of government in the state of nature, they are in a condition of _____.
11. In the state of nature, there is no _____.

12. The social contract, for Hobbes, requires that we deny our _____ to ourselves on the condition that others also do so, giving power to governmental authority.

13. Hobbes calls the coercive power that forces individuals to live by the social contract the _____.

14. The unity of persons in one governing body is called a _____.

15. The philosophy of _____ was to exert a great influence on Thomas Jefferson and the writing of the Declaration of Independence.

16. The architect of the natural law is _____.

17. Of all the rights embedded in the natural law, Locke attributes most importance to _____ rights.

18. What makes something "mine" when, at first, it belonged to everyone in principle is that my _____ mixes with it.

19. For Locke, some sort of government is necessary to avoid any _____ arising from individual transgressions of others when it comes to exercising power and punishing misdemeanors.

20. Locke does not give government supreme authority, but rather a _____.

21. Locke's social compact uses _____ as its rational foundation.

22. By allowing for certain _____ of power within government, Locke builds into his system certain checks and balances.

23. What can make an objective reading of Karl Marx difficult is a _____ hysteria hang-over, and people continuing to confuse Marxist theory with military dictatorships claiming to be communist.

24. Marx's theory of historical social development is based on the notion of dialectic formulated by _____.

25. Apart from the ideal of the communist state, societies are characterized by their internal _____.

26. According to Marx, there are basically five _____.

27. _____ is a byproduct of the capitalist mode of production.

28. When lifeless creations of man's labor are endowed with power and made objects of reverence and awe, _____ results.

29. _____ within the capitalist mode of production is a major contributor to alienation.

30. Bonus Question: After completing Chapter 6, I now conclude that philosophy has turned out to be one of the most interesting and personally useful courses that I have ever studied.

A. True
B. False

# SUMMARY OF MAJOR POINTS

1. What is the nature of political philosophy?
   • Different from politics and political science
   • A part of axiology
   • Overlaps with moral philosophy
   • Divisible into classical and modern theories
   • Political philosophers concerned with matters of justice, individual rights, freedom, state authority, political power, etc.

2. What are some classic and modern perspectives on political philosophy?
   • Plato's Republic
   • Hobbes's Leviathan
   • Locke's Social Compact
   • Karl Marx's Communist Utopia

3. How does Plato conceptualize society?
   • As a hierarchical class system
   • Philosopher rulers govern (gold class)
   • Auxiliaries execute and administer (silver class)
   • Artisans produce and deliver materially (bronze class)
   • Ideal society operates in harmonious balance

4. How, according to Plato, are societies corrupted?
   • Through social imbalance
   • Those who should follow lead, and vice versa
   • Passions and appetites are allowed to dominate
   • The unwise assume control, and people cease to perform their proper function
   • Conflicts arise between rich and poor
   • Disrespect for authority emerges

5. How were women treated in ancient Greece?
   * Plato allowed women full equality in the guardian classes.
   * Artisan women probably occupied traditional domestic roles.

6. How does Hobbes view human nature?
   * People are equal by nature with respect to bodily and mental capacities.
   * People are in constant competition and distrustful of each other.
   * People without government are in a condition of war.
   * Humans are solitary, nasty, selfish, and egoistic.

7. In what statements does Hobbes capture the natural laws of reason?
   * Basically two (though 19 discussed in *Leviathan*)
     1. "That every man, ought to endeavour Peace, as farre as he has hope of obtaining it; and when he cannot obtain it, that he may seek, and use, all helps, and advantages of Warre."
     2. "That a man be willing, when others are so too, as farreforth, as for Peace, and defence of himselfe he shalt think it necessary, to lay down this right to all things; and be contented with so much liberty against other men, as he would allow other men against himself."

8. What is Hobbes' Leviathan?
   * A coercive power to compel individuals to live by their covenant
   * A strong sanctioning body
   * Like a "Mortall God"

9. What is Locke's conception of the state of nature?
   * In nature, humans are free, but not licentious.
   * People are equal, independent, and possess the right to life, health, liberty, and possessions.
   * The state of nature is pre-political but not pre-social

10. To what natural right does Locke give special attention?
    * Property rights: precede society
    * State is created to protect property rights
    * Property rights given to us by God
    * Entitlements to property come from mixing our labor with objects

11. What function does the Lockean state play?
    * Fiduciary role
    * Protection of property rights
    * Resolving disputes between citizens
    * Avoidance of "inconveniences" regarding the punishment of wrongdoing

12. What are the basic structures of the state's power?
    * Legislative branch: power to make laws
    * Executive branch: power to enforce compliance to laws
    * Federative branch: power to make war and peace

13. How or why is Karl Marx considered a revolutionary threat?
    * His atheism is a threat to religionists and people of faith.
    * His dialectical materialism threatens philosophers, charging that ideas are simply products of socioeconomic conditions.
    * His theory threatens capitalism since he exposes its corruption and alienating effects.

14. Who influenced Marx's thinking?
    * Hegel with his concept of dialectic
    * Feuerbach and his materialism—reality is material, not spiritual (Hegel)
    * Comte de Sainte-Simon—economic conditions determine history (class conflict—rich versus poor)

15. What are the five historical periods of economic development according to Marx?
    * Primitive/communal
    * Slave
    * Feudal
    * Capitalistic
    * Socialist/communist

16. What does alienation mean? What role does it play in capitalistic modes of production?
    * Alienation is the experience of separation, difference, estrangement, powerlessness (from oneself, others, one's species-being, work).
    * One feels enslaved by machines originally made to serve humankind.

17. What contributes to alienation?
    * The dehumanizing capitalistic mode of production
    * Idolatry (making money your God)

- Fetishism of commodities (giving power to man-made objects and then adoring them)
- Division of labor (specialization)
- Making labor into a commodity that can be bought and sold

# SOURCE REFERENCES

## THOMAS HOBBES

**Copleston, Frederick,** *A History of Philosophy,* Vol. 5 (New York: Image Books, 1994).

**Hakim, Albert,** *Historical Introduction to Philosophy* (New York: MacMillan, 1987).

**Hobbes, Thomas,** *Leviathan,* Francis B. Randall, ed. (New York: Washington Square Press, 1964).

**Laslett, Peter,** "Social Contract" in *The Encyclopedia of Philosophy,* Vol. 7 (New York: Macmillan and Free Press, 1972).

**Matson, Wallace,** *A New History of Philosophy,* Vol. 2, *From Descartes to Searle,* 2nd ed. (Fort Worth: Harcourt College Publishers, 2000).

**Stumpf, S.E.,** *Philosophy: History and Problems,* 5th ed. (New York: McGraw-Hill, 1994).

**Titus, H., Marilyn Smith, and R.T. Nolan,** *Living Issues in Philosophy* (Belmont, CA: Wadsworth Publishing, 1995).

## JOHN LOCKE

**Copleston, Frederick,** *A History of Philosophy,* Vol. 5 (New York: Image Books, 1994), pp. 123–42.

**Locke, John,** *The Second Treatise of Government,* Thomas P. Peardon, ed. (Upper Saddle River, NJ: Prentice Hall/The Library of Liberal Arts, 1952).

**Scott-Kakures, Dion, Susan Castegnetto, Hugh Benson, William Taschek, and Paul Hurley,** *History of Philosophy* (New York: HarperCollins, 1993), pp. 280–85.

## KARL MARX

**Fromm, Erich,** *Marx's Concept of Man* (New York: Frederick Ungar Publishing, 1976).

**Lavine, T.Z.,** *From Socrates to Sartre: The Philosophical Quest* (New York: Bantam, 1989) pp. 261–320.

**Lawhead, William,** *The Voyage of Discovery: A History of Western Philosophy* (Belmont, CA: Wadsworth, 1966).

**Marx, Karl,** *Economic and Philosophical Manuscripts,* in Erich Fromm, *Marx's Concept of Man* (New York: Frederick Ungar Publishing, 1976).

———, *Capital,* Vol. 1, trans. Ben Fowkes (London: Penguin Books, 1990).

**Marx, Karl, and Friedrich Engels,** *Manifesto of the Communist Party (The Communist Manifesto)* (Moscow: Progress Publishers, 1952).

**Matson, Wallace,** *A New History of Philosophy,* 2nd ed., Vol. 2 (Fort Worth: Harcourt College Publishers, 2000).

**McInnes, Neil,** "Karl Marx" in *The Encyclopedia of Philosophy,* Vol. 5 (New York: Macmillan and Free Press, 1972).

**Soccio, Douglas,** *Archetypes of Wisdom: An Introduction to Philosophy,* 3rd ed. (Belmont, CA: Wadsworth, 1998), pp. 416–49.

**Taylor, A.J.P.,** "Introduction" to Marx and Engels, *Manifesto of the Communist Party* (Moscow: Progress Publishers, 1952).

**Wartenberg, Thomas,** Film review of "American Beauty" in *Philosophy Now* magazine, June/July, 2000, p. 44.

## PLATO

**Copleston, Frederick,** *A History of Philosophy,* Vol. 1, *Greece and Rome* (New York: Image Books, 1993).

**Fink, Hans,** *Social Philosophy* (London: Methuen, 1981).

**Honer, S., T.C. Hunt, and D.L. Okholm,** *Invitation to Philosophy,* 8th ed. (Belmont, CA: Wadsworth, 1987).

**Kenny, Anthony,** *The Oxford Illustrated History of Western Philosophy* (Oxford: Oxford University Press, 1997).

**Laslett, P., and P.W. Cummings,** "History of Political Philosophy," in *The Encyclopedia of Philosophy,* Vol. 6 (New York: Macmillan and Free Press, 1972).

**Lavine, T.Z.,** *From Socrates to Sartre: The Philosophic Quest* (New York: Bantam Books, 1989), pp. 54–66.

**Lawhead, William,** *The Voyage of Discovery: A History of Western Philosophy* (Belmont CA: Wadsworth, 1996).

**Plato,** *The Republic,* Jowett Translation (New York: Vintage Books, 1991).

———, *The Republic,* Desmond Lee Translation, (Harmondsworth, Middlesex, England: Penguin Books, 1955).

———, *The Republic of Plato,* trans. Allan Bloom (New York: Basic Books, 1968).

**Popkin, Richard, and Avrum Stroll,** *Philosophy Made Simple,* 2nd ed. (New York: Doubleday, 1993).

**Solomon, Robert,** *Introducing Philosophy: A Text with Readings,* 3rd ed. (San Diego: Harcourt Brace Jovanovich, 1985).

# PHILOSOPHY IN CYBERSPACE

**Political Philosophy/Political Theory**
http://www.library.ubc.ca/poli/theory.html
The Walter C. Koerner Library at the University of British Columbia presents a straightforward list of philosophy links.

**Introduction to Political Philosophy & Ideologies**
http://polisci.nelson.com/ideologies.html

At this site you can find many links to the lives and works of a wide range of important political philosophers.

**Political Philosophy Resources**
http://www.artsci.lsu.edu/poli/theoryx.html
This site at Louisiana State University provides comprehensive links to locate philosophical and historical documents.

# ENDNOTES

1. Stanley M. Honer, Thomas C. Hunt, and Dennis L. Okholm, *Invitation to Philosophy*, 8th ed. (Belmont, CA: Wadsworth, 1999), p. 208.
2. Anthony Kenny, *The Oxford Illustrated History of Western Philosophy* (Oxford: Oxford University Press, 1997) p. 275.
3. Robert C. Solomon, *Introducing Philosophy: A Text with Readings*, 3rd ed. (San Diego: Harcourt Brace Jovanovich, 1985).
4. Richard H. Popkin and Avrum Stroll, *Philosophy Made Simple*, 2nd ed. (New York: Doubleday, 1993), p. 59
5. Peter Laslett and Philip W. Cummings, "Political Philosophy, History of" in *The Encyclopedia of Philosophy*, Vol. 6 (New York: Macmillan and Free Press, 1967), p. 370.
6. Popkin and Stroll, *Philosophy Made Simple*, p. 61.
7. Ibid.
8. Frederick Copleston, *A History of Philosophy*, Vol. 1 (New York: Image Books, 1993), p. 224.
9. Popkin and Stroll, *Philosophy Made Simple*, p. 61.
10. T.Z. Lavine, *From Socrates to Sartre: The Philosophic Quest* (New York: Bantam Books, 1989), p. 57.
11. William Lawhead, *The Voyage of Discovery: A History of Western Philosophy* (Belmont, CA: Wadsworth, 1996), p. 76.
12. This expression is not actually used in the Alan Bloom, Jowett, or Desmond Lee translations of Plato, but by T.Z. Lavine. What the expression might lack in translation accuracy, it compensates for in poetic imagery. Hence, I borrow it from Lavine, *From Socrates to Sartre*, p. 57.
13. Plato, quoted in *From Socrates to Sartre*, Lavine, p. 59.
14. This point is underscored by Lawhead, *The Voyage of Discovery*, p. 77.
15. Plato says relatively little about the artisans/business class in *The Republic*. We assume from what he says and doesn't say that the artisans live under normal arrangements by comparison to the guardians, for whom family life and private property is prohibited. See Copleston, *A History of Philosophy*, p. 229.
16. Plato, *The Republic*, trans. Desmond Lee (Middlesex, England:Penguin Books, 1976), pp. 202, 432.
17. See Desmond Lee, "Translator's Introduction," in Plato, *The Republic*, p. 42.
18. Ibid., p. 184.
19. I thank professor Tom Robinson at the University of Toronto for clarifying why the translated expression "noble act of deception" is to be preferred over "noble lie" and "magnificent myth."

20. Plato, *The Republic*, pp. 205–6, 433e–434cd.
21. Ibid., Part Nine, Book Eight.
22. Copleston, *A History of Philosophy*, pp. 232–33.
23. Peter Laslett, "Social Contract," in *The Encyclopedia of Philosophy*, Vol. 7, pp. 465–67.
24. Wallace Matson, *A New History of Philosophy*, Vol. 2: "From Descartes to Searle," 2nd ed. (Fort Worth: Harcourt College Publishers, 2000), p. 333.
25. Albert Hakim, *Historical Introduction to Philosophy* (New York: MacMillan, 1987), p. 308.
26. Samuel Enoch Stumpf, *Philosophy: History and Problems*, 5th ed. (New York: McGraw-Hill, 1994), p. 225.
27. Harold, H Titus, Marilyn S. Smith, and Richard T. Nolan, *Living Issues in Philosophy* (Belmont, CA: Wadsworth, 1995), p. 32.
28. Lawhead, *Voyage of Discovery*, p. 239.
29. Thomas Hobbes, *Leviathan*, Francis B. Randall, ed. (New York: Washington Square Press, 1964), p. 84.
30. Ibid.
31. Copleston, *A History of Philosophy*, Vol. V, p. 34.
32. Hobbes, *Leviathan*, p. 34.
33. Ibid., p. 84.
34. Ibid., p. 85.
35. Ibid.
36. Copleston, *A History of Philosophy*, p. 35.
37. Hobbes, *Leviathan*, p. 87.
38. Ibid., p. 88.
39. Ibid.
40. Lawhead, *Voyages of Discovery*, p. 239.
41. Hobbes, *Leviathan*, p. 97.
42. Ibid., p. 98.
43. Ibid., p. 119.
44. Stumpf, *Philosophy: History and Problems*, pp. 224–34.
45. Copleston, *A History of Philosophy*, p. 42.
46. Ibid., pp. 42–43.
47. Hobbes, *Leviathan*, pp. 118–19.
48. Copleston, *A History of Philosophy*, p. 41.
49. These conditons are nicely summarized by Copleston, ibid.
50. Popkin and Stroll, *Philosophy Made Simple*, p. 70.
51. Matson, *A New History of Philosophy*, p. 379.
52. Popkin and Stroll, *Philosophy Made Simple*, p. 71.
53. John Locke, *The Second Treatise of Government*, Thomas P. Peardon, ed. (Upper Saddle River, NJ: Prentice Hall, 1952), p. 4.

54. Ibid., p. 5.

55. Copleston summarizing Locke's position, *A History of Philosophy*, p. 5.

56. Ibid.

57. Locke, *The Second Treatise*, p. 13.

58. Dion Scott-Kakures, et al., *History of Philosophy* (New York: HarperCollins, 1993), p. 282.

59. Locke, *The Second Treatise*, p. 7.

60. Ibid., p. 6.

61. P. Peardon, "Editor's Introduction," in Locke, *The Second Treatise*, p. xiii.

62. Ibid.

63. Hobbes, *Leviathan*, p. 87.

64. Locke, *The Second Treatise*, p. 71.

65. Ibid.

66. Ibid., pp. 98–99.

67. Copleston, *A History of Philosophy*, p. 129.

68. Locke, *The Second Treatise*, p. 20.

69. Ibid., p. 17.

70. Ibid., pp. 71–72.

71. Peardon, in Locke, *The Second Treatise*, p. xiii.

72. Locke, *The Second Treatise*, p. 57.

73. Ibid.

74. Stumpf, *Philosophy: History and Problems*, p. 273.

75. Locke, *The Second Treatise*, p. 55.

76. Peardon, "Editor's Introduction," p. xvii.

77. Popkin and Stroll, *Philosophy Made Simple*, p. 75.

78. Locke, *The Second Treatise*, p. 82.

79. Ibid., p. 83.

80. Popkin and Stroll, *Philosophy Made Simple*, p. 74.

81. Locke, *The Second Treatise*, p. 119.

82. Copleston, *History of Philosophy*, p. 138.

83. John Hallowell and Jene Porter, *Political Philosophy* (Scarborough: Prentice Hall Canada, 1997), p. 552.

84. Neil McInnes, "Karl Marx" in *The Encyclopedia of Philosophy*, Vol. 5, p. 172.

85. Quoted in Robert Payne, *Marx* (New York: Simon & Schuster, 1968), p. 155.

86. Erich Fromm, *Marx's Concept of Man* (New York: Frederick Ungar Publishing, 1976).

87. Matson, *A New History of Philosophy*, p. 498.

88. McInnes, "Karl Marx," p. 172.

89. Ibid.

90. Matson, *A New History of Philosophy*, p. 499.

91. Fromm, *Marx's Concept of Man*, p. vii.

92. Ibid., p. ix.

93. This point is highlighted by Lawhead, *The Voyage of Discovery*, p. 402.

94. McInnes, "Karl Marx," p. 173.

95. Marx, quoted in Matson, *A New History of Philosophy*, p. 503.

96. Lavine, *From Socrates to Sartre*, p. 207.

97. Ibid., pp. 209–10.

98. Medieval alchemists believed that "the philosopher's stone" was a symbol of something that could be found only within the psyche of man. It can never be lost or dissolved as it symbolizes something eternal that some alchemists have compared to mystical experience of God within one's own soul. See Carl Jung, ed., *Man and His Symbols* (New York: Dell Publishing, 1964), pp. 225–26. For Hegel, it was like a key opening the door to the mysteries of the universe.

99. A.J.P. Taylor, "Introduction," Karl Marx and Friedrich Engels, *The Communist Manifesto* (Moscow: Progress Publisher, 1975), p. 9.

100. Douglas Soccio, *Archetypes of Wisdom: An Introduction to Philosophy*, 3rd ed. (Belmont, CA: Wadsworth, 1998), pp. 420–21.

101. Marx, quoted in Lawhead, *Voyage of Discovery*, p. 402.

102. Soccio, *Archetypes of Wisdom*, p. 421.

103. Marx and Engels, *The Communist Manifesto*, pp. 40–41.

104. Soccio, *Archetypes of Wisdom*, p. 425.

105. Dion Scott-Kakures, Susan Castagnetto, Hugh Benson, William Taschek, and Paul Hurley, *History of Philosophy* (New York: HarperPerennial, 1993), p. 323.

106. Ibid., p. 323.

107. This point, along with the rest of the discussion here on the dialectical progression of historical epochs, is borrowed from Soccio, *Archetypes of Wisdom*, pp. 426–27.

108. This explanation of the transition from socialism to communism comes from the summary description found in Lawhead, *Voyage of Discovery*, p. 413.

109. Marx, *Economic and Philosophical Manuscripts*, in Fromm, *Marx's Concept of Man*, p. 107.

110. Karl Marx, *Capital*, Vol. 1, trans. Ben Fowkes (London: Penguin Books, 1990), p. 708.

111. Fromm, *Marx's Concept of Man*, p. 57.

112. Marx, *Capital*, pp. 461–62.

113. Marx, *Economic and Philosophical Manuscripts*, in Fromm, *Marx's Concept of Man*, p. 95.

114. Ibid., p. 103.

115. Ibid., pp. 98–99.

116. Thomas E. Wartenberg, film review of "American Beauty" in *Philosophy Now* magazine, June/July, 2000, p. 44.

117. Ibid., p. 44.

118. Marx, Economic and Philosophical Manuscripts in Fromm, *Marx's Concept of Man*, p. 99.

# APPENDIX

## Answers To Progress Checks

### Progress Check Chapter 1

1. wisdom
2. Western rational tradition
3. knowledge
4. practical use
5. depth
6. therapeutic value
7. instrumental
8. liberate
9. Hellenistic tradition
10. epistemology
11. axiology
12. foundational
13. logic
14. ethics
15. social/political philosophy
16. rational
17. Medicine Wheel
18. irrational leap
19. historical periods
20. conceptual analysis

### Progress Check Chapter 2

1. worldviews
2. Zeno
3. Socrates
4. Diogenes
5. ordered
6. synchronicity
7. courageous acceptance
8. nature
9. emotional detachment
10. existentialism
11. aphorisms
12. unorthodox
13. revolt
14. subjectivity, uniqueness
15. existence, essence
16. causal determinism

17. absurd
18. crowd
19. blame
20. Viktor Frankl
21. psychological hedonism
22. ethical hedonism
23. Aristippus
24. pleasure
25. self-control
26. immediate
27. Epicurus
28. enduring
29. *ataraxia*
30. natural
31. fear
32. virtue
33. friendship
34. vain
35. limits
36. suffering
37. craving
38. nirvana
39. Middle Way
40. ego

### Progress Check Chapter 3

1. factual, value
2. moral, nonmoral
3. groundless
4. arguments
5. rational disinterestedness
6. content, form
7. *modus ponens*
8. *modus tollens*
9. syllogisms
10. practical
11. inductive
12. inductive generalization
13. necessary
14. sound
15. premises
16. logical fallacies
17. *ad hominem*

18. straw man
19. two wrongs
20. appealing to authority

### Progress Check Chapter 4

1. epistemology
2. metaphysics
3. becoming
4. opinion
5. being
6. goodness
7. allegory of the cave
8. rationalist
9. Copernican revolution
10. deduction
11. methodological doubt
12. *cogito ergo sum*
13. wax example
14. John Locke
15. *tabula rasa*
16. complex idea, simple ideas
17. innate ideas
18. primary qualities, secondary qualities
19. Bishop Berkeley
20. God
21. perceiver
22. wrecking-ball
23. impressions, thoughts
24. self
25. causality
26. synthesis
27. active construction
28. sensibility
29. categories
30. pure reason

### Progress Check Chapter 5

1. teleology
2. soul
3. character
4. philosopher kings/rulers
5. democratic characters

6. utility
7. nature
8. sanction
9. hedonic calculus
10. is-ought
11. rational
12. good will
13. maxims
14. categorical imperative
15. hypothetical
16. ethical bias
17. post-conventional
18. care
19. rationality
20. similar
21. relation
22. God
23. will to power
24. slave morality
25. superman/*übermensch*
26. revaluation
27. ethical egoism
28. destructive
29. objectivist ethics
30. traders

## Progress Check Chapter 6

1. politics
2. axiology
3. aristocracy
4. *polis*
5. artisans
6. philosophical rulers
7. tyranny
8. women
9. altruism
10. war
11. objective morality
12. rights
13. *Leviathan*
14. commonwealth
15. John Locke
16. God
17. property
18. labor
19. inconveniences
20. feduciary role
21. consent
22. divisions
23. Cold War
24. Hegel
25. class conflicts
26. epochs of history
27. alienation
28. idolatry
29. division of labor
30. True/False

# PHOTO CREDITS

# INDEX

## A

A-B-C model, 54
absolute mind, 425
abstract universals, 67
absurdity, 62
Achenbach, Gerd, 18
active construction, 232
Adam and Eve, 170
Adler, Alfred, 63
aesthete, 86
aesthetic phenomenon, 345, 346
aesthetics, 24
African philosophers, 28
Age of Enlightenment, 204
alienated, 16
alienation, 429
    as a byproduct of capital-
        ism, 429–32
Allegory of the cave, 186–87
Alston, William, 39
altruism, 348
*American Beauty*, 435
American capitalism, 6
American Constitution, 409
American Philosophical
    Association, 18
American Philosophical
    Practitioners Association, 18
American Society for
    Philosophy, Counseling and
    Psychotherapy, 18
analytic
    judgments, 238
    propositions, 221
analytical philosophers, 32
Angeles, Peter, A., 39

*angst*, 75
Annas, Julia, 88, 89, 119
Anselm, St., 6,
    his ontological proof for
        God, 252–53
    profile, 250–51
antecedent, 247
antinomies, 247
Antisthenes, 48
antithesis, 424
aphorisms, 63
Apollo, 345
*aponia*, 88
appearance, 22, 178, 284
appetite, 283
*a priori*, 309
aristocracy, 386, 389
Aristotle, 401
artisans, 389
Aurelius, Marcus, 48, 51, 53,
    54, 56
    forms of intuition, 234
    statements, 222
Aquinas, St. Thomas, 6, 32,
    profile, 259–60
    his proofs for God, 253–58
argument
    and attitude adjustments,
        127–28
    benefits of, 128–29
    evaluating, 154–56
    nature of, 140
    unsound, 154
Aristippus of Cyrene, 84
aristocracy, 292

Aristotelian logic, 19, 23
Aristotle, 26, 86, 187, 191
*ataraxia*, 88, 89, 93
    impediments to, 90–92
atheists, 61
attachment, 100
attitude, 52
attitude adjustment, 10
Augustine, St., 32
Aurelius, Marcus, 17
authenticity, 72
autonomy, 317, 343
auxiliaries, 390
axiology, 21, 385

## B

bad-faith, 75
Bakunin, Mikhail, 420
Barrett, William, 119
beauty, 10
Beauvoir, Simone de, 32, 62, 66
becoming, 178
begging the question, 157
behaviorism, 25
being, 178
belief, 23
beneficiary, 348
beneficiary criterion
    of morality, 348
Bentham, Jeremy, 297, 298
Bercholz, Samuel, 119
Berkeley, Bishop George, 203,
    209–12
Berkowitz, Peter, 339
Bhagavad Gita, 361, 362–64

Blackham, H.J., 119
Blanshard, Brand, 11
Bodhi Tree, 98, 100
bodily health, 90
*bourgeois*, 428
Brandt, Richard, 83, 119
Brickell, Edie, 12, 16
British empiricism, 203–26
Buddha, 44, 97, 101, 104, 110, 111
Buddhism, 26, 31, 47, 97–113, 116
business class, 389

**C**

Campbell, Joseph, 25
Camus, Albert, 67
capitalism, 428
    after, 435–36
care, 28
Cartesian rationalist, 175
Castro, Fidel, 422
categorical imperative, 314–16
causal connection, 158
causality, 22, 214
    and constant conjunction, 220
    Hume's critique of, 218
    and necessary connection, 219
    and priority in time, 219
cause-and-effect, 204, 218
certainty, 192
change, 424
character, 6
character ethics, 282

character moralist, 281
character types, 288, 394
Chodorow, Nancy, 324
Christian ethics, 365–69
    and deontology, 367
    and revisionism, 367–68
    and virtue ethics, 368–69
Christianity, 344
Chrysippus of Soloi, 48, 50, 51
Chuang Tzu, 102
Cicero, 86
city state, 388
class conflict, 426
Cleanthes, 48, 51
*cogito*, 70, 230, 329
*cogito ergo sum*, 197, 199, 214
cold war, 422
collectivist thinking, 347
Collins, Patricia Hill, 226
commonwealth, 404, 406
communism, 421, 423, 424, 428
concentration, 105, 110–11
conceptual analysis, 32
conclusion, 150
Confucianism, 26
consequent, 144
    affirming the, 148
consciousness, 81
consent, 414
consequentialism, 298
content, 230
contiguity, 218
contingency, 71
Copernican revolution, 192
Copleston, Frederick, 39

copy, 216
cosmological determinism, 77, 78
cosmology, 52
cosmos, 247
courage, 391
courageous acceptance, 52, 74
covenant, 408
Crates, 48
craving
    as cause of suffering, 102–3
Crumbaugh, James C., 64
Cust, Kenneth, 18
customary morality, 342
cynic, 48, 49
Cynosarges, 48
Cyrenaic hedonists, 43

**D**

Dante, 126, 274
Darwin, Charles, 338
Das, Lama Surya, 108
Declaration of Independence, 409
deduction, 193
deductive arguments, 145–53
dehumanization of capitalism, 435
democracy, 392–94
democratic character, 287, 295–96
denial, 106
denying the antecedent, 145
denying the consequent, 145
deontological ethics, 308
deontologist, 281
deontology
    and Christianity, 367

Descartes, René, 70, 78, 189–202, 214, 237
    First Meditation, 193–94
    Second Meditation, 197–99
desires, 283
    natural, 90
    vain, 90
destiny, 50
determinism, 25, 74,
    economic, 81–82
    psychological, 79–81
    versus fatalism, 78–79
Dharma, 99, 104
dialectical materialism, 426
dialectical process, 425
dialogues, 63
Diogenes, Laertius, 48, 86, 343
disagreement, 125
discrimination
    powers of, 90
divided line theory, 178–80
division of labor, 388, 427, 433
division of power, 416
Dobson, Theodore, 320
Dostoyevsky, Fyodor, 67
Durant, Will, 21
duties
    to others, 313
    to ourselves, 313
duty
    for the sake of, 311–12
    not for the sake of, 311–12
    performed out of inclination, 312

**E**

*Economic and Philosophical Manuscripts*, 420
    excerpt from, 436–38
economic globalization, 6
Edwards, Paul, 39
ego, 104, 197
ego-impermanence, 178
egoistic rule of prudence, 404
egolessness, 105
ego-self, 103, 105
Ellis, Albert, 54
emotional detachment, 53
emotionalism, 350
emotional self-control, 18
emotions, 55
empiricism, 203
empiricist, 175
empty beliefs, 89
ends of life, 33
Engels, Friedrich, 420, 421
enneagram, 28, 30
Epictetus, 48, 50, 51, 55
Epicurus, 16, 86, 90, 93
epistemology, 21, 175
    Copernican revolution in, 233–34
epochs of history, 426
*esse est percipi*, 211
essence, 204
essence versus existence, 68–70, 74
ethical egoism, 299, 347
ethical hedonism, 83
ethical relativist, 308
ethics, 5, 21, 385

of altruism, 347
    collectivist, 26
ethnocentrism, 15
ethnophilosophy, 28
Euclid, 219
*eudaimon*, 53
*eudaimonia*, 52, 53
Eurocentrism, 27
Euthryphro, 128, 129
evil, 51
excessive passions, 55
existential atheist, 281
existential dilemmas, 18
existential free will, 75
existential frustration, 63, 68
existentialism, 47, 61–74, 116, 334
    Jean-Paul Sartre's, 19
existentialist ethics, 335
existentialist philosophers, 9
existential vacuum, 63, 68
experience, 11

**F**

factual premise, 150
factual statements, 140–141
faculty of sensibility, 235
faculty of understanding, 235
fascist, 61
fatalism, 76–77
fate, 50, 74, 78
fated, 50
feelings of compulsion, 221
feminine ethics, 320–33
feminine moralist, 281
fetishism of commodities, 432

Feuerbach, Ludwig, 425

fiduciary role of government, 414

first nations, 27

forms

    Kantian vs Platonic, 236

    theory of, 181–83

foundational/disciplinary philosophies, 21

Four Noble Truths, The, 97, 99–105

Four Signs, The, 98

Frankl, Viktor, 63, 68

freedom, 22, 52, 62, 76

    as absence of coercion, 76

    as freedom to, 67

freedom of choice, 71

free will, 74

Freud, Sigmund, 63, 79, 80, 93, 94, 274–75

friendship, role of in *ataraxia*, 93

Fromm, Erich, 420, 422, 431

functional explanation of morality, 283

**G**

Galbraith, John Kenneth, 153

Galileo, 190, 192

Garden, The, 86, 93

Garry, Ann, 39

Gautama, Siddhartha, 97–98

gentle force, 218

geocentric view of the universe, 191

German Association for Philosophical Practice, 18

Gilligan, Carol, 26, 322–26, 327

Glasser, William, 113

Glover, Jonathan, 126

God, 5, 6, 10, 22, 28, 50, 51, 68, 69, 74, 75, 79, 91, 92, 157, 214, 229, 247–48, 324, 405, 410

    the perpetual perceiver, 212, 217

    proofs for, 250

God is dead, 336

God's will, 52, 55

good and bad, 23

good life, the, 53

goodness, 10, 181

Good Will, concept of, 309–11

government, 380

    dissolution of, 417

Grant, George, 20

guardian class, 390

**H**

Hamlet, 275

handicraft, 433

happiness, 52, 101

Hassan, Riffat, 359

hedonic calculus, 301–2

hedonism, 47, 82–96, 116

    Cyrenaic, 84–85

    psychological versus ethical, 83

Hegel, Georg, 67, 424–26

Hegel's dialectic, 425

Heidegger, Martin, 66

Heine, Heinrich, 420

Heinz's dilemma, 323

heliocentric theory of the universe, 192

Hellenistic philosophy, 17, 88–89

Hellenistic tradition, 16

Heraclitus of Ephesus, 177, 282

heteronomy of the will, 317

Higgins, Kathleen, 39

higher-order principle, 155

Hindu ethics, 360–362

Hindu gurus, 31

Hinduism, 26

Hobbes, Thomas, 78, 79, 380, 400–409

    and his Leviathan, 404–6

    on laws of nature, 403–4

    profile, 400–1

    on social contract, 406

    and state of nature, 401–3

Hobbes' commonwealth, 383

Holbach, Baron d', 79

Homer, 345

Hoogendijk, Ad, 18

Hopi and space and time, 248–50

human existence, 22

human freedom, 71

humanitarianism, 61

human nature, 349

human rights, 6

Hume, David, 81, 203, 213, 229, 237

Hume's Fork, and types of reasoning, 221–23

Hurka, Thomas, 13–14

Hurley, Kathleen, 320

hypotenuse, 172

hypothetical moral dilemmas, 323

**I**

Ichazo, Oscar, 31

ideas, 214

association of, 218

innate, 207

origin of, 215–16

single and complex, 206–7

versus impressions, 215–16

identity formation, 324

idolatry and fetishism of commodities, 432

immanent, 51

imperatives, hypothetical versus categorical, 316

imperfect societies, 392–95

impermanence, 105

impiety, 49, 128, 129

impressions, 216

inclusive disjunct, affirming the, 147

individualism, 387, 414

individuality and subjective experience, 70

inductive logic

argument by analogy, 154

argument by inductive generalization, 154–55

argument from past experience, 153–54

informal logical fallacies

*ad hominem*, 158–59

appealing to authority, 161

circular reasoning, 159

guilt by association, 162

red herring, 161

slippery slope, 160–61

straw man, 159

two wrongs, 58

information age, 20

inner peace, 17

integrated mode of existence, 12

intelligible world, 182

interior freedom, 52

interpersonal, 62

intimacy, 325

intuition, 193

intuition, forms of, 234

Islam, 27

Islamic ethics, 357–59

is-ought fallacy, 21, 299

I Think, 197

**J**

Jagger, Alison, 26

James, William, 67, 140

Jaspers, Karl, 66

Jongsma, Ida, 18

Joseph McCarthy era, 422

Judeo-Christian tradition, 336

Judaism, 27

judgments, 52

analytic, 238

analytic *a priori*, 239

*a posteriori*, 239, 240

*a priori*, 240

distinction between analytic & synthetic, 241–43

synthetic *a posteriori*, 239

synthetic *a priori*, 239

types of, 238

justice, 6, 392

**K**

Kabbalah, 28

Kaczynski, Ted, 11

Kant, Immanuel, 26, 32, 228, 308, 313

and his synthesis of rationalism and empiricism, 229

Kantian categories of cause and substance, 237–38

Kantian formalism, 314, 328

Kantian structuralist, 175

*Kapital, Das*, 421, 423

Karma and rebirth, 112–13

Kennedy, J.F., 139

Kierkegaard, Søren, 28, 66, 68, 70, 324

knowledge, 10, 173, 179

*a priori* elements of, 234

and goods of the mind, 34

origins and limits of, 223

roles of reason and experience in, 190–233

Kohlberg, Lawrence, 320, 321, 323, 324, 325, 328

Kohn, Sherab, Chodzin, 119

Kopernik, Mikolaj Copernicus, 191, 192, 194, 233

**L**

LaHav, Ran, 39

laissez-faire capitalism, 353

Lauper, Cindy, 126

Lavine, T.Z., 182, 424

law of moral causation, 112

law of nature, 50

laws of association, 218

laws of nature, 403–4

Leibniz, Gottfried, 191

Leviathan, 380, 404–406, 409

life, 350

practical conduct of, 11

literary forms, 63

Locke, John, 203, 205–9, 229, 237, 380, 409–19

on government and political society, 413–14

and natural law, 410–11

and property rights, 411–12

and the right to punish, 411

and the right of self-preservation, 412

his Second Treatise of Gov't, 409

and social compact, 414

and the state of nature, 410–11

Locke's consensual democracy, 383

logic, 21

logical positivism, 204

logos, 50, 51, 63, 74, 77, 78,

logotherapy, 63, 68

Loomis, Mary E., 27, 39

Lucretius, 86, 203

Luther, Martin 194

## M

mad monkey of the mind, 31

Madonna, 25

Maholick, Leonard, 64

majority rule, 415

major premise, 150

male bias, in moral research, 320–22

*Manifesto of the Communist Party*, 421

manufacture, 433

Maoist conformity, 423

Marcel, Gabriel, 62, 66

Marinoff, Louis, 18

Marx, Karl, 6, 81, 380, 419–38

and dialectical materialism, 424–26

his metaphysics, 424–26

profile of, 419–21

Marxist alienation, 6

Marxists, 61

Marx's communism, 383

masculine ethics, 327

material substance, 211

matter, 230

matters of fact, 221

McVeigh, Timothy, 380

meaning of life, 85

meaning therapy, 63

Medicine Wheel, The, 27

medieval scholasticism, 192

meditation, 31

Menocceus, Letter to, 90, 94–6

mental gravity, 218

mental substance, 217

meta-ethicists, 23

metaphysical epistemology, Plato's, 176–88

metaphysical rubbish, 205, 209

metaphysics, 21, 22, 174,

Hume's rejection of, 216–18

and regulative function, 244–45

methodological doubt, Descartes's, 192–95

middle way, the, 97, 99

Mill, John Stuart, 32, 125, 143

mind, 36

minor premise, 150

mission in life, 68

*modus ponens*, 143–48

*modus tollens*, 145, 148

monist, 177

monistic universe, 50

Montaigne, Michel de, 66

Moose Mountain Medicine Wheel, 27

moral certainty, 309

moral evil, 52

morality, 10, 105

master vs. slave, 339–42

morality of care, 324

moral obligation, 23

moral reasoning development, 320

moral virtue, 284

Morris, Tom, 17–18

Morstein, Petra von, 18

Muhammad, 357, 358

Muslims, 358

mysticism, 350

## N

Naqshbandi Sufi order, 30

Naranjo, Claudio, 31

natural caring, 330

natural desires, 88

natural equality, 401

natural law, 410, 411

natural rights, 410

nature, 52, 350,

necessary, 218

negation, 72, 341

neo-mysticism, 350

new cases test, 155

Newtonian science, 204

Nietzsche, Friedrich, 26, 63, 66, 70, 334, 334–46

nihilism, 344

*nirvana*, 103–4

nobility of self-possession, 18

Noble Eight-fold Path, The, 97, 106–13

    right action, 108–9

    right concentration, 111–13

    right effort, 110

    right livelihood, 109–10

    right mindfulness, 110

    right speech, 107–8

    right thought/intention, 106

    right view, 106

nobles, 340

Noddings, Nel, 327–33

noetic, 68

noögenic neurosis, 63, 68

normative issues, 21

*noumena* versus phenomena, 244–45

Nussbaum, Martha, 16, 39, 88, 89,

**O**

objectivism, 346

objectivist, 281–82

objectivist ethics, 347–56

objects, qualities of primary and secondary, 208

oligarchic character, 287, 294–95

oligarchic state, 392, 394

one cared-for, 329

one-caring, 329

opinion, 6,10, 177

    versus argument, 139

Oracle at Delphi, 127, 288

oral tradition, 27

ordered universe, 50

other-as-beneficiary, 349

**P**

Panaetius of Rhodes, 51

parables, 63

Parmenides of Elea, 175

Pascal, Blaise, 66, 327

passion, 55, 283

Passmore, John, 9

peace, 404

peace of mind, 53

Pearsall, Marilyn, 39

perception, 22, 67, 180

perennial wisdom, 12

personal whim, 350

personhood, 22

*philos*, 9

philosopher, 8, 38

    closet, 8

    western rational, 38

philosopher king/ruler, 287, 288, 292–93, 390, 391

Philosopher's Hotel, 18

philosopher's profile, 9–10

critically minded, 9

curious, 10

detached and unbiased, 10

open-minded, 10

questioning attitude, 9

reasonable, 9

seekers of truth, 10

philosopher's stone, 424

philosophical consultants, 18

philosophical counselling, 18–20

philosophical enlightenment, 5

philosophical practitioners movement, 18

philosophical quest, 8

philosophical system–building, 67

philosophical worldview, 25

    freedom from, 90

philosophic contemplation, 35

philosophies of life, 6, 22, 40–115

philosophy

    analytic, 32

    approaches to, 26–32

    cash value of, 13–14

    continental, 32

    fields of, 21–25

    historical periods of, 32

    instrumental value of, 15

    intrinsic value of, 15

    masculine and feminine approaches to, 26

    practical value of, 12–16, 38

    rational versus non-rational, 28

relevance in an age of information and emerging technologies, 20–21

specialization, 38

therapeutic applications of, 16–20

and world philosophies, 26

philosophy and philosophers, caricatures, myths, and realities, 8

Piaget, Jean, 231, 322

Plato, 6, 26, 49, 67, 86, 139, 176, 177, 181, 214, 229, 387

and the realm of forms, 6

Platonic Character Type Index, 285–87

Platonic duality, 173

Plato's aristocracy, 383

Plato's character types, 288–96

Plato's class system, 389–92

Plato's republic, 386

Plato's teleology, 282

pleasure, 82, 84,

actual, 85,

intensity of, 84

kinetic versus static, 87–88

as leading to suffering, 101

momentary versus enduring, 86–87

potential, 85

polis, 388

political conservatives, 61

political philosophy, 6, 383

vs political science, 384–85

vs politics, 383, 384

political society and government, 413

Posidonius of Apamea, 51

power, 408

practical wisdom, 87

praise and blame, 23

prerogative power, 416

pride, 351

principle of utility, 298

principles of moral conduct, 23

productivity, 351

proletarian, 428

property rights, 411

*Proslogion*, 253

Proudhon, Pierre–Joseph, 420

Providence, 56, 74

prudence, 90, 311

pseudo-Marxism, 422

psychoanalysis, 81

psychological behaviorism, 25

psychological bias, 320

psychological egoism, 298

psychological honesty, 341

psychological wholeness, 27

pure and applied research, 15

pure reason, 245

purpose, 351

purpose of life, 52

Purpose of Life Test, The, 63–66

**Q**

Qur'an, 357

**R**

radical skepticism, 214–215

David Hume's 214–215

Rand, Ayn, 26, 82, 344, 387

rational approach, 9

rational disinterestedness, 127

rationality, 67, 351

rational justifications, 9

rational morality, feminist critics of, 9

rational objectivity, 28

rational selfishness, 347, 352–53

reality, 10, 22, 176, 284

reality testing, 106

realm of ends, 317

realm of forms, 67, 292

reason, 9, 243, 281, 351

reasonable, 9

reasoning, faulty and fallacious, 155–164

recurrent themes, 63

reflection, 206

reincarnation, 113

relation, 28, 329

relations of ideas, 221

religion

and ethics, 356–69

as opium of the people, 6

Republic, The, 176

resemblance, 218

resentment, 341

right and wrong, 23

right of nature, 403

right of self-preservation, 412

rights

earned or inherited, 10

basic, 10

right to punish, 411

Roman Catholic Ethics, 366–69

Russell, Bertrand, 32–39

## S

Sakyamuni, sage of the Sakyas, 97

Sambhava, Padma, 99

sanctions, 300

    Bentham's theory of, 299

Sangha, 99

Sartre, Jean-Paul, 32, 62, 63, 66, 72, 74, 75

Schurz, Carl, 420

scientific causal determinism, 77

scientific objectivity, 298

self, 103, 105, 245

    empirical, 245

    enlargement, 35

    logical, 246

    as transcendental unity of apperception, 246

self-control, 49

self-discipline, 49, 390

self-esteem, 351

self-evident principle, 193

selfishness, 347

self-knowledge, 27

self-mastery, 49, 338

self-overcoming, 338

self-sufficiency, 90

self-transcendence, 68

Seneca, 26, 48, 51, 55, 86

sensation, 206

sensible intuitions, 230

separation, 325

Shogan, Debra, 39

Sign of the Presence of God, 28

Simile of the Sun, 183–85

simple tastes, 90

Skinner, B.F., 25, 79

Snelling, John, 107

social classes, 393

social compact, 414

social contract, 380, 406

social contract theory, 399

social-political philosophy, 21

society, 349

Socrates, 5, 9, 48, 49, 127

Socratic humility, 128

Socratic method, 129

Solomon, Robert, 39

*sophia*, 9

Soul, 388

    parts of, 390

    Plato's vision of, 283

source, 51

sovereign, 406

space, 22, 234

Spinoza, Benedict, 190–91

spirit, 283, 391

spiritual enlightenment, 27

Stalin, Joseph, 392

Stalinist oppression, 423

state, 387

state of nature, 410

states of mind, 84

*stoa poikile*, 48

stoic apathy, 52

stoicism, 47, 48–61, 115

    and stress management, 54

stoic thinkers, 77–78

style, and Nietzsche, 346

subject and predicate, 238

subjective bias, 15

subjective experience, 67

subjective preference, 350

substance, 209

suffering, 58, 69, 100, 102–3, 105

Sufis, 358

Superman/Übermensch, 344–46

surplus value, 434

Swiftdeer, Harley, 27

syllogisms

    categorical, 149

    of class membership, 149

    disjunctive, 146, 148

    hypothetical, 146, 148

    practical, 152–53

synchronicity, 50

synthesis, 424

synthetic *a posteriori*, 222

## T

*tabula rasa*, 206, 207, 208, 230

tacit consent, 415

Taoism, 26

*tarachai*, 88

teleological model of universe, 77

teleology, 282

Teresa, St., of Avila, 5, 126

theists, 61

therapeutic philosophy, 50, 100

thesis, 424

things-in-themselves, 245

Thorndike, Edward, 80

thoughts, 216

Tillmanns, Maria da Venza, 39

timarchic character, 287, 293

time, 22, 234

timocracy, 392, 394

traders, 352

traditional (herd) morality, 342

tranquillity of the soul, 90

transcendental ideas, 245

Trudeau, Pierre Elliot, 387, 422

truth, 10, 23

    necessary and undeniable, 172

truths, self-evident, 10

twist of fate, 52

tyrannical character, 287, 296

tyrannical society, 392

**U**

*übermensch*, 345

ultimate life values, 23

ultimate reality, 22

understanding, 10

unfounded assumptions, 10

uniqueness of individuals, 67, 70

universalizability, 328

universalizability criterion, 155

unorthodox methods, 62

Upanishads, 361

utilitarian, 281

utilitarianism, 297

**V**

valid arguments, 6

validity, 153

valid reasoning, 143

value, 52

value judgments, 140–42

value premise, 150

values, 351

Vedanta, 361

Vedas, 361

virtue, 6, 92, 351

visible world, 181

**W**

war, 402

Watson, J.B., 80

Wax Example, The, 200–202

western rational tradition, 9

western thought, 26

White, Thomas, 23

Wilde, Oscar, 86

willful blindness, 102

will-to-meaning, 63

will-to-pleasure, 63

will-to-power, 63, 338

wisdom, 38, 105

    of the ages, 12

    and experience, 11

    and intelligence, 11

    and knowledge, 11

    lovers of, 9

    perennial, 11

    and sense of perspective, 11

Wittgenstein, Ludwig, 151

women

    the nature of for Plato, 396–99

    in Plato's republic, 395–96

**Z**

Zeno, 48

Zeus, 50

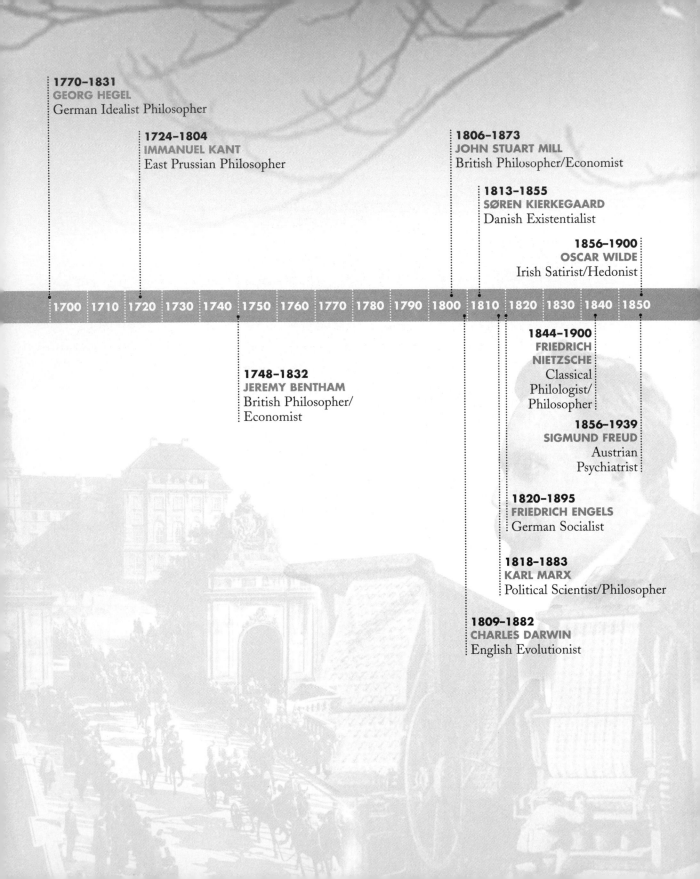

**1770–1831**
**GEORG HEGEL**
German Idealist Philosopher

**1724–1804**
**IMMANUEL KANT**
East Prussian Philosopher

**1806–1873**
**JOHN STUART MILL**
British Philosopher/Economist

**1813–1855**
**SØREN KIERKEGAARD**
Danish Existentialist

**1856–1900**
**OSCAR WILDE**
Irish Satirist/Hedonist

| 1700 | 1710 | 1720 | 1730 | 1740 | 1750 | 1760 | 1770 | 1780 | 1790 | 1800 | 1810 | 1820 | 1830 | 1840 | 1850 |

**1748–1832**
**JEREMY BENTHAM**
British Philosopher/
Economist

**1844–1900**
**FRIEDRICH NIETZSCHE**
Classical Philologist/
Philosopher

**1856–1939**
**SIGMUND FREUD**
Austrian Psychiatrist

**1820–1895**
**FRIEDRICH ENGELS**
German Socialist

**1818–1883**
**KARL MARX**
Political Scientist/Philosopher

**1809–1882**
**CHARLES DARWIN**
English Evolutionist